The Art of
Ancient Cyprus

Desmond Morris

The Art of Ancient Cyprus

with a check-list of the author's collection

Phaidon Press · Oxford
in association with Jonathan Cape

This book is dedicated to the late
James Bomford
whose generosity and wisdom first
led me into the world of the
visual arts

Phaidon Press Limited, Littlegate House,
St Ebbe's Street, Oxford.OX1 1SQ

First published 1985
© Phaidon Press Limited 1985

British Library Cataloguing in Publication Data
 Morris, Desmond
  The art of ancient Cyprus
  1. Art, Cypriote 2. Art, Ancient—Cyprus
  I. Title
  709'.39'37   N5430
  ISBN 0-7148-2280-9

Printed in Great Britain

Frontispiece: Detail of Pl. 185.

Note: All drawings and photographs are by the
author unless otherwise stated. Also, all the
objects illustrated photographically in this book
are in the author's collection and are being
published here for the first time. Objects
illustrated by drawings are from other sources and
have been published previously elsewhere.

Contents

Preface   6

I Epochs   7

II Vessels   15

The Pottery Wares   17

  1 Red Polished Ware   17
  2 Mottled Red Polished Ware   20
  3 Black-topped Red Polished Ware   20
  4 Red-and-Black Polished Ware   21
  5 Black-bottomed Red Polished Ware   21
  6 Reserved Slip Ware   24
  7 Black Polished Ware   24
  8 Black Slip Ware   25
  9 Drab Polished Ware   25
  10 Red-on-Black Ware   28
  11 Handmade White Painted Ware   29
  12 Base Ring Ware   32
  13 Cypro-Mycenaean Ware   33
  14 Cypro-Palestinian Bichrome Ware   33
  15 White Slip Ware   34
  16 Wheelmade Red Lustrous Ware   37
  17 White Shaved Ware   37
  18 Wheelmade White Painted Ware   40
  19 Bichrome Ware   40
  20 Black-on-Red Ware   41
  21 Bichrome Red Ware   41
  22 Wheelmade Black Slip Ware   44
  23 Wheelmade Black Slip Painted Ware   45
  24 Plain White Ware   45
  25 Wheelmade Red Ware   46

The Pottery Shapes   48

THE SIMPLE SHAPES   49
  1 Jug   49
  2 Bottle   65
  3 Flask   66
  4 Jar   67
  5 Bowl   70
  6 Dish   74
  7 Box   75
  8 Dipper   76
  9 Basket   77
  10 Strainer   77

THE COMPLEX SHAPES   78
  1 Ring Vessels   81
  2 Multi-Unit Vessels   85
  3 Subsidiary-Unit Vessels   104

III Representations   113

Human Forms   116

  1 Stump Figures   117
  2 Cruciform Figures   122
  3 Lactation Figures   133
  4 Ejaculation Figures   134
  5 Plank Figures   135
  6 Vessel-Shaped Figures   163
  7 Bone Figures   164
  8 Pubic Triangle Figures   166
  9 Snowman Figures   174
  10 Realistic Figures   182

Animal Forms   184

  1 Deer   185
  2 Cattle   190
  3 Equines   204
  4 Pigs   212
  5 Camels   214
  6 Sheep   216
  7 Goats   218
  8 Dogs   220
  9 Birds   222
  10 Snakes   230
  11 Other Species   233

Plant Forms   234

Inanimate Forms   250

Scenic Compositions   264

IV Decorations   291

Repertoires   292

Thematic Variation   322

Check-list of the Author's Collection   353
Bibliography   360
Acknowledgements   364
Restorations   364
Index   365

Preface

This book reflects an obsession with the art of ancient Cyprus which began in the summer of 1967. It started the moment I walked into Room Two of the Cyprus Museum in Nicosia and for the first time set eyes on the amazing objects produced 4,000 years ago by the Bronze Age inhabitants of the island. There I found vessels and figurines exuding a cheerful inventiveness of such warmth and intensity that I became immediately infatuated.

The rich playfulness of the Bronze Age Cypriot artists, their bold self-confidence in experimenting with novel shapes, their exuberant sense of sculptural humour and their imaginative verve in developing highly stylized forms were a revelation. It was hard to accept that these delightful works of art had originated as the sombre funerary accessories of some prehistoric burial ceremony, objects to be placed alongside the corpse in the cavity of a rock-cut tomb, never intentionally to be seen again. Their liveliness was at odds with their function. Their importance, it seemed to me, was more as works of art than as sacred trappings and I began to study them as such.

At the time, I was living in London where I was the Director of the Institute of Contemporary Arts and was deeply involved in the conceptual problems posed by the latest trends in twentieth-century art. I soon found that some of the questions I was asking in the modern context were equally valid in the ancient one. Problems of stylization, schematization, conventionalization, iconicity, abstraction and symbolic refinement threw up fascinating parallels between the artists of yesterday and today. The more I looked at the artefacts of prehistoric Cyprus, the more perfect they seemed for an extended investigation of the roots of human aesthetics. The difficulty I faced, living in England, was the lack of direct contact with the material.

This problem was solved by a visit to one of the London salerooms in the autumn of 1967. There, to my surprise, was a whole range of Cypriot antiquities—more than a hundred of them in a single sale. I decided to form a collection for serious study. I continued to add to this collection over the next fifteen years, by visiting the salerooms and art dealers of London, New York, Boston, Amsterdam and Paris. It now consists of over 1,100 items and represents the largest private collection of ancient Cypriot art outside Cyprus.

While I was assembling the collection it became clear to me that I had a duty to make it accessible to archaeologists. It is indefensible for private collectors to keep ancient artefacts if they are not prepared to make them available for examination by serious scholars. I let it be known that I welcomed such visitors, and they were soon pointing out to me that I could go a step further by publishing an illustrated catalogue of my collection. I agreed to do this as long ago as 1973, but when I started work on it I realized that it was falling short of my original goal. As a useful inventory for reference purposes it might be worthwhile, but it would hardly be the thesis on archaeo-aesthetics I had envisaged back in the 1960s.

My solution has been to produce a volume that is both at once. For archaeologists it can act as a catalogue of my collection because I have applied the strict rule that all objects illustrated photographically must be in the collection. Used in this way it can be treated as 'primary material' and act as a source of reference. For those interested in more theoretical questions and problems of aesthetics, it contains sections dealing with such issues as pattern repertoires and thematic variation. Finally, for those seeking a general survey of the art of ancient Cyprus, it provides an overall introduction to the subject by making use of drawings of artefacts outside my collection, as supplements to the photographs.

I Epochs

The story of ancient Cyprus has been divided into four major periods: the Stone Age, the Copper Age, the Bronze Age and the Iron Age. The crude dates for the start of each of these periods on the island are

Stone Age: 7000 BC
Copper Age: 4000 BC
Bronze Age: 3000 BC
Iron Age: 1000 BC

These approximate figures serve as a rough guide. More specific dates and dating controversies will be discussed later.

The Stone Age

Cyprus is an island lying in the Mediterranean less than fifty miles south of Turkey and less than seventy miles west of Syria. Greece and Egypt are just over 200 miles away. It is a large island covering 3,500 square miles, with a maximum length of 138 miles (from south-west to north-east). There are three main geographical features: the Troodos mountain range in the south-west, the long and narrow Kyrenia mountain range in the north-east, and, between them, the fertile central plain of the Mesaoria.

Today the island suffers from intense heat and drought during the summer months, but this was probably less severe in prehistoric times, when the land surface was much more densely wooded. Unfortunately for its climate, Cyprus became the main source of timber for ship-building for the whole of the eastern Mediterranean over many centuries. This and the spread of farming areas have gradually intensified the aridity of the hot summers, increasing evaporation, run-off and erosion, but even now the island remains a comparative paradise for human habitation, when considered alongside some of the other regions stubbornly populated by our early ancestors.

Bearing this in mind, it is surprising that no signs of Palaeolithic man have been found on Cyprus. The oldest known traces of human occupation have recently been dated to the last part of the eighth millennium BC (Todd, 1982), at a site in the south of the island called Kalavassos-Tenta. This means that the earliest Cypriots, on the present evidence, were Neolithic farmers.

It has been suggested that these first farmers arrived from the Levantine mainland, complete with their culture and their domestic animals, built small round houses with stone-rubble and mud-brick walls, and settled down on the virgin land, on the southern slopes a few miles from the sea. But we must be cautious of this interpretation. An alternative possibility is that there were much earlier inhabitants who gradually developed the culture we have unearthed at Tenta and elsewhere. Instead of being suddenly imported, it may have been slowly home-grown.

When considering such alternatives it is essential to remember that, with archaeological evidence, we are always dealing with tiny, almost random fragments of the past. A map of archaeological sites is not a map of human settlement, it is a record of where excavations and surveys have taken place. Although this is obvious enough, it is often overlooked in arguments about movements of early human populations. A lucky find, a new dig, an

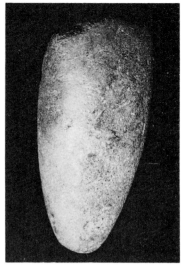

Pl. 1

Pl. 2

Pl. 3

Pls. 1 to 3 Neolithic stone hand-axes. *Andesite.*

1 *Length 15.7 cm (DM-ST-01).*
2 *Length 7.5 cm (DM-ST-02).*
3 *Length 8 cm (DM-ST-03).Cf. Dikaios 1953, Pl. LXXXIII.*

arbitrary preference of an individual archaeologist, can overnight change the whole picture.

This has certainly been the case in the story of early Cyprus. Up until the 1920s it was believed that even the Neolithic phase was missing from the island. Then a Swedish project unearthed the first evidence of it, on a tiny offshore island called Petra tou Limniti, in the north-west. In the 1940s attention was turned to the south coast, and the hillside settlement of Khirokitia was uncovered, revealing a major site of great importance that pushed man's 'arrival' on Cyprus back even further.

The Khirokitia people lived in small circular houses, used stone vessels and, with a singular lack of hygiene, buried their dead beneath the floor of their dwellings. They ate deer, sheep, goat and pig; also grain, lentils, beans, and peas. For some reason they artificially deformed the shape of their children's skulls. Among the precious possessions of the Khirokitians were imported Anatolian obsidian and Levantine carnelian, though how they obtained these is not known.

The date for this early settlement of farmers was originally given as the fourth millennium BC (Dikaios, 1953), but when accurate carbon-dating was carried out, this had to be radically altered to the sixth millennium BC. Now, with the latest evidence from nearby Tenta, the 'earliest' figure for Cypriot habitation has had to be raised yet again.

To sum up, since the 1920s, the 'earliest' occupation of Cyprus has risen dramatically from the third, to the fourth, to the sixth and finally to the eighth millennium BC. The obvious conclusion is that it will continue to rise as new sites are excavated and that it may well extend back into the Palaeolithic and even beyond. With an island as attractive as Cyprus visible from the surrounding mainland it seems inconceivable that early man should have ignored it for so long. The Khirokitians may eventually prove to be latecomers inheriting a long, indigenous tradition.

The 3,000-year-long Neolithic period, as it is known at present, is divided into two main phases, the major difference between them being the replacement of stone vessels with pottery. Careful studies of the later Neolithic sites, such as Ayios Epiktitos-Vrysi in the north and Sotira in the south, have revealed that, around the middle of the fifth millennium BC, new arrivals began to appear from the mainland. In addition to introducing painted and combed pottery, these newcomers also brought with them certain architectural innovations. At the hilltop settlement of Sotira, for example, rectangular, oval and irregular shaped houses occur as well as the more ancient, circular ones, and there was a separate cemetery sited lower down the hill, away from the main dwellings. Grapes and olives were added to the diet. Little contact with the outside world seems to have occurred during the course of this second phase of the Neolithic.

The Copper Age

At the end of the Neolithic, shortly after 4000 BC, there were violent earthquakes, followed by the abandonment of the old Neolithic II villages, and a major change in the pattern of settlement with the western part of the island, hitherto uninhabited, becoming the most important region. Stone and mud-brick buildings were given up in favour of lighter constructions based on circular hollows, possibly as a precaution against further earthquakes. More newcomers arrived on the island, mixing with the older inhabitants. It seems likely that some of these, coming from the Anatolian mainland north of Cyprus, were already experienced in metal-production, and for the first time a few metal objects appear on the island, heralding the start of the Chalcolithic, or Copper Age.

In truth, it is something of a joke to refer to this phase of Cypriot prehistory as a 'Copper Age', when the evidence for metal activity is assembled and examined with cold objectivity. The entire copper collection consists, so far, of (1) a fragment of a chisel; (2) a whole chisel; (3) a blade fragment; (4) a hook; and (5) a twisted spiral earring. That is all, from a period of nearly a thousand years, and there is no evidence whatever that any of these objects was locally made, rather than brought over from the mainland by one of the 'New Cypriots'. It might be argued that, on such a slender basis, it would be more scholarly to refer to the Cypriot Copper Age as Neolithic III, until some definite evidence of local copper production has been uncovered. It seems little short of what has been termed 'romantic archaeology' to set up a major cultural phase on the basis of five scraps of metal in a millennium.

This does not mean, of course, that there *was* no Copper Age on Cyprus—merely that the evidence for it remains to be established. It is entirely possible that the new immigrants from Anatolia may have cast envious metallurgical eyes on the strangely coloured outcroppings of metallic rock scattered over certain areas of the island's surface, and started in a modest way to mine for precious copper. Merrillees (in press) has put forward a persuasive argument in favour of early local copper production, pointing out that the complex business of roasting the copper ore was not necessary. A much simpler method of copper extraction, which does not involve a great deal of manpower or organization, would have been the leaching process of treating the ore with water. This would have posed little difficulty even for a technologically simple culture, and although it may have occurred late in what we call the 'Chalcolithic' phase, it may nevertheless have been a local invention rather than a foreign import.

One day we may find the facts to support this theory and at last give respectability to the 'Copper Age' title, but at the present time we know far too little of this crucial period in Cypriot prehistory to be sure about the speed with which the island's (later famous) copper industry developed. We do know, however, that the people living on the island in the fourth millennium BC had another intriguing cultural achievement to their credit—in the realm of the arts. This concerns the development of a highly refined and uniquely Cypriot artefact—the Cruciform Figurine (see p. 122). These miniature sculptures in polished greenstone show a remarkably rigid degree of stylization and a sophistication of shape and surface finish. Their uniformity and lack of mainland parallels reflect a local culture, especially in the western region of the island, which had developed a character of its own and a degree of independence from the repeated injections of mainland influence.

The Bronze Age

The end of the Copper Age and the transition to the important Bronze Age are not well understood. There appears to have been another major catastrophe of some kind, when, once again, many settlements were deserted. It may have been a plague of locusts, an intense drought or an epidemic of some kind. As yet we cannot be certain, and some authorities (Stanley-Price, 1979) scorn 'catastrophism' as a major source of cultural change: 'The context in which catastrophic explanations have usually been proposed is the apparently simultaneous abandonment of all sites of a phase ... [but] ... it is debatable whether any natural catastrophe could be so devastating as to cause abandonments on that scale ...' Instead, he believes that 'the "gaps" in the sequence that appear to require explanation in catastrophic terms may simply be artifacts of the taxonomies in force'.

Such a view, that emphasizes an inadequacy in archaeological knowledge as the explanation, must be given serious consideration, but in this particular case it is worth pointing out that wholesale abandonment of settlements is not so far-fetched for a small, probably superstition-ridden society faced with some dramatically baffling misfortune, such as an epidemic, a plague of locusts, or a massive earthquake. Such events could have sent a wave of panic through the early Cypriots, and, in seeking a magico-religious explanation, they may easily have settled for 'something evil' in their old ways, and felt a widespread need to move to new ground to appease the wrath of the angry gods. So, for the moment the question must remain open.

We do know, however, with some certainty, that disasters *were* taking place in Anatolia, a short distance to the north of Cyprus. There, early in the third millennium BC, marauding hordes were sweeping across the land, laying waste huge areas and creating a large, terrified refugee population. Part of this population appears to have made its way across the narrow, forty-four mile strip of sea to land on the northern coasts of Cyprus. There they moved inland along the Ovgos River valley to establish what has been called the Philia Culture. They brought with them from the mainland new styles of polished pottery, new forms of burial, and most importantly, a whole new technology of bronze metal production. The copper-rich foothills of the Troodos mountains in the west were soon to give them a special advantage, and the Cypriot Early Bronze Age became a period of cultural affluence which was reflected in the bold inventiveness of the ceramic art of this phase of the island's prehistory.

It would be wrong to think of this as an 'invasion', or a cultural 'take-over' of the island. The Anatolian pottery styles and wares

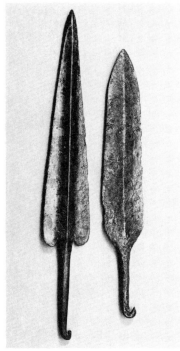

Pl. 4

Pl. 5

Pl. 4 Rat-tanged pointed blades. *Bronze.*

a(left) *Early to Middle Bronze Age. Length 27.5 cm (DM-ME-05).Cf. Catling 1964, Fig. 1, nos. 6 and 7, Fig. 2, nos. 1-6.*

b(right) *Late Bronze Age. Length 22.4 cm (DM-ME-06). Cf. Catling 1964, Fig. 13, nos. 3-7.*

Pl. 5 Pinch–spring depilatory tweezers. *Bronze. Early to Middle Bronze Age. Length 14.1 cm (DM-ME-17). Catling 1964, Fig. 5, no. 9.*

that these newcomers brought with them were quickly modified and transformed into something distinctly and uniquely Cypriot. Also, there is little evidence of violence or warfare, and the new arrivals seem to have joined peacefully with the indigenous population to forge the new Bronze Age culture of Cyprus.

Sadly, almost all our knowledge of this exciting period comes from the examination of the tombs and cemeteries of the Early Bronze Age. Of the settlements we know next to nothing, either because of bad luck in locating them, or because the buildings and villages constructed in this phase were architecturally of an unusually ephemeral nature. We know a great deal about the much earlier Neolithic settlements because of the liberal use of stones in the building at such sites as Khirokitia, but if the newcomers favoured lightweight, earthquake-safe huts, the remains of these flimsy dwellings must quickly have vanished, especially when built on sloping ground such as the foothills of the Kyrenia mountains. Bearing in mind that the island was much more thickly wooded in those days and that the climate was so hospitable, an all-wood construction for these settlements, perhaps augmented by stretched animal-skins, does not seem unlikely. In addition, the apparently peaceful atmosphere of the thinly populated island would also mean that heavier, defensive structures would not be needed. The discovery of tombs with mixtures of the new pottery alongside the older, Chalcolithic wares seems to underline the peaceful co-existence and mingling of the two populations. And the art produced by these quietly merging peoples also testifies to the happily creative and pastoral mood of the community. The violent elements (such as sacrifices and weapons) seen in their art by some observers are almost certainly misinterpretations, as will be discussed later.

During this Early Bronze Age, cultural affluence led to the provision of huge quantities of grave-goods to accompany the corpse. Pottery production flourished alongside the developing metallurgy, and we are lucky that large 'scenic vessels' (see p. 264) were produced, depicting the everyday activities of these prehistoric Cypriots. Because of the absence of other kinds of evidence, from settlement excavations or written records, these vessels are of especial importance in our understanding of the lives of these aesthet-

ically exuberant islanders.

Two significant imports at this stage were cattle (for the first time in the island's history) and tin (probably from Anatolia, but possibly from Mesopotamia) to add to the copper in the process of making the tougher bronze implements.

Painstakingly rock-cut tombs were hewn for the dead, with cave-like chambers approached by an entrance passage, and sealed by a large stone slab. During the thousands of years that have passed since these chambers were sealed, the island has experienced many major earthquakes. There were eighteen, for example, between AD 1911 and AD 1963 (according to Ambraseys, 1963). As a result, the contents of the tombs have often been badly shaken. Cracks have appeared in the tomb-walls and in many cases water has seeped in, filling the cavity with each winter storm and then draining out again. During this process, repeated time and again, unbroken vessels among the grave-goods must have bobbed about as the waters rose and fell, disturbing the neat arrangement within the tomb and destroying any hope of dating 'layers' of remains where there have been multiple burials. The extent of the jumbling up of artefacts in this way has not always been taken into account sufficiently, but despite the difficulties it creates we have by now a fairly clear picture of the major pottery sequences as the Bronze Age moves through its various phases.

The Early Bronze Age, once thought to have lasted for only two centuries, is now estimated to have stretched over almost a whole millennium—roughly the third millennium BC. It is dominated by polished ware pottery, usually Red Polished, but with many variants (see pp. 17-23). There then follows a transitional Middle Bronze Age of about three centuries' duration, during which the polished ware pottery goes into a steep decline, to be replaced by a Black Slip Ware, a Red-on-Black Ware, and, in particular, a White Painted Ware. The vessels become generally smaller and 'cosier', charming but less impressive. They are still handmade, although several wheelmade pottery imports have been found from this period, coming largely from the Syrian and Palestinian region. For some reason, the wheel, as a new invention, did not manage to make inroads on Cyprus at this stage of its prehistory despite the presence of these foreign examples.

The peaceful stability of the Early Bronze Age becomes disturbed during the Middle Bronze Age. Fortifications appear among the architectural features. As these are inland rather than coastal, they appear to be concerned with internal strife of some kind, rather than defence against foreign attackers or invaders. It is believed that, at times, the copper-rich west of the island was in a state of confrontation with the more agricultural east. There is no evidence that this ever developed into a state of war, but there was clearly tension and the threat of violence.

Architecture became much more ambitious, with rectangular, box-like shapes to the rooms, which were sometimes of an impressive size. One dwelling boasted a double storey, another had ten rooms. The walls were often much thicker, but were still built of the old materials—stone rubble at the base and then, above that, mud-bricks. The different rooms in a Middle Bronze Age house had different functions. In this respect, we have arrived at a period of prehistory when the domestic arrangements are starting to approximate to the modern condition.

Trade was beginning to increase with populations on the mainland. Among the imports of this period were horses and donkeys. A few depictions of equine-like animals have been found in the Early Bronze Age, but they were obviously rare then and did not become important before the end of the Bronze Age phase.

This state of affairs was to herald a period of major international significance for Cyprus—the Late Bronze Age. This was the time when metal production on the island grew and flourished as a vitally important prehistoric industry. Overseas trade reached new heights, and Cypriot pottery of this period has been found in large quantities on the mainland (see Merrillees, 1968). The period covered roughly the second half of the second millennium BC, and it can justly be described as the first truly urban period in the island's story, with large towns and cities such as Enkomi and Kition growing up in the coastal region. Trade and commerce, imports and exports, and a vigorous air of business and bustle were typical of this phase. Jewellery, faience and ivories were produced, under the influence of importations from Egypt, Syria and the Aegean.

The Bronze Age Cypriot potters at this stage made two distinctive wares—Base Ring Ware and White Slip Ware, but these were eventually joined by large quantities of Mycenaean vessels, as a more and more intrusive Greek presence appeared on the island. The Hellenizing process was not, however, a violent one. Friendly trading relations were maintained and even the old antagonisms between the eastern and western parts of the island were submerged in the new prosperity. In many ways, Cyprus was coming of age.

Many of the traders remained and settled on the island, adding their special skills to those of the indigenous population. The potter's wheel became a significant new feature. Before, it had been rejected, but now this important technological innovation was gradually accepted. It was during this phase that, for the Cypriots, prehistory became history, with the introduction of writing in the form of a Cypro-Minoan syllabic script (as yet undeciphered). This vital new trend began as early as the fifteenth century BC.

As the international fame of Cyprus began to spread it started to attract unwelcome attentions. The earlier visitors such as the Minoans and the Mycenaeans had been peaceful traders, but as the years passed pirates and raiders appeared on the scene, attracted by the rich pickings. Later, in the first part of the twelfth century BC, there was a massive influx of 'Sea Peoples', who devastated the coastal cities. After this, in the eleventh century BC, more and more Aegeans arrived, often as refugees, and settled on Cyprus, steadily increasing the Hellenic influence and leading eventually to almost complete Greek domination of the Cypriot culture.

Then, around 1050 BC, there was another moment of major disaster for the island. Huge earthquakes shook the land and destroyed the rebuilt cities such as Enkomi and Kition. They were largely abandoned and important new settlements were established at Salamis, Paphos and Soloi. The prehistoric Bronze Age was about to metamorphose into the historic Iron Age, Greek-inspired and culturally Hellenic.

The Iron Age

From around 1000 BC, the Cypriot scene changed radically. The Greek colonizers had brought with them their own cultural patterns, their religious beliefs and rituals, their architecture, their language and their ideas.

Pl. 6

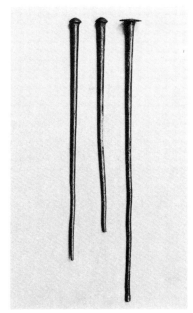

Pl. 7

Pl. 6 Pointed blades with pierced attachment holes. *Bronze. Early to Middle Bronze Age.*
a(left) *Length 21.5 cm (DM-ME-07).*
b(right, above) *Length 10.6 cm (DM-ME-14).*
c(right, below) *Length 8.7 cm (DM-ME-15). Cf. Catling 1964, Fig. 3.*

Pl. 7 Long Pins. *Bronze. Early to Middle Bronze Age.*
a(left) *Length 17.9 cm (DM-ME-22).*
b(centre) *Length 15.9 cm (DM-ME-25).*
c(right) *Length 21 cm. (DM-ME-21). Cf. Catling 1964, Fig. 5, no. 14.*

But they were not really interested in keeping political links with Greece itself. Instead they established what amounted to city-kingdoms where they were their own masters.

Following the switch from bronze to iron as the mainstay metal, and the therefore greatly reduced requirement for copper, the island declined rapidly in importance as a major trading centre. Pottery production remained high, however, and the first period of the Iron Age is known as the Cypro-Geometric, because of the abstract and highly geometrical designs on the typical, wheel-made White Painted Ware and Bichrome Ware.

During the roughly three centuries of the Cypro-Geometric period, ending in the middle of the eighth century BC, there was a major new intrusion into Cypriot culture in the form of the Phoenicians from nearby Tyre. They were the new super-merchants of the Mediterranean, seafaring salesmen and traders, who were setting up business centres all around the sea-coasts of the ancient world, and they could hardly ignore the island of Cyprus, right on their doorstep. They were not invaders, but rather infiltrators, and they soon established a number of important trading posts on the island, especially at Kition, where they moved in during the ninth century BC. They redeveloped the ancient city, built temples to Astarte and were soon busily introducing their unpleasant traditions of animal sacrifice, sacred prostitution and hard dealing. The question of just how far they colonized the island is still hotly debated, and earlier ideas that the extent of their take-over was impressive have recently been revised. It is now thought that they were very much the middlemen of Mediterranean trade rather than cultural colonizers. Their presence on Cyprus appears to have been maintained alongside that of the Greeks on the basis of a mutual wariness rather than out-and-out friendship or hostility.

Despite these revised ideas, there must have been a sufficient Phoenician presence to account for the fact that, towards the end of the Cypro-Geometric period, Cyprus had to pay tribute to Assyria. This seems to have come about because Phoenicia itself owed tribute to Assyria, and Cyprus as a Phoenician outpost was dragged into the same arrangement. This rather remote take-over bid for the island did not, however, involve any close contacts or cultural penetrations. The

subjugation of the local rulers of Cyprus to a foreign power was little more than a formality, although at a later date they did join the Assyrians in a military expedition against Egypt. But it was a sinister hint of what the future had in store for Cyprus, for, from this date on, the islanders would seldom be left in peace by foreign powers. It became a perpetual 'province', forever being lost and won by dominant nations in their bids for strategic territories. After the Assyrians it became Egyptian, then Persian, then Greek, then Ptolemaic, then Roman, then Byzantine, then Lusignan, then Venetian, then Turkish, then British until, at long last, in 1960, the island achieved its independence as part of the global trend towards de-colonization that gained momentum after the Second World War.

This book is not the place to pursue in any detail the endless bickerings and battles, power struggles and subjugations, which make up the early historic period of the island's long story. My concern is with the art of the island, and that, sadly, became increasingly influenced by foreign styles and techniques. The uniquely Cypriot art objects of the Copper and Bronze Ages find few parallels in the Iron Age. The introduction of the pottery wheel transformed ceramics from an art form into an industry, with the aesthetically blunting effect of mass-production lurking in the wings. The lovingly handmade vessels and figurines of the Bronze Age became the production-line products of the aggressive, urbanized Iron Age.

All was not lost, however. Despite the foreign influences, the Cypriot artists persisted in modifying and adapting their work and giving it, at least, a local flavour. The White Painted and Bichrome Ware of the Cypro-Geometric period blossomed in the next phase, the Archaic Period, from 700 to 475 BC. Abstract, geometric designs gradually lost ground to pictorial representations. Botanical and zoological subjects dominated, with lotus flowers and birds being among the top favourites for these new 'free-field' artists. So, although the vessels themselves may have become rather boring and repetitive in design, they survived aesthetically because of the decorations painted on them. The clay that had been converted into pieces of sculpture by the Bronze Age potters, as they fashioned their idiosyncratically shaped vessels, was now little more than a 'canvas' on which the Iron Age artists could paint their pictures.

Figurines did not fare much better. The delightful plank figures of the Bronze Age became slap-happy 'snowman' figures in the Iron Age—charming but casually clumsy.

As the Archaic period gave way to the Classic Period which ran from 475 to 325 BC, external influences on the art of Cyprus grew even stronger, and much that was produced was a poor imitation of mainland styles. With the following Hellenistic and Roman periods this process intensified, and even the local flavour that had been added to the foreign works in the past was greatly reduced. This is not to say that Cyprus was devoid of art, far from it. But it was so derivative that, if we are interested in that type of art, we would do better to turn to the central Greek and Roman products, rather than the provincial offshoots of distant colonies such as Cyprus.

I admit to a personal bias in making these statements. There may be those who find the earlier Bronze Age art objects too primitive for their tastes and would prefer even colonially diluted Greek and Roman artefacts. For them, I fear, the pages which follow will seem unusually biased towards the earlier phase of Cypriot art. My justification is that, whether my preference for the Bronze Age period is accepted or not it does remain the most truly Cypriot phase of the island's artistic history, when local innovations came to dominate more than at any other time. That alone justifies the large proportion of the book which is devoted to these early, prehistoric works of art.

There remains the question of precise dates for the various epochs and their sub-divisions. As already hinted, there have been—and still are—heated debates about certain of the dates. After studying more than twenty different published chronological tables, I have arrived at what I consider to be the best set of figures available at present.

Some comments are needed to justify these dates. The start of the Neolithic, given here as 7000+ BC, is higher than in any previous table because I have taken note of Todd's recent (1982) radiocarbon dates for Kalavassos-Tenta. Up until the mid-1970s the figure given was nearly always 5600 BC. It then rose to 7000 BC in the late 1970s and now requires a further increase. As mentioned earlier, it will doubtless soon require further increases as new evidence appears.

Cypriot Chronology

| NEOLITHIC | 7000+ to 4000 BC |
| CHALCOLITHIC | 4000 to 2500★ |

BRONZE AGE	
Early	
I	2700 to 2075
II	2075 to 2000
III	2000 to 1900
Middle	
I	1900 to 1800
II	1800 to 1725
III	1725 to 1650
Late	
Ia	1650 to 1575
Ib	1575 to 1475
IIa	1475 to 1400
IIb	1400 to 1325
IIc	1325 to 1225
IIIa	1225 to 1190
IIIb	1190 to 1150
IIIc	1150 to 1050

IRON AGE	
Cypro-Geometric	
I	1050 to 950
II	950 to 850
III	850 to 750
Cypro-Archaic	
I	750 to 600
II	600 to 475
Cypro-Classical	
I	475 to 400
II	400 to 325
Hellenistic	
I	325 to 150
II	150 to 50
Roman	
I	50 BC to AD 150
II	AD 150 to AD 250
III	AD 250 to AD 350

The authorities followed in this chronological table are as follows: Todd (1982) for the start of the Neolithic; Peltenburg (1981) for the Chalcolithic and the start of the Early Bronze Age; and Karageorghis (1982, Table A) for the remainder.

★ *This figure overlaps with the start of the next epoch because Chalcolithic settlements survived in parts of the island after the start of the Bronze Age.*

The start of the Chalcolithic is taken from Peltenburg (1981). Earlier tables gave 3000 BC and then 3500 BC for this point, but these figures are no longer acceptable in the light of what follows.

The start of the Early Bronze Age is the most controversial date of all. For a long time it was given as 2300 BC, until, in 1974, Mellaart, the Anatolian specialist, presented evidence for a much higher figure. Pointing out that the Philia Culture, which is the earliest manifestation of the Bronze Age in Cyprus, was time-linked to widespread destructions in Anatolia, leading to the exodus to Philia and other northern Cypriot sites, he insisted on a higher figure because of new information concerning corrected dates in Anatolia itself. These new facts, he says, 'suggest that the beginning of the Early Bronze Age in Cyprus would have occurred somewhere around 3100-3000 BC, if not even earlier'. Other calibrated dates, he adds, 'suggest that the Cypriote EBA ended soon after 2000 BC'.

Mellaart's drastic re-dating came as something of a shock to Cypriot specialists, who were slow to react. He was ignored by Brown and Catling (1975), Yon (1976), Karageorghis (1976), Merrillees (1977) and Tatton-Brown (1979). Then, in 1980, Gjerstad added his weight to the earlier figure, giving it as 3000-2900 BC, based on radiocarbon dating corrected by dendrochronological calibration. He quotes the exact figure as 2980 BC and it therefore seems reasonable to combine his figures with those of Mellaart, to produce a rounded date of 3000 BC for the start of the Early Bronze Age in Cyprus, assuming that their earlier dating is correct.

In his 1981 and 1982 publications, Karageorghis reacts to this problem by presenting two tables, A and B, and leaving it to his readers to make their own choice. Table A appeals to the more orthodox; table B to those who favour Mellaart and Gjerstad's datings. He also mentions the cunning diplomatic solution put forward by certain authorities who feel that the Philia Culture should be removed to the Chalcolithic age. In this way, Philia matches up with the new 'early' dates from Anatolia, without having to alter the now hallowed dating for the Cypriot Bronze Age. But to solve the problem by placing the Red Polished Ware of the Philia

Culture with the Chalcolithic, and separating it from the Red Polished Ware of the Early Bronze Age seems a trifle perverse. If the earlier figures really are correct, it is better to admit that mistaken dates have been repeated time and again, forget them and make a fresh start, defining the EBA of Cyprus as running from 3000 to 1900 BC. Were he alive today, this would bring a smile to the face of Sir John Myres who, long ago in 1914, gave the dates for the Cypriot Early Bronze Age as 'About 3000-2000 BC'. After much scholarship, by 1980 the wheel had turned full circle.

The debate did not stop there, however. Mellaart had second thoughts about his high dates, and Gjerstad's figure for the start of the Early Bronze Age was said to have been based on calibration errors. A modification was called for and Peltenburg (1981) suggested a date of 2700 BC for the start of the Cypriot Bronze Age. This is the one which is followed here, although I suspect we have not heard the last word on the subject.

The start of the Middle Bronze Age has been given variously as 1800, 1850, 1900 and 2000 BC. It seems safest here to follow Karageorghis (1982) with his compromise figure of 1900 BC.

After this there are very few differences of opinion about dates because there is more precise information available, and the discrepancies that do occur between the different tables are so trivial that they do not merit discussion here. For all these later dates I am following Karageorghis (1982).

II Vessels

A cynic once described archaeology as 'the study of second-hand crockery'. This joke definition underlines two important points. First, the ancient art we have available to us today does display a remarkably high proportion of pottery vessels. This is partly due to the fact that fired clay is so indestructible. Even when smashed to pieces, the vessels survive as pottery sherds that are easy to analyse. It is also partly due to the fact that most tomb goods were required to perform two functions: they had to be 'special' to honour the dead by their high quality, and they had to contain sustenance for the long journey to the other world. In other words there was a social pressure on mourners, when placing objects inside a tomb, to make their offerings both beautiful and at the same time capable of containing food or drink. This pressure led inevitably to a preponderance of carefully fashioned vessels, and it elevated ceramics into a much more dominant art form than it is today.

Second, the use of the word 'crockery' helps to emphasize the great difference between the ancient pottery vessels and the modern ones we use today. To the prehistoric potter, each vessel was like a hollow piece of sculpture, to be lovingly and individually shaped and decorated. Even after the advent of the wheel, the surface was still treated like a background for a special painting. As a result most of the ancient vessels that have come down to us can be treated as significant works of art, just as important as the figurines, idols and jewellery.

Despite this, many archaeologists tend to look upon ancient vessels simply as 'markers'. Instead of considering them in terms of archaeo-aesthetics, as works of art valuable for their own sake, they use them merely as convenient signs of cultural affinity, dispersal, movement and trade. I have heard it said that an ancient vessel without a provenance is 'of no archaeological value whatever'. This highlights the way in which the tail has come to wag the dog, in some archaeological circles. It is rather like students of Rembrandt telling us that the main value of his paintings lies in what they can tell us about the social life of seventeenth-century Holland, or, even more narrowly, about the chemistry of pigments. The most important feature of ancient works of art is that they *are* works of art. All other considerations, although they may be of enormous interest, are secondary.

With this in mind, it is worth asking who made the vessels and under what circumstances. Who *were* these early artists? Here it is necessary to make a distinction between handmade and wheelmade vessels. We know from anthropological studies of modern tribal communities that handmade pottery is typically produced by women and wheelmade pottery by men. It seems as if the process of handmaking pottery is somehow more akin to such activities as making and baking bread (kneading dough into special shapes = kneading clay; baking bread in oven = firing clay in oven) or decorating clothing (many of the incised and painted patterns are reminiscent of textile patterns), which are usually carried out by females. The social role of the pottery artist in early, pre-wheel communities is therefore essentially feminine.

Once the technology of the potter's wheel has arrived on the scene the process of making pots becomes more one of 'machine operation' and production-line efficiency, and the males take over the social role of pottery artists. The aesthetic qualities of the vessels suffer from this mass-production process, and they become more crudely 'run-of-the-wheel' objects. Now, their aesthetic value is transferred to the paintings upon their surfaces, and it is possible that many of these were also done by the women, in ancient times, as often happens today.

Despite this comparative evidence from many tribal studies, Cypriot archaeologists have persistently referred to the ancient artist of Cyprus as 'he'. For example: 'there may be instances when the potter simply wished to produce extraordinary and elaborately decorated vessels for *his* rich clients'. (The italics are mine.) This is Karageorghis (1982) writing about the exceptional vessels produced in the Early Bronze Age. He is not alone in this 'retrospective error', and even female archaeologists have recoiled from my suggestion that all the greatest and most original art to come out of the Cypriot soil (that is to say, the Early Bronze Age artefacts) were produced by women. What would seem obvious to an anthropologist seems somehow reckless to an archaeologist. Nevertheless I must insist, in this volume at least, on referring to all pre-Late Bronze Age potters as 'she'. To refuse to do this simply to follow tradition would be to fly in the face of the impressive indirect tribal evidence.

Strangely, once the idea of female prehistoric potters has been accepted, the nature of the Early and Middle Bronze Age vessels and figurines becomes easier to understand. Although their context is mainly funereal, they have about them a warm domesticity. The scenes shown on the larger vessels are essentially depictions of domestic village and farm life, with people performing their daily tasks—washing clothes, grinding corn, holding babies. There are no brave warriors, no signs of masculine status displays. These do not appear until after the wheel has arrived in Cyprus and the potters have become male—in the Late Bronze Age and the Iron Age.

What role did these early potters have in society? Again, looking at modern tribal comparisons, it seems likely that they were village specialists respected for their skills, who provided their services at two levels.

Ordinary, everday pottery would be produced rather simply, for house use, and in addition there would be 'special pieces' made for important funerals. Many of the tomb-goods are clearly not intended for everyday use. They are too elaborate for ordinary eating and drinking. In some instances, for example, the spouts point in different directions, so that it is impossible to pour from them in the usual way (see Figs. 26-8 and Pl. 164). They have clearly been designed to honour the dead by their inventiveness, complexity and ornateness.

It is relevant to add here the observations of Weinberg (1966), who compared pottery found at an early Cypriot settlement with that located in the nearby cemetery. He found that there was 'little correlation between the pottery from the two areas'. The settlement pottery was well fired and made in useful shapes. The cemetery pottery was less well fired, often too heavy for daily use, too elaborate in design, and 'too bizarre to be practical for domestic use'. He concludes that 'most, if not all, of the Early Cypriote pottery found in tombs, was made specifically for offerings in graves'. The difference in firing is interesting because it implies that the potters working on funeral pieces made them 'fancy but not tough', since they were intended for display but not for repeated use. In other words, they made them as beautiful as possible, but did not care whether they lasted beyond the one great 'burial meal'.

How surprised they would be, then, to find their works of art, carefully restored, sitting in the glass cases of our museums, thousands of years later, when all they had intended was to provide something as decorative and almost as ephemeral as a wreath of flowers on a modern grave. This may also explain why some objects, such as sheath-knives (see p. 257), were provided in the tombs in the form of pottery copies of the real implements. If less care was taken with the firing of tomb pottery, this meant that the villagers were, to some extent, acting out a scene for the deceased. They wanted to make a great show of the event of burying the body, but why waste time firing something very carefully when it was only going to be used once. Similarly, why waste a perfectly good sheath-knife, when the deceased would be just as happy with a pottery substitute?

The Pottery Wares

Before considering the specialized features of the ancient Cypriot vessels, it is necessary to recognize that we are dealing, not with a single ceramic tradition, but many. Each ceramic style, or ware, can be defined by a number of properties, which include:

1 The type of clay used.
2 The way it was worked into shape.
3 The kind of surface-covering applied.
4 The form of decoration added.
5 The manner in which it was fired.
6 The shape of the finished vessel.

There has been little consistency in naming the different wares. Sometimes one property is used, sometimes another, depending on which feature first caught the eye of the ceramic taxonomist. For example, property 3 was employed when naming such wares as Red Polished, Black Polished, Black Slip, Bichrome and Black-on-Red; property 6 was the basis for naming Base Ring Ware. But it must be remembered that these names are no more than convenient labels. In each case the un-named properties are also important and a ware can only be properly and fully defined by all its qualities. This explains why some people are puzzled to find, for example, a piece of Base Ring Ware that has no base ring. The explanation is that it possesses all the other properties of the ware and just happens to be exceptional in the one feature which was selected for the title of that particular ware.

In looking at the major Cypriot wares one by one, on the following pages, it is important to remember, therefore, that a number of features have been considered when classifying each piece. It should also be remembered that each of these major wares lasted for many years, usually for centuries, and there are inevitably a number of variant forms, differing only in minor ways. Inevitably this leads to the problem of deciding when a variant is important enough to be considered as a distinct ware. Wherever there are doubts or differences of opinion on such a point, these will be mentioned.

The earliest wares of all—those from the Neolithic and Chalcolithic periods—are extremely rare as complete vessels, and are excluded from this section. Bronze Age and Iron Age vessels, by contrast, are known in their thousands, and it is these that are discussed on the pages that follow.

1 Red Polished Ware

This is the dominant ware of the Early Bronze Age. The clay was covered with red slip which was then burnished to produce a high polish. Today, even in damaged vessels, this shiny polish usually survives, creating glinting highlights.

As already mentioned, the decorative examples of Red Polished Ware found in the tombs are rather poorly fired, compared with utilitarian pottery. Modern potters fire their vessels at 950° C, whereas the ancient ceramicists used less than 600° C for funerary ware (MacLaurin, 1980).

There are a number of variant forms of Red Polished Ware. Some of these appear to be local varieties—what might be called Red Polished 'dialects'—and others seem to be little more than individual idiosyncracies. Some authorities have favoured attempts to place these variants in a temporal sequence, as if one fashion was followed by another, but there is comparatively little to support this. Indeed, the process has included some rather unhappy misunderstandings, as MacLaurin (1980) has pointed out: 'Gjerstad carried on using Myres' nomenclature but refined this by introducing a typology into the system, terming the pottery Red Polished I, II, III, IV, which, for no apparent reason, came to be given chronological significance.' Certainly, today, most people imagine that RP II is later than RP I, and so on, and it is hard for some to believe that this was never intended to be the case. They were simply different types. It is better for the moment therefore to refrain from using such subdivisions, until the problem has been better resolved. Instead, to demonstrate the main varieties of Red Polished Ware, four major sub-divisions are presented here based on important differences in shape and decoration. This Red Polished 'family' has a number of close relations, with black areas added to the red. These could be treated as further variants but, for a number of reasons, they are being considered here as separate wares.

1a Philia Red Polished Ware

Pl. 8 *Early Bronze Age.*
a(left) *Bottle, flat base, plain. Ht. 12.3 cm (DM-PHRP-03).*
b(centre) *Incised jug with flat base, beak spout and small lug-handle. Motifs: multi-zigzag and open herring-bone bands. Ht. 19.5 cm. Formerly in the Bomford Collection (DM-PHRP-01).*
c(right) *Incised bottle, round base, two pierced holes together below rim. Motifs: multi-zigzag and open herring-bone bands, also batches of multi-lines on base. Ht. 10.9 cm (DM-PHRP-02).Cf. SCE IV. 1a, Fig. XCVIII, nos. 10 and 11.*

Pl. 8

1b Plain Red Polished Ware

Pl. 9 *Early Bronze Age.*
Left to right
a *Jug with round base.and round spout. Ht. 12.6 cm (DM-PRP-02).*
b *Bowl with round base, beak lug and trough spout. Diam. 10.8 cm (DM-PRP-29).*
c *Jug with nipple base, cutaway spout and paired, blunt projections near handle attachment-points. Ht. 27.5 cm (DM-PRP-12).*
d *Jar with tripod base and two vertical handles. Coarse finish. Ht. 13 cm (DM-PRP-15). Cf. SCE IV. 1a, Fig. CXXII, no. 16.*
e *Jug with round base and cutaway spout. Ht. 17.8 cm (DM-PRP-06).*

Pl. 9

Pl. 10

Pl. 11

1c Incised Red Polished Ware.

Pl. 10 *Early Bronze Age.*
Left to right
a *Jug with slightly flattened base, cutaway-beak spout and side-spout. Decorations include deeply incised circle motifs typical of the Dhenia region. Ht. 30.5 cm (DM-IRP-49).*
b *Bowl with round base and single pierced lug. Diam. 9 cm. (DM-IRP-57).*
c *Jar with flat base, and two pointed handles. Ht. 32.1 cm (DM-IRP-56).*
d *Bottle with slightly flattened base and one pierced lug. Ht. 4.8 cm (DM-IRP-51).*
e *Jug with tripod base, cutaway-beak spout and lugs front and rear. Incisions made with multi-pronged implement. Ht. 14.5 cm. Ink lettering on base reads 'Bt. of Percy Christian 1897' (DM-IRP-50).*

1d Relief-decorated Red Polished Ware

Pl. 11 *Early Bronze Age.*
a(left) *Jug with round base, cutaway-beak spout and twenty-five pierced lugs. Relief-work imitating cords threaded through lugs. Relief elements interspersed with incised multi-zigzags. Handle restored. Ht. 27 cm (DM-RRP-08).*
b(centre) *Bowl with slightly flattened base and four large lugs. Relief-work imitating cord suspension net. The cords are interspersed with circular bosses. Diam. 34.3 cm (DM-RRP-16). Formerly in the Brew Collection.*
c(right) *Jug with nipple base and cutaway-beak spout. Relief-work cords round neck and body. Ht. 28 cm (DM-RRP-13).*

a Philia Red Polished Ware

This is the controversial ware seen by some as the work of Anatolian refugees arriving from the north and settling peacefully on the island, making their own pottery in their traditional styles, with elegantly elongated jugs supported by flat bases (e.g. Catling, 1971). Others prefer to see it as an 'inbred regional phenomenon'—an example of 'the Cypriote potter's unique skill in copying the forms and styles of imported artefacts' which found their way to the island 'by trade or as souvenirs' (Merrillees, 1975). Nobody is denying an Anatolian influence, but whether the Philia Ware was the result of local potters copying exciting imports, or whether the Anatolian immigrants actually set up a pottery of their own on Cyprus, remains a point of heated debate. Until we know more, it is worth remembering that, whichever scenario is the true one, the development of Red Polished quickly became a uniquely Cypriot affair that left its Anatolian origins far behind.

b Plain Red Polished Ware

This is less common than might be expected, because the Early Bronze Age potters were such compulsive decorators, and could hardly bear to leave a vessel alone after shaping it. But some of the simpler shapes, especially the small, hemispherical bowls, do have a completely plain red surface. This is not so much a local ware as a 'simple vessel' anywhere.

c Incised Red Polished Ware

This is the most typical form of Red Polished Ware. The incised lines are usually of seemingly abstract patterns, cut into the clay at the point when it is 'leather hard', before firing. After the incisions have been made they are usually rendered more conspicuous by the addition of a white in-filling. This makes them stand out clearly against the dark red background.

d Relief-Decorated Red Polished Ware

Some potters favoured a raised form of decoration, producing relief-lines which are sometimes totally abstract and sometimes appear to imitate strings or ropes on the vessels' surfaces. Occasionally both relief and incised decoration appear on the same vessel, but this is uncommon, as if each artist has a personal preference for one decorative mode or the other.

2 Mottled Red Polished Ware

Some vessels are irregularly mottled in red and black patches. Usually the dominant colour remains red, with the smaller irregularities being the black. MacLaurin (1980) comments: 'The mottling on the vessels is haphazard, with no particular pattern ... It is the result of sulphides burning out of the wood, rather than ash falling on the vessel during firing.' She includes mottled vessels under her category of Medium Ware Vessels, as distinct from Fine Ware Vessels, where 'mottling is the exception'. Although it is certainly true that the mottling is rather random in design, it does not appear to be a mere 'unwanted accident' of firing. Instead it seems to represent a case of aesthetic serendipity—a lucky accident that becomes cultivated for its attractive effect. Stewart (1962, p. 226) remarks that 'none of the bowls in this mottled fabric have black tops and interiors', a comment that seems to imply that the mottling was associated with a distinct style and was avoided by others.

3 Black-Topped Red Polished Ware

Many of the Early Bronze Age potters preferred a two-tone effect of a more striking kind than crude mottling. The typical form which this took was 'red-below/black-above', usually with black interiors where the vessels were of the open type, such as bowls. Sometimes the switch from red to black occurred about halfway up the vessel, but with bowls it was usually the rim alone which was blackened. The visual effect is highly decorative, and as an aesthetic technique it seems to have been used by a number of very different Early Bronze Age pottery workshops. A similar effect is seen on many of the Egyptian pre-dynastic vessels, but the technique may well have been discovered several times in different places, and it is by no means certain that 'black-topping' was an Egyptian import.

4 Red-and-Black Polished Ware

This localized form of Polished Ware was first identified by Herscher (1973) on the basis of twenty-two items. At the time she was writing, the only known pieces in this ware were: fifteen long-necked bottles; three shallow bowls; two deep bowls; one fragment from a deep bowl; one spindle whorl. Since that time about 200 further examples of the ware have come to light. Of these, I have been able to acquire 171. They are of particular interest for incision-pattern analysis because, as Herscher pointed out, it is possible to identify individual potters, and this aspect of the ware is dealt with in detail in a later chapter (see p. 322).

All pieces in this ware are decorated with incision patterns of a characteristic kind. These patterns differ in a number of ways from those found on the more familiar Incised Red Polished vessels, which reflects either an isolation from other potters, or a deliberate opposition to their styles of decoration. The firing is also highly distinctive. The distribution of the red and black regions of the vessel surfaces is irregular but predictable. Its arrangement gives each vessel the two-tone effect of a fruit ripened on one side by the sun. In other words, the division between red and black is more or less vertical but not in any neat geometric fashion. Occasionally a vessel is found which appears to be all black or all red, but turning it around always reveals at least a small patch of the opposing colour somewhere on the surface. The majority of vessels, however, display a roughly 50/50 balance between the two colours.

Herscher places this ware in 'the early part of the Middle Bronze Age'. Stewart (1962) had called it Red Polished IV and referred it to Middle Cypriot II or III. It clearly disturbed Herscher to place it this late in the sequence and she put it back to Middle Cypriot I. Both of them were basing their dating, rather rashly, on a single vessel—the only one for which we have a definite tombsource. The bottle in question was found in Tomb 6 at Ayios Iakovos. This is a tomb which contained eleven skeletons and had suffered from serious flooding, so that there was a high chance of strata-jumbling. To date an entire ware on such a dubious basis was, to say the least, cavalier. Herscher feels the need to qualify her statement: 'This Red-and-Black Polished ware must date to Middle Cypriot I to (early) II. ... Yet none of the degeneration characteristic of Red Polished IV ware has occurred: the shapes are generally well formed, the slip is evenly applied and highly lustrous, the decoration is well planned, the motifs highly developed, and the design carefully executed.' Because it so ob-

viously fails to fit the 'tail-end' of the Red Polished era, it might be better, at this stage, to label it simply as a striking local variant and leave the dating of it until there is some hard evidence available. In the end, it may even prove to be *earlier* than much of the typical Red Polished Ware. For example, I have in my collection two tulip bowls in Red-and-Black Polished Ware, and tulip bowls are supposed to have vanished somewhere in the middle of the Early Bronze Age sequence. Clearly something is awry here, and extreme caution in dating is the most becoming posture at present.

It may seem strange that such an issue is debatable when 200 examples of this ware have been brought to light, but it must be emphasized that all except the one mentioned above have appeared, unprovenanced, on the antiquities markets in London, Paris and elsewhere. All unofficial clues point to an exclusively Karpasian ware restricted entirely to the north-east peninsula. The homogeneity of the ware suggests a single village source, possibly a group of closely linked families, sharing the same designs and motifs, but adding personal oddities of style in each individual case. (For a further analysis of these aspects of the ware, see p. 340.) On the present scanty evidence, I can see no good reason why these potters should not have been working at the same time as the typical Red Polished Potters further to the west. To be certain, we must await further serious excavation in the north-east which may, I fear, be some years away.

5 Black-Bottomed Red Polished Ware

This contrasts strikingly with the common Black-Topped Red Polished Ware. As yet it is extremely rare and hardly justifies a separate category, but I have included it here to draw attention to its existence and because I suspect that it may become more common when further excavation has taken place. In the case of the long-necked bottle, the whole of the neck is red and the whole of the body is black. With the bowls, the lower interior is black and all the other surfaces are red. The two-tone arrangement appears to be very carefully contrived and may even have been a deliberate attempt to create a conspicuous contrast with the popular and widespread Black-Topped form.

2 Mottled Red Polished Ware.

Pl. 12 *Early Bronze Age.*
Left to right, front
a *Bowl with flat base, single pierced lug. Diam. 13.6 cm (DM-MRP-20).*
b *Bowl with round base, single pierced lug. Diam. 9.7 cm (DM-MRP-12).*
c *Jug with round base, squat neck and side spout. Ht. 14.1 cm (DM-MRP-07).*
Left to right, back
d *Jug with pointed base, cutaway-beak spout and single pierced lug. Incisions on body, relief-work on neck. Ht. 18.2 cm (DM-MRP-08). A unique feature of this jug is its heart-shaped body.*
e *Bowl with stem base and four rim-lugs, one of which is pierced with two holes. The tall stem is hollow. Ht. 16.2 cm. Diam. 19.2 cm (DM-MRP-22).*

Pl. 12

3 Black-topped Red Polished Ware

Pl. 13 *Early Bronze Age*
Left to right, front
a *Bowl with tulip base and two lugs. Diam. 11.5 cm (DM-BTRP-20).*
b *Bowl with stem base and two pierced (opposing) holes at rim. The artist has created a black body on a red stem. Ht. 11.6 cm. Diam. 6.1 cm (DM-BTRP-23). This vessel appears to be unique.*
c *Bowl with round base and single pierced lug. Diam. 14.8 cm (DM-BTRP-16).*
Left to right, back
d *Bottle with round base and two pierced holes at rim. Ht. 13 cm (DM-BTRP-01).*
e *Bowl with round base and single pierced lug, plain. Diam. 12.2 cm (DM-BTRP-12).*
f *Bottle with round base, tall neck and pierced hole at rim. Motifs include incised dots in quadruple units, vertical running-diamonds and rare cruciform patterns. Ht. 16.7 cm (DM-BTRP-09).*

Pl. 13

Pl. 14

4 Red–and–Black Polished Ware.

Pl. 14 *Early Bronze Age.*
Left to right, front
a *Bowl with tulip base, trough spout and pierced lug. Diam. 10.7 cm (DM-RBP-166).*
b *Jug with round base and round spout. The handle has a square section. Ht. 13.8 cm (DM-RBP-01).*
c *Bowl with round base and two lugs. Diam. 10.1 cm (DM-RBP-160).*
Left to right, back
d *Bottle with round base and two vertical handles. Ht. 25.2 cm (DM-RBP-151). Only three examples of this type of two-handled bottle are known at present.*
e *Bottle with round base and two lugs. Ht. 24.4 cm (DM-RBP-150). This two-lugged vessel is unique.*
f *Bottle with round base. Ht. 21.1 cm (DM-RBP-23). More than 150 bottles of this type are known.*

Pl. 15

5 Black–bottomed Red Polished Ware

Pl. 15 *Early Bronze Age.*
a(left) *Bottle with round base and twin lugs. The artist has created a black body with a red neck. Ht. 18.7 cm. (DM-BBRP-01). This bottle is unique.*
b(right) *Bowl with round base, trough spout and three lugs. The interior of the bowl has a black bottom but the exterior is red. The lug opposite the spout is pierced and beak-shaped, but the other two lugs are flat and bi-lobed. This design converts the bowl into a bird-shaped vessel with the pierced lug as the head, the flat lugs as wings and the spout as the tail. Diam. 27.7 cm (DM-BBRP-02).*

6 Reserved Slip Ware

This comparatively rare form of Polished Ware demonstrates yet another way of achieving a two-tone effect. In this case, parts of the red slip are wiped away while it is still wet, revealing patches of the pale under-surface. After this the whole surface is polished and the end result is a 'trick' decoration in which the *negative* patches appear to be the *positive* pattern on the dark red surface. In some cases, the technique was improved by the addition of a pale slip first, which was allowed to dry, and then the application of the red slip over the top of this. When this dark red slip was wiped away, the pale buff under-slip was then revealed. In this way, the degree of two-tone contrast could be deliberately manipulated by the potter. For examples of this ware, see Stewart (1962), fig. CLI, and Yon (1976), fig. 23.

7 Black Polished Ware

In this ware the whole surface of the vessels is a shiny jet black. There are two restrictions: Black Polished objects are always small and almost always incision-decorated. Although moderately common, they are still much rarer than their red-coloured equivalents. Explaining the black coloration, Stewart (1962, p. 227) comments that this ware 'was clearly fired in a reducing kiln or under suitable conditions elsewhere'. Myres (1914, p. 20) explains that 'this black surface was produced by restricting the admission of air during the process of firing, and so reducing the rust-coloured oxide of iron to the black protoxide; some examples also show the presence of carbonyl absorbed from the fire.' MacLaurin (1980), however, after discussing the matter with a modern ceramic expert, comes to the following conclusion: 'it appears there were two ways in which to produce black-topped and black polished vessels. The first was to remove the vessel from firing at 400° C and to rub it with grass immediately; the second was to cover the vessel with grass, set it on fire and cover that with a layer of dung.' Whichever method the ancient potters used, they managed to produce some strikingly attractive small vessels, some of which could be accurately described as miniatures.

It could be argued that I should include this (and the other forms which display a red + black combination) as mere variants of the Red Polished family, and should not separate them as distinct wares. They are certainly closely related, and placing all the Early Bronze Age polished ware together under one umbrella would help to emphasize its unity. But traditional names die hard, and although it might be more correct to coin a new title and refer to the general family of polished vessels as 'Dark Polished Ware', this would mean introducing a major new term, which I am reluctant to impose on the literature.

It has been suggested that the Cypriot Black Polished Ware represents another Anatolian influence, this time from the Yortan Culture. Yortan is a town lying south-east of Troy, and the Bronze Age potters there produced huge quantities of Incised Black Polished Ware vessels (see Mellaart, 1966, fig. 39; Lloyd, 1967, fig. 4; and Ede, 1976, figs. 114 and 116.). It is quite possible that some of these found their way to northern Cyprus during the third millennium BC and inspired local Red Polished potters to try out a new colour. It is only necessary to compare the three Yortan examples illustrated on this page with the Cypriot Black Polished vessels shown overleaf, to realize how close the two styles were. But again it will probably be argued that the indigenous Cypriot potters were perfectly capable of experimenting with colour variants on their own, without any outside help, especially as there are so many different two-tone versions of red + black polished ware. As with the heated Philia debate, we lack enough hard evidence to be certain, one way or the other.

8 Black Slip Ware

Towards the end of the Polished Ware era— that is to say, at the beginning of the Middle

Pl. 16 Incised Black Polished Ware from Yortan in Anatolia. *Early Bronze Age.*
a(above) *Jug with tripod base and cutaway spout. Zoomorphic body. Length 7.5 cm (DM-YO-02).*
b(below) *Same description. Length 9.1 cm (DM-YO-03).*

Pl.17 Incised Black Polished Ware from Yortan in Anatolia. *Early Bronze Age. Jug with tripod base and cutaway spout. Barrel-shaped body. Ht. 6 cm (DM-YO-01). This ware shows a striking similarity to the Incised Black Polished Ware of Cyprus illustrated on p. 26.*

Pl. 16

Pl. 17

Bronze Age period—the high-quality, high-polish vessels give way to a cruder, dark slip ware. The surface is less attractive and the incision patterns become less imaginative, almost casual. Alongside this ware the final stages of the Red Polished sequence also show a similar crudity, the incised lines often being made in a slapdash, automatic way with multi-pointed instruments. Black Slip Ware is an appropriately crude name for this pottery because, as Astrom (1972) points out, the slip may be 'light or dark brown, reddish black or black', or even 'mottled red(-brown) and black'. The slip may be matt or lustrous and the clay varies from light brown, pinkish buff, buff, yellow or grey to greenish colour. The conclusion drawn from these comments and from a study of the pottery itself is that this is a rag-bag group of vessels, probably not a true type, but rather a collection of similar types resulting from the general decay of the Red Polished tradition.

This Black Slip Ware lasts through the Middle Bronze Age period and appears to provide the precursors to the important Base Ring Ware of the Late Bronze Age. Some Black Slip vessels (see Pl. 55b) show an incipient base ring and a surface which has a similar 'metallic' quality to the typical Base Ring Ware.

9 Drab Polished Ware

Sometimes difficult to distinguish from the last ware, this type of pottery comes exclusively from the south coast region of Cyprus and the south-west. Typically, the surface is buff-grey and heavily pock-marked, but there is much colour variation, from pale creamy-buff to orange to brown-black. Swiny (1981) describes the fabric as fine and very hard, 'fired to a high temperature for a short time'. He emphasizes that the core is a highly characteristic blue-grey colour and prefers to call this pottery Drab Polished Blue Core Ware, or simply Blue Core Ware. An objection to this new name has been made on the ground that a complete vessel would have to be broken to prove that it possessed a blue core, and that all titles for wares must be based on a typical *external* feature that is always visible. This makes sense, but nevertheless Swiny's pin-pointing of the blue core feature is of great value in identifying pieces of this ware.

Swiny also mentions that the incised decoration 'often consists of wavy or zig-zag bands with superimposed circles hanging from the shoulder. The use of hanging triangles filled with incisions is also common.' The problem with this is that very similar incised patterns can also be found on the late Incised Red Polished vessels and on Black Slip vessels. This sharing of motifs reflects how closely related these different wares are and underlines the difficulty in separating them neatly into different classes. Certain vessels in my collection have been identifed differently by different specialists, revealing the confusion which exists. It would seem that, at the tail end of the long Polished Ware tradition there were a number of potters who wanted to continue in the vague genre of 'incised polished monochrome', but who were no longer strict adherents of a particular technical process. They varied more freely their firing, their clay and their slip, but ended up with something approximating the great tradition of polished pottery of earlier centuries. In the end, we have a number of local, regional, or perhaps personal variations of technique which all aim at roughly the same kind of final result.

These, then, are the major categories of the Polished Ware tradition of Cypriot pottery, covering the centuries of the Early and Middle Bronze Ages. A number of other types have been recorded in the past, often on the basis of only a few vessels or fragments—ones that stubbornly refuse to fit in to a rigid taxonomy. But all the main subdivisions have been covered here.

Certain authorities will be unhappy that I have not reduced to mere variants of Red Polished such wares as Black Polished and Drab Polished, and it is only respect for traditional names that has prevented me from doing so. Some revision will have to be undertaken in the future, and this point was brought home to me by the acquisition of a group of small polished juglets, almost certainly made by the same individual potter. They were the same size, shape and texture and had the same 'sculptural' quality, but they were in five different colour forms. Taken singly, they would have been confidently classified as Plain Red Polished, Black Polished, Red-and-Black Polished, Black Slip, and so on. Seen together, they create more of a problem, reminding us that individual potters may play with different 'wares' as well as with different shapes.

6 Reserved Slip Ware

Pl. 18 *Middle Bronze Age. Bowl with round base, small vertical handle and one lug. Motif: single band of chevrons. Diam. 11.1 cm (DM-RS-01). Cf. Brown and Catling 1980, no. 26, Fig. 21; and Yon 1976, Fig. 23. Only four or five of these bowls are known.*

Pl. 18

7 Black Polished Ware

Pl. 19 *Early Bronze Age.*
Left to right, front
a *Bottle with round base and pierced lug. Ht. 6.1 cm (DM-BP-03). Cf. SCE IV. 1a, Fig. CLIII, nos. 1-4.*
b *Bottle with flat base and pierced lug. Ht. 5.4 cm. (DM-BP-06). Cf. SCE IV. 1a, Fig. LII, no. 1.*
Left to right, centre
c *Bowl with round base and one pierced lug. Diam. 10.2 cm (DM-BP-08). Cf. SCE IV. 1a, Fig. CLIV, nos. 1-10.*
d *Same description. Diam. 8.6 cm (DM-BP-07).*
e *Same description. Diam. 10.6 cm (DM-BP-09).*
Left to right, back
f *Bottle with flat base, pierced lug and cutaway spout. Ht. 9 cm (DM-BP-04). Cf. SCE IV. 1a, Fig. CLII, nos. 3-5.*
g *Jug with round base and round spout. Ht. 12.3 cm (DM-BP-02). Cf. SCE IV. 1a, Fig. CLII, no. 8, but this is not an exact parallel. The shape of the vessel shown here is identical with the typical Red Polished 'gourd juglets' discussed in Chapter IV.*

Pl. 19

Pl. 20

8 Handmade Black Slip Ware

Pl. 20 *Middle Bronze Age.*
a(left) *Jug with round base, wide neck and thumb-grip spur on handle. Decorated with bands of straight and wavy relief lines. Ht. 21.5 cm (DM-HBS-05). Cf. SCE IV. 1b, Fig. XXIX, no. 1.*
b(centre) *Jug with round base and round spout. Decorated with bands of straight and wavy incisions. Ht. 17.5 cm (DM-HBS-01). Cf. SCE IV, 1b, Fig. XXVI, no. 10.*
c(right) *Jug with round base, wide neck and thumb-grip spur on handle. Decorated with bands of straight and wavy incisions. Ht. 26 cm (DM-HBS-06). Cf. SCE IV. 1b, Fig. XXIX, no. 1.*

Pl. 21

9 Drab Polished Ware

Pl. 21 *Middle Bronze Age.*
a(left) *Jug with round base and cutaway-beak spout. Four relief 'ribs' and incised decorations. The off-white surface is unusual. Ht. 32.3 cm (DM-DP-07). Cf. Karageorghis 1973, Pierides no. 7 for similar shape.*
b(centre) *Jug with round base and squat neck. Simple incised decoration. Ht. 19.6 cm (DM-DP-03).*
c(right) *Jug with round base and cutaway-beak spout. Relief-work imitation cord hanging from neck and incised decoration. Ht. 23.4 cm (DM-DP-06).*

10 Red-on-Black Ware

In the Middle Bronze Age the great Red Polished tradition, with its shiny surface, its incisions and its relief decorations, its two-tone slips and its mottlings, was overshadowed by a new tradition of painted ware. The slip was now uniform and usually matt and the decoration was applied as painted lines. There were two main wares of this type: Red-on-Black Ware and White Painted Ware. The first of these was a speciality of the north-east of the island and was largely confined to the Karpasian peninsula.

Red-on-Black Ware has been described by Karageorghis (1982) as 'the debased, matt version of Red Polished'. It is true that it has several links with the very late forms of Red Polished Ware vessels, but it is wrong to think of it as just another variant of that ceramic family. The use of brushes to create linear, painted decoration places it in an entirely separate category. There are several variant forms:

a Red-on-Black Slip Ware

In this rather rare variety, the matt red lines are painted on to a slightly shiny, polished surface. The slip colour varies from black to grey and brown, sometimes with orange-red areas. If there were no red lines present the vessels would probably be identified as Black Slip Ware. In some ways this seems to be an intermediate form between the end of the Black Slip Ware and the start of the Red-on-Black Ware proper. Perhaps, because of this, it will be thought proper one day to label it as Proto-Red-on-Black Ware.

b Red-on-Black Painted Ware

This is the common, typical Red-on-Black Ware. The red lines are usually produced by a multi-pointed brush and the decoration covers almost the whole surface of the vessels, in a somewhat compulsive manner. Astrom (1972) has remarked on the *horror vacui* of these particular artists. On any particular vessel, the number of lines in the parallel-line 'units' is nearly always the same, indicating that the painter has used a single multi-brush throughout, unworried by the somewhat repetitious effect created.

In certain of these vessels the colours have proved rather fugitive, and in many cases the slip itself has flaked off in large patches. Sometimes only a trace of the original paint-

work remains to give a clue to the nature of the ware (see Pl. 188c).

Two other, rare variants of Red-on-Black are the Red-on-Red and Light-on-Dark, which are not illustrated here. The Red-on-Red has a polished slip of red-brown or pink colour, on which matt-finish lines have been painted in red-brown or purple. The Light-on-Dark has a lustrous slip with a red, brown, or black colour, on which lines of matt white paint have been added.

Similarities between these four kinds of Red-on-Black Ware and the Red Polished family of the Early Bronze Age are as follows:

1 During the late stages of the Red Polished tradition, the incised linear decorations became more careless and automatic. In the last of the Incised Red Polished vessels, the Black Slip vessels and the Drab Polished Ware, there is a frequent use of the multi-pointed decorating implement. This lazy way of producing batches of parallel lines is shared by these Late Red Polished variants and the typical Red-on-Black Ware.

2 The general effect of the lime-filled white lines on the incised Red Polished Ware is that of light decoration on a dark background. This is repeated (perhaps imitated?) on most of the Red-on-Black Ware vessels.

3 Some of the slips used by Red-on-Black Ware artists are polished and shiny, like the earlier Red Polished surfaces. This similarity is lost, however, on the most typical of the Red-on-Black Ware vessels, where the background is a matt, painted surface.

Despite these and other similarities, the Red-on-Black Ware must be considered as a separate major category because of its painted decoration, which links it to the next major category.

11 Handmade White Painted Ware

This is the dominant type of pottery in the Middle Bronze Age. There are many forms, but in all there is a painted pattern of dark lines on a pale slip surface. The most extreme form of this decoration displays a black on white contrast, but this is often muted by the use of off-white slips and off-black painted lines. The background slip colour varies from white to cream, to orange to red-brown, and the superimposed lines may be painted in red, brown or black.

The vessels are generally much smaller and more 'intimate' than the earlier Red Polished examples. There is a playful informality about them.

The name 'White Painted Ware' is unfortunate because this same title is given to a separate class of Iron Age Cypriot pottery, early examples of which already start appearing in the Late Bronze Age. This later ware was made on the wheel, which clearly distinguishes it from the handmade Middle Bronze Age ware.

Variations *within* the Middle Bronze Age White Painted Ware have been described in detail by Astrom in his 1957 monograph on the period. Rather awkwardly, he was caught in an ambivalent state of mind at the time he wrote his major work, and based his taxonomy on two conflicting systems—the sub-wares called White Painted I, II, III, IV, V and VI, and a series of decorative styles called Framed Caduceus, Pendent Line, Wavy Line, Latticed Diamond, String Hole and Cross Line. These two systems are 'married' to produce such cumbersome units as, for example, 'White Painted III-V String-hole Style'. In his own monograph on White Painted pottery in 1974, Frankel criticizes this system, pointing out that 'the types of variation are mixed in the classification, and the material is differentiated on the basis of any or all of the variables without consideration of their different significances'. He also agrees with Merrillees that the sub-ware groupings I-VI are unsatisfactory because 'they can neither be adequately differentiated nor effectively interpreted'. Both Frankel and Merrillees consider a design-based style classification to be of greater value when working within the major category of White Painted Ware. In this, they are switching from a temporal, technology-based sub-ware system to a regionally-defined style system. To put it another way, they are switching from the science of pot-making to the art of pot-decorating, as the basis for their classification.

This analysis based on aesthetic factors gets closer to the social reality of what was happening in Cyprus in the Middle Bronze Age. Local village or workshop pottery products were undoubtedly subjected to highly conservative decorative traditions, with set motifs being repeated again and again, and handed on from one generation to the next. Decorative inventiveness was expressed by constant variations in motif-combinations on each vessel, so that depite the motif-traditions it was possible to make each individual vessel a unique item.

It must be stressed, however, that there were few completely distinct regional differences. One motif might be preferred in one area, but would appear elsewhere also, giving each decorative unit a geographical range rather than an exclusive 'home base'. Frankel has studied some of these ranges and comes to the conclusion that 'it is possible to divide the island into a series of overlapping regions, each of which can be characterised by the greater popularity of specific design motifs …' Culturally, this can be caused either by the movement of finished vessels—as trade, gifts, souvenirs, loot or booty—or by the spread of the motif-makers themselves. Bearing in mind that the potters concerned were almost certainly women, the spread of traditional, local motifs could well be a reflection of a cultural out-breeding system between neighbouring settlements. Alternatively, it could be the result of minor short-distance migrations, or local hostilities.

This is not the place to go into detail, but a few of the major regional trends may be mentioned:

The Wavy Line Style is typical of the Karpasian Peninsula in the north-east.

The Pendent Line and Cross Line Styles are typical of the earlier vessels from the eastern regions of the island.

The Framed Broad Band Style is typical of the later vessels from the eastern regions.

A complex style favouring horizontal bands with double checker rows alternating with cross-hatched zigzags, diamonds or triangles is typical of the central regions of the island.

Angled cross-hatched checkers and diamonds are especially common in the Politico region.

A more formal, larger and heavier decorative style is popular on the north coast. A combination of cross-hatched panels and vertical wavy lines is common there, with broad bands as a basal element.

White Painted Ware is absent from the south and extreme west of the island.

10a Red-on-black Slip Ware

Pl. 22 *Middle Bronze Age.*
a(left) *Bowl with round base, trough spout and pierced lug. There are thick, short, paired wavy lines in red on both the inside and the outside of the vessel. Diam. 19.7 cm (DM-ROB-09).*
b *Jug with round base and round spout. Motifs: Vertical wavy lines and vertically joined ovals.*
Ht. 9.9 cm (DM-ROB-01). Both these crudely painted vessels are unusual and should perhaps be classified as 'Proto-red-on-black'.

10b Red-on-black Painted Ware

Pl. 23 *Middle Bronze Age.*
Left to right
a *Jug with flat base and wide neck. Flattened strap-handle with thumb-grip lug at top. Decoration applied with multi-point brush. Ht. 26.6 cm (DM-ROB-08). Cf. SCE IV.1b, Fig. XXXIV, no. 9.*
b *Jug with round base and round spout. Similar decoration. Ht. 20.5 cm (DM-ROB-06). Cf. SCE IV. 1b, Fig. XXXIII, no. 10.*
c *Bowl with round base, trough spout and small vertical handle. Similar decoration. Diam. 30 cm DM-ROB-10). This bowl was broken and repaired in antiquity, before it was placed in the tomb. Evidence of its repair consists of three pairs of drilled holes straddling the ancient crack.*
d *Jug with flat base and wide neck. Flattened strap handle with thumb-grip at top. Similar decoration. Ht. 28.9 cm (DM-ROB-07).*

Pl. 22

Pl. 23

11 Handmade White-painted Ware

Pl. 24 *Middle Bronze Age.*
Left to right, front

a *Jug with four stumpy legs, cutaway spout and eight pierced lugs. Ht. 20 cm (DM-HWP-29).*
b *Jug with round base, beak spout, two pierced lugs and a very small handle. Ht. 13.3 cm (DM-HWP-13).*

Second row
c *Flask with flared flat base. Ht. 21.5 cm (DM-HWP-36). Cf. SCE IV.1b, Fig. XVIII, no. 7, which is more complex but has the same base and decoration.*
d *Bowl with round base and wishbone handle. Diam. 10.6 cm (DM-HWP-48).*

Third row
e *Bottle with round base and two lugs. Ht. 7.4.cm (DM-HWP-30).*
f *Bowl with round base and handle. Diam. 7.8 cm (DM-HWP-49).*

Back
g *Bowl with round base, trough spout and pierced lug. Poorly shaped vessel. Diam. (narrow) 28.4 cm, (wide) 34 cm (DM-HWP-40). Cf. SCE IV.1b, Fig. XXXVII, no. 6, where it is called 'Composite Ware' because exterior is all black. But it is no more than a variant form of White-painted Ware.*

Pl. 24

12 Base Ring Ware

With the arrival of the Late Bronze Age two new wares came to dominate the Cypriot scene: Base Ring Ware and White Slip Ware. Both were widespread and they usually occurred together, rather than representing local differences of style. Also, both were exported in large numbers, reflecting the new international status of Cyprus as a trading culture of some importance.

Base Ring Ware is named for its shape, being the earliest ware to display a standing base formed by a ring applied to the lower part of the vessels. This means that it was intended for use on flat surfaces, a new feature of Cypriot pottery, the only notable exception being the flat-based Philia Red Polished Ware from the beginning of the Early Bronze Age, over a thousand years before. In the intervening period, the majority of the pottery vessels were given rounded bases, suggesting that they were either suspended in some way or were pushed into soft ground to make them stand up. The arrival of Base Ring Ware must be connected in some way with significant changes in local architecture and improved living quarters.

Base Ring Ware is handmade, well fired to a high temperature, giving it a metallic ring when struck, and with unusually thin walls. It is clearly the result of improved ceramic technology, but it is rather surprising that its eventual finish gives it a rather muted and sombre appearance. It is commonly covered with a dark, burnished slip of brownish-grey to black. An explanation for this somewhat grim surface has been sought in terms of 'imitation'. Myres (1914), who named the ware, says 'Base Ring Ware seems designed to imitate leathern forms, but some examples seem to show also the influence of metal vases'. A similar view was expressed as recently as 1981 by Karageorghis: 'The numerous metal vases which circulated round the island during the Late Bronze Age caused innovative potters to imitate them with vases whose surfaces had metallic qualities.' This may well be so, but an examination of some of the Black Slip Ware vessels of the Middle Bronze Age reveals that there was already a marked trend towards the type of finish used by the Base Ring Potters. In some cases (see Pl. 55b) there is even an incipient 'base ring' present on Black Slip vessels. So the similarity between the Base Ring Ware vessels and metal containers may be little more than an exploited coincidence.

There are several variants of Base Ring Ware. Accidental or deliberate overfiring has sometimes produced an orange-red form (see Pl. 25e) that lacks any resemblance to metallic prototypes. Some of the smaller vessels show incision patterns reminiscent of the Black Slip forerunners (see Pl. 25a). Others are completely plain and without any kind of decoration (see Pl. 79). One strange example (see Pl. 25d) is pure, matt white. It does not give the feeling of being a finished vessel, and yet it is undamaged and unworn. A special feature may give the clue as to its real significance. Its decoration style is that of a much larger vessel, and I suspect that it was used by the potter as a miniature model for making the bigger and more important jugs.

The two most common forms of decoration on this ware were Relief-bands and White-painted lines. It has become traditional to refer to these two types as Base Ring I and Base Ring II, but it would be misleading to assume that this necessarily indicates a temporal sequence. There is considerable overlap between the two in the Late Bronze Age time sequence (see Astrom 1972, p. 700), and they may simply represent two alternative styles.

The relief bands are uncomplicated except for a large, paired spiral that appears time and again as the main motif on the larger jugs. The earliest examples of this clearly show the design to be based on paired snakes, and later, more abstract examples are doubtless schematizations of this serpentine emblem, which almost certainly has some important symbolic significance (but see discussion under 'snake' on p. 230).

One curious feature of many of the jugs and juglets is their offset vertical axis. For some reason, as yet unexplained, nearly all the Base Ring Jugs lean backwards to a marked degree. This is a ceramic oddity for which I have been able to find no parallel.

Another oddity for which a bold explanation *has* been forthcoming is the striking resemblance between the shapes of the smaller juglets and (inverted) poppy-heads. These are the vessels that were exported in the largest numbers, and Merrillees (1968), who has studied this export trade in some detail, has postulated that their curious shape was their 'label', signalling their contents. Because of their poppy-head shape, he believes that they contained opium (for details see p. 237).

13 Cypro-Mycenaean Ware

Reflecting the internationalism of Cyprus in the Late Bronze Age, there are a number of striking imported influences in the ceramics of the period. Of these, perhaps the most important is the Mycenaean Ware. Huge quantities of this ware appeared in the island during the fourteenth and thirteenth centuries BC. At first it seems to have been enjoyed as a luxury import and then later, probably because of its high status, it became a subject for local imitation.

How this change from import to local product occurred has been the subject of much debate. There are those who feel that all the Mycenaean Ware found on Cyprus was imported from abroad, but the more commonly held view today is that the later examples were made on the island, either by immigrant Mycenaean potters working locally, or by indigenous potters copying the newly arrived styles.

Examining the vessels concerned it looks as though all three types of product were involved. First, there are many examples showing the typical Mycenaean clay and fabric; second, there are Mycenaean imitations of Base Ring Ware shapes; and third, there are Base Ring Ware imitations of Mycenaean shapes (see Pl. 110).

The typical Cypro-Mycenaean ware is made of a fine pale clay. The creamy-buff background colour of the vessels is decorated with linear designs or, on the larger examples, with pictorial panels. A glossy brown paint is used for these decorations, which, through extra firing, often becomes red.

Although occasional wheelmade vessels had appeared on Cyprus before the Mycenaean period, it is only with these new colonists that they appear in large numbers. In 1973 Astrom was able to publish a table of Mycenaean Ware found in Cyprus giving a total of 3,445 examples. Bearing in mind that this probably represents only a tiny percentage of the real total, it is clear that this was a major new ceramic input for the island. If the earlier, prehistoric pottery had received its influences from the north and the east, there was now to be a shift to the west and Greece as the major external pressure operating on Cypriot art and culture. The potter's wheel was there to stay, along with urban organization and technology. The Cypro-Mycenaean Ware heralds this new epoch.

14 Cypro-Palestinian Bichrome Ware

Among the minor pottery wares of the Late Bronze Age, this one is of particular interest. It appeared at the very beginning of the period, around 1600 BC, and was originally classified as an imported ware. Dikaios (1961) gives two possible sources: 'According to one theory this ware should be attributed to Southern Palestine but some archaeologists consider North Syria as its place of origin.' Amiran, in her 1970 monograph on the ancient ceramics of the Holy Land, places this pottery form in the Palestinian region. Called Palestinian Bichrome Ware, it is 'ascribed to a school of master potters and painters, working in one of the centers on the coast of Greater Canaan, somewhere between Ugarit in the north and Gaza in the south'. The vessels are wheelmade, unlike the typical Cypriot pottery, well fired and burnished and painted in red and black designs quite distinct from anything known on Cyprus.

Amiran mentions that this pottery, common all over the Holy Land, was exported to both Egypt and Cyprus. The argument for a foreign source appeared irrefutable and the ware was widely accepted as 'imported' for many years. Supporting this view was the observation that, had this wheelmade pottery been produced on the island, there was a strong chance that it would have revolutionized Cypriot ceramics a century or more before the arrival of the influential Mycenaean ware. Since this had not happened, the idea that the pottery had been manufactured on Cypriot soil was considered untenable.

Modern technology has intervened, however, and despite all the evidence to the contrary, recent neutron activation studies have proved that the so-called Palestinian Bichrome Ware found in eastern Cyprus is, in reality, locally made pottery. Artzy and his colleagues reported in 1976 that the wheelmade 'Bichrome Ware, considered by archaeologists to be Syro-Palestinian, was instead produced of Eastern Cypriote clay'. They also go on to claim that this ware is 'a variant ... of the Cypriote White Painted ware'. One is forced to accept the clay analysis, but this second point is hard to swallow. The feel of the ware as well as its decoration is so close to the mainland pottery, that it is difficult to accept it as anything but locally made ware produced by an immigrant potter.

12 Base Ring Ware

Pl.25 *Late Bronze Age.*
Left to right, front
a *Jug with round spout and incised decoration. Ht. 14.7 cm (DM-BR-10).*
b *Jug with round spout and painted decoration. Ht. 28 cm (DM-BR-01).*
c *Jug with round spout and painted decoration. Ht. 14.6 cm (DM-BR-19).*
Second row
d *Jug with round spout and relief decoration. Matt white finish. Ht. 14.7 cm (DM-BR-05).*
e *Jug with wide neck and long thumb-grip on handle. Orange-red finish. Ht. 17.3 cm (DM-BR-22).*
Third row
f *Bowl with deep body and tall handle. Ht. to top of handle 23 cm. Diam. of rim 16.7 cm (DM-BR-35). Formerly in the Cesnola Collection.*
g *Jug with round spout and relief decoration. Ht. 26.4 cm (DM-BR-04).*
Back
h *Jug with cutaway spout and relief decoration. Ht. 61.3 cm (DM-BR-25). This is the largest piece of Base Ring Ware known at present. Formerly in the Brew collection.*

Pl. 25

Pl. 26

13 Cypro-Mycenaean Ware

Pl. 26 *Late Bronze Age.*
Left to right
a *Jar with ring base and three handles. Vertical stripes on shoulders Ht. 15.2 cm (DM-CM-06).*
b *Jar with flat base, squat shape and three handles. Diagonal stripes on shoulders. Ht. 7 cm (DM-CM-12).*
c *Jar with ring base and three handles. Spiral motifs on shoulders. Ht. 17.7 cm (DM-CM-10).*
d *Bottle with ring base and two vertical handles. Chevron motifs below handles. Ht. 13.6 cm (DM-CM-02).*

14 Cypro-Palestinian Bichrome Ware

Pl. 27 *Late Bronze Age. Jug with ring base and wide neck. Ht. 30.5 cm (DM-CPB-02). Cf. Karageorghis 1976, Fig. 109.*

Pl. 27

15 White Slip Ware

The second major, indigenous Cypriot ware of the Late Bronze Age, which contrasts strikingly with Base Ring Ware, is the highly decorative and appealing White Slip Ware. Like Base Ring, it was in widespread use across the island and the two wares are often found together.

Essentially, White Slip Ware is a refinement of the White Painted Ware of the Middle Cypriot period. In both cases there is a pale slip on which dark—orange to black—linear patterns are painted. But with White Slip Ware, the slip is thicker and creamier, and the decoration applied to it shows a new spatial restraint and delicacy of touch. This appears to have given this handmade ware a special appeal, not only to modern eyes, but also to the people of the Late Bronze Age, and the vessels of this type were widely exported, to Syria, Palestine, Egypt and Greece.

The decorative patterns employed will be discussed later (see p. 312) in some detail, but it is worth pointing out here that earlier ideas concerning their imitation of leather stitching are no longer acceptable. This view was expressed by Myres in 1914; 'The forms ... seem to be wholly derived from leather-work ... The painted decoration ... consists essentially of simple bands, evidently intended to represent stitches or lacings.' He also considers that the handles of the vessels 'seem to imitate thin wooden laths'. He describes the White Slip Ware vessels, quite bluntly, as 'clay copies' of wood and stitched leather containers.

Although it is possible to see some resemblance between the White Slip vessels and stitched leather bowls and jugs, it is hard to accept this view today, now that we can see the smooth gradation from the later examples of Middle Bronze Age White Painted Ware to the earlier examples of Proto-White Slip Ware. Popham (1972) comments that 'this continuity ... seems to refute the once prevalent idea that White Slip wares were in imitation of leather vessels. This was based principally on the suggestive similarity of the decoration of ladder pattern bowls to stitching but it is now clear that this design is relatively rare in the early stages of this ware and probably in part owes its popularity to the general adoption of the multiple brush.'

A curious aspect of White Slip Ware is the strict limitation on the number of shapes used. The vast majority of all vessels are small hemispherical bowls equipped with a single horizontal handle of wishbone shape. In addition there are smaller numbers of juglets, tankards and a few larger bowls. The immense variety of shapes found in the Early and Middle Bronze Age wares has vanished, and for several centuries the White Slip potters, with immense conservatism, restrict themselves to these few simple shapes. Why this is so is not clear.

Three main stages are recognized:

a Proto-White Slip
This has thicker walls and a clumsier linear decoration than the later examples.

b White Slip I
This is the peak period for the ware, with the finest fabric and decoration. The walls are thinner and the linear decoration much more delicate. Sometimes there is a two-tone decoration, with some lines in red and others in black.

c White Slip II
The decoration becomes more automatic and gives the impression of being rather hurriedly mass-produced. Cross-hatched bands with broad borders come to dominate the decorative linear patterns and the individual lines lose their delicacy. The walls of the vessels are thicker again.

Perhaps the most appealing feature of these White Slip vessels is the way in which their decorators managed to overcome the *horror vacui* that is so widespread among prehistoric ceramicists. Instead of covering the whole surface of their bowls and tankards with a pattern of lines, they left large areas blank, restricting their decorations to carefully placed horizontal and vertical bands. In addition, they very often added a 'special motif' of a semi-abstract kind, which gave a decorative focus to their design. These special motifs were always slightly different and yet, when considered together, they form a family of designs with a distinctive quality that makes them immediately recognizable as being 'White Slip' (see fig. 536 on p. 318). This attractive thematic variation is discussed more fully in Chapter IV.

16 Wheelmade Red Lustrous Ware

This is another ware of foreign origin which found its way into Cyprus during the international trading era of the Late Bronze Age. Karageorghis (1982) says that it 'probably originated in Anatolia at the beginning of the Late Bronze Age but was current in Cyprus during the Late Bronze Age II period'.

There are only two popular shapes—the tall, thin *fusiform jug* and the flattened *pilgrim flask*, with one or three handles. The well-mixed and well-fired clay is covered with a slip which varies from buff to orange to red. The surface is nearly always burnished to produce a shiny, lustrous finish but falling short of a high polish.

The burnishing appears to have been done rather brutally, with a stick or a knife, so that it is possible, by rotating a vessel in a bright light, to see the direction of the burnish lines. On the fusiform jugs the burnish lines run vertically up the long slope of the body. On the pilgrim flasks they tend to radiate from the protruding centre of the body. This is clearly shown in the smaller of the two pilgrim flasks illustrated on the next page, where the burnishing process has left dark scratch marks on the surface of the vessel. On the handle of this same vessel, it is possible to see that there the burnishing marks are vertical. This is also the case on the neck, although in this region the marks are less obvious.

The pilgrim flasks have a 'lentoid shaped' body in which one side of the flattened shape protrudes more than the other, suggesting that the flask was intended to be worn with the flatter side against the body of its owner, or its owner's animal. In other words, these are likely to have been intended as travelling vessels. They certainly have about them a strictly functional air, rather than a decorative one, although their simple shapes are pleasing enough.

An interesting detail on many of these vessels is the 'pot-mark' placed at the bottom of the body of the fusiform jugs and at the lower end of the handles of the pilgrim flasks. Astrom (1972) mentions one fusiform jug that is an exception to this rule, being marked, like a pilgrim flask, at the base of the handle, and the example shown overleaf appears to be a similar exception, having a simple horizontal notch in this position. The smaller pilgrim flask overleaf is unmarked, but the larger one has a pot-mark which appears to consist of four inverted Vs. These marks seem to have been some kind of crude labelling system.

17 White Shaved Ware

This plain ware appears in Cyprus at about the same time as the Red Lustrous Ware (Late Bronze Age IB to IIB), but seems to have been provided with a highly fugitive slip, so that today almost all the vessels give the impression of being unadorned white. The special characteristic of this pottery is that the clay has been given a final shaping by trimming it, or 'shaving' it with a sharp knife.

Almost every example of White Shaved Ware is of one particular design—a small, spindle-shaped juglet with a sharply pointed base and a pinched mouth. The shaved markings left by the knife are clearly visible on the body, the handle and the neck.

We know that these vessels were made in Cyprus at Enkomi, because deformed examples have been found there which would not have been suitable for export to the island from the mainland. But examples are also common from both Syria and Palestine, and the original source of this handmade ware is not known for certain.

Astrom (1972) mentions that one example from Kourion displays a pot-mark, incised on the handle, consisting of a cross above a horizontal line. The specimen illustrated here (Pl. 28) also has a pot-mark: a bold horizontal line on the body, below the handle, and a fainter marking on the handle comprising a vertical line bordered above and below by horizontal lines, with a separate vertical line lower down the handle. As with the Red Lustrous examples, this appears to be a simple labelling device.

Pl. 28 White Shaved Ware.
Late Bronze Age. Jug with pointed base and pinched spout. Ht. 17.2 cm (DM-WSH-01). Cf. SCE IV.1c, Fig. LVIII, no. 7.

15a Proto-White Slip Ware

Pl. 29 *Late Bronze Age.*
a(left) *Bowl with round base and wishbone handle. Diam. 17.6 cm (DM-WSL-04). Cf. SCE IV.1c,*
Fig. LXXIX, no. 4.
b(right) *Bowl with round base and wishbone handle. Diam. 16.3 cm (DM-WSL-03).*

Pl. 29

15b White Slip Ware I

Pl. 30 *Late Bronze Age.*
a(left) *Jug with ring base and wide neck. Large thumb-grip on handle. Fine-line decoration.*
Ht. 20.3. cm (DM-WSL-01). Cf. SCE IV.1c, Fig. LXXXI, no. 8.
b(right) *Bowl with round base and wishbone handle. Diam. 18.5 cm (DM-WSL-05). Cf. SCE IV.1c,*
Fig. LXXX, no. 2.

Pl. 30

15c White Slip Ware II

Pl. 31 *Late Bronze Age.*
a(left) *Bowl with round base and wishbone handle. Diam. 17.7 cm (DM-WSL-09).*
b(right) *Jug with ring base and wide neck. Large thumb-grip on handle. Ht. 25.8 cm (DM-WSL-02).*

Pl. 31

16 Wheelmade Red Lustrous Ware

Pl. 32 *Late Bronze Age.*
a(left) *Flask with round base, round spout and vertical handle. There are black marks on the body from burnishing. Ht. 24.4 cm (DM-WRL-03). Cf. SCE IV.1c, Fig. LV, no. 1.*
b(centre) *Spindle-jug with ring base. A short horizontal line at the base of the handle may be a 'pot-mark'. Ht. 33.1 cm (DM-WRL-01). Cf. SCE IV.1c, Fig. LIV, no. 7.*
c(right) *Flask with round base, round spout and three handles. The zigzag incision at the base of the handle may be a 'pot-mark', identifying the potter. Ht. 33.3 cm (DM-WRL-02). Cf. SCE IV.1c, Fig. LV, no. 4.*

Pl. 32

18 Wheelmade White Painted Ware

This is the typical pottery of the Cypriot Iron Age, but it had already made its first appearance towards the end of the Late Bronze Age as Proto-White Painted Ware, in the twelfth century BC. In this early form there were still strong Mycenaean influences, and it was originally given the name of 'Submycenaean Ware'. But soon the strong Mycenaean intrusion was waning and being absorbed into Cypriot culture. The new technology of the wheel had become fully accepted, but many of the Mycenaean decorative elements had been submerged. The typically shiny painted surfaces were lost along with most of the imported motifs. The earliest examples of the new wheelmade Iron Age White Painted Ware display matt surfaces and geometric patterns more reminiscent of the much earlier Middle Bronze Age handmade ware. It was as though the ceramic offspring of the coupling between Cyprus and Greece showed the artistic features of the former combined with the technological features of the latter. This overstates the case, but it gives a rough idea of the way in which the new Iron Age pottery arose and then began to develop in the eleventh century BC, at the start of the Cypro-Geometric Period.

Gjerstad (1948) describes the change in the following words: 'The repertory of forms of Late Cypriot III pottery shows an initial fusion between Mycenaean, Cypriote, and Syro-Palestinian elements, and in the pottery of Cypro-Geometric I this assimilation has been accomplished.' Karageorghis (1981) sees the Early Iron Age (Cypro-Geometric) period as a time of 'the complete fusion of the Greek and indigenous Cypriot cultures, a process during which Cypriot styles often overwhelmed the Greek ...'

The White Painted Ware lasts for over 700 years, from the end of the Late Bronze Age in the eleventh century BC to the end of the Classic Period in 325 BC. During this long run it assumes many shapes and designs and appears in the tombs of Cyprus in vast quantities. Two main design styles have been recognized, which can be loosely termed 'rectilinear' and 'circle'. The first favours triangles, diamonds, rectangles and criss-crosses; the second favours groups of concentric circles, mechanically drawn.

The long White Painted series has been divided up for convenience into six major phases, and it is not until WP III that the circle style appears, after which it comes to dominate in WP IV and WP V, but then disappears again completely in WP VI.

19 Bichrome Ware

Rivalling the White Painted Ware for popularity during the Iron Age was a Bichrome Ware in which patches or lines of reddish-brown paint were added to the black, on the pale background. The clay and the slip were the same as in the White Painted Ware vessels, so that it is reasonably accurate to describe Bichrome Ware as White Painted Ware to which red paint decorations have been applied to give a more colourful end product.

Like White Painted Ware, the Bichrome Ware is divided into a number of phases. During the early phases, I and II, Bichrome is rare, but by III it has become much more popular and the number of vessels in the two wares are about equal. With phase IV, the Bichrome Ware has become the more common of the two. As before, at this stage, there are two distinct styles, the rectilinear and the circle. In both wares, the rectilinear style is largely confined to the eastern and southern regions of the island, while the circle style is found mostly in the western and northern.

It is during this phase IV that we see an explosion of 'free-field' pictorial painting on Bichrome jugs of the eastern type. (There are also some on the White Painted IV vessels, but the Bichrome share is something like 90 per cent.)

These free-field paintings, in which restrictive panels or zones are avoided and wide open spaces are left available for the depiction of birds, mammals, humans, flowers or trees, have been studied in great detail by Karageorghis and Des Gagniers (1974). Birds are undeniably the most popular subject and a selection of types is shown here on p. 229, figs. 372-80.

In the Western style, at the same time, the concentric circle motif runs riot. As Gjerstad puts it in his 1948 monograph: 'There is a veritable circle dance on the pots.'

By phase V, the popularity of Bichrome vessels has more or less swamped out the White Painted alternatives, which become quite scarce. The Eastern style shows a great blossoming of lotus flowers at this stage, while the Western style begins to show a decline in quality of the multi-circle motifs.

In the last phase, VI, there is a further decline in quality, as with the White Painted Ware.

20 Black-on-Red Ware

This delicate, attractive ware comprises mostly small juglets in a red-brown slip with a lustrous surface, on which simple geometric designs are painted in matt black. Its peak period is the end of the Geometric and the beginning of the Archaic period.

There has been some debate about its origin. Some authorities believe that it first came to Cyprus from the Syro-Anatolian region, and had nothing to do with the Phoenicians. Others see it as a Phoenician importation; still others label it as Syro-Palestinian. Palestinian archaeologists themselves refer to it as 'Cypro-Phoenician Ware'.

Being small, portable and attractive, these little Black-on-Red juglets have been found over a huge range in the lands surrounding Cyprus, and it appears to be anyone's guess as to where they first began. But one aspect does seem clear. After their initial importation into Cyprus in the Cypro-Geometric period, they were taken up and imitated by local Cypriot potters who used a much harder clay and finished them in a shinier surface. By the end of the Cypro-Geometric period they were being manufactured in large numbers on the island, and it is mostly these examples that have become scattered far and wide. If they began originally as Phoenician, then became transformed and improved in Cyprus and exported back in their new form to Phoenicia, the Palestinian name of 'Cypro-Phoenician' is entirely suitable for them.

The ornamentation of these vessels follows rather closely the Western or 'Circle' style of the White Painted and Bichrome Ware. At the end of the sequence, the very late examples of Black-on-Red Ware lose their typical concentric circle pattern, a change which parallels the change taking place in late White Painted Ware. It is as though, for the Cypriot potters of the Iron Age, the Black-on-Red Ware became just a third variant, alongside the more common White Painted and Bichrome Wares. It stands in relation to them rather as Black Polished did to Red Polished in the Early Bronze Age—more delicate, smaller and infrequent, as if, in both cases,

there was some special function involved—perhaps some valuable or scarce contents that required more delicate containers.

21 Bichrome Red Ware

The simplest way to describe Bichrome Red Ware is to call it Black-on-Red Ware with additional touches of white paint. The most descriptive title for it would be Black-and-White-on-Red Ware, but as this is unduly clumsy, it has instead been given a shorter, if slightly misleading name. It is misleading because it implies an intimate relationship with Bichrome ware, when its closest link is with Black-on-Red Ware. In fact, it is easy to confuse some pieces of Bichrome Red Ware with Black-on-Red Ware because the white additions are often rather fugitive.

The supplementary white colour, added to improve the decorative quality of the vessels, is always restricted to small zones highlighting certain selected elements of the painted patterns. Its most common use is in horizontal or vertical rings, where it is always combined with, and usually bordered by, black rings. Where pictorial elements are present—human figures, animals, flowers—the white paint is employed to touch up the images and intensify their impact. But on almost every vessel of this ware it is true to say that it is the black paint which is the basic, structural colour, defining the patterning, with the white added as a minor element.

This ware appears to be a slightly later development on Cyprus than the Black-on-Red, making its début at the end of the Cypro-Geometric period. It continues through the Cypro-Archaic phase and the Cypro-Classical.

One type of vessel could almost be called a 'speciality' of this ware. It is basically a ring-based, round-spouted jug, but it becomes metamorphosed into something more complicated by the addition of modelled figures. There are several types of elaboration, the most popular consisting of a small, realistically rendered female figure sitting on the shoulder of the jug, opposite the handle. The face of the figure looks straight ahead and the left arm is relaxed. The right arm, however, holds a jug by its handle. This is essentially a 'trick' vessel—a sculptural joke—because if the parent jug were tipped forward, any liquid it might contain would flow out of the pinched spout of the tiny model jug.

18 Wheelmade White Painted Ware

Pl. 33 *Iron Age.*
a(left) *Jar with ring base and two horizontally-attached handles. Ht. 19.2 cm (DM-WWP-99).*
b(centre) *Jug with ring base, basket handle and side spout. Ht. 12.6 cm (DM-WWP-47).*
c(right) *Jar with ring base, two horizontally-attached handles, one of which is surmounted by a concave 'cup-holder'. Ht. 18.1 cm (DM-WWP-106). Cf. Myres 1914, no. 400.*

Pl. 33

19 Bichrome Ware

Pl. 34 *Iron Age.*
a(left) *Jug with ring base and pinched spout. Ht. 33 cm (DM-BI-26).*
b(centre) *Jar with ring base, squat body and two horizontally-attached handles. Ht. 7.3 cm (DM-BI-53).*
c(right) *Jar with ring base and horizontally attached handles. Ht. 32 cm (DM-BI-51). Cf. SCE IV.1c, Fig. XLVIII, no. 11.*

Pl. 34

20 Black-on-Red Ware

Pl. 35 *Iron Age.*
Left to right, front
a *Jug with flat base and round spout. Ht. 12.4 cm (DM-BOR-05).*
b *Same description. Ht. 8.5 cm (DM-BOR-06).*
c *Jug with barrel-shaped body and round spout. Ht. 12.8 cm (DM-BOR-13).*
Left to right, back
d *Jug with pinched spout and ring base. Ht. 12.5 cm (DM-BOR-11).*
e *Jug with slender body, flat base and round spout. Ht. 9.7 cm (DM-BOR-08).*
f *Jug with flat base and round spout. Ht. 13.6 cm (DM-BOR-01).*

Pl. 35

21 Bichrome Red Ware

Pl. 36 *Iron Age.*
Left to right, front
a *Bowl with stem base and two horizontally-attached handles. Diam. 18.5 cm (DM-BIR-02).*
b *Dish with ring base and two rim-holes. No handles. Diam. 20.7 cm (DM-BIR-03).*
Left to right, back
c *Top half of jug with side-spout formed as a miniature jug held by a seated woman. Fragment. Ht. 15.1 cm (DM-BIR-04). Cf. SCE IV.2, Fig. LXVI, no. 8.*
d *Bowl with ring base and one horizontal handle. Diam. 15.1 cm (DM-BIR-01).*

Pl. 36

22 Wheelmade Black Slip Ware

This sombre ware was popular throughout the Cypro-Geometric Period. It was originally referred to as Cypro-Bucchero Ware because of its superficial resemblance to Etruscan Bucchero, but there is no true relationship and the misleading name has now been dropped. The only connection between the two is that they both imitate metal prototypes. It may even be that they copied similar metal jugs, because the Etruscans imported metal vessels from the East. But the pottery developed quite separately in the two cases. The original grouping of vessels under the heading of Cypro-Bucchero Ware included both Late Bronze Age and Early Iron Age examples, the former being handmade and the latter wheelmade. The vessels shared a special feature—the vertical ribbing or grooving of the body. But in other respects—clay, texture, finish—they were very different. It is now preferable to split them, with the earlier, handmade examples being considered as variants of Base Ring Ware, and renaming the later, wheelmade examples as Black Slip Ware.

23 Wheelmade Black Slip Painted Ware

Certain artists working in the Cypro-Geometric Period decided to produce 'hybrid' vessels—part Black Slip and part White Painted. This ware, called Black Slip Painted, nearly always shows the lower part of the body of jugs, jars and bowls finished in Black Slip and the upper part in White Painted decoration. Flat dishes have the outer area of the underside in Black Slip and the central zone in White Painted.

24 Plain White Ware

Throughout the Bronze Age and the Iron Age there are examples of plain unadorned White Ware vessels, though they are rarely of any special merit as works of art, being the utilitarian, poor relations of the more colourful ceramic products. Most of the shapes are the simplest designs for jugs, jars and bowls, but there is one particular shape that appears to be unique to Plain White Ware and that has some aesthetic appeal—the torpedo-shaped vessel—of which three examples are shown here.

22 Wheelmade Black Slip Ware.

Pl. 37 *Iron Age.*
Left to right, front
a *Jug with ring base and pinched spout. Ht. 12.6 cm (DM-WBS-12).*
b *Jug with ring base and round spout. Ht. 9.6 cm (DM-WBS-01).*
c *Jug with ring base and pinched spout. Ht. 15.5 cm (DM-WBS-06).*
Left to right, back
d *Jug with ring base and pinched spout. Ht. 20.7 cm (DM-WBS-16).*
e *Jar with ring base and vertical handles. Ht. 23.1 cm (DM-WBS-19).*
f *Jar with ring base and vertical handles. Ht. 12.5 cm (DM-WBS-20).*

Pl. 37

Pl. 38

23 Wheelmade Black Slip Painted Ware

Pl. 38 *Iron Age. Jar with ring base, wide neck and horizontal handles. Upper part white painted, lower part black slip. Ht. 17.8 cm (DM-WBSP-01).*

Pl. 39

24 Plain White Ware

Pl. 39 *Iron Age.*
Left to right, front
a *Jug with flat base and round spout. Ht. 14 cm (DM-PW-02).*
b *Jug with ring base and round spout. Ht. 14.3 cm (DM-PW-03).*
c *Bowl with flat base, no handles. Diam. 11 cm (DM-PW-13).*
d *Jug with flat base and round spout. Ht. 12 cm (DM-PW-01).*
Left to right, back
e *Torpedo-shaped jar with pointed base and round spout. Ht. 29.9 cm (DM-PW-09).*
f *Same description. Ht. 46.2 cm (DM-PW-07).*
g *Same description. Ht. 36.7 cm (DM-PW-08).*

25 Wheelmade Red Ware

Red Wares of one kind or another are popular throughout the Iron Age and beyond. Various examples are shown on these pages. They include (a) the ribbed vessels that were originally described as Red Bucchero Ware; (b) the Phoenician 'mushroom-mouthed' jugs and juglets which were imported into Cyprus and copied locally, some of the copies retaining only the shape and presenting it in local colours; (c) Hellenistic Red Slip jugs and (d) the Roman table ware called Terra Sigillata.

This completes a brief survey of the major Cypriot wares and some of the minor ones. Many of the minor wares have been omitted because they are of little aesthetic interest and

25a Wheelmade Red Ware, 'Bucchero-style'

Pl. 40
a(left) *Jar with ring base and two vertical handles. 'Bucchero-style' vertical stripes on lower body. Ht. 14 cm (DM-WRS-15).*
b(right) *Jug with ring base and pinched spout. 'Bucchero-style' markings on body. Ht. 17.2 cm (DM-WRS-09).*

Pl. 40

25b Wheelmade Red Ware, Phoenician-style.

Pl. 41
Left to right
a *Jug with ring base, round mushroom-shaped spout and carinated shoulder. Ht. 10 cm (DM-WRS-02).*
b *Same description. Ht. 8.5 cm (DM-WRS-04).*
c *Same description. Ht. 19.7 cm (DM-WRS-01).*
d *Same description. Ht. 8.7 cm (DM-WRS-03).*

Pl. 41

Pl. 42

25c Wheelmade Red Ware, Hellenistic

Pl. 42
Left to right
a *Jug with ring base and pinched spout. Relief ring around bottom of neck. Early Hellenistic.*
Ht. 12.7 cm (DM-WRS-11).
b *Jug with ring base and pinched spout. Base region is bare of red slip.*
Ht. 15 cm (DM-WRS-10).

Pl. 43

25d Wheelmade Red Ware, Roman

Pl. 43
Left to right
a *Jug with ring base and round spout. Shoulder region flattened. Sigillata Ware. Ht. 21.2 cm (DM-WRS-07). Inscribed on base: 'Lot 293, Cesnola Lawrence Coll. Mar. '88'. Cf. SCE IV.3, Fig. 22, nos. 22-3.*
b *Jug with ring base and round spout. Highly polished Sigillata Ware. Ht. 15.2 cm (DM-WRS-08). Inscribed on base: 'Cyprus. VA.4.HF', indicating that this vessel was formerly in the Hugh Fawcett Collection.*
c *Jug with ring base and round spout. Relief ring around bottom of neck. Sigillata Ware. Ht. 26.4 cm (DM-WRS-04).*

are often based on no more than a few isolated vessels, or even on a single vessel or a few fragments.

It is interesting that in each main period of the Cyprus story there are two outstanding wares:

EARLY BRONZE AGE:
  Red Polished
  Black Polished

MIDDLE BRONZE AGE:
  Red-on-Black
  Handmade White Painted

LATE BRONZE AGE:
  Base Ring
  White Slip

IRON AGE:
  Wheelmade White Painted
  Bichrome

In some cases they may have been triggered by foreign influences, but all eight categories reach their peaks of originality and aesthetic achievement as truly indigenous styles. Together they make Cyprus one of the most exciting ceramic centres in the world.

The Pottery Shapes

Only the simplest of ancient Cypriot vessels are purely functional in shape. In all other cases—the vast majority—functional considerations are tempered by the demands of ritual, art and sheer playful inventiveness. In extreme cases, art dominates function to the extent that the vessels are completely useless in their original, primary role as containers.

Yet, despite this powerful trend to convert simple utensils into individual works of art, the Cypriot potters felt the need to retain the original container-identity, even in the most extravagantly complex and bizarre examples. Instead of allowing themselves to create entirely new pottery shapes unrelated to ordinary vessels, they kept the vessel shapes as basic units and then began to build on them in various ways.

One method was to make the surface special with different kinds of firing, slip, polish or decorative patterns. Another was to modify the basic shape in such a way that, although it remained simple and functional, it acquired a new aesthetic quality. A third was to make a complex or composite vessel by multiplying the basic vessel-units. A jug, for example, suddenly sprouted two necks or handles; a jar divided into twin bodies; a bowl acquired double spouts. The units were the old, functional ones, but now, in *multi-unit vessels* they underwent a process of pluralization, as if they were cells in a growing organism. In this way, each vessel could become complex and special, while still being honest to the simple container units on which it was based.

A further type of elaboration was the addition of small, subsidiary units on a large one. A big jug would 'grow' small jugs or bowls on its shoulders, like some strange plant pushing out new shoots, or a *Hydra* reproducing by budding. Both the main vessel and the tiny, secondary ones were, in themselves, faithful to the original functional container-units, but in their combination as *subsidiary-unit vessels*, the Cypriot artist managed to create something complicated, original and exciting.

Only in one category did the early potters abandon completely any recognizably func-

tional vessel-unit. That was in the curious innovation referred to as *ring vessels*. Here, the fundamental unit has ceased to be a simple pot—a jug, a bowl, or a jar—and has become instead a hollow (or sometimes solid) ceramic ring with a mouth. There are often animal-head adornments or smaller vessels sprouting from the ring-shape to make the object more special.

Although examples of ring vessels are known from outside Cyprus—in Greece for instance—they appear to be a Cypriot invention that has travelled, rather than the other way around. They cover an enormous period in Cyprus, spanning more than 2,000 years, from the Copper Age to the Iron Age, yet for some reason they do not appear to have been very common at any stage. Precisely what triggered such an unusual design innovation and persuaded the Cypriot potters to break with their strong tradition of basing their experiments on simple-vessel units, is hard to say. The special (ritual?) significance of the ring-shape remains a mystery.

Before surveying the wide range of shapes found with ancient Cypriot vessels, it is helpful to list the basic functions which act as the starting points from which the potters depart on their creative journeys. In each case, the function is given on the left and is then followed by the names of vessels which might serve that function:

1	*Store:*	Bottle, Jug, Jar, Flask, Box *(Amphora, Pyxis)*.
2	*Pour:*	Bottle, Jug, Flask *(Oenochoe, Hydria)*.
3	*Drink:*	Bottle, Flask, Bowl, Cup *(Skyphos)*.
4	*Eat:*	Bowl, Dish, Plate, Platter.
5	*Dip:*	Ladle, Dipper, Spoon *(Kyathos)*.
6	*Mix:*	Bowl *(Krater)*.
7	*Cook:*	Bowl, Jar.
8	*Strain:*	Strainer.
9	*Display:*	Bowl, Jar, Dish, Plate, Pottery Basket.

There are other minor functions, but these

are the main ones and cover the bulk of the vessels made in ancient times. The names of some well-known Greek vessels have been added in brackets, because they are often used when Cypriot pottery is being discussed in English. This is a tradition I shall avoid wherever possible because it is frequently misleading. The Greek names were coined for specific types of vessels whose precise functions are known. For example, a *krater* was used for mixing wine and water; a *pyxis* was a box for cosmetics, and so on. When a Cypriot vessel with a shape that is reminiscent of these Greek types is encountered there is an unhappy tendency to label it with the Greek title, thus not only commenting on its resemblance, but also implying its function. To give one instance—when a large, melon-shaped pottery box is found in an Early Bronze Age tomb in Cyprus, it is automatically called a *pyxis*, suggesting that it was used for cosmetics, in the Greek way. But as far as I can tell there is not a scrap of evidence that any such function was involved. Indeed, it seems highly unlikely that such pottery boxes were used as *pyxides*, so it is better to avoid such terms. The only exceptions that could be made to this rule concern imported Greek pottery that is either unmodified by local potters, or modified in a minor way that does not obscure the specific Greek function.

The Simple Shapes

Many names for simple pottery shapes are used almost indiscriminately. In order to simplify and clarify the situation, I have reduced all simple shapes to ten basic types, as follows:

1	*Jug:*	*One-handled vessel with neck.* (To include: juglet, tankard, pitcher)
2	*Bottle:*	*Narrow-necked vessel with no handles or two handles.*
3	*Flask:*	*Sideways-flattened vessel.*
4	*Jar:*	*Symmetrical vessel with wide neck.* (To include: vase, beaker, urn, pot, *amphora*)
5	*Bowl:*	*Vessel with opening as widest part.* (To include: cup, basin, chalice, goblet)
6	*Dish:*	*Flat vessel.* (To include: plate, platter)
7	*Box:*	*Squat vessel with a lid.* (To include: *pyxis*)
8	*Dipper:*	*Squat vessel with tall handle.* (To include: ladle)
9	*Basket:*	*Open-work pottery bowl.*
10	*Strainer:*	*Vessel with group of punctured holes.*

This classification is deliberately over-simplified in order to create a small number of major categories, within which it is possible to group 'families' of vessel-shapes. The essence of the definitions is that they do not depend upon or rashly imply any kind of function for particular vessels. They are purely structural definitions, and when dealing with ancient pottery objects, this is the only safe system to use.

With this as a basis, it is now possible to survey the range of simple shapes found in ancient Cyprus, illustrated photographically with examples from the author's collection.

1 Jug

Jugs are common at all phases and in all wares. The two most useful elements for classification are the shape of the base and the spout. *Round bases* dominate during the Early and Middle Bronze Ages. *Ring bases* take over in the Late Bronze Age. In the Iron Age, *flat bases* and *ring bases* are the two common types.

Less popular base-types include the *pointed bases* which appear spasmodically from the Early Bronze Age to the Iron Age; the *nipple base*, a minor variant of the round base, which occurs in the Early and Middle Bronze Ages; the *barrel base*, another variant of the round base where the lower portion of the body of the vessel has the contours of a barrel lying on its side, and which appears in the Iron Age only. Finally there are rare examples of *tripod based* jugs, where round bases sprout three short stumpy legs. Tripod jugs appear to be confined to the Early and Middle Bronze Ages.

Spouts may be *round* (popular in all periods), *beak-shaped* or *cutaway* (both popular in the Bronze Age but not in the Iron Age) or *pinched* (popular in the Iron Age but not the Bronze Age). An additional *side-spout* appears occasionally (in all periods), a feature which separates the functions of filling and pouring.

1a Jugs with round bases

Pl. 44 Round spout

a(left) *Relief-decorated Red Polished Ware. Early Bronze Age. Decorated with bands around neck and short horizontal zigzag on shoulder. Ht. 38.3 cm (DM-RRP-02).*
b(right) *Plain Red Polished Ware. Early Bronze Age. With a short projection on the shoulder and a stylized face on the neck, comprising two pierced ears and a 'nose-lug'. Twin-spur thumb-grip on handle. Ht. 40.3 cm (DM-PRP-01).*

Pl. 45 Round Spout

a(left) *Mottled Red Polished Ware. Early Bronze Age. With two circular bosses on shoulder and two pierced ear-lugs on neck. Crude zigzag incision on handle. Ht. 34.2 cm (DM-MRP-01).*
b(right) *Relief-decorated Red Polished Ware. Early Bronze Age. With bands around the neck and shoulders. Ht. 18.4 cm (DM-RRP-03).*

Pl. 46 Round spout

a(left) *Mottled Red Polished Ware. Early Bronze Age. With curved vertical zigzags. Ht. 14.4 cm (DM-MRP-03).*
b(centre) *Incised Red Polished Ware. Early Bronze Age. With tall handle. Ht. 11.8 cm. (DM-IRP-36).*
c(right) *Mottled Red Polished Ware. Early Bronze Age. With simple, crude incisions on the neck, shoulders and handle. Ht. 16 cm (DM-MRP-02).*

Pl. 44

Pl. 45

Pl. 46

Pl. 47

1a Jugs with round bases

Pl. 47 Round spout
a(left) *Handmade Black Slip Ware. Middle Bronze Age. With flattened handle and incised decoration on the upper body. Dark red colour. Ht. 12.4 cm (DM-HBS-02).*
b(right) *Drab Polished Ware. Middle Bronze Age. With simple incisions including mechanically made circles. Ht. 10.2 cm (DM-DP-01).*

Pl. 48

Pl. 48 Round spout
a(left) *Drab Polished Ware. Middle Bronze Age. With incised markings. Ht. 8.5 cm (DM-DP-02).*
b(right) *Handmade Black Slip Ware. Middle Bronze Age. With most of the slip lost. Simple incisions including horizontal zigzags. Ht. 10 cm (DM-HBS-03).*

Pl. 49

Pl. 49 Round spout
a(left) *Red-on-black Ware. Middle Bronze Age. Ht. 17.8 cm (DM-ROB-04).*
b(centre) *Same ware. Ht. 14 cm (DM-ROB-02).*
c(right) *Same ware. Ht. 20.3 cm (DM-ROB-03).*

1a Jugs with round bases

Pl. 50 Round spout.
a(left) *Handmade White Painted Ware. Middle Bronze Age. Decoration includes vertical wavy lines. Orange paint. Ht. 22.5 cm (DM-HWP-01).*
b(centre) *Same ware, but with exceptionally tall neck and handle. Decoration unusually simple, vertical and horizontal wavy lines. Ht. 15 cm (DM-HWP-03).*
c(right) *Same ware. Decoration includes triangles alternating with circles. Black paint. Ht 19.5 cm (DM-HWP-02).*

Pl. 50

Pl.51 Round spout
a(left) *Handmade White Painted Ware. Middle Bronze Age. Black painted lines have almost vanished. Ht. 19.2 cm (DM-HWP-04).*
b(centre) *Same ware, but black painted lines remain strong. Tall handle. Ht. 9.2 cm (DM-HWP-06).*
c (right) *Same ware. Lines almost vanished. Ht. 17.7 cm (DM-HWP-05).*

Pl. 51

Pl. 52 Round spout
a(left) *Wheelmade White Painted Ware. Iron Age. Cruciform motif surrounded by circles and hatched triangles. Ht. 19 cm (DM-WWP-11).*
b(centre) *Same Ware. Horizontal bands only. Ht. 8.2. cm (DM-WWP-02).*
c(right) *Same ware. Decoration includes four sets of concentric circles on body. Ht. 12.4 cm (DM-WWP-06).*

Pl. 52

Pl. 53

Pl. 54

1a Jugs with round bases

Pl. 53 Round spout + side spout. *Relief-decorated Red Polished Ware. Early Bronze Age. With circular bosses, one on each side of body. Ht. 19.8 cm (DM-RRP-05).*

Pl. 54 Round spout + side spout. *Handmade White Painted Ware. Middle Bronze Age. Neck and side spout both rather short. Decoration faded. Ht. 14 cm (DM-HWP-07).*

Pl. 55

Pl. 55 Round spout + wide neck

a(left) *Incised Red Polished Ware. Early Bronze Age. Decorated with three-pronged instrument. Ht. 13.5 cm (DM-IRP-37).*
b(centre) *Black Slip Ware. Middle Bronze Age. Decorated with four-pronged instrument. Ht. 27.8 cm (DM-HBS-07). This vessel approaches Base Ring Ware in quality and has an incipient base ring in the form of an incised relief-band.*
c(right) *Handmade White Painted Ware. Middle Bronze Age. Handle with thumb-grip spur. Ht. 22.3 cm (DM-HWP-08). The shape of these three vessels is sometimes called 'tankard'.*

Pl. 56

Pl. 56 Round spout + squat neck

a(left) *Mottled Red Polished Ware. Early Bronze Age. Incised decoration includes four comb-figures (see p. 141). Ht. 11.8 cm (DM-MRP-04).*
b(centre) *Incised Red Polished Ware. Early Bronze Age. Ht. 7.4 cm (DM-IRP-39). Handle restored.*
c(right) *Same ware. Ht. 12 cm (DM-IRP-38). Handle restored.*

1a Jugs with round bases

Pl.57 Round spout + side spout + squat neck
a(left) *Mottled Red Polished Ware. Early Bronze Age. Decorated with single zigzag band below rim. Neck undifferentiated from body. Ht. 11.5 cm (DM-MRP-06).*
b(right) *Same ware. Decorated with single zigzag bands, one on neck and one on body. Ht. 13.5 cm (DM-MRP-05).*

Pl. 57

Pl. 58 Round spout + side spout + squat neck
a(left) *Drab Polished Ware. Middle Bronze Age. Decoration includes mechanically made circles. Ht. 17.9 cm (DM-DP-05). Spout restored.*
b(right) *Same ware. Ht. 20.4 cm (DM-DP-04). Spout restored.*

Pl. 58

Pl. 59 Round spout + side-hole. *Handmade White Painted Ware. Middle Bronze Age. Ht. 19 cm (DM-HWP-09). The side-hole permits the entry of air when liquid is being poured from the very narrow spout.*

Pl. 59

Pl. 60

Pl. 61

Pl. 62

Pl. 63

1a Jugs with round bases

Pl. 60 Beak spout. *Incised Red Polished Ware. Middle Bronze Age. Decorated with four-pronged instrument. Ht. 28 cm (DM-IRP-40). This vessel comes from the very end of the Red Polished series, in the Middle Bronze Age.*

Pl. 61 Beak spout

a(left) *Incised Red Polished Ware. Middle Bronze Age. Decorated with four-pronged instrument. Ht. 12.1 cm (DM-IRP-41).*
b(right) *Same ware. Decorated with minor zigzags and six lugs. Ht. 11 cm (DM-IRP-42). These small vessels, despite their Red Polished finish, are close to Drab Polished Ware.*

Pl. 62 Beak spout

a(left) *Handmade White Painted Ware. Middle Bronze Age. Very small handle. Decorated with orange lines. Ht. 12.7 cm (DM-HWP-12).*
b(centre) *Same ware. Lines red to black. Ht. 16.8 cm (DM-HWP-11).*
c(right) *Same ware. Lines black. The beak spout is flared at the sides. Ht. 14.2 cm (DM-HWP-10).*

Pl. 63 Cutaway–beak spout

a(left) *Relief-decorated Red Polished Ware. Early Bronze Age. Relief bands on neck and body interspersed with incised zigzag bands. Ht. 28.1 cm (DM-RRP-10).*
b(centre) *Same ware. Unusual relief decorations showing (apotropaic?) eye motif on front and back of body. Minor incisions on handle only. Dark red colour. Ht. 33 cm (DM-RRP-07).*
c(right) *Incised Red Polished Ware. Early Bronze Age. Decorated with vertical zigzags on neck and body. Ht. 28.6 cm (DM-IRP-45).*

1a Jugs with round bases

Pl. 64 Cutaway-beak spout

a(left) *Relief-decorated Red Polished Ware. Early Bronze Age. Bulbous neck with four relief bands. Four vertical zigzags on body. Ht. 37.2 cm (DM-RRP-09).*
b(centre) *Same ware. Two relief-bands on neck. Twelve raised studs on neck and body. Two wing-lugs and two horseshoe-lugs on shoulders. Ht. 44.4 cm (DM-RRP-06).*
c(right) *Plain Red Polished Ware. Early Bronze Age. Decoration confined to a few minor incisions on the twisted handle and three plain lugs. Ht. 36.1 cm (DM-PRP-04).*

Pl. 64

Pl. 65 Cutaway-beak spout

a(left) *Incised Red Polished Ware. Early Bronze Age. Ht. 14.1 cm (DM-IRP-43). Formerly in the Cesnola Collection.*
b(centre) *Plain Red Polished Ware. Early Bronze Age. Twisted handle . Seven plain lugs. Ht. 25.5 cm (DM-PRP-05).*
c(right) *Incised Red Polished Ware. Early Bronze Age. Ht. 17.5 cm (DM-IRP-44).*

Pl. 65

Pl. 66 Cutaway-beak spout

a(left) *Handmade White Painted Ware. Middle Bronze Age. Four lugs on body, three on neck. Also a thumb-grip on handle. Ht. 16.1 cm (DM-HWP-16).*
b(centre) *Same ware. One lug at base of neck. Ht. 23.3 cm (DM-HWP-17).*
c(right) *Same ware. No lugs. Strap handle. Ht. 15.1 cm (DM-HWP-18).*

Pl. 66

1a Jugs with round bases

Pl. 67 Cutaway-beak spout + side spout. *Incised Red Polished Ware. Early Bronze Age. Pierced lug at base of neck. Side-spout very long. Ht. 25.2 cm (DM-IRP-46).*

Pl. 68 Cutaway spout. *Incised Red Polished Ware. Early Bronze Age. Neck flares out widely towards spout. Four small pierced lugs on the edge of the spout and a large pierced lug at the base of the neck. Handle with thumb-grip. Ht. 29.3 cm (DM-IRP-48).*

Pl. 69 Cutaway spout. *Incised Red Polished Ware. Early Bronze Age. Ht. 15.1 cm (DM-IRP-47).*

Pl. 67

Pl. 68

Pl. 69

1a Jugs with round bases

Pl. 70 Pinched spout

a(left) *Handmade White Painted Ware. Middle Bronze Age. Tapering neck with the spout double-pinched. Large thumb-grip on handle. Complex painted decoration. Ht. 16.4 cm (DM-HWP-21).*
b(right) *Same ware. Rather wide neck and tall handle. Ht. 13.5 cm (DM-HWP-22).*

Pl. 71 Pinched spout

a(left) *Handmade White Painted Ware. Middle Bronze Age. Squat neck with tall handle. Simple decoration. Ht. 11 cm (DM-HWP-19).*
b(right) *Same ware. Squat neck with tall handle. Thumb-grip on handle and lug at base of neck. Decoration includes elements that look like a pair of staring eyes. This resemblance may be accidental, or it may indicate an apotropaic protective device. Ht. 13.7 cm (DM-HWP-20).*

1b Jugs with flat bases

Pl. 72 Round spout

Left to right
a *Handmade White Painted Ware. Middle Bronze Age. Only small area of base is flat.*
Ht. 10.2 cm (DM-HWP-23).
b *Bichrome Ware. Iron Age. The only red-painted area is the outside of the spout. Ht. 8.3 cm (DM-BI-02).*
c *Same ware. Ht. 12.7 cm (DM-BI-03).*
d *Same ware. Ht. 9.2 cm (DM-BI-01).*

Pl. 70

Pl. 71

Pl. 72

1b Jugs with flat bases

Pl. 73 Round spout + side spout

a(left) *Wheelmade White Painted Ware. Side spout short and tapering with fine aperture. Decoration shows six 'drooping leaves' in red paint. Ht. 11.6 cm (DM-WWP-16).*
b(right) *Bichrome Ware. Side spout tapering. Decoration most unusual for this ware. In addition to red and black lines there are large numbers of red and black dots and short dashes, filling in every available space on the body surface. Ht. 10.3 cm (DM-BI-08).*

Pl. 74 Pinched spout

a(left) *Handmade White Painted Ware. Middle Bronze Age. Flat base is at an angle so that the vessel leans backwards. Ht. 10 cm (DM-HWP-24).*
b(centre) *Same ware. Flat base crudely fashioned. Decoration includes vertical 'stripes' of eye motifs on lower body. Ht. 14.7 cm (DM-HWP-25).*
c(right) *Wheelmade White Painted Ware. Iron Age. Tall-bodied vessel with virtually no neck. Ht. 12.7 cm (DM-WWP-27).*

Pl. 75 Pinched spout

a(left) *Bichrome Ware. Iron Age. Pair of eyes on the pinched-in section of the spout. Two swastikas on the shoulders. Ht. 12.3 cm (DM-BI-12).*
b(centre) *Same ware. Decoration badly faded. Ht. 12.6 cm (DM-BI-15).*
c(right) *Same ware. Ht. 10.6 cm (DM-BI-16).*

Pl. 73

Pl. 74

Pl. 75

1c Jugs with pointed bases

Pl. 76 *Relief-decorated Red Polished Ware. Early Bronze Age. Big-bellied jug with relief ring at base of neck and four small protrusions on the body. The shortish neck has a cutaway-beak spout. Ht. 41.8 cm (DM-RRP-11).*

1d Jugs with nipple bases

Pl. 77 Beak spout. *Relief-decorated Red Polished Ware. Early Bronze Age. Relief 'cord' draped around neck and short cords hanging down the shoulders of the vessel, including some which are 'crossed over' or intertwined. Ht. 29.3 cm (DM-RRP-12).*

Pl. 76

Pl. 77

Pl. 78 Cutaway spout
Left to right
a *Plain Red Polished Ware. Early Bronze Age. Tall, slim, flaring neck. Egg-shaped body with large nipple. Handle with thumb-grip incisions in place of the more common spur or lug. These incisions are a rare case of pottery markings with a mechanical rather than a decorative function. Ht. 26.5 cm (DM-PRP-07).*
b *Same ware, but without the handle incisions. The surface is badly worn. Ht. 28.1 cm (DM-PRP-09).*
c *Same ware. Ht. 37.1 cm (DM-PRP-10).*
d *Same ware, with dark staining on surface. Ht. 24.4 cm (DM-PRP-11).*

Pl. 78

1e Jugs with ring bases

Pl. 79 Round spout

Left to right
a *Base Ring Ware, with dull black surface. Late Bronze Age. Ht. 13.8 cm (DM-BR-14).*
b *Same ware, with tall slender Syrian-influenced body shape. Ht. 15.9 cm (DM-BR-15).*
c *Same ware, plain. Ht. 13.7 cm (DM-BR-13).*
d *Same ware, with carinated shoulder. Ht. 13.1 cm (DM-BR-11).*

Pl. 79

Pl. 80 Round spout

Left to right
a *Base Ring Ware, relief-decorated. Late Bronze Age. Bucchero-style vertical ribbing of body. Ht. 14.2 cm (DM-BR-02).*
b *Same ware. Groups of body-stripes. Ht. 14.5 cm (DM-BR-07).*
c *Same ware. Groups of shoulder-stripes above horizontal bands. Ht. 13.3 cm (DM-BR-06).*
d *Same ware. Paired-spiral motif. Ht. 11.5 cm (DM-BR-08).*

Pl. 80

Pl. 81 Round spout

Left to right
a *Base Ring Ware, painted. Late Bronze Age. Ht. 12.2 cm (DM-BR-17).*
b *Same ware. Ht. 12.8 cm (DM-BR-18).*
c *Same ware. Ht. 15.4 cm (DM-BR-19).*
d *Same ware. Crude shape, lacking the widely flared spout and the tall neck. The paintwork is fugitive and only a few small traces remain. Ht. 10.2 cm (DM-BR-03).*

Pl. 81

1e Jugs with ring bases

Pl. 82 Round spout + wide neck

a(left) *Base Ring Ware. Late Bronze Age. Small 'tankard' vessel with a pair of relief-bands on the neck. Large thumb-grip spur on top of handle. Ht. 10.9 cm (DM-BR-23).*
b(right) *Same ware, but painted with white lines in place of relief decoration. Horizontal 'chain' motif on body. Large thumb-grip spur on top of handle. Ht. 10.9 cm (DM-BR-24).*

Pl. 82

Pl. 83 Cutaway spout

a(left) *Base Ring Ware, relief decorated. Late Bronze Age. Typical large jug with twin-spiral motif on the body. Ht. 39.8 cm (DM-BR-26). Formerly in the Lawrence Collection, this vessel was first sold at Sotheby's on 27 April 1892 and again on 23 February 1976.*
b(right) *Same ware, with similar relief decoration. Ht. 27.9 cm (DM-BR-27).*

Pl. 83

Pl. 84

1e Jugs with ring bases

Pl. 84 Pinched spout
a(left) *Handmade White Painted Ware. Middle Bronze Age (from the very end of the period). Ht. 13.7 cm (DM-HWP-27). Cf.Frankel 1983, no. 881.*
b(centre) *Same ware. Ht. 14 cm (DM-HWP-26). Cf. SCE IV.1b, Fig. XVI, no. 15.*
c(right) *Black Slip Ware. Middle Bronze Age (from the very end of that period). Incised pattern made with multi-pointed implement. Flattened handle. Ht. 15.9 cm (DM-HBS-08). Cf. SCE IV.1b, Fig. XXX, no. 14 and Frankel 1983, nos. 1235-6.*

Pl. 85

Pl. 85 Pinched spout
a(left) *Bichrome Ware. Iron Age. Concentric circles style. Ht. 24 cm (DM-BI-21)*
b(centre) *Same ware. Ht. 31.3 cm (DM-BI-29)*
c(right) *Same ware. Ht. 22.5 cm (DM-BI-28).*

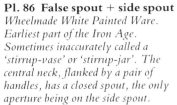

Pl. 86   Pl. 87

Pl. 86 False spout + side spout
Wheelmade White Painted Ware. Earliest part of the Iron Age. Sometimes inaccurately called a 'stirrup-vase' or 'stirrup-jar'. The central neck, flanked by a pair of handles, has a closed spout, the only aperture being on the side spout. Ht. 10.2 cm (DM-WWP-45). Cf. SCE IV.2, Fig. IV, no. 20.

Pl. 87 Basket handle + side spout. *Wheelmade White Painted Ware. Earliest part of the Iron Age. The central neck is topped by a basket handle. Ht. 13.8 cm (DM-WWP-46). Cf. SCE IV.2, Fig. IV, nos. 17 and 18.*

1f Jugs with barrel bases

Pl. 88 *Wheelmade White Painted Ware. Iron Age. This large jug with an almost spherical body has a complex motif below the handle. This motif may be a highly abstracted image of a bird (cf. Pl. 89 on this page). Ht. 39 cm (DM-WWP-50). Cf. SCE IV.2, Fig. XIII, nos. 6 and 7.*

Pl. 89 *Bichrome Ware. Iron Age. The motif opposite the handle appears to be a bird, shown flying upwards, with open beak, head, eyes, body, wings and forked tail. Ht. 33.7 cm (DM-BI-32). Cf. SCE IV.2, Fig. VIII, no. 10.*

Pl. 90 *Bichrome Ware. Iron age, The body is the shape and size of an ostrich egg lying on it side. There is a complex motif below the handle and another opposite it. They appear to be more than abstract adornments, but their meaning is obscure. Ht. 20 cm (DM-BI-31).*

Pl. 88

Pl. 89

Pl. 90

1g Jugs with tripod bases

Pl. 91 *Handmade White Painted Ware. Middle Bronze Age. Neck with narrow, round spout and side-hole. Ht. 18 cm (DM-HWP-28). Cf. SCE IV.1b, Fig. XIII, no. 12.*

Pl. 91

2 Bottle

Small pottery bottles were extremely popular in the Early Bronze Age, usually with two pierced holes near the mouth for a suspension cord, or for stopper-attachment. These vessels were typically without handles, but sometimes had a pair of small lugs. In the Middle Bronze Age the typical White Painted bottle had two small pierced lugs. Cypro-Mycenaean bottles had two small handles and a ring base. The small bottles of the Iron Age period were also normally two-handled, but favoured a flat base. Later on, in the Hellenistic period, the tall, slender Spindle Bottles became popular.

2a Bottles with round bases

Pl. 92 Without lugs

Left to right
a *Red-and-Black Polished Ware. Early to Middle Bronze Age. Not typical of this ware. Ht. 12.2 cm (DM-RBP-09).*
b *Same ware, but again this example is not typical. Ht. 16.5 cm (DM-RBP-08).*
c *Black-topped Red Polished Ware. Another problem vessel, with some characteristics of Black-topped Red Polished Ware and others of Red-and-Black Polished Ware. Ht. 17 cm (DM-BTRP-07).*
d *Same ware, but a more typical example. Ht. 15.8 cm (DM-BTRP-06).*
e *Same ware. Ht. 12.2 cm (DM-BTRP-03).*

Pl. 92

Pl. 93 With lugs
a(left) *Relief-decorated Red Polished Ware. Early Bronze Age. Plain spherical bottle except for snake-like relief motifs on the shoulders. Ht. 16.2 cm (DM-RRP-14).*
b(centre) *Red-and-Black Polished Ware. This vessel is red down one side and black down the other—the typical coloration of this ware, but its incision patterns are those of Incised Red Polished Ware. Ht. 12.5 cm (DM-RBP-07).*
c(right) *Mottled Red Polished Ware. Spherical vessel with four lugs on the*

body, two small and two very long and curved at the end. Ht. 15.1 cm (DM-MRP-09).

Pl. 94 With lugs
a(left) *Handmade White Painted Ware. Middle Bronze Age. Ht. 9.8 cm (DM-HWP-32).*
b(centre) *Same ware. Ht. 7 cm (DM-HWP-33).*
c(right) *Same ware. Ht. 9 cm (DM-HWP-31).*

2b Bottles with ring bases

Pl. 95 *Cypro-Mycenaean Ware. Late Bronze Age. Two vertical handles. Ht. 17.1 cm (DM-CM-01).*

2c Bottles with flat bases

Pl. 96
a(left) *Plain White Ware. Hellenistic Period. Spindle-shaped vessel. Ht. 17.2 cm (DM-PW-05).*
b(right) *Same ware, but with heavy black staining. Ht. 20 cm (DM-PW-04).*

Pl. 97
a(left) *Incised Red Polished Ware. Early Bronze Age. Ht. 10 cm (DM-IRP-52).*
b(right) *Black Polished Ware. Early Bronze Age. This type of vessel is sometimes called a 'feeder bottle' for a baby. Ht. 11.2 cm (DM-BP-05). Cf. SCE IV.1a, Fig. CLII, no. 16.*

Pl. 95

Pl. 96

Pl. 97

3 Flask

Flasks, by my definition, are vessels that have been flattened sideways, giving them a 'squashed' appearance. In the past the words 'bottle' and 'flask' have often been used interchangeably, but it is helpful to separate them because, traditionally, flasks were vessels that were carried about with their owners. Their squashed shape made them easier to transport in this way. For some reason they are absent from the Early Bronze Age period, but become common in the Middle Bronze Age where they are often festooned with pierced lugs for some sort of string attachment. In the Late Bronze Age they reappear as 'Pilgrim Flasks' and then re-surface again in the Iron Age as circular, two-handled vessels.

3a Flasks with round bases

Pl. 98

a(left) *Base Ring Ware. Late Bronze Age. Heavily flattened vessel in the 'pilgrim flask' style, probably borrowed from Wheelmade Red Lustrous artists by local Base Ring Ware potters. Single vertical handle. Heavy surface wear. Ht. 13.4 cm (DM-BR-28).*
b(right) *Handmade White Painted Ware. Middle Bronze Age. Heavily flattened vessel with beak spout and eight pierced lugs. Single, small vertical handle. Orange painted lines. Ht. 24 cm (DM-HWP-34).*

Pl. 99

a(left) *Bichrome Ware. Iron Age. Flattened circular vessel with two vertical handles. Ht. 9.6 cm (DM-BI-33).*
b(right) *Wheelmade White Painted Ware. Iron Age. Same shape. Ht. 13.9 cm (DM-WWP-54).*

Pl. 98

3b Flasks with flat bases

Pl. 100

Left to right
a *Handmade White Painted Ware. Middle Bronze Age. This minute, slender vessel appears to be the smallest one known from ancient Cyprus. It must either have been part of a model group, or a toy of a small child, or perhaps a container for some liquid so precious that only a few drops were carried. Ht. 6.7 cm (DM-HWP-39).*
b *Same ware. Ht. 9.9 cm (DM-HWP-37).*
c *Same ware. Ht. 21.5 cm (DM-HWP-35).*
d *Same ware. Ht. 9.3 cm (DM-HWP-38).*

Pl. 100

4 Jar

In the Early Bronze Age the most common form of jar is the round-based, two-handled variety, with the handles attached in the vertical plane. Some flat-bottomed ones also appear, and continue into the Middle Bronze Age. By the Late Bronze Age, jars have become rare as a vessel type, but in the Iron Age they occur again in large numbers, normally with a ring base. Horizontal handles rival vertically attached ones in popularity, and the size of many of the jars increases dramatically.

4a Jars with round bases

Pl. 101

a(left) *Incised Red Polished Ware. Early Bronze Age. The incised decoration is restricted to an unusual degree. Ht. 26.3 cm (DM-IRP-53).*
b(right) *Relief-decorated Red Polished Ware. Early Bronze Age. The base is slightly flattened, but functionally this remains a round-based vessel. Ht. 29.3 cm (DM-RRP-15).*

Pl. 102

a(left) *Incised Red Polished Ware. Early Bronze Age. The incised decoration includes four carefully drawn Comb Figures on the body, two under the handles and two opposite them (for details, see p. 141). Ht. 22 cm (DM-IRP-54).*
b(right) *Same ware. The base is slightly flattened, but functionally this remains a round-based vessel. Ht. 27.3 cm (DM-IRP-55).*

Pl. 103

Pl. 103

a(left) *Drab Polished Ware. Middle Bronze Age. Plain surface. Sharply pointed handles. Ht. 21.3 cm (DM-DP-13).*
b(right) *Same ware. Incised decoration typical of this ware. Ht. 23.2 cm (DM-DP-12). Although both these vessels have been identified as Drab Polished Ware, they show marked differences and reflect the lack of homogeneity in this group.*

4b Jars with flat bases

Pl. 104 *Wheelmade White Painted Ware. Iron Age.*
Large cylindrical vessel with slightly convex sides and two
horizontally attached handles. Squat neck. Body with
carinated shoulder. Ht. 28.1 cm (DM-WWP-56).
Cf. Karageorghis 1975, Alaas T.16, no. 16, for similar shape.

Pl. 105

a(left) *Bichrome Ware. Iron Age. Two horizontally attached handles.*
Ht. 10.3 cm (DM-BI-36).
b(right) *Same ware, but without lip to rim. Ht. 10.1 cm (DM-BI-37).*

Pl. 104

Pl. 105

4c Jars with nipple bases

Pl. 106 *Plain Red Polished Ware. Early Bronze Age. Giant jar with*
blunt nipple. Two vertical handles, each with an upward projecting
spur. The body and neck are completely plain but there are nine
shallow holes punched into each handle, front and back, three on the
spur, three on the upper handle and three on the lower. Ht. 63.5 cm
(DM-PRP-14). The weight of this huge vessel is ten kilograms.

4d Jars with pointed bases

Pl. 107 *Bichrome Ware. Iron Age. Ovoid vessel with two vertical handles. The*
'red' paint has a purple hue. Ht. 18.5 cm (DM-BI-39). Cf. jar of similar shape
from Alaas (T.6/8, no. 3) in RDAC 1977, Pl. XXXI.

Pl. 106

Pl. 107

Pl. 108

4e Jars with ring bases

Pl. 108
a(left) *Cypro-Mycenaean Ware. Late Bronze Age. Three horizontally attached handles. Shoulder panels decorated with cross-hatched lines. Ht. 16 cm (DM-CM-03).*
b(centre) *Same ware, but shoulder panels decorated with fish-scale motif. Ht. 16.2 cm (DM-CM-04).*
c(right) *Same ware, but shoulder panels decorated with two rows of tall Us. Ht. 17.3 cm (DM-CM-11).*

Pl. 109
a(left) *Cypro-Mycenaean Ware. Late Bronze Age. Three horizontally attached handles. Shoulder panels decorated with right-angled lines. Ht. 14.4 cm (DM-CM-07).*
b(right) *Same ware, but with shoulder panels decorated with spiral motifs. Ht. 12.7 cm (DM-CM-08).*

Pl. 109

Pl. 110

Pl. 110 *Base Ring Ware. Late Bronze Age. Three horizontally attached handles. Painted decoration of white lines. This is a rare example of a Base Ring artist imitating a typical Mycenaean jar shape. Ht. 11 cm (DM-BR-29).*

Pl. 111 *Wheelmade White Painted Ware. Iron Age. Large vessel with two horizontally attached handles. Raised stud at base of neck. Ht. 39.5 cm (DM-WWP-101).*

Pl. 112 *Bichrome Ware. Iron Age. Typical Bichrome shape, with two vertical handles, but with unusual decorative style for this ware. Ht. 18 cm (DM-BI-45).*

Pl. 113 *Wheelmade White Painted Ware. Iron Age. Large jar with two vertically attached handles. Ht. 44.8 cm (DM-WWP-95).*

5 Bowl

The typical bowls of the Bronze Age are small, hemispherical vessels which lack handles in the Early period, develop them in the Middle period and modify them into a wishbone shape in the Late period. Throughout this Bronze Age phase there are, however, much larger, so-called 'milk' bowls, usually with spouts and pierced lugs. Other medium-sized bowls with handles are also common. One uniquely Cypriot shape is the Early Bronze Age 'tulip bowl', which has a hemispherical interior, but a slightly pointed base. Tulip bowls are usually slightly larger than the more common hemispherical bowls and appear to have been a special local form of them, possibly with a specific function as containers.

It is usual to refer to the smallest bowls as 'cups', or, if they have stem-bases, as 'goblets', but this implies that they were drinking vessels, for which we have no hard evidence. They may have been placed in the tombs for this purpose, but it is also possible that they contained small food offerings.

5a Bowls with round bases

Pl. 114 No lugs
Black-topped Red Polished Ware. Early Bronze Age. Completely plain bowls of this kind are less common than might be expected. The typical, small hemispherical bowl usually has one or more lugs outside the rim. Diam. 9.6 cm (DM-BTRP-10).

Pl. 114

Pl. 115

Pl. 115 One lug
a(left) Mottled Red Polished Ware. Early to Middle Bronze Age. The incisions on this rather deep-bodied bowl suggest that it is late in the Red Polished series. Diam. 15.3 cm (DM-MRP-10).
b(right) Black-topped Red Polished Ware. Early Bronze Age. Diam. 10.5 cm (DM-BTRP-15).

Pl. 116 Two lugs
a(left) Red-and-Black Polished Ware. Early to Middle Bronze Age. This rather shallow bowl has two flat, square-ended lugs, one pierced with two holes, the other without holes. Diam. 18.4 cm (DM-RBP-161).
b(right) Same ware. A smaller bowl, with pointed lugs, one pierced and one unpierced. Diam. 10.7 cm (DM-RBP-157).

Pl. 116

Pl. 117 Four lugs
a(left) Incised Red Polished Ware. Early Bronze Age. Diam. 18.5 cm (DM-IRP-61).
b(right) Mottled Red Polished Ware. Early to Middle Bronze Age. Shallow bowl with four bi-lobed lugs, one of which has a pierced ring below it. Diam. 18.7 cm (DM-MRP-15).

Pl. 117

Pl. 118

Pl. 119

5a Bowls with round bases

Pl. 118 Lug + spout
a(left) *Red-and-Black Polished Ware. Early to Middle Bronze Age. Shallow bowl with a flat, square-ended lug pierced with two holes, opposite a short trough-spout. Diam. 22.2 cm (DM-RBP-164).* **b**(right) *Same ware. Diam. 17.2 cm (DM-RBP-163).*

Pl. 119 Horizontal handle
Black-topped Red Polished Ware. Early Bronze Age. Long lug opposite handle. Incisions unusually crude and casual. Diam. 15 cm (DM-BTRP-19).

Pl. 120 Horizontal handle
White Slip Ware. Late Bronze Age. Diam 18.6 cm (DM-WSL-07). Cf. SCE IV.1c, Fig. LXXXII, no. 7 (WS IIA).

Pl. 121 Vertical handle
a(left) *Handmade White Painted Ware. Middle Bronze Age. Diam. 11.5 cm (DM-HWP-41). Cf. SCE IV.1b, Fig. XVI, no. 6.* **b**(right) *Same ware. Diam. 5.9 cm (DM-HWP-43).*

Pl. 122 Two vertical handles
Incised Red Polished Ware. Early Bronze Age. The vertically flattened, pierced handles appear to be 'overdeveloped' lugs. Diam. 18.4 cm (DM-IRP-64).

Pl. 121

Pl. 122

Pl. 123

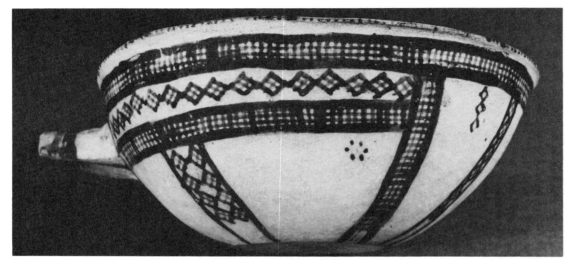

Pl. 124

5b Bowls with flat bases

Pl. 123

a(left) *Plain Red Polished Ware. Early Bronze Age. This shape is rare in the Red Polished series and because of its flat base it has been considered that this small bowl should be placed with the Philia group, but there seems some doubt about such a step. Diam. 11.2 cm (DM-PRP-34).*
b(right) *Handmade Black Slip Ware. Middle Bronze Age. Carefully incised bowl with two opposing holes pierced below rim. Diam. 9.2 cm (DM-HBS-09). Formerly in the collection of the Rev. V. E. G. Kenna. Cf. Ohnefalsch-Richter 1893, Fig. 34c and CLXXI, no. 14. The bowl shown here is almost identical with the 1893 one and its locality can therefore safely be guessed as Ayia Paraskevi.*

Pl. 124 *White Slip Ware. Late Bronze Age. Flat-bottomed bowls in this ware are far less common than the hemispherical form. Diam. 14.3 cm (DM-WSL-06). Formerly in the Cesnola Collection. Cf. SCE IV.1c, Fig. LXXXIII, no. 5.*

5c Bowls with tulip bases

Pl. 125

a(left) *Black-topped Red Polished Ware. Early Bronze Age. One lug opposite a small trough spout. Omphalos base. The black area extends down most of the outside of the vessel. Diam. 11 cm (DM-BTRP-22). Cf. Stewart and Stewart 1950, Pl. XIV (Vounous T.105, no. 16).*
b(right) *Same ware. There are two pairs of lugs, one pair of which almost constitute short trough spouts. The 'red' area of this tulip bowl is a faded yellow colour. Diam. 14.2 cm (DM-BTRP-21).*

5d Bowls with conical bases

Pl. 126 *Red-and-black Polished Ware. Early to Middle Bronze Age. This conical 'cup' with a pierced hole near its base appears to be unique. Diam. 11.2 cm (DM-RBP-167).*

Pl. 125

Pl. 126

5e Bowls with ring bases

Pl. 127 *Wheelmade White Painted Ware. Iron Age. Two horizontally attached handles. Checkerboard decoration. Diam 23.6 cm (DM-WWP-114).*

Pl. 128
a(left) *Base Ring Ware. Late Bronze Age. Small bowl with single pierced lug and no handle. Diam. 10.7 cm (DM-BR-34).*
b(right) *Same ware. Horizontal wishbone handle. Fired to red finish. Diam. 10.5 cm (DM-BR-33).*

Pl. 127

Pl. 128

5f Bowls with stem bases

Pl. 129 *Incised Red Polished Ware. Early Bronze Age. A small hemispherical cup on a short stem. Four rim-lugs. Diam. 9 cm. Ht. 8.2 cm (DM-IRP-65). Cf. Dikaios 1940, Pl. XIIe (Vounous T.9, no. 55).*

Pl. 130 *Handmade White Painted Ware. Middle Bronze Age. The decoration has almost completely faded, but a few traces remain of dark red lines on the pale background. Diam. 6.9 cm. Ht. 6.4 cm (DM-HWP-50).*

Pl. 131 *Mottled Red Polished Ware. Early to Middle Bronze Age. Diam. 10.3 cm. Ht. 12 cm (DM-MRP-23).*

Pl. 132 *Bichrome Ware. Iron Age. Decoration includes swastika motifs. Diam. 12.2 cm (DM-BI-58).*

Pl. 129

Pl. 130

Pl. 131

Pl. 132

5g Bowls with tripod bases

Pl. 133 *Mottled Red Polished Ware. Early to Middle Bronze Age. Small cup on very tall stem with tripod base. Diam. 7.2 cm. Ht. 14.3 cm (DM-MRP-24).*

Pl. 134 *Black-topped Red Polished Ware. Early Bronze Age. Single pierced lug. Although hemispherical bowls of this type are common, it is extremely rare for them to be supplied with a tripod base. Diam. 10.4 cm (DM-BTRP-24).*

Pl. 133

Pl. 134

6 Dish

The flat dish is a late arrival on Cyprus, being absent from the indigenous Bronze Age repertoire. It arrives eventually as a Greek import, establishing itself firmly in the Geometric Period at the beginning of the Iron Age. It then remains common for a long period, especially in the two-handled, paint-decorated version. There is also a rare three-handled type and a one-handled form with a finger-like projection opposite the handle.

These dishes appear most frequently in White Painted Ware, but are also seen in Bichrome and in mixed wares involving Black Slip.

Most of the ancient dishes are about the size of modern dining plates, but one is known (see Pl. 135a) which is of huge proportions—so cumbersome, in fact, that it snapped in two in ancient times and had to be repaired before it was placed in the tomb. The paired repair holes are clearly visible.

6 Dishes

Pl. 135

a(left) *Wheelmade White Painted Ware. Iron Age. This giant, three-handled dish appears to be the largest one known. It is so cumbersome that it was broken and repaired in antiquity. Pairs of ancient, drilled holes can be seen along the line of the original cracks, where the broken parts were tied together before the object was placed in the tomb. Diam. 51.1 cm (DM-WWP-126).*
b(right) *Bichrome Ware. Iron Age. This small, two-handled dish is shown here alongside the large one to give some idea of the former's proportions. Diam 10.2 cm (DM-BI-69).*

Pl. 136 *Wheelmade White Painted Ware. Iron Age. Three-handled dishes of this type are rare compared with two-handled ones. Diam. 27 cm. (DM-WWP-127).*

Pl. 137 *Wheelmade White Painted Ware. Iron Age. Typical two-handled dish. Diam. 22 cm (DM-WWP-131).*

Pl. 138 *Wheelmade White Painted Ware. Iron Age. One-handled dish. Opposite the handle is a slightly tapering spike. Diam. 19 cm (DM-WWP-173).*

Pl. 135

Pl. 136

Pl. 137

Pl. 138

7 Box

Large, egg-shaped pottery boxes are a special and unique feature of the Cypriot Early Bronze Age. They are made in incised Red Polished Ware and have small, flat lids of a 'rounded rectangular' or oval shape. A flat-bottomed form of box has been found but is rare. The egg-shaped version is also known from a White Painted example in the Middle Bronze Age (see p. 205, Fig. 329). After this, these interesting objects seem to disappear altogether from the art of ancient Cyprus.

Surveying the literature, I have been able to locate a total of 25 of these boxes (usually listed under the name *pyxis*), to which can be added three from my own collection. This total of 28 includes a number of examples with special embellishments projecting from the 'shoulders', as follows:

A	a	Plain Egg Shape	17
B	a	+ Two Miniature Bowls	1
	b	+ Two Human Figures	2
	c	+ Two Humans and Four Birds	1
	d	+ Two Deer and Two Birds	1
	e	+ One Bull and One Bird	1
	f	+ One Human and One Bird	2
	g	+ Two Humans on Horse-Necks	1
C	a	Plain Flat-Bottomed Shape	2

7 Boxes

Pl. 139 *Incised Red Polished Ware. Early Bronze Age. Large box with lid missing. Length 24.2 cm. Ht. 13.4 cm (DM-IRP-66).*

Pl. 140 *Incised Red Polished Ware. Early Bronze Age. Small box with lid missing. Large, horizontally attached handle on one side. Length 15.1 cm. Ht. 12.6 cm (to top of handle) (DM-IRP-67).*

Pl. 139

Pl. 140

Pl. 142　　　Pl. 143

Pl. 142 *Incised Red Polished Ware. Early Bronze Age. Box-lid of oval-rectangular shape with two flattened lugs. Length 12.5 cm (DM-IRP-71).*

Pl. 143 *Incised Red Polished Ware. Early Bronze Age. Box-lid of oval shape with no lugs. Beneath the lid is a ridge which kept it in place when it was covering the aperture of its now missing box. Length 18.6 cm (DM-IRP-70).*

Pl. 141 *Incised Red Polished Ware. Early Bronze Age. Large box with rectangular lid. At one end of the oval aperture stands a human Plank Figure, with short, protruding arm-buds. At the other end is the figure of a bird. Length of box: 32.7 cm. Length of lid: 12.9 cm (box DM-IRP-68; lid DM-IRP-69). This box has been reconstructed from fragments, but the basal area is completely missing. Cf. Karageorghis 1976, no. 61 (Pierides Collection).*

8 Dipper

Squat vessels with tall handles are another Bronze Age speciality and do not appear to survive into the Iron Age. They occur in Red Polished Ware and in White Painted Ware and may have their handles attached either vertically or horizontally. There is only one handle to each vessel and it appears to have been used to facilitate dipping down into a liquid held in a larger vessel, or possibly into some sort of food solid such as seed or grain stored in a large jar. Some examples may be no more than small cups with abnormally exaggerated handles, but it seems justified to include all of them here, on structural grounds.

In the past, these vessels have often been classified as 'ladles', but I have been forced to adopt the more general word 'dipper' because two of the examples in my collection are too big to be thought of as simple ladles.

8 Dippers

Pl. 144

a(left) *Incised Red Polished Ware. Early Bronze Age. Heavy-walled vessel with cutaway spout and tall, strong, vertical handle. Ht. 38.5 cm (DM-IRP-72).*

b(right) *Mottled Red Polished Ware. Heavy-walled vessel with cutaway spout and tall, strong, vertical handle. Single lug on neckbase opposite handle. Ht. 25 cm (DM-MRP-25).*

Pl. 144

Pl. 145

a(left) *Handmade White Painted Ware. Middle Bronze Age. Horizontally attached handle which rises in the vertical plane. Ht. 100 cm (DM-HWP-52).*

b(right) *Same ware. Ht. 90 cm (DM-HWP-51).*

Pl. 145

9 Basket

Pottery baskets are comparatively rare. Only a few examples have been published and they are all confined to the Iron Age, appearing there in both White Painted Ware and Bichrome Ware. Gjerstad (1948) believes that they imitate 'plait-work prototypes', but he is not so certain about their origin, commenting that they 'seem to be derived from the corresponding open-work kathaloi, which appear in Proto-Geometric Greek pottery, and continue in the Geometric period and subsequently. On the other hand, open-work vessels of this kind have been found in Palestine already in the Late Bronze Age, and the type seems therefore to be ultimately of Oriental derivation, but more and safely dated specimens must be found in the Orient before the question can be definitely settled.'

Pl. 146 *Wheelmade White Painted Ware. Iron Age. An open-work 'bowl' with fourteen triangular apertures. Unusually large example. Diam. 27 cm (DM-WWP-177). Cf. SCE IV.2, Fig. XIII, no. 3.*

10 Strainer

There appear to be three forms of strainers—that is, perforated vessels which enable liquids (or perhaps also fine solids) to pass through, while larger solids are held back. The first appears in the Late Bronze Age, where it is referred to as a 'Side-spouted Strainer in Tankard Form' by Astrom (1972). In this case, the perforations are in the flat top of the vessel, suggesting that something was squeezed down onto the strainer and the juice which collected inside it was then poured out of the side-spout.

A second form consists of a shallow bowl with holes in the lower, central region. A third takes the form of a jug with a perforated plate inside the spout.

Pl. 147

Pl. 148

Pl. 149

10 Strainers

Pl. 147 a(left) *Wheelmade White Painted Ware. Iron Age. Vessel with ring base, round spout and cutaway side-spout. At the base of the side-spout is a disc perforated with three strainer holes. Ht. 14.1 cm (DM-WWP-179).*
b(right) *Same ware, but with deeper cutaway on side-spout and with six strainer holes. Ht. 15.8 cm (DM-WWP-178). Cf. SCE IV.2, Fig. XIII, no. 19.*

Pl. 148 *Black-on-red Ware. Iron Age. Vessel with ring base round spout and cutaway side-spout. At the base of the side-spout is a disc per-forated with four strainer holes. On the neck below the round spout is a human face. The face has a modelled nose and chin and painted eyes, eyebrows and lips, converting the strainer-jug into a 'vessel-shaped figure' (see also p. 159) (DM-BOR-21).*

Pl. 149 *Handmade Black Slip Ware. Middle Bronze Age. Round-based strainer-jug with disc at top of round spout, perforated by three holes. Minor incisions on handle and shoulders. Ht. 19 cm (DM-HBS-10).*

The Complex Shapes

Among the thousands of pottery vessels that have been recovered from the ancient tombs of Cyprus, there are some that stand out as 'special items' because of their complex shapes. Of course, the majority of the simple shapes were also made 'special' by the early artists. This was done by adding a unique decorative pattern to each vessel, preparing the surface texture and colour in a particular way, exaggerating the simple contours in one direction or another, applying relief elements to the surface, or in rare cases adding modelled figures to the shoulders of jugs and jars, or the rims of bowls. All these devices helped to make individual vessels placed in the tombs more important, but by the further addition of complexity of shape a whole new realm of embellishment possibilities was opened up.

In embarking on this more ambitious form of experimentation, the artists concerned restricted themselves to three main themes: the *ring vessel,* the *multi-unit vessel* and the *subsidiary-unit vessel.* In each case a great deal more work was involved in the production of the object, and the special value of the vessel when placed in the tomb seems to have been that it was 'costly' (in time if nothing else), and therefore represented a high-order offering to the deceased, rather like a specially large wreath on a grave today.

In seeking ways of increasing the impact of a tomb-offering, the potters used their playful ingenuity to create some fascinating composite ceramics. Within the three main themes mentioned, they explored all sorts of compositional possibilities, giving their aesthetic curiosity full reign. At the level of the 'main theme', however, their exuberant playfulness was held firmly in check. It was as if each of the three had some kind of powerful attraction for them.

The ring-vessel theme is the hardest to understand. It does not appear to have some other vessel shape as a precursor or prototype. It erupts suddenly in the Chalcolithic and then re-surfaces in the Early Bronze Age, the Middle Bronze Age, the Late Bronze Age and the Early Iron Age. This span of several thousand years is impressive but it does give rise to the question as to whether we are dealing with a single, continuing phenomenon, or several independently emerging ones. The Chalcolithic example, for instance,

is a solitary specimen consisting of a plain ring-shape on three short legs. It looks like a circular stand for a large, round-bottomed jug, bowl or jar. Indeed, this is probably all it was, and to seek some arcane symbolic significance in its shape may well be misguided.

By the Early Bronze Age, however, matters have become more complicated. There, the ring vessels are typically surmounted by several miniature bowls. The effect is a circle of tiny vessels. Sometimes the ring on which they stand is on short legs, sometimes it lies on the ground. The strangest aspect of these Red Polished ring vessels is that some of them are hollow and the small bowls are connected to the hollow space inside the pottery ring by basal apertures. This curious feature creates a problem for those writers who rejoice in the affectation of referring to these Cypriot artefacts by the Greek name of *kernos.* It also makes it difficult to understand their function. To explain this it is necessary to make a brief diversion into the sphere of the true *kernos* of ancient Greece.

Athenaeus gives us the following definition: '*Kernos,* a vessel made of earthenware, having in it many little cups fastened to it, in which are white poppies, wheat, barley, pulse, vetch, ochroi, lentils; and he who carries it after the fashion of the carrier of the *liknon,* tastes of these things, as Ammonius relates in his third book on Altars and Sacrifices.' Later, he mentions other contents of the small cups: sage, beans, spelt, oats, a cake, honey, oil, wine, milk, sheep's wool unwashed. Harrison (1903) comments: 'Such a vessel might well be called a *separator* ... the kernos [was] a vessel in which various sorts of grain could be kept separate. The *Kernophoria* was nothing but a late and elaborate form of the offering of first-fruits.'

In other words, the Greek *kernos* was a device for carrying and offering to the gods a wide variety of samples of different crops and products at a religious festival. The more products, the higher, presumably, the status of the offerer, and Lacey (1967) records that this particular status display often became excessive: 'These kernoi have sometimes eight, eleven, nineteen, twenty or even as many as twenty-five small vases. They are often found in tombs in Crete, and one found at Mallia near Herakleion has no less than forty-one small vases.'

This is pluralization run riot, and no Cypriot vessel has ever attained such numbers.

The maximum number of units in a Cypriot composite vessel is, as far as I know, nine (see Pl. 163). But the most important difference is in the internal structure of the Greek and Cypriot ring vessels. The hollow Cypriot rings with their connecting bowls are clearly not intended as *separators* and therefore cannot be given the name of *kernos*. The resemblance must be seen as superficial. Since it must have been rather difficult to fabricate the hollow connections for the small bowls, it follows that there must have been some special reason for providing this feature. Solids would easily clog, so the contents must have been liquid. Why then would it have been so important to ensure that the liquid levels in the cups found the same level, which would be the only effect of the ring-tube connection? The only answer seems to be that these particular vessels were employed as multiple oil lamps. Even this seems a little contrived, but other explanations make even less sense, unless a mystical interpretation is invoked.

In magical and symbolic terms, the ring has always stood for eternity. As Cirlot (1962) puts it: 'Like every closed circle, the ring is a symbol of continuity and wholeness. This is why (like the bracelet) it has been used both as a symbol of marriage and of the eternally repeated time-cycle.' If one sees the inclusion of ring vessels in ancient Cypriot tombs as part of a magico-religious process, then it might make sense to connect the cups on the ring and thereby create a mystical ring of liquid within the vessel, perhaps symbolizing the eternal life which the mourners hoped for after entombment.

Leaving these speculations and moving on to the Middle Bronze Age does not help much. There, a new form of ring vessel appears on the scene to confuse matters further. This is the vertical ring—a hollow, ring-shaped flask with a single spout and a handle attached to it. This form continues through into the Iron Age, varying little as it goes except for one handle versus two, or round spout versus beak spout. It defies explanation unless one accepts simple aesthetic playfulness, or arcane mystic symbolism.

A third form of ring vessel is the horizontal spouted-ring with basket handle. This begins its run in the Early Bronze Age Red Polished Ware, continues through the Handmade White Painted Ware of the Middle Bronze Age and the Base Ring Ware of the Late Bronze Age to end with the Wheelmade White Painted and Bichrome Wares of the Iron Age. Along the way, it adopts animal and human heads to adorn the spout. Miniature jars, birds, and pomegranates occasionally sit on the ring itself and, once in a while, a second head-spout is added. This type is nearly always hollow, but its function as a container often seems to be almost perfunctory—as though it is a ritual necessity that has become a chore. Increasingly now, the focus of attention is in the animalized nature of the vessel. Where there are small jars on the ring these may once again act as food or liquid containers, or they may simply be decorative.

Viewed together these ring vessels do not look like a homogeneous group with a single tradition, unless that tradition has to do with the mystical significance of the circle as a symbol of eternity. Functionally they clearly differ widely from one another and they should certainly not be referred to by the name *kernos*, which is misleading.

With the second major theme for complex vessels—the multi-unit vessels—there is a multiplication of some aspect of the object—its neck, its body, its handle or its spout. There are two-necked and three-necked jugs; jars and jugs with from two to seven joined bodies; multiple bowls of from two to nine units; large bowls with twin spouts; and jugs with duplicated or multiple handles.

The motto here seems to be: 'keep faith with the old, simple shapes, but let them breed'. It is possible to identify the simple vessels clearly in every multiple example. The word *kernos* has even been extended to include these multi-unit vessels, but it is more inappropriate than ever here. The majority of the Cypriot multi-unit vessels do not permit a separation of different contents. Twin-necked jugs can pour a double jet but internally there is only one space for the liquid. Many of the three- and four-bodied jugs have their bodies fused to a single spout. Some two-necked vessels have spouts at opposite ends, making pouring virtually impossible. Certain two-bodied jugs have one connected on top of the other with only one spout for pouring. Only the multi-bowl examples could be construed as belonging to a *kernos* type, and these may indeed have held separated, varied offerings. But since they are only one special part of a general trend towards pluralization, they cannot be considered as providing a general functional explanation. That must be sought elsewhere.

Here we seem to be driven back again to the 'playful inventiveness' explanation. There is no other way to describe the repeated urge to multiply the basic units of the Cypriot vessels. If there is some mysterious ritual significance it seems lost to us forever. The vast majority of these multi-unit vessels come from the prehistoric period of the Bronze Age and we therefore have no written records to help us. Searching desperately for a ritual function for the 'fused' vessels—those with several bodies but only one spout—the only idea that comes to mind is one of symbolic mixing. Each body of the vessel might be a token display of one essential ingredient. A three-bodied jug, therefore, would be symbolically displaying a triple-ingredient liquid, and so on. But this is grasping at straws. The twin-necked jugs might have been designed for some special twin-jet pouring ritual, but this also seems far-fetched. Until there is some specific evidence to support such ideas, it is better to accept the simpler proposition that we are dealing with creative exuberance, and enjoy the remarkable results of it that have survived down the millennia for us to see.

The third main theme, that of subsidiary-unit vessels, throws up similar problems and the explanation may be the same, but there are certain features that should be mentioned. All these vessels—big ones with tiny ones sprouting out of them—belong to the Early or Middle Bronze Age period. Unlike the other two main themes, they lack a long life span. Also, the 'offspring' vessels that sit on the shoulders or rims of the large ones are nearly always of a particular type—cutaway-beak jugs and shallow bowls—as though they are representing, not small versions of the large ones, but some kind of 'ritual set' such as a milk bowl and a pouring jug, for instance. There are examples (see Pl. 172) where, even though the parent vessel has a round spout, the small juglet has a cutaway one. It is as if the artists are deliberately making the point that the parent vessel is not really a parent at all, but merely a kind of platform on which to display the 'ritual set'. Indeed, in one case, the artist does away with the parent vessel altogether and instead places the 'ritual set' on a kind of offering table. This makes it look very much as though, with subsidiary-unit vessels, we are dealing with a special display, in miniature, model form, of an important 'liquid rite'—a sacred ablution, an offering to the gods of milk, food, wine or water in some kind of libation ceremony, a primitive baptismal ceremony, or perhaps a seasonal drinking celebration to give thanks for the first milk of the year, the first wine, or even rain after a drought.

There is no way we can choose between these alternatives at present. Future discoveries of scenic pottery artefacts may give us additional clues, but for now we can only speculate. What we can say, however, is that the repeated emphasis on two kinds of subsidiary vessels, to the exclusion of others, and regardless of the nature of the parent vessels, does strongly suggest that a ritual significance is intended here. It is even possible that the miniature vessels perched on the rings of the ring vessels may be part of the same phenomenon.

Having said this, however, we must never lose sight of the possibility that *all* these complex shapes are, without exception, playful inventions of the ancient potters of Cyprus with no hidden meanings and no mystical symbolisms. They may simply represent the artists' way of having fun with clay, on occasions when considerations of hard-wearing, everyday use were unimportant and fancy embellishments were at a premium for purposes of mourner status-display.

Before illustrating each of the three main themes of the complex vessels, it will be helpful to present a brief classification of the types that have been traced so far. It should be made clear that this is not an attempt at a comprehensive survey. Without making a special search, I have merely recorded all the examples I have come across over the years. The total so far is 279—57 ring vessels, 188 multi-unit vessels, and 34 subsidiary-unit vessels. Of these, 27 are in my own collection and all of these are illustrated photographically. A representative selection of the others is shown as drawings.

1 Ring Vessels (57)

1 HORIZONTAL (44)

a Plain Ring (11)

1 No miniature vessels attached (1)
The ring stands on three short legs. Chalcolithic. *Example traced:* Red-on-White (1).

2 With miniature vessels attached (8)

With three legs, four legs or no legs and with three, four, or five bowls. One vessel has three bowls + a cutaway-spout jug. Early Bronze and Iron Age. *Examples traced:* Incised Red Polished (1); Plain Red Polished (5); Mixed—Incised Red Polished and Handmade White Painted (1); Black-on-Red (1).

3 With miniature vessels and figurines attached (2)

With three legs or four legs and two or four bowls + two human couples or quadrupeds. Early Bronze Age. *Examples traced:* Plain Red Polished (1); Mixed—Plain Red Polished and Handmade White Painted (1).

b Simple-Spouted Ring (7)

1 No miniature vessels, but basket handle (7)

With no legs, three legs or four legs. Early, Middle and Late Bronze Age. *Examples traced:* Relief-decorated Red Polished (1); Handmade White Painted (5); Wheelmade White Painted (1).

c Zoomorphic-Spouted Ring (26)

1 No miniature vessels and no basket handle (2)

No legs and with bull-headed spout. Late Bronze Age to Early Iron Age. *Examples traced:* Wheelmade White Painted (2).

2 With miniature vessels but no basket handle (2)

No legs or three legs; two or three jars. Late Bronze Age. *Examples traced:* Base Ring (1); Cypro-Mycenaean (1).

3 No miniature vessels, but basket handle (3)

No legs. Human, goat or other animal-headed spout. One with snake along handle. Late Bronze Age. *Examples traced:* Base Ring

(2); Wheelmade White Painted (1).

4 Miniature vessels and basket handles (15)

No legs, with one four-legged exception. Spout usually bull-headed, but may also show a goat or some other animal—even birds. One example has two animal spouts, one a bull and one a goat. From one to four jugs, jars or bowls stand on rings. All Late Bronze Age to Early Iron Age. *Examples traced:* Base Ring (1); Wheelmade White Painted (14).

5 Miniature vessels, basket handles and figurines (4)

No legs. Goat or bull spouts. With one, two or three jugs or jars on ring. Also one or two modelled pomegranates on each ring and, in one case, a modelled bird. Late Bronze Age and Early Iron Age. *Examples traced:* Wheelmade White Painted (3); Bichrome (1).

II VERTICAL (13)

a One Handle (5)

1 Pinched spout (2)

Middle Bronze Age and Iron Age. *Examples traced:* Handmade White Painted (1) and Wheelmade White Painted (1).

2 Round spout (3)

Middle and Late Bronze Age and Early Iron Age. *Examples traced:* Drab Polished (1); Wheelmade White Painted (1); Bichrome (1).

b Two Handles (8)

1 Round spout (8)

Late Bronze Age to Early Iron Age. *Examples traced:* Wheelmade White Painted (6); Black Slip Grooved (1); Bichrome (1).

1a Horizontal ring, plain

Fig. 1 *Plain ring on three legs. Decorated with horizontal bands, checker-board and primitive meander pattern. Vessel restored from fragment. Red-on-white Ware. Chalcolithic. From Ambelikou-Ayios Georghis. See Dikaios 1962, p. 144. Described as a 'tripodic ring stand', this unique object stands apart from other Cypriot Ring Vessels, both in date and in the simplicity of its design.*

Fig. 2 *Ring on three legs with three small hemispherical bowls attached to its upper surface equidistantly, a bowl positioned above each leg. Incised decoration with band of horizontal diamonds. Incised Red Polished Ware. Early Bronze Age. From Lapithos (Tomb 322, Chamber D, no. 1). Ht. 20 cm. Diam. 19.5 cm. See Buchholz and Karageorghis 1973, p. 145, no. 1502. This is one of eight bowl-carrying Red Polished rings found at north coast sites such as Lapithos and Vounous, some with legs and some without.*

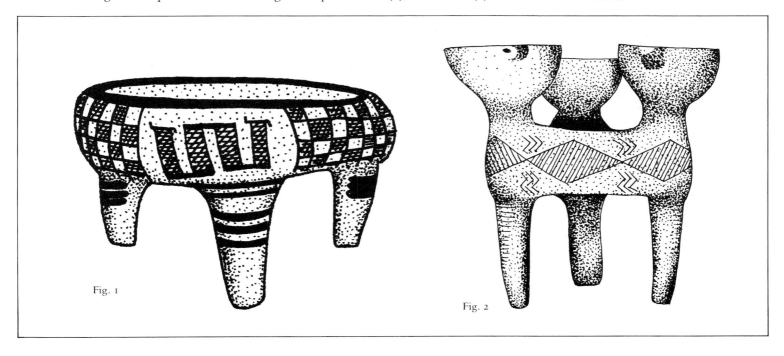

Fig. 1

Fig. 2

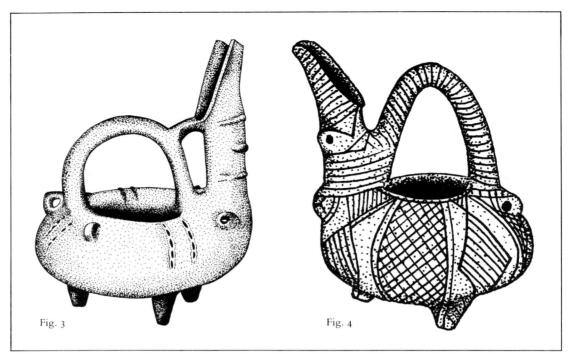

Fig. 3   Fig. 4

Ib Horizontal ring, simple spouted

Fig. 3 *Ring on three legs with cutaway-beak spout and basket handle. Simple, rope-like relief decorations on body and neck of spout. Relief-decorated Red Polished Ware. Early Bronze Age. From Vounous (Tomb 56). See Schaeffer 1936, Pl. XIX, no. 2. This is the*

earliest example of a Spouted Ring Vessel, a style which becomes popular in later periods. This particular specimen could be used as an efficient pouring jug, unlike many of the later examples.

Fig. 4 *Ring on three stump-feet with cutaway-beak spout and basket handle. Parallel lines on neck and spout, and cross-hatched panels alternating with vertical diamonds on*

body of ring. White Painted Ware. Middle Bronze Age. No provenance: purchased in Cambridge and now in the Ashmolean Museum, Oxford. Ht. 15.5 cm. See Brown and Catling 1980, p. 104, no. 29. One of five White Painted examples of Spouted Rings from the Middle Bronze Age period, this example appears to be a direct descendant of the Early Bronze Age example (Fig. 3).

Ic Horizontal ring, zoomorphic-spouted

Pl. 150 *Simple hollow ring with bull-headed spout in front and loop handle behind. Wheelmade White Painted Ware. Late Bronze Age to Early Iron Age. Maximum dimension (from bull's mouth to handle) 27.8 cm. Outside diameter of ring 21.3 cm (DM-WWP-180).*

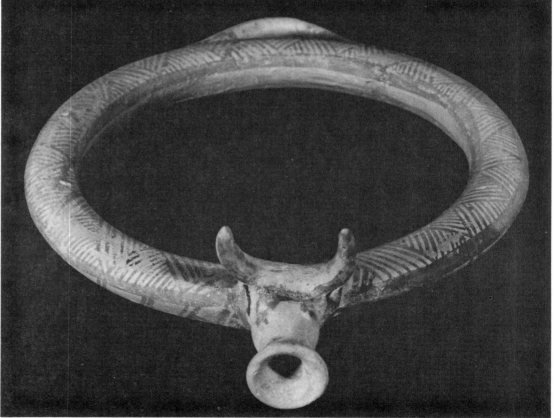

Pl. 150

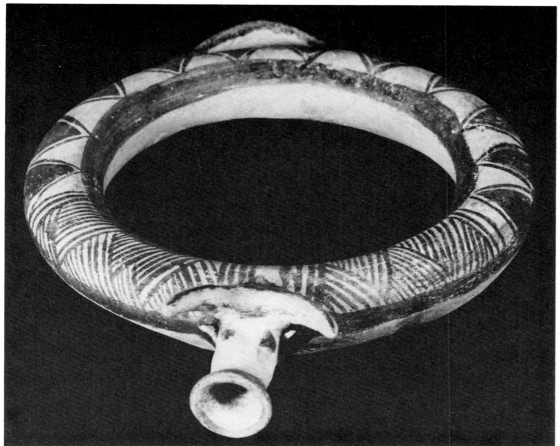

Pl. 151

1c Horizontal ring, zoomorphic-spouted

Pl. 151 *Simple hollow ring with bull-headed spout in front and loop handle behind. Wheelmade White Painted Ware. Late Bronze Age to Early Iron Age. Outside diameter of ring 20.8 cm (DM-WWP-181).*

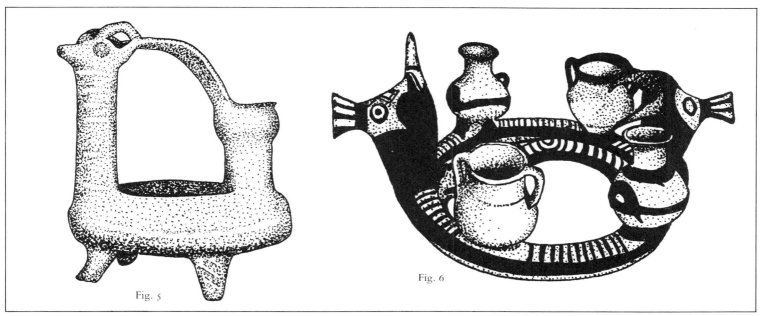

Fig. 5

Fig. 6

Fig. 5 *Ring on four flattened feet, with two vertical projections, one ending in a goat-headed spout, for pouring, and the other in a bowl-shaped aperture, for filling. The two projections are joined by a flattened, basket handle to which the goat's backward sweeping horns are also connected. Decorated with simple white blobs and bands. Base Ring Ware. Late Bronze Age. No provenance. Pierides Collection,* Larnaca. Ht. 12.5 cm. See Astrom 1972, p. 190. One of several Base Ring Ware Ring Vessels, this appears to be the earliest example of an animal-headed spout. Astrom calls it a ram, but from the backward sweeping horns it seems more likely to have been a goat. It is too highly stylized to be certain.

Fig. 6 *Complex ring, without legs but with four miniature jars and two animal-head spouts growing from its upper surface. There is a basket handle connecting the two animal heads, one representing a bull and the other a goat, both with pierced, trumpet-mouths. The jars are in two opposing pairs, one pair with vertical handles and the other with horizontal handles. Decoration is with simple bands and parallel lines. White* Painted Ware. Geometric Period. From Rizokarpaso, Anavrysi (Tomb 1). Now in Cyprus Museum, Nicosia (1937/V-1/3). This is an unusually large example. Diam. 30 cm. Ht. 19.8 cm. With this vessel and other similar ones from the Early Iron Age, the ring-theme reaches its most complex form of expression, before vanishing completely from the Cypriot scene.

1C Horizontal ring, zoomorphic-spouted

Pl. 152 *Hollow ring with goat-headed spout in front and small, jar-like neck behind, the two connected by a basket handle. To left and right, standing on the ring, are two pomegranates painted in red. Other painted decoration is in black. Bichrome Ware. Late Bronze Age to Early Iron Age. Maximum dimension (goat's mouth to far rim) 22.8 cm. Outside diam. of ring 19.3 cm (DM-BI-74). Similar pomegranates appear on the ring vessel shown in SCE IV.2, Fig. XV, no. 2.*

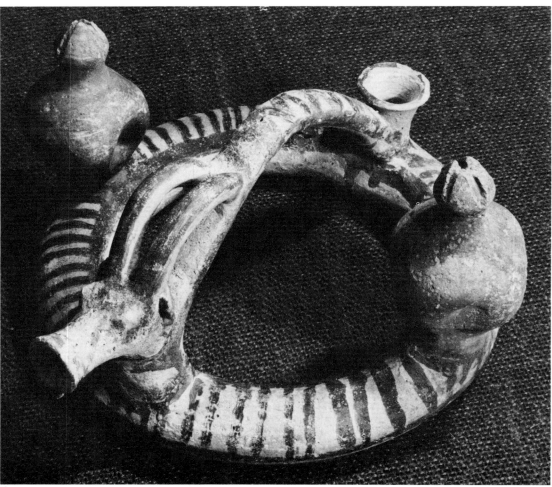

Pl. 152

II Vertical ring

Pl. 153 *Hollow ring with two small handles, one on each side of the short, round-spouted neck. Simple decoration of rings and criss-cross lines. Wheelmade White Painted Ware. Late Bronze Age to Early Iron Age. Diam. of ring 16 cm (DM-WWP-182).*

Fig. 7 *Ring with pinched spout and single handle. Decoration in groups of parallel lines, interspersed with wavy lines. White Painted Ware. Middle Bronze Age. Probably from Ayios Iakovos; now in the Pierides Collection, Larnaca. Ht. 24.5 cm. This example appears to be a precursor of the vertical ring vessels known from the Late Bronze Age and the Early Iron Age. Like the early examples of the horizontal ring vessels, its existence proves that the ring theme was present in Cyprus long before the arrival of the Mycenaeans.*

Fig. 7

Pl. 153

2 Multi-Unit Vessels (188)

I MULTI-NECK (48)

a Two Neck (48)

1 Twin neck (42)

The necks rise, side by side, from the body of the jug. Confined to the Early and Middle Bronze Age. *Examples traced:* Incised Red Polished (20); Relief-decorated Red Polished (6); Plain Red Polished (3); Mottled Red Polished (1); Incised Black Polished (1); Drab Polished (2); Black Slip (1); Handmade White Painted (8).

2 Opposing neck (5)

The necks arise from the opposite ends of the jug. Confined to the Early Bronze Age. *Examples traced:* Incised Red Polished (5).

3 Fused twin neck (1)

The necks rise, side by side, from the body of the jug but then fuse to form a single spout. Middle Bronze Age. *Example traced:* Handmade White Painted (1).

b Three Neck (4)

The necks rise together from the body of the jug. Early Bronze Age. *Examples traced:* Incised Red Polished (3); Plain Red Polished (1).

II MULTI-BODY (89)

a Two Body (53)

1 Horizontal link (43)

The two bodies are joined horizontally. Early Bronze Age to Iron Age. *Examples traced:* Incised Red Polished (8); Relief-decorated Red Polished (1); Plain Red Polished (3); Black Slip (1); Red-on-Black (1); Handmade White Painted (3); Base Ring (24); Wheelmade White Painted (1); Bichrome (1).

2 Vertical link (10)

The two bodies are placed one above the other. Early Bronze Age. *Examples traced:* Incised Red Polished (9); Handmade White Painted (1).

b Three Body (20)

1 Horizontal link (19)

The three bodies are joined horizontally. Wide distribution from Chalcolithic to Iron Age. *Examples traced:* Chalcolithic Red-on-White (1); Incised Red Polished (5); Relief-decorated Red Polished (1); Plain Red Polished (1); Black Slip (1); Red-on-Black (1); Handmade White Painted (4); Wheelmade White Painted (3); Bichrome (1).

2 Vertical link (1)

The three bodies are placed one above the other. Middle Bronze Age. *Example traced:* Handmade White Painted (1).

c Four Body (14)

1 Horizontal link (2)

The four bodies are arranged in a square at one level. In one example the necks connect to form a single spout. Early and Middle Bronze Age. *Examples traced:* Incised Red Polished (1); Handmade White Painted (1).

2 Horizontal + vertical link, square(2)

The four bodies are arranged two at the lower level and two at the higher level, forming a vertical square. Early Bronze Age. *Examples traced:* Incised Red Polished (2).

3 Horizontal + vertical link, pyramid (8)

The four bodies are connected with three in a triangle at the lower level and one placed centrally above them, topped with a single spout. Early and Middle Bronze Age. *Examples traced:* Incised Red Polished (7); Handmade White Painted (1).

d Seven Body (2)

1 Horizontal link (1)

The seven bodies connected in a row with seven separate necks. Iron Age. *Example traced:* Wheelmade White Painted (1).

2 Horizontal + vertical link, pyramid (1)

The seven bodies are arranged three at lower level, three more slightly above and inside them and one, centrally, on top. Early Bronze Age. *Example traced:* Incised Red Polished (1).

III MULTI-SPOUT (9)

a Two Spout (9)

1 Twin spout (8)

The two spouts project side by side from the rim of the bowl. Early Bronze Age. *Examples traced:* Relief-decorated Red Polished (5); Plain Red Polished (1); Black-bottomed Red Polished (1); Reserved Slip (1).

2 Opposing spout (1)

The two spouts project from opposite sides of the bowl. Early Bronze Age. *Example traced:* Plain Red Polished (1).

IV MULTI-BOWL (34)

a Two Bowl (6)

The two bowls are joined side by side. Early and Middle Bronze Age. *Examples traced:* Plain Red Polished (3); Handmade White Painted (3).

b Three Bowl (5)

The three bowls are joined horizontally to form a triangle. Early Bronze Age to Iron Age. *Examples traced:* Incised Red Polished (2); Plain Red Polished (1); Handmade White Painted (1); Bichrome (1).

c Four Bowl (17)

The four bowls are joined horizontally in a square, sometimes at low level, sometimes higher. Early and Middle Bronze Age. *Examples traced:* Incised Red Polished (14); Plain Red Polished (1); Mottled Red Polished (1); Handmade White Polished (1).

d Five Bowl (1)

Three of the bowls are arranged as a lower level triangle, with two more at higher level, Middle Bronze Age. *Example traced:* Handmade White Painted (1).

e Six Bowl (3)

The six bowls are arranged as a rectangle at low level, or round a central handle, or with four as a low-level square with two at high level. Early Bronze Age. *Examples traced:* Incised Red Polished (1); Plain Red Polished (2).

f Seven Bowl (1)

Six bowls arranged in a circle around a central one. Early Bronze Age. *Example traced:* Plain Red Polished (1).

g Eight Bowl (2)

Seven bowls arranged in a circle round a central one, or six bowls arranged in a circle round a central one, with an eighth one on top of the handle. Early Bronze Age. *Examples traced:* Plain Red Polished (2).

h Nine Bowl (1)

Eight bowls arranged in two rows with a ninth one centrally placed at the base of the handle. Early Bronze Age. *Example traced:* Plain Red Polished (1).

V MULTI-HANDLE (2)

a Two Handle (2)

Two handles to jug arranged one above the other.(Ordinary two-handled jugs or jars with *opposing* handles not included here.) Early Bronze Age and Iron Age. *Examples traced:* Red Polished (1); Wheelmade White Painted (1)

b Six Handle (1)

Bowl with six handles projecting upwards from outside its rim. Early Bronze Age. *Example traced:* Black-topped Red Polished (1).

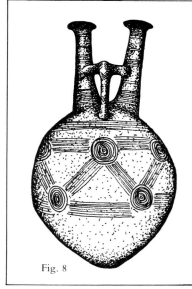

Fig. 8

Fig. 9

Fig. 10

Fig. 11

1 Multi-neck vessels

Figs. 8-17 Twin-necked jugs with round spouts. *Round or flat bases. A variety of handle-styles employed to link and strengthen the paired necks. Red Polished Ware. Early Bronze Age. All except Fig. 14 are decorated with incision patterns: bands of parallel lines, multi-zigzags, and concentric circles. Fig. 14 has minimal relief decoration, with raised 'buttons'.*

Fig. 8 *Vounous (Tomb 9, no. 161). Ht. 55 cm. Dikaios 1940, Pl. XXVa.*

Fig. 9 *Vounous (Tomb 15, no. 43). Ht. 56 cm. Dikaios 1940, Pl. XXIIIc.*

Fig. 10 *Vounous (Tomb 12, no. 94). Ht. 58 cm. Dikaios 1940, Pl. XXVd.*

Fig. 11 *Vounous (Tomb 46a, no. 23). Ht. 58 cm. Dikaios 1940, Pl. XXVc.*

Fig. 12 *Lapithos (Tomb 302a, no. 22). Ht. 25 cm. Stewart 1962, Fig. XCV, 10.*

Fig. 13 *Lapithos (Tomb 323, no. 10). Ht. 14 cm. Stewart 1962, Fig. XCV, 5.*

Fig. 14 *Lapithos (Tomb 308, no. 11). Ht. 48 cm. Stewart 1962, Fig. LXXXII, 8.*

Fig. 15 *Anoyira. Ht. 63 cm. Stewart 1962, Fig. LXXIII, 1.*

Fig. 16 *Anoyira. Ht. 62 cm. Stewart 1962, Fig. LXXIII, 2.*

Fig. 17 *Near Erimi. Ht. 44 cm. Stewart 1962, Fig. LXXIII, 3. Figs. 8-14 are from the north coast, Figs. 15-17 from the south coast region. Figs. 8-11 appear to have been made by a single Vounous artist; similarly, Figs. 15-17 seem to be the work of a single south coast artist.*

See also Pls. 154-7 on pp. 96-8.

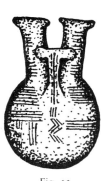

Fig. 12

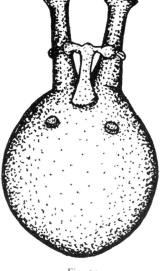

Fig. 13

Fig. 14

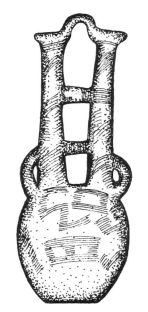

Fig. 15

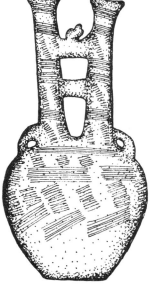

Fig. 16

Fig. 17

1 Multi-neck vessels

Fig. 18 A unique twin-necked jug with one cutaway spout and one round spout. *Relief-decorated Red Polished Ware. Early Bronze Age. From Lapithos. Now in Cyprus Museum, Nicosia. Ht. 57 cm. See Des Gagniers and Karageorghis 1976, Pl. XXX, 4.*

Figs. 19-25 Twin-necked jugs with cutaway-beak spouts. *Round or flat bases. Five from the Early Bronze Age, in Red Polished Ware; and two from the Middle Bronze Age, one in Drab Polished (Fig. 22) and one in White Painted Ware (Fig. 25).*

Fig. 19 *Vounous (Tomb 161, no. 8). Ht. 69.5 cm. Stewart and Stewart 1950, Pl. LI.*

Fig. 20 *Vounous (Tomb 161, no. 10). Ht. 71.2 cm. Stewart and Stewart 1950, Pl. LII.*

Fig. 21 *No provenance (now in Nat. Mus., Stockholm). Ht. 11 cm. Stewart 1962, Fig. LXXI, 9.*

Fig. 22 *No provenance (private collection). Ht. 21.5 cm. Ede 1982, no. 6.*

Fig. 23 *No provenance (now in Ashmolean Mus., Oxford). Ht. 24.5 cm. Brown and Catling 1975, Pl. V.*

Fig. 24 *Dhenia (?) (now in Hadjiprodromou Collection, Famagusta). Ht. 20 cm. Des Gagniers and Karageorghis 1976, Pl. XXXII, 1.*

Fig. 25 *Agos Iakovos (Tomb 6, no. 1). Ht. 24.2 cm. Astrom 1972, Fig. VII, 11.*

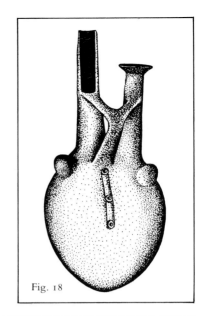

Fig. 18

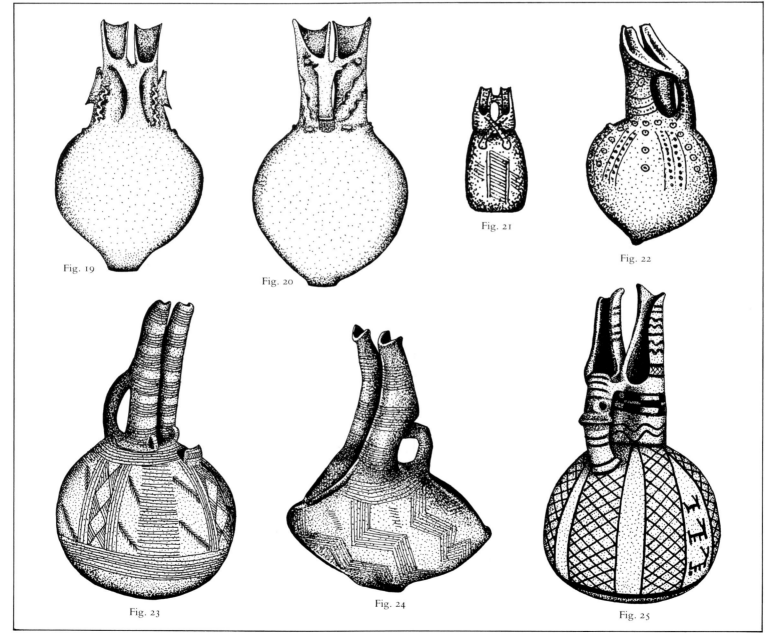

Fig. 19

Fig. 20

Fig. 21

Fig. 22

Fig. 23

Fig. 24

Fig. 25

Fig. 26

Fig. 27

Fig. 28

1 Multi-neck vessels

Figs. 26-8 Jugs with two opposing necks. *The necks emerge from either end of the low bodies which have their long axis in the horizontal plane. Red Polished Ware. Early and Middle Bronze Age.*

Fig. 26 *No provenance (private collection). Ht. 13.6 cm. Sotheby's 11 July 1983, no. 271.*

Fig. 27 *No provenance (private collection). Ht. 22.8 cm. Ede 1976, no. 8.*

Fig. 28 *No provenance (Ashmolean Mus., Oxford). Ht. 9 cm. Frankel 1983, no. 138.*

Figs. 29-32 Triple-necked jugs. *Red Polished Ware. Early Bronze Age.*

Fig. 29 *No provenance (private collection). Ht. 21.5 cm. Ede 1982, no. 3.*

Fig.30 *Vounous (Tomb 47, no. 85). Ht. 54 cm. Dikaios 1940, Pl. XXVb.*

Fig. 31 *Vounous (Tomb 37, no. 114). Ht. 32 cm. Dikios 1940, Pl. XXVf.*

Fig. 32 *Kyrenia. Ht. 31 cm. Karageorghis 1969, Pl. 45.*

Fig. 29

Fig. 30

Fig. 31

Fig. 32

II Multi-body vessels

Figs. 33-6 Twin-bodied vessels linked in the horizontal plane. *This simple form of pluralization is common from the Early Bronze Age to the Iron Age, but is most frequent in the form of Late Bronze Age Base Ring Ware double-poppy juglets. The majority of these are linked by a tall vertical handle, but one (Fig. 34) is known with a smaller horizontal handle.*

Fig. 33 *No provenance (Cyprus Museum, Nicosia). Ht. 11 cm. Buchholz and Karageorghis 1973, no. 1587.*

Fig. 34 *No provenance (Cyprus Museum, Nicosia). Ht. 13.5 cm. Buchholz and Karageorghis 1973, no. 1590.*

Fig. 35 *Vounous (Tomb 8, no. 97). Ht. 24 cm. Dikaios 1940, Pl. XXXIIb.*

Fig. 36 *No provenance (Cyprus Museum, Nicosia). Ht 15 cm. Buchholz and Karageorghis 1973, no. 1561.*
The Early Bronze Age Red Polished example (Fig. 35), and the Middle Bronze Age White Painted one (Fig. 36) are both close to multi-bowl vessels in shape, but since their apertures are not their widest part they must technically be called double-bodied jars.

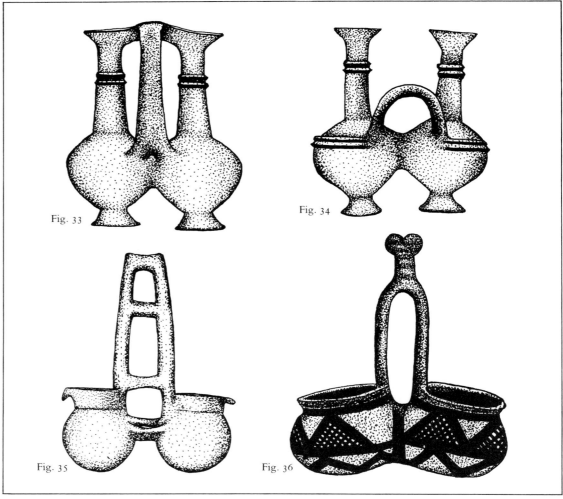

Fig. 33

Fig. 34

Fig. 35

Fig. 36

Figs. 37-42 Twin-bodied vessels linked in the vertical plane. *This rare form is restricted to Red Polished (Figs. 37-41) and White Painted Ware (Fig. 42) from* the Early Bronze Age. *Essentially these vessels consist of a small jug sitting on top of a large jug. To put it another way, each of the larger jugs has grown a juglet-shaped spout.*

Fig. 37 *Lapithos (Tomb 322d, no. 10). Ht. 43 cm. Stewart 1962, Fig. LXXI, 10.*

Fig. 38 *Lapithos (Tomb 314a, no. 1). Ht. 23 cm. Stewart 1962, Fig. LXXI, 11.*

Fig. 39 *Lapithos (Tomb 319b, no. 34). Ht. 30 cm. Stewart 1962, Fig. XCVII, 4.*

Fig. 40 *Vounous. Ht. 27 cm. Dikaios 1940, Pl. XIVa.*

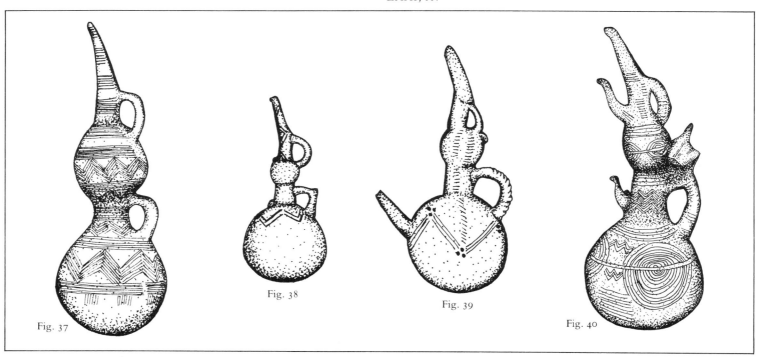

Fig. 37

Fig. 38

Fig. 39

Fig. 40

II Multi-body vessels

Fig. 41 *No provenance (Lowie Museum, Berkeley, California). Ht 11.2 cm. Karageorghis et al. 1974, no. 1.*

Fig. 42 *Vounous (Tomb 5, no. 14). Ht. 39 cm. Dikaios 1940, Pl. XLIc.*

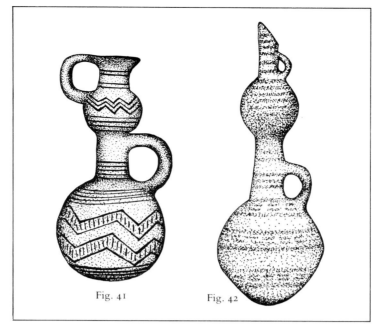

Fig. 41   Fig. 42

Figs. 43-50 Triple-bodied vessels linked in the horizontal plane. *In some, the vessels have separate openings, but in others the necks fuse to form a single opening. Most examples are Early Bronze Age Red Polished Ware, but others are in Middle Bronze Age wares such as White Painted (Fig. 48), Red-on-black (Fig. 49) or Black Slip (Fig. 46).*

Fig. 43 *No provenance (Lowie Museum, Berkeley, California). Ht. 18.3 cm. Karageorghis et al. 1974, no. 19.*

Fig. 44 *Vounous (Tomb 9, no. 73). Ht. 16 cm. Dikaios 1940, Pl. XXXIId.*

Fig. 45 *Evdimou (Hadjiprodromou Collection, Famagusta). Ht. 17 cm. Des Gagniers and Karageorghis 1976, Pl. XXXV,1.*

Fig. 46 *Toumba tou Skourou (Tomb 1, no. 301). Ht. 13.8 cm. Vermeule 1974, Fig. 34b.*

Fig. 47 *Vounous (Tomb 15, no. 50). Ht. 47 cm. Dikaios 1940, Pl. XXXIb.*

Fig. 48 *No provenance (Pierides Collection, Larnaca). Ht. 14 cm. Buchholz and Karageorghis 1973, no. 1544.*

Fig. 49 *No provenance (Cyprus Museum, Nicosia). Ht. 19.5 cm. Buchholz and Karageorghis 1973, no. 1543.*

Fig. 50 *Vounous (Tomb 13, no. 85). Ht. 38 cm. Dikaios 1940, Pl. XXXIa.*

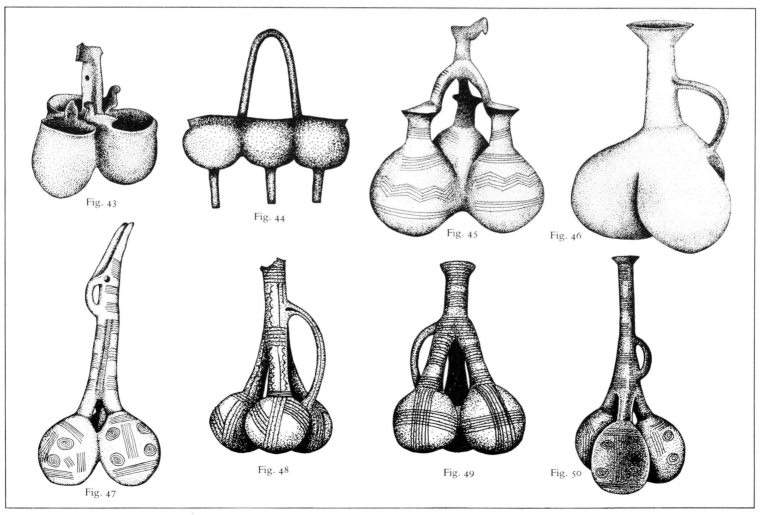

Fig. 43   Fig. 44   Fig. 45   Fig. 46

Fig. 47   Fig. 48   Fig. 49   Fig. 50

Fig. 51

II Multi-body vessels

Fig. 51 A unique triple-bodied vessel, linked in the vertical plane. *White Painted Ware. Middle Bronze.Age. From Galinoporni. Hadjiprodromou Collection, Famagusta. Ht. 37 cm. See Karageorghis 1976, no. 90.*

Fig. 52 Four-bodied vessel linked in the horizontal plane. *Red Polished Ware. Early Bronze Age. From Vounous. Schaeffer 1936, Pl. XIX, no. 1. This type is rare, and the example shown here is unique in that it is made up of a quartet of small bottles with closed mouths. This means that it is a pottery imitation of a multiple vessel,* rather than the vessel itself. Schaeffer (1936) suggests that the bottles are based on pomegranate shapes, and this may have been a method of 'labelling' their contents. The alternative possibility, namely that they are models of pomegranates and should be considered as skeuomorphs rather than vessels (see p. 250) seems unlikely because of the way they are fused together and are supplied with a basket handle.

Figs. 53–4 Four-bodied vessels consisting of twin juglets placed on top of twin juglets. *Two examples are known, both from the Early Bronze Age, in Red Polished Ware. In one (Fig. 53) there is a pair of criss-cross handles linking the upper juglets; in the other (Fig. 54) there are four separate, small vertical handles, one per body (not visible in the drawing here). Fig. 54 is unusual in having mixed spouts, one round and one cutaway, reminiscent of vessel Fig. 18.*

Fig. 53 *Lapithos (Tomb 314b, no. 62). Ht. 18 cm. Stewart 1962, Fig. LXXI, 12.*

Fig. 54 *No provenance (Ashmolean Museum, Oxford). Ht. 19 cm. Brown and Catling 1980, no. 18.*

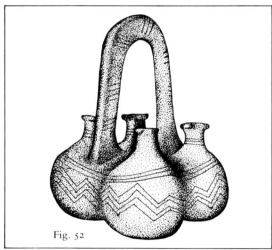

Fig. 52

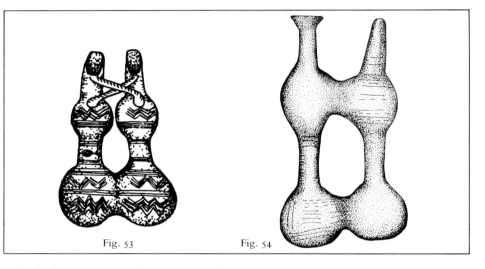

Fig. 53   Fig. 54

Figs. 55–61 Four-bodied vessels with a trio of bodies linked horizontally, their necks rising to enter the base of a fourth jug situated centrally above them. *Seven of the known examples are from the Early Bronze Age in Red Polished Ware, and the eighth (Fig. 60) is from the Middle Bronze Age in White* Painted Ware (see also Pl. 159). All have cutaway-beak spouts. The only shape variant is found in Fig. 61, where the upper body of the pyramid sits directly on the three lower ones, without the usual three intervening necks.

Fig. 55 *Vounous (Tomb 38, no. 39). Ht. 42.5 cm. Des Gagniers and Karageorghis 1976, Pl. XXIX, 2.*

Fig. 56 *Vounous (Tomb 15, no. 29). Ht. 38 cm. Dikaios 1940, Pl. XXXId.*

Fig. 57 *Vounous (Tomb 9, no. 149). Ht. 18 cm. Dikaios 1940, Pl. XXXIc.*

Fig. 58 *Katholiki, Limassol (Limassol Museum). Ht. 24.4 cm. Des Gagniers and Karageorghis 1976, Pl. XXIX,4.*

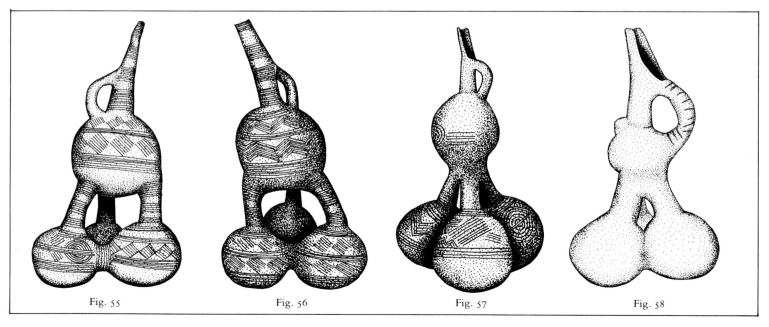

Fig. 55   Fig. 56   Fig. 57   Fig. 58

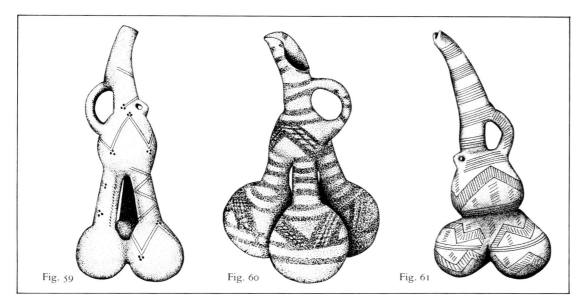

Fig. 59　Fig. 60　Fig. 61

Fig. 59 *Vounous. Schaeffer 1936, Pl. XVIII,1.*

Fig. 60 *Toumba tou Skourou (Tomb 6, no. 77). Ht. 12.5 cm. Vermeule 1974, Pl. 34a.*

Fig. 61 *No provenance (Nicholson Museum, Sydney). Ht. 22 cm. Hennessy 1979, Pl. 49.*

Fig. 62 A unique multiple vessel, having seven bodies linked horizontally, with seven necks and fourteen handles. *From Kition (Tomb 11, no. 130). See Karageorghis 1975, no. 57. This is an extreme case of the fusing together of simple flasks of Bichrome Ware in the Cypro-Geometric period. Several examples are known where two or three such flasks are joined together as one, but this is the only case where the process was taken to the extreme of connecting seven units.*

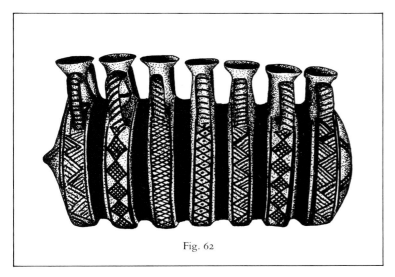

Fig. 62

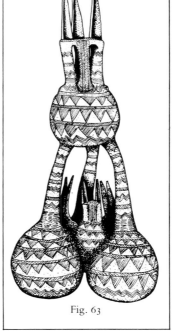

Fig. 63

Fig. 63 Seven-bodied vessel. *This extraordinary vessel takes the Cypriot pluralization process to a zenith of complexity. The trio of lower bodies have smaller ones on their inner shoulders, forming another trio. Each of these inner bodies is triple-necked, with long cutaway-beak spouts. The elongated necks of the three lower bodies rise to join the base of an upper body which also boasts three necks of similar design. From Vounous (Tomb 19, no. 16). Dikaios 1940, Pl. XXXIIc. With a height of 83 cm this is easily the largest of the complex vessels of Cyprus.*
For multi-spout vessels see Pl. 162, p. 100.

Figs. 64-6 Two bowls. *Red Polished Ware (Figs. 64-5) and White Painted Ware (Fig. 66). Early and Middle Bronze Age. These always have a centre handle which helps to strengthen their fusion.*

Fig. 64 *Vounous (Tomb 22, no. 38). Ht. 20 cm. Dikaios 1940, Pl. XXVIc.*

Fig. 65 *Vounous (Tomb 137, no. 22). Ht. 25.4 cm. Stewart and Stewart 1950, Pl. LXXVIIa.*

Fig. 66 *No provenance (Loch Collection, Ontario Museum, Toronto). Ht. 8 cm. Leipen 1966, no. 35.*
See also Pls. 163-7, pp. 101-3.

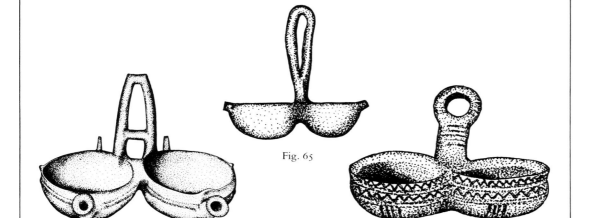

Fig. 65

Fig. 64　Fig. 66

IV Multi-bowl vessels

Figs. 67-8 Three bowls. *Red Polished Ware. This type of multiple vessel is known from the Early to the Late Bronze Age. The elegant, long-stemmed Fig. 68 has a close parallel in a triple-bowl of the early Cycladic period from Naxos, and it has been suggested that this reflects a Cycladic influence. Bearing in mind the dominance of the multi-unit theme in Cyprus, it seems more likely that the opposite is the truth and that the Cycladic vessel shows a Cypriot influence.*

Fig. 67 *Lapithos (Tomb 7). Ht. 14 cm. Buchholz and Karageorghis 1973, no. 1505.*

Fig. 68 *Polemidhia (Limassol Museum). Ht. 21 cm. Tatton-Brown 1979, no. 65.*

Figs. 69-74 Four bowls. *Red Polished Ware (except for Fig. 74, which is early White Painted Ware). Early Bronze Age. The most common form has the four bowls resting on the ground with a tall handle rising from the middle of them. This is usually flattened and in some cases (see p. 153) may boast human figures growing from its upper edge.*

Fig. 69 *Vounous (Tomb 19, no. 5). Ht. 30 cm. Dikaios 1940, Pl. XXVIIa.*

Fig. 70 *Vounous (Tomb 9, no. 84). Ht. 30 cm. Dikaios 1940, Pl. XXVIIb.*

Fig. 71 *Vounous? (Cyprus Museum, Nicosia). Ht. 31 cm. Karageorghis 1980, no. 29.*

Fig. 72 *Vounous (Tomb 8, no. 91). Ht. 19 cm. Dikaios 1940, Pl. XXVIb.*

Fig. 73 *Lapithos (Tomb 322d, no. 6). Ht. 42.5 cm. Buchholz and Karageorghis 1973, no. 1508.*

Fig. 74 *Vounous (Tomb 12, no. 25). Ht. 25 cm. Dikaios 1940, Pl. XLIb.*

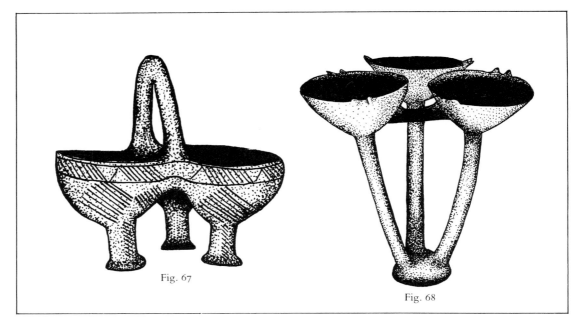

Fig. 67

Fig. 68

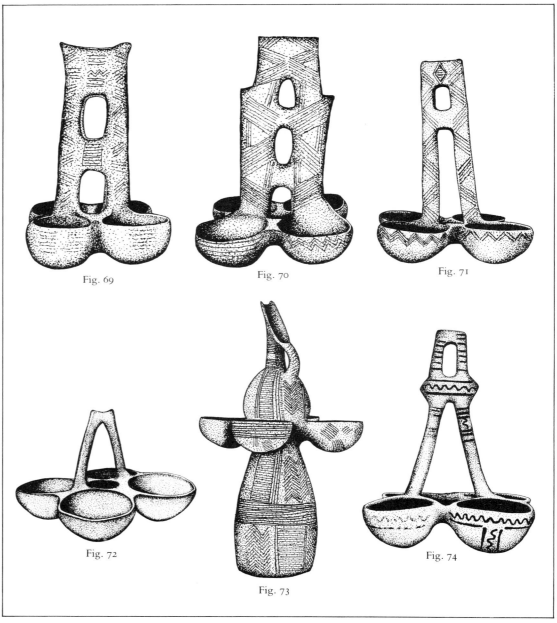

Fig. 69

Fig. 70

Fig. 71

Fig. 72

Fig. 73

Fig. 74

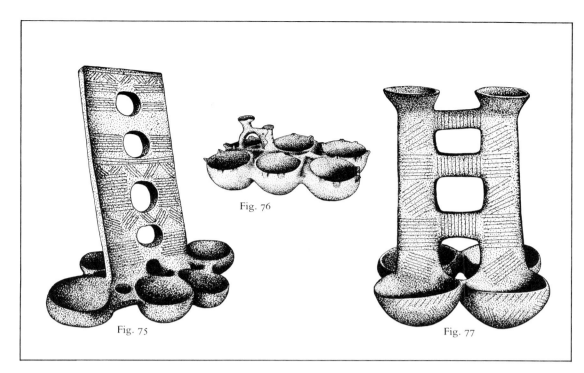

Fig. 76

Fig. 75

Fig. 77

IV Multi-bowl vessels

Figs. 75-7 Six bowls. *Red Polished Ware. Early Bronze Age. These are extensions of the more common four-bowl vessel. In one case, the extra two bowls are added on at either end of the base of the tall handle (Fig. 75); in another (Fig. 76) the six bowls are arranged as a rectangle, but most of the central handle is broken away, so that it is impossible to guess its full height or shape; and in another (Fig. 77) the ordinary four-bowl design is amplified by the addition of two extra, smaller bowls on top of the tall central handle.*

Fig. 75 *Vounous (Tomb 76). Ht. 30 cm. Schaeffer 1936, Fig. 13.*

Fig. 76 *No provenance (Lowie Museum, Berkeley, California). Surviving ht. 30 cm. Karageorghis et al. 1974, no. 16.*

Fig. 77 *No provenance (private collection, London).*

Figs. 79-80 Eight bowls. *Red Polished Ware. Early or Middle Bronze Age. Fig. 79 has a ring of seven small bowls with pointed bases, around a central bowl, and Fig. 80 has six small bowls round a central one, but with an additional, eighth bowl on top of a tall handle. Fig. 79 has lost most of its handle and, like Fig. 78 has only two short handle-stumps surviving. In Fig. 80, where the vessel is entire, the upper bowl has a small human figure clinging to its own small handle.*

Fig. 79 *No provenance (Lowie Museum, Berkeley, California). Surviving ht. 7.4 cm. Karageorghis et al. 1974, no. 18.*

Fig. 80 *No provenance. Ht. 22.6 cm. Karageorghis et al. 1974, no. 17.*

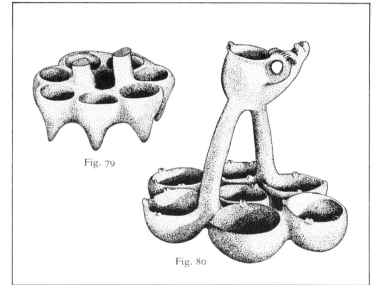

Fig. 79

Fig. 80

Fig. 78 Seven bowls. *This unique vessel consists of a ring of six bowls surrounding a central, seventh one. A central handle has been broken away and survives only as two short stumps. Plain Red Polished Ware. Middle Bronze Age. Surviving ht. 8.1 cm. (Lowie Museum, Berkeley, California). Karageorghis et al. 1974, no. 17.*

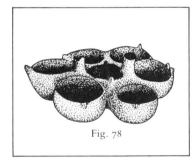

Fig. 78

v Multi-handle vessels

Figs. 81-2 Two handles. *The two surviving examples are separated in time by centuries and yet have a similar design concept, with the handle divided into two loops. Fig. 81 is in Red Polished Ware from the Early Bronze Age, and Fig. 82 is in Black-on-Red Ware from the Iron Age.*

Fig. 81 *Dhenia (Fitzwilliam Museum, Cambridge). Ht. 22 cm. Stewart 1962, Fig. XCVIII, 9.*

Fig. 82 *No provenance (Cyprus Museum, Nicosia). Gjerstad 1948, Fig. XXV, 12.*

Fig. 81

Fig. 82

1 Multi-neck vessels

Pl. 154 Twin-necked jug with round base and round spouts.
The necks connected by a divided vertical handle. No incision markings. Mottled Red Polished Ware. Early Bronze Age. Ht. 23 cm (DM-MRP-26). Cf. SCE IV.1a, Fig. LXXXII, no. 8.

Pl. 155 Twin-necked jug with round base and cutaway-beak spouts. *There are four vertically-pierced lugs on the body and two horizontally-pierced lugs on each neck. Each neck has its own, separate vertical handle, with thumb-grip.*

The incised decoration includes broad, dot-filled stripes with interior vertical zigzags. Handmade Black Slip Ware. Middle Bronze Age. Ht. 19 cm (DM-HBS-11). Cf. SCE IV.1b, Fig. XXVI, no. 12, for single-necked vessel with similar decorative elements.

Pl. 156 Twin-necked jug with pointed base and beak spouts.
There are two small, horizontally-attached handles, one in front of the necks, with a small bird perched upon it, and one behind the necks. In addition, there is the main, vertical

handle, which divides into two to connect the twin necks. At the point where it divides there is a zoomorphic thumb-grip in the shape of an animal head with open mouth. The presence of this head converts the divided section of the vertical handle into animal 'horns'. On either side of the necks is a model of a bird on a stem which rises from the shoulder of the vessel. One of these birds has a flattened body, the other's is circular. In addition there is some relief-decoration and groups of incised dots. Drab Polished Ware. Middle Bronze Age. Ht 38.6 cm (DM-DP-14).

Pl. 155

Pl. 154

Pl. 156

1 Multi-neck vessels

Pl. 157 Fused-twin-neck jug with flat base, cutaway-beak spout and single vertical handle. *The two necks fuse at the point where the handle meets them, to end in a single spout. There are three pierced lugs on the front of the necks and one at the base of the handle. There is also a thumb-grip on the handle. Handmade White Painted Ware. Middle Bronze Age. Ht. 35 cm (DM-HWP-53). Formerly in the Joseph Mueller Collection, Switzerland.*

Pl. 157

Pl. 158

II Multi-body vessels

Pl. 158

a(left) **Two-bodied jug, one body on top of the other.** *The upper body has a handle, but the lower one does not. The upper body has a neck with a cutaway spout, the lower one has a round base. Incised Red Polished Ware. Early Bronze Age. Ht. 28.6 cm (DM-IRP-74).*
b(right) *Same description, except that both bodies have a handle and a pierced lug. The lower body has a flattened base. Ht. 27.3 cm (DM-IRP-73). Formerly in the Bomford Collection.*

Pl. 159

Pl. 159

a(left) **Four-bodied jug of 'pyramid' type.** *The necks of the three, round-based bodies slope towards one another and enter the base of a single jug above them. The upper body, which has a beak spout, is the only one with a handle. Incised Red Polished Ware. Early Bronze Age. Ht. 24 cm (DM-IRP-75). Cf. Schaeffer 1936, Pl. XVIII, 1.*
b(right) **Three-bodied jug with the bodies arranged in a horizontal triangle.** *Their necks slope towards one another to fuse in a single, round spout. Handmade White Painted Ware. Middle Bronze Age. Ht. 15.7 cm (DM-HWP-54). Cf. Buchholz and Karageorghis 1973, no. 1544.*

II Multi-body vessels

Pl. 160 Twin-bodied vessel. *Each body has a ring base and a round spout, but they share a central vertical handle. Base Ring Ware. Late Bronze Age. Ht. 10.2 cm (DM-BR-20).*

Pl. 161 Triple-bodied vessel. *Three flasks with twin handles, round bases and round spouts, are fused together in the horizontal plane. Bichrome Ware. Iron Age. Ht. 9.7 cm (DM-BI-75). Cf. SCE IV.2, Fig. XXIII, no. 14.*

Pl. 160

Pl. 161

III Multi-spout vessels

Pl. 162 Twin spouted bowl.
Four rim-lugs, the one opposite the spouts being large and pierced. The two cutaway spouts are effectively 'bridge spouts'. Black-bottomed Red Polished Ware. Early Bronze Age. Diam. 27.5 cm (DM-BBRP-03).

Pl. 162

IV Multi-bowl vessels

Pl. 163 Nine-bowl vessel with central handle. *Eight of the bowls are arranged in two rows of four and the ninth is centrally placed, slightly raised up, under the handle. This multi-unit vessel has more units than any other known at present. Plain Red Polished Ware. Early Bronze Age. Maximum length 34 cm (DM-PRP-38). Handle restored.*

Pl. 163

Pl. 164

Pl. 164 Two-bowl vessel with central loop handle and opposing spouts. *Because the spouts point in opposite directions, efficient pouring is impossible. Plain Red Polished Ware. Early Bronze Age. Length 31 cm. Ht. 16.2 cm (DM-PRP-37).*

Pl. 165 Four-bowl vessel with the quartet of small bowls on top of a tall central stem with a tripod base. *This appears to be a unique vessel with no exact parallels yet known. Mottled Red Polished Ware. Early Bronze Age. Ht. 25.4 cm (DM-MRP-27).*

Pl. 165

Pl. 166

IV Multi-bowl vessels

Pl. 166 Four-bowl vessel with tall, flattened central handle.
The handle is pierced by three apertures, one above the other. The bowls are arranged, one in front, one behind, and two flanking the handle. This is an unusual arrangement for this type of vessel. It is more common for the four bowls to be arranged two in front and two behind (as in Pl. 167a). Incised Red Polished Ware. Early Bronze Age. Ht. 32.2 cm (DM-IRP-77).

Pl. 167
a Four-bowl vessel with tall, flattened central handle. *The handle is pierced by three apertures. The bowls are arranged, two in front and two behind the handle. Incised Red Polished Ware. Early Bronze Age. Ht. 31.5 cm (DM-IRP-76).*
b *Same description, but with only the flattened handle surviving. The points of attachment of the four bowls are clear and indicate that this vessel, when complete, was of the same form as Pl. 167a. Ht. 21.4 cm (DM-IRP-78). Cf. Stewart and Stewart 1950, Vounous T.143, nos. 61 and 69.*

Pl. 167

V Multi-handle vessels

Pl. 168 Tulip bowl with six vertical handles around its rim. *One handle has an unusual face on its flattened tip, the mouth and eyes being rendered with the same circular motif. Because of its flattened shape and its eyebrows, this appears to be a human face. An imaginative interpretation of this vessel sees it as a kind of 'loving cup', with a different person drinking from each space betweeen adjacent handles. This interpretation was suggested by the fact that the incised band between the handles shows a different pattern in each segment. Black-topped Red Polished Ware. Early Bronze Age. Diam. (at rim) 16.3 cm. Ht. (to top of handles) 18.8 cm (DM-BTRP-25). The basal region of the bowl and parts of three handles restored. No exact parallels known.*

Pl. 168

3 Subsidiary-Unit Vessels (34)

I MAIN VESSEL WITH MINIATURE BOWLS ATTACHED (21)

a Two Bowls (13)

Two small bowls are attached to the shoulders of a jug or the rim of a parent bowl, either directly, or on stalks. In four cases the parent vessel is a stemmed bowl. Of the three parent jugs, one is beak-spouted, one round-spouted and one side-spouted. Early to Middle Bronze Age. *Examples traced:* Incised Red Polished (7); Plain Red Polished (3); Relief-decorated Red Polished (2); Drab Polished (1).

b Three Bowls (6)

Three small bowls attached to the shoulders of a jug or the rim of a parent bowl. In one case the parent vessel is a stemmed bowl. The four parent jugs are all round-spouted and bowls are arranged in the same way on each: one on either side of the handle and one opposite it. Early Bronze Age. *Examples traced:* Incised Red Polished (3); Relief-decorated Red Polished (3).

c Four Bowls (2)

Four small bowls attached to the rim of a large bowl. Early Bronze Age. *Examples traced:* Incised Red Polished (1); Plain Red Polished (1).

II MAIN VESSEL WITH MINIATURE JUGS ATTACHED (3)

a Two Jugs (1)

Two small, cutaway-beak-spouted juglets are attached to the shoulders of the parent jug, which has a similar spout. All three spouts face in the same direction, with the two juglets on either side of the handle of the parent vessel. Early Bronze Age. *Example traced:* Philia Red Polished (1).

b Three Jugs (1)

Three small, cutaway-spouted juglets sit on the shoulders of a round-spouted parent jug, one juglet on either side of the parent handle and one opposite it. Early Bronze Age. *Example traced:* Incised Red Polished (1).

c Four Jugs (1)

Four small cutaway-spouted juglets are arranged around the shoulders of a large round-spouted jug. Early Bronze Age. *Example traced:* Relief-decorated Red Polished (1).

III MAIN VESSEL WITH MINIATURE BOWLS AND JUGS ATTACHED (8)

a One Bowl and One Jug (2)

A small bowl and a cutaway-beak-spouted juglet are attached, one on either side of the neck of a parent jug, the latter with cutaway-beak or round spout. Early to Middle Bronze Age. *Examples traced:* Mottled Red Polished (1); Drab Polished (1).

b Two Bowls and One Jug

Two small bowls are attached on either side of the vessel with a juglet frontally placed between them. In two cases the parent vessel is a cutaway-beak-spouted jug and the juglet attached has a similar spout. In one case, the main jug is round-spouted and so is the juglet. In the fourth instance the parent vessel has become a vertical tube topped by a narrow platform on which the three miniature vessels are displayed, as if on an 'offering table' Early and Middle Bronze Age. *Examples traced:* Incised Red Polished (1); Plain Red Polished (1); Drab Polished (2).

c One Bowl and Two Jugs (1)

Two small cutaway-spouted juglets are attached on either side of the neck of a large jug (of which the spout is missing), with a small bowl frontally placed between them. This is the reversed arrangement of (b) above. Early Bronze Age. *Example traced:* Relief-decorated Red Polished (1).

d Three Bowls and Two Jugs (1)

A complex vessel with two small bowls on either side of the neck of the round-spouted parent jug, a cutaway-beak-spouted juglet perched on the main handle, and, frontally placed opposite this handle, a small modelled bench on which sit a human couple, with a cutaway-beak-spouted juglet perched at one end of the bench and a small bowl at the other. Early Bronze Age. *Example traced:* Relief-decorated Red Polished (1).

IV MAIN VESSEL WITH MINIATURE JARS ATTACHED (2)

a One Jar (1)

The jar is perched on top of the handle of a multi-unit vessel with four basal bowls. Early Bronze Age. *Example traced:* Incised Red Polished (1).

b Two Jars (1)

The two jars are perched on the handles of a parent jar whose wide neck has been converted into a human face by the pierced ears. Middle Bronze Age. *Example traced:* Late Incised Red Polished (1).

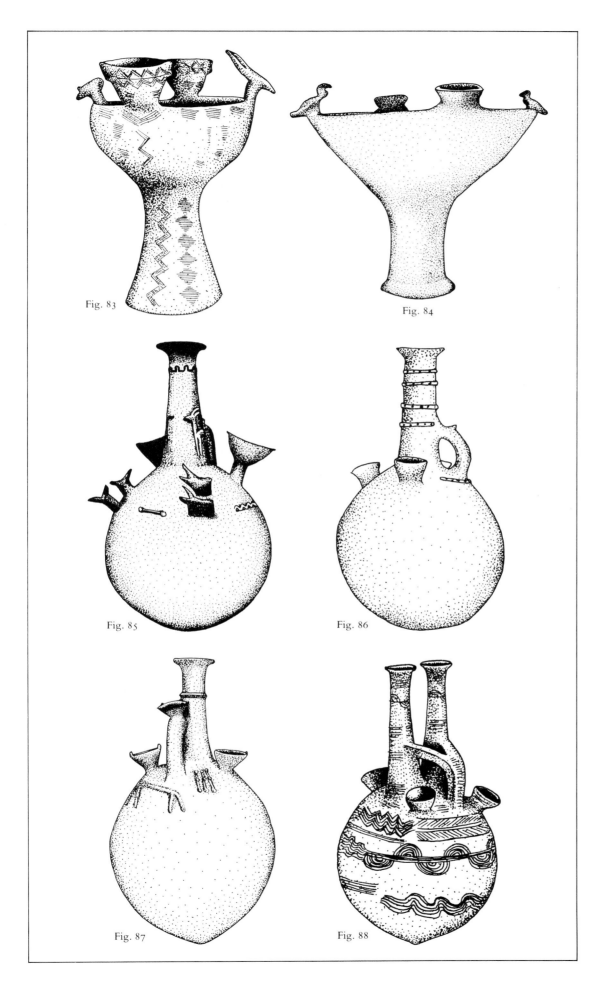

Fig. 83

Fig. 84

Fig. 85

Fig. 86

Fig. 87

Fig. 88

1 Main vessel with bowls attached

Fig. 83 Long-stemmed bowl with two small tulip bowls on the rim. *Also protruding from the rim of the parent bowl is a pair of horned animal heads. Incised Red Polished Ware. Early Bronze Age. From Vounous (Tomb 111, no. 1). Ht. to rim 36.9 cm. Stewart and Stewart 1950, Pl. LXXXI.*

Fig. 84 Long-stemmed bowl with two small bowls on the rim. *Two modelled birds also perching on rim. Plain Red Polished Ware. Early Bronze Age. From Vounous (Tomb 8, no. 17). Ht. 26 cm. Dikaios 1940, Pl. XVIb.*

Fig. 85 Large, round-spouted jug with two small, stemmed bowls attached to its shoulders, *one on either side of the handle. On the opposite shoulders are two pairs of modelled bulls and on the neck there is a further pair of horned animals, probably goats, in relief. Relief-decorated Red Polished Ware. Early Bronze Age. From Kochati. Now in the Pierides Collection in Nicosia. Ht. 55 cm. Des Gagniers and Karageorghis 1976, Pl. XXV, 1.*

Fig. 86 Large, round-spouted jug with three small bowls attached to its shoulders, *one on either side of the handle and a third opposite the handle. Relief-decorated Red Polished Ware. Early Bronze Age. From Lapithos (Tomb 322e, no. 28). Ht. 67 cm. Stewart 1962, Fig. LXXXIII, 3.*

Fig. 87 Large, round-spouted jug with three small bowls attached to its shoulders, *one on either side of the handle and a third opposite the handle (not visible in this drawing). On top of the handle is a fourth bowl. There is also a long-legged animal depicted in relief on the body of the parent vessel. Relief-decorated Red Polished Ware. Early Bronze Age. From Lapithos (Tomb 3, no. 13). Ht. 59 cm. Des Gagniers and Karageorghis 1976, Pl. XXIV, 1.*

Fig. 88 Large, twin-necked, round-spouted jug with three small bowls attached to its shoulders, *one on either side of the handle and a third opposite the handle. Incised Red Polished Ware. Early Bronze Age. No provenance. Private collection. Ht. 56 cm. Sotheby's Catalogue, 12 December 1983, no. 290.*

1 Main vessels with bowls attached

Pl. 169 Large jug with nipple base, cutaway-beak spout and a pair of subsidiary bowls, *one on either side of the handle. The handle itself has a large thumb-grip that has grown into a bull's head. Also, on the shoulder of the jug, opposite the handle, is a modelled figure of a standing bull. There are incised dots around the base of the jug's neck. Drab Polished Ware. Early to Middle Bronze Age. Ht. 44.3 cm (DM-DP-15).*

Pl. 169

III Main vessels with
bowls and jugs attached

**Pl. 170 Large jug with nipple
base, cutaway-beak spout, a
pair of subsidiary bowls on
either side of the handle and a
subsidiary jug oppposite it.**
*The thumb-grip on the handle has
developed into an animal's head.
There are incisions on the jug's neck
and upper body. Drab Polished
Ware. Early to Middle Bronze Age.
Ht. 48 cm DM-DP-16).*

Pl. 170

I Main vessel with bowls attached

Fig. 89 Single-handled parent bowl with three small bowls protruding from its rim, *one on either side of the handle and a third opposite it. Crudely incised Red Polished Ware. End of the Early Bronze Age or the beginning of the Middle Bronze Age. No provenance. Pierides Collection, Larnaca. Ht. 17 cm. Karageorghis 1973, no. 4.*

Fig. 90 Long-stemmed bowl with three small tulip bowls on the rim, *alternating with modelled animals. Incised Red Polished Ware. Early Bronze Age. From Vounous (Tomb 160a, no. 17). Ht. to rim 52.7 cm. Stewart and Stewart 1950, Pl. LXXXIV.*

II Main vessel with juglets attached

Fig. 91 Large jug with cut-away spout carrying two juglets of similar design on its shoulders, *on either side of the parent vessel's handle. Incised Philia Red Polished Ware. Early Bronze Age. From Philia-Vasiliko (Tomb 3, no. 8). Ht. 36 cm. Dikaios 1962, Fig. LI, 11.*

Fig. 92 Large round-spouted jug with three juglets attached to its shoulders. *The unusual, horizontally attached handle is not connected to the neck. The juglets have cutaway spouts (only two are visible in this drawing). There is one on either side of the main handle and a third opposite it. Each juglet is connected to the neck of the parent vessel by a horizontal bar. On top of the main handle there is a small modelled figure of a bull. Crudely incised Red Polished Ware. Early Bronze Age. From Margi/Kochati. Hadjiprodromou Collection, Famagusta. Ht. 24 cm. Des Gagniers and Karageorghis 1976, Pl. XXIV, 4.*

Fig. 93 Large, round-spouted jug with four small juglets arranged equidistantly around the shoulders. *Relief-decorated Red Polished Ware. Early Bronze Age. From Vounous (Tomb 37, no. 38). Ht. 58 cm. Dikaios 1940, Pl. XIXe.*

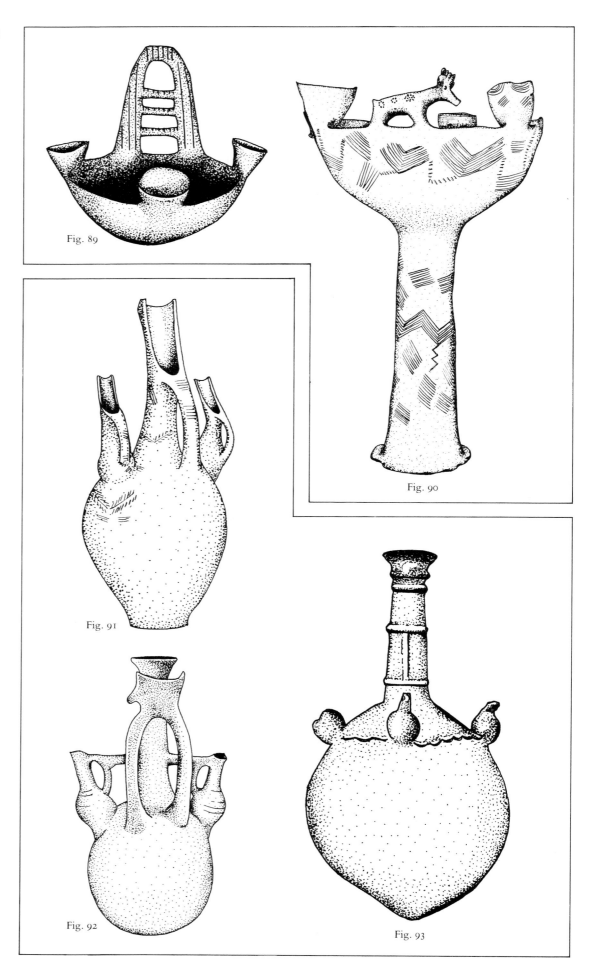

Fig. 89

Fig. 90

Fig. 91

Fig. 92

Fig. 93

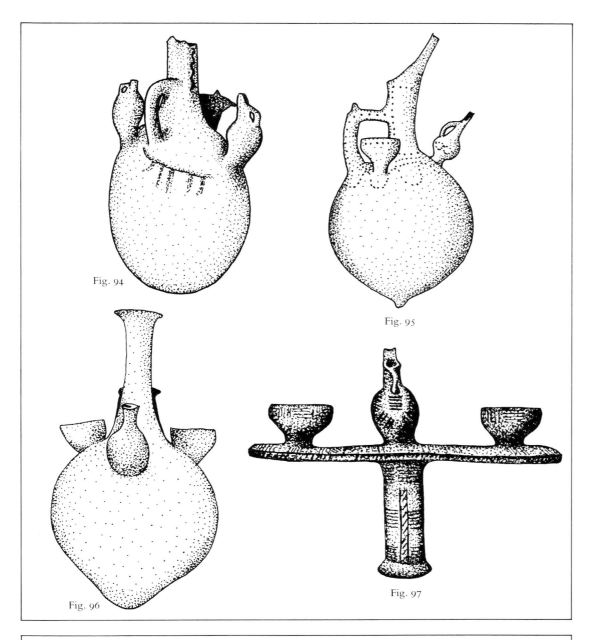

Fig. 94

Fig. 95

Fig. 96

Fig. 97

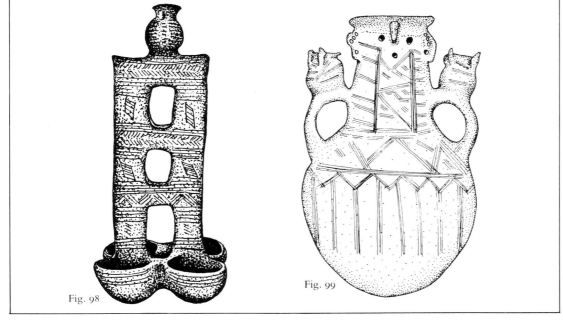

Fig. 98

Fig. 99

III Main vessel with bowls and juglets attached

Fig. 94 Jug with broken neck, two cutaway-spouted juglets, one on either side of the handle, and one small bowl opposite it. *A long-legged animal, probably a stag, is depicted in relief on the body of the main vessel. Relief-decorated Red Polished Ware. Early Bronze Age. No provenance. Ashmolean Museum, Oxford. Ht. 23.3 cm. Frankel 1983, no. 1254.*

Fig. 95 Jug with cutaway-beak spout and nipple base with two small bowls, one on either side of the handle, and a juglet opposite it. *Incised Red Polished Ware. Early Bronze Age. From Krysochous. MacLaurin 1980, Fig. 121, 2.*

Fig. 96 Large, round-spouted jug, with two small bowls, one on either side of the handle, and a round-spouted juglet opposite it. *Plain Red Polished Ware. Early Bronze Age. From Vounous (Tomb 16, no. 26). Ht. 56 cm. Dikaios 1940, Pl. XXIIIa.*

Fig. 97 *Here the parent vessel has been reduced to a tubular pillar topped by a long narrow table on which sit a central juglet and a pair of small bowls. This unique object stresses the special nature of the group of small subsidiary vessels as a kind of 'ritual set', rather than as merely decorative excrescences. Incised Red Polished Ware. Early Bronze Age. From Vounous (Tomb 9, no. 63). Ht. 17 cm. Dikaios 1940, Pl. XXXIIIb.*

IV Main vessel with jars attached

Fig. 98 *This is both a four-bowl Multi-unit Vessel and a one-jar Subsidiary-unit Vessel, the multiple bowls being at the base of the tall handle and the subsidiary jar at the top. Incised Red Polished Ware. Early Bronze Age. From Vounous (Tomb 7, no. 29). Ht. 38 cm. Dikaios 1940, Pl. XXVIIc.*

Fig. 99 Two-handled jar with two jars attached to the handles. *The upper neck has been metamorphosed into a human face, with pierced ears, modelled nose, and incised eyes and mouth. The handles, in effect, become transformed into shoulders and arms, with the two small jars sitting on them. Late Incised Red Polished Ware. Middle Bronze Age. From Yialia. Hadjiprodromou Collection, Famagusta. Ht. 37 cm. Des Gagniers and Karageorghis 1976, Pl. XXII, 3.*

III Main vessels with
bowls and jugs attached

**Pl. 171 Large jug with nipple
base and beak spout, bowl on
one side of the handle and a
jug on the other.** *In relief on the
front of the neck of the parent vessel
is a bull's head, showing eyes,
nostrils and mouth. Projecting on
either side of the neck above this head
are upward-curved projections, now
broken, which were originally the
horns of the bull. Below the neck, on
the shoulder of the vessel, is a pair of
crossed snakes shown in relief. In
addition, there is an incised decorative
element on the neck showing a 'cross-
over' pattern. Drab Polished Ware.
Early to Middle Bronze Age.
Ht. 37.3 cm (DM-DP-17).*

Pl. 171

III Main vessels with bowls and jugs attached

Pl. 172 Large jug with pointed base and round spout, a bowl on one side of the neck and a jug with a cutaway spout on the other. *These small vessels are placed on top of tall stems which arise from the shoulders of the parent vessel and are stabilized by bridges to the main neck. This strange arrangement has led the artist to omit a handle for the parent vessel. Mottled Red Polished Ware. Early Bronze Age. Ht. 48.1 cm (DM-MRP-28).*

Pl. 172

Complex Vessels: Conclusion

Although composite and multiple vessels are known from other ceramic traditions outside Cyprus, it is true to say that the Cypriot artist remains the supreme exponent of these complex shapes. The 279 examples I have been able to trace undoubtedly represent only a fraction of the output in ancient times. Indeed, their frequency of occurrence on the island is so high compared with elsewhere, that it is tempting to think of the Greek and other mainland examples as being derivatives of a Cypriot tradition, rather than the other way round.

Scanning the illustrations assembled here, it is clear that the complex themes were far more than local or personal idiosyncracies. Almost every category and sub-category spanned more than one ware, and usually more than one period. To take one example: the large jug with small vessels sprouting from its shoulders. This is known from the very early Philia Red Polished Ware, through to the much later Drab Polished Ware, a 'theme life-span' lasting for something like a thousand years. The idea of perching miniature vessels on the bodies of large ones is so uncommon in the history of world ceramics, that it is hard to think of it as having been re-invented several times on one small island. The obvious conclusion must be that the 'subsidiary-unit' concept must have become a Cypriot tradition, fostered and handed on from centre to centre. Whether this was a purely stylistic tradition originating from an individual 'quirk' and then becoming embedded in Cypriot 'ceramic thinking', or whether it started out as a pottery portrayal of some sort of ritual procedure, is a problem that remains to be resolved.

In simple—physical—functional terms, the majority of the vessels illustrated here are of little use. Attempting to pour, for example, from the subsidiary-unit jugs would create unusual problems. If the miniature juglets and bowls were filled with liquids or solids, these would be spilled as soon as the the parent vessel was tipped up. In some cases, where there is a hole in the base of the miniature vessels, leading through into the interior of the parent vessel, it would perhaps have been possible to pour from all exits at once, when tipping the parent jug, but such an attempt would at best be messy, and would lack the sort of formal elegance required by ritual procedures. The same is true of ring vessels with little jars on top of their hollow rings. And with the exception of multi-bowl vessels, the multi-unit creations of Cypriot potters nearly all lack any practical value.

Their real value, in most cases, seems to be ostentation. The mourner who placed a six-unit vessel in a tomb was perhaps being six times as respectful as someone who merely offered a common or garden single-unit vessel. The status-conscious individual could, of course, have used other methods. He could have presented six separate vessels, or one vessel six times the normal size, or a single small vessel of unusually brilliant finish or elegant contours. Instead, in the Cypriot context, the channel chosen was the composite pottery construction, and it was this one that gave the local artists the greatest chance to demonstrate their ceramic cheekiness and exuberance. It was a trend that resulted in some of the most flamboyant and remarkable examples of prehistoric art, although it has to be admitted that they are not to everyone's taste. Ceramic experts such as Charleston (1968), for example, take a dim view of them aesthetically. Discussing the prehistoric pottery of the Near East he comments: 'It was only in Cyprus that the relative conservatism inherent in plain pottery was broken ... Much of the Early Bronze Age pottery of Cyprus is heavy and technically inferior ... At times ... the artist in a fit of virtuosity could create such bizarre pieces as that illustrated. [He shows a four-bowl and a seven-body example of multi-unit vessels.] The product is completely without use and almost totally without artistic merit ...'

Such a stern criticism of Cypriot complex vessels is unfair. It springs from the academic ceramicist's tendency to place a high value on austere restraint in vessel contours—an almost minimalist approach to pottery shapes. If there is to be complexity it is permissible only in surface decoration. Happily, most of us do not suffer from these narrow prejudices and we are free to enjoy the bizarre designs and complex shapes of ancient Cypriot pottery without imposing any old-fashioned bias. We can now see them for what they are—extraordinary flights of ceramic fancy, which even Charleston had to admit do 'serve to demonstrate the potter's complete mastery of his material'. And, whatever he may say, their merit, as prehistoric works of art, is considerable.

III Representations

Many of the pottery vessels found in the ancient tombs of Cyprus are adorned with representations of humans, animals, plants or inanimate objects. Sometimes these forms are added as small, modelled figures protruding from the bodies of vessels, or perched on their rims; sometimes they are painted or incised as part of the decorative pattern; and sometimes the vessel itself is transformed into a human or animal figure by making the body of the vessel into the body of the person or creature depicted.

There are interesting differences here. Small, modelled figures protruding from vessels or perched on their rims are common only in the Early and Middle Bronze Age. During this same phase it is extremely rare to find representational figures depicted as part of the incised or painted decoration. Of the thousands of decorated vessels known from the Early and Middle Bronze Age, only a handful display incised or painted figures on their surfaces. The exception to this near-taboo on 'surface-figures' is the depiction of long-legged ungulates of one kind or another on Relief-decorated Red Polished Ware. Why the Relief-artists were less inhibited in this respect than the Incisers or the Painters, is hard to say, because it is just as easy, if not easier, to draw a deer with a sharp point or a paint-brush, as it is to apply it with strips of relief-work clay.

Another intriguing difference concerns the bias towards animal, rather than human shapes, when converting a vessel into a figure of some kind. Vessels that grow human heads, with the belly of the vessel becoming the belly of the figure, are rare compared with animal-shaped vessels, and this applies at all stages. There seem to be two reasons for this: first, if an artist is going to depict a human form, she or he is more likely to present it as a terracotta figurine, rather than as a metamorphosed vessel. Second, many of the animal-shaped vessels are clearly intended to show, not the living animal, but its *askos*, or wine-skin pelt. This can be told from the odd shape of the body and the near-absence of legs. In other words, animals are popular as transformed vessels because they themselves had been transformed into vessels, in real life.

Painted representations as part of the decorative pattern on vessels did not become popular until the Late Bronze Age, when they arrived as a Mycenaean introduction of major importance to the island. From this point onwards, Cyprus was to enjoy centuries of painted figures on jugs, jars, bowls and dishes. The old inhibitions about painted images were swept aside. Even at this stage, however, there were many potters who still restricted themselves to geometric patterns. Although they must have been aware of the pictorial images of their contemporaries, they clung to the old-style concentric circles, checker-boards, diamonds, criss-crosses, bands and stripes. How they resisted the temptation to add a few of the charming birds, lotus flowers, or mammals that had become so popular, is hard to imagine, unless, for them at least, some sort of pictorial taboo still existed.

Up to this point mention has been made only of representations *on* vessels. But vessels, although dominating the scene where tomb-goods are concerned, were not the only offerings in the rock-cut resting places of the ancient Cypriots. In addition, there were sometimes pottery figurines depicting humans or animals, or small models of such things as sheath-knives, horns, furniture, boats or chariots. These were rare, when compared with the vessels, but there are enough of them to force us to ask serious questions about their role in the burial proceedings. To pose the questions properly, it is necessary to probe the more fundamental problem of why *anything*—vessel, figurine or model—should be placed with the corpse in the rock chamber. A number of theories have been put forward in the past and they can be summarized briefly as follows:

1 To provide the deceased with a meal to sustain him or her on the journey to the other world.

2 To provide offerings for the gods, to be presented by the deceased on arrival in the next world, so that he or she will be welcome there.

3 To provide offerings for the gods from the mourners themselves, so that their friend, the deceased, will be made welcome in the next world.

4 To provide the spirit of the deceased with food and drink inside the tomb.

5 To provide gifts for the deceased to appease him or her and thus prevent any harm to the living.

6 To share a last meal with the deceased (assuming that the mourners first ate and drank from the vessels and then left them in the tomb at the end of the funeral celebrations).

7 To prevent the deceased from returning to collect his or her belongings (assuming that the tomb-goods belonged to the deceased in life).

8 To remove memories of the deceased (assuming the same).

9 To prevent anyone else using the deceased's possessions (assuming the same).

Only the first three of these hypotheses require a belief in deities and an afterlife. Most of the others demand no more than a feeling that the deceased still has some sort of power in relation to the living. Such imagined powers do not necessitate any formal religious concepts, merely the refusal to accept that,

after death, the human being becomes totally inert.

It seems likely that ideas on this subject changed as ancient Cyprus moved from the prehistoric to the historic. Perhaps the earliest tomb-offerings reflect no more than belief in 'ghosts' or 'spirits', which had to be helped, or humoured, or kept at bay. There is certainly no evidence of anything more complex from the prehistoric phases. Later, as Cyprus became urbanized, specific religious cults and practices did, of course, develop, and the reasons given for offering tomb-goods may then have been more directly related to the 'other world' and its dominant figures. But it is a mistake to argue retrospectively from this period back to earlier, more primitive days. It is frustrating that we have so little to go on from those days, but it only clouds the issue to transport advanced ideas backwards through time without any real supporting evidence. Sadly, this is done all too frequently, as we shall see later, and the 'Retrospective Error' is one of the most common faults of modern archaeology.

Having made these points about the possible functions of tomb offerings, it becomes clear that caution is needed in interpreting the role of the pottery figurines and small pottery models which were occasionally added to collections of vessels. It is all too easy to slip into the mode of thought which ascribes to them some holy or sacred qualities. They *may* have had such properties, but this is far from certain.

The small human figures provide a good example of how the Retrospective Error can become rigidly entrenched. When such prehistoric figurines were first unearthed in various countries by the early archaeologists they were referred to simply as 'dolls' or 'figures'. But, as Ucko (1968) points out: 'Very shortly, however, Sir Arthur Evans became a firm follower of the view that such figurines were prototypes of the later Mother Goddess, Ishtar, or Great Mother ...' The prehistoric Cypriot figurines soon became labelled in the same way and, to this day, are unhesitatingly referred to as 'Mother Goddesses'. This wildly speculative interpretation of the significance of prehistoric Cypriot figurines is made by hard-nosed archaeologists who, on other topics, would demand extreme caution. What has happened, of course, is that the term 'Mother Goddess' has been repeated so frequently and over such a long period that it has become hallowed by tradition and is no longer questioned. I propose to question it. First, though, what does it mean?

To call a small human figure found in a tomb a 'Mother Goddess' or an 'Idol' implies that it is a representation of an early deity. The presumption is that a likeness of the deity was placed with the deceased to protect the body from evil influences. But where is the evidence for the worship of a deity in prehistoric Cyprus? There are no temples to the Great Goddess, no remains of huge effigies, no models of the faithful attending her shrine, nothing, not a scrap of hard evidence to support her existence on the island at an early date. All we have is a large number of strange little figurines from tombs and occasionally from excavated settlements.

Ucko (1968), who is also highly sceptical about the blanket use of the term 'Mother Goddess', points out that such figurines could, in reality, have had a number of other possible meanings. He is dealing with artefacts from other cultures, but his remarks are just as valid for prehistoric Cyprus. He lists the following:

1 MOURNER FIGURINES. *Figurines placed in the tomb to provide mourners to accompany the deceased.* Figurines carrying offerings or playing musical instruments would be the most obvious candidates for this category. Less obvious, but equally important, are female figures shown holding their breasts, as this was an ancient mourning posture (and not a sexual posture as is so often supposed). The hands held to the head was another mourning posture, sometimes seen in small figurines. Pottery substitutes for widows or loved ones, to accompany the dead, also belong to this category.

2 SERVANT FIGURINES. *Figurines placed in the tomb to provide servants for the deceased.*

3 PERSONAL FIGURINES. *Figures placed in the tomb because they were of special importance to the deceased during his or her lifetime.* Ucko (p. 429) lists the following possibilities: 'a figure used during the initiation ceremony of the deceased; a twin figure representing the deceased's previously dead twin brother or sister; a vehicle for sympathetic magic treasured because it had fulfilled its purpose; or the agent of a sorcerer which had to be buried with the sorcerer concerned to rid the surviving family from any suspicion of hav-

ing harboured a sorcerer in the family'. He adds that 'children may have been buried with one or more of their favourite dolls, and it is even possible that adults too may have been buried with their childhood loves'. This idea of including personal 'toys' in the tombs would help to explain why some of the ancient figurines were made in the form of animal rattles (see Pls. 241 and 242). It should be remembered that we have no idea whether the Cypriot pottery figurines were clothed or dressed in some way when they were placed in the tomb—which would make them more doll-like.

In making his analysis, Ucko was concerned with prehistoric figures from Egypt, Crete, Greece and the Near East, so that caution must be used when applying his comments to ancient Cyprus. But his insistence on examining a variety of possible functions for the small human figurines found from prehistoric times provides a valuable lesson for Cypriot studies. His final conclusion, regarding the figurines he studied, is particularly relevant. He says that, with a few exceptions, 'no evidence has been found to support the view that they represented a Fertility Goddess although some may well have been associated with a desire for children'.

This last distinction is an important one. It is my own conclusion, after a detailed study of the Cypriot figures, that their most important function was as Fertility Figurines, but not as Fertility Goddesses. In other words I am suggesting that they come into the category of 'personal objects previously used for sympathetic magic'. I hasten to add that this does not apply to *all* the ancient Cypriot figurines, but only to certain major categories of them during the earlier, prehistoric periods. I agree with Ucko that it is wrong to attempt to place many different kinds of tomb figurines into a single functional category, and it seems highly likely that, especially in later phases, there were several distinct functions involved, along the lines he mentions. But the most famous of the early Cypriot figurines do, I believe, fall into the general area of what, in modern tribal studies, is referred to as 'fertility charms'.

It is important to explain why this interpretation places them outside the 'Mother Goddess' category. The essential feature of Mother Goddess idols is that they stand for a great Earth Mother who is responsible for the fertility, not merely of an individual, but for the whole community. She guides and guards the fertility of women, domestic animals and crops in an all-embracing role as a sacred protectress. Her own fecundity becomes symbolic of the fecundity of the whole culture and its environment. She is a powerful figure to be worshipped and appeased.

There is nothing about the early Cypriot figurines to hint at such a deity. They are all rather small and many are tiny. They are not particularly common and many tombs are without them. They were worn or carried by women, because we have several examples depicting this (see Figs. 150 and 211). Because of certain features, which will be discussed later, they appear to have been personal 'good luck charms', worn to increase the chances of giving birth. Today, suffering from over-population, it is hard for us to understand how important successful breeding was to these early islanders. If a modern female were to wear a lucky charm, it would probably be in the shape of a contraceptive pill, to help her *avoid* breeding. But for the prehistoric Cypriot female, the opposite was undoubtedly the case. The protection she needed was against infertility, and the small figurines she wore, around her neck or tucked into her clothing, were there to provide her with a little magical assistance.

These fertility charms took several forms. They could work their magic by showing:

1 a stylized form of pregnancy;
2 a stylized form of parturition;
3 a swaddled baby;
4 a baby in a cradle;
5 a mother holding a baby;
6 a mother suckling a baby;
7 a phallus.

All these forms are represented in the art of ancient Cyprus, and in surveying the various types of human representation on the pages which follow, these themes will be returned to time and again.

After the prehistoric period, during the Late Bronze Age and the Iron Age, there arises an entirely new kind of representation, with warriors and soldiers, horsemen and shield-carriers, musicians and worshippers. The figurines placed in the tombs take on new meanings and a totally different interpretation is required. But this should not surprise us for, with the passing of time, the island had become a very different place. The burial rituals of placing bodies in rock-cut tombs may have survived, but the tomb-goods accompanying the body now reflect a quite different cultural attitude, with warfare and specifically masculine pursuits coming to dominate the earlier reproductive themes.

Human Forms

Scanning the whole range of human forms as depicted by the artists of ancient Cyprus, it soon becomes clear that there is a strongly favoured type of stylization in each period. There are many intermediates, minor trends and idiosyncratic pieces, but depite this variability, there is one major style that typifies each main epoch. These dominant themes in human representation can be summarized as follows:

1 Neolithic	Stump Figures
2 Chalcolithic	Cruciform Figures
3 Early and Middle Bronze Age	Plank Figures
4 Late Bronze Age	Pubic Triangle Figures
5 Iron Age	Snowman Figures

As will become clear, this is a gross oversimplification, but it does serve as a useful crude guide to the shifts of emphasis in depiction of the human figure as the centuries pass. These shifts have to do with basic changes in aesthetic tradition, and, before describing them in detail, it is necessary to clarify certain terms and set out a few definitions.

The one feature that all these ancient figures have in common is that they do *not* present a realistic image of the human form. Without exception they all show some kind of deliberate modification of the natural object on which they are based. Not so long ago, such modifications were looked upon as inept and sadly lacking in artistic merit. Myres, for example, writing in 1914, refers to 'the childish clumsiness of the early handmade figures, in all periods of the Bronze Age'. Again, speaking of Bronze Age figurines, he comments, 'these first attempts are clumsy and barbaric.' Late Bronze Age figurines he attacks as 'peculiarly gross and unpleasing'. For him, clearly, skilled art does not begin until Classical times, with the more realistic portrayals of Greece and Rome.

Today a very different view prevails. It is now felt that Myres and others like him completely misunderstood the nature of the aesthetic process involved in the making of ancient figurines. The artists concerned were not attempting to reproduce natural shapes. They were engaged instead on a much more intriguing task—that of exploiting a natural shape for symbolic purposes. This involved several distinguishable processes, as Lorblanchet (1977) has pointed out.

Schematization. This is the process of modifying a natural object to emphasize its significant features. The artist decides, consciously or unconsciously, which features are important in a particular context and then exaggerates those, while reducing or eliminating other features he or she considers insignificant. I have referred to this as 'Stimulus Extremism' (Morris, 1977, p. 276), commenting that 'this double process heightens the impact of the selected features. Irrelevant features are eliminated or played down and the magnified elements therefore appear even more striking.' This is not an aesthetic process. It is based on the psychological significance of the selected elements, not their beauty.

Stylization. This is the process of modifying a natural object for decorative purposes. Unlike schematization, this does have an aesthetic basis. A stylized figure has its natural shape changed to enhance its rhythm, its proportions, or its texture, or some other such property. As Lorblanchet (1977) puts it: 'In stylization the model is not so important as the free use of the image with decorative intent.'

Stereotyping. As a result of the development of a traditional form of stylization, one often sees a stereotyping of the images, where one particular 'shape-style' is almost slavishly repeated, time and again. In such instances, the artist satisfies his or her urge for individual expression by varying small details, while keeping to the main stereotype. Stereotyping eventually led to the introduction of models, moulds and mass production.

Formalization. This is the process by which complex natural shapes become simplified during the artistic process. The subtle shape of the human head, eye, or breast, for example, becomes formalized as a circle.

Abstraction. This is formalization taken to an extreme. When natural shapes are modified to such a degree that they can no longer be related back to their origins, they are said to be abstract. This process had already begun back in the Palaeolithic, and there are many abstract signs on the cave walls which defy interpretation. It is not that they are purely decorative and have no specific meaning, but that the process of abstraction has obscured their symbolic significance.

These processes are not clearly separated from one another. They overlap and merge into one another in every example of ancient art. But by teasing them apart as I have done here, it helps to clarify the complex nature of the modification that takes place every time the human form is represented as a carved, modelled, drawn or painted figure.

1 Stump Figures

I am defining a Stump Figure as one in which the body extremities are reduced to mere stumps. This is a crude definition which brings together the stone-carved figurines of the Neolithic period in Cyprus and also includes certain of the Chalcolithic examples.

Sadly this is a small category, comprising only about two dozen figures, few human representations having survived from the Stone Age period. But although small in size and in number, they nonetheless comprise an extremely interesting group. They can be conveniently sub-divided into four sub-categories:

a Stump Figures with rounded outlines.
b Stump Figures with phallic heads.
c Stump Figures with folded arms.
d Stump Figures with protruding arms.

These sub-categories are based on important features, rather than on period or locality. This is not the usual way of presenting them, but it is adopted here because it helps to draw attention to the way in which certain themes have dominated the thinking of the ancient artists.

a Stump Figures with rounded outlines
There are six examples in this group, four of them Neolithic and two Chalcolithic. The Neolithic ones all come from Khirokitia and show a remarkable degree of simplification.

1a Stump Figures with rounded outlines

Fig. 100 *Khirokitia. Diabase. Neolithic. Ht 9.1 cm. Dikaios 1953, Pl. XCV.*

Fig. 101 *Khirokitia. Andesite. Neolithic. Ht 9 cm. Dikaios 1953, Pl. XCV.*

Fig. 102 *Khirokitia. Diabase. Neolithic. Ht 14.5 cm. Dikaios 1953, Pl. XCV.*

Fig. 103 *Khirokitia. Andesite. Neolithic. Ht 15.8 cm. Dikaios 1953, Pl. XCV.*

Fig. 104 *No provenance (Cyprus Museum). Picrolite. Chalcolithic. Ht. 3.2 cm. Spiteris 1970, p. 23.*

Fig. 105 *No provenance. (Cyprus Museum). Picrolite. Chalcolithic. Ht. 3.5 cm. Spiteris 1970, p. 23.*

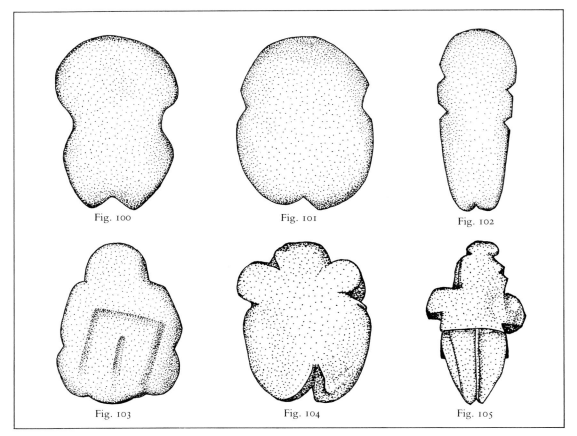

Fig. 100   Fig. 101   Fig. 102

Fig. 103   Fig. 104   Fig. 105

The first (Fig. 100) is a flat piece of diabase ground to a slight polish, with two indentations to make a 'waist' and one below to separate two leg-stumps. The upper half of the figure does service as a combined head and chest, as in the cephalopod shape universally favoured by small children (see Morris, 1962). There are no features or details of any kind. The second example is similar, except that it is made of andesite and is more circular in shape (Fig. 101). The third is more slender and has an additional pair of indentations providing the figure with a neck (Fig. 102). The fourth also has a distinct separation between the head and the body (Fig. 103). This one has a special additional feature, however, namely grooved lines representing outlandishly enlarged female genitals. The curved outline at the base of this figure, between the leg-stumps, suggests a heavily swollen belly.

The two Chalcolithic examples (Figs. 104-5), made out of picrolite (sometimes called steatite), have similar rounded outlines, but the 'arm-stumps' are slightly more protrusive. They are much later, but display the same 'swollen body' tradition.

The schematization of the figures in this group stresses the abdomen of the human form. Face, arms, legs, hands, feet, hair and breasts are all reduced or eliminated totally. The result is a visual symbol of pregnancy, emphasized in one case by an indication of distended female genitals. This strongly suggests that they were made and carried as fertility charms by women wishing to become mothers.

b Stump Figures with phallic heads

There are five obvious candidates for this sub-category. The first (Fig. 106) is made of andesite and comes from Khirokitia. It is armless, with leg-stumps and a broad, swollen trunk. There is a clearly marked head and neck, with slight cavities representing the eyes and mouth. In shape, however, the head is strongly reminiscent of the glans penis, giving the figure a double symbolism and emphasizing both the reproductive female (swollen body) and the reproductive male (phallic head and neck). A more blatant example (Fig. 107) comes from the Neolithic settlement at Sotira. This one dispenses altogether with facial features and shoulders and simply places a phallus on top of a pair of leg-stumps. The leg-stumps themselves are rounded off in such a way that they acquire a double symbolic role, both as broad female thighs and as testicles for the 'penis-head'. The extreme schematization here creates an image of intense sexuality. Very similar, but less intense, is the much smaller figure from the Neolithic settlement of Ayios Epiktitos Vrysi (Fig. 108).

A recent, accidental discovery in a field near Sotira (Fig. 109) provides another variation on the intense reproductive theme. This remarkable and unique figure, probably also Neolithic, shows an erect phallus sprouting directly from a pair of seated female legs. The whole of the female's trunk, neck and head has been transformed into the stiffly erect penis, giving this figurine, once again, a powerful double image.

the breasts. At first sight this gives the bizarre impression that the artist, unsatisfied with a double gender for the figure, had given it in addition two sets of female genitals. At second sight it becomes clear that the upper incisions are meant to represent a pair of pointed drooping breasts with their tips touching. This displays a visual inventiveness of which many modern artists would be proud. Between the two Vs the stomach is clearly shown to be swollen, and this, coupled with the enormously wide hips, serves to emphasize the fecundity of this female image.

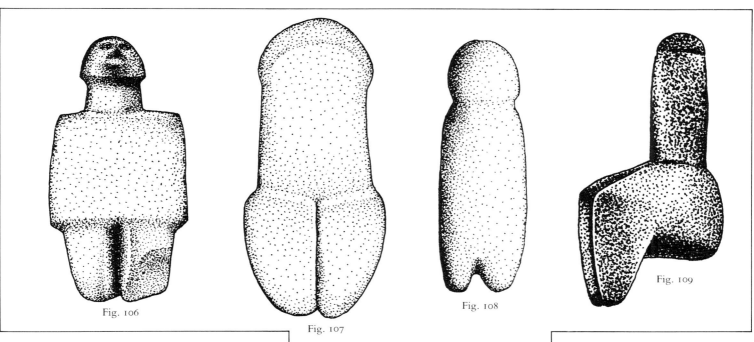

Fig. 106

Fig. 107

Fig. 108

Fig. 109

Even more remarkable is the famous 'Lemba Lady' (Fig. 110) discovered by Peltenburg in 1976. This, at 36 cm the largest of the early figurines, presents another extraordinary double image, having a voluptuous female body surmounted by a powerfully phallic neck and head. It was found, not in a tomb, but in the debris of a destroyed building. It is too large to have been carried on the body and was undoubtedly a fertility figure associated with a particular dwelling or family. Made of limestone, it has a greater affinity with the earlier, Neolithic pieces, rather than the typical picrolite objects of the Chalcolithic, but in date it belongs to the later epoch, having been fixed by Peltenburg at around 3000 BC. In terms of stylization it boasts one of the boldest and most original of design echoes ever displayed by a nude figurine, namely two split-V motifs, one above the other, standing for the female genitals and

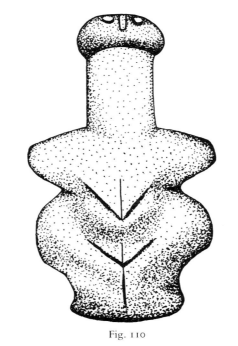

Fig. 110

1b Stump Figures with phallic heads

Fig. 106 *Khirokitia. Andesite. Neolithic. Ht. 19 cm. Dikaios 1953, Pl. XCV.*

Fig. 107 *Sotira. Limestone. Neolithic. Ht. 16.5 cm. Dikaios 1961, Pl. 91;106.*

Fig. 108 *Ayios Epiktitos Vrysi. Neolithic. Ht. 7.2 cm. Peltenburg 1975, Pl. VI.*

Fig. 109 *Sotira Arkolies. Limestone. Neolithic. Ht. 16.1 cm. Swiny and Swiny 1983, Pl. VI, 1-4.*

Fig. 110 *Lemba. Limestone. Chalcolithic. Ht. 36 cm. Peltenburg 1979, Pl. XI, 1.*

1c Stump Figures with folded arms

Fig. 111 *Paphos district. Picrolite. Chalcolithic. Ht. 4 cm. Crouwel 1978, no. 12.*
Fig. 112 *Paphos district. Picrolite. Chalcolithic. Ht. 6 cm. Karageorghis 1969, Pl. 33c.*
Fig. 113 *Paphos district. Picrolite. Chalcolithic. Ht. 5.6 cm. Karageorghis 1969, Pl. 33a.*
Fig. 114 *Lemba Lakkous. Limestone. Chalcolithic. Ht. 17.3 cm. Peltenburg 1980, p. 58.*

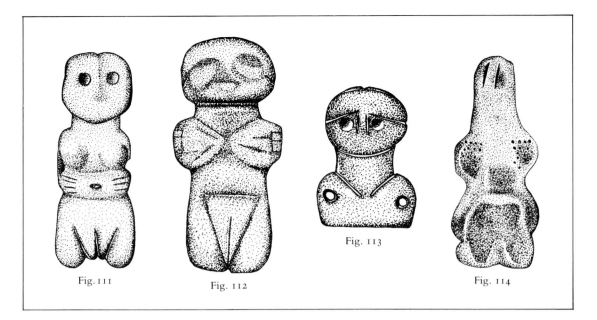

Fig. 111   Fig. 112   Fig. 113   Fig. 114

c Stump Figures with folded arms

This group of four figures is entirely Chalcolithic. The arms and legs are reduced to stumps, but there are sculptural suggestions that the artists intended the arms to be folded back against the body. In the first, a small picrolite figurine from the Paphos district (Fig. 111), incisions on either side of the swollen belly suggest fingers clasping that region of the body, as if to draw attention to its pregnant condition. Beneath the belly, between the well separated leg-stumps, is a conspicuous rendering of outsized female genitals. The face boasts big eye-sockets and a sculptured nose; at the back of the head, hair is shown by incision markings. The second example (Fig. 112) is similar in design, but the breasts are hidden by the folded hands and the pubic triangle is even larger. In the third example (Fig. 113) the lower part of the body is missing altogether and there are no incisions indicating the position of the hands, but Vagnetti (1974) is sufficiently confident of this figure's affinity with the previous two to classify it as 'type with hands holding breasts'. She feels that the two holes drilled through its chest are meant to indicate arms wrapping around and back on to the body.

Unlike these three, which are in picrolite, the fourth (Fig. 114) is in limestone and was found at Lemba by Peltenburg. Its arms, which are stumplike, appear to be folded down to the sides of its powerfully swollen belly. The figure is shown in a seated posture. There are two crude, vertical slits for eyes and some curious incised dots on each shoulder apparently depicting some sort of shawl or cape. If they do indeed represent an article of clothing, it must be of very special significance, since it is the only one visible on this or any other Stump Figure. (This question of a special shawl will arise again in other figurine categories.)

d Stump Figures with protruding arms

Arm stumps that protrude from the side of the body are rare among Neolithic figures, but two Stone Age examples do exist where this feature is present. The first (Fig. 115) is a sizeable but rather crude, legless figure from Petra tou Limniti. Arm-buds on this example appear to have been worn down somewhat, but even with greater protrusion they would still probably be greatly abbreviated as upper limbs. The second example (Fig. 116) has more distinct stumps, with a strongly tapering contour. Its facial features are extremely odd, with mournful, 'drooping' eyes and eyebrows. This Neolithic andesite figure is from Ayia Mavri in the Paphos district.

The other examples in this sub-category are all from the Chalcolithic period and made from picrolite. Three of them (Figs. 117-19) are from Maroni, Souskiou-Vathyrkakas, and Klavdhia respectively, and have short, squat bodies with stump arms and legs. Figs. 117 and 118 display facial features, but Fig. 119 has instead a pierced head and was clearly worn as a suspended object on the body of its owner.

Finally, Figs. 120 and 121 are two Stump Figures that provide a valuable link between this and the next category (Cruciform Figures). They are both made of picrolite and have short, flange-shaped arm-buds, but their general body shape is longer, more slender and more elegant than the typical Stump Figure. Except for their abbreviated arms they are very much like the classical Cruciform Figures for which the Cypriot Copper Age is famous. The first (Fig. 120) was found by Peltenburg at Kissonerga Mylouthkia, near to Lemba, and he dates it at roughly 3500 BC (see Peltenburg, 1980, 1982). He believes that it is intermediate between the earlier Neolithic figures and the later Chalcolithic cruciform ones. This is an important point because it means that, if Cypriot precursors for the Cruciform figures exist, they cannot be viewed as a sudden arrival or importation.

Looking for additional support, Peltenburg (1982) discovered a small figurine (Fig. 121) in the Birmingham Museum which is a further link in the chain, being intermediate between Fig. 120 and the typical Cruciform Figures. It has a longer neck than Fig. 120 and a head shape that places it even closer to its long-armed successors. The problem for Peltenburg, however, was that the figurine arrived at the Birmingham Museum from the Wellcome Collection which, as he says, 'is largely of Egyptian origin'. Despite this he was convinced that the figure was from Cyprus and provided a vital link in the development of the cross-shaped figures. He was correct. It has since been possible to trace the object to a photograph published by Cesnola in 1881. In the fifth plate of his volume called *Cyprus Antiquities* it is clearly visible, although very small, and has a label beside it with the number 22 (in mirror image). Since the entire Cesnola collection originated in Cyprus, there is now no doubt that this important figurine comes from the island and heralds the next, remarkable category—the Cruciform Figures.

1d Stump Figures with protruding arms

Fig. 115 *Petra tou Limniti. Neolithic. Ht. 18-25 cm. Dikaios 1962, Fig. XIV, 1.*

Fig. 116 *Ayia Mavri. Andesite. Neolithic. Ht. 16 cm. Buchholz and Karageorghis 1973, no. 1689.*

Fig. 117 *Maroni. Picrolite. Chalcolithic. Ht. 3.8 cm. Cook 1979, p. 5, b.*

Fig. 118 *Souskiou-Vathyrkakas. Picrolite. Chalcolithic. Ht. 7.7 cm. Vagnetti 1980, Pl. I, 1.*

Fig. 119 *Klavdhia. Picrolite. Chalcolithic. Ht. 2.9 cm. Cook 1979, p. 5, a.*

Fig. 120 *Kissonerga Myloutha. Picrolite. Chalcolithic. Ht. 5.8 cm. Peltenburg 1982, Pl. I, 1.*

Fig. 121 *No provenance (Birmingham Museum). Picrolite. Chalcolithic. Ht. 6.4 cm. Peltenburg 1982, Pl. I, 3.*

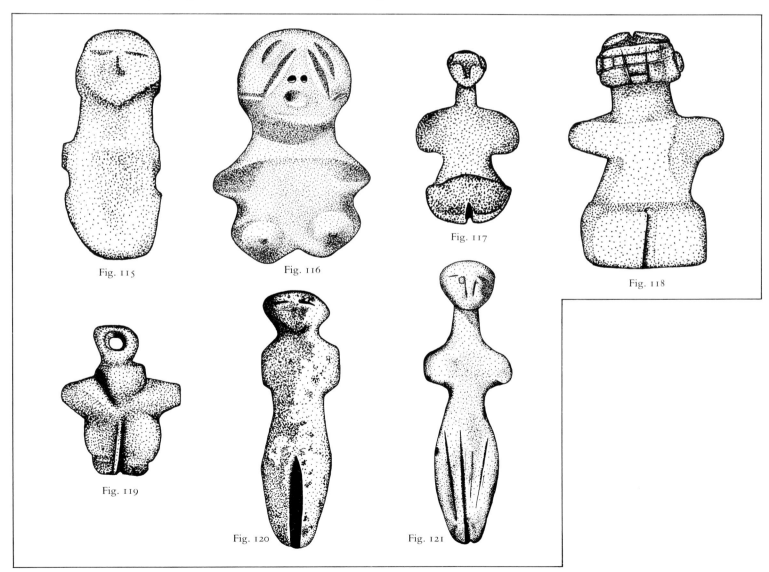

Fig. 115

Fig. 116

Fig. 117

Fig. 118

Fig. 119

Fig. 120

Fig. 121

Fig. 122 *Birth scene from ancient Egypt (Ptolemaic period) showing mother in squatting posture with outstretched arms. From a bas-relief at the temple of Hermonthis. (After Ploss and Bartels.) A stylized version of this posture is shown on the Cruciform Figures of Chalcolithic Cyprus.*

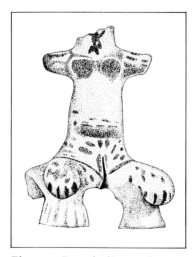

Fig. 123 *Recently discovered Cypriot figurine of a pregnant female about to give birth. She is seated on a birth-stool with her legs wide apart. Around her neck she wears a crude image of herself. Kissonerga Mosphilia. Red-on-White Ware. Chalcolithic. Peltenburg 1984, Pl. XX.*

2 Cruciform Figures

I am defining a Cruciform Figure as a small, picrolite, Chalcolithic human form in the shape of a vertical cross. In a typical example, the body is tall and slender, with a long neck surmounted by a head that tilts slightly backwards. The legs and feet are clearly shown and are tightly bent in a sitting or squatting position. The figures are either sexless or with small breasts in relief. The arms are the most characteristic feature of this category of figure. They are stretched out sideways stiffly and are full-length, usually with formally squared-off ends showing no differentiation of wrists, hands or fingers. There is nothing like them in any other prehistoric culture, the nearest approach being the Christian crucifixes that became popular several millennia later. Their symbolic significance, however, is totally different, and not immediately apparent. Once again it has to do with fertility.

Whereas the Stump Figures stood for pregnancy, the Cruciform Figures stand for the act of parturition. Many of them were pierced to be worn as pendants. Some were found as miniatures on necklaces. The unpierced ones were small enough to be carried on the body, tucked into clothing. It is my contention that they were worn exclusively to encourage, by sympathetic magic, a new birth. To achieve this they had to possess some kind of symbolic features that represented the act of parturition. The way they do this is not obvious today because, in modern times, our culture has been conditioned by the medical profession into thinking that the correct position for giving birth is lying down. This posture creates an appropriately ritualistic doctor-patient relationship and turns an expectant mother into a conventional hospital inmate, but it also puts an appalling strain on her body, for she must push her baby out *horizontally* with no assistance from gravity. Few 'primitive' societies would behave so stupidly. As we know from artefacts as far apart as ancient Mexico and ancient Egypt, the normal delivery posture for the human female was sitting or squatting, usually with other females supporting her arms. The Egyptian hieroglyphic for birth shows just such a squatting posture, and an early drawing by Witkowski (in Ploss and Bartels, 1935, Vol. II, p. 751) depicts a formal presentation of a birth scene from the Ptolemaic period, with the mother in a bent-legs, arms-raised-wide-and-supported posture (see Fig. 122). A recently discovered Cypriot figurine (Fig. 123) presents a similar posture, with a pregnant female sitting, legs apart, on what appears to be a birth-stool. Such stools, or 'parturition chairs', were popular in the ancient world and survived in many countries until quite recent times.

Clearing one's mind of modern medical techniques and concentrating instead on these more ancient methods of aiding birth, the posture of the Cruciform Figures at last makes sense. They show (1) the tightly bent legs of the correct human birth posture; (2) the arms flung wide for support; (3) the head tilted back as the mother strains to deliver the child. To wear a small figurine displaying such a posture must surely have meant only one thing—the desire on the part of the wearer to give birth herself.

Viewing them in this light, the true function of the famous Cruciform Figures of Cyprus becomes clear. Their repeated labelling as 'Mother Goddess' figures—small, portable versions of some giant effigy worshipped by the Copper Age Cypriots—is, I believe, a piece of romantic speculation, and a serious Retrospective Error.

Having said this, it is only correct to consider what possible alternative explanations could be put forward. Seeking support for the Mother Goddess explanation, it could be argued that the sitting posture of the legs is meant to reflect the dominant, seated position of a powerful personage. Further, the widespread arms can be interpreted as a welcoming, embrace-invitation signal given symbolically by a queen or a goddess to her followers. The upturned face could be seen as a lofty gaze of the omnipotent one. Furthermore, in defence of the goddess, it could be pointed out that not one of the many Cruciform Figures found so far (and there must be about a hundred of them by now) shows the slightest sign of pregnancy. Their trunks are slim and elegant. No swollen bellies are to be found.

Until further evidence is forthcoming (perhaps more ancient wall paintings like the fragment found at Tenta recently), there is no way of reaching an indisputable conclusion. The choice between 'Birth Charm' and 'Mother Goddess' remains a matter of personal taste. The apparent objection to the parturition explanation, in the shape of the slender, un-pregnant figures is less worrying than it might at first appear. In the Egyptian drawing (Fig. 122) the female giving birth is not swollen with child because, as is clearly visible, the baby has just been successfully delivered. If the Cypriot figures also stand for birth, then they too presumably depict the moment *after* a successful birth, when the mother has just experienced that sudden, magical return to a slender outline.

Another small anti-goddess quibble: If the goddess is gazing upwards with her back-tilted head, what is she gazing up *at*? A goddess, surely, would symbolically gaze down, not up.

Merrillees (1980), summarizing his findings concerning Cypriot Bronze Age human representations, comments: 'Though Cypriote prehistory is not without its converts to the Mother Goddess faith, none of the figures, static or operative, has any attributes of an extraordinary supernatural quality.' The same may be said of these earlier Chalcolithic representations.

Having made these general points, it now remains to examine the various sub-groupings of the Cruciform Figure category. They are as follows:

a Plain body with bent legs and no face.

b Plain body with bent legs and facial features.

c Plain body reduced to flat shape with no features.

d Plain body with wide pelvis, no legs and no face.

e Body adorned with necklace with cruciform pendant.

f Body with hands, one up and one down.

g Body with segmented arms and chest.

h Body with segmented arms.

i Body with diagonal segmented bands on arms.

j Body with one hand segmented.

k Body with arms transformed into horizontal figure.

l Double body, one on top of the other.

m Triple body, joined at the feet.

Fifty of these figures are illustrated here, being roughly half the total known at present. All the major types are shown, those figures omitted being for the most part repetitions of types a, b and c.

a Plain body with bent legs and no face
This can be considered as the basic form of the Cruciform Figure. It differs little from the Stump Figures in Figs. 120 and 121, except for the lengthening of the arms, the tightening of the bend in the legs, and the

2a Plain body with bent legs and no face

Fig. 124-31 *Picrolite. Chalcolithic.*
Fig. 124 *No provenance (Pierides Collection). Ht. 9 cm. Karageorghis 1973, no. 1.*
Fig. 125 *No provenance (Pierides Collection). Ht. 7.5 cm. Karageorghis 1973, no. 2.*
Fig. 126 *Salamiou. Ht. 4 cm. Vagnetti 1975, Pl. I,3.*
Fig. 127 *Kathikas. Ht. 4.4 cm. Vagnetti 1975, Pl. I,4.*
Fig. 128 *No provenance. Ht. 4.8 cm. Thimme 1977, no. 577.*
Fig. 129 *Souskiou-Vathyrkakas. Ht. 4.4 cm. Vagnetti 1980, Pl. VII,21.*
Fig. 130 *Kythrea. Ht. 6.4 cm. Vagnetti 1974, Pl. V,4.*
Fig. 131 *Souskiou-Vathyrkakas. Ht. 4.9 cm. Vagnetti 1974, Pl. V, 4.*

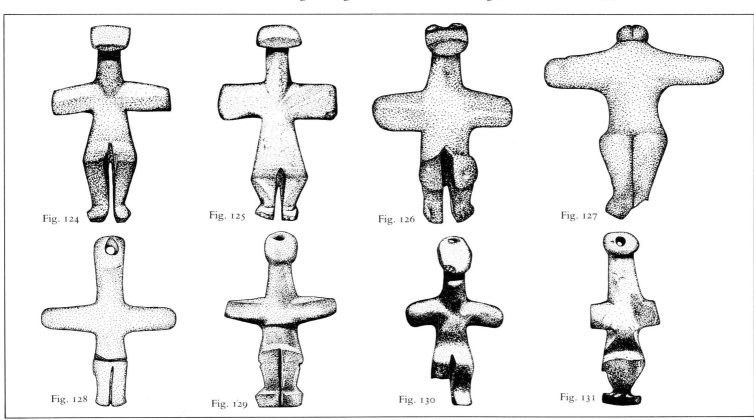

Fig. 124   Fig. 125   Fig. 126   Fig. 127

Fig. 128   Fig. 129   Fig. 130   Fig. 131

2b Plain body with bent legs and facial features

Figs. 132-5 *Picrolite. Chalcolithic.*
Fig. 132 *No provenance (de Menil Collection, Houston). Ht. 8.4 cm. Thimme 1977, no. 572.*
Fig. 133 *Souskiou-Vathyrkakas. Ht. 8.3 cm. Vagnetti 1980, Pl. IV, 13.*
Fig. 134 *Lemba Lakkous. Ht. 5.8 cm. Peltenburg 1979, Pl. XI, 2.*
Fig. 135 *No provenance (Cyprus Museum). Ht. 8.8 cm. Vagnetti 1975, Pl. I, 1.*

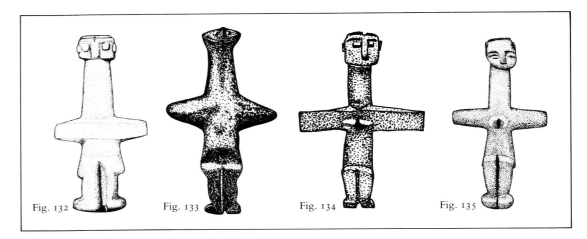

Fig. 132   Fig. 133   Fig. 134   Fig. 135

differentiation of the feet.

Eight examples are shown here, four with their heads pierced for suspension and four with unpierced heads. Like all Cruciform Figures, they are made of picrolite, and come from the west of the island. They are all small, varying in size from 4 cm to 9 cm. In colour, they vary from green to grey to brown.

Their smoothed surfaces, shunning all anatomical details, are strongly reminiscent of the austerely restrained depictions of the human form so well known from the Cycladic region. In both cases facial details are eliminated, but the arm positions are completely different (folded in the Cycladic figurines). It is true that the Cypriot and Cycladic figures date from roughly the same period of the Chalcolithic, but there is no evidence that one group influenced the other, and the similarities may well be superficial.

Where the provenance is known, all but one of this category come from within twenty miles of Paphos. The source of the attractive stone for making these figurines was in the foothills of the Troodos Mountains, which means that the exception, Fig. 130, said to have come from Kythrea, must have been carried a long way from its original home.

The one oddity of shape in this group concerns the head of Fig. 127, which is a mere stump. Vagnetti (1975) has suggested that 'the head was probably broken and reworked into its present shape; the incised line at the base of the neck could have been intended for suspension.' This suggests that the original head was perhaps pierced rather than solid and that its original suspension hole was broken through, demanding a new type of suspension attachment. It also hints at the prolonged use of the figurine by its owner,

involving wear and damage.

b Plain body with bent legs and facial features

Similar to the last group except for the addition of a face. Fig. 132 shows a typical 'cruciform facial design'. Incisions in the soft stone are worked away until the features show as low relief. The nose is rectangular and the eyes are square to rounded. Ears, hair and large eyebrows are also indicated. All these features are formalized in a cubist manner— that is to say, the subtle biological shapes are reduced to simple geometric units, and the head itself is squared off. This type of face re-appears frequently on other Cruciform Figures, with only minor variation, and seems to be a strong local tradition, if not the work of a single artist.

The second of the four examples of this category shown here, Fig. 133, represents a different type. The facial features are not squared off in the typical cubist style; incised nostrils are shown; the upturned face is tri-angular in shape; the outstretched arms are pointed instead of having the usual blunt ends; and the calf muscles of the legs are bulging. These details set it slightly apart from the typical cruciform images. Only one other example has similarly tapering arms (Fig. 160), and the calf muscle detail is not found elsewhere. The head is so atypical that Vagnetti (1974) is driven to the conclusion that 'the small triangular face seems to wear a mask'. This hardly seems justified but it underlines the oddity of this particular figure.

The other two examples in this category (Figs. 134-5) both display breasts, a feature seen in only ten of the fifty figures illustrated here. They are not rendered with any degree of realism and appear almost apologetically on the slender bodies.

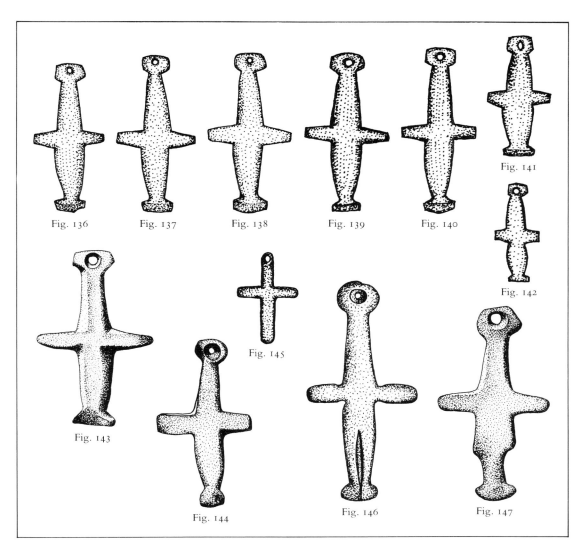

Fig. 136
Fig. 137
Fig. 138
Fig. 139
Fig. 140
Fig. 141
Fig. 142
Fig. 143
Fig. 145
Fig. 144
Fig. 146
Fig. 147

2c Plain body reduced to flat shape with no features

Figs. 136-47 *Picrolite. Chalcolithic.*

Figs. 136-42 *All from Paphos district. Ht. 1.8 to 3.8 cm. Crouwel 1978, Pl. IV, 1-8.*

Fig. 143 *Souskiou-Vathyrkakas. Ht. 2.5 cm. Vagnetti 1980, Pl. IX, 34.*

Fig. 144 *Souskiou-Vathyrkakas. Ht. 3.4 cm. Vagnetti 1980, Pl. IX, 29.*

Fig. 145 *No provenance. Ht. 2.7 cm. Christie's catalogue, 27 April 1976, lot 80.*

Fig. 146 *No provenance. Ht. 8.1 cm. Christie's catalogue, 27 April 1976, lot 83.*

Fig. 147 *Souskiou-Vathyrkakas. Ht. 2.8 cm. Vagnetti 1980, Pl. IX, 28.*

c Plain body reduced to flat shape with no features

Although this is the most common type of Cruciform Figure, with roughly fifty examples known at present, it should not be thought of as the 'basic type', but rather as a crudely simplified version of the cruciform style. It is clear from the Stump Figure precursors that the typical Cruciform Figure did not grow from a tiny, simple cross, but from a more complex, humanoid shape by a process of arm extension. These starkly reduced, flat images must therefore be looked upon as degenerate Cruciform Figures rather than primal ones.

All the many examples of this category are faceless and lack any details. Almost all are pierced for suspension and there is strong evidence, in the shape of two reconstructed necklaces from Souskiou (Tomb 3, nos. 6 and 7) (see Karageorghis 1976, nos. 28 and 30), that this particular type was intended to be worn in groups. In other words, what they lacked in quality they made up for in quantity. Perhaps if they were, as I am suggesting, fertility figurines, they were made up into a necklace as a request for a large family.

The typical figurine in this category has its neck, body and legs simplified to a flattened 'cigar' shape, with the legs completely fused in the majority of cases. Large feet remain a dominant feature in almost every case. In a few examples such as Pl. 173 and Fig. 145, the reduction of detail is so extreme that both head and feet are eliminated, resulting in what amounts to a crude geometric cross. To Christian eyes, these small pendants are immediately reminiscent of a crucifix, and it is strange to think of ancient Cypriots wearing such adornments several millennia before the birth of Christ.

Of the twelve examples shown, the first seven all come from the Allard Pierson Museum in Amsterdam (Figs. 136-42). They have no provenance and the same is true of the others, except for Figs. 143, 144 and 147, which come from Souskiou-Vathyrkakas.

Pl. 173 Highly formalized Cruciform Figure in the shape of a simple cross. *A suspension hole is drilled through the top section of this figure, which was clearly meant to be worn round the neck. Used as an adornment in this way it must have looked remarkably like a modern crucifix—several millennia before the birth of Christ. Pale green picrolite. Chalcolithic period. Ht. 4 cm. (DM-ST-07).*

2d Plain body with wide pelvis, no legs and no face

Fig. 148 *No provenance (Cyprus Museum). Picrolite. Chalcolithic. Ht. 6.6 cm. Vagnetti 1979, Pl. XII, 1.*

Fig. 149 *No provenance (Cyprus Museum). Picrolite. Chalcolithic. Ht. 6.4 cm. Vagnetti 1979, Pl. XII, 2.*

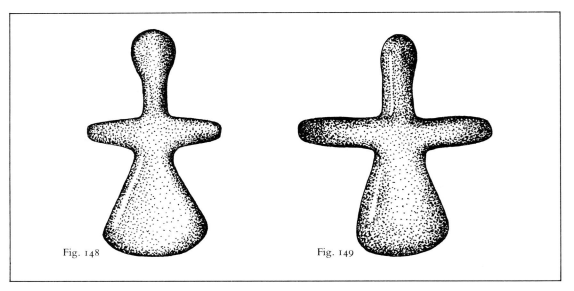

Fig. 148   Fig. 149

2e Body adorned with necklace with cruciform pendant

Fig. 150. *Yiala. Picrolite. Chalcolithic. Ht. 15.6 cm. Karageorghis 1962, Pl. III, 2.*

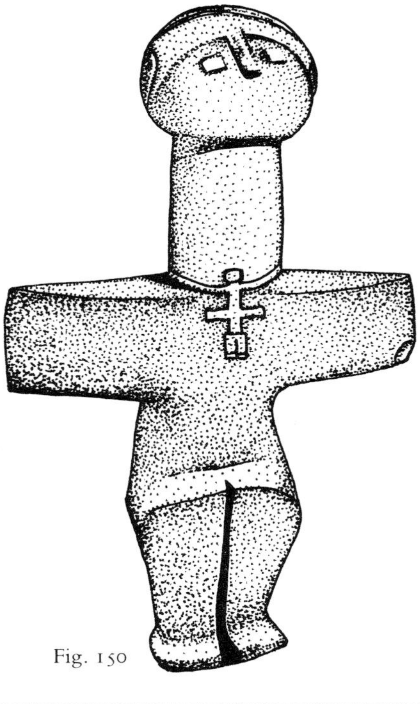

d Plain body with wide pelvis, no legs and no face

Only two examples of this type are known. They first appeared in a Christie's catalogue (27 April 1976, lots 81 and 82) and were acquired by the Cyprus Museum. Vagnetti (1979) accepts them as undoubtedly Cypriot 'on the basis of the raw material', but points out that they have a strong resemblance to certain marble figurines from Anatolia. The obvious conclusion is that they 'form an important link between Cyprus and Anatolia, as they confirm the existence of early cultural connections'. What is not clear, however, is which way the influence travelled. The long tradition of Cypriot figurines seems so well established that it seems more probable that Cyprus exported the idea of outstretched-arms figurines to Anatolia. In general, Anatolian figurines are much more closely related to Cycladic forms than to Cypriot ones, and seem to have little influence on Cypriot styles in other respects. But these two figures (Figs. 148-9) do create a problem because their lower body shape is so unlike anything else from the Cypriot Chalcolithic. For the moment it is impossible to decide whether this shape was imported or exported.

e Body adorned with necklace with cruciform pendant

The single example of this type (Fig. 150) is the most accomplished and impressive of all the prehistoric stone carvings from Cyprus. It is similar to the ordinary b. type except for the fact that it is twice the average size and carries around its neck a band from which hangs a pendant of the typical a. type of figurine. This band and its pendant are shown in careful relief so precise that the bent-leg posture is clearly indicated. Of particular interest is the fact that the pendant is not of the pierced head type. It is attached to the necklace band *below* its head, strongly suggesting that all cruciform figurines were worn around the neck, whether pierced or unpierced. (Type d. is a possible exception here, having narrow heads.)

The large size of this example suggests that (like the Lemba Lady, Fig. 110) it was a dwelling-based charm rather than a personal body-charm. Even so, it cannot be seriously considered as a deity figure, since no self-respecting goddess would need the protection of her own image hanging from her neck. If,

Fig. 150

on the other hand, the fertility charm interpretation is accepted, this splendid figure is a
representation of a woman giving birth while
wearing a protective charm around her neck
—a sculptural proof of the efficacy of such
pendants, for those who believed in them.

f Body with hands, one up and one down

The two examples of this curious arm posture (Figs. 151-2) known so far defy any certain interpretation. They both come from
Souskiou-Vathyrkakas, and Vagnetti (1980)
refers to the arms in the following words:
'flat arms ending with hands set one up and
the other down in swastika postion'. This is
purely descriptive and provides no explanation for this strange hand position. If, as I
have suggested earlier, the arms of these
figures are flung wide seeking support during
the act of giving birth, then this category
may represent asymmetrical support, with
one hand pressing down on something and
the other holding onto something. But if this
is so, it is a curious feature to have included
in such a stylized figurine. Another speculative suggestion comes from miming the posture. If this is done, with the knuckles of both
hands frontally positioned, one hand pointing
up and one down, you find yourself acting
out the posture of someone holding an imag-
inary baby. Could it be that these figures
were miming the desire of the wearer, namely to hold a real baby in the arms?

g Body with segmented arms and chest

Another enigmatic motif is the covering of
the whole horizontal element (='arms and

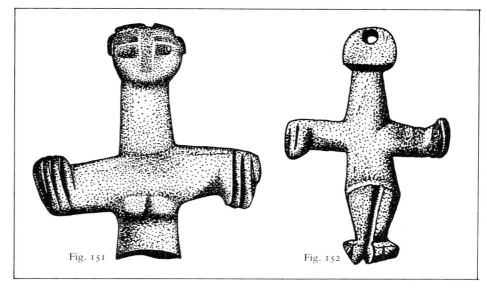

Fig. 151   Fig. 152

chest') with a double row of segmentations.
This lattice pattern of deep incisions is not
uncommon and six examples are shown here
(Figs. 153-8). In one case (Fig. 157) the lattic-
ing also covers the face and the feet, where it
appears to be an abstracted version of the
facial features and the toes. Because of this
degree of abstraction, Vagnetti (1980) concludes that the pattern on the arms 'probably
indicates the fingers'. This is possible but
unlikely, since the abstract 'fingers' run right
across the chest region as well. An alternative
speculation is that the net-like pattern that
has settled on these figures is meant to depict some kind of body veil or shawl—a garment of some kind that was associated with
birth or some other significant social event.
Neither explanation is particularly convincing. A third suggestion, that the segments are
feathers and the arms are wings, charming
though it is, seems even more unlikely.

2f Body with hands, one up and one down

Fig. 151 *Souskiou-Vathyrkakas.
Picrolite. Chalcolithic. Ht. 4.7 cm.
(but the lower part is missing).
Vagnetti 1980, Pl. II, 5.*
Fig. 152 *Souskiou-Vathyrkakas.
Picrolite. Chalcolithic. Ht. 3.4 cm.
Vagnetti 1980, Pl. VI, 20.*

2g Body with seg- mented arms and chest

Fig. 153 *Souskiou-Vathyrkakas.
Ht. 3.6 cm. Vagnetti 1980, Pl. VI, 16.*
Fig. 154 *Souskiou-Vathyrkakas.
Ht. 3.4 cm. Vagnetti 1980, Pl. VI,
18. (The height of this figurine is
incorrectly given as 0.4 cm in
Vagnetti 1980.)*
Fig. 155 *Souskiou-Vathyrkakas.
Ht. 3.4 cm. Vagnetti 1980, Pl. V, 17.*
Fig. 156 *No provenance (Cyprus
Museum). Ht. 3.5 cm. Spiteris
1970, p. 23.*

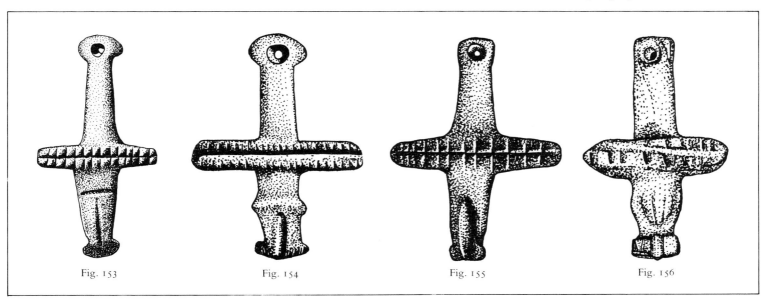

Fig. 153   Fig. 154   Fig. 155   Fig. 156

2g Body with seg-mented arms and chest

Fig. 157 *Souskiou-Vathyrkakas. Picrolite. Chalcolithic. Ht. 4 cm. Vagnetti 1980, Pl. III, 6.*

Fig. 158 *Paphos district. Picrolite. Chalcolithic. Ht. 4.8 cm. Crouwel 1978, Pl. V, 1.*

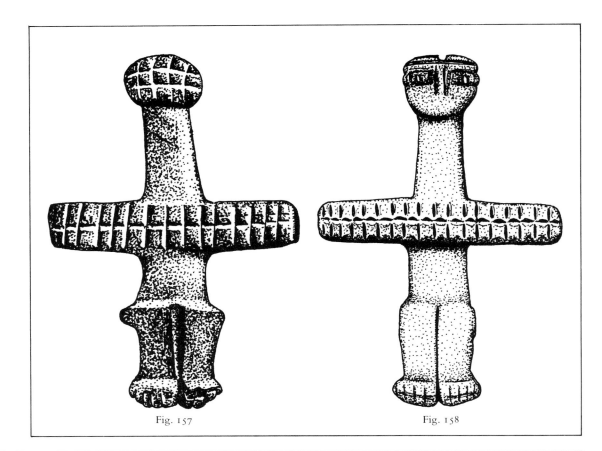

Fig. 157   Fig. 158

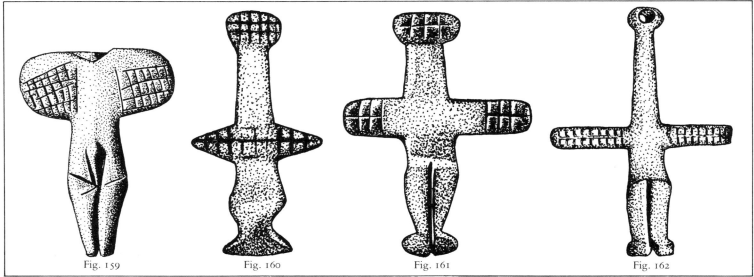

Fig. 159   Fig. 160   Fig. 161   Fig. 162

2h Body with seg-mented arms

Figs. 159–62 *Picrolite. Chalcolithic.*

Fig. 159 *Kissonerga Mythlouthkia. Peltenburg 1980, p. 58.*

Fig. 160 *Souskiou-Vathyrkakas. Ht. 3.9 cm. Vagnetti 1980, Pl. III, 8.*

Fig. 161 *Souskiou-Vathyrkakas. Ht. 4.7 cm. Vagnetti 1980, Pl. III, 7.*

Fig. 162 *Souskiou-Vathyrkakas. Ht. 8.3 cm. Vagnetti 1980, Pl. V, 14.*

h Body with segmented arms

Four examples of this type are shown here (Figs. 159-62). They are similar to the last, except that the lattice pattern stops short of the chest region, giving the impression of fi-gures with 'quilted arms'. The first, Fig. 159, is an unusually early one, discovered recently at Kissonerga Mylouthkia by Peltenburg (1980). He dates it at 3500 BC, and it may well be a precursor of the later, more typical lattice-arm types. Its legs are only slightly bent and the feet and head are missing. The arms are massively flattened out and, in this case, do look remarkably like wings, reviv-ing momentarily the old idea that these figu-rines represent some kind of flying, super-natural being. A less romantic interpretation would see these flattened, net-covered arms as shawled or clothed in some sort of special cape or cloak. Peltenburg identifies this fig-ure as male, suggesting that the pelvic lump is a broken penis, but figurines with this type of genital detail, from other cultures, are of-ten clearly female in gender, the apparent penis shape being a sculptural rendering of the female labia (see Thimme, 1977, no. 246).

i Body with diagonal segmented bands on arms

The two existing examples of this intriguing category strengthen the view that the 'quilting', lattice, or net-like patterns of g. and h. are in fact some kind of reticulated or openwork adornment, as though the artists are stating, 'these figures wore something special'. Of the two figures shown here, the first, Fig. 163, is fairly typical of the cruciform style and appears to be by the same artist as Fig. 132. Its only unusual feature is the pair of diagonal sashes draped over its arms.

The second, Fig. 164, is quite exceptional. It is in a Swiss private collection and was not published until 1977 (see Thimme, no. 573). It appears to be the only Cruciform Figure not made of picrolite, having been carved from a large piece of limestone. At 39.5 cm in height it not only dwarfs all other Cruciform Figures, but is even larger than the stump-armed 'Lemba Lady' discovered by Peltenburg. It is described as having 'a monumental presence' and was clearly intended as a dwelling-based figure of some importance. Typical cruciform features include the widely stretched arms, the long neck, the neatly relief-rendered hair, ears and nose, the tightly bent legs and the shape of the feet. Atypical features are the bored pupils of the eyes, the more realistic shaping of the head and face, and the triangular,

pendulous breasts with touching tips. The diagonal arm-bands are reduced in width here, looking like a double-segmented cord, or rope. It is precisely this double-segmented pattern which is enlarged to cover the whole frontal surface of the arms of the smaller, picrolite figurines. It is tempting to suggest that on this larger figure it was possible for the artist to make an accurate rendering of the 'segmented sash' and that, when smaller versions were being manufactured, the artists were unable to reduce the scale of the sash appropriately. Not wishing to omit it, they were forced to show it out of proportion, covering a larger area than would have occurred in real life.

The breasts of this female figure are strongly reminiscent of the pointed breasts of the Lemba Lady, only here they are sculptured, whereas there they were merely incised. The breast shape depicted is so idiosyncratic and unusual that it strongly suggests a close relation between these two major figures. They are certainly not the work of the same artist, but they do seem to be following some special local tradition in breast motif. In the case of Fig. 164, the artist concerned has cleverly used the angle of the diagonal sashes on the arms to continue the outside line of the breasts, a design device revealing aesthetic sophistication of a surprising degree.

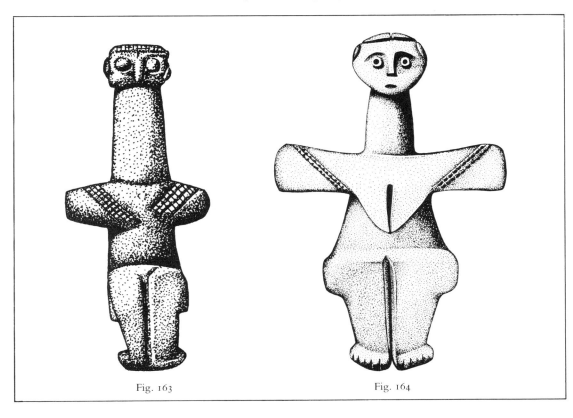

Fig. 163   Fig. 164

2i Body with diagonal segmented bands on arms

Fig. 163 *No provenance (Cyprus Museum). Picrolite. Chalcolithic. Ht. 13.5 cm. Karageorghis 1962, Pl. III, 1.*

Fig. 164 *No provenance (private collection, Switzerland). Limestone Chalcolithic. Ht. 39.5 cm. Thimme 1977, no. 573.*

2j Body with one hand segmented

Fig. 165 *Souskiou-Vathyrkakas. Picrolite. Chalcolithic. Ht. 7.3 cm. Vagnetti 1980, Pl. II, 4.*
Fig. 166 *Souskiou-Vathyrkakas. Picrolite. Chalcolithic. Ht. 7.3 cm. Vagnetti 1980, Pl. I, 2.*

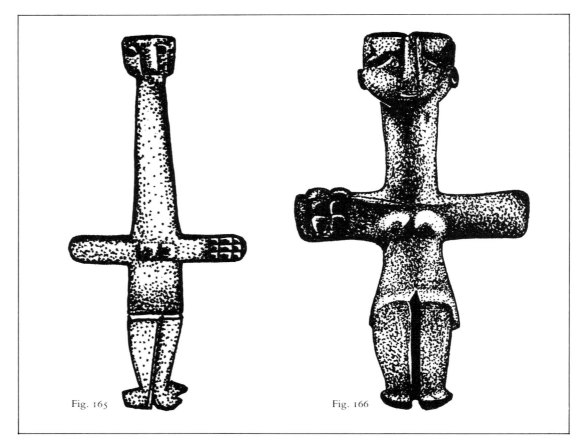

Fig. 165   Fig. 166

j Body with one hand segmented

The two known examples of this category form a link between h. and k. The first, Fig. 165, has a 'quilted' or latticed left hand, with incision marks exactly like earlier examples. Fig. 166, on the other hand (literally), has quilting so protrusive that it gives the arm the appearance of having a 'head' with cubist features. As will emerge in the next section (k.), the transformation of the arms into a horizontal body is far from being a wild speculation, and category j. may well represent a precursor of this trend. It is significant that both these figures have breasts, as do all those in the next group, suggesting that there is a link between 'arms-with-a-head' and maternity. This point will be developed below.

k Body with arms transformed into horizontal figure

Here, the widespread arms have become converted into a second bent-leg body with all the typical features and details of the usual Cruciform Figure. These strange 'double' figures are unique to Cyprus and four have so far been discovered, all of which are illustrated here. One is broken, but they are all clearly of the same type and possibly by the same artist. The 'dominant' figure, that is,

the one with a longer body and larger head and feet, is always female with a clearly depicted pair of breasts. The smaller, horizontal figure has no gender, although it always has the same hairstyle and facial features as its vertical companion. This may suggest that it is female, but more probably means that the degree of formalization employed exceeds any gender differentiation in the head region.

There are four possible explanations of these double figures. First, they may simply represent a 'trick' design where arms become bodies and bodies become arms, as the object is turned in the hand. Such devices occur throughout the whole history of art as playful examples of ambivalent imagery. Since both the 'bodies' here have bent legs, the double figurine could simply be a magical double-strength charm, with two birth figures for the price of one. Second, they may specifically represent a desire for twins, each birth figure squatting to produce its own baby. A variant of this is to see it as a charm demanding two children, but not necessarily at the same time.

Third, there is the possibility that we are dealing with figure stylization of such a rigid kind that the horizontal figure is only depicted in the typical cruciform shape because of the fixed tradition. In reality, it may repres-

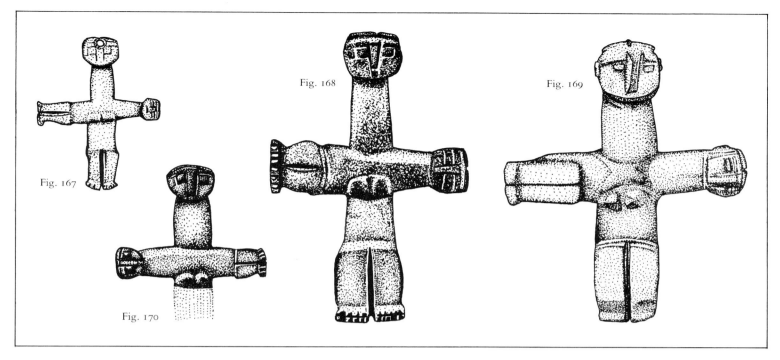

Fig. 168

Fig. 169

Fig. 167

Fig. 170

ent a quite different kind of figure, namely a baby held in the arms of its mother. This makes sense of the high frequency of breasts on the vertical elements of these figures. Of the total of fifty Cruciform Figures illustrated here, only three out of the forty-two with 'simple arms' have breasts, while seven out of eight of the 'complex arms' examples (f, j. and k.) have them clearly shown. In other words, this type of figure shows an image of maternity (baby + breasts), while the others show an image of parturition. However, although the horizontal figures are slightly smaller than the vertical ones, they are still rather massive as 'babies' and this interpretation is by no means certain.

Fourth, the two figures are seen as a 'cross' in the mating sense as well as the structural sense. Here the horizontal figure is seen as the male 'crossing' (=copulating) with the vertical female. This could be a way of adding sexual activity to the bent-leg symbol of parturition, giving it another form of 'double strength' as a magic charm. One difficulty here is that the figures are in the wrong relationship to one another. Students of ancient signs have long referred to the cross as a symbol of 'union of the sexes', but here is the way Cooper (1978) summarizes its properties: 'the vertical line is the celestial, spiritual and intellectual, positive, active and male, while the horizontal is the earthly, rational, passive and negative female, the whole cross forming the primordial androgyne'. The Cypriot figurines simply will not fit this

symbolism, since the strong, vertical figure is female and the weaker, horizontal one is (supposed to be) male.

Russell (1981) takes a slightly different view, seeing the cross as a kinship signal representing, not the mating of a particular male and female, but of the males of one tribe or community mating with the females of another group, in an outbreeding system. She writes: '... the pre-Christian cross can be a visual symbol of a symmetrical mating system, just as we speak of cross-breeding. This appears for instance, from a small cross made of steatite, found in a Copper age site in Cyprus. It is made of the body of a man laid across the body of a woman, which is slightly the thicker of the two, indicating a matrilineal system.' In other words, she explains the dominant size and posture of the female as a reflection of a female-dominated society. On this interpretation, ancient Cyprus was populated by small, passive, horizontal males and large, active, vertical females. Only in this way can the 'primordial cross symbolism' be satisfied. This is entirely possible, but it would be more convincing if the horizontal figures carried some positive, anatomical evidence of being masculine.

Each of the four explanations has something in its favour, and each has weaknesses. For the moment the only answer is to return an open verdict and await the results of further excavations of Chalcolithic sites in Cyprus.

2k Body with arms transformed into horizontal figure

Figs. 167-70 *Picrolite. Chalcolithic.*
Fig. 167 *Paphos district. Ht. 3.9 cm. Crouwel 1978, Pl. IV, 10.*
Fig. 168 *Souskiou-Vathyrkakas. Ht. 8.3 cm. Vagnetti 1980, Pl. IV, 10.*
Fig. 169 *Paphos district. Ht. 9.3 cm. Karageorghis 1969, Pl. 33.*
Fig. 170 *Souskiou-Vathyrkakas. Ht. 4.7 cm. Vagnetti 1980, Pl. IV, 11.*

2l Double body, one on top of the other

Fig. 171 *Paphos district. Picrolite. Chalcolithic. Ht. 7.5 cm. Crouwel 1978, Pl. IV, 3.*

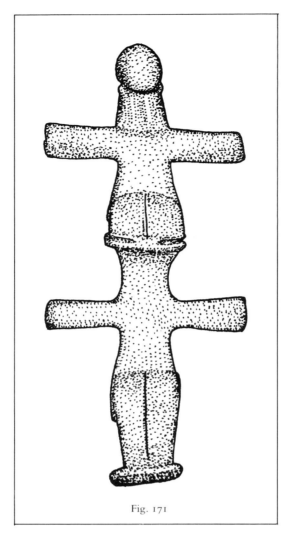

Fig. 171

2m Triple body, joined at feet

Fig. 172 *Souskiou-Vathyrkakas. Picrolite. Chalcolithic. Ht. of the two surviving elements 2.2 and 2.1 cm. Vagnetti 1980, Pl. III, 12.*

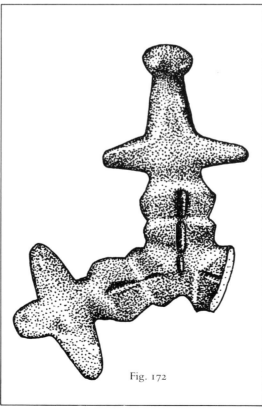

Fig. 172

l Double body, one on top of the other

This rare category, based on a single exceptional example (Fig. 171) in the Allard Pierson Museum in Amsterdam, shows one figure perched on the top of the head of another, slightly larger one. Both have the typical, sharply bent legs and the stiffly outstretched arms with blunt ends. Both have polished picrolite surfaces with no incised details.

There is a parallel to be found in a Cycladic carving which shows a similar double-figure arangement (see Thimme, 1977, no. 257) but with a much smaller figure, presumably meant to be a child, on the top of the head of a larger figure. Both have the folded arms typical of the Cycladic tradition. Crouwel (1978) does not think that this parallel is significant in terms of influence or contact. He considers it accidental: 'It shows no more than that artists in different areas independently came upon the same idea of shaping two figures—presumably belonging closely together and quite possibly mother and child—out of one piece of stone.'

A choice has to be made here between artistic playfulness and symbolic significance. Is this another case of Cypriot inventiveness or does the double figure again stand for some specific social event, desire or relationship? Most of the explanations given for the previous category also apply here, with the exception of the fourth, which requires the cross motif as an integral part of the 'crossing' concept. Again, no final answer can be given.

m Triple body, joined at the feet

This remarkable and unique object shows three Cruciform Figures (one of which is largely broken away and missing), connected to one another by the feet and spread out equidistantly at angles of 120 degrees. One figure has a distinct head and the other does not, but it is impossible to tell which is the odd-one-out without seeing the missing unit. This strange composition from Souskiou-Vathyrkakas creates a new problem of interpretation. As a kinship symbol it could represent the coming together of three tribes; sexually, it could indicate a *ménage-à-trois*—a husband with two wives, or vice versa; as an aid to fertility it could be a greedy demand for triplets or a family of three children; or it could be yet another example of Cypriot creative exuberance.

3 Lactation Figures

Two unusual Chalcolithic terracottas require a special category of their own. They can be defined as 'figures showing a female squeezing milk from her breasts'. One is almost complete, the other fragmentary. Only the complete one shows clearly what is happening, but the fragmentary one is so similar in its surviving detail that it almost certainly depicts the same act.

The complete figure, now in the Louvre, shows a woman with a distinctive hairstyle, sitting with her legs stretched out straight in front of her. On her knees is a large, shallow bowl into which she appears to be squirting milk from her breasts. Her arms are bent and each hand is pressing a breast. When the figure is viewed in profile it is clear that she is aiming her pendulous breasts at the bowl, as she squeezes them. Both breasts are covered in incision markings—horizontal lines alternating with rows of dots. Almost identical markings appear on the breasts of the fragmentary figure, suggesting that it is by the same artist, or at least from the same village. As there are no incision markings elsewhere on the bodies of these females, it is hard to see the breast patterns as part of an overall decorative device. Instead it seems more likely that they represent something specific in the way of body decoration, such as painting, scarification or tattooing.

Caubet (1974) is in no doubt about the significance of these figures. She says that they provide unequivocal confirmation of the importance accorded to the fertility cult in the early part of the Chalcolithic period. This certainly seems the most obvious interpretation. The female depicted is seen in a state of maternity, performing an act of self-milking, presumably to offer up the milk she is collecting in her bowl for some symbolic ceremony celebrating fecundity.

Obvious though it is, such a view cannot go unchallenged. Eibl-Eibesfeldt, in his behaviour studies of remote tribes, discovered that, in moments of acute stress, females would grab and squeeze their breasts. If they happened to be lactating at the time, the result was that they sometimes squirted jets of milk several feet in front of them. In ancient historic times, clothed women were often said to clutch or clasp their breasts at moments of great anguish. Ucko (1968) is more specific: ' ... the Pyramid texts of historic Egypt make it clear that the holding of the breasts is one of the accepted ways in which to depict mourning ... and has nothing to do with the expression of fertility.' So it is possible that the Cypriot Lactation Figures show, not a great Mother Goddess, but the mourning widow of the deceased, offering her milk as a symbol of bereavement.

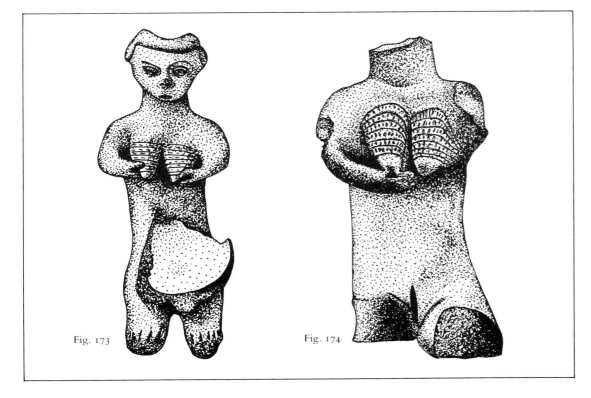

Fig. 173   Fig. 174

3 Lactation Figures

Fig. 173 *No provenance (Louvre Museum). Terracotta. Chalcolithic. Ht. 12.9 cm. Caubet 1974, Pl. VII.*
Fig. 174 *Alaminos. Terracotta. Chalcolithic. Ht. 15.2 cm. Caubet 1974, Pl. VII.*

4 Ejaculation Figure

Fig. 175 *Souskiou(?). Terracotta. Chalcolithic. Ht. 36 cm. Karageorghis 1981, Pl. 15.*

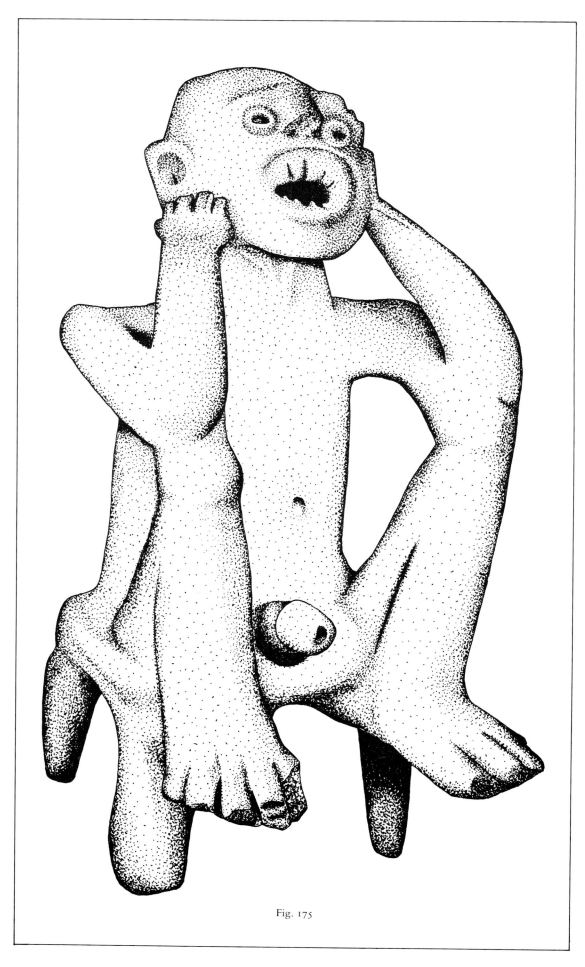

Fig. 175

4 Ejaculation Figure

At the present time only a single figure belonging to this category is known, but it is such an impressive terracotta that it fully deserves its special status. It is the largest terracotta known from the Chalcolithic, having a height of 36 cm, and is unlike anything else found in Cyprus. It depicts a naked male sitting on a stool, with his knees bent and his elbows resting on them. His hands clasp the sides of his slightly upturned head and his open mouth gives his face an expression of great tension. The artist has added one extraordinaary detail. The neck muscles are shown in distinct relief, indicating a moment of straining muscle contraction. (This is not clear in published photographs of the figure, but easily detected if the original is viewed in different light.) Such attention to anatomical detail is remarkable and contrasts strongly with the degree of stylization and schematization in other prehistoric Cypriot figures. It must mean that it was of particular importance to show this male at a moment of great physical strain and body tension.

What could such a posture mean? The most obvious interpretation, that the man in question was suffering from acute constipation, can be quickly discarded. An alternative, that he was engaged in some kind of 'Primal Scream'—perhaps calling on the almighty for assistance—is more attractive and would account just as well for the bulging neck muscles. But Karageorghis (1981) has provided what must surely be the true answer: 'Through a perforation at the top of the head one may pour a liquid which flows through the conspicuous tubular penis. This may have been a tribal act connected with fertility.' It also explains perfectly the bulging neck muscles and the open mouth. The straining tension of the figure is almost certainly the posture of male orgasm. The artist has shown the male at the very moment of ejaculation, and has even provided the technical facility for this crucial act of fertility to be symbolically performed as part of some ancient ceremony. It is easy to imagine the figure being carried around from field to field to perform its seminal libation and magically fertilize the crops, for example, or to envisage it in operation at rituals to encourge human fertility.

It is perhaps worth mentioning that this figure also underlines a curious case of archaeological sex discrimination. Had the person depicted been female she would instantly have been dubbed a Mother Goddess or a Fertility Goddess. Because he is male it would therefore be logical to refer to him as a Father God or a Fertility God, but needless to say this is not done. He is simply a 'Seated Figure'. This reflects the rigid thinking that sees these early prehistoric periods as totally dominated by Earth Mothers and Goddesses. The deity is not allowed to undergo the sex change until much later in the human story. In such a pattern of thought, the Great Ejaculator from the Copper Age of Cyprus is something of an embarrassment.

These comments are not intended to imply that this remarkable statue should be considered as representing a male god. They are merely meant to expose the ease with which certain interpretive words become fixed and hallowed beyond logic by archaeological tradition.

5 Plank Figures

Plank Figures are so called because they are completely flattened, rectangular in shape, and usually lacking in limbs or body extremities. In number they are about as common as the Cruciform Figures, although there may be many unrecorded examples scattered across the world as they are greatly sought after by collectors. Their dramatically simplified shape makes them particularly attractive to twentieth-century eyes.

Plank Figures dominate the Early and Middle Bronze Ages in the way that the Cruciform Figures dominated the Chalcolithic period. Whereas there were intermediate forms providing a link between the Neolithic Stump Figures and the Chalcolithic Cruciform Figures, it is generally accepted that there is no such bridge between the Cruciform and the Plank Figures. The arrival of Plank Figures as the new 'fashion' for depicting the human figure is seen as the result of foreign influences imported from the mainland north of the island. Flourenzos (1975) comments: 'It seems that the Cypriote plank-shaped idols have their model in the south Anatolian region. Plank-shaped idols have been produced in the south-east region of Asia Minor since the Chalcolithic times ... These idols appeared as a new element in Cypriote material culture, which have no predecessor in the local Chalcolithic period.'

Pl. 174 *Highly simplified Plank Figure of the Shoulder Figure type, found on Lanzarote in the Canary Islands. Stone. Arrecife Museum, Lanzarote.*

Although this statement was perfectly justified on the basis of published information at the time, it is no longer valid. Cypriot Plank Figures from the Chalcolithic have now come to light.

During recent years a number (at least twelve) of pale green picrolite figurines from the Cypriot Chalcolithic have appeared in the London salerooms and galleries. Almost all of these have disappeared into private collections and can no longer be traced, but it is known that at least three of them were flat, plank-shaped figures. One was obtained and is illustrated here (see Pl. 175). It is quite clear from this that the Chalcolithic artists on the island, although favouring the cruciform shape, were not averse to experimenting with other images of the human form. Indeed, several of the other figurines, ones that can no longer be traced, were also of non-cruciform shapes, suggesting that we may be in for some surprises when further Chalcolithic sites are excavated.

The fact that the Cypriot Chalcolithic can now offer us examples of picrolite Plank Figure precursors means that it is no longer necessary to seek outside inspiration for the Bronze Age flowering of this type of figurine. It is certainly true, as Flourenzos says, that similar figures were being produced in Anatolia (and, for that matter, in the Cyclades), but we can no longer be sure that they are essential to the development of the Cypriot Plank Figures. It is a possibility, but no longer a certainty.

It is worth mentioning here that I have been able to trace the Plank Figure shape to a prehistoric culture as far away as Lanzarote in the Canary Islands (see Pl. 174), and similar 'Plaque Figures' are well known from prehistoric sites on the Iberian peninsula (see Savory, 1968). Cles-Reden (1961) has suggested that they 'seem to be related', but they are so distant geographically that this is rather far-fetched. I am only mentioning them here to underline the way in which cubistically simplified human figures can easily end up with striking resemblances that are purely accidental and reflect no cultural connection or any influence in either direction. It is entirely possible that the Cypriot and Anatolian Plank Figures developed independently of one another.

It is preferable to leave the question of the symbolic significance of Plank Figures until the different types have been described and illustrated. Suffice it to say here that their unusual appearance was probably not due simply to aesthetic and stylistic considerations, but had to do more with schematization. In other words, I am suggesting that the *way* in which the ancient artists simplified the human figure had more significance than has hitherto been realized. To give a single example, I am proposing that if legs are not shown on a Plank Figure this is not because they interfered with the aesthetic line of the figure but more probably because they were not important and perhaps not even visible on the kind of person being represented.

With this thought in mind, here is a simplified classification of Plank Figure types. This is based more on shape than ware. The Plank Figure tradition is expressed variously in stone and terracotta; in free-standing figures and in small figures attached to or growing out of vessels; in Early Bronze Age Red Polished Ware and in Middle Bronze Age White Painted Ware; it lasts from the start of the Bronze Age until the Mycenaean intrusion in the Late Bronze Age, when another strikingly different style of human representation sweeps it away and completely replaces it. I am less concerned here with a precise time sequence for the Plank Figures, than with a separation into different classes of the basic images being portrayed by the Cypriot artists. Clearly, with the whole range of Cypriot Plank Figures, we are dealing with a continuum, a single tradition, and since the provenance of many of the pieces is unknown it is better to concentrate on the artistic intention of the pieces rather than to play a guessing game with the smaller steps of their cultural sequence.

Plank Figures

a Shoulder Figures
b Comb Figures
c Slab Figures
d Multi-neck Figures
e Parental Figures
f Cradle Figures
g Vessel-attached Figures
h Legged Figures
i Long-eared Figures

This covers most of the human representations of the Early and Middle Bronze Ages, but there are some exceptions, which escaped the general 'flattening' process, and these will be dealt with separately later.

a Shoulder Figures

These are the 'classic' Plank Figures. The head and neck are shown as a small rectangle, placed on top of a large rectangle which represents the rest of the body. The legs and feet are never differentiated from the lower body. An occasional interference with the formal outline appears at the sides of the head in the form of two small, protruding ears. They are pierced for earrings, but none of these have survived the passage of time. In typical examples there are incision patterns depicting head-bands, necklaces and wide belts; also facial markings, hair, eyes, eyebrows, nostrils and mouths. The nose is shown in relief. In addition, there is usually a

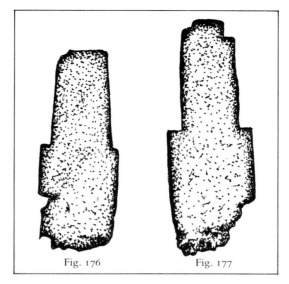

Fig. 176   Fig. 177

5a Shoulder Figures with plain surfaces

Fig. 176 *Vounous (Tomb 2, no. 14). Gypsum. Early Bronze Age. Ht. 22 cm. Dikaios 1940, Pl. XXXIIa.*

Fig. 177 *Vounous (Tomb 2, no. 15). Gypsum. Early Bronze Age. Ht. 25 cm. Dikaios 1940, Pl. XXXIIa.*

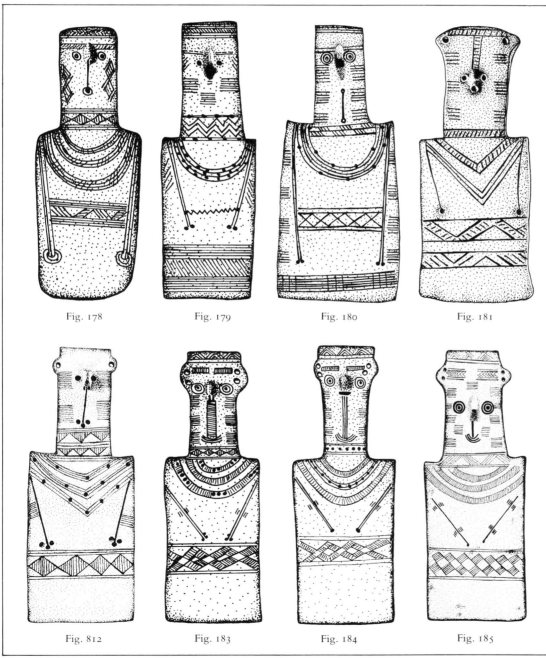

Fig. 178   Fig. 179   Fig. 180   Fig. 181

Fig. 812   Fig. 183   Fig. 184   Fig. 185

5a Shoulder Figures with incised details

Figs. 178-85 *Red Polished Ware. Early Bronze Age.*

Fig. 178 *Lapithos (Tomb 201). Ht. 27 cm. Flourenzos 1975, Pl. II, 1.*

Fig. 179 *No provenance (Cyprus Museum). Ht. 22 cm. Flourenzos 1975, Pl. II, 2.*

Fig. 180 *Vounous. Schaeffer 1938, Pl. XX, 1.*

Fig. 181 *Vounous. Schaeffer 1938, Pl. XX, 2.*

Fig. 182 *No provenance (Louvre Museum). Ht. 27.5 cm. Hennessy 1979, Pl. 48.*

Fig. 183 *No provenance (Liveris Collection). Ht. 28.3 cm. Flourenzos 1975, Pl. II, 5.*

Fig. 184 *Vounous. Ht. 28 cm. Des Gagniers and Karageorghis 1976, Pl. LVI, 2.*

Fig. 185 *No provenance (Cyprus Museum). Ht. 26.2 cm. Des Gagniers and Karageorghis 1976, Pl. LVI, 1.*

pair of diagonal lines sloping downwards and inwards on the front of the body. These lines have nearly always been interpreted as arms, but closer examination throws some doubt onto this, as will be discussed later. Finally, on a few of the 'classic' figures there is a small pair of breast-buds. The majority, however, give no hint of gender. Despite this they have nearly always been labelled as female figurines, presumably to enhance the ubiquity of the Mother Goddess image. Merrillees (1980), with typical outspokenness, will have none of this: ' ... a majority of figures lack any identifiable sexual criteria, primary or secondary ... The assertion by Frankel and Tamvaki that "all known plank idols are female", to which des Gagniers and Karageorghis also subscribe, is not supported by the evidence and cannot be allowed to pass unchallenged. It should also not be overlooked that the small breasts represented could be men's.' As will become clear later, this caution is crucial in seeking an interpretation of the meaning of Plank Figures.

Of the ten examples illustrated here, two are atypical and eight are typical. The two oddities (Figs. 176-7) are carved from stone and have plain surfaces with no facial or other details. Made from gypsum, they were found by Dikaios in Tomb 2 at Vounous. A vessel with typical terracotta Plank Figures attached to it was discovered in the same tomb. A few other stone-carved Plank Figures do exist, but these are the only two in the classic 'shoulder' shape, with the head/neck rectangle narrower than the body/legs rectangle.

Of the eight typical, terracotta examples (Figs. 178-85) five have pierced ears and three are earless. Five have an enigmatic vertical line beneath the nose—a feature so exaggerated that it must have some special significance. Merrillees (1980) describes this peculiar feature as follows: 'The lines of the nostrils and philtrum exerted a particular fascination on the artist, who sometimes artificially elongated them downwards.' It seems inconceivable that the human philtrum (the small hollow between the nostrils and the upper lip, which stucturally possesses a vertical element) should be given such disproportionate importance. Also, it is clear in some cases, such as Fig. 184, that the mouth comes *above* the vertical line. This would make the line into an exaggerated chin-cleft, which is almost as improbable. I will defer my own interpretation of the line until the discussion on p. 162.

Further examples of Shoulder Figures are illustrated in colour on pp. 146-7.

b Comb Figures

Comb Figures constitute a special category of Shoulder Figures so controversial that it is safer to treat them as a separate group. Few other authors would even consider them as human figures at all. For a variety of reasons they have been referred to in the past as 'combs', 'brushes', or 'forks', but new evidence now suggests that they may all be highly abstracted, pendant versions of Plank Figures.

In shape, they differ in proportion from the typical Shoulder Figures. The necks are taller and thinner and the bodies are wider and more square. In typical examples, the lower body is incised with a row of vertical lines. These lines have been interpreted as (a) *teeth* on wide, long-handled combs; (b) *bristles* on wide brushes like those used by modern house-decorators; or (c) *prongs* on a wide fork implement of some kind. If the Comb Figures (as I am calling them for convenience) are, in reality, not some skeuomorphic imitation of a common utensil, but a highly formalized representation of a Plank Figure, then, of course, the vertical lines on the lower body become the *pleats* of a skirt.

I admit that my interpretation seems improbable and that pottery combs for tomb-use would make economic substitutes for real

Pl. 175 Comb Figure, *with suspension hole and decoration in the form of shallow, drilled holes (on both sides of the pendant). This and other similar Chalcolithic pendants reveal that the Comb Figure shape was aleady being worn on Cyprus at a very early date. Pale green picrolite. Chalcolithic. Ht. 4.4 cm (DM-ST-08).*

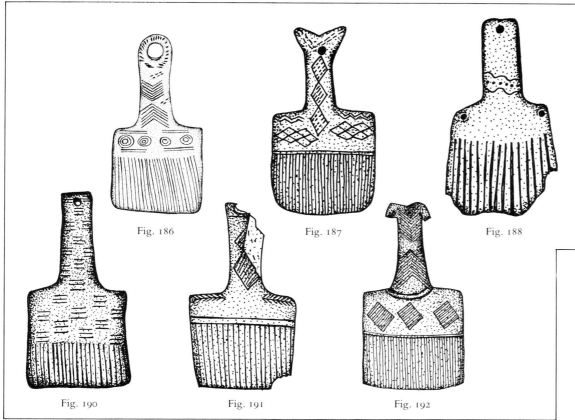

Fig. 186   Fig. 187   Fig. 188   Fig. 189

Fig. 190   Fig. 191   Fig. 192

5b Comb Figures

Figs. 186-92 *Red Polished Ware. Early Bronze Age.*

Fig. 186 *Vounous. Schaeffer 1938, Pl. XXI, 1.*

Fig. 187 *Vounous (Tomb 121, no. 42). Ht. 13.4 cm. Stewart and Stewart 1950, Pl. XCVIc.*

Fig. 188 *Vounous (Tomb 131a, no. 26). Ht. 13.9 cm. Stewart and Stewart 1950, Pl. XCVIe.*

Fig. 189 *Vounous (Tomb 121, no. 43). Ht. 9.9 cm. Stewart and Stewart 1950, Pl. XCVId.*

Fig. 190 *Vounous (Tomb 9, no.27). Ht. 14.5 cm. Dikaios 1940, Pl. XXXVIIIc.*

Fig. 191 *No provenance (Cyprus Museum). Ht. 10 cm. Buchholz and Karageorghis 1973, no. 1710.*

Fig. 192 *No provenance (Cyprus Museum). Ht. 11.5 cm. Flourenzos 1975, Fig. 3a.*

combs that had been laboriously cut from bone or antler, or even wood. We may eventually find a real comb of the appropriate shape to support the comb-theory, but in the meantime it seems to me that the human-figure hypothesis should be given a hearing.

I mentioned earlier that, back in the Chalcolithic period, there were a few unpublished Plank Figures in green picrolite. These have the proportions, not of the classic Plank Figure, but of the Comb Figure. The one illustrated here (Pl. 175) confirms this. It also shows that, at this stage, incised dots were the decorative motif, rather than vertical lines, so that it is difficult to call this example a 'comb'. Instead it appears to be another schematized version of the human body, constrasting with the then dominant cruciform shape. It is as if the human figure is reduced to a slender head and neck surmounting a grossly broad body. This smacks of a pregnancy figure and it is equipped with a suspenson hole at the top of the neck, suggesting that it was worn around the neck by its owner.

Moving on now into the Bronze Age, we find a number of pottery objects (Figs. 186-92) of a very similar shape, but with the addition of what I believe to be a wide pleated skirt. Again there is a suspension hole at the

top of the slender neck, the hole replacing the facial features and thus 'dehumanizing' the image. (It will be recalled that suspension-hole Cruciform Figures also lost their facial features. In their case, however, the arms and legs were sufficiently specific as human attributes to remove any doubts about the true nature of the figures.)

The superficial resemblance of these Comb Figures to native combs, distemper brushes, or heavy forks was, however, enough to throw observers off the scent. What was needed was some kind of more 'humanized' Comb Figure, to give the vital clue.

The problem was to find a Comb Figure that was not a pendant and therefore had its face area available for the display of undeniably human features. Since all the terracottas of Comb Figures *were* pendants, this seemed an impossible quest. Then, at Christie's in London on 14 December 1983, a large Cypriot Red Polished jug was put on sale, described as having a 'relief moulded idol figure under each handle'. The vessel was illustrated in colour (p. 41 of the catalogue) and the photograph clearly shows one of the relief figures. It is a Comb Figure with a unmistakable face.

Close-up photographs of the 'idols' were made and the drawings of them shown here

5b Comb Figures with human faces

Figs. 193-4 *Red Polished Ware. Early Bronze Age. No provenance. Christie's catalogue, 14 December 1983, lot 275. The two figures appear as relief decoration on a large, round-spouted jug. Fig. 193 is clearly visible in the illustration on p. 41 of the catalogue, but Fig. 194, on the other side, is hidden from view. Ht. (of jug) 49.5 cm; estimated height of figures, approximately 12 cm.*

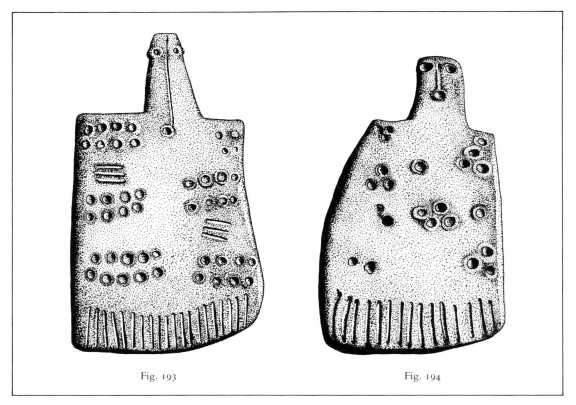

Fig. 193   Fig. 194

give the details of both figures (Figs. 193-4). Each has a pair of eyes, a vertical 'nose-line', and a circular mouth. Groups of large, stabbed dots appear over the bodies, and there is a row of vertical lines across the lower region of each body, as in the typical Comb Figures, creating the impression of a pleated skirt. On one figure (Fig. 193) there is, in addition, a pair of triple-horizontal incisions that appear to represent hands pressed

to the body. These large, relief figures strongly suggest that the faceless, pendant 'combs' are, in reality, human figures worn as pregnancy charms. With this in mind, a search was made for other examples of Comb Figures portrayed as reliefs, or incised on vessels or figurines, where suspension holes would not be needed and facial details might appear.

The results of this search were disappoint-

Figs. 195-204 *Examples of incision motifs in the shape of Comb figures, which appear on Red Polished Ware objects of the Early Bronze Age. Fig. 201 is on a tulip bowl in the Louvre Museum, but all the rest are to be found on the backs or fronts of Plank Figures.*

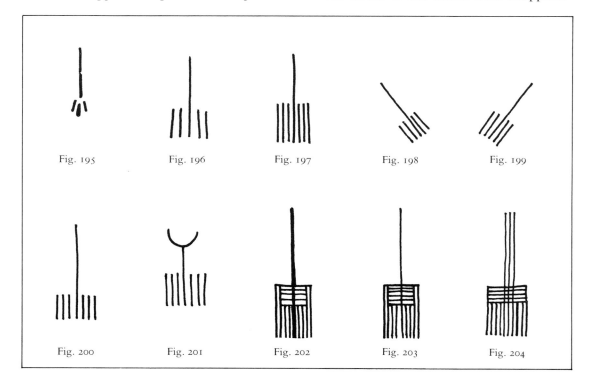

Fig. 195   Fig. 196   Fig. 197   Fig. 198   Fig. 199

Fig. 200   Fig. 201   Fig. 202   Fig. 203   Fig. 204

ing. A number of Plank Figures did show themselves to be Comb Figure wearers, sometimes on the front of the body, but usually on the back. Sadly, however, the Comb Figures incised on the Plank Figures were so tiny that no details of any kind could be shown. (See Figs. 195-200, 202-4, and Pl. 176, g and h.) Several examples of larger, incised Comb Figures were discovered on Red Polished vessels (see Pl. 176 a-f, and Fig. 201), but even here there was no sign of any human face or arms. The only other Comb Figure formed as a relief comes from Margi (Tomb 1, no. 9c) (see Karageorghis, 1958, Pl. XI, e). It is shown on a fragment of a large Red Polished bowl but it has no face. The fact that it is shown as being the same size as a long-legged animal placed next to it, is suggestive but no more.

The only exception appeared on a Red Polished jar from Kition (Tomb 8, Area I) published by Karageorghis in 1974. Here there were four Comb Figures complete with heads and arms (See Figs. 205-6). Karageorghis described them in the following words: '… four anthropoid motifs resembling female(?) figures wearing long skirts. In fact they may also be taken as brush motifs, with the arms and other details springing from the handle of the brush.' He must be forgiven for hedging his bets,

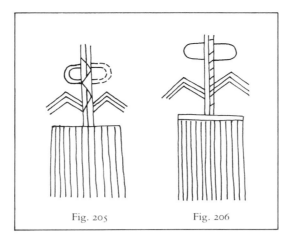

Fig. 205   Fig. 206

because the evidence was, and is, ambivalent. Even with the striking new examples of Comb Figures with faces, we still cannot be certain that all Comb Figures are formalized human figures. It is also possible that combs or brushes really were of some great ritual significance to the early Cypriots and that, occasionally, they 'humanized' them with faces, out of a playful inventiveness. Finally, however, it is the Chalcolithic example (Pl. 175) that brings me down on the 'human side' of the argument, because this pendant was made at a time when skeuomorphic objects simply were not part of the culture. I suspect that we will find more examples of this shape from the earlier period and that they will settle the matter.

Figs. 205-6 *Incision motifs in the shape of Comb Figures, on a Red Polished Ware jar from the Early Bronze Age. They appear to have arms and heads. Kition (Tomb 8, area 1). Karageorghis 1974, Pl. CXI.*

Pl. 176 *Comb Figures that appear as incised motifs on various Early Bronze Age vessels and figures*
a,b *From a small squat-neck jug in Mottled Red Polished Ware (see Pl. 56a).*
c,d *From a jar in Incised Red Polished Ware (see Pl. 102a).*
e,f *From a fragmentary juglet in Incised Red Polished Ware (DM-IRP-30).*
g,h *From the backs of the Plank Figures shown in Pls. 178 and 179 respectively.*

Fig. 207

5c Slab Figures

Fig. 207 *Red Polished Ware. Early Bronze Age. The lid of a pottery box has been transformed into a figure by the addition of a face. Nose in relief, eyes and mouth incised. No provenance (private collection, Germany).*

5c Slab Figures with folded arms

Figs. 208-10 *Red Polished Ware. Early to Middle Bronze Age.*
Fig. 208 *No provenance (Metropolitan Museum, New York). Ht. 16.8 cm. Karageorghis 1976, no. 100.*
Fig. 209 *No provenance (Louvre Museum). Ht. 18.4 cm. Caubet 1971, Pl. II, 2. (The height of this figure is incorrectly given as 118.4 cm in Caubet 1971.)*
Fig. 210 *No provenance (Cyprus Museum). Ht. 24.5 cm. Des Gagniers and Karageorghis 1976, Pl. LIX, 1.*

c Slab Figures

A third category of Plank Figure has the head, neck and body of roughly the same width, so that the general outline of the flattened form is that of a long slab. In human terms this means that the figures lack any differentiation of shoulders.

This type appears to be slightly later than the classic Shoulder Figures, extending from Early Bronze Age Red Polished Ware to the late Red Polished Ware of the Middle Bronze and even the White Painted Ware of this later period.

It can be looked upon either as a degeneration of the classic plank form, or as a purification of it, according to taste.

The simplest example is a pottery box-lid which has been given a smiling face (Fig. 207). There are no arms, legs, or any other features, other than incised eyes and mouth, and the usual relief nose.

A second variation (Figs. 208-10) has folded arms rendered in relief and, in two cases, strangely flat-topped ears. In both instances the ears are pierced for earrings and on Fig. 210 these are indicated in relief. All three examples show some kind of ornamentation on top of the head—either a hairstyle or a hat.

A third form has protruding arm-stumps (Figs. 211-14). These stumps bend downwards to varying degrees, from a slight curve to a right-angled bend. Again, there are the oddly flat-topped ears—in three of the four cases illustrated. Also, the tops of the heads show hair or hat decoration. One figure (Fig. 211) wears a Comb Figure, apparently suspended from a heavy necklace.

The final variation of this type is the purest—an almost blank, vertical slab of pottery or stone, with minimal details. The first (Fig. 215) is made of Red Polished Ware, has a pair of downwards curving arm-stumps and protruding ears pierced for earrings. That is all. No eyes, nose, mouth, breasts, adornments, costume, or any kind of incisions. For some reason the artist has reduced the human figure to its simplest expression. One possible explanation is that the figure was originally 'dressed' or decorated in some way with fugitive material, all traces of which have long since disappeared. It certainly seems curious that, of all the facial features, only the ears should have survived. The second (Fig. 216) is made of alabaster and, apart from a more sharply rectangular shape, is very similar to the pottery version. The third and final one shown here (Fig. 217) is exceptional in that it is both the simplest one ever found and also the biggest. In fact,

Fig. 208   Fig. 209   Fig. 210

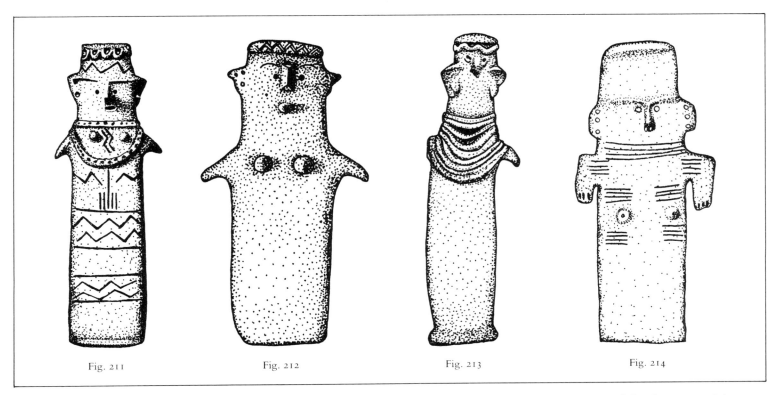

Fig. 211   Fig. 212   Fig. 213   Fig. 214

at 61 cm in height it towers over all other Plank Figures. It arrived in London from Greece in 1975 and was sold at Sotheby's on 14 July (lot 216). It was purchased by a Swiss dealer and is now in a Swiss private collection. Made from a single large slab of limestone, it was described by Sotheby's as having 'two small projections forming the arms, two holes to either side of the rectangular head'. They were cautious about

identifying the holes, but Merrillees (1980) was less inhibited and described the figure as having 'two holes drilled through either side of its top part close to the edges, representing the eyes ...' I have doubts about this interpretation, especially when Fig. 217 is studied alongside Fig. 215 and Fig. 216. It seems much more likely that, like them, the big figure has arms and *ears*, not eyes. The holes are too far apart for eyes and seem to be

5c Slab Figures with protruding arm-stumps

Figs. 211-14 *Red Polished Ware. Early to Middle Bronze Age.*

Fig. 211 *No provenance (Louvre Museum). Ht. 28 cm. Caubet 1971, Pl. II, 1.*

Fig. 212 *No provenance (private collection, Japan).*

Fig. 213 *No provenance. Ht. 17.8 cm. Sotheby's catalogue, 4 April 1977, lot 120.*

Fig. 214 *No provenance (Cyprus Museum). Ht. 22.7 cm. Spiteris 1970, p. 33.*

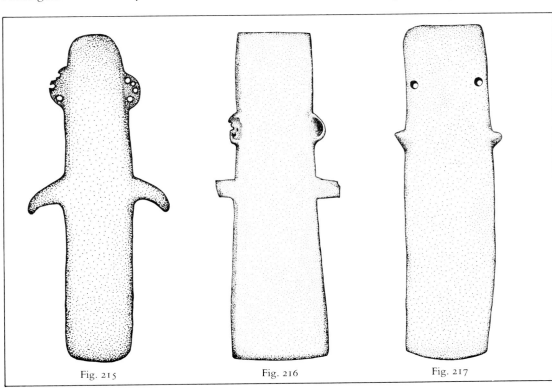

Fig. 215   Fig. 216   Fig. 217

5c Slab Figures without faces

Figs. 215-17 *Early to Middle Bronze Age.*

Fig. 215 *Limassol-Katholiki. Red Polished Ware. Ht. 34 cm. Des Gagniers and Karageorghis 1976, Pl. LIX, 2.*

Fig. 216 *No provenance (private collection). Alabaster. Ht. 18.8 cm. Christie's catalogue, 3 April 1973, lot 147.*

Fig. 217 *No provenance (private collection, Switzerland). Limestone. Ht. 60.3 cm. Thimme 1977, no. 571.*

another case of providing apertures for some important ritual objects, such as gold earrings. Again, it seems likely that something (a skull? a freshly killed animal head?) was hung in the facial region of the great figure, or that it was decorated in some special way for some specific event. But this is idle speculation and we may instead be dealing with a remarkable purification of the human image on the part of the Cypriot artists.

Further examples of Slab Figures are illustrated in colour on p. 150.

d Multi-neck Figures

There is a small group of multi-necked Plank Figures, all in Red Polished Ware, dating from the Early Bronze Age.

Most are two-necked (Figs. 218-25), but a few are three-necked (Figs. 226-7). Their main source appears to be Lapithos on the north coast, where they were probably the work of one, or a few artists, intent on developing the classic Plank Figure motif in a new and more complex form. One (fig. 218) shows the twin heads and neck completely separated from one another down their whole length, but in all the others there is some kind of join between the two verticals, providing greater strength. Incision decoration is much like that on the normal, one-necked Plank Figures.

5d Plank Figures with two necks

Figs. 218-225 *Red Polished Ware. Early Bronze Age.*

Fig. 218 *Dhenia. Ht. 28.5 cm. Des Gagniers and Karageorghis 1976, Pl. LVII, 1.*

Fig. 219 *No provenance (Geneux Collection, Geneva). Ht. 27.9 cm. Thimme 1977, no. 574.*

Fig. 220 *Lapithos (Tomb 21). Flourenzos 1975, Pl. III, 1.*

Fig. 221 *No provenance (Cyprus Museum). Ht. 23.8 cm. Spiteris 1970, p. 33.*

Fig. 222 *No provenance. Ht. 21.7 cm. Flourenzos 1975, Pl. III, 2.*

Fig. 223 *Lapithos (Tomb 21). Ht. 26.5 cm. Flourenzos 1975, Pl. III, 3.*

Fig. 224 *Lapithos (Tomb 18). Ht. 24 cm. Des Gagniers and Karageorghis 1976, Pl. LVII, 2.*

Fig. 225 *Lapithos (Tomb 14). Ht. 22 cm. Flourenzos 1975, Pl. III, 6.*

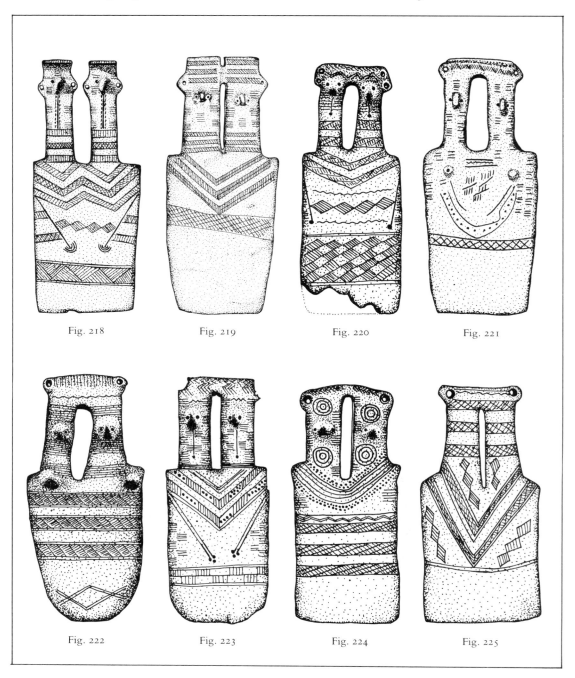

Fig. 218   Fig. 219   Fig. 220   Fig. 221

Fig. 222   Fig. 223   Fig. 224   Fig. 225

In most of these multi-neck examples, there are two sets of facial features, prominently displayed, but in the case of Fig. 224 these are greatly reduced and almost inconspicuous among the incised concentric circles. The ears remain strongly represen -ted however, with large pierced holes. In Fig. 225 these holes survive even more dramatically, but the faces have now vanished completely. As with some of the Slab Figures, ears are surprisingly more important than eyes. Fig. 226 tries a different configuration. Here it is hard to see the earring holes for what they are because they have come to dominate the figure so much that they inevitably give the impression of being a pair of staring, round eyes, with smaller darker nostrils below them. This is a deception. The 'nostrils' are the true eyes of the single face that sits on top of the central neck. The large 'eyes' are part of an enormous pair of ears. On fig. 227 even the small, central face has disappeared and this three-necked terracotta shows the same degree of schematization as the two-necked Fig. 225. Once more, the earring holes are the last to go in the move towards abstraction.

It is tempting to conclude from this that earrings were of some very special significance in the lives of these Bronze Age Cypriots. Their unfortunate absence from all these figurines today suggests that, for tomb purposes, the original gold(?) ones were replaced by some non-lasting substance, in order to hold on to the precious metal for other uses.

The significance of the doubling or trebling of the necks may have to do with the production of magic figures asking for twins, triplets, or a future family of two or three children, as in the case of the double and treble Cruciform Figures. Or it may have been simply a local creative whim—part of the general trend towards pluralization that was so popular with Bronze Age vessels.

e Parental Figures

During the Early and Middle Bronze Age, the period dominated by the Plank Figure style, there appears from time to time a representation of parental care. Typically this takes the form of an adult figure holding a tightly swaddled baby in its arms, with the baby's head close to the left-hand side of the parental chest.

This addition of an infant to the Plank

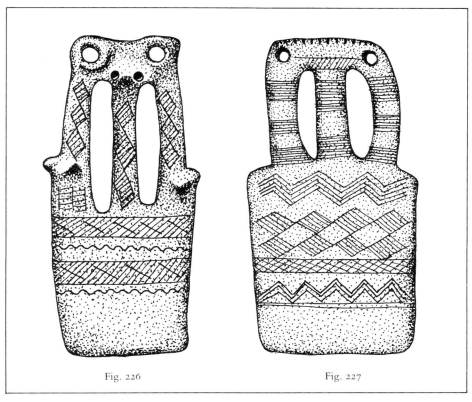

Fig. 226   Fig. 227

Figure shape causes stylization problems because it clashes with the powerful trend to produce a completely flattened human form. The baby protrudes forward and also requires one or both parental arms to be modelled in the round to embrace it. The result has a curious, hybrid appearance, rather as if a cut-out drawing were shown holding a small sculpture. It is clear that the baby is an after-thought grafted on to an already well-entrenched plank-shaped tradition.

Six examples are illustrated here (Figs. 228-33). Four can be described as mothers-with-babies, because the parental figure has breasts. One is sexless and one is male. Two of the figures are in the classic Shoulder Figure style; one is a seated figure which, although flattened, is modelled in a slightly more realistic style; two are Slab Figures; and one—the male—is an incredibly elongated and rather tubular figure in White Painted Ware from the Middle Bronze Age, which has a conspicuous penis.

In those cases where the infant figure is complete it is clear that the style of swaddling employed was important enough to be portrayed with some accuracy. The baby is stiffly swaddled on a heavily hooded cradle-board. The ring-shaped hood is open at the top, providing a powerful protection for the baby's head without reducing air circulation. This type of cradle-board, popular in certain

5d Plank Figures with three necks

Fig. 226 *No provenance. Red Polished Ware. Early Bronze Age. Ohnefalsch-Richter 1893, Pl. XXXVI, 3.*
Fig. 227 *No provenance (Ashmolean Museum). Red Polished Ware. Early Bronze Age. Ht. 19 cm. Frankel 1983, no. 152.*

5a Shoulder Figures

Pl. 177 *The classic Shoulder Figure type. The breasts and nose are shown in relief. The eyes consist of incised holes, each hole being surrounded by a semicircle of white dots. The mouth is a horizontal slit. The figure is wearing headgear, a neck-band, some kind of shoulder-cape and a skirt. Two inward-sloping diagonal lines on the body each end in a drilled hole, and between these two holes is a mysterious horizontal bar. No arms are indicated (it being clear from Pl. 179 opposite that the diagonal lines do not, as is usually claimed, represent arms). Incised Red Polished Ware. Early Bronze Age. Ht. 20.3 cm (DM-IRP-79).*

Pl. 177

Pl. 178

5a Shoulder Figures

Pl. 178 *The nose is shown in relief. The eyes are two incised holes, with heavy eyebrows above them. The mouth is a horizontal slit immediately below the nose. Beneath the mouth is a long vertical line leading down to an incised hole which could easily be mistaken for a rounded mouth, were it not for the presence of the slit mouth above. Incised decoration includes a neck-band, a hanging necklace and a skirt-band. A pair of diagonal lines on the front of the body, easily mistaken for arms, end in incised holes. On the back of the figure, hair is indicated by vertical zigzags, below which hangs a small 'Comb Figure' (see p. 141). Incised Red Polished Ware. Early Bronze Age. Ht. 10 cm (DM-IRP-81).*

Pl. 179 *Similar in all details to Pl. 178, with one important exception: namely, the presence of a pair of arms in relief. These arms are folded on to the chest and are depicted in addition to the pair of diagonal lines ending in incised holes. This confirms that the diagonal lines, found on so many Plank Figures, are not meant to represent arms, but some other feature, probably part of the special costume. Incised Red Polished Ware. Early Bronze Age. Ht. 12.5 cm (DM-IRP-80).*

Pl. 180 *The nose, breasts and head-gear are in relief. In addition, arm-buds and pierced ears protrude from the sides of the flat body. The eyes and mouth are indicated by incised holes. Painted decoration, although faded and damaged, reveals the presence of a neck-band and a skirt-band. Handmade White Painted Ware. Middle Bronze Age. Ht. 14.8 cm (DM-HWP-55). This appears to to be the only Shoulder Figure known in White Painted Ware.*

Pl. 179

Pl. 180

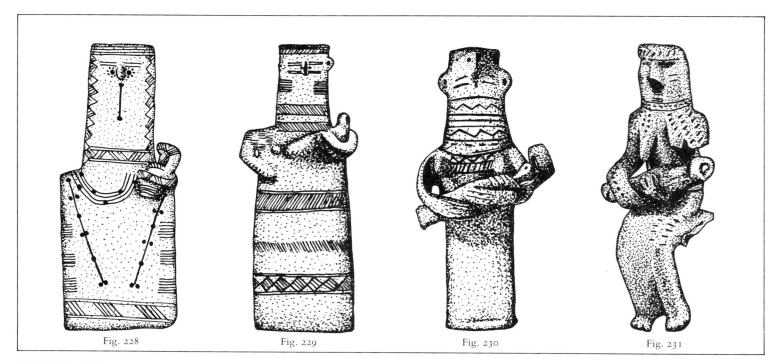

Fig. 228   Fig. 229   Fig. 230   Fig. 231

5e Parental Figures

Figs. 228–31 *Red Polished Ware. Early to Middle Bronze Age.*

Fig. 228 *Lapithos. Stewart 1962, Fig. 94, 2.*

Fig. 229 *No provenance (British Museum). Ht. 26 cm. Cook 1979, Pl. 10a.*

Fig. 230 *No provenance (Louvre Museum). Ht. 15.5 cm. Caubet 1971, Pl. II, 3.*

Fig. 231 *No provenance (Cyprus Museum). Ht. 12.2 cm. Des Gagniers and Karageorghis 1976, Pl. LX, 2.*

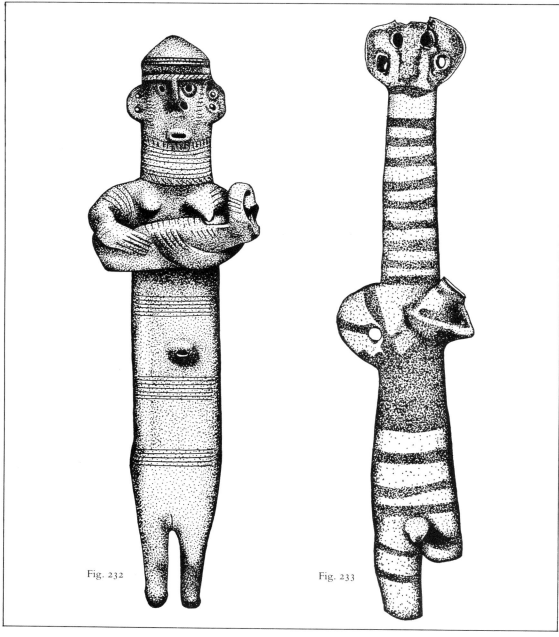

Fig. 232   Fig. 233

5e Parental Figures with elongated bodies

Fig. 232 *No provenance (Oriental Institute of Chicago). Red Polished Ware. Early Bronze Age. Ht. 36.4 cm. Des Gagniers and Karageorghis 1976, Pl. LX, 1.*

Fig. 233 *No provenance (Pierides Collection, Larnaca). White Painted Ware. Middle Bronze Age. Ht. 24.5 cm. Karageorghis 1973, no. 16.*

tribal cultures in recent times, is a compromise between soft swaddling clothes and a large, solid cradle. It is essentially a mobile cradle enabling the parent to carry the child on the back and then, if necessary, remove it for a while and leave the child in it without risk.

It might be argued that these figures with babies depict a mourning parent carrying a dead baby in a kind of funeral shroud. This would explain the placing of such figures in the tombs, but it overlooks the fact that, in one case at least, the baby is being breast-fed (Fig. 232). It seems more likely that this is yet another example of fertility figures made to encourage breeding by magical means, the successful ones being kept as prized possessions and then placed in the tomb alongside the previous owner.

The male figurine (Fig. 233) is most unusual and, as far as I know, is the earliest example from any culture depicting paternal behaviour in this way. In function, this may have been made to assist a man who was having difficulty in producing offspring. Its

existence creates yet another problem for the Mother Goddess theory.

Two other Middle Bronze Age examples (Figs. 234-5) present a slightly different image. One is complete and the other, although fragmentary, is broken off in such a way as to suggest that it displayed a similar posture. The complete one (Fig. 234) shows a female figure, not holding the baby, but with the infant lying across her knees. Part of the arch of the cradle-board hood is still visible, but most of it has been broken away and lost. The mother is not even touching the baby, but instead raises her arms in shock, adoration, or anticipation of reaching out towards it. The mother's face is blackened and, although this could certainly be another scene of parental care, there is a strange mood about the piece, as though the baby is dead and the mother is mourning it. This is an ambiguous piece and it would be a mistake to lump it with other obviously maternal examples. As Ucko (1968) warned, 'Old World prehistoric figurines may not be homogeneous' in their purpose.

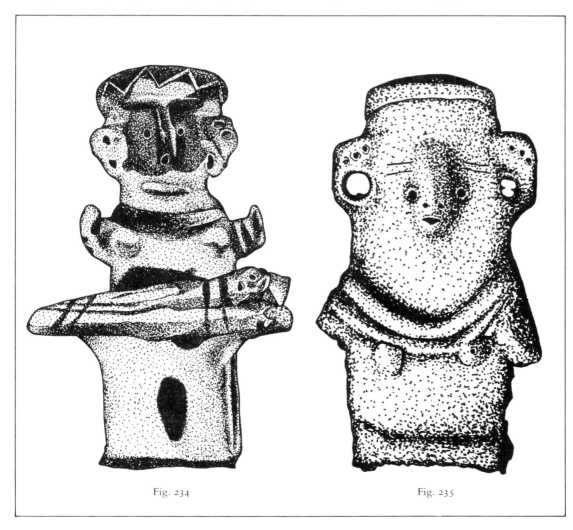

Fig. 234

Fig. 235

5e Parental Figures with infant on knees

Fig. 234 *No provenance (Metropolitan Museum, New York). White Painted Ware. Middle Bronze Age. Ht. 10.2 cm. Karageorghis 1976, no. 102.*

Fig. 235 *No provenance (Louvre Museum). Red Polished Ware. Middle Bronze Age. Ht. 12 cm. Caubet 1971, Pl. II, 4.*

5c Slab Figures

Pl. 181 *Incised Red Polished Ware. Early Bronze Age.*

a(left) *Female figure with nose and breasts shown in relief. Arm-buds and pierced ears protrude from the side of the flattened body. The arms are curved downwards. Eyes, eyebrows, mouth and nostrils are shown as incisions. Other incised decorations include headgear, neck-band, skirt and some kind of cape over the arms.*

On the back of the figure, vertical wavy lines depict the hair. Ht. 18.8 cm (DM-IRP-83). Lettering in red ink on the back reads: 'Lawrence Coll. Sotheby, Lot 525. Apr. 1892. p. 818'.

b(centre) *Female figure with nose, breasts, chin, headgear and hair in relief. Arm-buds and ears with pendant earrings protrude from the sides of the body. Eyes, mouth, nostrils and*

nipples are indicated by simple incisions. The incised decorations include a wide neck-band, some kind of cape over the right shoulder, and vertical wavy lines representing hair on the back of the head. Ht. 19.4 cm (DM-IRP-84).

c(right) *Genderless figure with nose shown in relief. Beneath the nose is a pair of incised nostrils. The eyes are shown as incised spots above the*

nose. Each eye consists of a central hole surrounded by a ring of similar holes. (This 'ring-of-holes' eye-motif can also be seen in Pls. 177 and 183.) The arms of this Slab Figure project sideways horizontally from the body and are decorated with incised holes. Apart from a hint of some kind of headgear, there are no other details of this highly simplified figure Ht. 17.6 cm (DM-IRP-85).

Pl. 181

Pl. 182

Pl. 182

a(left) *Unusually small Slab Figure. The nose is shown in relief and large ear-flaps protrude from the side of the 'head'. The eyes are indicated by incised holes, as is the genital cleft, indicating that the figure is female. There appears to be some kind of headgear and, below the nose, a horizontal row of dots suggesting a neck-band. Incised Red Polished Ware. Early Bronze Age. Ht. 4.4 cm (DM-IRP-86).*

b(centre) *Figure with nose shown in relief and arm-buds protruding outward and downward. The eyes and mouth are indicated as simple*

incisions and other incised decoration includes a conspicuous neck-band. Incised Red Polished Ware. Early Bronze Age. Ht. 6.9 cm (DM-IRP-82). Lower body restored. This figure appears to have been broken away from the shoulder of a pottery box. Cf. the human figure in Pl. 141.

c(right) *Figure with nose and arms shown in relief. Fingers indicated by incisions. Headgear shape reminiscent of Syrian figurines. Large, pierced ears protrude from the sides of the head. Handmade White Painted Ware. Middle Bronze Age. Ht. 6.2 cm (DM-HWP-60).*

Pl. 183

Pl. 184

5g Vessel-attached Figures

Pl. 183 *Shoulder Figure type, protruding from the bodies of round-spouted jugs. Incised Red Polished Ware. Early Bronze Age.*

a(left) *Jug. Ht. 21.2 cm (DM-IRP-87).*
b(right) *Jug. Ht. 18.5 cm (DM-IRP-88). The figure on this jug has arm-buds and its eyes are made from circles of incised dots.*

Pl. 184 *Human face on the outside of the rim of a shallow bowl. The face, with nose in relief and incised eyes and nostrils, is clearly a 'humanized' rim-lug in origin. Mottled Red Polished Ware. Early Bronze Age. Diam. 23.2 cm (DM-MRP-29).*

5f Cradle Figures

Figs. 236-40 *Early to Middle Bronze Age.*

Fig. 236 *No provenance. Red Polished Ware. Ht. 19 cm. Flourenzos 1975, Pl. III, 5.*

Fig. 237 *No provenance. Red Polished Ware. Ht. 16.5 cm. Karageorghis 1973, no. 12.*

Fig. 238 *Ayia Paraskevi. White Painted Ware. Ht. 18 cm. Astrom 1972, Fig. 16, no. 15.*

Fig. 239 *No provenance (Louvre Museum). White Painted Ware. Caubet 1977, p.3.*

Fig. 240 *Ayios Iakovos(?). White Painted Ware. Ht. 11 cm. Karageorghis 1973, no. 14.*

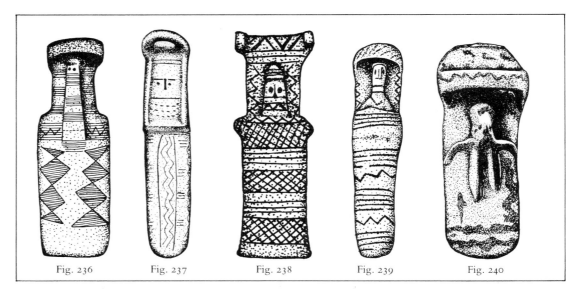

Fig. 236   Fig. 237   Fig. 238   Fig. 239   Fig. 240

f Cradle Figures

As an apparent extension of the Parental Figures, there also appears a type of Plank Figure in which the 'plank' has become the stiff board of the cradle. The whole figure is now the baby, lying in its cradle, but presented in a more flattened form. Five examples are shown here, two in Red Polished Ware from the Early Bronze Age (Figs. 236-7) and three in White Painted Ware from the Middle Bronze Age (Figs. 238-40). The protective arch is shown in all cases, but in one case (Fig. 238) it is damaged and largely broken away. Four of the babies are depicted snugly tucked in their swaddling clothes, but one of them (Fig. 240) is allowed a little more freedom, with both arms and legs visible.

The most obvious function of these infant figurines is that of encouraging a future birth. The mother carries on her body the image of the baby she hopes soon to hold in reality. Others may see this as a sacred depiction of the infant Goddess, but as before there is nothing convincing to support such a view.

One intriguing feature of these cradle figures is that in outline shape they echo the two basic types of Plank Figure—Shoulder and Slab. The two Red Polished examples show this clearly. Fig. 236 has the typical outline of a classic Shoulder Figure, while Fig. 237 is a typical Slab Figure. This gives rise to the thought that perhaps *all* Plank Figures are meant to be shown in a swaddled condition. This would explain the widespread absence of legs and feet, since they would be invisible inside the tightly wrapped swaddling clothes. It would also explain why, in contour and in lack of genitals, the Plank Figures are so sexless. Even when breasts are shown they are very small. But to interpret the typical Plank Figures as highly stylized portrayals of *babies*, attractive as this idea is in terms of figurine function, is unconvincing. The existence of plank-mothers holding babies contradicts it. But such thoughts do lead on to the idea that perhaps the highly stylized shape of the typical Plank Figures is based on something similar to swaddling. In other words the legs and feet were not omitted schematically because the artists had no interest in them but because these limbs were invisible beneath some sort of covering. Three possibilities come to mind—a marriage costume, a maternity smock, or a burial shroud. In each case the body might well be encased in a special kind of garment which concealed the lower limbs completely. This would explain the wide outline of the figurines, an outline which conceals the natural curves of the human body. It would also explain why most of the Plank Figures are so well adorned with decorative belts and necklaces—they were 'dressed up' for some special occasion. The fact that some of the Plank Figures are holding babies tends to eliminate costumes of marriage or death, and points to maternity. It could be argued that, if a female is shown holding a baby, she would hardly need a fertility figurine showing her dressed in a special, loose maternity costume, but it must be remembered that these mother and child figurines are extremely rare compared with ordinary Plank Figures and that there is nothing strange about an occasional mother wanting to encourage a second baby quickly after the first one, and using an image of a pregnant female holding an earlier baby to indicate this.

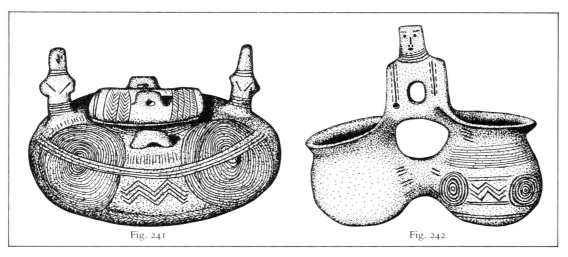

Fig. 241   Fig. 242

5g Vessel-attached Figures

Fig. 241 *Margi. Red Polished Ware. Early Bronze Age. Ht. 19.5 cm. Karageorghis 1973, no. 9.*

Fig. 242 *Vounous (Tomb 71). Red Polished Ware. Early Bronze Age. Schaeffer 1936, Pl. XVII, 1.*

g Vessel-attached Figures

Up to this point all the figures discussed have been small sculptures or terracottas, but there is a distinct class of Plank Figure which consists of various forms of 'outgrowth' from pottery vessels. The precise shapes of these Vessel-attached Figures is often strongly influenced by the way they join on to or merge into their vessels, but the basic style of the figure is usually clearly defined, making it possible to relate it to one of the terracotta types. For example, on a few of the many Red Polished gourd-shaped jugs there is a diminutive Plank Figure, of the classic Shoulder Figure type, protruding from the body of the vessel, opposite the handle (see

Pl. 183). Apart from its small size and the fact that its lower edge joins a curved surface, such a figurine is identical with the larger terracottas in shape, proportion and style of incised decoration. In other cases, the resemblance is not so clear. In many instances, the human figure has become reduced to no more than a face shown in relief on some part of a jug, bowl (Pl. 184) or jar (Pl. 186).

Special categories of Vessel-attached Figures that deserve attention include:

1 Figures mounted on the shoulders of egg-shaped pottery boxes

Four examples are known, three of them almost certainly by the same artist. In two

5g Vessel-attached Figures, as handles of four-bowl vessels

Figs. 243-5 *Red Polished Ware. Early Bronze Age.*

Fig. 243 *Vounous. Ht. 36 cm. Dikaios 1940, Pl. XXVIIIa.*

Fig. 244 *Vounous. Ht. 37 cm. Dikaios 1940, Pl. XXVIIIb.*

Fig. 245 *Vounous (Tomb 48, no. 2). Ht. 46 cm. Dikaios 1940, Pl. XXVIId.*

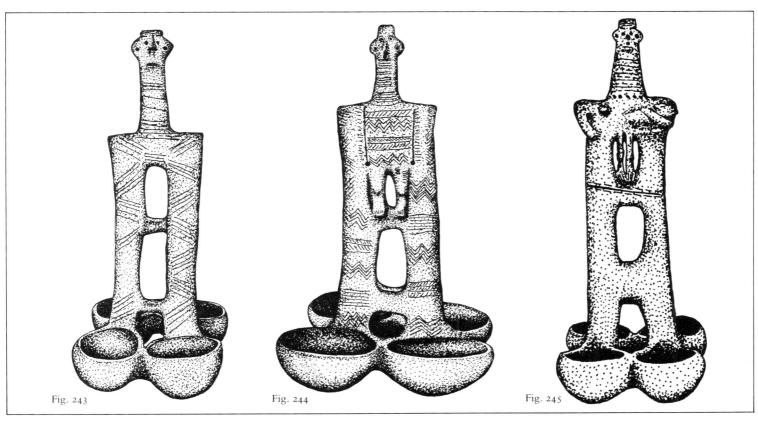

Fig. 243   Fig. 244   Fig. 245

Pl. 185

5g Vessel-attached figures

Pl. 185 *The figure rises from the handle of a five-bowl Multi-unit Vessel. The face, with a startled expression, shows nose and headgear in relief and eyes, eyebrows, nostrils and mouth as incisions. Two short arm-buds protrude forward at the point where the figure divides into two to allow for an aperture for lifting or hanging the vessel. Below this point there is a pair of breast-like bowls flanking the main stem and three further bowls forming a tripod base. Handmade White Painted Ware. Middle Bronze Age. Ht. 29.8 cm (DM-HWP-56). A unique vessel. The closest approximations to it are the Early Bronze Age examples shown in Figs. 243-5.*

Pl. 186 *Large jar sprouting a head and neck from the top of its body, both front and rear. Each head is adorned with headgear and neck-band in relief. The nose is also shown in relief and pierced ears protrude from the sides of the head. Circular incisions form the eyes and the mouth. The jar itself is provided with what appear to be a pair of pierced ears, a pointed nose and a relief-work necklace. If these interpretations are correct, then it was conceived as a Vessel-shaped Figure itself, depicted as wearing two small effigies, one on the front of its neck and one on the back. Drab Polished Ware. Middle Bronze Age. Ht. 31.6 cm (DM-DP-18).*

Pl. 186

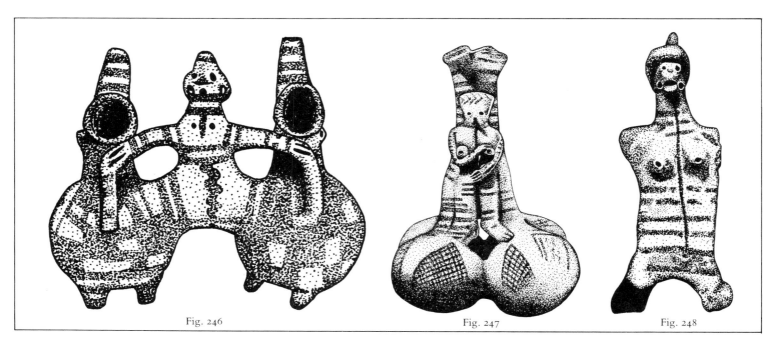

Fig. 246   Fig. 247   Fig. 248

5g Vessel-attached Figures

Figs. 246-8 *White Painted Ware. Middle Bronze Age.*

Fig. 246 *Lapithos, Vrysi tou Barba (Tomb 21). Ht. 11.5 cm. Buchholz and Karageorghis 1973, no. 1556.*

Fig. 247 *Angastina (Tomb 2, no. 8). Ht. 13 cm. Karageorghis 1976, no. 86.*

Fig. 248 *No provenance (Pierides Collection, Larnaca). Ht. 10.5 cm. Belgiorno 1980, no. 9.*

cases a single human Slab Figure is shown opposite a bird (see Pl. 141). In a third, two similar human figures are shown, one on each side of the box aperture (Fig. 241). In the fourth, probably by a different artist, there are two humans facing one another across the aperture and one of them is holding a baby.

2 Figures as handles of multi-unit vessels
Nine examples are illustrated here. The first (Fig. 242) is a Red Polished Shoulder Figure surmounting a two-jar vessel. Because of its role as a handle, the flat body of this figure has been pierced with a large hole. A similar, but more elaborate piercing can be seen in the next three (Figs. 243-5), where the four-bowl vessels have tall handles which are transformed into Shoulder Figures with two apertures each. In the case of Fig. 245, there is a baby held in the left arm and, in addition, a pair of disproportionately small legs dangling from below the main figure.

Similar examples can be found in the later, White Painted Ware from the Middle Bronze Age. Fig. 246 shows a small human figure straddling a two-bodied vessel and Fig. 247 depicts a woman adorning the handle of a four-bodied vessel. Fig. 248 is a related figure which, although fragmentary, seems to have been attached to a similar kind of multi-unit vessel. The most remarkable example, however, is the one shown in Pl. 185. This is a late White Painted version of the Red Polished type shown in Figs. 243-5, with a tall, pierced handle rising from a trio of small bowls and surmounted by a plank-face and a

pair of forward-curved arm-stumps. Halfway up the vessel is a unique feature—a pair of additional bowls on either side of the handle shaft which inevitably take on a breast-like role. No other vessel from any period has this particular configuration.

Another unique vessel, a multi-handled tulip-bowl (see Pl. 168), has one of its six handles flattened into a human face of a type not found elsewhere. The mouth and eyes are depicted as three large, circular depressions, each ringed by an incised circle. The effect is a dramatic expression of remarkable intensity, and I have been unable to find any exact parallel for it.

3 Figures in relief on large vessels
These are extremely rare and only a few are known. Two have been mentioned already in the section on Comb Figures (see Figs. 193-4). More appear on a large fragmentary jug of Red Polished Ware published by Karageorghis in 1969 (no. 59), where he comments: 'decorated around the body with pairs of human figures in relief'. The figures in question are of the Slab type, with protruding arm-stumps curving slightly downwards.

The only other case I know appears on the shoulder of a large round-spouted jug of Red Polished Ware (see Pl. 187). This is a remarkably inventive design of a kind I have only encountered before in the Chancay pottery of Peru. The artist depicts the human figure straddling the top of the body of the jug, so that the arms appear on one side of the vessel's neck and the head, trunk and feet appear on the other. A casual glance at this jug does not reveal the presence of a human form on it. It is only when the jug is turned round and round that it emerges. Looking at the front of the vessel, opposite the handle, there is a raised lump on which rest two feet with three incised toes to each foot. Above these is a flat, slab-shaped body with incised markings and, above that again, there is a head made from a pierced lug. The whole of this part of the human figure is framed by an incised, dotted line. On the far side of the vessel's neck, on either side of the handle, there are two very long arms ending in three-fingered hands. These arms and hands are also rendered in low relief and decorated with incised lines. The whole figure melts into the vessel in such a way that it becomes part of the general decoration, an unobtrusive but undeniable presence.

4 Figures modelled around the rims of large bowls
These will be considered separately under the heading of Scenic Compositions. Suffice it to say here that in almost all scenic examples, the style of depicting the human form changes from a predominantly plank-shape to a more rounded figure. It is still obvious that these small human shapes are closely related to the Plank Figure tradition, but they lack the sharply flattened stylization because

they are nearly always engaged in some sort of activity that requires a more rounded form.

h Legged Figures
The vast majority of Plank Figures show no differentiation of the legs or feet, but in the Middle Bronze Age short legs do begin to appear on a few figures, and four of them are illustrated here. The first (Fig. 249) is a rare example of a Red Polished Slab Figure with legs and feet. It is sexless, but wears an elaborate necklace and what appears to be some kind of large hat with a narrow brim. The protruding arms are bent sharply back against the sides.

The second figure (Fig. 250) is in White Painted Ware and, despite its small breasts, has been identified by some as depicting a bearded man. An alternative explanation is that it is a very long-faced woman. The most interesting detail of the decoration of this figure is the indication of a cloak or cape of some kind slung over the right shoulder. This also occurs on a number of incised Red Polished Plank Figures and is clearly visible on Fig. 229 and Pl. 181b. As those are both female figures, it seems likely that the right-shoulder-cape was some special kind of garment worn by women, which makes the

5h Legged Figures

Figs. 249-52 *Middle Bronze Age.*
Fig. 249 *Akaki. Red Polished Ware. Ht. 22.2 cm. Des Gagniers and Karageorghis 1976, Pl. LIX, 3.*
Fig. 250 *Nicosia-Ayia Paraskevi. White Painted Ware. Ht. 34 cm. Karageorghis 1976, no. 83.*
Fig. 251 *No provenance (Cyprus Museum). White Painted Ware. Ht. 18.7 cm. Tatton-Brown 1979, no. 73.*
Fig. 252 *No provenance (Cyprus Museum). White Painted Ware. Karageorghis 1976, no. 96.*

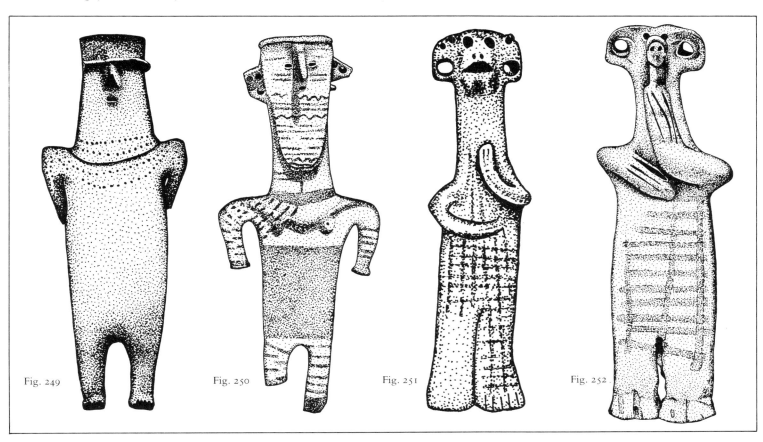

Fig. 249   Fig. 250   Fig. 251   Fig. 252

5g Vessel-attached Figures

Pl. 187 *Large jug, with the figure straddling the jug, lying on its back. Its head is formed from a pierced lug at the base of the neck opposite the handle. Its flat, slablike figure is shown in relief, with its feet resting on a large spherical body-lug. The upward stretched arms of the figure begin on the far side of the jug's neck and spread across the vessel's body, passing either side of the jug-handle. Incisions on the feet and hands clearly indicate the toes and fingers. This is the only example of a neck-straddling figure of this type in Cypriot art. Relief-decorated Red Polished Ware. Early Bronze Age. Ht. 51 cm (DM-RRP-18).*

Pl. 187

Pl. 188

Pl. 189

6 Vessel-shaped Figures

Pl. 188

a(left) *Tulip bowl converted into a human head by the addition of a pair of eyes, with eyelashes and a smiling mouth. The handle of the vessel forms the protruding nose. The bowl has an omphalos base. Incised Red Polished Ware. Early Bronze Age. Diam. 10 cm. Ht. 10.3 cm (DM-IRP-89).*

b(centre) *Bottle with round base, round spout and two pairs of pierced rim-holes; converted into a humanoid shape by the addition of a pair of large pierced ears and a strongly protruding nose at the base of the neck. Handmade Black Slip Ware. Middle bronze Age. Ht. 12 cm (DM-HBS-12).*

c(right) *Jug with four short legs and a round spout, the neck transformed into a human face with nose in relief. Eyes, nostrils and circular mouth incised. Large, protruding ears with heavy circular earrings. Red-on-black Ware. Middle Bronze Age. Ht. 19.6 cm (DM-ROB-11). Almost all the paintwork has been lost but sufficient traces remain to identify the ware.*

Pl. 189 *Handmade White Painted Ware. Middle Bronze Age.*

a(left) *Jug with round base and round spout, converted into humanoid shape by the transformation of the large thumb-grip into a big-nosed face. The eyes indicated by incisions. Ht. 16.8 cm (DM-HWP-58).*

b(centre) *Large flask converted into humanoid shape by the addition of eyes, nose and ears to the short neck. The eyes are drilled holes passing through the neck-wall, the protruding ears are pierced through with single earring-holes, and the small nose is shown in relief. The vertical flask-handle joins the face at the point where the mouth would be. Ht. 26.1 cm (DM-HWP-57). Base restored.*

c(right) *Jug with round base and round spout. There is no face on the neck of this vessel, but the two huge pierced ears with large circular earrings successfully convert it into a humanoid shape, even without the help of facial features. Ht. 14.8 cm (DM-HWP-59). I am following Karageorghis (1981, Pl. 37) in calling this last piece White Painted Ware, but perhaps a more correct name would be Handmade Bichrome Ware, since the artist has deliberately employed two contrasting colours in her paintwork (as distinct from firing one part of the decoration to red and another to black, as often happens in White Painted Ware—see Pl. 189b).*

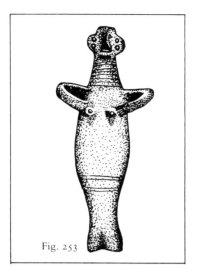

Fig. 253

5i Long-eared Figures

Fig. 253 *With curvaceous body. Black Slip Ware. Middle Bronze Age. No provenance (Metropolitan Museum, New York). Ht. 26 cm. Myers 1914, no. 2004.*

Figs. 254-8 *Plain White Ware (except for Fig. 255, which is in Red Slip Ware). Middle Bronze Age. No provenance (the five figures were found together and are now in the Severis Collection, Nicosia). Karageorghis 1975, A1-5.*

Fig. 254 *Ht.13.2 cm.*
Fig. 255 *Ht.13 cm.*
Fig. 256 *Ht.17.7 cm.*
Fig. 257 *Ht.14.5 cm.*
Fig. 258 *Ht.16.5 cm.*

gender of Fig. 250 more likely to have been feminine.

Figs. 251 and 252 are clearly the work of a single artist. These flattened, White Painted figures with folded arms and huge ears differ from one another in one strange detail. Fig. 251 is bare-faced, but the left hand of Fig. 252 is holding a small mask up to cover its own, much larger face. Its own eyes can just be seen peeping out over the top of the mask, and the strangest aspect of this curious figure is that the mask has normal, realistic facial proportions, while the real face behind it is grotesquely distorted. The reason for this rather sophisticated joke is not clear. The only other possible explanation of this figure is that it is meant to be a parent holding a baby up in front of its face to show it to a companion. If this was the intention, it failed, because the mask image is much stronger.

i Long-eared Figures

This is a small group of figures from the Middle Bronze Age that herald the new wave of human representation styles about to arrive in the Late Bronze Age. Although they are slightly flattened from front to back, their bodies are much more rounded than the typical Plank Figures and they barely justify inclusion in this category.

The first (Fig. 253) is an old Cesnola piece excavated in the nineteenth century and now in the Metropolitan Museum in New York. It is unique in being the only incised human figure of this type in Black Slip Ware. Its head and neck remain true to the old Slab Figure tradition, but its ears, arm position, and curvaceous body contours with a widening pelvic region, relate it strongly to the Pubic Triangle Figures of the Late Bronze Age. In short, it is an intermediate.

The other five figurines (Figs. 254-8) were found together and constitute intermediates of a slightly different kind. Here the figures are more slab-like and relate to the earlier style, but there are conspicuous genital markings which link with the Pubic Triangle Figures of the period yet to come. The eyes of two of the figures are surrounded by circles made up of incised dots, and this is a characteristic of earlier Plank Figures (see Pls. 177, 181c and 183b), but the long pierced ears are typical of the Late Bronze Age figures of the future. Again, these are intermediate figures and Karageorghis (1975) sums them up as follows: 'The group of five terracotta female figures offers an important link for the typological evolution from the plank-shaped idols to the fully developed types of the Late Bronze Age.'

This classification of Bronze Age Plank Figures into nine major types inevitably in-

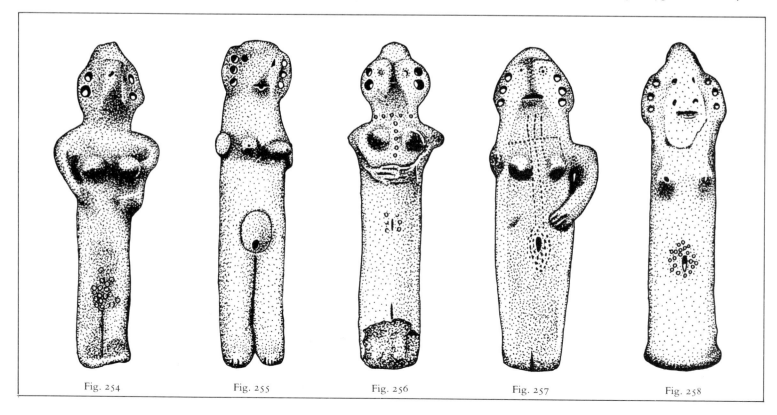

Fig. 254   Fig. 255   Fig. 256   Fig. 257   Fig. 258

volves over-simplification. Despite this, it serves a useful purpose when one attempts to detect trends in style and emphasis during the Early and Middle Bronze Age periods. The *Shoulder, Slab* and *Multi-neck Figures* together form a fascinating group of small terracottas, dominated by a geometric urge to 'square-off' the curves of the human body and transform it into an almost robot-like shape. The mysterious *Comb Figures* are clearly closely related, but have become even more dehumanized. The *Parental* and *Cradle Figures* reflect a strong preoccupation with fertility and reproduction on the part of the Bronze Age artists. The *Vessel-attached Figures* reveal the close link that existed between the tomb pottery and the human figurines. Plank Figures repeatedly appear as embellishments on a variety of vessels, adding their symbolic significance—whatever that might be—to the items in question. It is perhaps too easy simply to say that the Cypriot artists were being 'playful' when they added Plank Figures to tomb vessels in this way. The manner of the addition—the way in which the figure was merged into the shape of the vessel, or was shown growing out of it like some organic development—could certainly be explained as playfully inventive, but the original decision to add a Plank Figure must have had a more specific significance.

Finally, there are the late examples of *Legged* and *Long-eared Figures*, only slightly flattened and already moving out of the long tradition of geometric plaques and on to the more sexual and curvaceous shapes of the Late Bronze Age.

Looking back on this whole array of Plank Figures, there remains the question of their symbolic meaning. Apart from their flatness and their rectangularity, what are their main characteristics? To answer this, sixty examples were analysed feature by feature. The sixty chosen were Incised Red Polished Ware figures of the Shoulder, Slab and Multi-neck types, and the ten most frequently occurring features are shown in Fig. 259. They are expressed as percentages. The most popular element was the nose, appearing on 85 per cent of the sixty figures, and the second most popular was a pair of eyes—on 83 per cent. But natural features by no means dominate. The third most frequent motif was the decorative neck-band (73 per cent), and the fourth was head-gear (68 per cent). Natural and decorative features continue to

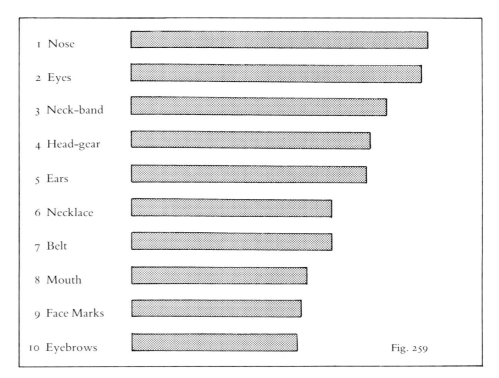

Fig. 259

share the honours as one moves down the scale. The final score is five-each:

Natural Features	Decorative Features
Nose	Neck-band
Eyes	Head-gear
Ears	Necklace
Mouth	Belt
Eyebrows	Facial Markings

The fact that body adornments are given equal prominence with anatomical features confirms my earlier suggestion that Plank Figures represent individuals who are decked out for some special occasion. Indeed, the costume seems to be of more importance than the body beneath it. All the most popular biological features are confined to the facial region. Details of the rest of the body hardly register. The only exceptions are small breasts (38 per cent) and abbreviated arm stumps (28 per cent). Male (0 per cent) and female (3 per cent) genitals are almost non-existent, as are legs, feet, buttocks, hips, knees and waists. Indeed, the lower half of the Plank Figures is so perfunctory as to suggest that it might have been slid, thrust or tucked into something, when in use. None of these figures will stand up on its own. Museums have to construct special stands for them to keep them erect. So what was their position when they were made? Were they placed in small cradles, like dolls, and kept inside dwellings? Were they tucked into special slots on women's clothing and worn

Fig. 259 *Percentage of Plank Figures showing various details (from 60 examples).*

on special occasions, or even day by day? Were they kept upright by being thrust into soft ground and if so where? Were they made purely for placing in a tomb, flat on their backs alongside the deceased? The only clue comes from the Comb Figures which certainly were worn. But perhaps Comb Figures were the pierced, wearable versions of ordinary Plank Figures.

I have already admitted my bias favouring the fertility charm interpretation of prehistoric Cypriot figurines, and the Bronze Age Plank Figures do seem to replace the Chalcolithic Cruciform Figures and the Neolithic Stump Figures in this role. As before there are twin versions and triplet versions. There are also mother-and-baby and baby-in-cradle versions. The conclusion seems inescapable. And yet there is something so un-sexual about these stocky little figures that one is left with nagging doubts. Could they after all be *substitute figures*—effigies of widows placed in their husbands' graves to accompany them in death, thereby avoiding the unhappy entombment of the real widows? Could the babies in cradles be substitutes of surviving infants placed in tombs with their dead mothers?

The only clue to this possible function comes from the curious 'vertical mouth-lines' and 'diagonal arm-lines'. Incised lines running downwards under the nose (seen on 32 per cent of Plank Figures) are too long to be normal facial features, even in an exaggerated form. It is more likely that these lines portray some kind of long pin or costume slit. The same is true of the pair of inward-sloping diagonal lines that appears on 37 per cent of Plank Figures. These have nearly always been referred to as arms, but the Plank Figure shown in Pl. 179 contradicts this, since it has a normal pair of relief-rendered arms and, below them, a pair of the diagonal lines. Also, they do not have any of the usual attributes of arms seen on other figurines from any part of the ancient or modern world. They are unnaturally thin, fingerless, handless and elbowless. Also, they often have strange markings alongside them or at their ends which hint at tucks and folds. In short, they appear to be another costume feature which, like the vertical face 'slit', hints at some sort of shrouding or swaddling that wraps up and encases the body.

The key difference between the two interpretations—fertility figures or substitute entombment figures—is that on the first they were personal objects used during lifetime, and on the second they were specially and exclusively made for the burial. We should be able to settle this argument when, eventually, there have been extensive excavations of Early Bronze Age settlements. To date, almost all our information concerning the period comes from tombs alone, hence the dilemma.

6 Vessel-Shaped Figures

During the Early and Middle Bronze Ages almost all representations of the human form adopted the Plank Figure style, or something approaching it. Figures in the round were extremely rare during this period (although this was not the case with animal figurines). There were only two exceptions—the tiny models of people that appear on large Scenic Vessels (see below, p. 264), and a small group of hollow Vessel-shaped Figures. These have features related to Plank Figures, but are much too three-dimensional to be classed with them.

This type of figure develops out of the Vessel-attached category, where small human faces are placed as decorations on the rims, necks or handles of bowls, jugs or jars. By a small extension of this process, the vessel *becomes* a figure. The vessel neck becomes the human neck, the vessel belly becomes the human belly, the vessel legs become the human legs, and so on. It is surprising that this device, so popular in the pottery of many other cultures, should be so rare in such an inventive ceramic tradition as that of Cyprus. A mere handful of cases are known, of which several are illustrated here. The most dramatic is a big-bellied jar-figure in Red Polished Ware, now in the Sèvres Museum near Paris (Fig. 260). Its arms are clasped around its swollen abdomen, with its distended navel, and give a strong impression of a gravid female about to give birth. This appears to be the only early example of such a complete transformation. Other Red Polished examples are less extensive in their metamorphosis.

The tulip bowl in Pl. 188a, for example, has only become human by the minimum of modification—the mere addition of eyes, eyelashes and a smiling mouth, which automatically convert the handle into a nose and the whole vessel into a human head.

The large jars illustrated in earlier sections (Pl. 186 and Fig. 99) which have ears and faces on the necks become bulging human bodies without the addition of other anatomical details such as arms or legs. And the round-spouted vessels in Red-on-black Ware (Pl. 188c) and Black Slip Ware (Pl. 188b) also become humanized by the mere addition of facial elements to their tall vessel-necks.

In the White Painted Ware of the Middle Bronze Age there are similar modifications. The jug illustrated here (Fig. 261) has a more elaborately transformed neck, giving it a striking head and face; also two small conical breasts and a pair of arm stumps growing out of its upper body. On its left shoulder, near the neck, there are the remains of small feet, presumably once part of a child figure being held by the main jug-figure.

The Pierides Collection in Larnaca possesses a remarkable twin-figure jug (Fig. 262) in which a pair of faces have been added to the necks, and short arm-stumps project from the shoulder of the joined, 'Siamese-

Fig. 260

Fig. 261

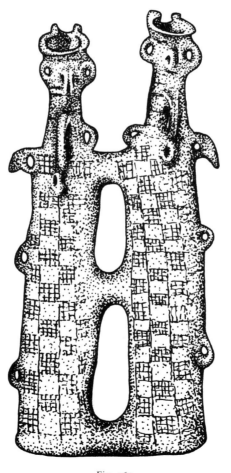

Fig. 262

6 Vessel-shaped Figures

Fig. 260 *No provenance (Sèvres Museum). Red Polished Ware. Early Bronze Age. Ht. 20.5 cm. Hennessy 1979, no. 47.*

Fig. 261 *Morphou. White Painted Ware. Middle Bronze Age. Ht. 23.5 cm. Vermeule 1974, Fig. 48.*

Fig. 262 *No provenance (Pierides Collection, Larnaca). White Painted Ware. Middle Bronze Age.*

twin' bodies. A similar idea, but based on a single-bodied flask, is shown in Pl. 189b. Here, the modification is minimal, but effective. Only ears and eyes have been added, with the handle making a rather unconvincing nose. In Pl. 189a, a small juglet has been humanized by the addition of a face to a vertical extension of the handle.

In almost all these cases there is an inevitable hint of pregnant bellies because of the shape of the vessels, and the potters themselves may have been inspired by the 'pregnant' feel of the vessels they were making, to convert their jugs and jars into female forms. In so doing they were acting out the age-old concept that sees all vessels as the universal symbol of the womb.

7 Bone Figures

The conversion of animal long bones into human figures has been practised in many cultures and at many times. In Cyprus this art form is rare, but a small number of incised animal bones has come to light, and nine of them are illustrated here.

The contours of the bones are little changed, the impact of the image coming almost entirely from the face, positioned at the end of a long, slender 'neck'. The eyes are shown as geometrically precise circles, usually with an inner circle and always with a central incised spot. The mouth is depicted with two or three horizontal lines. Curved eyebrows are always conspicuously present, either as single lines, double lines, or double lines with diagonal hatching between them. A V-shaped 'necklace' hangs below the face of three of them. Ornamental headgear is present above each face. In two instances this headgear appears to have hair sweeping downwards and outwards through it, as though the horizontal part of the headgear is meant to be some kind of headband holding the hair in place.

In many respects these Bone Figures are strongly reminiscent of the Bronze Age Plank Figures (see Figs. 183-5, where the facial details are so similar). It is easy to imagine the same artists trying their hands at both terracottas and decorated bones. Unfortunately for this hypothesis, the five examples which have a known provenance (Figs. 263-7) were all found at Salamis where they were associated with other items that date from the much later Cypro-Archaic

7 Bone Figures

Fig. 263 *Salamis (Tomb 9b, 4). Ht. 6.5 cm.*

Fig. 264 *Salamis (Tomb 9b, 3). Ht. 8.5 cm.*

Fig. 265 *Salamis (Tomb 17, 2). Ht. 6.5 cm.*

Fig. 266 *Salamis (Pyre A, 19a). Ht. 6.5 cm.*

Fig. 267 *Salamis (Pyre A, 19). Ht. 13 cm. For Figs. 263-7 see Karageorghis 1970.*

Fig. 268 *Private collection, London.*

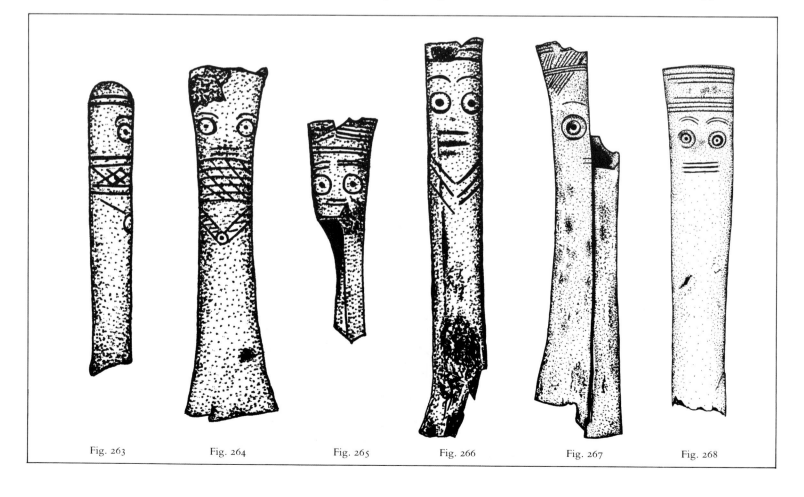

Fig. 263   Fig. 264   Fig. 265   Fig. 266   Fig. 267   Fig. 268

Period in the Iron Age. Three were found in tombs (Figs. 263-5) and two were discovered in the remains of a pyre (Figs. 266-7).

Either the similarity between the Bone Figure facial design and that of the Early Bronze Age Plank Figures is purely coincidental, or the bone figures were prized, ancient possessions of the Cypro-Archaic people who gave them up as tomb and pyre offerings. They may well have come across Early Bronze Age tombs when making new tombs and, inside them, found these strange bone images. Endowing them with magical properties, they may have kept them and then later sacrificed them as burial offerings.

There are three small shreds of evidence to support this far-fetched idea. First, one of the Bone Figures (Pl. 190c) has green copper or bronze stains inside the hole near its base, suggesting that it was in some way fixed to a larger object by a metal pin. In the Cypro-Archaic period these stains would be more likely to be from iron. Second, Bone Figures of this type were being made on the nearby Palestinian mainland in the Early Bronze Age. Third, the facial patterns of the Cypriot Bone Figures are not only very much like those of the Plank Figures, but they are also very *unlike* facial features being employed by artists in the Archaic period.

Only when one of these bones has had a section removed for laboratory dating will we be certain of the true affinity of these rare figures.

Pl. 190

7 Bone figures

Pl. 190 *Bone figures with faces and headgear. Trimmed and polished long bones have been converted into human figures by the addition of incised lines.*

a(left) *Eyes as concentric circles, mouth as three horizontal lines, nose as three vertical lines, and heavy eyebrows shown as curved parallel lines with diagonal hatching inside. The forehead is scored by three horizontal lines. Ht. 14.6 cm (DM-BO-01).*
b(centre) *Eyes as concentric circles, mouth as two horizontal lines and heavy eyebrows as curved parallel lines with diagonal hatching inside. The forehead is scored with horizontal lines, above which there is a band of zigzag elements suggesting headgear of some kind. Ht. 17.9 cm (DM-BO-03).*
c(right) *Same description, except for a variation in the headgear motif. Ht. 16.5 cm (DM-BO-02). There are traces of copper residue around the hole at the base of this figure, as though it was attached to something in its original role.*

8 Pubic Triangle Figures

In the Late Bronze Age, Cypriot artists made a radical change in the way they represented the human figure. The most obvious shift was from the rectangular outline to the curvaceous. The typical Late Bronze Age figurine showed a human form that had wide hips, tapering thighs, differentiated feet on tiptoe, a conspicuous, incised triangle of pubic hair, pointed breasts, spindly arms curved back to the chest, a tapering neck, large 'button' eyes in relief with a ring around them, a sharply protruding nose, and protruding ears.

Within this general category minor variations can be found, but there is far less individuality than there was in the earlier phases of the Bronze Age. For some reason, stricter rules seem to have been laid down as to what a human figurine should look like.

A large number of these figurines has been found, and it is a striking fact that, with only two exceptions, they are all obtrusively female. This is another strong constrast with the earlier phase of the Bronze Age, where the typical figure was biologically almost sexless. It has been suggested that the reason for this shift of emphasis was due to an imported Syrian influence. Astrom (1972) comments: 'It is evident that the Cypriote figurines are derived from the old type of figurine which started in Mesopotamia in the third millennium. Here we can see how the Cypriotes took over an old oriental type … giving it their own individual characteristics.' Karageorghis (1981) is more specific: 'This type of figure originated in Syria and may be connected with Astarte, the divinity of fertility.'

It is certainly true that there is a strong similarity between Syrian female figurines and those of Cyprus during this period. In particular they share the massive pubic triangle, the widely jutting hips and the sloping thighs. Also, they have in common the 'button' eyes, the large ears and the protruding, beak-like noses. This is too much to be put down to coincidence and a strong link between Cyprus and Syria must be accepted. Yet, despite this, there is never any doubt about whether a particular figurine comes from the island or the mainland. The Cypriot females have a unique quality of their own. It is as though the Cypriot artists were told of the special features I have listed above and

were then left to make their own version without ever seeing the original. I am not saying this is precisely what happened, but it certainly seems to have been the case that after the initial influence the island artists went their own way, without further reference to their mainland counterparts.

The function usually suggested for these particular figures is that they were substitute figures placed in the tombs as female companions for the deceased, possibly to provide a painless replacement for a wife who was less than enthusiastic about the idea of premature entombment in the service of her dead husband. The concept of a journey to the other world and of an afterlife was, by now, probably widely popular. The intense sexuality of the female figurines does not necessarily contradict this 'mourner' role for them. As mentioned earlier, the posture of hands to breasts was a special mourning gesture, and it is striking that all the figures are depicted with down-turned feet, as if they are lying on their backs. (The alternative— that they are standing on tiptoe—makes little sense.) If the blatant display of the pubic triangle seems more lusty than bereaved, perhaps they were anticipating a long trip. The deceased might appreciate a few diversions.

Against this interpretation must be put the observation that many of these figures are shown suckling their babies. Their huge, child-bearing hips and their maternal condition could easily be the result of another phase of the 'fertility charm' story proposed earlier. Alternatively, at this stage in the ancient history of Cyprus, there is no reason to suppose that a more organized form of religion was absent from local culture, and the Pubic Triangle Figures may have been the first true 'Mother Goddesses' on the island. At present we have no way of choosing between these different views.

There were two main styles in the Late Bronze Age depiction of the human form. Both were in Base Ring Ware and about the same size and colour, but several features differed between them. They are summarized below. To give the two types labels, I have chosen two diagnostic features: Headgear and earrings. The thick-necked Headgear Figures have a completely flattened top to the head and their ears are squashed downwards by the tightly fitting hat. Even though the headgear is barely differentiated, it always has this marked effect of pushing the ears down to a startling degree. The thinner-necked Earring Figures have huge, vertical, flanged ears pierced several times for earrings. There are no intermediates between the two. They seem to represent rival traditions, with the Earring Figures being closer to the Syrian prototype.

PUBIC TRIANGLE FIGURES

Headgear Figures	Earring Figures
Large flat top to head.	Small top to head.
Ears point down.	Ears vertical.
Ears unpierced.	Ears pierced for earrings.
Nose sharper and more pointed.	Nose deeper and more rounded.
Nostril slits common.	Nostrils absent.
Mouth slit common	Mouth absent.
Pointed chin.	No chin.
Neck thick.	Neck thinner.
Painted neck-band.	Incised neck-band.
Baby in arms rare.	Baby in arms common.
Pierced navel common.	Navel rare.
Hips wide.	Hips wider.
Pubic triangle painted.	Pubic triangle unpainted.

The following categories have been traced:

a Headgear Figures

1 Simple vertical figures (Figs. 269-72 and Pls. 191-3)

About thirty of these have been published and there are undoubtedly many more. They are all without a babe-in-arms and almost all of them are shown clasping their hands to their bodies just below the breasts, but not actually touching them. In two unusual cases (with rather broader faces) the arms are down at the sides of the body.

2 Seated figures (Figs. 273-5)

Six examples are known, and in all cases the figures are similar to those above, except for the fact that they are in a seated posture with two legs of a stool protruding from the region of the buttocks.

3 Seated figure with baby (Fig. 276)

This is the only Headgear Figure in a maternal pose. The highly simplified figure of the baby is shown feeding at the left breast.

4 Figures wearing skirts (Fig. 277)

Only five examples of these 'Astarte Bottles' appear to have been published. The head, neck, arms, breasts and upper body are typical of the Headgear Figures, but the legs have become invisible beneath a floor-length, patterned skirt. Also, on top of the head there is a small bowl which serves as the opening of the bottle.

5 Figure holding bull (Fig. 278)

The single example of this category is un-

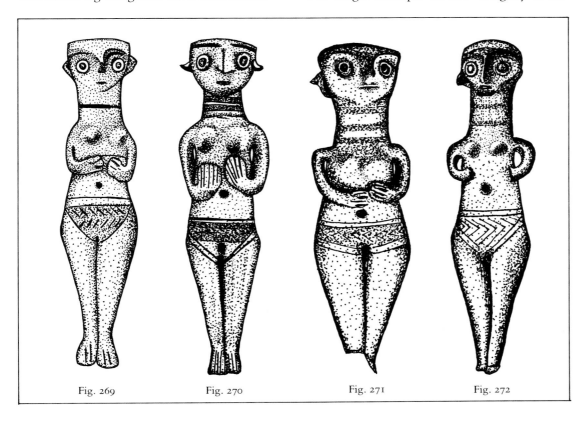

Fig. 269   Fig. 270   Fig. 271   Fig. 272

8 Headgear Figures

Figs. 269-72 *Base Ring Ware. Late Bronze Age.*

Fig. 269 *No provenance (Pierides Collection, Larnaca). Ht. 22.5 cm. Karageorghis 1973, no. 27.*

Fig. 270 *Dromolaxia. Ht. 21.2 cm. Admiral 1982, Pl. III, 1.*

Fig. 271 *No provenance (Louvre Museum). Ht. 19.8 cm. Caubet 1971, Pl. IV, 2.*

Fig. 272 *No provenance (Louvre Museum). Ht. 21.5 cm. Caubet 1971, Pl. IV, 1.*

8a Headgear Figures

Pl. 191 *Smaller than usual, this figure has its body flattened. The legs are missing, but the pubic triangle survives to show that its interior is plain and lacks the usual 'pubic hair' incision motif. In other respects the figure is typical, with the flat headgear pressing the ears downwards and the arms clasped to the chest beneath the breasts. Base Ring Ware. Late Bronze Age. Ht. (of surviving section) 9 cm (DM-BR-37).*

Pl. 191

Pl. 192 *Another small example, this one is perhaps the least typical. Unusual features are: ears which are not pressed downwards by the flat headgear; less beak-like nose; less pointed chin; arms which are placed akimbo instead of below breasts; incised neck-band and necklace. Base Ring Ware. Late Bronze Age. Ht. 13.5 cm (DM-BR-38). The feet are missing.*

Pl. 192

Pl. 193 *Typical example, with flat-topped headgear; ears pressed downwards; beaky, pointed nose; roundel eyes; pointed chin; thick neck; hands below breasts; pierced navel; large pubic triangle with 'pubic hair' incisions; feet in tiptoe posture. There are faint traces of black paint in the region of the neck and the pubic triangle. Base Ring Ware. Late Bronze Age. Ht. 19.1 cm (DM-BR-36).*

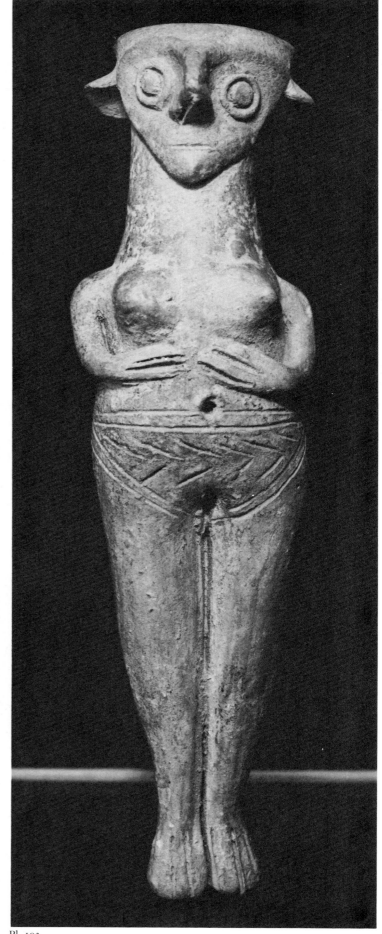

Pl. 193

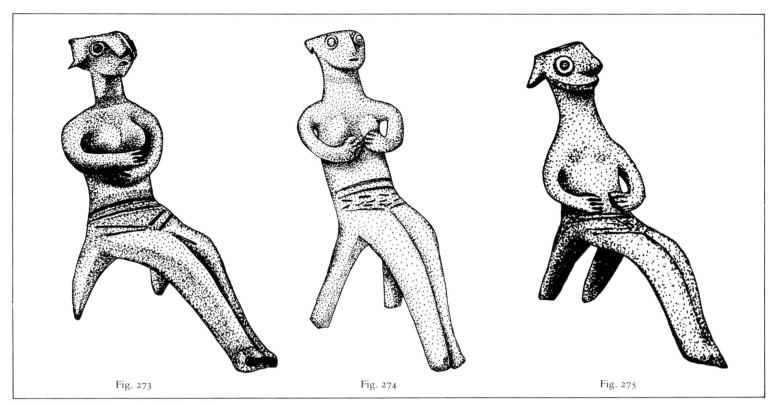

Fig. 273   Fig. 274   Fig. 275

usual in that the figure has no breasts and a conspicuous penis. It is shown grasping the right horn of the bull with both hands. Both bull and man face in the same direction. It has been boldly stated that 'the animal is intended for sacrifice'. This may be true and there were undoubtedly animal sacrifices on frequent occasions during this epoch, but it is also possible that the man is shown engaging in bull-jumping, bull-wrestling or some other sort of dangerous sport. Alternatively,' he could simply be a farmer leading his bull, or, at the other extreme, the spirit of man engaging some taurine symbol of power. We simply have no way of settling this matter at present.

6 Figure riding horse (Fig. 279)
This remarkable figure, shown sitting side-saddle on a horse, was discovered as recently as 1979. Like the last one it appears to be male, although Karageorghis seems to be of two minds about it. In 1980 he says, 'the male sex is shown in relief', but in 1981 he comments, 'the sex of the rider is not indicated.' The problem is that the 'genital bulge' is rather small and it is risky to label a figure as masculine in such a predominantly feminine genre. However, there are no breasts present and this suggests that the figure really is male. Like the previous one, he is provided with a bar of dark paint above the genital region, indicating pubic hair, but

Fig. 276

8a Headgear Figures

Figs. 273-6 *Seated Figures. Base Ring Ware. Late Bronze Age.*

Fig. 273 *Katydhata. Ht. 9.5 cm. Buchholz and Karageorghis 1973, no. 1727.*

Fig. 274 *No provenance. (Ashmolean Museum, Oxford). Ht. 10 cm. Karageorghis 1975, Pl. VIII, 1.*

Fig. 275 *Psilatos. Ht. 10.5 cm. Karageorghis 1975, Pl. VII, 7.*

Fig. 276 *No provenance (Nationalmuseet, Copenhagen). Ht. 8.6 cm. Karageorghis 1975, Pl. VII, 6.*

Fig. 277 *Figure with skirt. Base Ring Ware. Late Bronze Age. No provenance (Ashmolean Museum, Oxford). Ht. 13.3 cm. Brown and Catling 1980, Fig. 44.*

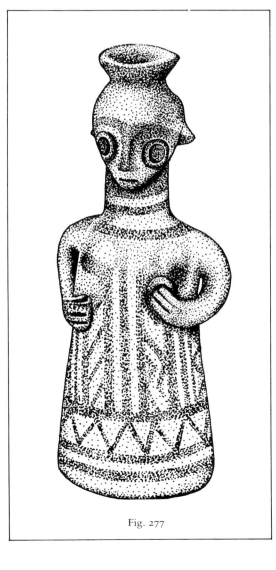

Fig. 277

8a Headgear Figures

Figs. 278-9 *Figures with animals. Base Ring Ware. Late Bronze Age.*
Fig. 278 *Man with bull. Kazaphani. Ht. 12 cm. Karageorghis 1976, no. 162.*
Fig. 279 *Man on horse. No provenance (Cyprus Museum). Ht. 15.8 cm. Karageorghis 1980, Pl. XVII, 1.*

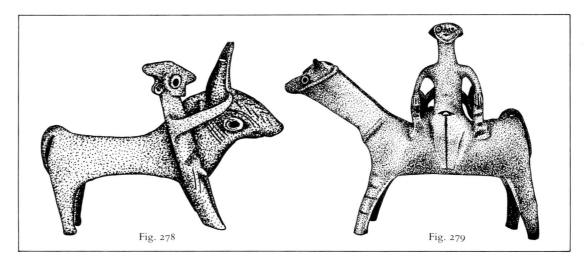

Fig. 278   Fig. 279

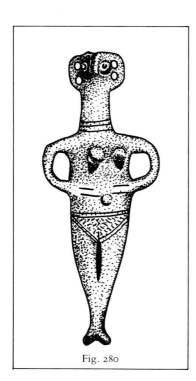

Fig. 280

8b Earring Figures

Fig. 280 Slender type. *Base Ring Ware. Late Bronze Age. No provenance (University of California, Robert Lowie Museum). Ht. 20.9 cm. Karageorghis et al. 1974, Fig. 30.*

Pl. 194 Slender type. *The head and breasts are missing, the arms are held in the akimbo posture. There is a large pubic triangle on the slender pelvis, with a zigzag 'pubic hair' motif. The feet are shown on tiptoe. Base Ring Ware. Late Bronze Age. Ht. 14.6 cm (DM-BR-39).*

not a full pubic triangle. The 'rider' is ignoring the horse with both his eyes and his hands. It is as if the animal has become part of an ornate throne on which the important figure is sitting in splendour. He is certainly no traveller, unless the journey is a purely symbolic one, or he is being attended by careful, but invisible horse-handlers, who are controlling the animal while he gazes off sideways into space.

b Earring Figures

1 Slender vertical figures
Although Earring Figures typically have very wide hips, one or two examples are known where the whole body is much more slender. In this type, the arms curve further away from the body so that the hands come to rest on the sides of the trunk and lower down than usual (see Fig. 280 and Pl. 194).

2 Simple vertical figures
Earring Figures without babies are comparatively rare, but a number are known, including the extremely wide-hipped one shown in Pl. 195. They stand in a similar posture to the Headgear type, with their arms bent round so that their hands clasp the front of the body just below the breasts.

3 Vertical figures with baby
This is the most common type of Earring Figure. About twenty have been published and a number of others are known to exist. The baby is always held on the left side of the chest, near to the mother's heart. The infant is usually shown sitting up, with its head out of contact with the mother's body (see Figs. 281-6), but in the three examples shown in Pls. 196-8, the baby is feeding at the left breast. Pottery earrings, varying in number from one to four, have survived in at least nine cases.

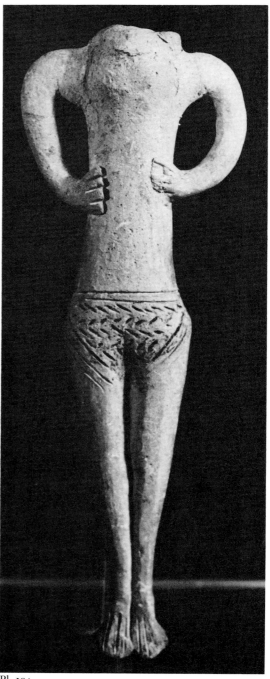

Pl. 194

8b Earring Figures

Pl. 195 *This large figure with greatly widened hips is characteristic of its type except for the fact that it is not holding a baby in its left arm. The huge ears are each pierced twice. There is a neck-band and necklace, indicated by incisions. The prominent breasts are pointed. The arms are clasped to the body just below the breasts and there is a large pubic triangle with interior 'pubic hair' motif. The tapering legs end in poorly formed feet. Base Ring Ware. Late Bronze Age. Ht. 20.7 cm (DM-BR-43).*

Pl. 195

Pl. 196

Pl. 197

Pl. 198

8b Earring Figures

Pl. 196 *Female suckling a baby at her left breast. The mother's large ears are pierced twice for earrings. Above the pointed nose and roundel eyes are clearly marked eyebrows. There is a neck-band but no necklace. Although the legs are missing, it is clear that there is a large pubic triangle with interior 'pubic hair' motif. Base Ring Ware. Late Bronze Age. Ht. (of surviving section) 11.2 cm (DM-BR-42).*

Pl. 197 *Female suckling a baby at her left breast. Smaller than usual, this figure has an exceptionally short chest and belly region, the pubic triangle reaching almost up to the breasts. Base Ring Ware. Late Bronze Age. Ht. 13.5 cm (DM-BR-40). Head restored.*

Pl. 198 *Female suckling a baby at her left breast. The mother's large ears are each pierced three times for earrings. Eyebrows are present as incision marks. There is a neck-band but no necklace. There is more detail than usual on the baby: its nose, eyes and ears are shown and its arms are clasping the mother's chest. The pubic triangle shows the typical 'pubic hair' motif. Base Ring Ware. Late Bronze Age. Ht. 19.2 cm (DM-BR-41). The feet are restored.*

Figs. 281–6 *Figures holding babies. Base Ring Ware. Late Bronze Age.*

Fig. 281 *Hagios Theodoros Soleas, Alonia (Tomb 2). Ht. 18.5 cm. Buchholz and Karageorghis 1973, no. 1722.*

Fig. 282 *No provenance (Cyprus Museum). Ht. 14 cm. Buchholz and Karageorghis 1973, no. 1723.*

Fig. 283 *No provenance (Cyprus Museum). Ht. 21 cm. Karageorghis 1969, Fig. 78.*

Fig. 284 *No provenance (Louvre Museum). Ht. 20.5 cm. Caubet 1971, Pl. IV, 5.*

Fig. 285 *No provenance (Louvre Museum). Ht. 18.5 cm. Caubet 1971, Pl. IV, 7.*

Fig. 286 *Tyr. Ht. 24 cm. Caubet 1971, Pl. IV, 3.*

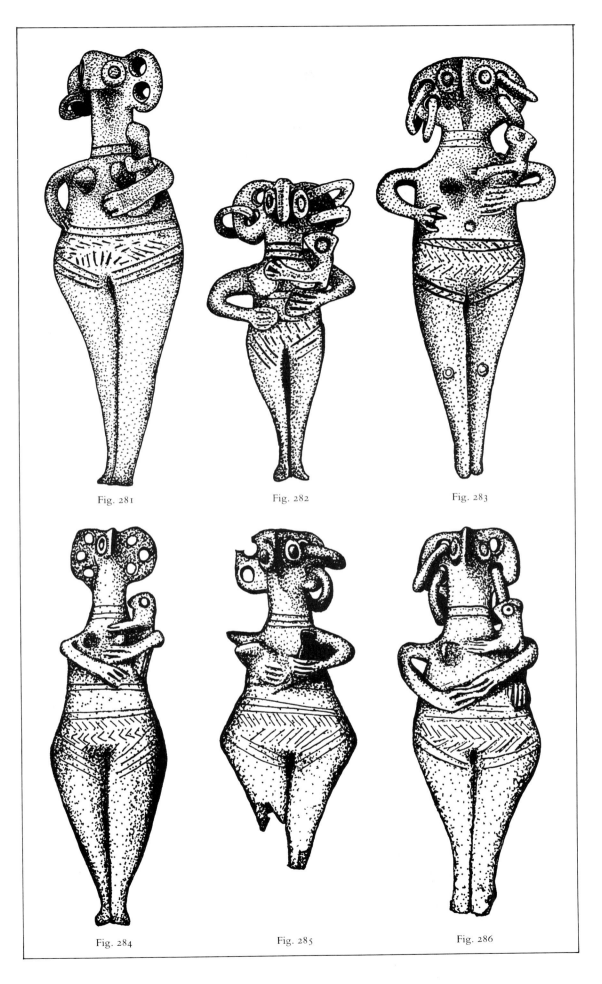

Fig. 281

Fig. 282

Fig. 283

Fig. 284

Fig. 285

Fig. 286

8b Earring Figures

Fig. 287 *Figure playing tambourine (or carrying a circular loaf of bread as a food offering). Base Ring Ware. Late Bronze Age. No provenance (Louvre Museum). Ht. 12 cm. Caubet 1971, Pl. IV, 4.*

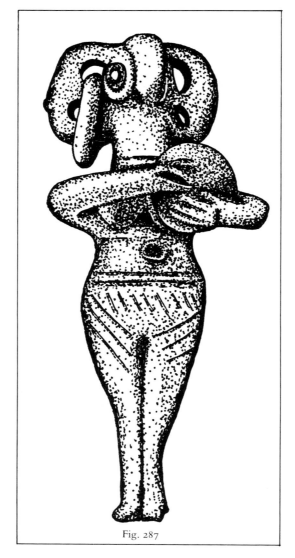

Fig. 287

4 Vertical figure with tambourine

A unique figure in the Louvre shows a typical Earring Figure holding to her left breast not a baby but a tambourine. Tambourines are common later on, in the Cypro-Archaic period (see p. 179) where they are held in the arms of Snowman Figures, but this Louvre figurine is the only example known from the Bronze Age. (The possibility that the 'tambourine' might in fact be an offering in the shape of a circular loaf of bread has also been mentioned.)

9 Snowman Figures

With the arrival of the Iron Age 3,000 years ago, the lovingly made figurines of the prehistoric period give way to the mass-produced Snowman Figures that will dominate for centuries to come. Hundreds of these small figurines have been unearthed, and the majority are casually made with minimal aesthetic content. True, large terracottas and important statues do appear from time to time, but it is the crudely made 'snowmen' that are typical of the epoch.

Despite this change, some of the better Iron Age figurines do manage to retain the vigour and humour so typical of the Cypriot ceramic tradition, and a number of examples are illustrated here.

A survey of the different types of Snowman Figure soon reveals a shift of emphasis in the type of person depicted. Mothers holding babies are now a rarity. They are replaced by worshippers, musicians, offering-bearers and warriors. These trends first appear at the end of the Bronze Age, where several important bronze statues of warrior figures and some small terracottas of females in postures of worship arrive on the scene, but they do not become common until the Geometric and Archaic periods that follow. Clearly the function of these figures is changing, and they can no longer be discussed in the same terms as the prehistoric fertility charms.

Because they exist in such huge numbers, no attempt is made here to conduct a comprehensive survey. Instead, a sample of some of the most popular types will be given. A simplified classification is as follows:

  a Figures with both arms raised.
  b Figures with outstretched arms.
  c Figures with arms held straight at the sides.
  d Figures with arms clasped to chest.
  e Figures with one arm clasped to chest.
  f Necklace figures.
  g Musician figures.
  h Figures carrying food or drink.
  i Figures carrying an animal.
  j Figures carrying a child.
  k Masked figures.
  l Warrior figures.
  m Mounted figures.

a Figures with both arms raised

Like all Snowman Figures, these have a crudely cylindrical body with a slightly flared base for support. The arms are raised so that the hands are at about eye level or slightly below it. The palms, where indicated, face forward. Breasts are usually shown in relief. The head is typically tilted back as if the figure is gazing skywards. Some kind of headgear is indicated in most cases.

Nicolaou (1979) expresses a widely held view when he comments that 'it is unlikely that this type of figure derived from the

Mycenaean type or from earlier figurines in Cyprus. So that the sudden appearance in the Island, in the eleventh century BC, of a type common in Crete suggests that it was introduced from that island.' The main difference between the Minoan originals and their Cypriot copies is that the Cretan females are shown with a narrow waist that flares out into a wide skirt. In the Cypriot examples the waist is never differentiated in this way. But the posture of the arms is very similar in the two cases, especially when one compares the Minoan figures with the earlier Cypriot examples (see Figs. 288-9). In both there is a distinct bending at the elbows. This detail is

lost in the later, Archaic figurines (see Pl. 199), where everything is simplified and the arms become upward curved stumps with no elbow angle visible.

The uplifted arms and slightly upturned face are typical of the pose of an early worshipper. It is as if the figure is reaching up to the deity, a much more ancient gesture than the palm-to-palm posture of prayer that is in use today. It clearly identifies the figures as worshippers *of* a deity rather than the deity herself but despite this obvious interpretation, this type of Snowman Figure is often misleadingly referred to as the 'goddess with uplifted arms'.

9a Figures with both arms raised

Figs. 288-9 *Early Iron Age.*
Fig. 288 *No provenance (Pierides Collection, Larnaca). Bichrome Ware. Ht. 23.5 cm. Karageorghis 1973, no. 71.*
Fig. 289 *Morphou-Toumba tou Skourou. White Painted Ware. Ht. 16 cm. Karageorghis 1969, no. 101.*

Fig. 288

Fig. 289

Pl. 199

9a Figures with both arms raised

Pl. 199 *Female figures with tall, frontally flattened headgear. Some with breasts, some without. Facial features restricted largely to nose and ears. Only faint traces of black and red paint surviving. Bichrome Ware. Iron Age.*

Left to right
a *Ht. 17.7 cm (DM-BI-77).*
b *Ht. 18 cm (DM-BI-76).*
c *Ht. 11.3 cm (DM-BI-80).*
d *Ht. 16.7 cm (DM-BI-78).*
e *Ht. 16.5 cm (DM-BI-79).*

9b Figures with outstretched arms

Pl. 200 *Male figure, bearded and helmeted, with backward tilted head. A suspension hole pierces through the helmet. Two more holes pierce the rim of the figure's short skirt. From these a pair of legs originally hung, but they are missing. White Painted Ware. Early Iron Age. Ht. 12.7 cm (DM-WWP-183).*

Pl. 200

b Figures with outstretched arms

A type popular in the Cypro-Geometric period shows a bearded figure wearing a helmet and with his arms spread wide as if greeting someone or offering an embrace (see Pl. 200 and Figs. 290-2). The most likely interpretation is that these figures are offering their embraces, not to a human companion, but to their deity. The lower part of the body is bell-shaped and pierced with two holes, one on each side. This suggests that they were once fitted with moveable legs, but sadly no legs have survived.

c Figures with arms held straight at the sides

A rigid posture of figures 'standing to attention' is sometimes seen (Pl. 201), but whether this has any special significance or is simply a perfunctory design of a formal type is not clear. It has the effect of reducing the objects to crude metaphors for the human figure.

d Figures with arms clasped to the chest (Pl. 202)

This common posture was probably popular, not so much because of its symbolic gestural message, but because it was simple to make and the folded arms were less easily broken off or damaged. It is possible, however, that it is meant to present the chest-clutching action of the mourner discussed earlier. If this is the case, then, these figures may safely be interpreted as small mourner-substitute figures.

e Figures with one arm clasped to chest

This is a variant of the last type and may be interpreted in the same way. In some cases the other arm is raised (Pl. 203a), but it may also be lowered (Pl. 203b). The clasp + raise examples appear to be a compromise between types 9a and 9d, with the figure uplifting an arm to the deity while at the same time clutching the chest in mourning.

f Necklace figures

One group of Snowman Figures shows individuals wearing heavy necklaces which are so emphasized that they must have had some special status significance (see Pl. 204). Characteristically these figures have a second adornment in the shape of a matching neckband. They tend to have long hair beneath their heavy headgear and are usually holding offerings or playing musical instruments.

Fig. 290   Fig. 291   Fig. 292

Pl. 201

9b Figures with outstretched arms

Figs. 290-2 *Early Iron Age.*
Fig. 290 *Rizokarpaso-Latsia. Ht. 9 cm. Christou 1972, Pl. XXVI, 17.*
Fig. 291 *Rizokarpaso-Latsia. Ht. 10 cm. Christou 1972, Pl. XXVI, 46.*
Fig. 292 *Rizokarpaso-Latsia. Ht. 11.7 cm. Christou 1972, Pl. XXVI, 45.*

9c Figures with arms held straight at sides

Pl. 201 *Statuesque figure with headgear. Formal posture with no expressive elements. Limestone, with traces of red paint. Iron Age. Ht. 18.2 cm (DM-ST-23).*

g Musician figures

Many of the Snowman Figures are shown in the act of playing some kind of musical instrument. The most popular is the tambourine (see Pl. 205a-f and Pl. 206), but harps and pipes (Pl. 205g) are also known.

h Figures carrying food and drink

A number of examples have been found in which the figure is depicted offering a plate

9d Figures with arms clasped to chest

Pl. 202 *Crudely modelled features. Faint traces of paint. Bichrome Ware. Iron Age.*

Left to right
a *Ht. 14 cm (DM-BI-83).*
b *Ht. 13.5 cm (DM-BI-86).*
c *Ht. 13.1 cm (DM-BI-87).*
d *Ht. 14.7 cm (DM-BI-84).*
e *Ht. 14.2 cm (DM-BI-85).*

Pl. 202

9e Figures with one arm to chest

Pl. 203

a(left) *Figure with left arm to chest and right arm raised. Faint traces of paint. Bichrome Ware. Iron Age. Ht. 14 cm (DM-BI-88).*
b(right) *Figure with right arm to chest and left arm down by side. Tall conical headgear. Traces of painted stripes on body. Bichrome Ware. Iron Age. Ht. 16 cm (DM-BI-89).*

9f Figures with heavy necklaces

Pl. 204

a(left) *Figure with heavy headgear, neck-band and necklace. Faint traces of paint. Bichrome Ware. Iron Age. Ht. 19 cm (DM-BI-90).*
b(right) *Figure with heavy neck-band and necklace, the left hand holding a bowl in front of the chest. Traces of paint. Bichrome Ware. Iron Age. Ht. 17.6 cm (DM-BI-91).*

Pl. 203

Pl. 204

Pl. 205

Pl. 206

9g Figures with musical instruments

Pl. 205 *Tambourine players. Traces of paint. Bichrome Ware. Iron Age.*

Left to right

a *Ht. 15.2 cm (DM-BI-96).*
b *Ht. 15 cm (DM-BI-94).*
c *Ht. 14.1 cm (DM-BI-95).*
d *Ht. 17.6 cm (DM-BI-97).*
e *Ht. 16 cm (DM-BI-93).*
f *Ht. 15.5 cm (DM-BI-92).*
g *Flute player, upper section only. Traces of paint. Ht. (of surviving section) 6.2 cm (DM-BI-99).*

Pl. 206 *Tambourine player. Tambourine is held flat to the chest. The figure is bearded and has the head tilted back. There is a suspension hole drilled through the conical headgear. Two more holes pierce the flared 'skirt', presumably for the attachment of movable legs. The paintwork has survived well. Bichrome Ware. Iron Age. Ht. 13.7 cm (DM-BI-98). It is possible that this figure and the other 'tambourine players' above are, in reality, carrying food offerings in the shape of circular loaves.*

of food or carrying a jug of liquid. This may be symbolic of an offering to the gods, or for the deceased in the case of a burial.

i Figures carrying an animal

This is a rare category and may represent a sacrificial offering, or the bringing of food as a simple sustenance offering for the gods or the deceased.

j Figures carrying a child

Again, this is rare during the Iron Age, but a few examples do exist.

k Masked figures

A handful of examples are known in which the human figures are depicted wearing animal masks. Usually they are portrayed at the moment of taking off or putting on the mask, their hands raised to hold it. This was no doubt done to make it clear that the figures in question *were* human and not some mythological man–animal. The animal in question is nearly always the bull. These figures have been interpreted by different authors as representing priests, worshippers or dancers, but all agree that they are meant to symbolize some kind of ritualistic performance.

l Warrior figures

The arrival of male warriors as art objects began back in the Late Bronze Age, from which period a few large and important bronzes have been discovered showing muscular figures wearing horned helmets and in one case brandishing a spear and a shield. This introduction of war and fighting as a subject for human figurines was a completely new departure, and it grew in popularity during the Iron Age epoch which followed. Some of the best of the Snowman Figures belong to this category, often adorned with bright bichrome colours, helmets, beards and painted shields (see Pl. 209). Some, such as the damaged figure shown in Pl. 208, have a small vertical hole pierced into the top of the helmet, suggesting that a special decoration,

9l Warriors

Pl. 207 *Bearded, helmeted figure, wearing heavy shoulder pads. All traces of paint lost, but probably Bichrome Ware. Iron Age. Ht. 10.3 cm (DM-BI-100).*

Pl. 208 *Short figure wearing a crestlike helmet. A vertical hole is drilled into the top the helmet, presumably for the insertion of a plume. There is also a pierced hole at the bottom of the flared 'skirt'. Traces of paint survive on the lower section. Bichrome Ware. Iron Age. Ht. 10.2 cm (DM-BI-101).*

Pl. 207

Pl. 208

such as a feather or a military emblem of some kind, was added.

m Mounted figures

Bearded figures are often shown mounted on horses (Pls. 210, 235 and 236, and Figs. 332–8) or other animals (such as goats, see Fig. 355). Many of these are extremely crudely formed, but a few are carefully made and brightly coloured, and it is these that are among the finest of the small Iron Age figurines.

Another attractive type of mounted figure is found peeping over the rim of decorated chariot-models. Again, there are crude, poorly made examples of this subject—many of them—but the handful of carefully made 'small-figure-in-a-large-chariot' examples are particularly appealing (see Pl. 211). Whether these are meant to represent a particular charioteer, or whether they are models of magical chariots to provide the deceased with a vehicle for transportation to the other world is not clear. The scale of the diminutive human figure in the relatively vast chariot suggests the latter interpretation.

Pl. 209

9l Warriors

Pl. 209 *Bearded figure wearing a conical helmet and carrying a circular shield. The head is tilted back. The lower body flares out into a 'skirt' in which two holes are drilled, presumably for the attachment of movable legs. The paintwork has survived well. Bichrome Ware. Iron Age. Ht 12.8 cm (DM-BI-102).*

9m Mounted Figures

Pl. 210 *Horse-riders. The riders' legs are not depicted. Their hands cling to the horses' necks. Conical headgear is worn. Traces of paint survive. Bichrome Ware. Iron Age.*
a(left) *Ht. 12.5 cm (DM-BI-110).*
b(right) *Ht. 14 cm (DM-BI-111).*

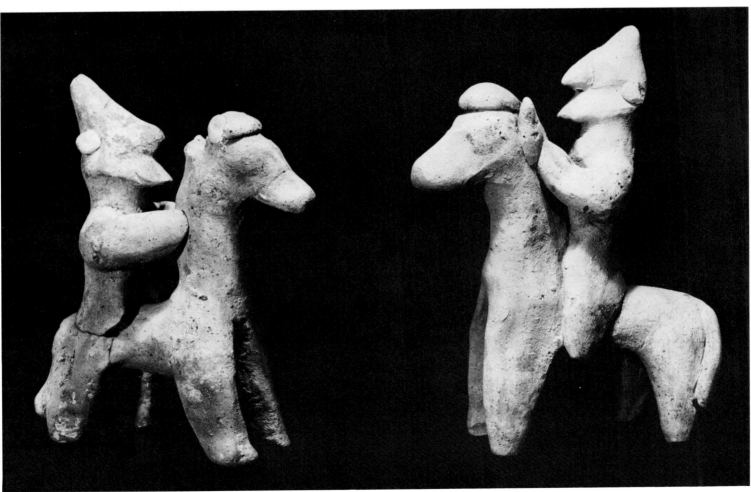

Pl. 210

9m Mounted Figures

Pl. 211 *Chariot-rider. The tiny figure of the rider is dwarfed by the huge chariot, suggesting that it is meant to represent a supernatural chariot to carry him to the other world, rather than a real one. Bichrome Ware. Iron Age. Ht. 23.2 cm (DM-BI-103).*

Pl. 211

10 Realistic Figures

The final phase of human representation in the ancient art of Cyprus sees the arrival on the island of the more realistic styles of Greece and Rome (see Pl. 212), with the human figure portrayed in naturalistic proportions and with features lacking the high degree of stylization and schematization so typical of the earlier epochs. At this stage, we are dealing with what amounts to 'colonial art', and although beautiful examples have been found on the island in large numbers, there is little specifically or uniquely Cypriot about them and they will not be pursued here.

10 Realistic Figures

Pl. 212 *Large, bearded human head. Red terracotta. Ht. 30 cm (DM-RT-01). This head must once have belonged to an almost life-size statue.*

Pl. 212

Animal Forms

1 Deer

Figs. 293-6 *Deer figures with antlers. Incised Red Polished Ware. Early Bronze Age.*

Fig. 293 *Vounous (Tomb 160a, no. 11). Ht. 8.7 cm. Stewart and Stewart 1950, Pl. XXIV, 11.*

Fig. 294 *No provenance (University of California, Robert Lowie Museum). Ht 15.2 cm. Karageorghis et al. 1974, no. 6.*

Fig. 295 *No provenance (Sèvres Museum). (MNC 10 689).*

Fig. 296 *No provenance (Ashmolean Museum, Oxford). Ht. 17 cm. Brown and Catling 1975, Pl. VI.*

Although animal representations were extremely rare in the Cypriot art of the Neolithic and Chalcolithic periods, they became common in the Bronze Age and the Iron Age. The main focus of interest was on the domesticated species. Wild animals and mythological beasts attracted less attention. This preference is not surprising because, being a small island, Cyprus did not offer a dramatic indigenous fauna to inspire the ancient artists. Apart from bats, there were only eight species of wild mammals available: the Cyprian moufflon or wild sheep, the fox, the hare, the long-eared hedgehog, the shrew, the rat, the mouse and the spiny mouse. Of these, only the moufflon was ever to figure in the early art of the island. Even the representations of the moufflon must be treated with extreme caution, since the early settlers brought domestic sheep with them

and a domestic ram would be indistinguishable from a male moufflon in the stylized art of the Bronze Age.

Domestic animals brought to the island by man in the Neolithic period were the Mesopotamian fallow deer, the pig, the goat and the sheep. During the Bronze Age, cattle, camels, horses, donkeys and dogs were added.

There are 313 species of birds on Cyprus and, although early artists were far from specific in portraying avian subjects, it is clear that vultures, eagles, ducks, pigeons or doves, partridges and song birds were all depicted.

The island also has venomous snakes, various lizards including chameleons, also tortoises, frogs and toads. Of these, only the snake figures importantly in the ancient art of the island.

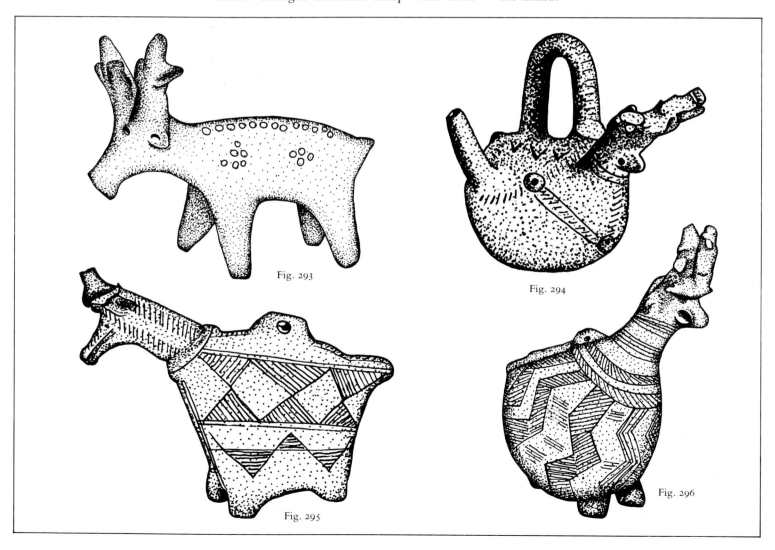

Fig. 293

Fig. 294

Fig. 295

Fig. 296

1 Deer

The deer of ancient Cyprus was *Dama meso-potamica*, the Mesopotamian fallow deer, a close relative of the common fallow deer so well known today from the parks and zoos of Europe. The two forms differ most conspicuously in the shape of the antlers. The Mesopotamian species has a greater flattening in the lower part of the antlers, but lacks the distal palmation so characteristic of the common fallow. The natural range of the Mesopotamian deer was Iran and Iraq, but today it is almost extinct. Fortunately, a breeding herd has been established at the Kronberg Zoo in West Germany, where they are being carefully studied (see Pls. 213 and 214).

As in all deer species, except the reindeer, the female lacks antlers. This creates a difficulty if an artist wishes to portray a female deer, since its shape is not sufficiently distinctive. The novel solution is to produce what has been called a 'female stag'. In other words, antlers are provided to label the creature as 'deer' and then the female gender is signified either by showing the animal suckling its young (see Pl. 298 and Fig. 299), or by a deliberate omission of the prominent male 'adam's apple' (see Pl. 215), or by the depiction of a pair of antlered animals, one with and one without a conspicuous penis (see Fig. 302). The one ancient artist who did bravely attempt something more zoologically correct (see Fig. 297), failed, at least, to convince modern authors, who have referred to her figure of a female deer simply as 'animal-

Pl. 213

Pl. 214

1 Deer

Pl. 213 *The male Mesopotamian Fallow Deer (Dama mesopotamica). This is the species of deer which lived on Cyprus. It is extremely rare today, but a small breeding herd has been established in a West German Zoo (photo by courtesy of Kronberg Zoo).*

Pl. 214 *The female Mesopotamian Fallow Deer (photo by courtesy of Kronberg Zoo).*

Fig. 297 *Female deer figure. Incised Red Polished Ware. Early Bronze Age. No provenance (Cyprus Museum). Ht. 16 cm. Buchholz and Karageorghis 1973, no. 1524.*

Fig. 298 *Deer with small animal on neck. Because the small animal has lost its head, it is impossible to decide whether the artist intended it to represent a dog attacking the deer, or a young fawn jumping playfully on its parent's body. The former seems more likely. White Painted Ware. Middle Bronze Age. The paint has largely worn away. No provenance (Pierides Collection, Larnaca). Ht. 14 cm. Belgiorno 1980, no. 11.*

Fig. 297

Fig. 298

1 Deer

Pl. 215 *Stag from a scenic vessel (see p. 265). The body is marked with rows of spots and there is a distinctively large, male 'adam's apple'. The four legs rise directly from the shoulder of the parent vessel. The jug on which it stands is intermediate between Late Red Polished Ware and Drab Polished Ware. Early to Middle Bronze Age. Ht. of stag 10.5 cm (DM-DP-36).*

Pl. 216

a(left) *Stag from a large vessel. This small deer figure was clearly once attached to the shoulder or rim of a large vessel, probably a pottery box of the kind shown in des Gagniers and Karageorghis 1976, Pl. XVII, no. 1. The animal is given no legs, being connected to the parent vessel by a central stem. Incised Red Polished Ware. Early Bronze Age. Ht. 5.7 cm (DM-IRP-91).*
b(right) *Same description, except that the deer is larger and includes the detail of a prominent 'adam's apple'. Ht. 9.6 cm (DM-IRP-90).*

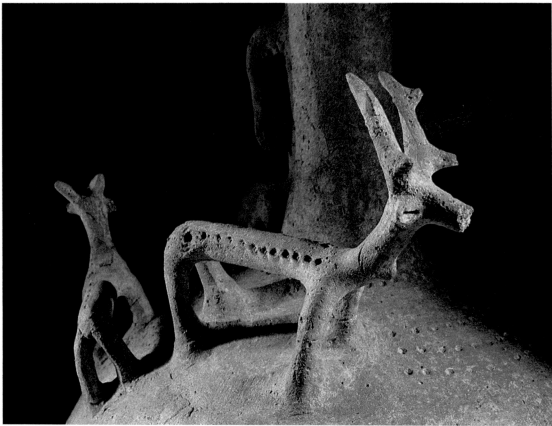

Pl. 215

Pl. 216

Pl. 217

1 Deer

Pl. 217
a(left) *Stag figure with hollow body and circular aperture on chest. The globular body has three stump-legs and a small loop handle in the middle of the back. Handmade White Painted Ware. Middle Bronze Age. Ht. 15 cm (DM-HWP-61). Antler tips restored.*
b(right) *Stag's head. Handmade White Painted Ware. Middle Bronze Age. Ht. 5.3 cm (DM-HWP-62).*

Pl. 218 *Deer figure. Solid figurine with nose, antlers, eyes and tail painted in black. Also 'ladder-pattern' decoration on legs and chest. White Painted Ware. Early Iron Age. Ht. 15 cm (DM-WWP-184).*

Pl. 218

1 Deer

Figs. 299–306 *Deer shown as relief decoration or as incision motif (Fig. 306) on Early Bronze Age, Red Polished vessels.*

Fig. 299 *Female 'stag' suckling young fawn. Vounous. Spiteris 1970, p. 41.*

Fig. 300 *Stag with lowered head. Christie's catalogue, 14 June 1978, lot 71, Pl. 17.*

Fig. 301 *Stag with conspicuous penis. Vounous (Tomb 65). Schaeffer, Pl. XI, 1.*

Fig. 302 *'Pair' of deer. Vounous (Tomb 39, no. 8). Dikaios 1940, Pl. XIXb.*

Fig. 303 *Stag with penis. Sèvres Museum (MNC 10 6903).*

Fig. 304 *Deer from same vessel as Fig. 302.*

Fig. 305 *Simplified deer image. Vounous (Tomb 11, no. 9). Karageorghis 1976, no. 54.*

Fig. 306 *Deer as incised motif. Vounous (Tomb 15, no. 60). Dikaios 1940, Pl. XXIIb.*

Fig. 299   Fig. 300   Fig. 301

Fig. 302   Fig. 303

Fig. 304   Fig. 305   Fig. 306

shaped', 'theriomorphic', or 'zoomorphic'.

Deer bones were particularly common at Neolithic sites such as Khirokitia, Sotira and Erimi. In some places they constituted as much as 75 per cent of the animal remains. Yet the Neolithic artists ignored them (as far as we know at present). In the Early Bronze Age, however, they became extremely popular, either in the form of an *askos* or a figurine (see Figs. 293–7), or as an attachment to the rim or shoulder of a vessel (see Pls. 290–1 and Figs. 90 and 307–9), or as a relief decoration (see Figs. 299–305), or occasionally as an incised decoration (see Fig. 306). These Red Polished Ware examples are the most common form of deer representation to be found in ancient Cyprus, but a number of fanciful depictions also appear in the White Painted

Ware of the Middle Bronze Age (see Pl. 217 and Figs. 298, 310 and 311). After this, they lose their popularity and become almost un-recorded in the art of the Late Bronze Age (although we know that deer bones were still associated with Late Bronze Age sites). Pottery figurines of deer are equally rare in the Iron Age, the example shown here in Pl. 218 being a rare exception. Deer do, however, figure in the free-field style paintings of this late period, and Karageorghis and des Gagniers (1974) have traced seventeen examples.

The most hotly debated topic with regard to Cypriot deer is whether they were in-digenous or were introduced by Neolithic settlers. The geological evidence is against them having been there since very early times, so they must have swum to the island or been carried there by man (see Watson and Stanley-Price, 1977). If they did swim it must have been comparatively recently, since the Cypriot remains show none of the changes associated with adaptation to a small island habitat. They are indistinguishable from the mainland bones. The human factor seems almost inevitable. This is underlined by the fact that the nearest mainland deer—as far as swimming is concerned—were not Mesopotamian fallow deer, but the common fallow deer of Anatolia. The species that did arrive in the Neolithic was a more remote one from the Persian region, and this strongly suggests that the settlers involved were coming from the east rather than the north. It also implies a considerable degree of domestication, but this is not surprising when one considers how easily the fallow deer has been domesticated in European parks in recent centuries.

How did the early Cypriots exploit their deer population? Zeuner (1958) suggests that they were domesticated 'either for religious purposes only or for meat supply also'. He emphasizes their sacred role by adding, 'it is believed that fallow deer ... represented with their white spots the starlit sky, and that for this reason they became the attribute of the goddess of the moon.' Halstead (1977), studying the deer remains at the Late Bronze

Age site of Kouklia, is puzzled by the large proportion of adult deer bones present. He comments: 'If they were raised for meat, the large percentage of adults here marks a most inefficient pattern of exploitation.' He concludes that they 'seem to have been wild and hunted in a real sense. Although there is both archaeological and historical evidence for the taming of deer as pets or as draught animals, they offer no secondary product which justifies their being kept in large numbers.' This is not entirely correct. Reindeer are milked regularly and there is no reason why fallow deer females should not have been exploited in a similar way. The Kronberg Zoo reports that female Mesopotamian fallow deer give milk from May to August—just the period of the year when Cyprus experiences its greatest shortage of drinking water. Of course, some deer may have gone wild and may have been hunted for meat, but others may well have been kept for summer milking, especially during the earliest periods of habitation when cattle seem to have been absent. Further evidence to support this idea is presented later (see p. 265). No doubt as cattle became more and more important during the Bronze Age, the deer were gradually phased out and allowed to run wild. This would account for the sharp decline in deer images in the Late Bronze Age and the corresponding increase in cattle images.

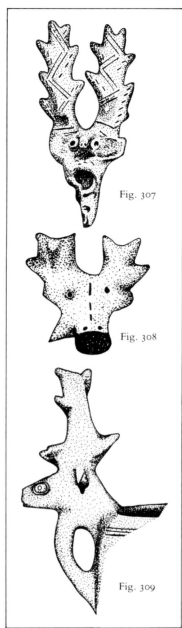

Fig. 307

Fig. 308

Fig. 309

Fig. 310   Fig. 311

1 Deer

Figs. 307-9 *Antlered deer's heads as vessel-attachments. Incised Red Polished Ware. Early Bronze Age.*
Fig. 307 *Ohnefalsch-Richter 1893, Pl. XXXVI, 7.*
Fig. 308 *Vounous. Stewart and Stewart 1950, Pl. XCd.*
Fig. 309 *Karageorghis 1976, no. 66.*

Figs. 310-11 *Deer figures with antlers. White Painted Ware. Middle Bronze Age.*
Fig. 310 *No provenance (Louvre Museum). Ht. 16.5 cm. Hennessy 1979, Pl. 65.*
Fig. 311 *No provenance (Metropolitan Museum, New York). Ht. 14.6 cm. Myers 1914, no. 221.*

2 Cattle

The evidence for cattle in Cyprus before the start of the Bronze Age is almost non-existent. Nothing is known from Khirokitia, Sotira, Erimi or Dhali-Agridhi, the only large animals there being the deer. A solitary cattle bone was reported from the early north coast site of Ayios Epiktitos Vrysi, but it was so outnumbered by deer, sheep and goat bones that it was little more than an oddity and certainly does not reflect a significant presence of bovids on the island prior to the dawn of the Bronze Age.

Pl. 219

2 Cattle

Pl. 219 *Bull motifs on a large bowl with stem base. Modelled figures rise from the rim of the bowl, as follows: A bull shown standing on four legs. A pair of opposed, bucranial poles, with bulls' heads perched on the top of very long stems. A vulture. A pair of shallow, subsidiary bowls on short stems. This unique vessel displays both types of early bull motif, alongside one another. Plain Red Polished Ware. Early Bronze Age. Ht. 34.5 cm. Rim diam. 30 cm (DM-PRP-39).*

Pl. 220 *Bucranial jug. A round-based jug with a tall neck topped by a bull's head. The side-spout becomes transformed into a phallic display. There is a tail-stump at the back of the 'body'. Incised Red Polished Ware. Early Bronze Age. Ht. 24 cm (DM-IRP-93). Horn-tips restored.*

Pl. 220

With Vounous the whole scene changes dramatically. Cattle have arrived in force. Peltenburg (personal communication, 1974) comments: 'Their sudden appearance in domesticated form at Early Bronze Age Vounous certainly could be taken as an importation, especially when one considers all the other artefactual evidence for a very close connection at this juncture between Cyprus and Anatolia where cattle, as a domesticated species, were already known for millennia.'

It seems as if the new settlers from the north brought with them, not only their new pottery styles, but also their favourite animals—both in their practical and their symbolic roles, for there were more than cattle bones left behind. In addition, there were many images of cattle, as figurines, decorations on vessels, and as elements of scenic compositions (see pp. 285-6).

These cattle images do not seem to have been totemic, however, for they do not compete with the images of the already well-established deer. Indeed, there are certain vessels on which both deer *and* cattle appear,

and there is a Red Polished figurine in the Ashmolean (Brown and Catling, 1980, no. 22) which has a stag's head at one end and a bull's head at the other. Brown and Catling comment: 'The combination of both bull and stag suggests an exceptional interest in potency.' Their idea appears to be that the masculine heads of two large ungulates combine as a 'male power' symbol of double strength. Whether the symbolism of this power was primarily concerned with fertility or with protection is difficult to resolve, but whichever way it is taken, the essential feature of the role of these horned and antlered heads is that, instead of being emblematic of particular social groups or factions, they are carrying much the same message as one another, that message being embodied in the powerful masculine nature which they share, rather than in their differences. In other words, when cattle arrived on the scene, they added to the deer as forceful images, rather than competed with them. In another Ashmolean piece, a large Red Polished bowl with modelled animals around its rim (Brown and Catling, 1980, no. 17), there are goats

2 Cattle

Pl. 221 *Standing bull. Solid figurine with short, stocky legs. Incised Red Polished Ware. Early Bronze Age. Length 11.6 cm. Ht. 5.3 cm (DM-IRP-92).*

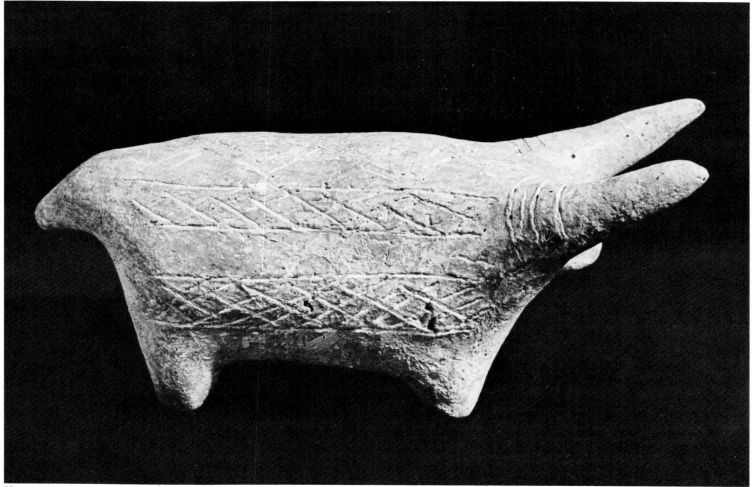

Pl. 221

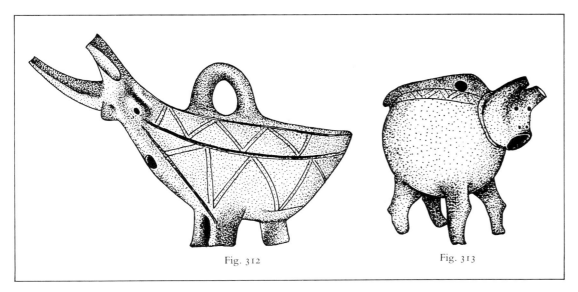

Fig. 312   Fig. 313

2 Cattle

Figs. 312-13 *Bull figures. Red Polished Ware. Early Bronze Age.*
Fig. 312 *No provenance (Cyprus Museum). Ht. 23 cm. Karageorghis 1971, Fig. 51.*
Fig. 313 *No provenance (University of California, Robert Lowie Museum). Ht. 11.4 cm. Karageorghis et al. 1974, no. 15.*

mixed with deer, suggesting that almost any powerful horned head will do and that the specific type of ungulate involved is almost irrelevant.

If one surveys the different kinds of cattle image used in the Early Bronze Age, it soon emerges that there are two distinct types. These can be called the 'Standing Bull' and the 'Bucranial Terminal'. Pl. 221 and Figs. 312-15 represent the Standing Bull category. As isolated figurines these are comparatively rare, but they are quite common as elements in scenic compositions such as ploughing scenes (see pp. 285-6). They seem to be representing the bull in its more docile, domesticated role. But the Bucranial Terminals are another matter. These consist of a bull's head protruding from the rim or neck or shoulder of a vessel (see Pls. 219, 220 and

222, and Figs. 316-25) and their role is more aggressively masculine. Triple bucrania appear on scenic models from Vounous (Fig. 495) and Margi (Figs. 496-7), where three bulls' heads are placed on top of three poles or pillars set side by side on some sort of wall. They tower over the tiny human figures, implying that they were high up and dramatically conspicuous.

Two examples deserve special mention. The bucranial jug (Pl. 220) adds to the virility and power of its symbolism with a strongly phallic spout. The effect is a bull rampant with sexual energy. The large bowl with modelled figures on its rim (Pl. 219) is a remarkable example of a Red Polished Ware creation which presents both types of cattle image on the same vessel. There are two towering bucranial 'poles', two subsidiary

Figs. 314-15 *Bull figures. Red Polished Ware. Early Bronze Age.*
Fig. 314 *Soloi. Ht. 13 cm. Buchholz and Karageorghis 1973, no. 1525.*
Fig. 315 *No provenance (Cyprus Museum). Ht. 8.6 cm. Des Gagniers and Karageorghis 1976, Pl. XLVIII, 1.*

Fig. 314   Fig. 315

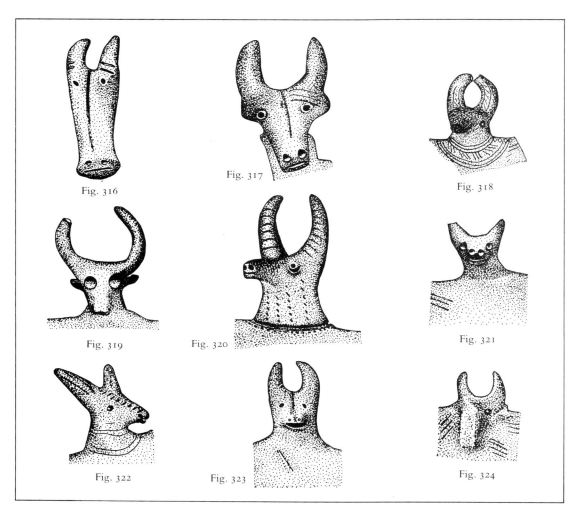

Fig. 316

Fig. 317

Fig. 318

Fig. 319

Fig. 320

Fig. 321

Fig. 322

Fig. 323

Fig. 324

2 Cattle

Figs. 316-25 *Bucranial terminals attached to Red Polished Ware vessels. Early Bronze Age. Figs. 316-24 all from Vounous.*

Fig. 316 *Tomb 160a, 17. Stewart and Stewart 1950, Pl. XCf.*

Fig. 317 *Tomb 160a, 17. Stewart and Stewart 1950, Pl. XCe.*

Fig. 318 *Tomb 117a. Peltenburg 1981, no. 311.*

Fig. 319 *Tomb 160a, 13. Stewart and Stewart 1950, Pl. XCIId.*

Fig. 320 *Tomb 160b, 12. Stewart and Stewart 1950, Pl. XCIb.*

Fig. 321 *Tomb 153, 1. Stewart and Stewart 1950, Pl. XCa.*

Fig. 322 *Tomb 81b, 9. Stewart and Stewart 1950, Pl. XCIIe.*

Fig. 323 *Tomb 153, 1. Stewart and Stewart 1950, Pl. XCb.*

Fig. 324 *Tomb 153, 10. Stewart and Stewart 1950, Pl. XCIIb.*

Fig. 325 *No provenance (Hadjiprodromou Collection, Famagusta). Karageorghis 1976, no. 66.*

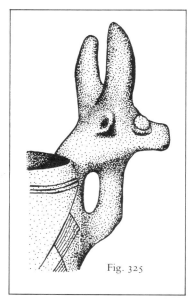

Fig. 325

Pl. 222 *Tulip bowl with two bucranial lugs on rim. The base of the bowl is pierced with a horizontal hole. Black-topped Red Polished Ware. Early Bronze Age. Diam. 16 cm (DM-BTRP-26).*

Pl. 223 *Protective bucrania on present-day Mediterranean buildings. In rural areas of islands such as Malta, Gozo and elsewhere, the horns, skulls, or modelled heads of bulls are placed high up on walls or roofs to protect the inhabitants from the Evil Eye and other hostile elements, a tradition that has persisted since the Neolithic period. (Photographs taken in Malta in 1983.)*

Pl. 222

Pl. 223

bowls, a vulture and a standing bull, spread out round the rim at roughly equal intervals. It is as if the artist is making it absolutely clear that the bucranial elements are not merely stylized bulls, but are categorically distinct from the bull that is shown in a normal bovine posture. The only other object that makes this distinction is the famous 'sanctuary' scene from Vounous (see Fig. 494). There, Standing Bulls are shown in pens as part of the busy scene, and, in addition, up on the wall at one side, there is a triple Bucranial Terminal.

These two artefacts provide clear evidence that the Bucranial Terminals are not simply schematic simplifications of bulls, but instead are some special kind of 'displayed bulls' heads'. To understand the significance of this it is necessary, for a moment, to look beyond Cypriot shores.

From the earliest Neolithic times, the mainland cultures surrounding Cyprus have revered the bull. They admired its strength in more than one way, as Conrad (1959) has pointed out: 'In addition to the docile, plough-pulling steer they were familiar with two other types of bulls: the ferocious aurochs of the mountain country, and the semi-domesticated though dangerous stud bull. In each of these types they found something to admire, something to praise ... As the lord of battle, the strength and savagery of the wild mountain bull stood unchallenged. As the lord of reproduction, the stud bull was supreme. And, as lord of the plants, the great fertility of the steer was unquestioned.'

In his monumental work on *Zeus*, Cook (1914) records a Sumerian text written down at about the same time as the bull was entering Cypriot culture. The Sumerian bull-god's name was *Enlil*:

> O Enlil, Councillor, who can grasp thy
>   power?
> Endowed with strength, lord of the
>   harvest lands!
> Created in the mountains, lord of the
>   grain fields!
> Ruler of great strength, father Enlil!
> The powerful chief of the gods art thou,
> The great creator and sustainer of life!

As a symbolic figure, the bull therefore represented *power* because of its size and wild savagery, *animal fertility* because of its impressive mating acts, and *crop fertility* because of the way the ox-plough opened the earth for the early farmers. Deified, this made the bull the ideal protector of men, livestock and crops respectively. And it was this Great Protector that the new settlers from the north brought with them to Cyprus at the start of the Bronze Age. It is rather surprising that the local fallow deer stag was not immediately overwhelmed as a symbolic image by this awesome import, but he was so well entrenched on the island as part of the fauna, that he managed to hold out for at least the first part of the Bronze Age, sharing the honours with the taurine 'arriviste'.

The diagnostic feature of the bull in his role as Great Protector was his magnificent pair of horns. They became his sign, and to make this sign was to invoke his aid. The simple gesture of forming a horned hand, by extending the forefinger and the little finger while keeping the other digits bent, became widely used in the ancient world as a protection against the Evil Eye. Amulets of hands making this gesture have been worn for thousands of years. In a recent survey (Morris et al., 1979) we found that they are still in use in many countries today.

A more direct way of calling up the protective power of the bull spirit is to erect a pair of horns or a bull's head on top of a pole or a wall. Jutting defiantly into the sky, they symbolically challenge the evil forces that may be threatening the livestock or crops in the nearby fields, or the human inhabitants of the dwelling on which they are placed. Such practices have been operating from the Neolithic (see Mellaart, 1967) to the present day (see Pl. 223) around the lands of the Mediterranian region. Mellaart found the Neolithic town of Çatal Hüyük in Anatolia full of protective horn-signs: '... a single bucranium may be found in a house, whilst rows of bucrania are confined to shrines, where they may also be painted.' On the island of Malta, the ancient practice has survived the passage of time and is still strongly in evidence today. In rural districts everywhere one can find, high up on buildings and walls, protective bucrania, sometimes modelled or sculptured, but usually made of natural horns. The function is still the same, explicitly to protect the inhabitants from evil forces.

When these modern Maltese examples on p. 195 are compared with the ancient Cypriot Bucranial Terminals on p. 194, the similarity is striking. The amusing difference is that the Maltese are devout Christians, and there is a delightful irony in their recourse to the protective powers of the ancient bull-figure. The symbolic bull of ancient times eventually became institutionalized into a Horned God, complete with rituals of worship, temples and priests. It was this deity that the Christians opposed and converted into the Horned Devil, who then became the evil enemy. But his old protective powers refused to be extinguished, and modern Christians still call upon him for help whenever they make the *cornuta* hand-sign or erect a pair of horns on their farmhouse.

Returning now to ancient Cyprus, it seems almost certain that the Cypriots of the Early Bronze Age were using bulls' heads in a similar way, probably placing pairs of real horns on top of poles or dwellings as protective devices. The pottery bucrania adorning rims and shoulders of bowls and jugs were almost certainly ceramic echoes of this practice, and the triple bucrania shown in

model form (and discussed in a later chapter, see p. 284) were undoubtedly accurate portrayals of bulls' heads *in situ* on dwellings.

It is possible that these horns were thought to belong to a bull-god and that he was worshipped with all the trappings of a true religion. Archaeologists tend to refer to them as important elements 'in the religion of early Cyprus'. But we have no direct evidence that this was so and it may well be overstating the case. We know that the Sumerians had deified the bull at about the same time, and the mystical trappings of their beliefs may have been imported to Cyprus along with the cattle. Alternatively, the use of protective bucrania may have been little more than a simple superstition (as in present-day Malta), without any complex religious organization to accompany it. Until we have more extensive knowledge of Early Bronze Age settlements, we must keep an open mind,

2 Cattle

Pl. 224 *Standing bull. Hollow figurine with aperture at 'tail'. Four short stump-legs. Small loop-handle in the middle of the back. Pierced lugs form a pair of ears. Handmade White Painted Ware. Middle Bronze Age. Length 8.6 cm. Ht. 8.4 cm (DM-HWP-66). Old label on base indicates that this figure was formerly in the Cesnola Collection.*

Pl. 224

2 Cattle

Pl. 225 *Standing bull. Hollow figurine with aperture on chest. Three short stump-legs. Small loop-handle in the middle of the back. Handmade White Painted Ware. Middle Bronze Age. Length 14 cm (DM-HWP-64). Horn-tips restored.*

Pl. 225

Pl. 226 *Standing bull. Hollow figurine with aperture in middle of back. The aperture is connected to the tail by a loop handle. Four short legs. The small horns and general proportions of this figure suggest that it may be a cow, but as no udder is shown it is safer to see it as a variant of the many bull figures. Handmade White Painted Ware. Middle Bronze Age. Length 17.8 cm (DM-HWP-65). Old label on base indicates that this figure was formerly in the Cesnola Collection.*

Pl. 226

2 Cattle

Pl. 227

Pl. 227 *Standing bull. Hollow figurine with aperture in the form of a cutaway-spouted 'tail'. Two lugs on either side of the tail-base. Loop handle in the middle of the back. Four short legs. A flat face with large, incised eyes and a nose formed from a pierced lug. Strongly inward curved horns and a pair of small, backward-turned ears. Handmade White Painted Ware. Middle Bronze Age. Length 15.6 cm (DM-HWP-63).*

Pl. 228

Pl. 228 *Standing bull. Hollow figurine with aperture emerging as a round-spouted neck from the back of the animal's head. The head itself is reduced to little more than a pair of horns. The spout is joined to the middle of the back by a large loop handle. Three short, stump-legs. A down-curved tail, pressed to the rear end of the body. Red-on-Black Ware. Middle Bronze Age. Length 18.4 cm (DM-ROB-12). Paintwork worn.*

2 Cattle

Pl. 229

a(left) *Standing bull. Hollow figurine with aperture on back of neck. Loop handle from rear of aperture to middle of back. A second aperture forms the mouth of the animal. A large nose-ring is indicated on top of the snout. Traces of painted decoration. Base Ring Ware. Late Bronze Age. Length 13.2 cm (DM-BR-47).*
b(right) *Same description, but without the nose-ring. Length 10.8 cm (DM-BR-45).*

Pl. 230 *Jug with ring-base and round spout, the latter connected by loop-handle to a bucranial side-spout. Painted decoration. Base Ring Ware. Late Bronze Age. Ht. 20.8 cm (DM-BR-21).*

while freely admitting that the bull was an important image at this stage of Cypriot prehistory.

In the Middle Bronze Age there are still many small, cattle-shaped jugs to be seen, in White Painted Ware (Pls. 224-7) and Red-on-black Ware (pl. 228), but there is nothing particularly fierce or impressive about them, and the protective bucrania have already vanished from vessels.

With the arrival of the Late Bronze Age, however, the bull image reasserts itself. Dozens of vigorous Standing Bull figurines have been excavated, in both incised and painted Base Ring Ware (see Pls. 229, 231, and 232). Some have noses pierced for rings (Pls. 229a and 231), indicating that these are domestic bulls that can be led by man. This implies the fertility symbolism of the stud bull, rather than the protective symbolism of the all-powerful bull. It is significant that, during this epoch, the Base Ring Ware artists favoured two special images: *female humans* (see pp. 166-74) and *male cattle*. Men and cows were shunned. This preoccupation with the manufacture of many figures of women and bulls implies that they were, in a sense, a 'pair'—the symbols of female and male fertility respectively.

The Bucranial Terminal makes a comeback during this Late Bronze period, appearing as a bull-headed spout on a number of Base Ring jugs (see Pl. 230). At least nine of these have been published and, judging by their variety of shape and detail, they were not the idiosyncratic work of a single artist, but constituted a standard theme throughout the Base Ring phase of Cypriot pottery. Towards the end of the Late Bronze Age, bronze bulls were also made in some numbers, and the animal was clearly a dominant theme again in this period, so much so that gold earrings were worn in the shape of bulls' heads (see Pl. 233a). These are best known from Enkomi and Kition. This bull-earring tradition lasted well into the Cypro-Classical period (see Pl. 233b).

In the Iron Age the bull image survived, appearing and reappearing as Bucranial Terminals on ring vessels, and on Bichrome Ware jars (with horns acting as handles). The bull was also moderately popular as an element in the free-field paintings of this period. Karageorghis and des Gagniers (1974) traced twenty-five examples. But perhaps the most attractive form of bull image is that found on a series of hanging wall brackets (see Pl. 234) which re-create the Early Bronze Age mood of a protective bull's head fixed high upon a building.

Pl. 229

Pl. 230

2 Cattle

Pl. 231 *Standing bull. Hollow figurine with aperture on back of neck. Loop handle from rear of aperture to middle of back. A second aperture forms the mouth of the animal. A large nose-ring is indicated on top of the snout. One ear is shown open and one half-shut. Painted decoration. Base Ring Ware. Late Bronze Age. Length 15.1 cm. Ht. 13.6 cm (DM-BR-46).*

Pl. 231

Pl. 232 *Standing bull. Hollow figurine with aperture on back of neck. Loop handle from rear of aperture to middle of back. Rather pointed nose. Painted decoration is unusually well preserved. Base Ring Ware. Late Bronze Age. Length 17.7 cm. Ht. 12 cm (DM-BR-44).*

Pl. 232

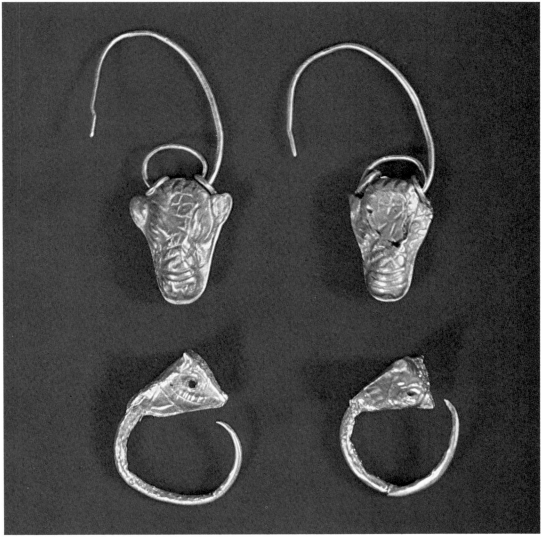

Pl. 233

2 Cattle

Pl. 233

a(above) *Pair of bull's-head earrings. Decoration includes nostrils, eyes and ears. There are two apertures on top of the head, the loops of wire emerging from them symbolically representing the horns. On the forehead is a distinctive cross-within-a-circle motif. Gold. Late Bronze Age. Head lengths 1.8 cm (DM-ME-49). Cf. Murray 1900, Pl. X, nos. 234 and 403, which show identical forehead motifs.*
b(below) *Pair of bull's-head earrings. Decoration includes pair of short horns, forelock and inset blue eyes. Gold. Cypro-Classical Period. Head length 1.4 cm (DM-ME-50). Cf. Pierides 1971, Pl. XXI, nos. 8 and 9.*

Pl. 234

Pl. 234 *Hanging bracket lamp-stand with bull's head decoration in relief. The bull's eyes with eye-lashes. The lower part of the bracket is missing. Bichrome Ware. Iron Age. Ht. (of surviving section) 17.1 cm (DM-BI-104). Cf. Karageorghis 1969, Fig. 55.*

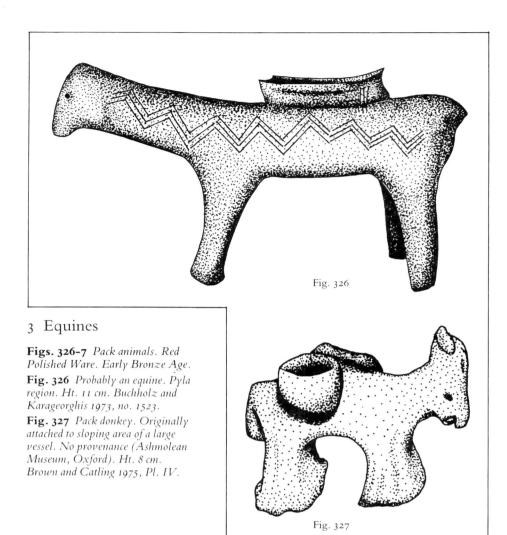

Fig. 326

3 Equines

Figs. 326-7 *Pack animals. Red Polished Ware. Early Bronze Age.*
Fig. 326 *Probably an equine. Pyla region. Ht. 11 cm. Buchholz and Karageorghis 1973, no. 1523.*
Fig. 327 *Pack donkey. Originally attached to sloping area of a large vessel. No provenance (Ashmolean Museum, Oxford). Ht. 8 cm. Brown and Catling 1975, Pl. IV.*

Fig. 327

3 Equines

Horses and donkeys became important domesticated animals on the mainlands around Cyprus in the early part of the Bronze Age. Mules had also become common by 2500 BC. Earlier claims that the first equines domesticated in the region were in fact onagers (see Zeuner, 1963) have recently been refuted (Clutton-Brock, 1981).

Unfortunately, the equine images left to us by the Bronze Age Cypriot artists are so formalized that it is impossible in most cases to tell which species is being represented. The vital diagnostic features, such as the ears and tail, are usually missing or so reduced that they cannot be trusted for species identification.

It is clear, however, that some sort of equines had arrived by the Early Bronze Age, and there are several images of them to be found among the Red Polished Ware vessels and figurines. One of these (Fig. 326) has a long equine neck but a ridiculously small head, and its identity, even as a generalized equine, is doubtful. But on its back there is a concave pad which appears to be intended as the holder for a heavy burden of some kind—a large water jar, for instance, or food bundle. If this is a pack animal, then what could it have been other than an equine? The

Fig. 328 *Horse wearing a halter. White Painted Ware. Middle Bronze Age. No provenance (Musée d'Art et Histoire, Geneva). Ht. 8 cm. Karageorghis 1975, Fig. 3.*

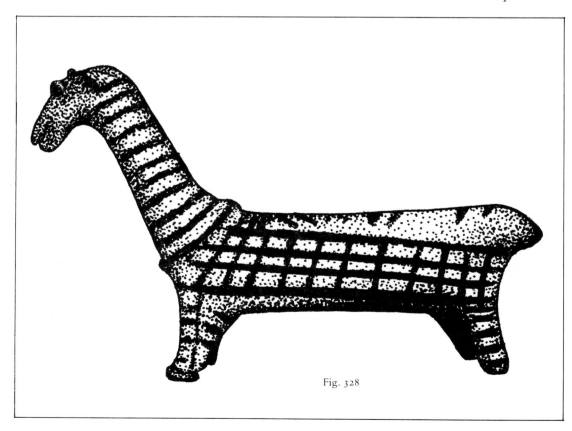

Fig. 328

only other possible interpretation is that it is meant to be a camel, but this seems even less likely.

More convincing is the little pack animal with two panniers in the Ashmolean Museum (see Fig. 327). Brown and Catling (1975) and Frankel (1983) agree that this must be a donkey, and despite the absence of detail its general bearing seems to indicate this. Another donkey-like animal can be seen on the famous 'Margi Bowl' (Fig. 488), where it is also shown carrying panniers. The extraordinary feature of this last equine is that, in addition to the burden of its panniers, it is also carrying two human figures. This must make it the earliest example of *riding* in the history of art. We are so familiar with riding today that we overlook the fact that it was a comparatively late development in man's long relationship with equines. The first exploitation was to kill and eat them, then to use them as pack and draught animals for shifting heavy burdens and for drawing chariots. The chariot became the high-status form of transportation for centuries, and it was not until the Iron Age that horse-riding became popular and eventually rendered the chariot obsolete in warfare.

In the Early Bronze Age in Cyprus, oxen were the draught animals (see Fig. 499). Their immense strength compensated for their slow movements, and it is clear that equines were not brought into the island in enough numbers to oust the cattle from their traditional role. As pack animals, however, the equines do seem to have made a start during this period.

By the Middle Bronze Age we have the first hint of a Cypriot horse being used for traction rather than carrying. A White Painted Ware animal figurine in the Geneva Art Museum (see Fig. 328) has been identified as a horse by Karageorghis (1975) because it has a 'ridge round the base of the neck'. This ridge almost certainly indicates a thick collar of the type worn by a horse pulling a heavy weight. This is an isolated example, however. The only other White Painted Ware horses appear on a large box-shaped vessel which has a horse's head protruding from each end. To each horse's neck clings a small human figure (see Fig. 329). Again, this is an amazingly early example of equine riding, well ahead of its time.

With the arrival of the Late Bronze Age, the horse becomes more frequent as a subject for Cypriot artists. There are at least ten Base Ring Ware horse figurines, two with front-facing riders and two with what can only be described as 'side-saddle-thrones' (Fig. 330). Here, once more, Cyprus seems to be ahead of the rest of the world in its use of the horse as an animal on which to ride.

In the last part of the Late Bronze Age, the horse is in evidence again in the Proto-White Painted Ware of the period (see Fig. 331).

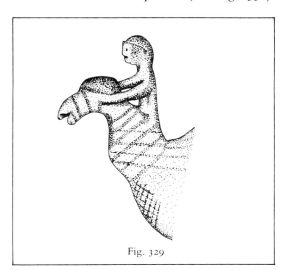

Fig. 329

3 Equines

Fig. 329 *Horse with rider, attached to an ovoid pottery box. White Painted Ware. Middle Bronze Age. Vounous (Tomb 64). Ht. (of whole vessel) 23.5 cm. Schaeffer 1936, Pl. XXII, 2. A similar figure is attached at the other end of this vessel.*

Fig. 330-1 *Horses with 'side-saddle' seats. Late Bronze Age.*

Fig. 330 *Base Ring Ware. No provenance. Karageorghis 1975, Fig. 2.*

Fig. 331 *Proto-White Painted Ware. No provenance (Ashmolean Museum, Oxford). Ht. 22.7 cm. Catling 1974, Pl. XVI, 1-5. This important figure is known as 'The Bomford Horse-and-Rider'.*

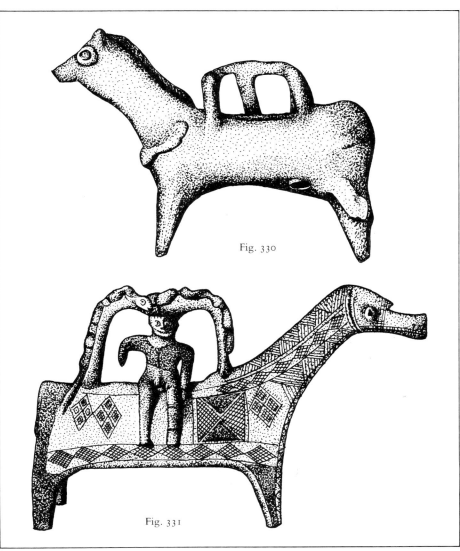

Fig. 330

Fig. 331

3 Equines

Pl. 235 *Horse with stiff mane. Bearded rider holding on to mane with hands. Elaborate painted decoration. Bichrome Ware. Iron Age. Ht. 19.5 cm (DM-BI-113).*

Pl. 236 *Horse with stiff mane. Bearded rider holding on to mane with hands. Elaborate painted decoration. Bichrome Ware. Iron Age. Ht. 20 cm (DM-BI-112).*

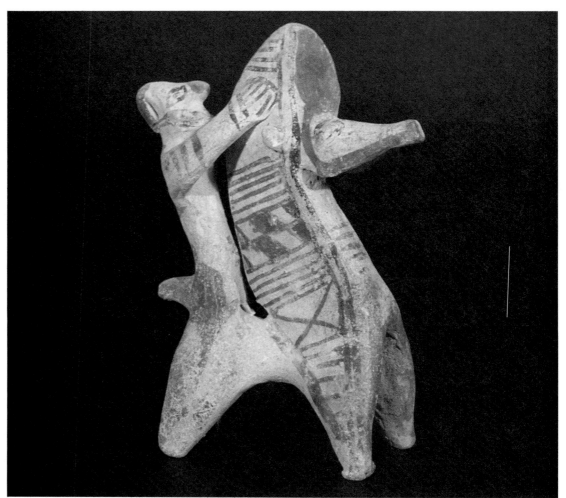

Pl. 235

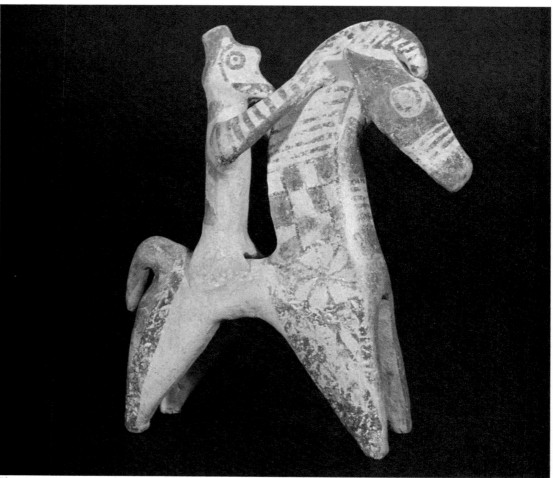

Pl. 236

Pl. 237

3 Equines

Pl. 237
a(left) *Horse with two front legs and a single central back leg. Some painted decoration surviving. Bichrome Ware. Iron Age. Ht. 12.3 cm (DM-BI-106).*
b(right) *Same description. Ht. 10 cm (DM-BI-105).*

Pl. 238 *Horse with stiff mane. There may once have been a rider, as is usual with such horses, but this seems unlikely because the red paint marks run along the back of the animal. Bichrome Ware. Iron Age. Ht. 20.5 cm DM-BI-108).*

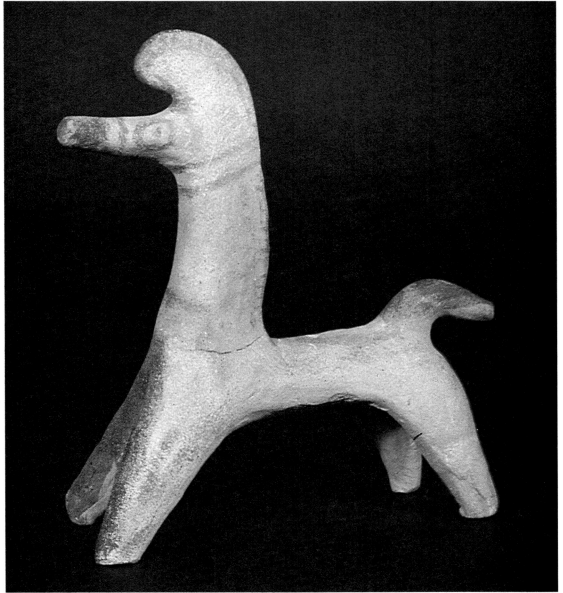

Pl. 238

3 Equines

Figs. 332–9 *Iron Age horse-and-rider figures. In Fig. 339 the rider has been lost but traces of his hands are still visible on the mane of the animal.*

Fig. 332 *White Painted Ware. No provenance (Cyprus Museum). Ht. 13.6 cm. Tatton-Brown 1979, no. 194.*

Fig. 333 *No provenance. Ht. 29.5 cm. Christie's catalogue, 18 October 1972, lot 78, Pl. IV.*

Fig. 334 *Bichrome Ware. No provenance (Louvre Museum). Ht. 13.5 cm. Hennessy 1979, Pl. 118.*

Fig. 335 *Bichrome Ware. No provenance (Cyprus Museum). Ht. 21 cm. Karageorghis 1962, Pl. XXXI.*

Fig. 336 *Bichrome Ware. No provenance (Cyprus Museum). Ht. 21 cm. Karageorghis 1977, no. 61.*

Fig. 337 *Bichrome Ware. No provenance (Cyprus Museum). Dikaios 1961, Pl. 30, no. 6.*

Fig. 338 *Bichrome Ware. No provenance (Museum of Fine Arts, Boston). Ht. 22.5 cm. Vermeule 1972, no. 26.*

Fig. 339 *Bichrome Ware. No provenance (Royal Ontario Museum, Toronto). Ht. 20.7 cm. Leipen 1966, no. 143.*

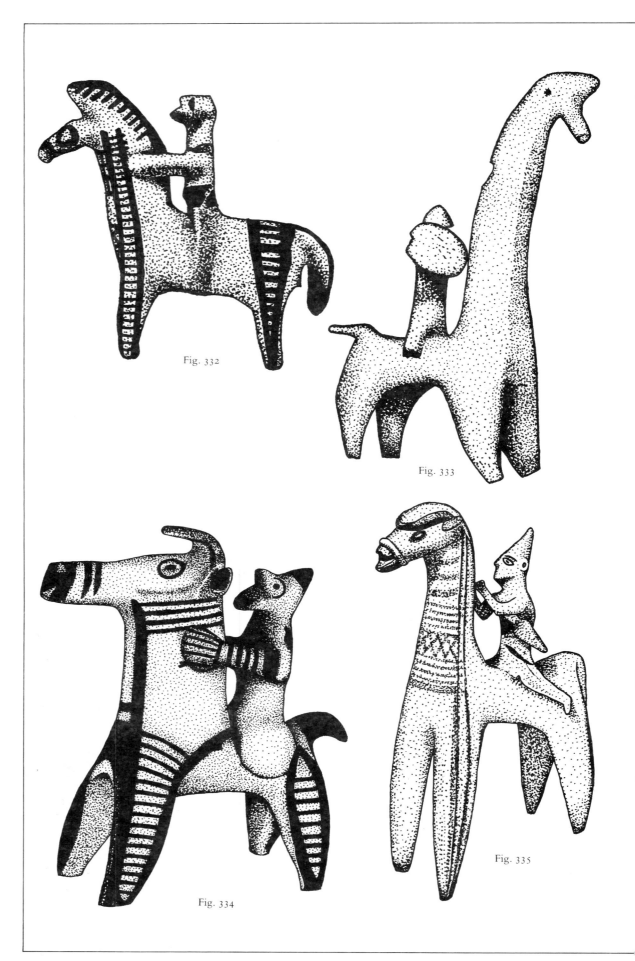

Fig. 332

Fig. 333

Fig. 334

Fig. 335

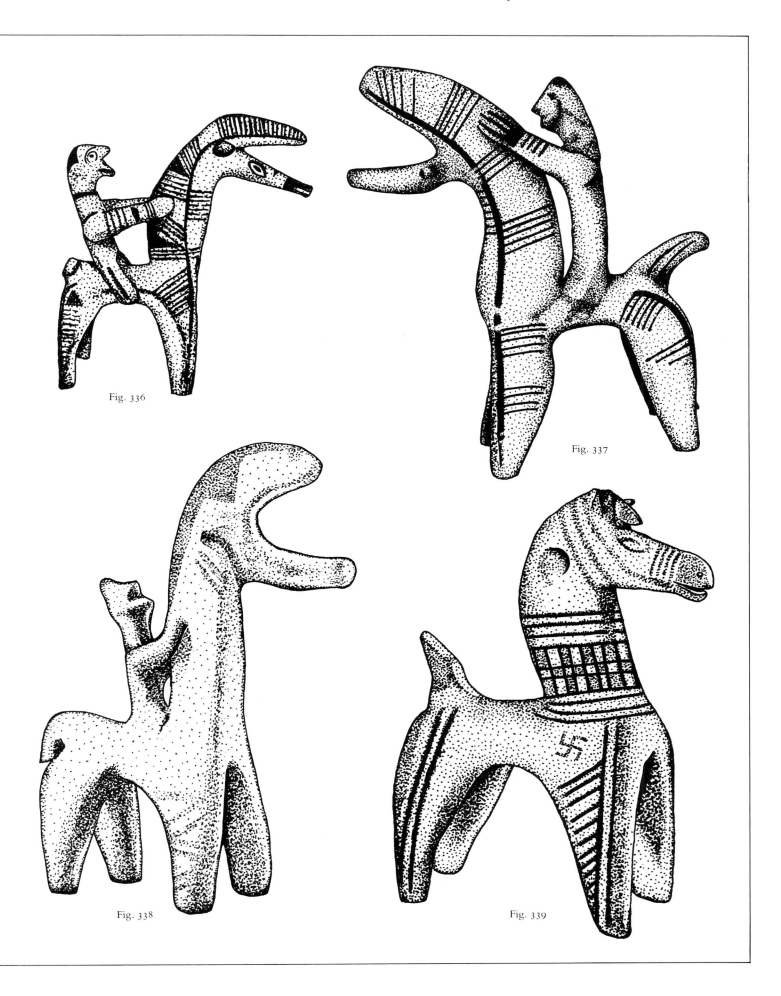

Fig. 336

Fig. 337

Fig. 338

Fig. 339

3 Equines

Fig. 340

The tradition of sitting 'side-saddle' is continued, although the 'throne' has now become a symbolically snake-festooned arch over the rider's head. Catling (1974) comments that, if this was a tomb offering, 'it is just conceivable we see the dead man himself, setting out on the journey to the next world, with the snakes that remind us of immortality ...' Whether the sideways posture on the back of the horse was an imaginative concept devised specifically for the great journey to the afterlife, or whether it was based on a real posture adopted perhaps by high-status in-

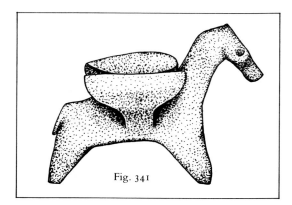

Fig. 341

dividuals in Cypriot society, is hard to say, but the latter seems more likely.

It is during the next epoch, the Iron Age, that the horse really comes into its own. In sheer numbers it is far and away the most popular mammal for artists to portray. The basic theme of Cypriot figurines has moved away from fertility to warfare, and the horse appears both as a chariot draught-animal (Fig. 340) and as a warrior's steed. Ten examples of mounted horses are shown here (Pls. 235-6 and Figs. 332-9) from the many that are known. They are occasionally in White Painted Ware, but more often in attractive Bichrome colours. They reveal several intriguing features about the way horses were ridden in these early days. There were no proper saddles and no stirrups. The riders are all shown clinging on to the manes of their mounts, and it is significant that at this stage in the horse's history, these manes were still stiffly upstanding, as in wild equines.

It is amazing that this ungainly manner of sitting astride a moving horse was tolerated.

3 Equines

Pl. 239

Pl. 239 *Pack donkey with harness straps on neck and head. On the animal's back there is a large pannier—a huge basket or jar. No trace whatever of any pigment is present on this figure and it seems likely that it was never painted. Plain White Ware. Iron Age. Length 12.3 cm. Ht. 11 cm (DM-PW-25). An old label on this figure suggests that it was formerly in the Cesnola Collection, and four similar ones are to be found illustrated in Cesnola 1881.*

It seems inconceivable that man's ingenuity could not quickly invent the necessary equipment to facilitate fast riding, and it is tempting to think of the lack of saddle and stirrups as a mere formalization on the part of the artist concerned. We know that this is not so, however, from written instructions on horsemanship from an even later period. In the fourth century BC, Xenophon requests that the rider 'whether on the horse's bare back or on a cloth ... should sit ... as if he were standing upright with his legs somewhat apart; for thus he will cling more firmly to the horse with his thighs ...' It is an amazing fact that neither Alexander the Great nor Julius Caesar knew of the stirrup. Their great victories were made with horsemen all gripping their steeds with their thighs. As Clutton-Brock (1981) points out, they must indeed have been supreme riders—almost like centaurs—'How else could a man ride a galloping horse, manage all the accoutrements of primitive metal armour, carry spare weapons and hurl a javelin, all without stirrups?' As far as we can tell, stirrups did not

arrive (apparently from the Orient) until several centuries after the close of the Roman period. So the horsemanship depicted by the figurines of Iron Age Cyprus was quite different from modern riding and much more difficult and hazardous.

Iron Age horses without riders are comparatively rare in Cypriot art. Examples such as that shown in Fig. 339 originally had a rider but he has since been lost. Only the imprint of his hand on the stiff mane survives. Other riders have been similarly broken away, but there are a number of large (Pl. 238) and small (Pl. 237) riderless horses which appear to be intact. It has been suggested that they were placed in graves as substitutes for the sacrifice of highly valued real horses.

Pack horses and donkeys are still depicted from time to time in the Iron Age, although they are even less common than riderless horses. Their tomb role has been interpreted as pack animals carrying provisions for the long journey to the other world (Pl. 239 and Fig. 341).

4 Pigs

4 Pigs

Fig. 342 *Probably a pig. Picrolite. Chalcolithic. No provenance (private collection).*

Fig. 343 *Long-snouted pig with bristly back. Incised Red Polished Ware. Early Bronze Age. Vounous (Tomb 160a, no 22). Ht. 6 cm. Stewart and Stewart 1950, Pl. XXIVa, 22.*

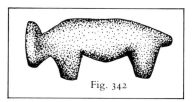
Fig. 342

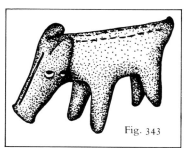
Fig. 343

Pl. 240 *The body is hollow underneath. The eyes are depicted with black paint, the ears and tail are modelled. On the body, four black stripes alternate with three broader, red stripes. The nose is almost touching the ground. Bichrome Ware. Iron Age. Length 7 cm. (DM-BI-114).*

Pigs were domesticated as early as 7,000 BC at Jericho, on the nearby mainland, and had been brought to Cyprus by 6,000 BC. Remains have been found at the Neolithic sites of Khirokitia, Erimi and Sotira.

As domestic animals, pigs have certain advantages and disadvantages that set them apart from the other ungulates popular with early farmers. Their advantages are that they are easy to herd, so that they can be allowed to roam freely in woods or forests near to human settlements, with only a young swineherd in charge of them; that they will find their own food when herded in this way; and that they can adapt to being penned in to a pigsty if close confinement is required. Their disadvantages are that they supply a much narrower range of products than the other ungulates, being used almost exclusively for meat; and that they refuse to be driven over long distances.

This last point explains why there have

been such strong taboos over the eating of pork among certain peoples. Because pigs would not travel well they were useless to nomadic groups and became exclusively associated with settled farmers. Nomads therefore came to despise the pigs, and it is no accident that the ancestors of the anti-pork cultures, the Jews and the Arabs, were early nomads.

A small island is no place for nomads, however, and the settled islanders obviously took to pork from their earliest times on Cyprus. Even so, the pig never seems to have been immensely popular. Its remains are found throughout the ancient epochs of the island's story, but always at a level of secondary importance. The same is true of the images of pigs in the ancient art of Cyprus. They are there from the earliest times, as figurines, right through to the Roman period, but never in any numbers and never as the subject for major works. This is probably

Pl. 240

Figs. 344-5 *Bichrome Ware. Iron Age. From Salamis.*

Fig. 344 *Tomb 13, no. 35. Ht. 4 cm. Karageorghis 1970, Pl. LXXV.*

Fig. 345 *Tomb 51, Dr. 1. Ht. 5.2 cm. Karageorghis 1970, Pl. CXXIX.*

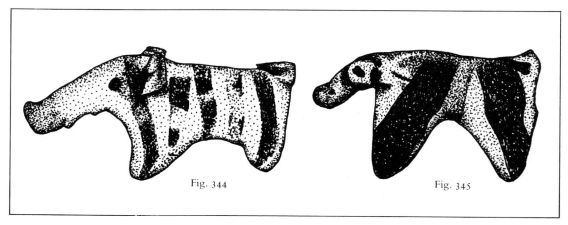
Fig. 344   Fig. 345

due to the fact that, although delicious to eat, pigs lack any great symbolic value. Although creatures of great charm and intelligence to those who know them well, they lack the emblematic dignity of the more powerful, horned and antlered beasts or the impressive speed and grace of the long-legged equines and antelopes. The usefulness of pigs to early, schematizing artists is therefore somewhat limited.

From the Chalcolithic phases we have only one or two animal carvings in pale green picrolite that might just be pigs, but the identification is dubious. The most likely candidate is shown in Fig. 342. In the Red Polished Ware of the Early Bronze Age there is one undeniable pig from Vounous (Fig. 343), with incised markings that may be intended to indicate a bristly back.

From the Iron Age there are two small Bichrome pigs from Salamis (Figs. 344-5). A similar one, but with a more hippo-like shape, is shown in Pl. 240.

For some reason, the pig was not favoured by the free-field painters of Iron Age vessels. The only example traced is from a Cypro-Archaic jar found at the village of Goudhi, near Marion in the Paphos district. Here the animal portrayed appears to be a wild boar, rather than a domesticated pig. Its hair bristles conspicuously (see Fig. 346). The beast is part of a panel the rest of which shows two savage carnivores hemming it in from either side. Karageorghis (1979) interprets this tentatively as 'the chasing of a wild boar by two dogs', although he admits that 'the fierce looking dogs and the boar with his

head lower to the ground do not succeed in producing a scene of action.'

A little later on, in the Hellenistic period, the pig becomes rather more popular, in the form of small pottery rattles (see Pls. 241-2). Each is provided with a clay pellet inside its rotund body, and the function of these charmingly toy-like figurines appears to have beeen that of children's playthings, perhaps placed in the tombs of infants to keep them amused on the long journey to the other world. Cesnola acquired at least nine of these, illustrating them in his 1881 album of Cypriot Antiquities. The three illustrated here are from that collection and have spent the last century in the Pitt Rivers Museum in Dorset, until it was closed down and dispersed through sales at Sotheby's in recent years.

4 Pigs

Fig. 346 *Wild boar(?) with bristling back, depicted as a painting on a Bichrome Ware jar. Iron Age. From Goudhi, south of Marion. Ht. (of vessel) 29.5 cm. Karageorghis 1979, Pl. XIII, 5.*

Fig. 346

Pl. 241 *Pig with trumpet mouth. Hollow figure with mouth as aperture. The animal was used as a rattle, there being a spherical clay pellet inside it. There are large erect ears, four short stump-legs and a short, fat tail, On the back are two short crests, one behind the other. Incision marks run outwards and backwards from each erect crest, suggesting bristling. It is possible that the animal represented is a wild boar rather than a domesticated pig. Red Slip covers the front half of the body but the remainder is left as Plain White Ware. Cypro-Classical or Hellenistic Period. Length 10.8 cm (DM-WRS-25). Formerly in the Cesnola Collection.*

Pl. 242

a(left) *Pig with trumpet mouth. Details as for Pl. 241, except for the absence of Red Slip. The body is longer. Plain White Ware. Length 15 cm (DM-PW-26).*
b(right) *Same description, but with longer nose and longer front-crest. Plain White Ware. Length 15 cm (DM-PW-27). Both these figures were formerly in the Cesnola Collection. For others see Cesnola 1881.*

Pl. 241

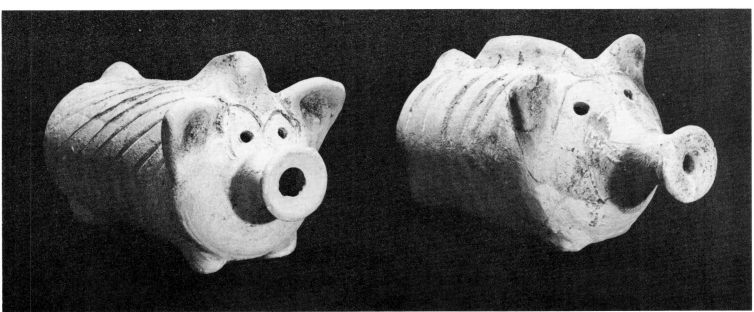

Pl. 242

Pl. 243 *Head of a living camel, showing the characteristic bump on top of the head, which is exaggerated by the ancient artists in the figures below, and on the opposite page.*

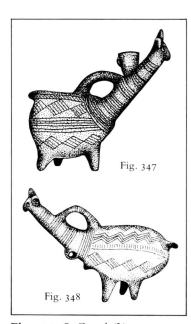

Fig. 347

Fig. 348

Figs. 347-8 *Camels(?).*
Fig. 347 *Red Polished Ware. Early Bronze Age. No provenance (Cyprus Museum). Ht. 14 cm. Buchholz and Karageorghis 1973, no. 1527.*
Fig. 348 *Black Polished Ware. Early Bronze Age. No provenance (Cyprus Museum). Ht. 15.3 cm. Buchholz and Karageorghis 1973, no. 1526.*

5 Camels

Camels arrived rather late on the domestication scene. According to Clutton-Brock (1981) there is nothing before the third millennium BC that suggests human control of this species. She records that 'camel dung was identified from the site of Shar-i Sokhta in central Iran which has been dated to approximately 2,600 BC ... This is the earliest evidence for domestic camels that has so far been documented.'

The evidence from Cyprus about the early use of the camel there is confusing. Over a hundred years ago, Cesnola (1877, p. 282) was cheerfully reporting a profusion of camel bones in the ancient tombs of the island, adding: 'I should here state, that in most ancient tombs, whether at Dali, Aghios Photios, Paphos, or Amathus, I have often found teeth of animals, especially of camels.'

In the present century, more careful excavation techniques have failed to support this early enthusiasm for a camel-strewn Cyprus. Indeed, camel bones have been something of an archaeological rarity. Gjerstad (1962, p. 75) recorded camel remains from an Early Bronze Age tomb at Katydata, and his discovery has been quoted and re-quoted by later authors. Although it was only a single instance it has been generalized in the retelling. For example, Hill (1940), commenting on the Cypriot Bronze Age burial customs, says: 'The offerings which were buried with the dead included ... domestic animals, horse, camel and dog, which were killed and laid with their master to serve them in the next world'. This bold statement begins to look a little shaky when Gjerstad's Katydata field notes are examined. Referring to the tomb in question (T69), these notes state: 'Among the bones there are some which seem to be an animal—especially a backbone and one head ... length of neck 0.70 m ... The animal seems to have a long neck.' Zeuner (1963) is highly sceptical about this, commenting that the Gjerstad camel is 'an example of how positive statements can develop from vague factual reports. He continues: 'The bones are no longer traceable ... It can safely be said that this case is quite inconclusive. At best, parts of a camel were thrown into the pit at a time unknown, but more probably the animal was not a camel.'

To be fair to Gjerstad, an animal with such a long neck is difficult to explain if it is not a camel. But even if Zeuner's scepticism is justified, it remains true that the Katydata 'camel' is a solitary piece of evidence for the earlier part of the Cypriot Bronze Age and should be treated with caution for that reason alone. Later in the Bronze Age, camel teeth were found at Toumba tou Skourou (Astrom, 1972), but the evidence for this species remains poor for a long period.

What are we to make of this? Perhaps Cesnola was right and camels were common in ancient Cyprus, but were largely restricted to parts of the island from which we do not yet have good archaeological material for modern osteological examination. This is not unreasonable when one recalls that the island was much more heavily wooded in earlier days. Stewart (1962) remarks that the presence of camels on Cyprus would indicate 'an extension of scrub country' in the Bronze Age period. This extension might well have occurred in places where we do not have plentiful animal bones from tombs to study.

Alternatively, perhaps camels were present but were not considered suitable for inclusion among tomb offerings. They may have been exclusively employed for heavy work as beasts of burden, but not eaten, thus setting them outside the orbit of ceremonial food offerings at burials. A third possibility is that camels were present in very small numbers— a domestication oddity on the island—and of little significance in the cultural life of the early Cypriot farmers.

So far, only the bones of camels have been considered as evidence, but what of the artefacts? Are there any camel images to help us? Until very recently the answer had to be negative. The only exception was a small White Painted figurine from the Middle Bronze Age, at the Ashmolean Museum (Frankel, 1983, no. 206) which was recorded as 'Zoomorphic vessel. (Camel?).' It has a very long neck with a characteristically cameline curve in it, and a reasonably camel-like head with ears (see Fig. 349). A similar figurine (Fig. 350; Frankel, 1983, no. 1135) lacks the ears and has a slightly more bird-like body, with the result that it is labelled as 'Long-necked creature, perhaps a bird'. But bird-like bodies can be deceptive in Cypriot art. Even antlered stags and horned bulls often have bird-like bodies. The shape is a stylistic convention more than an anatomical statement. To identify these early animal images it is necessary to concentrate on details

Pl. 244

such as wings, necks, ears, horns, antlers, beaks and faces, and to ignore the general body shape. Even the absence of the camel's hump cannot be taken too seriously. The specific features to look for, with camels, are the long bent neck and the camel-shaped head. On this basis, both these small Ashmolean figurines could well be camels.

There are a number of other long-necked animal figurines that could be placed in this category, but none is totally convincing. Two well-known Incised Polished Ware examples from the Early Bronze Age (Figs. 347-8) deserve a brief mention, because they include an additional cameline feature. In both cases, as well as a long neck and an eared head, they display a curious, central projection on the top of the head. It is so obtrusively rendered in both animals that it is hard to overlook it or write it off as artistic whim or error. It seems clear that the artist concerned was deliberately drawing attention to a large 'bump' on the top of the head of animal she was portraying. The camel's profile has just such a bump, albeit far less exaggerated (Pl. 243). It would seem therefore that these two figurines, usually referred to simply as 'zoomorphic', were intended to represent camels in the Early Bronze Age period. Just as antlers were enlarged on images of deer, so the 'bump' was enlarged on

the head of these camels, to emphasize their identity.

One of these two figurines is described as carrying a small bowl on its neck (Fig. 347), but this is a curious position for such a burden, and an alternative explanation seems more likely. Several pottery funnels are known from this period (see Pl. 284), and if these figures are seen not as representations of living animals but as stylized images of animal-shaped wine-skins, then the 'bowl' on the neck becomes a more sensible funnel, thrust into the neck for filling the *askos* with liquid. The body shapes also make more sense if seen as wine-skins rather than parts of living animals.

The most convincing of all the early camel images, however, is the one shown in Pl. 244. This is from the Middle Bronze Age and there is just enough pigment left on its surface to reveal that it is from the Red-on-Black Ware tradition of this period. The shape of its neck and head is so strongly cameline that it is hard to see it as anything else. So it would seem that domestic camels were, after all, present in Bronze Age Cyprus, making them among the earliest examples known from anywhere in the world. They may only have played a minor role, because of the nature of the island habitat, but they were there.

5 Camels

Pl. 244 *Camel figure with highly characteristic neck posture and typical bump on top of the head. The figurine rests, not on legs, but on a ring base. The figure is hollow, with a round spout on the back acting as the sole aperture (the animal's mouth and eyes not being pierced through to the interior). Almost all paintwork has worn away, but a few faint lines remain to reveal the ware. Red-on-Black Ware. Middle Bronze Age. Length 19.5 cm (DM-ROB-13).*

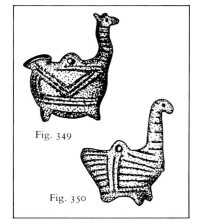

Fig. 349

Fig. 350

Figs. 349-50 *Camels(?). White Painted Ware. Middle Bronze Age.*
Fig. 349 *No provenance (Ashmolean Museum, Oxford). Ht. 8.9 cm. Frankel 1983, no. 206.*
Fig. 350 *Kouklia(?). Ht. 9.1 cm. Frankel 1983, no. 1135.*

6 Sheep

6 Sheep

Fig. 351 *Ram seen in plan view as an incised motif on a deep bowl. Red Polished Ware. Early Bronze Age. Vounous (Tomb 91, no. 14). Ht. (to rim of bowl) 17.2 cm; (of ram motif) 8.6 cm. Stewart and Stewart 1950, Pl. XCIIIa.*

Fig. 352 *Ram figure. Incised Red Polished Ware. Early Bronze Age. No provenance (University of California, Robert Lowie Museum). Ht. 12.6 cm. Karageorghis et al. 1974, no. 9.*

Fig. 353 *Ram figure in White Painted Ware. Middle Bronze Age. No provenance (Museum of Fine Arts, Boston). Ht. 16.1 cm. Vermeule 1972, no. 6.*

Sheep were probably the first ungulates ever domesticated by man. There is evidence that this step had already been taken by the eighth millennium BC, on the mainland to the east of Cyprus. According to one view, domesticated sheep were taken across to Cyprus by the very earliest settlers, who made their way from the Levant a millennium or so later. These sheep, or some of them, soon ran wild on the island and reverted to the feral type known today as the Cyprian moufflon. The wild ones were hunted and the tame ones were farmed, from that point onwards, providing Cypriots with a major source of food down the ages.

This view has been put forward by Watson and Stanley-Price (1977) who base their argument on the lack of evidence for the earlier presence of wild sheep on the island and the probable inability of sheep to swim to Cyprus from the mainland at some ancient date before man's arrival.

A different view is expressed by Fisher, Simon and Vincent (1969) in *The Red Book* that examines rare species and their present-day status. They state categorically that 'The moufflon is the only large wild mammal native to Cyprus'. Zeuner (1963) comments, 'Cyprus is an outpost of the oriental mouf-

flon, and one wonders whether it was ever taken into domestication', again supporting the idea that it was an indigenous species.

Whichever view one favours, the fact remains that sheep were of major importance as a food source in prehistoric Cyprus. The Khirokitians ate them in numbers, only deer being more popular, judging by remains. Sheep bones were twice as common as goat bones. According to Dikaios (1953), the sheep bones of Khirokitia differed in no way from those of the present-day wild Cyprian moufflon.

The male moufflon has heavy, sickle-shaped horns. The female is hornless. The animals, whether native or introduced, were very common and widespread on the island in ancient times. Even as late as the medieval epoch, they were still common in the mountains and foothills right across Cyprus. But then, although fleet of foot, they began to fall prey more and more to huntsmen who were often aided by cheetah or packs of hounds. With the advent of modern firearms the numbers sank dramatically until, by 1937, the entire Cypriot population of moufflon had been reduced to a mere fifteen animals in one small herd in the Paphos Forest. Modern conservation has now rescued the herd from

Fig. 351

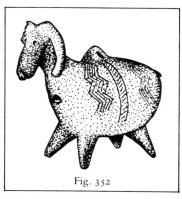

Fig. 352

Fig. 353

Pl. 245

6 Sheep

Pl. 245 *Ram figure. Hollow figure with raised tail acting as the aperture in the form of a cutaway spout. Loop handle on back. Tightly curved horns above forward bent ears. Eyes and mouth are incised holes, but not penetrating to the interior. Four very short 'leg-buds' and the grossly swollen, almost spherical body indicate that this animal is being portrayed as a liquid-carrying skin, full to capacity. Handmade White Painted Ware. Middle Bronze Age. Length 12.1 cm. Ht. 11.2 cm (DM-HWP-67). Formerly in the collection of Sir Francis Cook.*

extinction and it is believed that the numbers have risen to somewhere between 100 and 200 animals.

The sheer numbers of sheep bones found in excavations seem to suggest that farming must have been taking place on an impressive scale. Hunting alone could hardly account for the quantities involved, bearing in mind the primitive weapons available to prehistoric Cypriots and the difficult terrain in which the free sheep were living. At the Bronze Age site of Kalopsidha, for instance, Gejvall (in Astrom, 1966) reported that 94.6 per cent of the animal remains were sheep. Furthermore, 77 per cent of the sheep remains (that is, 642 out of 833 bones) were of sub-adult or infantile animals. In other words, the inhabitants preferred lamb to mutton and were clearly using sheep as major meat producers. There can be no doubt, therefore, that by this time, sheep were fully domesticated and Zeuner's reservations on the subject can be forgotten.

In the art of ancient Cyprus, the distinctive curved horns of the ram appear early at the beginning of the Bronze Age, at Vounous. There, ram's heads are seen protruding from rims of vessels in a similar manner to the bucrania discussed earlier in the section on cattle. In addition, an incised motif in the shape of a ram seen from above (Fig. 351) appears as part of the decoration on one vessel. This has previously been interpreted as a human figure wearing a ram's head mask, but its four legs with cloven hooves suggest that it is more probably a plan view of the animal itself.

Ram figurines in Red Polished Ware are rare, but one is shown here in Fig. 352. They are more common in the Middle Bronze Age White Painted Ware, and two attractive examples are illustrated (Pl. 245 and Fig. 353). The species remains a popular subject right through the Iron Age, especially in the form of small Bichrome Ware figurines such as Fig. 354. From the seventh to the fifth century BC, Cyprus saw the introduction of sacred ram cults. Vermeule (1974) comments: 'Just as the rustic sanctuaries of Greece ... featured ... votives of Hermes as god of the flocks ... so the thoroughly agrarian or pastoral areas of Cyprus ... could produce works of art in which the lofty, regal images imported from Egypt (Ammon) and the Syrian coast (the ram-headed god Baal-Hamman) were brought into relationship with simple, local aspirations.'

Fig. 354

Fig. 354 *Ram figure. Bichrome Ware. Iron Age. No provenance (Pierides Collection, Larnaca). Ht. 10 cm. Karageorghis 1973, Pl. 75.*

7 Goats

The goat rivals the sheep as the earliest ruminant to be brought under control by man. Expert opinion differs as to which came first, but it seems fairly certain that the goat was more important to man in the early stages. Clutton-Brock (1981) comments: 'Although there may be evidence from radiocarbon dating that the domestication of sheep preceded that of goats it is quite clear from many sites from which their remains have been retrieved that the goat was more commonly kept as a supplier of meat at this earliest period than sheep.' Furthermore, the goat was a valuable source of milk and remained dominant in this role until cattle arrived on the scene.

Whereas sheep are grazers, goats are browsers, and their ability to find food in a variety of harsh environments and to survive on a poor diet in appalling conditions made them the ideal species for early exploitation by man. Although the exact location is not known, somewhere on the mainland east of Cyprus around 8,000 BC they came under human control, and were among the earliest animal importations to the island, accompanying the first settlers there. Goat remains have been found at the Neolithic sites of Khirokitia, Sotira and Erimi, and they were clearly of importance on Cyprus throughout the prehistoric period—as they are to this day.

By the Early Bronze Age there were already two distinct breeds of goat present on Cyprus. Red Polished Ware jugs from this period show relief figures of both the scimitar-horned goat (see Schaeffer, 1936, Pl. XIII, 1, from Vounous) and the spiral-horned goat (see Karageorghis, 1976, no. 65, from

7 Goats

Fig. 355 *Man riding goat, holding on to its horns (but right horn and arm missing). Bichrome Ware. Iron Age. No provenance (private collection).*

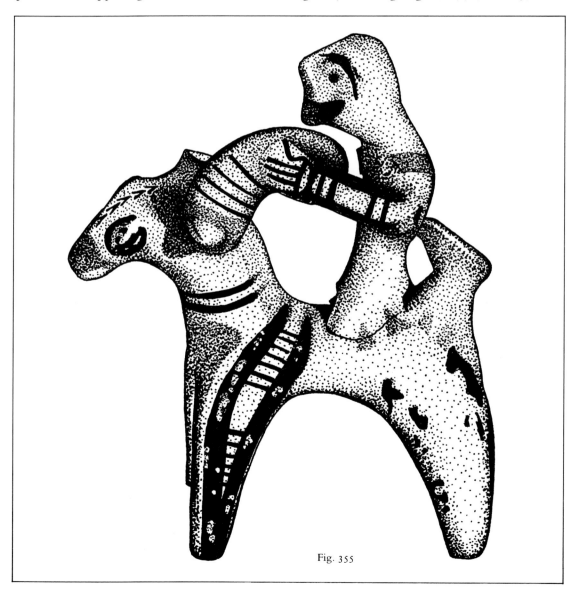

Fig. 355

Kochati). Certain authors have suggested that there were, in fact, two distinct species of wild goats involved in the development of the domestic animal, giving rise to these two types of horn-shape. The bezoar goat (*Capra aegagrus*) comes from Asia Minor and the Middle East and has scimitar-shaped horns. The markhor (*Capra falconeri*) has spiralled or screwed horns and hails from further east, from Kashmir to Baluchistan. But, attractive though this idea is, there seems little doubt that all domestic goats stem from the bezoar goat species, and that the domestic animals with spiralled horns are merely a variant of that species produced by artificial human selection, rather than separate descendants from the markhor.

The goat appears rarely in the art of the Middle Bronze Age but makes a strong return in the Late Bronze Age, always now in the scimitar-horned version. It appears as a terminal on a Base Ring Ware ring vessel (see Fig. 5) and on a large number of early Wheel-made White Painted and Bichrome Ware vessels, where the curving, backward-sweeping horns connect with the basket-handle (see Pl. 246). This device continues on into the Early Iron Age (see Fig. 357).

Sometimes these horned heads are so formalized that it is difficult to tell whether the artists specifically intended to portray goats, but there are two clues that prove helpful in such cases. The bezoar goat possesses two characteristic features that it passed on to its domestic descendants: the lateral compression of the anterior surface of the horns, forming a sharp 'leading edge' or anterior keel; and the inter-ramal beard beneath the chin of the male. The sharp edge to the front of the horns is visible in all four examples illustrated here (Pl. 246 and Figs. 355-7), and in all but Fig. 355 there is also a clear suggestion of the beard, albeit somewhat abbreviated for sculptural purposes.

The most remarkable goat figure of all is the Bichrome Ware example (Fig. 355) illustrated here, in which the animal is shown with a human rider on its back. Despite the absence of a beard on this animal, there is no doubt that it is meant to be a goat rather than some other, larger ungulate, because, if examined frontally, the sharp edge and lateral compression of the horns are strikingly portrayed. This figurine is odd because it represents a fantasy ride, which is most unusual in Cypriot art.

Pl. 246

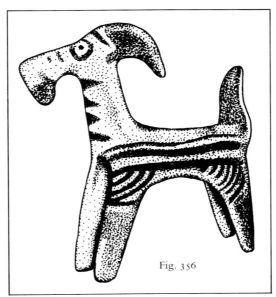

Fig. 356

7 Goats

Pl. 246 *Goat's-head spout with distinctive beard and backward curving, parallel horns. On ring vessel (see Pl. 152 on p. 84 for details). Bichrome Ware. Late Bronze Age to Early Iron Age (DM-BI-74).*

Fig. 356 *Goat figure. Bichrome Ware. Iron Age. No provenance (Museum of Fine Arts, Boston). Ht. 13.4 cm. Vermeule 1972, no. 25.*

Fig. 357 *Goat-headed spout on a Bichrome Ware jug. Iron Age. No provenance (Metropolitan Museum, New York). Ht. (of jug) 20 cm. Hennessy 1979, Pl. 105.*

Fig. 357

8 Dogs

Long before any ungulates were brought under human control, the domestication of the dog had begun—somewhere in the region of 12,000 years ago. All 400 breeds of modern dogs are descended from the wolf. Both species, man and wolf, were co-operative hunters and young wolf cubs reared by prehistoric tribes (originally to fatten them for food, no doubt) eventually came to join their foster parents in the hunt. Their use in this context quickly changed their role from prey to hunting companions. Judging by dog bones found at Neolithic Cypriot sites, the first settlers on the island brought these companions with them when they crossed over from the neighbouring mainland.

It is intriguing that the dog reported from the Neolithic site of Sotira, by Dikaios (1961) is described as 'fox-terrier size'. Already, at this early stage, the original wolf body had been considerably modified by selective breeding, indicating a fairly advanced stage of domestication.

By the dawn of the Cypriot Bronze Age,

dogs were beginning to appear occasionally as pottery figurines, in Red Polished Ware (see Figs. 358-9), and these too look much smaller and more friendly than their wolf ancestor. The ears are floppier, the jaws weaker and the legs shorter. These may well be exaggerations based on purely stylistic modifications, especially where the shortening of the legs is concerned, but nevertheless it is clear that the artists were not setting out to portray the dog as a powerful, savage beast. He already has the look of 'man's best friend' about him.

The same is true of a popular Bronze Age canine motif where dogs are shown playfully jumping up the side of jugs or jars. These little dog-handles run right through from the Red Polished Ware of the Early Bronze Age to the White Painted and Black Slip Ware of the Middle and Late Bronze Ages. Vermeule (1974) recorded that the Middle-to-Late Bronze Age town of 'Toumba tou Skourou produced dozens of these otherwise rare White Painted tankards with dogs climbing the waist in front to act as an extra handle'. She was so impressed by their liveliness that she could not resist referring to two of them as a 'yelping sheep dog' and a 'peaceful house dog'.

Dogs become popular again with Cypriot artists in the Iron Age, when they reappear as friendly little canine figurines in Bichrome Ware (see Figs. 360-5), especially at Salamis (Karageorghis, 1970), and in Plain White Ware (see Pl. 247).

8 Dogs

Figs. 358-9 *Red Polished Ware. Early Bronze Age.*

Fig. 358 *No provenance (Sèvres Museum).*

Fig. 359 *Nicosia-Ayia Paraskevi. Ht. 4 cm. Karageorghis 1976, no. 73.*

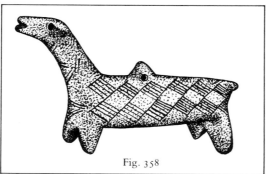

Fig. 358

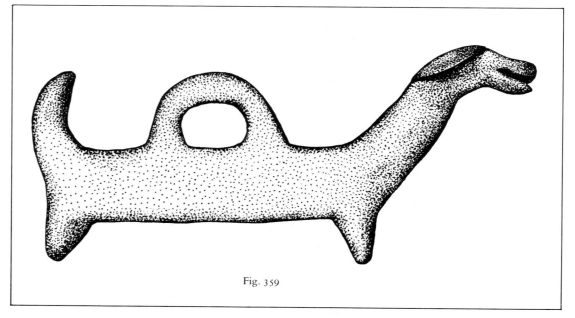

Fig. 359

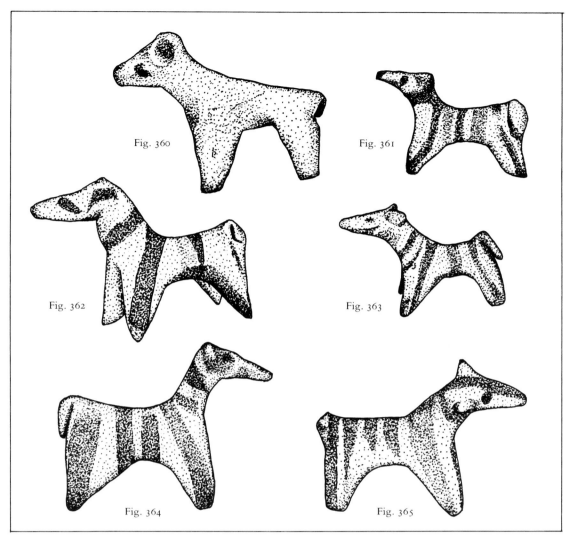

8 Dogs

Figs. 360–5 *Bichrome Ware. Iron Age. From Salamis.*

Fig. 360 *Tomb 10, no. 37. Ht. 5.2 cm. Karageorghis 1970, Pl. LXVII.*

Fig. 361 *Tomb 102, no. 1. Ht. 6 cm. Karageorghis 1970, Pl. CLXXV.*

Fig. 362 *Tomb 56, no. 1. Ht. 6.7 cm. Karageorghis 1970, Pl. CXXXVIII.*

Fig. 363 *Tomb 85, no. 10. Ht. 7.2 cm. Karageorghis 1970, Pl. CLXVI.*

Fig. 364 *Tomb 27a, no. 8. Ht. 7 cm. Karageorghis 1970, Pl. CIX.*

Fig. 365 *Tomb 42, Dr. 2. Ht. 7 cm. Karageorghis 1970, Pl. CXXVI.*

Pl. 247 *Dog with pointed snout, erect ears and down-curving tail. No trace of pigment survives, although the figure may once have been painted. Plain White Ware. Iron Age. Length 10.5 cm (DM-PW-28).*

Pl. 247

9 Birds

Pigeons, chickens, geese and ducks have been domesticated from early times, and pigeons and geese, in particular, seem to have come under human control from the Neolithic onwards. It is hard to be specific, however, because the smaller bird bones do not survive as well as the tougher mammalian bones discussed earlier. So, for this group of animals, more is to be learnt from the work of ancient artists than from skeletal material.

The earliest representations of birds in Cypriot art are to be found in the Red Polished Ware of the Early Bronze Age. Here they seem to be forever alighting on the rims of bowls or the shoulders of jugs and jars, but they never appear, at this stage, as free-standing figurines in their own right. The only non-attached examples in this period are a few vaguely bird-shaped juglets (see Pl. 253). In this respect they are different from mammals such as cattle and deer, which appear both as vessel-attached figures and as independent figurines.

Unfortunately the bird images created in ancient Cyprus are so formalized that it is usually impossible to identify the species involved, and equally impossible to decide whether the birds portrayed are wild or tame. Their generalized shape might be interpreted as anything from eagle to pigeon, and

9 Birds

Pl. 248 *Bird figures, detached from the rim or shoulder of large vessels. With flattened areas to represent wings. Incised decoration on upper surfaces, but no eye or beak details on head. Incised Red Polished Ware. Early Bronze Age.*
a(left) *Length 8.3 cm (DM-IRP-94).*
b(right) *Length 8.2 cm (DM-IRP-95).*

Pl. 249 *Vulture figure, on rim of large vessel (for details of which see Pl. 219 on p. 190). Plain Red Polished Ware. Early Bronze Age. (DM-PRP-39).*

Pl. 248

Fig. 366

Fig. 366 *Vulture on rim of Red Polished Ware bowl. Early Bronze Age. No provenance (Cyprus Museum). Des Gagniers and Karageorghis 1976, Pl. XV, no. 2.*

Pl. 249

any attempt to be more specific would be futile.

One exception to this rule concerns a few Red Polished Ware birds that have a distinctly vulturine shape (see Fig. 366 and Pl. 249). Here, the curve of the neck and the general outline of the body are sufficiently characteristic to venture a guess that, in these cases at least, the artists were intent on portraying the 'bird of death'. Vultures, so unpopular today for their association with carrion, had a much more powerful, mystical image in ancient times because of their appearance in the sky whenever a dead body was present. They figure importantly in the Neolithic town of Çatal Hüyük in nearby Anatolia (Mellaart, 1967), where wall paintings show huge vultures pecking at headless human corpses, and they also play a significant role in the mythology of ancient Egypt. Furthermore, Cyprus does boast an indigenous vulture—the Griffon Vulture—which can still occasionally be seen flying around the peaks of the mountain ranges. These huge birds, with their impressive wing span of over two metres, can hardly have failed to catch the imagination of the early Cypriots, and it is

Pl. 250

not surprising to find them represented on tomb vessels so closely associated with death.

One bewildering feature of the birds created by the artists of ancient Cyprus is that they sometimes appear to be quadrupedal. Because of this it is easy to mis-identify

9 Birds

Pl. 250 *Three bird figures on shoulders of large, twin-necked jug (for details of which see Pl. 156 on p. 97). Drab Polished Ware. Middle Bronze Age (DM-DP-14).*

Pl. 251 *Tulip bowl with two bird-headed lugs on rim. Incised Red Polished Ware. Early Bronze Age. Ht. of bowl 17.2 cm. Diam. 17.4 cm (DM-IRP-97).*

Pl. 251

Pl. 252

them. The small animal perched on the shoulder of the Red Polished Ware gourd jug in Pl. 252 gives a first impression of being some strange kind of mammal, because of the apparent arrangement of its legs. But closer examination reveals that the artist has simply perched a small bird on a pierced lug. This makes the lug look like front and back legs instead of a resting place. Similarly, the bird-shaped juglets shown in Pls. 256-7 on p. 226 may have three or even four short, stumpy legs, but these have been provided more as 'stands' for the vessels than as anatomical statements.

Key elements that help to identify these early, highly stylized birds *as* birds are not the legs but the beaks, tails and wings. Some, like Pls. 255 and 256b, have long beaks and clearly defined wing-stumps projecting from the side of the body. These features alone are diagnostic and the oddity of other elements, such as the barrel-shaped body of one or the button-ears and forelegs of the other, should not be allowed to deflect from an avian identification.

Other bird-vessels, such as Pls. 256a, 257b and 257d, have wing patterns painted on them as part of the body decoration. Still others, such as Pl. 257c, although highly formalized and almost abstract, reveal their avian nature by the presence of a pair of spiky projections on the flanks, which are the last stylized remains of the wings.

9 Birds

Pl. 252 *Bird-shaped lug on shoulder of round base, round spout jug. The bird is sitting on a pierced lug which wrongly gives the impression that it has four legs. Incised Red Polished Ware. Early Bronze Age. Ht. of jug 21.6 cm (DM-IRP-96).*

Pl. 253

a(left) *Bird-shaped jug with round base, short neck with cutaway spout, loop handle on back, and short tail. Decorated with crude incisions. Mottled Red Polished Ware. Early Bronze Age. Ht. 11.6 cm (DM-MRP-30).*

b(right) *Bird-shaped jug with flat base, long neck with beak spout, loop handle on back and short tail. Decoration is both relief and incised. Same ware. Ht. 14.5 cm (DM-MRP-31).*

Pl. 253

Pl. 254

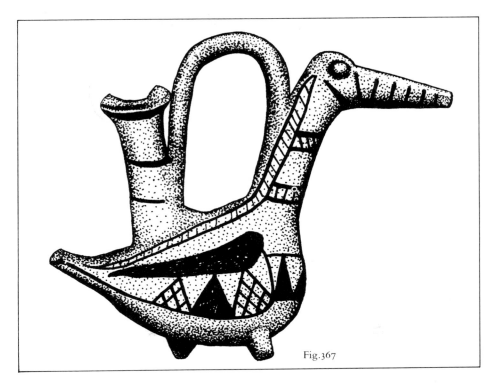

Fig.367

Birds were popular with Cypriot artists in all epochs. After the Red Polished Ware birds of the Early Bronze Age (see Pls. 248–53 and Fig. 366), there were White Painted Ware examples in the Middle Bronze Age (see Pl. 256), White Shaved 'owls' and Proto-White Painted bird-jugs in the Late Bronze Age (see Pls. 254–5 and Fig. 367), and Bichrome and White Painted bird-juglets in the Iron Age (see Pl. 257). Even in these later stages, how-

ever, the terracotta bird figurine (as distinct from the bird-shaped juglet) remained a rarity. Only a handful of examples appear to have been published, of which Figs. 368–71 are typical.

In addition to these three-dimensional birds, there was a great explosion of bird paintings in the Iron Age. White Painted Ware and Bichrome vessels display bird motifs time after time. In their major study of

9 Birds

Pl. 254 *Owl-shaped rattle with pointed base, vertical handle and two pierced holes for eyes. Decoration of simple black lines. White Shaved Ware. Late Bronze Age. Ht. 9.8 cm (DM-WSH-02). Cf. Myres 1914, no. 387; also Loch 1966, no. 48.*

Fig. 367 *Long-billed bird. Proto-White Painted Ware. Late Bronze Age. No provenance (Metropolitan Museum, New York). Ht. 16.4 cm. Karageorghis 1975, Pl. X, 2.*

Pl. 255 *Bird-shaped jug. The barrel-shaped body has two short, stubby wings projecting from its sides. On the back is a tall neck with a round spout and a loop handle behind it. The side-spout at the front of the vessel has been converted into the bird's neck by the addition of a clumsy beak. The whole vessel is crudely shaped and its transformation into a bird is primitively executed. Proto-White Painted Ware. Late Bronze Age. Ht. 17.3 cm. Max. length 22.7 cm (DM-WWP-185).*

Pl. 255

Pl. 256

Pl. 257

9 Birds

Pl. 256 *Bird-shaped figures. Handmade White Painted Ware. Middle Bronze Age.*

a(left) *Hollow body with single aperture on back in form of pinched spout. Loop handle behind spout. Four very short stump-legs. Eyes and mouth shown as incisions. Bump on top of head makes this figure reminiscent of the camel in Pl. 244, but the shorter neck, the forked tail and the way in which the painted decoration suggests a pair of wings, indicate that this is meant to be an avian figure. Length 13.5 cm. Ht. 11.5 cm (DM-HWP-69).*

b(right) *Hollow body, the aperture being a circular hole in the chest region. A small loop handle on the back and a pair of wing-stubs projecting from the sides of the body. Four splayed out legs. Pointed tail and beak. What appear to be the eyes are in fact the nostrils. The larger, button eyes are placed on top of the head. Almost all signs of painted lines have worn away. Length 11.6 cm (DM-HWP-68).*

Pl. 257 *Bird-shaped figures*
Back, left to right
a *Three legs, strap-handle on back and trumpet-mouth. Body hollow with aperture in round spout behind handle. Eyes shown in relief. The whole body covered in geometric patterns. Proto-White Painted Ware. End of the Late Bronze Age. Length 16.5 cm. Ht. 12.1 cm (DM-WWP-186). Formerly in the Bomford Collection.*
b *Three legs. Body hollow with apertures in mouth and in round spout on the back. The spout with loop handles in front and behind. Painted decoration includes eyes and wings. Bichrome Ware. Iron Age. Length 16.5 cm (DM-BI-115).*

Front, left to right
c *No legs. The head is reduced to a pinched spout, providing the aperture for the hollow interior. No facial features are shown. Wings are represented by a pair of protruding spikes. Bichrome Ware. Iron Age. Length 15.8 cm (DM-BI-116).*
d *No legs. The head is reduced to a pinched spout, providing the aperture for the hollow interior. Painted eyes are present on the rim of the spout. Wings are represented by painted motifs. Bichrome Ware. Iron Age. Length 20.8 cm (DM-BI-117).*

Pl. 258 *Bird painting, on side of bowl with stem base and two horizontal handles. Black-on-Red Ware. Iron Age. Diam. 13 cm (DM-BOR-19).*

Pl. 259 *Bird-shaped glazed dish. Glazed in pale blue and white, with feathers indicated by black lines. On either side of the dish a bird's wing is shown and, in the centre, a group of body feathers. At the top, the dish is cut away to form the bird's head, with an eye shown in relief. The beak is strangely shaped, widening out at its tip, where it curves back to touch its own body, as if the bird is preening itself. This curving back of the beak forms an aperture by which the dish could be hung on a wall-peg. The back is plain but glazed. This curious dish, for which there are no parallels, is said to have been found in a fourth-century BC, Cypro-Classical II tomb in Cyprus. Diam. 19.7 cm (DM-GL-01).*

9 Birds

Pl. 260 *Bird paintings on the shoulders of a jug with ring base and round spout. Twisted handle. Three birds painted in red on buff background. Wheelmade White Painted Ware. Hellenistic period. Ht. 22.4 cm (DM-WWP-32).*

Pl. 260

the 'free-field' style of vessel-painting in this period, Karageorghis and des Gagniers (1974) devote no fewer than 221 pages to bird examples. The total number of bird-decorated vessels is 294. They divide up into the following wares:

Bichrome:	87 per cent
White Painted:	10 per cent
Black-on-Red:	2 per cent
Bichrome Red:	1 per cent

The vast majority belong to the sub-ware labelled Bichrome IV (188 out of the 294 vessels).

This means that the bird-decorated bowl illustrated here in Pl. 258 is a comparatively rare type, there being only six other Black-on-Red Ware examples listed by Karageorghis and des Gagniers.

Nine examples of painted birds from the huge number known are shown in Figs. 372-80. These demonstrate that it is in the wings that there are the greatest variations of style, from 'sprouting feathers' in Figs. 372-3, to 'flowing scarves' in Figs. 378-9.

Benson (1975), who has made a particular study of the earliest examples of Cypriot bird-painting, sees this trend, which erupted at the end of the Bronze Age, as an essentially imported phenomenon. He comments that 'the native inhabitants at this time did not, in effect, have the habit of depicting birds on their pottery; yet they were in close contact with cultures which did, viz., the Mycenaeans (and even Minoans), Syrians, and, ultimately, Philistines. In the historical process by which the culture of the Mycenaean settlers amalgamated with that of the native population, the practice of adding birds to the decoration of vases apparently had its origin.' This is undoubtedly the case (see Vermeule and Karageorghis, 1982), but with the passage of time, as so often happened, the Cypriot artists began to bring their own stylistic humour and liveliness to bear on yet another foreign import.

Figs. 368-71 *Small terracotta figures of birds. Iron Age.*

Fig. 368 *White Painted Ware. Rizokarpaso-Latsia. Christou 1972, Pl. XXVI, 15.*

Fig. 369 *Bichrome Ware. Salamis (Tomb 27a, no. 9). Ht. 6 cm. Karageorghis 1970, Pl. CIX.*

Fig. 370 *White Painted Ware. Rizokarpaso-Latsia. Ht. 6.8 cm. Christou 1972, Pl. XXVI, 16.*

Fig. 371 *Bichrome Ware. Soloi, Ht. 9.2 cm. Karageorghis 1972, no. 62.*

Fig. 368

Fig. 369

Fig. 370

Fig. 371

Fig. 372

Fig. 373

Fig. 374

Fig. 375

Fig. 376

Fig. 377

Fig. 378

Fig. 379

Fig. 380

Figs. 372–80 *Bird motifs painted on Bichrome Ware vessels. Iron Age. From Karageorghis and Des Gagniers 1974, Group XXV. No provenance is known with certainty.*

Fig. 372 *d8 (Louvre Museum).*
Fig. 373 *a4 (Kolokossides Collection, Nicosia).*
Fig. 374 *a6 (Museum of Fine Arts, Boston).*

Fig. 375 *g5 (Cyprus Museum).*
Fig. 376 *g12 (Cyprus Museum).*
Fig. 377 *e3 (Cyprus Museum).*
Fig. 378 *g23 (Kolokossides Collection, Nicosia).*

Fig. 379 *g18 (Cyprus Museum).*
Fig. 380 *g36 (Cyprus Museum).*

Pl. 261

10 Snakes

Pl. 261 *Snake decoration on large jug with round base and round spout. Handle with small thumb-spur. 'Baker's stick' motifs on shoulder of jug (Cf. Pl. 303 on p. 272) and serpentine motifs running up the long neck. Relief-decorated Red Polished Ware. Early Bronze Age. Ht. 36.3 cm (DM-RRP-01).*

Pl. 262 *Snake decoration on large jug with round base and round spout. Handle with large thumb-spur and, opposite it, a very large lug—almost another handle. The serpentine motifs run up the shoulders of the vessel, inside panels formed by parallel lines. Relief-decorated Red Polished Ware. Early Bronze Age. Ht 52.1 cm (DM-RRP-04).*

Pl. 262

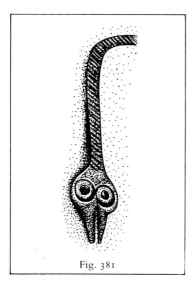

Fig. 381

10 Snakes

Fig. 381 *Detail of a snake relief-decoration motif on a Proto-Base Ring Ware vessel. Late Bronze Age. No provenance (British Museum). Ht. (of vessel) 27.5 cm. Hennessy 1979, Pl. 76.*

10 Snakes

Cyprus once had the reputation of being infested with poisonous snakes, and although this was a wild exaggeration, the local fauna does include one highly venomous species, the Levant viper *(Vipera lebetina)*. This, the largest of the Mediterranean vipers, which can grow up to 1.5 metres in length, must always have played a dangerous and important role in the lives of the ancient Cypriots. It is not surprising therefore to find snake motifs appearing on prehistoric vessels.

Many of the Red Polished jugs and bowls of the Early Bronze Age period display an undulating, serpentine pattern, and two typical examples are shown on the previous pages (Pls. 261-2). These relief-rendered motifs are widely accepted as representing snakes, and it is highly likely that they do so, but a word of caution is necessary. None of the Early Bronze Age snake motifs actually displays a snake's head at one end of the undulating relief line. The most convincing example (on a Vounous jug, Tomb 87a, no. 2) has very snake-like curves and is patterned with spots, but it still lacks the head which would make it totally convincing. It could be argued that all these 'undulating relief-line' motifs are instead (a) abstract design elements, (b) symbols of some other natural element, such as a winding river, or (c) an undulating tassel or rope motif. I am not suggesting that one of these seems more likely, but it would be reassuring if an Early Bronze Age snake image with a convincing head could be unearthed at some point in the future, to lend support to the widely accepted serpentine interpretation.

This is particularly important because (as we shall see on p. 283) the vertical undulating relief-lines on the famous Vounous 'Model of a Sacred Enclosure' (Fig. 495) have been imaginatively exploited as the key element in that remarkable scenic composition. Dikaios (1940) put forward the idea 'that the ceremony represented in the Vounous enclosure is mainly intended for the chthonian deities whose attribute is the snake'. If the two small, vertical 'squiggles' on the wall of this model are to be used as the basis for building a major concept of prehistoric Cypriot snake-gods and snake-worship, then we had better be certain that they really *are* snakes. Their accurate description by Dikaios does little to help. The 'snakes' appear between three buc-

ranial figures, shown in relief on the wall. Of these figures, Dikaios says: 'their hands are extended and joined to one another, and from where they are joined hangs a snake.' A more logical but less exciting interpretation is that, if an undulating line hangs down from the point where two hands are joined, that line represents the free end of a rope binding the two hands together. Dikaios compares the 'enclosure snakes' with two other 'snakes' that hang down below the heads of two bulls on a large Vounous bowl (Tomb 36, no. 10), but this hardly assists his case, because again an undulating line below an animal's head logically suggests the free end of a rope that has been placed around its neck.

These objections are merely a reminder of the need for caution and are not to be given too much weight. It is well known (see Morris and Morris, 1965) that the snake was a powerful symbolic element in the thinking of early human societies on a worldwide scale. It was indeed multi-symbolic. Because it shed its skin it was thought to 'rise again from the dead' and therefore symbolized reincarnation, resurrection, immortality and the perennial renewal of life through death. Individuals may come and go but the spirit of the race lives forever in the serpent. Because snakes appear to come from inside the earth and slither back into it again, they were thought to represent 'the underworld powers of dead ancestors' (Harrison, 1903). Because of its (literally) ever-open eyes, the snake was seen as an ever watchful guardian and protector, who would strike down an enemy intruder. Because of its rising head and its long, legless shape, it was also given phallic properties which made it a symbol of virility, fertility and fecundity.

These and other symbolic equations mean that snakes were well qualified for use in ancient Cypriot ceremonies involving magical beliefs and superstitions. In fact, these reptiles had so many qualifications that it is hard to decide which one was operating in the Early Bronze Age, when all we have to go on is a collection of serpentine squiggles. However, if the association with bucrania is significant, then it would seem reasonable to suppose that the snake and the bull were joined together as 'Great Protectors'. This would bring the Cypriot snake symbol into line with the well-known Minoan one. As Hutchinson (1962) has pointed out, the Minoan 'snake had probably nothing to do with the snakes that appear in underworld cults in classical Greece. It was the house snake and was fed and revered as the genius, the guardian angel of the house, according to a very widespread superstition.' In such a role, the snakes on the prehistoric Cypriot tomb vessels would be there as protective devices, guarding the deceased and his provisions from harmful elements. And the snakes shown on the wall of the Vounous enclosure scene would be there to protect the community depicted in the model—an additional defence to that provided by the bucranial horns.

The snake image virtually disappears in the Middle Bronze Age but reasserts itself strongly in the Late Bronze Age. Here it appears in a special form on the bodies of Base Ring Ware jugs, and, for the first time, a convincing snake's head is present (see Fig. 381). These relief-rendered serpents always appear in pairs, one on each side of the jug handle. As the Late Bronze Age advances, these twin snake motifs gradually change, the two snake heads coming closer together until they merge as one, as if in the artists' imagination the snakes are mating. From this point the motif becomes increasingly abstract and reaches a point where it would be indecipherable, were it not for the existence of the earlier, more obviously serpentine examples (see Fig. 538).

The most realistic snakes in the art of ancient Cyprus are to be found on a group of complex vessels from the end of the Late Bronze Age and the beginning of the Iron Age (see Strand, 1974, p. 43 and Karageorghis, 1975, Pls. LXXVIII and LXXX). These are in Proto-White Painted Ware and show well-proportioned snakes carefully modelled on the handles or bottoms of the vessels. The snakes are spotted or banded and have clearly defined heads. In each case they are associated with a horned head that appears to be that of a goat, with backward sweeping horns and a short beard.

11 Other Species

In addition to the animals discussed above, certain other species do appear from time to time in the ancient art of Cyprus, in minor roles. The lion is portrayed a few times, from the Late Bronze Age through to the Cypro-Archaic and beyond. Although the Cypriots themselves will not have encountered it, the

lion was, of course, present in those days on the neighbouring mainlands. People arriving on the island will have brought memories of it, or perhaps even images of it, with them. (For lions, see Karageorghis, 1975, Pl. X,1; Catling, 1964, Pl. 43a; Karageorghis, 1970, no. 43; Karageorghis, 1979, Pl. XII,1; Karageorghis, 1973, no. 76, where the Pierides figurine is wrongly called a dog, despite the presence of a leonine mouth, a black mane and a tufted tail; and Karageorghis and des Gagniers, 1974, Pls. XIV,1 and XIV,2.)

At the other end of the scale, there are three delightful little frog figures modelled inside complex bowls from the end of the Late Bronze Age. These bowls have main spouts in the shape of horned-animal heads and display the 'trick feature' that, if water is poured into the mouth of the horned head, it emerges from the mouth of the frog lying on the bottom of the bowl. (For frogs, see Pieridou, 1966, Pl. IV,8; Pieridou, 1971, Pl. XII,4; Karageorghis et al., 1974, Fig. 51.)

The only other small animals portrayed are the tortoise (in the form of a Bichrome terracotta, Iron Age, see Karageorghis, 1973, no. 77) and the hedgehog (a Late Bronze Age animal-shaped vessel from Maroni, see Johnson, 1980, no. 11). The latter is so stylized, however, that the identification cannot be certain. Its face and body shape are more reminiscent of a chameleon than a hedgehog, and the absence of a long tail may simply be artistic license (see Fig. 382).

On the free-field painted vessels of the Iron Age period there are also a number of marine creatures—fish, octopus, squid and dolphin (see Karageorghis and des Gagniers, 1973).

Fig. 382 *Hedgehog or chameleon? A Late Bronze Age animal figure of doubtful identity, from Maroni (Tomb 14). Length 18.3 cm. Johnson 1980, no. 100.*

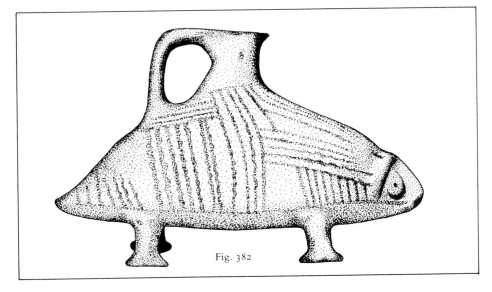

Fig. 382

Pl. 263

Pl. 264

Pl. 263 *Rosettes on large jar. These simple rosettes are among the earliest found on Cypriot vessels, dating from the very beginning of the Iron Age. Wheelmade White Painted Ware. Early Iron Age. Ht. 51 cm (DM-WWP-97).*

Pl. 264 *Tendril motifs on large, squat jar. Bichrome Ware. Iron Age. Ht 25.2 cm (DM-BI-46).*

Pl. 265 *Terracotta pomegranate rattle. Iron Age. Length 11.5 cm (DM-RT-26). Cf. Karageorghis 1981, no. 53, for a similar shaped pendant.*

Pl. 265

Plant Forms

Plant motifs arrive late in the art of ancient Cyprus. During the prehistoric period, they are almost non-existent as decorative or symbolic designs. The only major influence of botanical forms during this phase is on the shape of certain of the vessels. During the Early Bronze Age, many of the jugs and juglets in Red Polished Ware are referred to as 'gourd jugs' or 'gourd juglets'. The inference is that the potters imitated the shape of gourds when fashioning their vessels and that this occurred because natural gourds were themselves used as vessels. This idea can be traced back as far as Perrot and Chipiez in 1885, who wrote: 'Another shape scarcely known out of Cyprus is the gourd form of bottle, which may have been suggested to the potter by some of those calabashes which are to be found in nearly all hot countries. Some flagons turned on this model are among the best established and most original of Cypriot industrial products.' Myres (1914) takes this idea further, commenting that these globular vessels are 'designed in imitation of the neck and wooden handle of a gourd bottle. The peculiar form of the handle ... imitates a handle made of pieces of bent wood inserted in the neck and shoulder of a gourd bottle. Broken examples of such pottery usually show that the potter has imitated not only the external form, but the actual process employed by the gourd-bottle maker.'

For some, this concept of specific imitation of gourds in pottery, right down to small details, goes too far. They prefer the idea of a 'vague influence', rather than deliberate copying. But if modern tribal examples of decorated gourds are examined, the similarities are remarkable. In Chappel's (1977) work on *Decorated Gourds of North-eastern Nigeria* the colour plates reveal that not only the shapes but also the colours and textures of the gourds are amazingly reminiscent of Cypriot Red Polished Ware. Furthermore, the gourd artists always incise their decorations, either by cutting them into the soft surface of the gourd, or by burning them in with a fine poker. They do not paint them. This provides a strong hint as to why the Early Bronze Age artists confined themselves almost entirely to brownish-red, polished, globular bodied, round-bottomed vessels which were so frequently decorated with incised patterns but never with painted ones. It also suggests that there was probably a well-developed tradition of incised decorated gourds on the island, in addition to the pottery tradition.

The gourd species in question is the Bottle Gourd *(Lagenaria vulgaris)*, and it is still in use as a functional drinking vessel in the Mediterranian region today. It is also sold, in both incised and plain form, as a decorative object. The example shown in Pl. 266 was purchased in Cyprus in the 1960s and makes a striking comparison with the Early Bronze Age vessel beside it. (For further details of gourd vessels, see Organ, 1963.)

The second plant to influence early Cypriot pottery is the poppy head, according to an imaginative hypothesis by Merrillees (1968). His basic assumption is that Base Ring Ware juglets 'owe their morphological origin to a common organic prototype, viz., the seed capsule of the opium poppy plant *Papaver somniferum)*'. He carried out experiments with capsules cut from the stems of living plants found in Cyprus. With these 'it proved

Pl. 266 *A modern Cypriot gourd compared with an ancient Cypriot 'gourd bottle'. The close similarity of shape is undeniable but it is not certain whether the early artists were specifically imitating gourds or were merely influenced by their shapes. The bottle shown here is one of the type discussed in the final chapter. Red-and-Black Polished Ware. Early Bronze Age. Ht. 23.2 cm (DM-RBP-80).*

Pl. 266

possible, by paring down the stem, to produce a strap handle, and, by incising the surface, to release the latex and create a pattern which might have inspired the ornamental designs on the juglets' bodies.'

Merrillees believes that this imitation of the poppy head shape by Late Bronze Age Cypriot potters had a practical function. They were not seeking botanical inspiration for purely decorative purposes, they were *labelling* the contents of their vessels: '... the juglets were modelled on the opium poppy head to advertise the substance they held, and ... it was primarily for their contents that they were imported by Egypt.' He believes that this explains the lack of variation in the shapes of these Base Ring Ware vessels. Their design conservatism was to ensure that their 'label' was not mis-read.

Support for this theory might be expected from chemical analysis of the contents of these juglets, if any traces survived, but there is little help from this direction. Tests carried out at Sydney University did reveal traces of an 'opium derivative' in a few juglets, but other investigations totally failed to find such evidence. For the moment we must therefore return an open verdict on the Merrillees theory. At the very least, we must be grateful to it for alerting our attention to the intriguing question of how ancient potters *did* label the contents of their vessels. Perhaps a number of other shapes also carried specific messages about their contents.

A third plant shape that appears as a pottery motif in ancient Cyprus is the pomegranate. Here the representation is accurate enough to remove any doubts. Modelled pomegranates appear as early as the Late Bronze Age, on certain of the ring vessels (see Pl. 152 on p. 84) and continue through into the Iron Age, both on ring vessels and as independent objects such as rattles (Pl. 265) or pendants (see Karageorghis, 1981, no. 53, from Amathus, Tomb 332, no. 12).

Unfortunately, the pomegranate has enjoyed such a rich and varied symbolic life in different cultures that we cannot be certain what its specific meaning was to the ancient Cypriots who fashioned or wore its image. Judging by comments in Leach (1975), we may be dealing with yet another fertility charm: 'Because of its very numerous seeds, the pomegranate has been through the ages, a symbol of fertility, in Chinese, Persian, Semitic, Greek, and Roman lore. Chinese

women offer it to the goddess of mercy when praying for children, especially sons. The pomegranate is often credited with being the forbidden fruit of the Garden of Eden ...' Cooper (1978) also stresses a similar interpretation, but both authors mention the following additional symbolic roles played by the pomegranate at different times and in different places: wealth, hope, immortality, rejuvenation and regeneration. However, on balance, it is true to say that its most popular role is as a symbol of fertility, fecundity and abundance, and this has to be the most likely interpretation of the examples from ancient Cyprus.

Moving from sculptural shapes to painted designs, there are three plant motifs which figure significantly on Iron Age Cypriot vessels: the tendril, the rosette and the lotus.

Tendrils occur in a rather rigidly formalized version on a number of Bichrome jars (see Pl. 264 and Gjerstad, 1984, Fig. XLVIII, no. 10). They may point upwards or downwards and often lean off at an angle from the vertical. They are multilinear and show a single tight curl at the tip.

Rosettes appear from the very beginning of the Wheelmade White Painted Ware tradition (see early example on Pl. 263) and assume a variety of forms, eighteen popular examples

Pl. 267 *A dried poppy head compared with a 'poppy juglet'. It is claimed that the poppy-like shape of the small jug acted as a 'label' indicating that the vessel contained opium. The juglet shown here is relief-decorated Base Ring Ware. Late Bronze Age. Ht. 11.5 cm (DM-BR-09).*

Pl. 267

Pl. 268 *Simple lotus pattern in the painted decoration of a large, flat-based, round-spouted jug. Although found in Cyprus, this jug shows powerful foreign influences. Whether it was made in Cyprus by a immigrant potter or was imported from abroad has not yet been established (see p. 33). Clay analysis may settle this point but whatever the result, this vessel must stand at present as the earliest known example of the lotus motif in Cyprus. Cypro-Palestinian Bichrome Ware. Beginning of the Late Bronze Age. Ht. 41.7 cm (DM-CPB-01). Cf. Amiran 1970, no. 142.*

Pl. 269 *Highly stylized lotus design incorporated into the decoration of a large jar. Horizontally attached handles and ring base. Bichrome Ware. Iron Age. Ht. 36.6 cm (DM-BI-50).*

Pl. 268

Pl. 269

of which are given on p. 241 (Figs. 383-400). Whether the use of this simple floral pattern is merely decorative and it is being used solely for its geometric qualities, or whether it is meant to convey some deeper symbolic significance, is hard to say. The problem is that, as with the pomegranate, it has been given more than one traditional meaning. And that is an understatement. At various times and places it has been seen as a symbol of: wisdom, perfection, paradise, passion, time, eternity, life, death, fertility, virginity, the unknown, the mystery of life, completion, beauty, grace, happiness, voluptuousness, sensuality, seduction, love, creation, charm, mortality, sorrow, pain, blood, martyrdom, resurrection, the unattainable, unity, joy, desire, innocence, purity, chastity, prosperity, consummation, silence and secrecy. Although this far from exhausts the list, it would be foolish to continue. It is complex symbols of this kind that give the study of symbolism a bad name, allowing investigators to pick and choose interpretations at will, to suit the needs of the moment. As there is no supporting evidence to guide us in the case of the ancient Cypriot rosettes, the only appropriate response is to label them as 'floral decorations' and leave the matter there until ancient texts can be found to support a specific symbolic usage.

The third painted design—the lotus—suffers a similar fate. Indeed, the rosette is sometimes seen as 'the lotus viewed from above'. But there is one overriding symbolic tradition where the lotus is concerned, namely the idea of creation and renewal.

The lotus in question is the Water Lily, *Nymphaea lotus*, and is not to be confused with the Lotus Tree (probably *Zizyphus jujuba*) the fruit of which was consumed by the 'lotus eaters' to bring forgetfulness, nor the Nelumbo, *Nelumbium speciosum*, of the East which was sacred to the Hindus.

Nymphaea lotus is the lotus of the Nile and its image spread to Cyprus, either directly or indirectly, from ancient Egypt, where it was the symbol of the recurring fertilization of the land by the great river. Three visual elements were involved: the spreading petals of the great, open flower, facing upward to the sun; the closed, pointed buds yet to open; and the large floating leaves. These elements were the starting point for an explosion of Cypriot inventiveness (see pp. 242-8).

The earliest representation of the lotus known from ancient Cyprus is the extremely simplified pattern on the large jug shown in Pl. 268. This unique vessel may have been imported to the island from Egypt, or from the neighbouring Palestinian coast, or it may have been made in Cyprus by a potter strongly influenced by foreign designs. It is supposed to have been found with the jug of Cypro-Palestinian Bichrome Ware (Pl. 27) shown on p. 35, and must tentatively be ascribed to that ware. There is a jug in Amiran (1970) which appears to be intermediate between these two and may indicate a stronger link between them (see Amiran, 1970, photo 142).

One thing is certain. The jug in Pl. 268, which must be dated to the very beginning of the Late Bronze Age, around 1600 BC, did not start a fashion in lotus design on Cyprus. Centuries were to pass before this floral motif was to reappear and become a popular feature. It was in the Cypro-Archaic period that the lotus flowered on the island's vessels.

Two trends are evident in the stylistic modification of the lotus plant by the Cypriot artists. One is an increasingly ornate elaboration of the elements of the basic motif, as in Figs. 424-30 and 445-8, and the other is a geometricizing of the botanical shapes until they become almost abstract to the untrained eye. Gjerstad (1948) commented on this latter development, relating it to the long tradition of abstract pattern-making in the earlier art of Cyprus. 'The strength of the geometrical tradition and the geometricizing tendency of the Cypriote ceramists are well illustrated by the transformation of the floral motives into geometric designs. The transformation of the lotus flower is particularly instructive ...' (p. 64).

Six Cypro-Archaic vessels are shown here, bearing lotus designs of varying degrees of stylization (see Pls. 269-75). The bowl in Pl. 272 shows the least modified representation and the bowl in Pl. 271 shows the most extreme form of geometric reduction.

In order to give some idea of the range of variation of lotus designs in the Cypro-Archaic period, a collection of fifty-six examples is presented here. They have been arranged, very roughly, under nine headings, on the basis of certain visual elements. It would be wrong to read too much into this arrangement—it is a matter of convenience more than a serious classification.

At its most ornate the lotus rears up to

Fig. 383   Fig. 384   Fig. 385

Fig. 386   Fig. 387   Fig. 388

Fig. 389   Fig. 390   Fig. 391

Fig. 392   Fig. 393   Fig. 394

Fig. 395   Fig. 396   Fig. 397

Fig. 398   Fig. 399   Fig. 400

Figs. 383–400 *Variations on the rosette motif, from White Painted and Bichrome Ware vessels. Iron Age.*

Figs. 383–4 *Karageorghis 1962, Pl. XXV.*

Fig. 385 *Spiteris 1970, p. 103.*

Fig. 386 *Myres 1914, Cesnola no. 688.*

Fig. 387 *Spiteris 1970, p. 110.*

Fig. 388 *Gjerstad 1948, Pl. XLIX, 11.*

Fig. 389 *Karageorghis 1970, Pl. CCLVI.*

Fig. 390 *Karageorghis et al. 1974, Fig. 65a.*

Fig. 391 *Gjerstad 1948, Pl. XXXV, 4.*

Figs. 392–3 *This volume, p. 234.*

Fig. 394 *Peltenburg 1981, no. 466.*

Fig. 395 *Karageorghis 1965, Pl. 6.*

Figs. 396–400 *Karageorghis and Des Gagniers 1974, Pls. XXVd12; XXVg54; SXXVc2; SXXIV, 15; XXVh2.*

Pl. 270

Pl. 271

Pl. 270 *Living lotus flower. The model on which the many, often highly stylized, lotus motifs are based.*

Pl. 271 *The lotus motif reduced to no more than a pair of almost abstract lotus leaves, on a stem base bowl. Bichrome Ware. Iron Age. Diam. 14.3 cm (DM-BI-59).*

Pl. 272 *The lotus motif in its less stylized form, on a stem base bowl. Bichrome Ware. Iron Age. Diam. 20 cm (DM-BI-60). Cf. SCE IV.2, Fig. XXXI, no. 14b.*

Pl. 272

Pl. 273

Pl. 274

Pl. 273 *Lotus motif reduced to lotus leaves, on a pinched spout jug. Wheelmade White Painted Ware. Iron Age. Ht. 14 cm (DM-WWP-22).*

Pl. 274 *Lotus motif reduced to lotus leaves, on a squat ring base jar. Bichrome Ware. Iron Age. Ht. 10.8 cm (DM-BI-52).*

Pl. 275

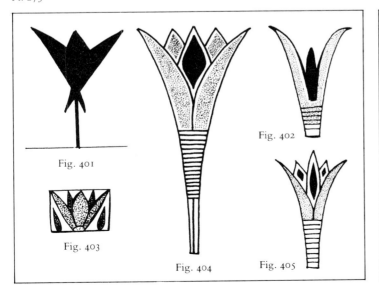

Fig. 401

Fig. 403

Fig. 402

Fig. 404

Fig. 405

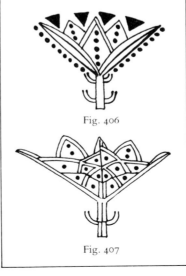

Fig. 406

Fig. 407

Simple lotus

Figs. 401-2 *Karageorghis and Des Gagniers 1974, Pls. SXXIV, 13; XXVf6.*
Fig. 403 *Karageorghis 1970, no. 57.*
Figs. 404-5 *Karageorghis and Des Gagniers 1974, Pls. XXVc6; XXVf6.*

Dotted lotus

Figs. 406-7 *Karageorghis and Des Gagniers 1974, Pl. SVI, 1.*

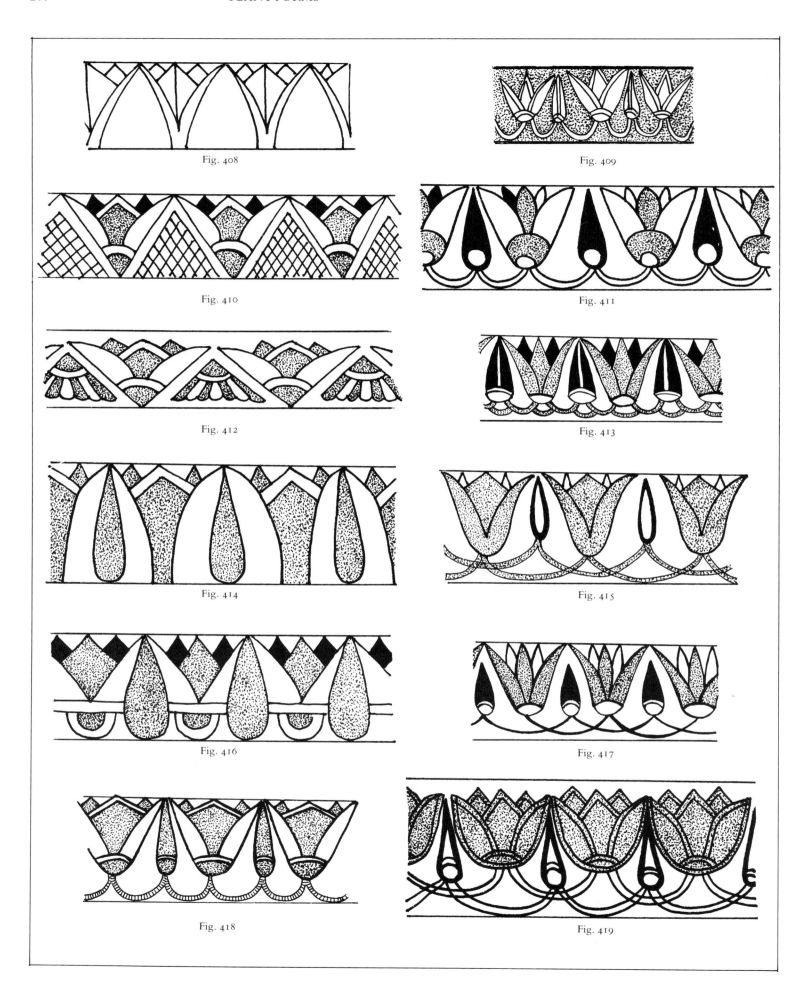

Fig. 408

Fig. 409

Fig. 410

Fig. 411

Fig. 412

Fig. 413

Fig. 414

Fig. 415

Fig. 416

Fig. 417

Fig. 418

Fig. 419

Lotus frieze

Fig.408 *Gjerstad 1948, Fig. XXXIX, no. 16.*

Fig. 409 *Karageorghis 1978, Pl. XLVII.*

Fig. 410 *Karageorghis 1973, no. 55.*

Fig. 411 *Karageorghis and Des Gagniers 1974, Pl. VI, 6.*

Fig. 412 *Karageorghis 1973, no. 53.*

Fig. 413 *Karageorghis 1970, Pl. CCLVI, 13.*

Fig. 414 *Karageorghis and Des Gagniers 1974, Pl. III, 3.*

Fig. 415 *Karageorghis 1970, Pl. CLXXVI, 6.*

Fig. 416 *Karageorghis 1973, no. 52.*

Figs. 417-18 *Karageorghis 1970, Pl. CCXXIII, 8; CCL, 5.*

Fig. 419 *Karageorghis and Des Gagniers 1974, Pl. VIII, 10.*

Line-leaf lotus

Figs. 420-3 *Karageorghis and Des Gagniers 1974, Pls. SXXVb9; XXIVa20; XXVf24; XXVf7.*

Tendril-leaf lotus

Figs. 424-30 *Karageorghis and Des Gagniers 1974, Pls. XVIa1; XXVh15; XVIa2; XXVe16; XIIa1; XXVe10; XXVe6.*

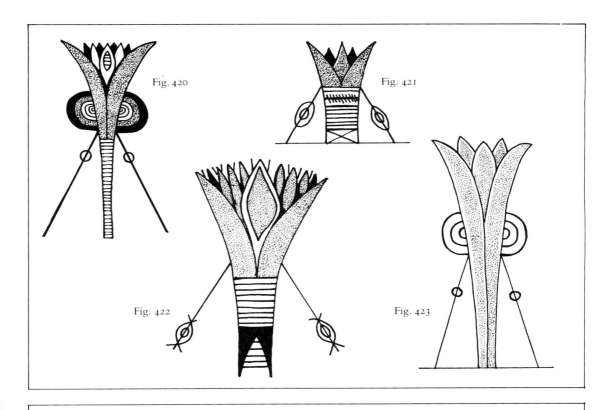

Fig. 420

Fig. 421

Fig. 422

Fig. 423

Fig. 424

Fig. 425

Fig. 426

Fig. 427

Fig. 428

Fig. 429

Fig. 430

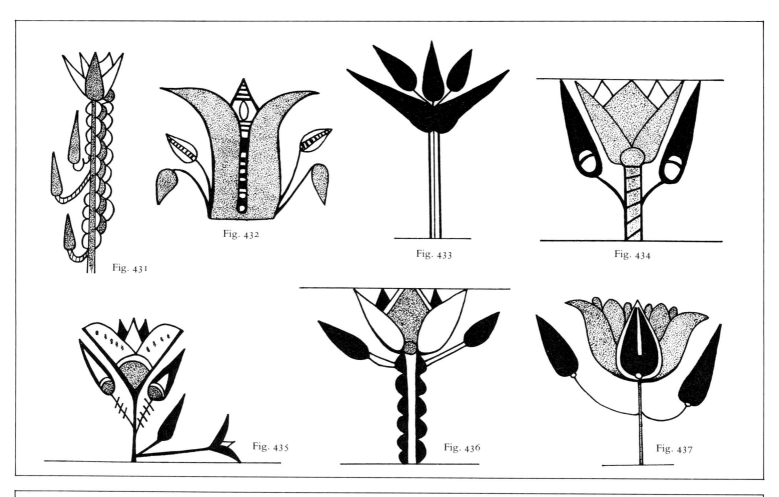

Fig. 431

Fig. 432

Fig. 433

Fig. 434

Fig. 435

Fig. 436

Fig. 437

Fig. 438

Fig. 439

Fig. 440

Fig. 441

Fig. 442

Fig. 443

Fig. 444

Budding lotus

Figs. 431-7 *Karageorghis and Des Gagniers 1974, Pls. VIII, 1; SXXVf3; p. 514; XIIa2; XXVh9; XXVe17; X, 3.*

Drooping-sepals lotus

Figs. 438-40 *Karageorghis and Des Gagniers 1974, Pls. XVIa3; VI, 10.*
Fig. 441 *Spiteris 1970, p. 102.*
Fig. 442 *Astrom 1968, p. 81.*
Figs. 443-4 *Karageorghis and Des Gagniers 1974, Pls. VIII, 10; XXVf3.*

Heavy-leaf lotus

Figs. 445-8 *Karageorghis and Des Gagniers 1974, Pls. VIII, 5; VIII, 8; XXVb23; XVIII,10.*

Semi-circle-leaf lotus

Figs. 449-53 *Karageorghis and Des Gagniers 1974, Pls. XXVf15; XXVh15; XXVf13; XXVf17; XXVe12.*
Fig. 454 *Karageorghis 1973, no. 54.*
Figs. 455-6 *Karageorghis and Des Gagniers 1974, Pls. XXVb24; XXVb29.*

Fig. 445

Fig. 446

Fig. 447

Fig. 448

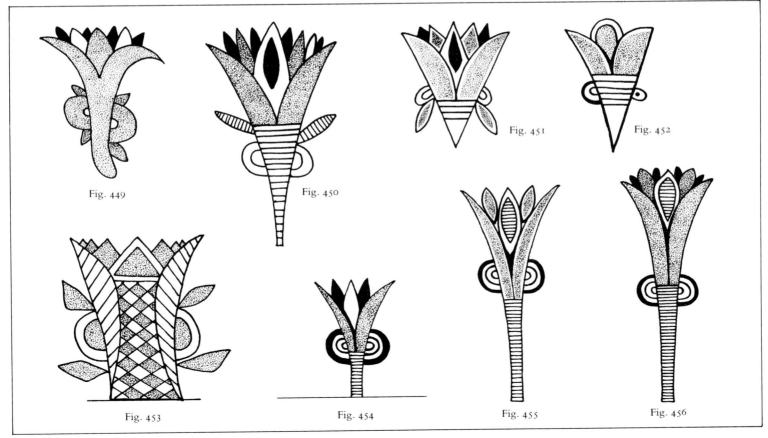

Fig. 449

Fig. 450

Fig. 451

Fig. 452

Fig. 453

Fig. 454

Fig. 455

Fig. 456

Pl. 276 *Simple inverted lotus motif on a pinched spout jug. Bichrome Ware. Iron Age. Ht. 11.1 cm (DM-BI-13).*

become a 'sacred tree'. The artists, still employing the original water-lily motifs, convert the plant into a huge, fantastic tree, usually flanked by deer or large birds which appear to be feeding upon it.

At the other end of the scale, the lotus patterns decay to the simplest splodges of paint. This process begins with an inversion of the usual motif (see Pl. 276), so that the triple-petals of the flower point downwards. The next step is for them to lose their characteristic overlapping design (see Pl. 277) and then, finally, to lose even their triple-unit feature (see Pl. 278). In these later stages, many examples of which have been found at Salamis, the downward strokes of the brush have sometimes been referred to as leaves or even feathers, but their lotus-petal derivation, if distant, nevertheless seems clear enough.

Pl. 276

Pl. 277 *The trefoil lotus motif in decline as a 'drooping leaf' pattern, on pinched spout jugs. Bichrome Ware. Iron Age.*
a *Ht. 17.8 cm (DM-BI-17).*
b *Ht. 16.7 cm (DM-BI-18).*

Pl. 277

Pl. 278 *The drooping leaf pattern simplified to eliminate the trefoil element. The down-strokes are now separate from one another. Wheelmade White Painted Ware. Iron Age. Ht. 11.5 cm (DM-WWP-15).*

Pl. 278

The rosette and the lotus dominate the botanical scene on Iron Age vessels to such an extent that other plant motifs are allowed to play only a minor role. One, however, deserves brief mention and that is the conifer.

A motif apparently meant to indicate a tall, thin, conifer tree, with down-sloping branches, occurs on a number of free-field vessels. It sometimes appears alone (Pls. 279-83), but is often shown alongside a bird or ungulate, as if labelling the animal as a forest species. Some authors have interpreted this motif as an arrow, but this seems unlikely because (a) it is usually vertical, (b) it is not aimed at the animals, and (c) it differs in design from the arrows shown in archers' bows of similar vessels. Brown and Catling (1975) refer to it as a 'stylized tree', and there seems to be no reason to doubt them.

Pl. 279

Pl. 280

Pl. 281

Pl. 279 *Simple 'fir-tree' motif on ring base bowl. Wheelmade White Painted Ware. Iron Age. Diam. 13.7 cm (DM-WWP-117).*

Pls. 280-3 *Simple 'fir-tree' motifs on jugs with pinched spouts. Wheelmade White Painted Ware. Iron Age.*
Pl. 280 *Ht. 16.3 cm (DM-WWP-19).*
Pl. 281 *Ht. 25.5 cm (DM-WWP-36).*
Pl. 282 *Ht. 12.7 cm (DM-WWP-20).*
Pl. 283
a(left) *Ht. 13.8 cm (DM-WWP-21).*
b(right) *Ht. 12.3 cm (DM-WWP-18).*

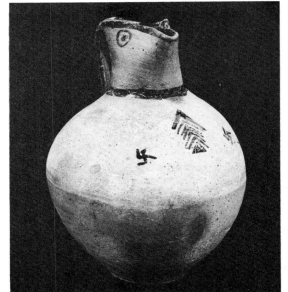

Pl. 282

Pl. 283

Inanimate Forms

Representations of inanimate forms are of two types. First, there are inanimate elements in scenic compositions. In ploughing, baking and washing scenes, for example, there are pottery representations of ploughs, ovens and water troughs respectively. These will be dealt with in the next section (see p. 264), where the scenic compositions are examined as a whole.

Second, there are inanimate forms represented as independent subjects in their own right. There are two sub-categories here: skeuomorphs and models. The difference is that the skeuomorphs are life-size and the models are greatly reduced in size.

A skeuomorph is defined by Bray and Trump (1970) as 'an object which in its shape or decoration copies the form it had when made from another material or by another technique'. Strictly speaking, all 'gourd jugs' are skeuomorphs because in their design they copy the natural gourd shape. But a distinction has to be made here between 'general influence' and 'deliberate imitation'. The gourd jugs, and also the Base Ring Ware vessels which have been influenced by metal prototypes or perhaps by poppy-head shapes (see p. 237), come in to the former category and are omitted from this section. Here, only deliberate imitation is considered.

There appear to be three reasons for placing an imitation object in an ancient tomb:

1 Because the original object is too precious to be disposed of in this way. A cheap copy is made from clay and the original—in gold or bronze, or some other valuable substance—is kept for future use by the mourners.

Another version of this, known from Egypt, involved the placing of worthless substitutes in a tomb to deter tomb-robbers and thereby allow the deceased to lie in peace, without fear of violent disturbance.

2 Because the original object is too ordinary to be offered as part of a solemn ritual. Here, the opposite applies. The mourners would know that items made of leather, gourd-shell, wood, or horn must have a short life-span. Their personal experience during their own lifetime would have told them this. If they imagined that the journey to the 'other world' was to be a lengthy one, then this may have prompted them to produce something more permanent for the deceased, in the way of pottery imitations.

Alternatively, the consideration may simply have been to offer up something a little more 'special' than an old gourd-shell or leather object. The pottery copy may not have been seen as 'longer-lasting' so much as 'better-quality' and therefore more appropriate for a ritual occasion. Indeed, special pottery versions of ordinary household goods, created specifically and exclusively as tomb-offerings, may have had more 'magical' significance.

3 Because the original object is too big to be placed in a tomb. This is the 'model' category, where a miniature of some large object is placed in the tomb because the original will not fit. If the deceased is to be provided with a vehicle to ease the journey to the 'other world', then this is usually scaled down for practical purposes. Model boats and model chariots fall into this category. To provide the deceased with a seat or throne for comfort in the other world may also prove too difficult in the confined space of a rock-cut tomb, so that small model chairs and thrones are also sometimes encountered among the tomb-goods.

An alternative and completely different explanation for finding small models in ancient tombs is that they are, in reality, no more than the toys of deceased children, placed with their bodies to provide playthings to relieve the boredom of the lengthy trip to the afterlife. It is difficult to decide between this and the previous explanation for the presence of models, but intuition favours the former explanation

With these thoughts in mind it is interesting to draw up a list of the kinds of inanimate objects copied in terracotta, both as skeuomorphs and as models, in the tombs of ancient Cyprus. It is a curious collection:

Skeuomorphs
1 Leather container (4+)
2 Gourd funnel (4+)
3 Wooden spoon (1)
4 Wooden stool (1)
5 Wood, bone, or metal plaque (1)
6 Wood-and-hair brush?
7 Bone or wood comb? (7+)

8 Wood or metal mouth-cover (1)
9 Wooden spindle (2)
10 Spindle whorl (many)
11 Animal horn (10+)
12 Metal-and-wood sheath-knife (10+)
13 Leather knife-sheath (11+)

Models
14 Boat (19+)
15 Chariot (10+, excluding chariot groups)
16 Water-cart (4+)
17 Chair (2+)

All these have been copied in terracotta and presented to the dead in the tombs of ancient Cyprus. The thirteen skeuomorph types are all from the Early Bronze Age, in Red Polished Ware or Black Polished Ware. The four model types have a wider range, stretching from the Bronze Age to the Iron Age.

The numbers shown above give a rough idea of the rarity of the different subjects. An extensive search has not been carried out, so that all the figures should be treated as on the low side. Even so it is clear that some subjects are much more popular than others. Several appear to be unique, idiosyncratic choices, while others belong to a minor tradition. But even the most favoured among them are extremely rare when compared with ordinary tomb vessels. The mystery to be solved is why, if skeuomorphs occur at all in the Early Bronze Age, they do not occur much more frequently; and why, if models occur at all in the Late Bronze Age and the Early Iron Age, they, too, do not appear in much larger numbers, to match the huge quantities of jugs, jars and bowls. What was so special about the deceased in these particular cases that warranted placing imitation objects in the tombs, when most ancient corpses were despatched to the other world with only food and drink in a collection of pottery vessels? It is not as though the imitation objects can be put into the category of 'bodily adornment'. Beads, necklaces, rings,

1 Leather containers

Figs. 457–8 *Skeuomorphic pottery vessels imitating 'skin bags'. Incised Red Polished Ware. Early Bronze Age.*
Fig. 457 *No provenance (Cyprus Museum). Ht. 34 cm. Spiteris 1970, p. 27.*
Fig. 458 *Margi(?). Ht. 17.5 cm. Belgiorno 1980, no. 22.*

Fig. 457   Fig. 458

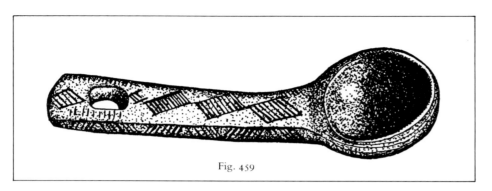

Fig. 459

3 Wooden spoon

Fig. 459 *Skeuomorphic pottery imitation in Black Polished Ware. Early Bronze Age. Kochati. Length 13.2 cm. Karageorghis 1973, Pl. 13.*

4 Wooden stool

Fig. 460 *Skeuomorphic pottery imitation in Incised Red Polished Ware. Early Bronze Age. Ayios Demetrios, near Kythrea. Ht. 14 cm. Des Gagniers and Karageorghis 1976, Pl. XL, 2.*

earrings and other jewellery and costume adornments are easy to understand; so are weapons in bronze or iron. But to send a loved one to the afterlife equipped with such unlikely items as terracotta copies of funnels, horns, stools and spindles does seem a trifle eccentric. There has to be some special explanation which at present remains hidden from us.

One possible explanation is that each of these objects had a personal significance for the deceased beyond its mundane use. Just as today someone might wish to be buried with a lucky mascot that meant a great deal to them during life, so the owner of the wooden stool might have considered it to have had magical significance for him (or her) and insisted on being buried with an image of it.

Alternatively, these objects may have had, not a personal meaning to the deceased, but some tribal, ritual significance. The sheath-

knives may have been of a particular type used in certain formal ceremonies by, say, a tribal elder. When such an individual died, he would be accompanied by a copy of such a knife.

Perhaps the truth is that these inanimate objects were not rare at all, but that nearly all of them were placed in the tombs in their original materials and have long since rotted away.

Examining each of the seventeen types in turn, the following brief comments can be made:

1 Leather container

A number of Bronze Age vessels are reminiscent of skin bags. Many of the small animal-shaped *askos* figures appear to be representations of wine-skins or water-containers, rather than of the live animals themselves. But it is frequently difficult to be certain as to whether this is a case of stylization or not. There are, however, several outstanding examples of indisputable skeuomorphs where the potter has deliberately tried to give the impression of a leather bag or basket, complete with imitation bumps and bulges. All those known are in Red Polished Ware and come from the Early Bronze Age. Three are illustrated here, two of 'shopping bag' design (see Figs. 457-8) and one designed like a leather jug with a bulbous pouch of a body, stiffened at the top by an imitation wood frame (Pl. 284a).

2 Gourd Funnel

It is clear from the photograph of the gourd shown on p. 236 that it is an easy matter to fashion an excellent funnel. If the gourd is cut through twice, once near the stalk and once at the widest part of its spherical 'body', two useful objects are immediately created. One is a simple, hemispherical bowl and the other is a funnel-shaped section that can be put to great use in transferring liquids to narrow-necked jugs, jars or wine-skins. Several pottery imitations of these gourd funnels have come to light in recent years, of which the one shown on p. 258 (Pl. 284b) is the best example.

3 Wooden spoon

A single example is known (Fig. 459). Made in Incised Black Polished Ware, it has a large suspension hole, a simple, flat handle with parallel sides, and a round bowl. It is believed

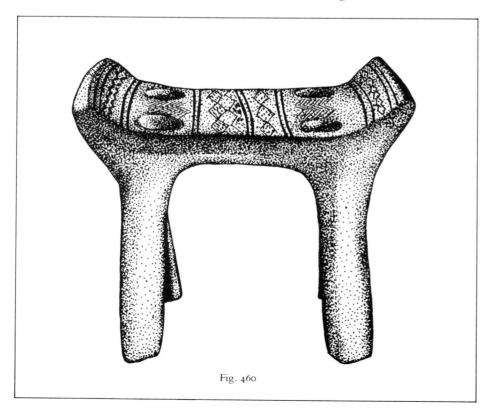

Fig. 460

to have come from Kochati and is now in the Pierides collection at Larnaca. It is possible that this should not be classed as a skeuomorph and that this is the original spoon or ladle rather than a copy of it. But it is doubtful if this type of pottery utensil would have been strong enough for ordinary use, and it seems much more likely that the original was made of carved wood.

4 Wooden Stool

Like the spoon, this is a unique object. Des Gagniers and Karageorghis (1976) refer to it as a table, in which case it would have to be considered as a model rather than a skeuomorph. But the design is much more like that of a small stool, with the ends up-turned to make sitting more comfortable. If it is a stool, then it is life-size and should be called a skeuomorphic imitation rather than a small model. The potter has left no doubt about the fact that it was originally made of wood, by including four circular bosses, protruding through the upper surface, one above each leg (Fig. 460).

5 Wood, bone or metal plaque

Another unique skeuomorph, this appears to imitate a decorative plaque that was worn round the neck. The plank figure shown on p. 146 (Pl. 177), bears an incised motif which may reveal the way in which such a plaque was used as an article of adornment. If this is the case, then in its original publication (Karageorghis et al., 1974, fig. 10) it was shown upside down. I have inverted it here to show two suspension holes on the upper side and five 'tassel holes' in the projections on the lower side. It is made of Incised Red Polished Ware, from the Early Bronze Age (Fig. 461).

6 Wood-and-hair brush?
7 Bone or wood comb?

These two categories might be expected here because the terracottas shown on p. 139 (Figs. 186-92) have previously been designated either as brushes or combs. If one of these interpretations is correct and I am wrong to think of them as highly modified plank figures, then they must, of course, be classed as important Early Bronze Age skeuomorphs.

8 Wood or metal mouth-cover

This is a unique and puzzling terracotta object. More than twenty mouth-covers of similar shapes, but always in metal, have been found. Murray et al. (1900) published a large number of these, from Late Bronze Age Enkomi. Nearly always in gold, and sometimes clearly carrying the outline of human lips in relief, they appear to have been used to cover the mouth of the corpse before burial. This may have been done for purely decorative reasons, adding extra richness to the funeral adornments, or it may have been part of a superstitious belief concerning the need to mask or close the orifice. The strange feature about the Incised Black Polished mouth-cover shown here in Pl. 288 is that it seems to be so much ahead of its time. All the others occur in the Late Bronze Age, suggesting a temporary custom of mouth-covering at that point. Brown and Catling (1980) point out that they are characteristic of LC II, are confined to Enkomi and Kition, and are exclusively Cypriot in occurrence. Yet here is one being used centuries earlier. The only explanation seems to be that the Early Bronze Age mouth-covers were usually made in some impermanent material such as wood and that, although the tradition lasted right through the Bronze Age era, it was not until a period of affluence in the Late Bronze Age II epoch that a permanent material such as gold or silver was employed. The solitary terracotta from the Early Bronze Age shown here must then be viewed as an isolated oddity, where a potter, instead of a wood-carver, was commissioned to fashion a mouthpiece for a particular burial, revealing to us that the custom is much more ancient than was previously believed.

9 Wooden spindle

Two Early Bronze Age spindles have been found (Figs. 462-3), both at Vounous. These are almost certainly terracotta copies of wooden originals, rather than the originals themselves. A tapering wooden stick with an attached spindle whorl would have been the

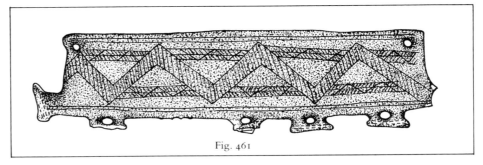

Fig. 461

5 Wood, bone or metal plaque

Fig. 461 *Skeuomorphic pottery imitation in Incised Red Polished Ware. Early Bronze Age. No provenance (University of California, Robert Lowie Museum). Ht. 8.8 cm. Karageorghis et al. 1974, no. 10.*

9 Wooden spindles

Figs. 462-3 *Skeuomorphic imitations in Incised Red Polished Ware. Early Bronze Age.*
Fig. 462 *Vounous (Tomb 92, no. 6). Length 20.7 cm. Stewart and Stewart 1950, Pl. Cd.*
Fig. 463 *Vounous (Tomb 29, no. 52). Length 20.3 cm. Dikaios 1940, Pl. LVI, 6.*

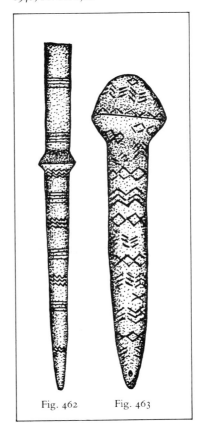

Fig. 462   Fig. 463

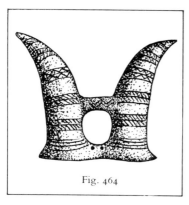

Fig. 464

11 Animal horns

Fig. 464 *Pottery imitation of two curved horns, in Incised Red Polished Ware. Early Bronze Age. No provenance (University of California, Robert Lowie Museum). Ht. 15.5 cm. Karageorghis et al. 1974, no. 8.*

Fig. 465 *Pottery imitation of single horn in White Painted Ware. Early Bronze Age. Vounus (Tomb 18, no. 32). Ht. 14 cm. Dikaios 1940, Pl. XLIa.*

Figs. 466–72 *Pottery imitations of single horns in Incised Red Polished Ware pottery. Early Bronze Age.*

Fig. 466 *No provenance (Ashmolean Museum, Oxford). Ht. 22.2 cm. Brown and Catling 1980, no. 20.*

Fig. 467 *Vounous (Tomb 36, no. 109). Ht. 27 cm. Dikaios 1940, Pl. XXXVIIIa.*

Fig. 468 *Vounous (Tomb 36, no. 96). Ht. 31.8 cm. Dikaios 1940, Pl. XXXVIIIb.*

Fig. 469 *Vounous (Tomb 132, no. 55). Ht. 27.8 cm. Stewart and Stewart 1950, Pl. XCVIb.*

Fig. 470 *Vounous (Tomb 164a, no. 61). Ht. 27.5 cm. Stewart and Stewart 1950, Pl. XCVIa.*

Fig. 471 *Vounous (Tomb 9, no. 61). Ht. 12 cm. Dikaios 1940, Pl. XXXVIIIe.*

Fig. 472 *Vounous (Tomb 9, no. 105). Ht. 15 cm. Dikaios 1940, Pl. XXXVIIIb.*

simplest and most useful form of spindle for early weaving. A terracotta version would probably have been too fragile. Pieridou (1967) comments: 'Spinning in Cyprus was probably made by the "supported hand spindle" which is easy and speedy work, the spinner rolling the spindle on her thigh to twist it. The spindle used was a rounded stick of wood or metal with a pointed end and a hook on top for holding the yarn; the whorl was placed at the head or a little lower on the stem of the spindle. This type of spindle can be seen on the terracotta models of spindles found in Cyprus from the Early Cypriote I-III periods.' It is clear from the costumes indicated on the Early Bronze Age figurines that weaving was an important element in village life, and it is highly likely that many spindles were placed in the tombs of weavers. Most of these must have been in the original wood and soon decayed, but these two terracotta skeuomorphs have survived to reveal their design.

10 Spindle whorl

Large numbers of spindle whorls have been found in Bronze Age tombs. For a selection, see Pl. 285. Most of those surviving are made of terracotta, but there are also examples in stone, bone and metal. It is possible that the terracotta ones were 'originals' rather than skeuomorphic copies, but they do not seem to show the wear one might expect if they had been used repeatedly during daily life. Singer et al. (1954) have shown that the use of whorls as weights for the spindle-sticks was common throughout much of the ancient world, and there is nothing unusual about the Cypriot ones.

11 Animal horn

The making of imitation animal horns in the Early Bronze Age appears to have been popular for superstitious reasons. If pairs of horns were erected on walls as protective devices, then it would follow that the deceased might also benefit from an apotropaic horn placed alongside the body in the tomb. Terracotta copies of horns have been found in a number of Vounous tombs; others are known with no provenance, but probably also come from Vounous. Ten examples are shown here. Eight are single horns in Incised Red Polished Ware (Pl. 287 and Figs. 466-72), one is a single horn in Early White Painted Ware (Fig. 465), and one is a double horn in Incised Red Polished Ware (Fig. 464). The double horn appears to be just that; in

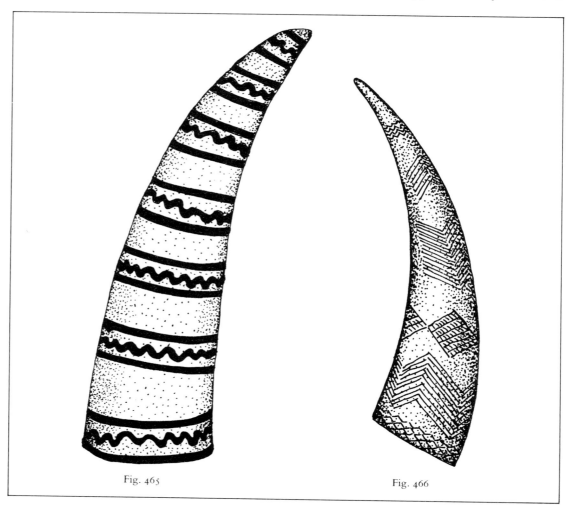

Fig. 465   Fig. 466

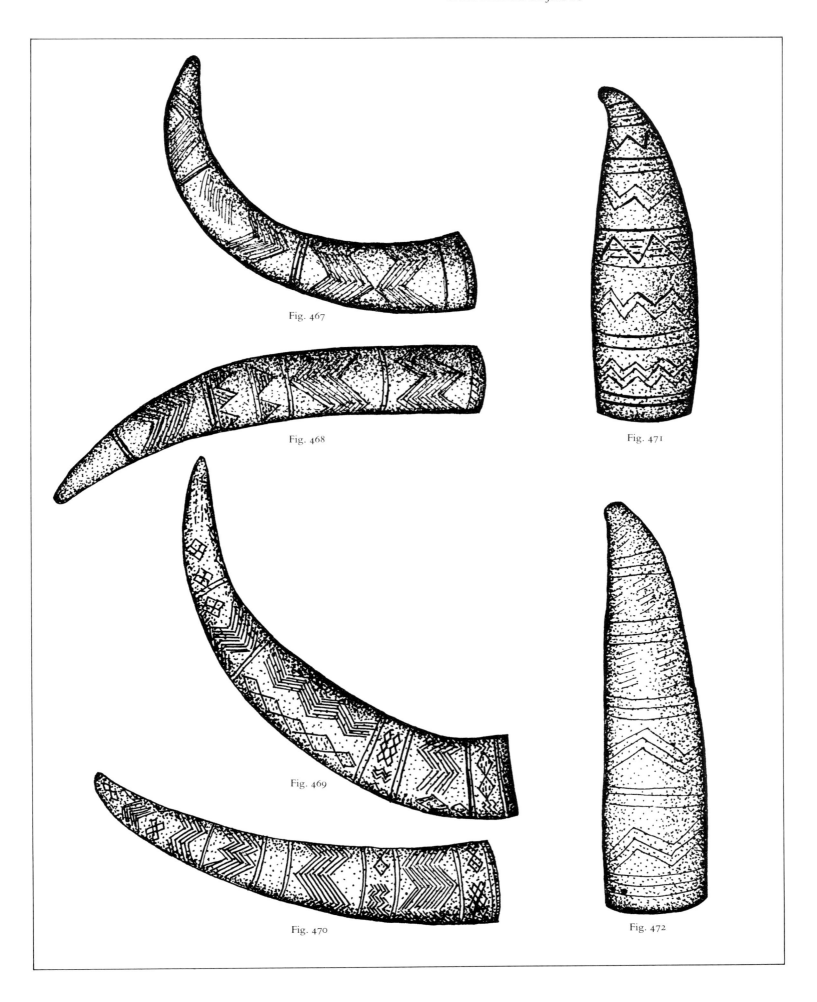

Fig. 467

Fig. 471

Fig. 468

Fig. 469

Fig. 470

Fig. 472

other words, it is not a pair of horns but two single horns artificially joined together, presumably to give double-strength protection. It is perhaps relevant that small horns made of gold, silver or other substances are still worn as protective amulets today in certain Mediterranean countries.

12 Metal-and-wood sheath-knife
13 Leather knife-sheath

One of the most popular skeuomorphic subjects is what has been referred to in the past as the 'dagger and sheath'. This title has been particularly unfortunate and misleading because it implies that we are dealing with a stabbing weapon, worn by Early Bronze Age Cypriots to be used against human opponents in aggressive encounters. There is no other way of interpreting the word 'dagger'. Although this is a faint possibility, there is no shred of evidence that the Cypriots of the period went armed in this way, or that they needed to do so. It is much more likely that the implement in question was a general purpose sheath-knife, employed mainly in connection with skinning animals, cutting meat and other farming tasks. Like any such knife it could easily be used in human clashes, but until there is some evidence that this was its primary role, it is wrong to give it the specific functional name of 'dagger'. This is yet another example of the 'retrospective error' in archaeology. Later on, from the Late Bronze Age into the Iron Age, armed warrior figures became a popular subject for Cypriot artists, but in the Early Bronze Age warriors and soldiers are conspicuous by

their total absence from the art repertoire. It is unlikely that they would be represented solely by a handful of imitation daggers. (Real bronze weapons did, of course, occur in the tombs of this early period—see Pl. 4 on p.10—but the function of these weapons was more likely to have been animal-hunting rather than warfare.)

I have been able to trace a total of ten sheath-knives and eleven sheaths. The example shown in Pl. 286 is perhaps the best preserved and most elegantly fashioned. There is little variation in the sheaths. Two more are shown, for comparison, in Figs. 473-4. Knife design does vary slightly more, however, especially in respect of the two lateral lobes, or projecting guards (see Figs. 475-9). As with the skeuomorphic horns, those pottery knives and sheaths which have a known provenance all come from Vounous.

Although there may be some doubt as to whether certain other terracottas are 'originals' or copies, there can be no such indecision in the case of these knives. A pottery knife is totally functionless in real life, either for cutting or stabbing, and here, at least, we must be dealing with skeuomorphic 'counterfeits', deliberately made as substitutes for use as tomb offerings. It seems likely that in this instance the original article was too precious to be 'wasted' on a corpse. If such an explanation is accepted however, it remains to be explained why it was that, in many tombs, real bronze blades *were* found with the dead. Perhaps the sheath-knives copied in terracotta were of some special tribal signifiance and the originals had to be retained for further use;

13 Sheaths

Figs. 473-4 *Skeuomorphic pottery imitations in Incised Red Polished Ware of the leather originals. Early Bronze Age.*

Fig. 473 *Vounous (Tomb 45, no. 14). Ht. 26 cm. Dikaios 1940, Pl. XXIXa.*

Fig. 474 *No provenance (Ashmolean Museum, Oxford). Ht. 17 cm. Brown and Catling 1980, no. 21.*

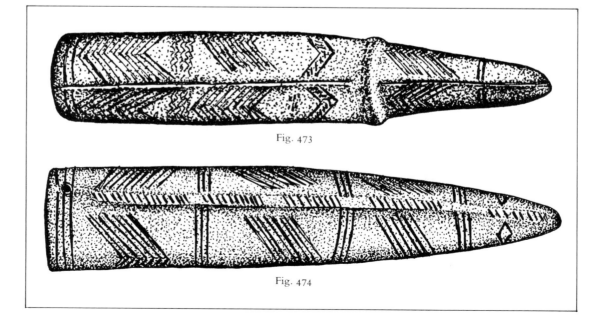

Fig. 473

Fig. 474

12 Sheath knives

Figs. 475-9 *Skeuomorphic pottery imitations in Incised Red Polished Ware of metal and wood originals. Early Bronze Age.*

Fig. 475 *Vounous (Tomb 145, no. 6). Ht. 18.3 cm. Stewart and Stewart 1950, Pl. XCVIIId.*

Fig. 476 *Vounous (Tomb 132, no. 56). Ht. 17.5 cm. Stewart and Stewart 1950, Pl. XCVIIc.*

Fig. 477 *Vounous (Tomb 114, no. 9). Ht. 18.3 cm. Stewart and Stewart 1950, Pl. XCVIIa.*

Fig. 478 *Vounous (Tomb 45, no. 15). Ht. 19 cm. Dikaios 1940, Pl. XXIXa.*

Fig. 479 *No provenance (Ashmolean Museum, Oxford). Ht. 15.4 cm. Brown and Catling 1980, no. 21.*

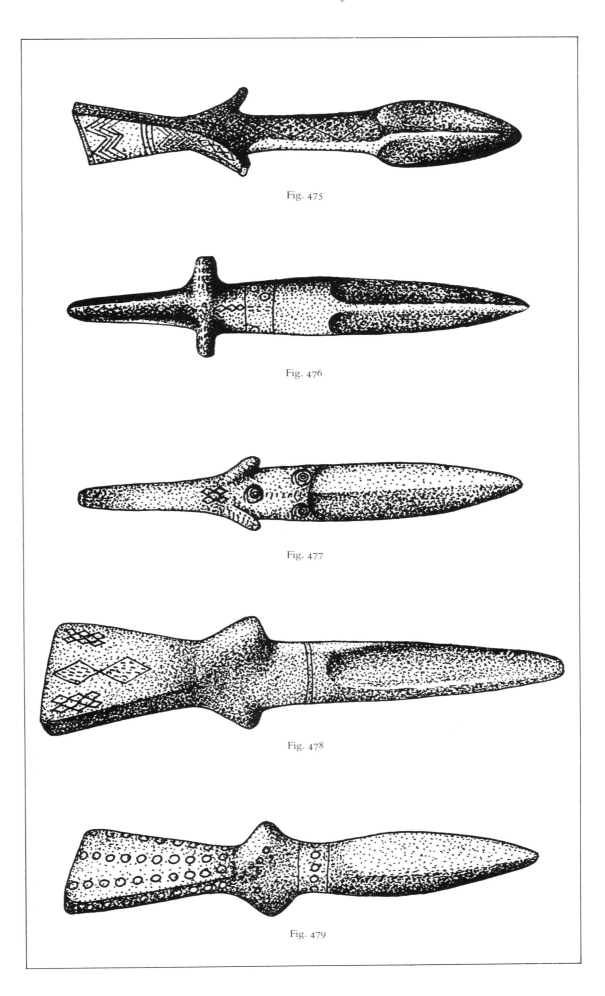

Fig. 475

Fig. 476

Fig. 477

Fig. 478

Fig. 479

Pl. 284

a(back) *Jug with round base and round spout imitating a leather and wood original. Incised Red Polished Ware. Early Bronze Age. Ht. 30.8 cm (DM-IRP-98).*
b(front) *Pottery funnel imitating a gourd original. An efficient funnel could be made simply by cutting the body of a gourd in half and using the stem as a spout. This would have been of great value for filling animal-skins with liquid. Mottled Red Polished Ware. Early Bronze Age. Ht. 15.7 cm (DM-MRP-32).*

Pl. 285 *Spindle whorls. Seventeen examples in Drab Polished Ware, each with a slightly different incision pattern. Sixteen of the spindle whorls have the typical bi-conical shape, but the seventeenth has a more complex, waisted shape. This waisted 'hour-glass' example does not appear to have any parallels. Middle Bronze Age. Ht. (of waisted example) 5.5 cm (DM-DP-19). Ht. (of other examples) 3 to 4.5 cm (DM-DP-20-35).*

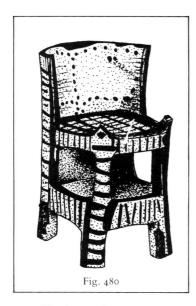

Fig. 480

17 Chair or throne

Fig. 480 *Pottery model in White Painted Ware. Early Bronze Age. No provenance (Glasgow Museum). Ht. 18.6 cm. Peltenburg and Karageorghis 1976, Pl. XVIII, 4.*

or perhaps corpses with terracotta knives represented the 'economy burials' of the community.

14 Boat

Model boats appear as early as the Middle Bronze Age (see Fig. 504 on p. 288), but they do not become popular until the Late Bronze Age and the Early Iron Age. A number of examples are shown in Murray et al., (1900, Fig. 164) and five others are illustrated here (Pl. 289 and Figs. 483-6). They usually take the form of simple canoes, pointed at both ends, sometimes empty and sometimes with a small human figure inside clinging on hopefully as if waiting for a suitable current to sweep him away to the afterlife.

15 Chariot

An example of a chariot model was shown in Pl. 211 on p. 182. At least ten of these are known, most with a tiny figure peering over the rim, completely out of scale with the vehicle in which he is riding. The implication here is that this is a special, magical, *giant*

chariot suitable for the mystical journey to the other world, rather than a down-to-earth chariot for everyday use. (Excluded here are the extremely common Iron Age chariot groups with rider and horses, where the inanimate element is of secondary importance.)

16 Water-cart

Very similar to the model chariots, but always lacking a human figure, are the two-wheeled carts in which the body of the vehicle has become transformed into a huge liquid-container of some kind. These have been rather optimistically referred to as 'wine-carts', but it seems more reasonable to suppose that, at this scale, their task was to transport water on an island which, during the summer months, can suffer from serious drought. Four of these have been published, of which two are shown in Figs. 481 and 482. Their symbolic tomb-function was presumably to provide the deceased with a mobile water supply for his long journey. Like the chariots, these models are confined to the Iron Age.

17 Chair

Models of chairs are rare and only a few appear to have been published. The most interesting one is in the Glasgow Museum (see Peltenburg and Karageorghis, 1976, p. 88) and is shown here in Fig. 480. It is in White Painted Ware and is believed to belong to the Early Cypro-Geometric period at the very start of the Iron Age. It is essentially a 'high-chair' and may have been a throne of some kind, but this is pure conjecture. Peltenburg and Karageorghis comment that 'the dots of paint on the concave part of the backrest may denote decorative rivets or inlaid discs ...'

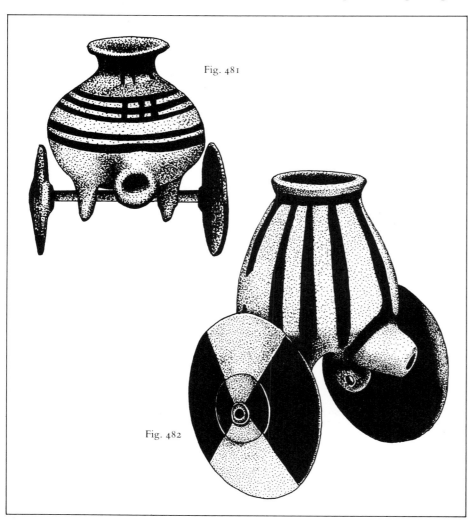

Fig. 481

Fig. 482

16 Water carts

Figs. 481-2 *Pottery models in Bichrome Ware. Iron Age.*
Fig. 481 *Nicosia. Ht. 12 cm. Karageorghis 1977, no. 43.*
Fig. 482 *No provenance (Pierides Collection, Larnaca). Ht. 20 cm. Karageorghis 1973, Pl. 69.*

14 Boats

Figs. 483–6 *Pottery models. Late Bronze Age to Iron Age.*

Fig. 483 *Salamis (Tomb 104, no. 5). Length 10.5 cm. Karageorghis 1970, Pl. CLXXVI, 5.*

Fig. 484 *Salamis (surface find, 35). Length 9.5 cm. Karageorghis 1970, Pl. XLII, 35.*

Fig. 485 *Maroni (Tomb 7, no. 60). Ht. 14 cm. Johnson 1980, Pl. XVI, 60.*

Fig. 486 *Kazaphani (Tomb 2b). Ht. 23 cm. Buchholz and Karageorghis 1973, no. 1719.*

Fig. 483

Fig. 484

Fig. 485

Fig. 486

Pl. 286 *Sheath knife and sheath. The knife is usually referred to as a 'dagger', but there is no evidence that it was used for stabbing rather than cutting. The careful incision decorations are complex in their pattern variations. Black-topped Red Polished Ware. Early Bronze Age. Knife length 21 cm. (DM-BTRP-27). Sheath length 21.6 cm (DM-BTRP-28).*

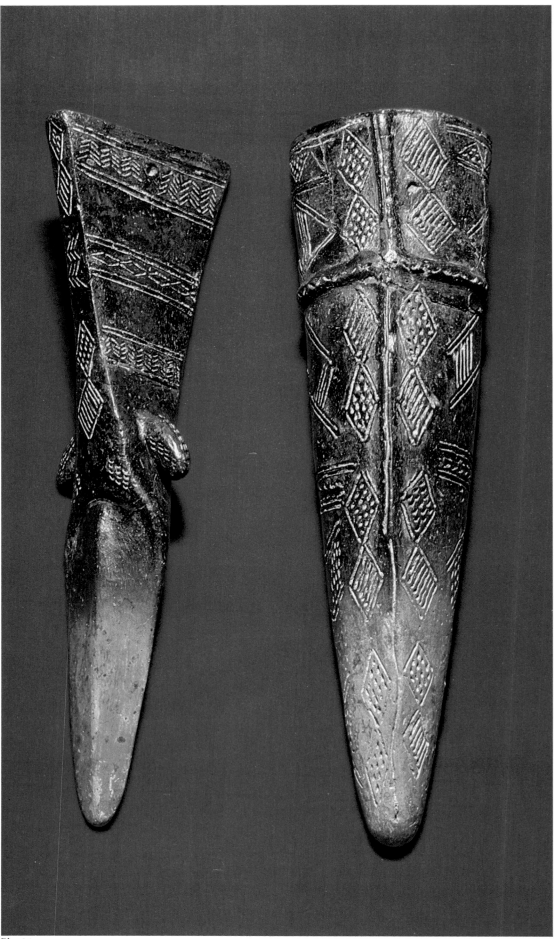

Pl. 286

Pl. 287

Pl. 287 *Animal horn. Hollow, with two pierced holes on rim. (For other examples, see p. 255.) Incised Red Polished Ware. Early Bronze Age. Length 10.2 cm (DM-IRP-102).*

Pl. 288

Pl. 288 Pottery mouth-cover. *This unique object appears to be a ceramic imitation of a wooden (?) covering that was tied over the mouth of the corpse when it was placed in the tomb. This is the only example to survive from the Early or Middle Bronze Age. By the Late Bronze Age, gold is used, and a number have survived from that later period. The inner surface is curved to fit the lips. The outer surface has a groove to take a fine tie-cord. In the central section this groove is open, but at either end it is covered to ensure that the cord did not slip. Both surfaces are decorated with zigzag and diamond motifs. Black Polished Ware. Early Bronze Age. Length 10.1 cm (DM-BP-10).*

Pl. 289

Pl. 289 Small model of a boat. *The decoration includes parallel diagonal lines on one side which suggest long oars. Bichrome Ware. Iron Age. Length 9.7 cm (DM-BI-118).*

Scenic Compositions

By far the most interesting works of art to survive from the prehistoric period of Cyprus are those which depict scenes from daily life. This is because, by definition, we have no written records from this early phase of the island's story, and any artefacts which depict human activities are therefore of great value.

Scenic compositions are great rarities. As we have already seen, the vast majority of representations show human beings, animals, plants or inanimate objects as single units. Even where several appear together on a vessel it is the general rule for them to remain separate entities. Each figure stands where it is in its own right and does not interact with the others.

In scenic works of art, this formal *juxtaposition* is replaced by operational *composition*. Actions are performed. Events occur. At the simplest level these may amount to no more than a mother holding a baby or a man riding a horse. Simple interactions of this kind have been dealt with already in other sections. At a more complex level, diverse elements are grouped together in more unusual ways, and it is these that are discussed here.

There are twenty examples of Scenic Compositions from the prehistoric period, all from the Early and Middle Bronze Ages. They take several forms:

1 Large Red Polished Ware bowls with small modelled figures all around the outside of the rims. Six of these are known at present. Four come from Margi and one from Kalavassos. The other one has no provenance. In each case, scenes from ordinary daily life are shown, providing us with something like a 'strip cartoon' of prehistoric village activities.

2 Large Polished Ware jar with small modelled figures all around its 'shoulders'. The solitary example has no provenance. As before it displays everyday scenes and commonplace activities.

3 Modified Red Polished Ware bowl, with flat bottom and side-aperture, containing scenic composition inside its walls. A unique object and the most complex yet discovered, this has been interpreted in the past as depicting a religious ceremony of some kind. If this is so then it is out of step with the other Scenic Compositions, all of which show everyday events.

4 Red Polished Ware jugs with groups of modelled figures protruding from their 'shoulders'. Six of these jugs are known, five in Red Polished Ware and one in Drab Polished Ware. Four are from Vounous, one from Lapithos and one is without provenance. Humans and animals are depicted in scenes from everyday life.

5 Terracotta models. In another six cases, the artists have abandoned vessels altogether as the stage for setting their scenes, and have placed their figures on a slab of pottery instead. In one special case the 'vehicle' for the grouped figures has become a simple ship.

In addition, there are several intermediate examples, where, although some kind of activity is occurring, it is really too simple to be called 'scenic'.

Looking at these Scenic Compositions as a whole, it seems likely that their function as tomb offerings was to equip the deceased with possessions that would make them feel more 'at home' by providing them with familiar scenes from their past lives. Whether the selection of topics in each case was related to the specific activities of the deceased, or whether they were simply intended to remind them of village life in general, is not clear. Some scenic pieces depict only one activity, such as ploughing, which might have been thought especially appropriate for a dead ploughman, but others show a whole variety of tasks being performed.

One intriguing feature of these Scenic Compositions is that they present human figures in the round. This contrasts strikingly with the most characteristic element of distortion that occurred in almost all the *single* human figures produced during the Early and Middle Bronze ages, namely the complete flattening of the forms. The scenic figures, busily grinding corn, washing clothes, ploughing furrows,or kneading dough, are *not* plank figures. This strengthens the suggestion made earlier that the flatness of the plank figures had some special, functional significance. Rendering the human figure two-dimensional was not an all-embracing stylistic rule for the period.

The twenty examples of prehistoric Scenic Compositions are as follows:

1	The Deer-milking Jug	No provenance	DM Collection
2	The Oxford Bowl	Margi?	DM Collection
3	The Margi Bowl	Margi	Cyprus Museum (CM)
4	The Sèvres Bowl	No provenance	Sèvres Museum
5	The Pierides Bowl	Margi	Larnaca
6	The Hadjiprodromou Bowl	Margi	Famagusta
7	The Kalavassos Bowl	Kalavassos, Panayia Church Area, Tomb 36	CM
8	The Sèvres Jar	No provenance	Sèvres Museum
9	The Vounous Bowl	Vounous, Tomb 22, no. 26	CM
10	The Bucrancial Wall (with crossbar)	Kochati	CM
11	The Bucranial Wall (no crossbar)	Kochati	CM
12	The Ploughing Scene	Vounous, SS, no. 1	CM
13	The Ploughing Jug	Vounous, Tomb 37, no. 9	CM
14	The Grinding Jug	Vounous, SS, no. 7	CM
15	The Washing Scene	No provenance	Louvre
16	The Couple-with-Panniers Scene	No provenance	Louvre
17	The Ship-with-Crew Scene	No provenance	Louvre
18	The Couple-on-a-Bench Scene	Lapithos, Tomb 429c, no. 22	CM
19	The Trough Jug	Vounous, Tomb 111, no. 8	Birmingham Museum
20	The Trough-and-Jar Jug	Vounous, Tomb 164a no. 13	CM

The first two are being published here for the first time. The others are well known but have never been brought together before as a distinct category. Brief details of the scenic elements will be given in each case, for comparative purposes.

In the case of the large bowls with figures all around the outside of the rims, the same sequence is followed in each case. The bowl is visualized seen from above with the spout at 12 o'clock and the elements are numbered off in a clockwise direction starting from one o'clock.

1 The Deer-milking Jug

This remarkable vessel was purchased at a Christie's sale in London on 11 July 1973 (lot 87). Several similar ones were purchased at about the same time (and they are illustrated here on pp. 97, 106, 107 and 110). There is also one in the Pierides Collection in Larnaca (see des Gagniers and Karageorghis, 1976, Pl. XXIV, no. 3) that appears to have been made by the same artist. However, the Deer-milking Jug is the only one of this group to show a Scenic Composition. The others show subsidiary vessels or animals placed on the shoulders, but their is no 'group effect'.

The jug itself is 44.2 cm high, with a round bottom and an almost perfectly spherical body. The tubular neck flares slightly as it reaches the cutaway-beak spout. The vertical handle, which is attached low down on the long neck, has a prominent, vertical thumbgrip. There is some surface wear on the body and the neck. The ware is intermediate between the late and rather inferior Red Polished IV and Drab Polished Ware. Although the vessel has no provenance it seems likely that it came from somewhere in the south-west of the island.

The scenic group is placed on the shoulders of the jug. If the vessel is viewed from above, with the handle pointing to 12 o'clock, the elements are arranged clockwise in the following order:

1 *Three curved rows of incised dots,* running from the bottom of the handle, around the shoulder of the jug to the legs of the first animal figure. The upper, middle and lower rows have nine, ten and eleven dots respectively.

2 *A modelled stag* standing sideways on to

Pls. 290, 291 *Deer-milking scenic composition on the shoulders of a large, round-based jug. For details see text (DM-DP-36).*

Pl. 290

Pl. 291

the neck of the jug, with its head end nearer to the handle. Its maximum height to the tip of its antlers is 10.5 cm. Its legs rise smoothly from the surface of the vessel, with no differentiation of feet. Its tubular body has a row of incised dots running down each flank. There is a prominent 'adam's apple' at the front of its long neck, indicating that the artist was aware of this as a specifically male characteristic for this species. There are two large ears protruding horizontally from the sides of the head. The long antlers each show three points.

3 *A modelled quadruped* standing sideways on to the neck of the jug and pointing in the opposite direction from the stag. This animal is slightly lower down the shoulder of the jug, further away from the neck. Its maximum height is 7.5 cm. Its legs and body are similar to those of the stag, but slightly smaller. The rows of incised dots on its body are fainter. The shape of its head, neck and ears are the same as those of the stag, with two exceptions. It lacks the 'adam's apple' on the throat and its antlers are much smaller, with a single point. The artist appears to be attempting to portray a female deer, and is signalling this fact by the absence of the male 'adam's apple'. It is clear from earlier discussions that artists in ancient Cyprus often gave antlers to female deer to indicate the species, even though this is anatomically incorrect. Antlered females are portrayed suckling their fawns (see Fig. 299), so there is no need to be surprised that this female deer is shown with small antlers.

4 *Two curved rows of incised dots,* running from the region of the deer, around the shoulder of the parent jug to the legs of the stool of the next figure (no. 5). The upper and lower rows have seven and eight dots respectively.

5 *A human being sitting on a low, rectangular, four-legged stool,* facing away from the handle of the jug. The height from the bottom of the stool leg to the top of the figure's head is 13.5 cm. The head was missing and has been restored. The neck is long and thinner than the body. The arms hang awkwardly from the shoulders. They point downwards and do not touch the body at any point. The hand region is flattened and three incised lines indicate the fingers. The trunk of the body is excessively long. It is slim and tubular, like that of the stag's and is attached to the neck of the jug by a supporting strut at the back.

The legs are bent and apart, to allow space for a small model of a jug to be placed on the ground between them. The jug model is supported and held in place by a curved ridge that runs between the feet of the human figure. The jug model itself shows a round-bottomed jug with a vertical handle. Its spherical body is marked with incised dots. The top of its neck is damaged so that it is impossible to be sure about its spout-shape. The surface of the stool on which the figure is sitting curves up slightly on either side, making it a perfect model of the full-sized stool illustrated on p. 252 (Fig. 460).

6 *A model of a large milk bowl,* placed below the human figure's right hand. It is attached to the shoulder of the parent jug by a stalk.

7 *A single ring of incised dots* running around the base of the neck of the parent jug.

Together these elements make up what appears to be a deer-milking scene, with a human being shown sitting on a low milking stool, equipped with a milk jug and a milk bowl. Of the two deer, the male is shown pointing away from the figure on the stool, while the female appears to be approaching, as if the artist is trying to suggest that the stag is not involved, but his female is.

If this is the correct interpretation, then this is the first evidence we have that the Mesopotamian Fallow Deer was employed as a milk-supplying animal. Such usage is well known for reindeer and there is no reason why, once a year, the ancient Cypriots should not have exploited their deer in this way. For those who favour religious scenarios it is not unreasonable to suggest that this annual deer-milking had some sacred connotation and that the liquid obtained was put to some ritual use. Alternatively, obtaining milk in this way may simply have been one of the ordinary, seasonal domestic activities of these Bronze Age farmers.

The only other possible explanation of the scenic composition on this jug is that the deer are about to be killed and their blood ceremonially collected in the jug and the bowl. Although this remains a possibility, the milking interpretation is favoured because of the special positioning of the male and female deer. It is interesting in this connection that this vessel, when illustrated in the Christie's catalogue, showed *both* animals pointing away from the seated figure. When the jug had been purchased it was closely examined and found to have been badly restored. Removal of the female deer revealed that it had been stuck on backwards. It was quite clear, during its careful re-restoration, that, from the slope of its legs, it was meant to be facing the human figure and it was replaced in its correct position. It was this discovery that strengthened the milking interpretation, although it must be admitted that this must remain tentative until we have additional evidence to support it, from other sources.

There is one other strange feature of this jug which deserves brief mention. Around the neck, just below the spout, there is a broad *impressed* band about 1.2 cm wide. It is very faint and the impression is very slight, but under a lens it is clear that something was tied firmly around the neck of the vessel at this point, when the clay was only leather-hard. The material used has left some very small horizontal striations in one area.

2 The Oxford Bowl

This important vessel was purchased from a London dealer in March 1972. It had previously been offered to the Ashmolean Museum, but negotiations had broken down and the dealer had removed it from the museum, refusing to discuss it further with them. I then acquired it.

It seems that the dispute had arisen partly because of the strange condition of the bowl. Its surface was extensively covered with what appeared to be two kinds of pale deposit, one whiter than the other. Close examination revealed that, although the darker of the two deposits was ancient and genuine, the whitish one was modern and had been applied to cover over a number of cracks and breaks in the pottery. It is a well-known 'dealer's trick' to conceal vessel damage in this way, and in the case of this large bowl suspicions went further. It was felt that perhaps the object had been assembled from fragments of different vessels, with the artifical 'deposit' being smeared over the surfaces to conceal this fact. This suggestion was hotly denied by the dealer, and in the end he proved to be correct. Careful removal of all the deposit, both ancient and modern, revealed that the bowl was, in reality, all from one original and that this was more than 90 per cent complete. All that the false deposit had been doing was concealing a number of fractures.

The Oxford Bowl is one of six known examples of Scenic Compositions in which many small figures are shown protruding from around the outside of the rims of very large deep bowls in Red Polished Ware. Each one provides a fascinating 'strip cartoon' of village life in the Early Bronze Age, with many different activities being portrayed. Other large bowls of similar shapes and the same ware, but without these scenic additions, are also known, so it looks as though these six were 'special' ones, made perhaps by a single artist or group of artists who wanted to provide something 'extra' as a tomb offering. As already mentioned, three of the six came from Margi, in central Cyprus, and one came from Kalavassos, slightly further south (eighteen miles away, to be precise). The Oxford Bowl was thought to have come from Margi, but there was of course no proof of this. The sixth example has no provenance. On this basis, the big, scenic bowls begin to look like a 'Margi speciality'.

The Oxford Bowl is 38.3 cm high, from base to rim, with a maximum height of 42.5 cm to the top of the handle. Its deep hemispherical shape has a flattened bottom, so that it stands firmly on a flat surface without support. There is a heavy, vertical handle which divides into two before joining the rim of the vessel. Opposite this handle are twin spouts with round apertures pointing straight up. Originally, these twin spouts were connected to one another by a short bar, but this has been broken away and lost. Each spout was also connected to the rim of the vessel by a short bar, but only a small trace remains today.

The scenic composition is arranged around the outside of the rim. If the vessel is viewed from above, with the twin necks pointing to 12 o'clock, then the elements of the composition are arranged clockwise in the following order:

1 *A seated figure leaning up aginst the side of one of the spouts.* It has no facial details, but it is clear from the way it is leaning back against the surface of the spout that it is meant to be relaxing. Its arms are held over its lap and something is clasped in its hands. It is impossible to decide what is being held but it gives the impression of being a food object.

2 *A horizontal ledge bearing three small, conical lumps.* A highly simplified human figure stands in front of the left-hand lump. These cones look like loaves of bread. We know

Pl. 292

Pls. 292–302 *The Oxford Bowl.*
For details see text (DM-RRP-19).

Pl. 293   Pl. 294   Pl. 295

Pl. 296   Pl. 297

Pl. 298

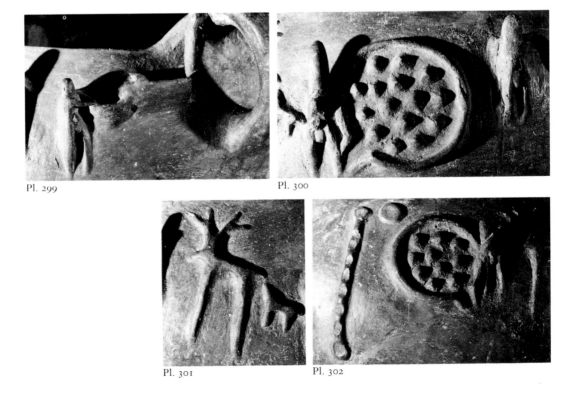

Pl. 299

Pl. 300

Pl. 301

Pl. 302

Pl. 303 *'Baker's stick' boards, reminiscent of relief motifs seen on Early Bronze Age vessels, are still offered for sale in Cypriot antique shops (photograph taken near Larnaca, 1982).*

that in Early Egypt there were two shapes of bread loaves—the conical or pyramid type and the flat, round type. According to Neuburger (1930), '... the loaves of pyramidal shape were prepared for purposes of worship; this is the origin of the name later given to the Pyramids.' It is dangerous to translate from Egypt to Cyprus, but it is tempting to think of the Cypriot pyramid loaves as special products for sacred use—possibly at burials such as the one in which the Oxford Bowl itself was placed in its tomb.

3 *Another horizontal ledge, this time with three human figures bent over it busily working.* The only anatomical details surviving on these highly simplified figures are large ears and, in one case, a pair of arms. A small lump is placed on the ledge in front of each figure, and the impression is that they are kneading dough into shape to make loaves.

4 *A single figure standing on a ledge in front of an oven.* The human figure appears to be reaching out towards the entrance of the oven, as if putting something in it or taking something out. On the left side of the oven there is a basin. This strengthens the idea that this is a bread oven. Neuburger (1930) mentions that early ovens often had '... small water containers half built into the façade which perhaps contained the water with which the surface of the bread was moistened in order to obtain a good crust.' Wetting the half-baked loaves, he explains, makes their crusts shine brightly. So it would seem that the Early Bronze Age Cypriots preferred their loaves crusty and shiny.

5 *A single human figure seen working at some unidentifiable task.* The figure is slightly lower than the previous one.

6 *Three flat, circular discs,* shown in relief. They are arranged in a horizontal row and give the impression that the figure working below them has made three flat loaves and placed them ready for baking.

7 *A standing figure holding a large pestle.* The pestle is being ground down into a basin-shaped mortar, and this figure is clearly intended to be depicted in the act of grinding corn to make the flour for the bread.

Moving round to the other side of the handle:

8 *A vertical pipe running down into a trough which in turn runs down into a bowl.* A human figure stands to the left of the bowl with his hands resting on its rim. Unlike all the fig-

ures on the other side of the parent vessel, this figure is conspicuously male.

9 *A solitary male figure standing on its own.* Again, male genitals are distinct, even though there are no facial details.

10 *A large, circular ridge inside which are fifteen conical lumps,* similar in shape to the pyramid loaves on the other side of the parent vessel. In the bottom left-hand part of the circular ridge there is an aperture representing some kind of opening to the space inside the circle. To the left of this opening, so close that he is touching the side of the circular ridge, stands another conspicuously male figure.

11 *An antlered deer* facing to the left, rendered in relief lines, followed by a small quadrupedal animal. It is impossible to identify the species intended for the small animal. It is either a dog pursuing the deer, or a fawn following it.

12 *A second, large circular ridge with conical lumps inside it.* This time there are only ten lumps, and the circle of the ridge is slightly smaller. The male figure stands to the right in this case, and the opening in the circle faces towards the bottom right.

13 *A single, round, flat disc,* high up near the rim of the parent vessel. This looks like an isolated flat loaf, similar to the three shown on the other side of the bowl.

14 *A long vertical 'stick'* rendered in relief, with seven small hollows down its length and a larger circular hollow at its swollen lower end. At the top is what looks like a flat, fan-shaped handle. This object is strongly reminiscent of the long baker's sticks (see Pl. 303) used until recent times for placing bread in ovens in Cyprus. Such sticks can still be seen offered for sale in the island's antique shops.

This brings the bowl full circle, and it now remains to attempt to interpret the more obscure elements described above. My first inclination was to describe it as 'The Bakery Bowl' and to see all the elements as being related to the one activity of bread-making. But I knew from the other scenic bowls that it was not necessary to imagine that a single pursuit had to be shown. In several instances it was clear that this was not the case. The possibility remained that perhaps bread-making was only one of the activities taking place here.

One clue comes from the curious division of the sexes. On one side all the human figures have conspicuous male genitals. On the other side no gender signs are present. The suggestion from this is that one side of the bowl shows male activity and the other female. Divided up in this way, it is clear that the females are baking bread. They are seen grinding the corn, kneading the dough, shaping the loaves, baking them in an oven and, perhaps, (in figure one) enjoying eating the bread they have made.

But if this is the case, what are the males on the other side doing? One is seen collecting something in a bowl from a pipe-fed trough, and this could, of course, be water to make the dough, or for the glazing basin next to the oven. But it could also be for many other purposes. The two males guarding or operating the strange circular discs full of conical lumps could be bakers tending their ovens. The ovens here could be seen in section, each with its roof removed to reveal the pyramid loaves baking inside it. The presence of the long 'baker's stick' suggests that the men in question had to use some such implement to place the loaves inside the oven and then to regain them after baking. The antlered deer seems oddly out of place unless the small animal following it is meant to be a fawn, in which case, despite the antlers, the adult may be intended as a milk-giving female. Milk, of course, was commonly used as an ingredient in bread making.

But although this interpretation gave coherence to the subject matter of the Oxford Bowl it seemed curiously unsatisfactory. In particular, the idea that the ancient artist should have shown a bread oven in a sideways view on one side of the parent vessel and in plan view on the other, seemed odd. Also, if ovens were being used for baking on both sides of the bowl why were males active one side and females on the other? A possible explanation here could have been that this was related to the two kinds of loaves being produced. If the ancient Cypriots followed the Egyptian pattern, then there was a possibility that the females baked the ordinary day-to-day flat loaves, while the men alone were responsible for the production of the sacred pyramid loaves. Supporting this is the fact that the shapes inside the male 'ovens', seen in section, are conical. Also, the female oven on the other side of the bowl is next to three flat loaves.

At this point, however, the neat division breaks down, for the female side of the bowl also shows a row of conical, pyramid loaves on a ledge, and there is a single flat loaf on the male side. It is still possible that the whole of the scenic composition of the Oxford Bowl does portray bread-making, but a search for an alternative explanation for the male activities cannot be abandoned.

The strange male 'ovens', shown in section, pose the greatest problem. The deer between them adds to the confusion. One proposal was that this section of the composition represents some kind of animal trapping. The small animal behind the stag is seen as a dog driving the deer and the circular 'ovens' are interpreted instead as some kind of trap or stockade, with hunters guarding the entrances. But this also lacks conviction.

A more convincing argument was put forward recently by Robert Merrillees, who suggested that the male side of the bowl could be taken as a depiction of metal production—specifically, of copper leaching. The technical definition of leaching is the dissolving, by a liquid solvent, of soluble material from its mixture with an insoluble solid. In ancient Cyprus this would have meant leaching crude copper ore with water

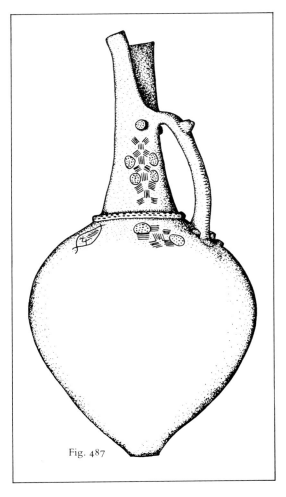

Fig. 487

Fig. 487 *A large Red Polished Ware jug from Vounous, Early Bronze Age, with incised motifs of a special kind. They appear to be schematic rather than abstract. If the lump-filled rings on the Oxford Bowl represent copper-leaching enclosures, as Merrillees has suggested, then the dot-filled circles on this jug almost certainly show a series of similar enclosures. Vounous (Tomb 164a, no. 45). Ht. 77.4 cm. Karageorghis 1962, Pl. VII.*

to produce a copper-rich sludge. This sludge or leachate could then be allowed to dry out in specially designed troughs and the precipitate collected and used for metal production through smelting.

Merrillees envisages the Bronze Age Cypriots collecting copper ores and stacking them in piles in the open, probably on a sloping surface. Exposed for months to the winter rains, the soluble copper salts would be washed out of the crude ore and down into some kind of drainage pit. The sludge slowly collecting there would then be thickened by drying out in troughs and the resultant mass could be used for smelting to create an impure form of copper. From this, more refined copper could then be made.

If this process is now related to the 'male scene' on the Oxford Bowl, it fits the details rather well. While the females busily make bread on the other side of the bowl, the males stand around supervising the leaching process, which involves about as much activity as watching paint dry. The two large circular 'ovens' are now more comfortably explained as leaching enclosures, where piles of crude ore have been placed on the ground and surrounded by a low, protective wall. When the rains fall, the copper salts are washed out and down to the aperture in the circular ridge. There, they are collected in some kind of pit and transferred to troughs for drying out. This last stage in the process is shown in no. 8 on the male side of the bowl, where a vertical pipe (the drainage pit?) empties into an open trough at the far end of which is a bridge-spout over a large bowl. The bowl is tended by a male figure. Merrillees suggests that the bridge indicates that the trough was dammed at that end to encourage the slowly collecting sludge to dry out. Then, when it had become sufficiently concentrated, the block would be removed and the concentrate would be allowed to flow into the bowl, held here by the male figure. This would then be taken off for smelting and further treatment.

This is a most ingenious and attractive interpretation and seems to offer the best explanation to date. Its only weaknesses are that it does not explain the presence of the stag and the small animal behind it or the long 'baker's stick' to the left of the 'leaching enclosures'. But what it does do admirably is to add to all the other daily activities portrayed in the various Scenic Compositions

from the Bronze Age, the crucial but previously missing one of metal production. It would be surprising if such a vital part of early Cypriot life was completely omitted from the representations of the prehistoric period.

3 The Margi Bowl

This is the first of the large Margi bowls to be discovered. It was found by villagers at a site called Pappara, about half a mile east of Margi Village, and taken to the Cyprus Museum by the village constable in 1942. It was published in detail after the war, by Karageorghis (1959).

The lower part of the bowl is completely missing, but the vital area around the rim, where the Scenic Composition occurs, is almost complete (Fig. 488). The height of the surviving part is 26.2 cm and the width is 35.7 cm. Like the Oxford Bowl, it has twin spouts, connected to one another and to the rim. But these spouts are much lower, almost in a horizontal position. As before, there is a strong vertical handle opposite. In common with all these large bowls, the vessel is made of Red Polished Ware from the Early Bronze Age, but it is of a much darker, browner colour than the others.

All around the outside of the rim there is a crowded circle of small, modelled figures. The Scenic Composition has even more elements than the Oxford Bowl, twenty in all. With the spouts pointing to 12 o'clock and reading clockwise, these elements are as follows:

1-9 *Nine human figures, apparently seated on a long bench* (but perhaps standing), facing the rim of the bowl and with their arms stretched out to touch the bowl surface. They are busily working at some task, and Karageorghis believes this to be the grinding of corn. Just above them on the surface of the bowl near the rim is a broad, discontinuous rope pattern. This is missing on the other side, so it seems to be more than merely decorative, but its significance is not clear. This group of nine figures takes up the whole of one side of the bowl, from spout to handle.

10 *A damaged quadruped animal figure,* perched on top of the tall handle. It may have been a bull, but it is no longer possible to be certain.

11-13 *A group of three human figures.* The

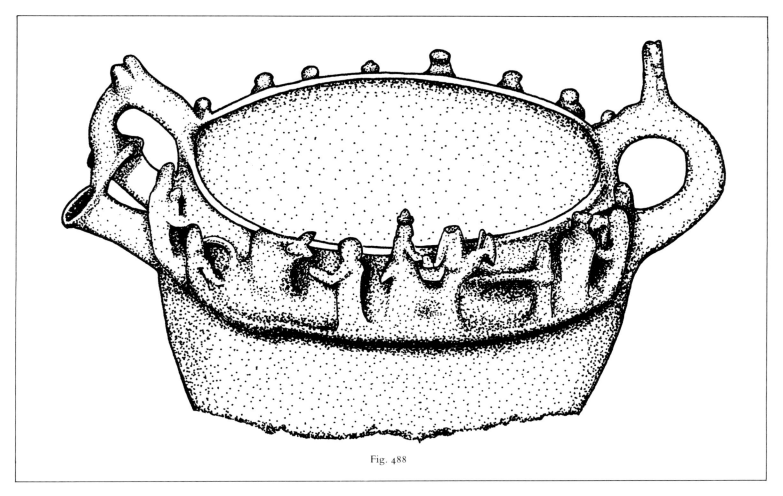

Fig. 488

central one, carrying an oblong object in the left arm, faces the bowl. It is flanked by two others, half turned towards it, with their arms stretched forward to touch a flat object which is marked with dots. The held object seems too small to be a baby, and it is thought that this trio, too, is engaged in corn grinding.

14 *A human figure facing the bowl* (similar to figures 1 to 9 on the other side).

15 *Two figures seated on the back of a pack animal*. They face one another. Between them, across the animal's back, is a double basket, and Karageorghis (1958) suggests 'that they may represent street vendors such as are to be seen even today in Cypriot villages'.

16, 17 *A human figure with arms outstretched towards a bull*, as if controlling it. The figure and the bull face one another.

18 *A human figure, apparently seated, facing a small oven*, presumably in the act of baking bread.

19 *A human figure facing the bowl, with a baby on its chest*. This appears to be a mother and child representation.

20 *An animal-shaped projection* from the top

of the vertical connection which links the twin spouts to the rim. This has been even more badly damaged than its opposite number (no. 10) and little now remains of it.

This bowl may, as Karageorghis suggests, represent general scenes of daily life, or it may perhaps be more specifically concerned with a single activity—bread-making. If some of the elements are given only slightly different interpretations, then they can all be seen as part of one major activity. For instance:

The figure with the bull may be ploughing a field for the planting of corn. The two figures on the pack animal may be transporting the corn to the corn-grinders. The group of three figures together (nos. 11 to 13) may be fashioning loaves of bread. The figure supposedly holding a baby (no. 19) and standing next to the oven, may be holding loaves of bread. With these few adjustments (not unreasonable in view of the extreme simplification of the figures) the whole composition becomes transformed into a 'bakery scene'. This interpretation is by no means certain but it must be considered as a serious possibility.

Fig. 488 The Margi Bowl. *For details see text. Karageorghis 1958, Pl. XIa, c.*

4 The Sèvres Bowl

This large, flat-bottomed bowl has suffered severe surface damage and a section of the rim is missing. It is clear, however, that it once displayed a complex Scenic Composition. It is difficult to make out the remnants of this, but close examination of the vessel in the basement of the Sèvres Museum, outside Paris, revealed the following details:

The bowl, no. MNC 10690, is in Red Polished Ware of the Early Bronze Age. Around the outside of the rim is a segmented rope design in relief. Two tassels of this hang down, one on either side of the two horizontal handles. There is no spout. If the handle on the right (in Fig. 489) is pointing at 12 o'clock, then reading clockwise the compositional elements are:

1 *A relief ring enclosing five circular lumps.* There are two possible interpretations. Following the Merrillees concept, this would represent copper-leaching and would be an enclosure containing five small piles of crude copper ore. But there is no drainage exit at the lower end of this enclosure. This may be due to greater simplification and formaliza-

tion by the artist. Alternatively this element may stand for a container full of loaves of bread, or even a bread oven seen in section.

2 *Ditto, but with six lumps inside the ring.*

3 *Ditto, but with five lumps inside the ring.*

4 *A crudely depicted quadruped* with a pair of vertical horns. This is presumably a bull. It is facing towards the right, with its head close to element no. 3.

5 *A human figure working at some kind of trough.* She (?) is positioned above the rings and the bull, and is facing the parent bowl. It is clear that three other similar figures were once seen working alongside this lone survivor, but they have been broken away and lost. They appear to be a 'corn-grinding' group similar to the ones discussed earlier, but they could equally well be washing clothes or performing some other manual task.

6 *Two patches* (to the left of the last group), the first circular and the second rectangular, which show that modelled figures of some kind once projected from the surface there.

7 *An oven,* of the type already described for other vessels, but with its attendant baker missing.

8 *The remains of a quadruped* facing to the left, rendered in relief.

9 *The remains of a quadruped.* On the other side of the second handle, a large section of the rim is missing, but four long, quadruped legs have survived beneath it, indicating that a large animal once stood there in relief.

10-15 *Six more relief rings containing circular lumps* (4, 7, 5, 4, 4, and 4 lumps respectively). As before, these run across the body of the bowl at a lower level, while above them is:

16 *Another group of four human figures facing the bowl, working at a trough or ledge of some kind.* Badly damaged again, but clearly meant to represent the same kind of work activity as element no. 5.

17 *The remains of an oven,* similar to element no. 7.

18 *A large quadruped* of some kind with very long legs, facing to the left.

The curious feature of this bowl is that the two sides are basically similar, even down to the detail of having one long-legged animal on the right, facing right, and one on the left, facing left. But there is no attempt to copy the same arrangement of elements slavishly.

Fig. 489 The Sèvres Bowl. *For details see text.*

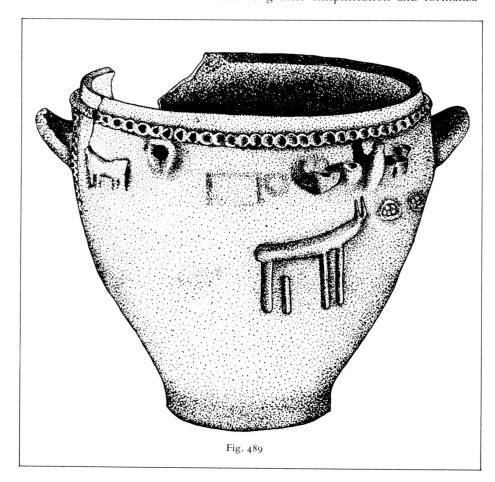

Fig. 489

The rings, for instance, are arranged in a different way, and there are twice as many on one side as the other. It is as if the artist is portraying two similar scenes, rather than one scene twice over. They may represent bread-making or copper-leaching, but the vessel is too badly preserved to say more.

5 The Pierides Bowl

This scenic bowl (Fig. 490) has an unusually deep, conical body, with a flat base. There are twin spouts set at roughly 45 degrees, joined to one another by a bar and to the rim of the vessel by two more bridge-bars. Opposite is a powerful, vertical handle. There is a rope-like relief-band running around the outside of the rim, punctuated with indentations at roughly regular intervals. The vessel is 45.5 cm high and is in Red Polished Ware. From the Early Bronze Age period, it was found in Margi and is now in the Pierides Collection in Larnaca.

The scenic elements, reading clockwise from the spouts, are as follows:

1 *A trough-like object,* badly damaged. The remains of two human legs can be seen, but the figure is lost.

2 *A pair of human figures* facing outwards from the vessel. The left-hand figure is much taller and larger than its companion. Both wear headgear and they appear to be 'wrapped' together by a broad band, but there is another, vertical band between them. They give the impression of a couple being 'paired' in some way, perhaps at a ceremony of some kind. Alternatively, with a little artistic licence, they could represent a married couple in bed together.

3 *A heavily pregnant female,* facing away from the bowl. A small vertical groove indicates the female genitals.

4 *Another trough, with one surviving pyramid loaf of bread on it.* This element is badly broken, with the result that it has been misidentified in the past as a bird. (It is just possible that it represents a pack animal and that the loaf of bread is in a pannier on its back, with almost all the animal's body broken away.)

5 *A figure grinding corn in two troughs.* The figure faces towards the first, smaller, of the two troughs and has what appears to be a pestle thrust into it. This figure is also broken and something is missing from it.

6 *A female figure in the act of giving birth.* She is facing away from the parent vessel and is wearing headgear. Across her upper body there is a wide band, as if some form of constriction is being applied to help the birth. (This band has been described before as a 'collar round neck', but it is too low for a collar.) The genitals are represented by a vertical groove through which a pellet of clay is appearing. This pellet is clearly meant to be the baby's head emerging.

On the other side of the handle are:

7 *A couple of human figures,* facing away from the bowl. Again, they both wear headgear and are positioned close to one another. To their right is a small trough or container of some kind with a large pestle resting in it. There are two rows of incised dots on the front of the larger of the two figures.

8 *A baby in a cradle or swaddling-board.* It is shown at an angle, as if hung up in a tree while the parents work.

9 *A row of figures standing working at a table.* All are badly broken and only four of the original six survive.

10 *An oven with a glazing trough beside it* and a pair of leg stumps below it revealing where the 'baker' stood before being broken away. There is a second pair of surviving leg stumps nearby indicating that another human

Fig. 490 The Pierides Bowl.
For details see text. Karageorghis 1973, Pl. 8.

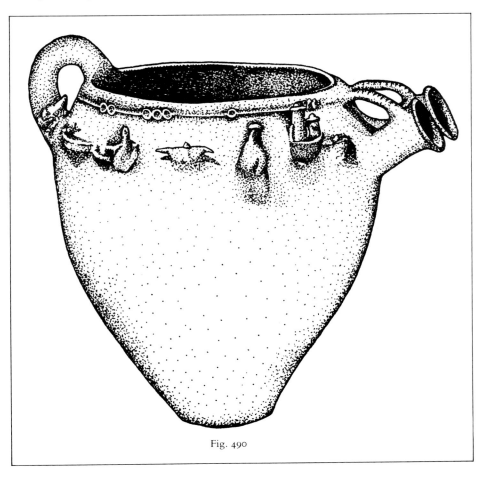

Fig. 490

figure was also present in the original scene. The sequence of elements on the Pierides Bowl is fascinating because, if read in the order given here (which is the reverse of the one previously published), it looks like a deliberate time sequence. A couple are paired off (element 2), the female becomes pregnant (3) and then gives birth (6). Next we see the couple with an implement near them, suggesting they have returned to work (7) while their baby is snugly protected in its cradle nearby (8). Interspersed with this sequence are scenes of work (1, 4, 5, 9 and 10), mostly to do with bread-making and involving the grinding of corn, the making of loaves and the baking of them in an oven.

It has to be admitted that this interpretation makes a few intuitive leaps, and the scenario outlined here is by no means certain. It does, however, seem highly likely, and makes this Pierides Bowl of especial interest because of its apparent depiction of married life in the Early Bronze Age.

6 The Hadjiprodromou Bowl

This is the most spherical of all the large Scenic Bowls, with a round bottom (Fig. 491). Like the others, it has twin spouts with a connecting bar and a handle-bridge to the rim of the vessel. Opposite it, as usual, is a massively powerful, vertical handle. This bowl is from

Fig. 491 The Hadjiprodromou Bowl. *For details see text. Des Gagniers and Karageorghis 1976, Pl. XI, 1.*

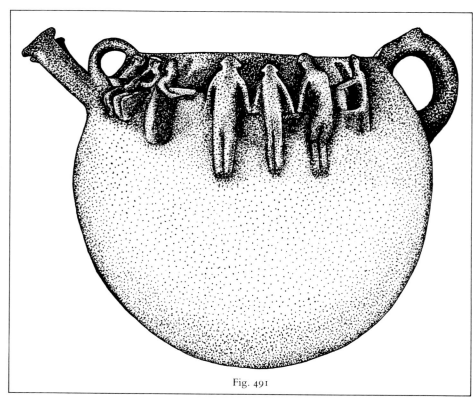

Fig. 491

Margi and, like the others, is in Red Polished Ware, from the Early Bronze Age. It is in the Hadjiprodromou Collection in Famagusta, but has not been seen for ten years, since that city became isolated by Turkish troops. Its height and diameter are the same—38 cm.

The scenic elements around the outside of the rim, reading clockwise from the spouts, are as follows:

The first side, from spout to handle, has lost its figures, but it is clear from the remains that they depicted a scene not unlike that on the other side, where all the elements survive. These consist of:

1 *A human figure grinding corn with a pestle.* The figure is slightly turned towards the one on its left.

2-4 *Three human figures* facing the body of the bowl. They seem to be kneeling at a trough and are engaged either in food production or the washing of clothes. Their arms are held forwards into the trough and, whatever the precise nature of their task, they are all hard at work with their heads bent forward in concentration.

5 *A slightly smaller figure* facing to the right, looking at the three workers. It holds something towards them in its arms. The object may be a bowl or a food object—or perhaps a pile of clothes.

6 *A pair of figures* facing away from the body of the bowl. They are both wearing headgear and one appears to be holding a baby.

Again, this is a domestic scene of industrious figures carrying out their daily tasks. There is nothing whatever about this scene to suggest anything sacred or ceremonial. Routine, daily activities dominate the subject-matter.

7 The Kalavassos Bowl

This is the last of the 'Six Scenic Bowls' and was the most recent one to be discovered. It was found in the summer of 1978 when a rescue operation was mounted to salvage the contents of a group of Bronze Age tombs in the middle of Kalavassos village. A mechanical digger had started to prepare the ground for some new shops which were to be built just to the east of the Panayia Church, when ancient tombs were uncovered. In Tomb 36, the large scenic bowl was discovered. It has been described by Todd (1979) as being 'Red

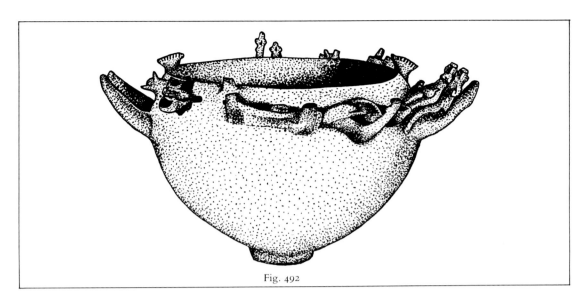

Fig. 492

Fig. 492 The Kalavassos Bowl.
For details see text. Todd 1979, p. 59, Fig. 9.

Polished III Mottled Ware' and is dated by him to the Middle Bronze Age. It is doubtful, however, whether this bowl is much later than the others described above. They all probably come from the period when the Early Bronze Age passes over into the Middle Bronze Age. The height of the Kalavassos Bowl is only 27.2 cm (maximum) and the diameter is 28.5 cm. It is slightly shallower than the others in shape, and has a small, flattened and slightly protruding base. It lacks spouts; instead it has a pair of opposing, horizontal handles like the Sèvres Bowl. The Kalavassos Bowl is now in the Cyprus Museum in Nicosia.

Starting with the handle seen on the right of the drawing (Fig. 492) and proceeding clockwise, there are the following elements:

1 *A birdlike shape on the rim of the bowl,* above the handle.

2 *An embracing couple sitting on a bench* which is perched on the handle of the parent vessel. Both figures wear headgear and the female holds a jug with a cutaway spout on her lap.

3 *A complex trough system,* with a long section connected to a basin by a pouring spout. Inside the basin there appears to be another cutaway-spouted jug. A further jug is on the right of the basin. The lower part of a human figure is positioned inside the trough and outside it another figure is bending over the side, with both hands on the edge. A further figure stands in front of the basin.

4 *The lower part of a human figure,* standing near the rim of the parent bowl.

5 *A pack animal carrying two baskets across its back,* badly damaged and fragmentary.

6 *An ox.* Originally this was probably one of a yoked pair but its partner has been lost.

7 *A birdlike shape on the rim* above the other handle.

8 *Marks indicating that a human figure stood near a bench of some kind.* Nothing remains of this element, except the scars on the surface of the bowl.

9 *A long trough with several human figures working at it.* Originally there seem to have been six of them, but they are damaged and only one survives in a complete form. She has breasts, suggesting that this is a female group. They are bending forward and appear to be grinding corn or washing clothes.

10 *The lower part of a human figure, standing behind a large bowl containing a lumpy shape.* The contents could be either dough or a pile of washing.

11 *Another female, working at an oven.* Next to the oven is a bowl containing a grooved implement of some kind.

The suggestion has been put forward that the first side of this bowl shows a scene of wine-making and the second side depicts bread-making. It is proposed that there is some division of labour with males making the wine and females making the bread. This may well be true, but there is insufficient detail to be certain. This particular vessel may be showing several different activities on each side, rather than two coherent patterns of production. It is impossible to be certain, but one important fact does emerge, namely that this is yet another Scenic Composition in which the general subject is 'daily life'. Again, there is nothing sacred or ceremonial taking place, merely the busy work tasks of the ordinary village people.

8 The Sèvres Jar

This large jar is encircled with small figures modelled on its shoulders. Its Scenic Composition is similar in feeling to those on the six big bowls described above. The jar has two vertical handles and a small, flattened base protruding from the bottom of its globular body. It is in Red Polished Ware, from the Early Bronze Age and is 61 cm high. Originally in the collection of a French diplomat called Boysset, who was stationed at Larnaca in the 1890s, it is now in the basement of the Sèvres Museum in Paris, where I was able to examine it.

Reading clockwise from the handle on the right of the drawing (Fig. 493), the elements of the composition are as follows:

1 A female with prominent breasts, leaning back against the parent vessel, with a cutaway-spouted jug held in front of her.

Fig. 493 The Sèvres Jar. *For details see text. Hennessy 1979, Pl. 45.*

Fig. 493

2 A group of four females working at a trough. The one on the right is missing, but the others are complete. They have conspicuous breasts and wear some kind of headgear, like all the figures on this side of the vessel. They are working at something with their hands, leaning forward to do so. They are either kneading dough or washing clothes.

3 A mother holding a swaddled baby, leaning against the centre of the neck of the parent vessel. She has a bowl at her left side into which a cutaway-spouted jug on her lap is tipping.

4 A standing female figure facing a large bowl, with her arms outstretched towards it. She is below and to the right of the previous figure and stands facing towards the body of the parent vessel.

5 An oven with a glazing bowl close beside it. The 'baker' figure in front of it has been broken away and only the pottery scar remains.

On the other side of the parent vessel:

6 A roughly circular ridge enclosing ten pyramid-shaped lumps. At the lower side of the ring there is an opening with side-walls. This element is very similar to nos. 10 and 12 on the Oxford Bowl and must be interpreted in the same way. In other words, this element must either be a section through an oven showing ten pyramid-shaped loaves baking inside it, or a copper-leaching enclosure as suggested by Merrillees.

7 A male figure wearing conspicuous headgear, positioned to the left of no. 6 and close to it. The arm nearer the 'oven' or leaching enclosure is stretched out and down towards the opening at its lower side. As with the Oxford Bowl, he appears to be in charge of the oven/enclosure.

8 A second male, also facing away from the parent vessel, with legs spread and arms folded across the front of his body. As with the previous male, the conspicuous penis emphasizes the gender of this figure to such an extent that it was obviously important to the artist to underline the division of labour on the two sides of the parent vessel. This again repeats the arrangement on the Oxford Bowl.

9 A large jar standing on the ground, with two opposing handles.

10 An enclosure with a bridged trough leading down into a large basin via a pointed spout. At each of the four corners of the trough there is the stem of something that has been broken away, but it is impossible to guess precisely what is missing.

The similarity between the Sèvres Jar and the Oxford Bowl is striking. It is clear that, if it was not created by the same artist, then the two artists involved must have been in close contact with one another and followed a very similar pattern. Whether one interprets both as 'bakery bowls' or both as 'bakery females plus copper-leaching males', it is clear that the two vessels must ultimately be interpreted in the same way. On the present evidence I favour Robert Merrillees's explanation to my original one. My main reason for this is that I find it hard to accept that a prehistoric artist would present a bread oven in two totally different styles—one in side view, tended by a female, and one in plan view section, tended by a male—on the same parent vessel. It seems certain that we are dealing here with two separate and distinct activities, and the fact that pyramid loaves and small piles of copper ore are both likely to have been depicted as 'conical lumps' should not be allowed to confuse the issue.

To sum up, it seems likely that the (female) artists who created these remarkable Scenic Compositions were setting out to show the great industry of the prehistoric women of Cyprus, always busily grinding, kneading, washing, baking and giving birth, while their males preoccupied themselves with high status metal-production and spent most of the day sitting around watching copper concentrates dry out from sludge.

9 The Vounous Bowl

The Vounous Bowl (Fig. 494) is the most extraordinary and complex of all the Scenic Compositions of the prehistoric period in Cyprus. It is unique is that it shows a busy scene *inside* the bowl instead of around the outside of the rim. To make this possible, the artist has modified her large bowl in two ways. She has flattened its base to provide a level stage on which her modelled figures can be arranged and she has converted the spout into a wide aperture representing a large doorway or entrance.

Inside this modified bowl a busy scene of village life is portrayed, with twenty-seven distinct elements. The bowl, which had suffered considerable damage in the tomb, is made of Red Polished Ware from the Early Bronze Age period. Its diameter is 37 cm. but its height is only 8 cm.

Before describing the elements one by one,

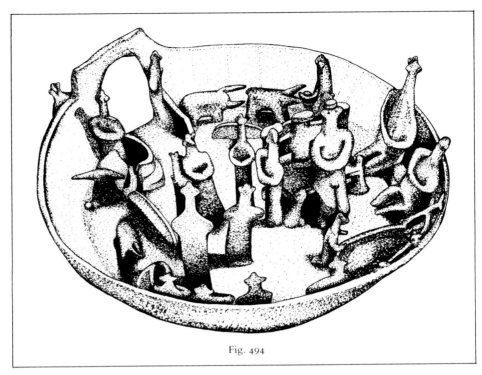

Fig. 494

Fig. 494 The Vounous Bowl. *For details see text. Dikaios 1940, Pl. VII.*

it is important to mention the way in which the significance of this scene has been interpreted in the past. It is nearly always referred to as either a 'Sacred Enclosure' or a 'Circular Sanctuary', and the moment recorded by the artist is said to be a religious ceremony of some kind. This interpretation can be traced back to a paper read by Dikaios, its discoverer, at the First International Congress of Prehistoric and Protohistoric Sciences in London in 1932, and published in 1934. In it he stated his belief that the 'sacred enclosure' model reveals that '... there already existed in Cyprus, in the Early Bronze Age, a well-developed cult of the Mother Goddess, associated with the Snake God and the Divine Bull, with separate temple-sites and organized ceremonies including dances, disguises, masques and sacrifices'. When Dikaios published the Vounous Bowl in detail in 1940, he pursued this interpretation further, making much play of 'a cult of chthonian and fertility deities' and of 'rites and sacrifices performed in special enclosures'. This approach has been copied by virtually all later authors and the concept of the Vounous Bowl as representing a religious ritual in a holy sanctuary has itself gradually become sacred to Cypriot archaeology. Indeed, it has become so firmly entrenched that today nobody questions it. Yet it has obvious weaknesses.

The most glaring fault is that it is so out of step with the mood of all the other Scenic Compositions from the prehistoric period.

As we have seen, and as we shall see, the abiding rule of these works is that they portray ordinary people engaged in ordinary, everyday tasks. This is their great charm and gives them their special interest.

Secondly, the religious interpretations of the elements in the Vounous Bowl composition are based on a number of imaginative leaps only barely supported by the evidence. The whole scene can be viewed in a much simpler way, and this is how it will be described here.

First, the 'enclosure' itself. The circular shape has been taken as real, but the comparative evidence is against this. Nobody has suggested that the scenes around the rims of the big bowls described earlier represent human activities arranged in a great ring. It is accepted there that the distribution of the elements is secondary to the shape of the vessels on which they are placed. It is logical to assume the same for the Vounous Bowl. The scene there is circular because the artist has decided to place it inside a circular bowl, not because it represents a circular enclosure. Indeed, it is unlikely that it represents an enclosure of any kind. It is much more reasonable to assume that it is simply a peaceful village scene, with people standing around talking at the end of another busy day. The walls of the bowl become transformed into the walls of the village dwellings where necessary; a doorway is added by removing the spout of the bowl; and a small figure supposedly peeping daringly, or cheekily, into the holy of holies, is probably no more than someone looking *out* of a window. The fact that the majority of the figures sitting or standing around are males hardly clashes with the sex ratio of figures seen today in a typical Cypriot village square. The (female) artist who made this bowl seems to be saying that when the males get home from a hard day's work watching the copper sludge dry out, they proceed to gather in earnest groups at the centre of the village to engage in their other arduous daily task of exchanging gossip. (It may well have been criticisms of this kind that led early males to convert their private chatter into the mumbo jumbo of religion, but there is no evidence that this status-enhancing mystification process had begun at this stage.)

If the Vounous Bowl is viewed from above, with the 'entrance door' facing to 12 o'clock, then the separate elements, taken in clockwise direction around the outside, and followed by the central features, are as follows:

1 *A human figure standing beside the doorway.*

2 *An ox in a pen.*

3 *An ox in a pen.*

4 *A standing female figure holding a baby in the crook of her left arm, looking at the oxen in the pens.*

5 *A male figure standing looking at the female with her baby.*

6 *A figure with arms folded, sitting on a bench against a wall.*

7 *Ditto.*

8 *A vertical pole shown in relief against the wall, with a bull's head (or model of a bull's head) on top of it.*

9 *Ditto.*

10 *Ditto.* These three bucranial poles are connected to one another by horizontal bars. From the centre of each bar hangs a vertical squiggle which has been interpreted as a snake, but which could also be a dangling rope or tassel (see Fig. 495).

11 *A figure with arms folded, sitting on a bench against a wall.*

12 *Ditto.* There is a space between 11 and 12 which may be deliberate or may indicate that a seated figure there has been broken away and lost.

13 *Another seated figure with folded arms* and, close by it:

14 *Ditto.*

15 *Ditto.*

16 *An ox in a pen.*

17 *An ox in a pen.*

18 *A human figure standing in the corner of the ox-pen behind the second ox.*

19 *A human figure attached to the outside of the wall of the bowl, with its head peering down on the scene below.*

In the central area there is:

20-5 *A circle of six, inward-facing standing figures with arms folded.* Seen from directly above it is clear that this is not a perfect circle that would be expected if the figures were engaged in some formal rite or dance. It is the casual circle of an informal group of friends.

26 *A male figure wearing distinctive headgear, seated on a large and impressive chair.* Like the others, he has folded arms.

27 *A figure kneeling in front of a low wide trough,* reaching out its arms as if to take something from the trough or put something into it. This semicircular trough could be

meant to contain water, animal food, or even small animals of some kind, but no indication of its contents remains to help us.

These are the elements of the Vounous Bowl described in an objective manner, with as little interpretation as possible, and it should be clear that, on this basis, it is more likely that the scene depicted is one of ordinary village life than some high ceremonial. However, since more romantic interpretations have been proposed in the past it is only fair to mention them. They are as follows:

The figures on either side of the entrance are seen as guardians of the sacred enclosure, keeping out the uninitiated.

The oxen in their pens are awaiting sacrifice.

The infant held by the female is 'probably for sacrifice'.

The folded arms of many of the figures represent an attitude of prayer.

Several figures 'show the phallus, symbolizing fertility'.

Male figures guard the 'sacrificial bulls' which are sacred animals 'representing the Divine Bull'.

The circle of six figures is 'either dancing or engaged in some sacred action'.

The male sitting on a large chair is 'enthroned and wearing a crown'. He is the 'High Priest' with his arms crossed in front 'as a sign of reverence'.

The kneeling figure has his hands bent forward in prayer, or adoration.

The figure on top of the wall is an uninitiated individual trying to sneak a look at the mysteries being performed inside the sanctuary.

The most sacred part of the enclosure 'where the mystic ceremony is being performed' is the area of the triple-bucranial construction which one author described as 'three conventional figures performing a sacred dance, joining hands and holding snakes', the snakes being symbols of the Snake God.

All the figures in the sacred enclosure are 'seeking to partake of the power which is represented by the attributes'.

These are typical phrases used to describe this particular Scenic Composition. The wording has been selected from a variety of publications on the subject of the Vounous Bowl and nothing has been added or caricatured.

The best that can be said for these imaginative comments is that they *may* be true but that, assembled together here and compared with the hard evidence, they do seem a little over-enthusiastic. I remain convinced that a more domestic interpretation is nearer to the intention of the artist.

More specifically, there is no sign of any sacrifice taking place or any special location for such an act. The folded arms posture is more likely to be an artist's gestural device for showing a state of non-working or relaxation, rather than some imagined posture of prayer. The kneeling figure's arms seem to be active rather than engaged in some gesture of adoration. He appears to be *doing* something at the trough, not worshipping at it. The bucranial poles behind the trough, as already discussed in the animal section of this book, are probably protective signs placed on the outside of a building, based on a simple superstition. The 'High Priest' need be no more than the village 'head-man'. The two pairs of oxen have probably been penned up for the night after a hard day in the fields, yoked to the plough.

This way of seeing the Vounous Bowl brings it into line with the other Scenic vessels and makes it much easier to understand as part of a fascinating group of Early Bronze Age representations.

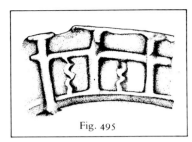

Fig. 495

Fig. 495 *Detail of the Vounous Bowl showing the triple bucranial element with two hanging tassels, ropes or snakes. Karageorghis 1970, Pl. V.*

10 The Bucranial Wall (with cross-bar)

This Scenic Composition (Fig. 496) is not a modified vessel but a model in the shape of a plaque on a small stand. On the section of wall depicted there are three bucranial poles joined by two cross-bars. The poles themselves are rectangular in section and are topped either by bulls' heads or by models of bulls' heads. Two up-curved hooks protrude from the wall, one above each cross-bar, and there is another pair of similar hooks behind the wall in the same positions. On the ground below the central pole is a large jar, and standing to its left, facing it, is a small female figure. An area of flat ground is included in the model which enables it to stand up without support.

This terracotta is in Red Polished Ware and comes from the Early Bronze Age cemetery in the region of Kochati/Margi. It was found there by looters in the late 1960s and was subsequently acquired by the Cyprus

Fig. 496 Bucranial Wall with cross-bar. *For details see text. Karageorghis 1970, Pl. I.*

Fig. 497 Bucranial Wall—no cross-bar. *For details see text. Karageorghis 1970, Pl. III.*

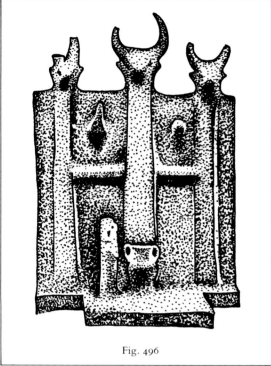

Fig. 496

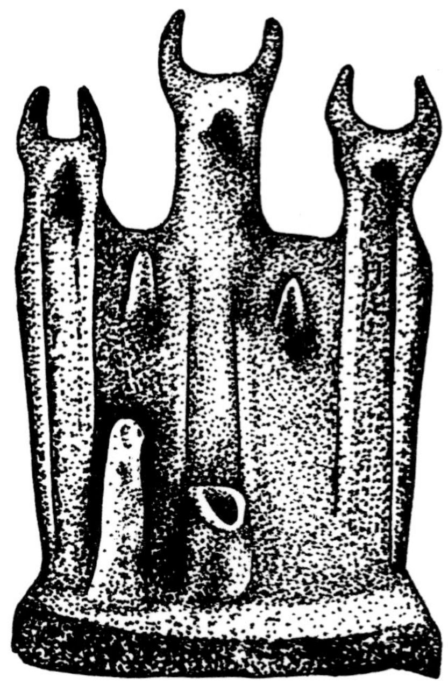

Fig. 497

Fig. 498 *Bucranial wall model from Kalopsidha. Although damaged, its significance is now clear. Karageorghis 1970, Pl. V.*

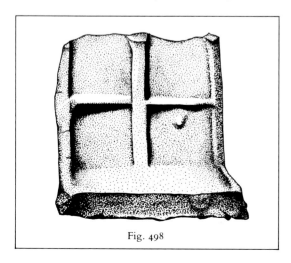

Fig. 498

Museum, being published in full by Karageorghis in 1970. Its height is 19 cm. to the top of the panel and the thickness of the wall is 1 cm.

Karageorghis interprets this terracotta as follows: 'There is no doubt that here we have a standard representation of a sanctuary, consisting of three idols or *xoana*, fixed on a wall crowned with bull's heads.' He is less certain about the female, commenting, 'Is she supposed to pour libations? Or did she bring the amphora itself as a gift?'

There is no question that this composition does represent some kind of ancient, superstitious practice, probably of a protective kind, as discussed earlier, but whether it is part of some more elaborate religious system remains to be seen. Only when Early Bronze

Age settlements have been excavated in Cyprus in more detail will we be in a position to answer this question.

11 The Bucranial Wall (no cross-bar)

This model (Fig. 497) is very similar to the last one and was found at the same time and comes from the same source. Its main differences are that it lacks the two cross-bars and that there are no up-curved projections on the back of this wall. It is slightly smaller, its height being only 14 cm. to the top of the panel.

A third model along similar lines, but with much less detail (Fig. 498), was found at Kalopsidha (Tomb 5) as long ago as 1894. It consists of no more than a vertical panel, 17 cm. high, with a flat floor area projecting in front of it. On the panel are three vertical, rectangular poles with two cross-bars joining them, but the tops are broken away and the heads are missing. Seen in the light of the two new bucranial walls, this old terracotta now has more significance. It is clear that it, too, was a model of a similar subject. All three are closely related to the triple-bucranial section of the Vounous Bowl and suggest that raising bulls' heads on top of poles was a common practice in the Early Bronze Age, as it still is today on the walls of village buildings in Malta.

12 The Ploughing Scene

This is another important terracotta that has abandoned the use of a vessel to support its Scenic Composition. Instead the ploughing figures are presented on a small, five-legged table-top (Fig. 499). This terracotta was discovered by Dikaios at Vounous and published by him in detail in 1940. It is in Red Polished Ware and from the Early Bronze Age. Its length is 41 cm.

It was first unearthed by looters who found the table section. Then Dikaios excavated the looted tomb carefully and was able to locate the rest of it in the form of scattered fragments. It was reassembled and is now in the Cyprus Museum in Nicosia. It consists of the following elements:

1 *A pair of yoked oxen pulling a plough.*

2 *A human being standing behind the plough,* presumably the ploughman.

3 *A second pair of yoked oxen behind the first pair,* also pulling a plough.

4 *A second ploughman.*

5 *A pair of human figures standing facing one another,* positioned on the left-hand side of the ploughing group. Between them they carry a horizontal object, either a grain trough or a grain-filled cloth, for sowing seeds where the plough has already passed.

6 *A pack animal,* behind the sowing couple. The saddle or pannier has been lost but the traces of its attachment remain.

7 *Another human figure,* behind the pack animal, facing in the same direction as the ploughmen.

As Dikaios points out, this scene is not too difficult to interpret: 'Such scenes are frequent in modern Cyprus, where quite often the whole of the family camps under a tree near the field where the male member of the family may be ploughing. Frequently one of the grown-up children serves, with a donkey, as carrier of provisions, grain, water, or any other necessary object.' He analyses the plough in some detail, describing it as 'composed of a yoke resting on the bulls' necks, a straight beam, a handle which curves at the top, and a share beam which is partly stuck into the earth'. He considers that this early type of plough was entirely made of wood.

Fig. 499 The Ploughing Scene. *For details see text. Dikaios 1940, Pl. IX.*

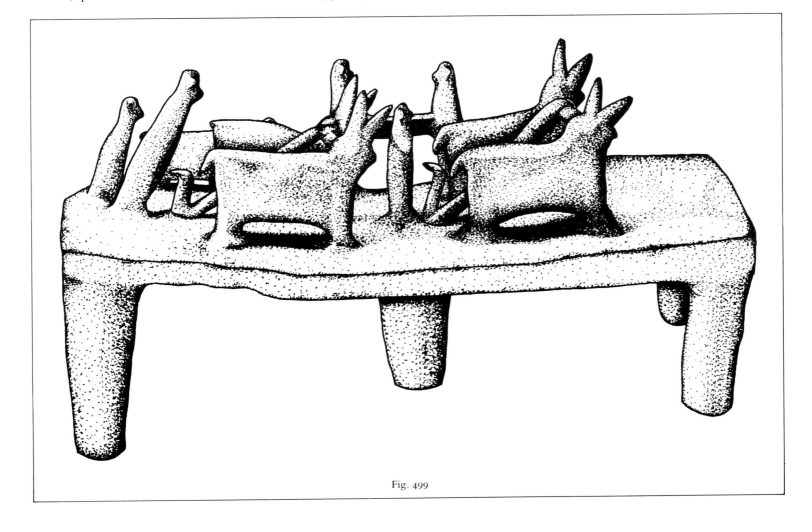

Fig. 499

13 The Ploughing Jug

A similar scene to the last one, probably by the same artist, appears on the shoulder of a large Red Polished Ware jug (Fig. 500). This was also found by Dikaios at Vounous but is less impressive than it might appear at first glance. The jug in question was fragmentary and the ploughing scene was badly damaged. Only the two oxen and their yoke survived. Their horns were missing, as was the plough and the figure of the ploughman, but Dikaios could see where they had once stood.

Using a little artistic licence he reconstructed the scene, with the ploughing terracotta as a model.

14 The Grinding Jug

This domestic scene on the shoulder of a fragmentary, twin-necked jug from Vounous (Fig. 501) was also found by Dikaios. As before, it is in Red Polished Ware from the Early Bronze Age and again it has been heavily restored. The scene shows four human figures bent over a trough, busily at work grinding corn (or perhaps washing clothes?). When found, only one of the four figures was complete. The other three sur-

vived only as leg-stumps, but have been rebuilt. This scene is strikingly similar to several elements on the large Margi bowls, revealing the close connections that must have existed between the two centres.

15 The Washing Scene

Yet another scene of daily domestic labours. Seven figures surround a deep trough with a ledge down one side of it (Fig. 502). Five of the figures, adorned with headgear and elaborate neck-bands, are working with both hands pressing down on something (presumably wet clothing). At the left-hand end of the trough a sixth figure, slightly taller than the rest, faces the workers with an infant held in its arms. Both the mother(?) and the child wear the same kind of heavy headgear and neck-band. At the right-hand end of the trough is a seventh figure, smaller than the rest, which holds a large jug in its arms, presumably to replenish the water in the trough.

It is this Scenic Composition that throws some doubt on the Dikaios identification of the previous scene as 'grinding corn'. The groups of side-by-side figures bent over a long ledge or trough in Scenic Composition no. 14 and also on some of the large bowls,

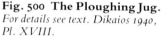

Fig. 500 The Ploughing Jug. *For details see text. Dikaios 1940, Pl. XVIII.*

Fig. 501 The Grinding Jug. *For details see text. Dikaios 1940, Pl. XXI.*

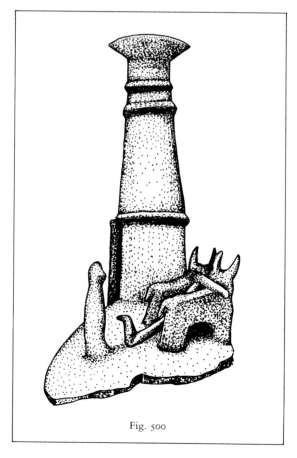

Fig. 500

Fig. 501

may in reality be depictions of washing rather than grinding.

This washing scene is in Red Polished Ware from the end of the Early Bronze Age. It is in the Louvre Museum, Paris, and has no provenance. The height is 13 cm. and the length 27.7 cm.

16 The Couple-with-Panniers Scene

An agricultural scene (Fig. 503) with a row of twelve large baskets, ready for loading on to pack animals, or shortly after having been unloaded from them. At either end of the terracotta stands a human figure. They face one another, a male at the left end and a female at the right. Like the last terracotta,

Fig. 502

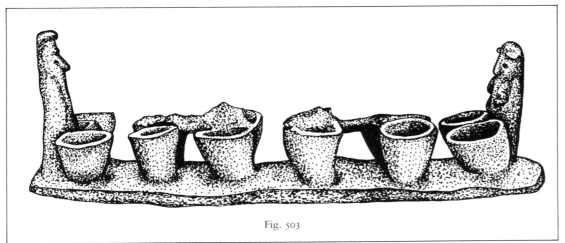

Fig. 503

Fig. 502 The Washing Scene. *For details see text. Hennessy 1979, Pl. 50.*

Fig. 503 The Couple-with-Panniers Scene. *For details see text. Caubet 1971, Pl. III, 2.*

this one is in Red Polished Ware from the end of the Early Bronze Age, has no provenance and is in the Louvre Museum. Its height is 11.8 cm and its length 32 cm.

This composition has been misinterpreted in the past. The baskets have been called 'deep conical bowls', but it is obvious from the way that they are yoked together in groups that they are intended to be slung over the backs of pack animals. As pottery bowls they would be unduly heavy, and it is much more likely that they are meant to represent the pannier baskets depicted in other Scenic Compositions. In the Margi Bowl, for example, a pack animal is shown carrying such baskets and also, significantly, two human riders.

It has been suggested that this scene depicts a 'cult' activity involving the making of offerings. The more obvious explanation, that it represents a simple domestic scene of a farmer and his wife out in the fields carrying

out one of their many daily tasks is, for some reason, less appealing. (It should be explained that the word 'cult' is often used when the urge to provide a religious explanation for an ancient work of art greatly exceeds the factual evidence available.)

17 The Ship-with-crew Scene

This is the earliest example found so far of a Cypriot boat (Fig. 504). Unlike all the other Scenic Compositions, it is in White Painted Ware from the Middle Bronze Age. Its provenance is unknown and it is now in the Louvre Museum. Its length is 25 cm. and its height 15 cm. Considering its fragility, it is in a remarkable state of preservation.

Around the sides of the boat are ten figures, eight humans and two birds. Starting with the figure on the far side with its arm up to its head, they are as follows (reading clockwise):

Fig. 504 The Ship-with-Crew Scene. *For details see text. Astrom 1972, Fig. 16, no. 13.*

Fig. 504

1 *A human figure clinging on to the edge of the boat with its left hand and holding on to its hat with its right hand.*

2 *A bird figure perched on the side of the boat (obscured in this view of the scene).*

3 *A human figure with arms akimbo and its head tilted strongly to its right.*

4 *A tall-headed figure clinging to the pointed end of the boat with its right hand and to the side with its left. It is possible that this figure is intended to be shown in the act of steering the boat from the rear.*

5, 6 *An embracing couple, holding on to the boat and to one another at the same time. They are leaning backwards.*

7 *Another bird figure perched on the side of the boat.*

8 *A human figure with arms akimbo.*

9 *A human figure clasping what appears to be the prow of the boat. Staring intently forward, this figure gives the impression of guiding the progress of the boat through the water.*

10 *A large-headed figure holding on to the side of the boat with both hands.*

The artist has put a great deal of movement into this group of figures. There is nothing formal about their postures. Instead, they are arranged in such a way that there is a hint of a 'rough crossing' about the scene. Tilting, leaning and clinging on, the crew and/or passengers appear to be making a slightly hazardous journey. Whether this is a symbolic journey to the next world, as has been suggested in the past, or whether it is a re-enactment of a crossing from the mainland to Cyprus, is impossible to say.

18 The Couple-on-a-bench Jug

This huge jug from Lapithos (Fig. 505), now in the Cyprus Museum, is 71 cm. tall. It is in Red Polished Ware, from the Early Bronze Age. It is essentially a Subsidiary-unit Vessel, with small bowls and cutaway-spouted jugs on its shoulders, but it is included here because it also depicts an attractive, if simple, scene of two women sitting on a bench.

The fact that in this 'couple' both figures have prominent breasts, is unusual. Couples appear on a number of vessels and scenic terracottas, but they are typically male + female, suggesting that pair-bonding was a norm for early Cypriots. This is so on the Pierides Bowl, for example, and on two other vessels shown here, a box with a modelled lid (Fig. 507) where a couple lie in bed together, and a twin-necked jug (Fig 506) where a male embraces a female as they stand together.

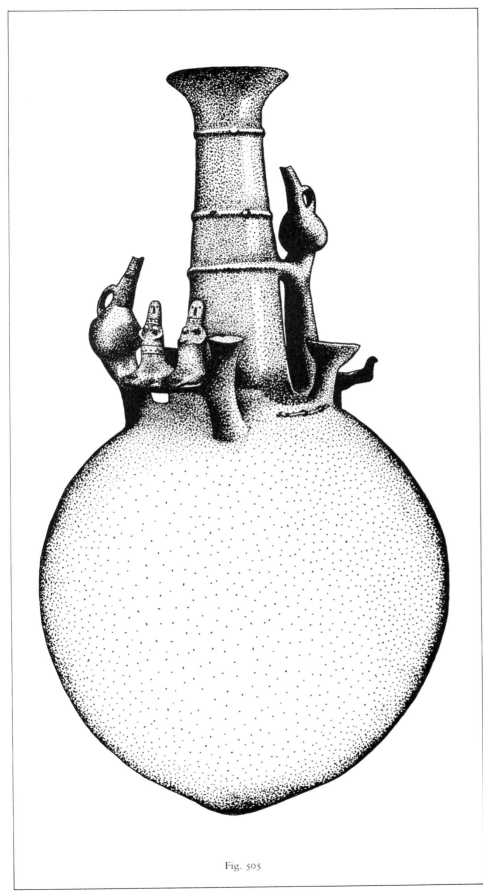

Fig. 505

Fig. 505 The Couple-on-a-Bench Scene. *For details see text. Des Gagniers and Karageorghis 1976, Pl. XXIII.*

Fig. 506

Fig. 506 *Twin-necked jug with embracing couple. Relief-decorated Red Polished Ware. Early Bronze Age. Vounous (Tomb 19, no. 10). Dikaios 1940, Pl. XIXd.*

Fig. 507

Fig. 507 *Couple lying side by side, shown in relief on lid of pottery box. Red Polished Ware. Early Bronze Age. Vounous (Tomb 37, no. 84). Dikaios 1940, Pl. XXXVa.*

Fig. 508

Fig. 509

19 The Trough Jug

This unusual, wide-necked jug from Vounous (Fig. 508) boasts no living figures in its Scenic Composition. Instead it has a complex model of a trough system, emptying into the parent vessel. The open trough is supported by two forked uprights, and by the side of the trough at the point where it passes over the rim of the parent vessel is a tiny model of a cutaway-spouted jug. At this point the trough itself is equipped with a bridge and then ends in a point as if ready to pour something into the parent jug. Robert Merrillees has suggested that this is a depiction of the sludge concentration phase of copper production (see discussion on p. 274).

This remarkable jug, in Incised Red Polished Ware of the Early Bronze Age, was originally described (inevitably) as a 'Cult Vessel', but Merrillees's more down-to-earth interpretation is far more convincing. The height of the jug is 26.9 cm. (to the rim).

20 The Trough-and-jar Jug

A similar but more complex vessel (Fig. 509), this appears to have been made by the same artist as no. 19. It is also from Vounous and in the same ware, but is larger, having a height of 32.8 cm. Here, instead of a trough emptying into the parent vessel, there is one modelled on the side of the jug and emptying

into a miniature replica of it. The trough is supported on a special stand, has a bridge spout and is positioned below a model of a cutaway-spouted jug which is depicted in the act of pouring.

In effect, this is a different version of the same scene as depicted in no. 19. As before, it was originally called simply a 'Cult Vessel', with no explanation of the nature of the scene represented. The Merrillees explanation applies here with equal validity.

These, then, are the twenty Scenic Compositions of the prehistoric period in Cyprus. They are relentlessly secular in subject-matter and infused throughout with a charming informality and domesticity. It is this that gives them, not only their special appeal, but also their unusual importance as depictions of everyday life of ordinary people at a very early date. The subject-matter they dwell upon strengthens the idea that they are entirely the work of female artists. The more usual male subjects—hunting, warfare, rituals and ceremonies—are missing. There are no huntsmen, warriors, priests or kings. Instead, the daily grind, both metaphorically and literally, is shown in its many facets. The picture that emerges is one of a settled community with village chores taken care of by the females, metal-production by the males and agricultural work in the fields by whole families together.

IV Decorations

The art of ancient Cyprus is lively and imaginative, not only in its development of fabrics and wares, complex shapes and stylized images, but also in its surface decorations. From the very beginning, the pottery of the island has been covered in linear patterns and motifs that have added another basic element to the aesthetic appeal of the work of the local artists.

In the very earliest days—the Neolithic and the Chalcolithic—the pottery decorations are painted, usually with a red pigment on a whitish background, but so little material has survived from these periods that it is impossible to carry out any detailed analysis. Even the fragmentary evidence that has been unearthed is, however, sufficient to reveal an already sophisticated use of complex geometric motifs.

It is when we come to the Early Bronze Age that the material first becomes rich enough for proper study. Here, the technique has switched from painting to incision, and there are literally thousands of examples of pottery vessels covered with networks of incised linear patterns. The lines, cut into the still soft surface of the clay with a simple, pointed tool, are often filled with white after firing, making them attractively conspicuous against the dark, polished surface of the pottery, which is typically dark red or black.

This incised ware dominates the whole of the Early Bronze Age period and survives through into the earlier part of the Middle Bronze Age, where it is gradually replaced by another phase of painted decoration. Here the linear patterns return to the earlier mode of placing dark lines—red, brown or black—on a whitish background. The vessels in general grow smaller during this period and the patterning becomes more crudely reticular, although many different styles and motifs are still detectable.

During this Middle Bronze Age phase there also arises a Red-on-Black form of decoration in the north-east of the island, where an attempt is made to prolong the 'light line on dark background' style of the earlier incised ware. The linear patterning of this Red-on-Black work is, however, lacking in motif differentiation, consisting largely of multilinear criss-crossing of a rather mechanical kind.

A more exciting form of decoration emerges on the White Slip Ware of the Late Bronze Age. This pottery appears to be a refinement of the Middle Bronze Age White Painted Ware, with the whitish background becoming a thicker, richer and generally finer surface, on which dark-line patterns are painted with greater inventiveness and spatial restraint.

Parallel with this attractive White Slip Ware in the Late Bronze Age, there is the darker and more austere Base Ring Ware. Growing, it seems, out of the degenerating Black Slip Ware of the Middle Bronze Age, it becomes a striking and impressive new art form of the Late Bronze Age potters, but relies for its impact more on shape and texture than decorative pattern. The earlier examples of Base Ring Ware continue the incision tradition of the Black Slip Ware, but as time passes these incisions become combined with relief bands and lines. Eventually, with the later Base Ring Ware, relief lines and incisions give way to rather crudely applied white lines in simple patterns.

At this point in the decorative sequence there is the explosive arrival on the scene of the pictorially decorated vessels of the Mycenaeans and the technological upheaval of the introduction of the potter's wheel. As the Bronze Age gives way to the Iron Age, White Painted Ware once again becomes the dominant form of pottery, but now it is subjected to the mechanical impositions of the wheel, rendering it less personal. The geometrically improved shapes lose a great deal of their playful individualism and their attractive idiosyncrasies. Alongside this development there is a similar change in the quality of the decorative patterns. Bands and circles of dark lines are now also made by mechanical means, their mathematical perfection robbing them of a great deal of the human warmth of the earlier, hand-drawn patterns of the Bronze Age.

It is important to remember the change in sex of the potter at this stage. The earlier vessels had been made by women in a simple domestic setting. They created and decorated their works of art much as they would have prepared and decorated food, or clothing, giving a gentle, personal informality to the task. But now, with the introduction of a special 'pottery machine' and the mystique of technical equipment, the males take over and turn what had been a lovingly executed art-form into a mass-production business.

However, although the decorative lines themselves are now coldly mechanical, their arrangement and combination on the individual vessels continues to be subjected to considerable creative variation. It is still unusual to find two alike. The artist's inventiveness may be restricted by machine-production, but it is not eliminated.

As the Iron Age centuries pass, the increasingly precise geometric decoration employed seems to leave something to be desired, and a more expressive, new style of Free-field Pictorial painting eventually arises to challenge it. This first begins to surface in the Geometric Period, echoing the pictorial panels of the Mycenaean phase of the Late Bronze Age. But then, in the ensuing Archaic Period, it becomes stronger and more regionalized, with its centre of activity in the south and east of the island. There, decorative pictorial images of lotus flowers, birds, bulls, horses, gazelles and humans abound, as deftly painted additions to the vessels. In the north and west, by contrast, the tightly geometric patterns of compass-drawn circles and mechanically applied multi-linear bands remain the dominant motifs.

Despite these occasional eruptions of pictorial decoration in the Mycenaean and the Archaic phases, it remains true to say that, viewed over the long term, from the Neolithic to the Hellenistic, the decorations of the ceramics of ancient Cyprus have been dominated by abstract linear patterns of one kind or another, either incised or painted on the surface of many different kinds of vessels.

Repertoires

To study the range of decorative patterns employed by the ancient Cypriot artists, the repertoires of three major styles have been analysed: the *Incised Polished Ware* of the Early Bronze Age, the *White Painted Ware* of the Middle Bronze Age and the *White Slip Ware* of the Late Bronze Age. Between them, these three wares cover nearly 2,000 years—roughly the second and third millennia BC—and they represent a remarkably persistent rejection of pictorial imagery. Pictorial images are so stubbornly suppressed that it is tempting to argue for some kind of cultural taboo, of the sort found in Islamic art from the eighth century AD onwards where, according to the sayings of the Prophet, 'Angels do not enter a house which contains ... an image', and 'On Resurrection Day God will consider image-makers as the men most deserving of punishment.' But a strict prohibition of a religious kind is hard to accept for two reasons. Firstly, human and animal figures are common throughout the Bronze Age in the form of terracottas, animal-shaped vases and relief additions to vessels. So there is no overall ban on their production and it is difficult to imagine how a ban could have applied to surface decoration alone. Secondly, there is a handful of Bronze Age vessels, out of the many thousands discovered, which do display human or animal forms as part of the incised or painted decoration (see p. 141, Fig.

205 and p. 188, Fig. 306). The fact that such rarities exist at all suggests that there was no binding prohibition with regard to pictorial images. These rare exceptions make the general rule even more difficult to explain. The answer must lie in the positive significance of the abstract patterns employed, rather than in the negative elimination of pictorials. This implies that the motifs hold some kind of specific meaning for the artists. This may or may not involve symbolism. For example, a multiple zigzag motif may carry a hidden message, such as water, snake or ploughed field. But it may equally well carry an emblematic message without the involvement of a symbolic equation. As a simple geometric pattern, it may have become so strongly associated with a local community that to use it as a decorative device is simply to identify oneself with that community. In other words, a multiple zigzag becomes an 'abstract traditional' motif, repeated time and again without anyone ever questioning its meaning. Whether it originally had a symbolic meaning or arose purely as an abstract, geometric pattern, is no longer relevant in such a case. It has now become abstract through repetition and its significance is that of being locally traditional. But before pursuing this aspect further, here first are the repertoires of the three main styles analysed:

Incised Polished Ware

1 Horizontal Bands (Fig. 510)

These are extremely common and appear on the vast majority of vessels, usually as borders above and below other motifs. By far the most common type is no. 2, the *Plain Multi-linear Band*. The number of lines varies from two to as many as ten, but only one example is shown here. The *Plain Single Line* is by contrast extemely rare. A more popular variant is the *Broken Multi-linear Band* (no. 3). The *Diagonally-hatched Band* is also common (no. 5). Other variants include bands with segmented markings (nos. 6, 7, 8, 10, 11, 12, and 27), also combinations of short dashes arranged in various ways (nos. 15 to 21). The *Wavy Line* (no. 14) is rare. *Herring Bone* and *Feathery* patterns occur occasionally (nos. 22-7) and an odd restriction applies to no. 22—the *Open Herring Bone Band*. This seems to be found almost exclusively on Philia Ware pottery.

2 Vertical Stripes (Fig. 511)

These are much less common than the Horizontal Bands because the general decorative trend in the Early Bronze Age is *around* the vessel rather than down it. Stripes tend to break up this arrangement and are frequently avoided altogether. When they do occur they show similar motif details to the horizontal bands, but the multi-linear forms are no longer the most frequent. The favourites here are the *Open Diagonally-hatched Stripe* (no. 33) and the *Dash-bordered Line* (no. 37), with the *Closed Diagonally-hatched Stripes* (no. 31) also common. Surprisingly, the *Meander* motif (no. 48), usually thought of as a later Greek import, already appears at this phase of Cypriot pottery. A number of vessels from the north-east of the island show a *Segmented Feather* motif (nos. 51-3) which gives the impression of a tree-like design, but it is doubtful whether this imagery was specifically intended as representational.

3 Horizontal Zigzags (Fig. 512)

Like the straight horizontal bands, these are very common, especially the *Plain Multi-linear Horizontal Zigzag* (no. 58). Indeed the zigzag and its variants appear to constitute the most widespread and most basic of all decorative patterns in the Early Bronze Age. Many minor variants occur, often differentiated by the use of small 'fillers' between the zigs and the zags.

Special types of zigzag favoured are the *Half-filled Zigzag* (nos. 63 and 64), where half of the trough or peak of the zigzag pattern has hatching or dotting that creates the impression of a horizontal series of triangles; the *Thick-and-thin Zigzag* (nos. 65 and 66), where the zigs are broad and the zags are narrow; and the *Dot-capped Zigzag* (no. 69), where the lines are capped at their upper and lower points by trios of small incised dots.

4 Vertical Zigzags (Fig. 512)

Plain Multi-linear Vertical Zigzags (no. 71) and *Closed Hatched Vertical Zigzags* (no. 72) are common in certain parts of the island but rare elsewhere. In general, the central regions favour the horizontal zigzags, while the vertical versions are restricted more to the north-east and the south coast regions. Somewhere between the centre of the north coast and its extreme eastern end, there must be some kind of 'motif-frontier', where the plane of the popular zigzag pattern switches from

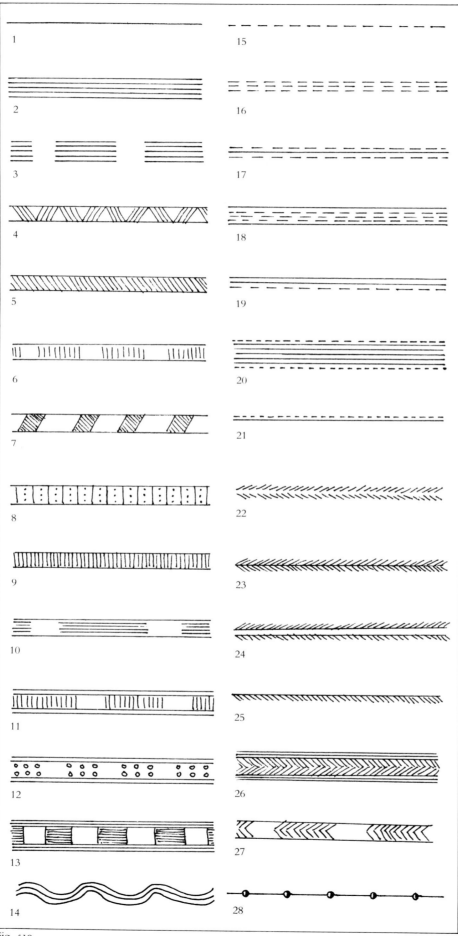

Fig. 510

almost exclusively horizontal to almost exclusively vertical. Down on the south-west coast there is also a shift to the vertical zigzag, but here it typically alternates with Multi-linear Stripes (see p. 27).

5 Horizontal Diamonds (Fig. 513)
Bands of diamonds are rare as borders, but widespread in one form or another as 'main display motifs' occupying the central area of an incision pattern on a vessel. Diamond bands are essentially elaborations of the basic zigzag. If two zigzag bands criss-cross one another, they form the diamond shapes automatically, and this is probably how they were developed in the first place. Once formed, the diamonds can then act as independent units (as in nos. 89 and 91-4).

6 Vertical Diamonds (Fig. 513)
Vertical stripes of diamond motifs are comparatively rare, although I have been able to find twenty different varieties (nos. 99-118). Most of these seem to occur only a few times, and some are unique to a single vessel.

7 Isolated Diamonds (Fig. 514)
On a number of vessels, especially those from the Karpas peninsula in the extreme north-east of the island, there are special, isolated diamond motifs of large size, frequently with internal patterns. These typically occur on the convex 'display panel' area of the vessels. These figures are sometimes sufficiently idiosyncratic to provide identities of individual potters (see p. 344 for further discussion). Diamond motifs nos. 134 and 138 are exceptions, in that they are much smaller and normally appear as 'fillers' rather than as 'main motifs'.

Fig. 510 *Horizontal Bands on Incised Polished Ware of the Early Bronze Age.*

Fig. 511 *Vertical Stripes on Incised Polished Ware of the Early Bronze Age.*

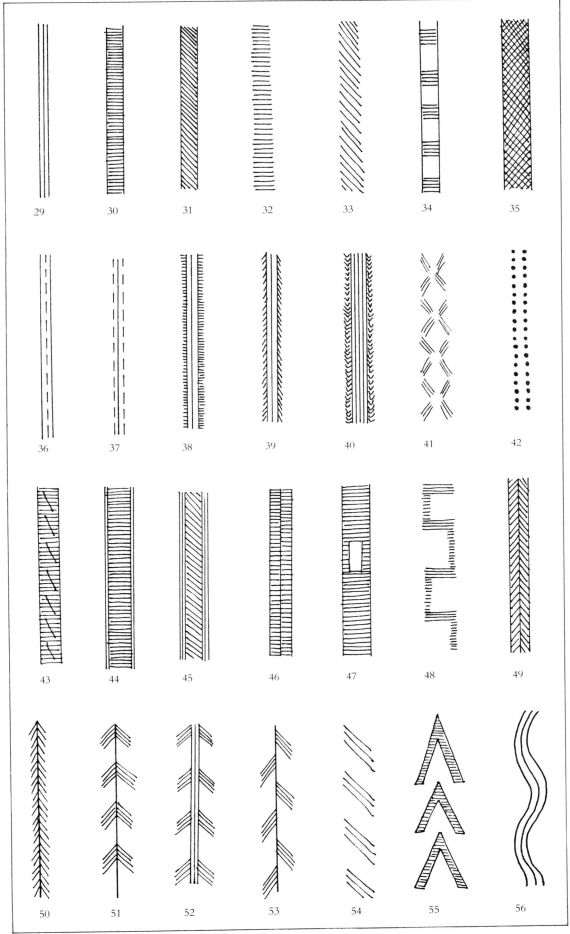

Fig. 511

Fig. 512 *Horizontal Zigzags and Vertical Zigzags on Incised Polished Ware of the Early Bronze Age.*

Fig. 512

Fig. 513 *Horizontal Diamonds and Vertical Diamonds on Incised Polished Ware of the Early Bronze Age.*

Fig. 513

Fig. 514 *Isolated Diamonds on Incised Polished Ware of the Early Bronze Age.*

Fig. 514

8 Circular Motifs (Fig. 515)

The most typical circular motif of the Incised Polished Ware is the *Concentric Circles* form (no. 150). This is extremely common on pottery from the central regions of the island, but seems to be absent in the extreme northeast. Down on the south-west coast it is largely replaced by small, simple circles (nos. 143-5), which are formed mechanically by the pressing in of some hollow circular device. All the larger circular motifs during this period are, however, made freehand. In the case of the neatly drawn Concentric Circles, this freehand action requires considerable expertise, as anyone who has tried to copy these circles will soon have discovered. Why the Early Bronze Age artists should have favoured so strongly a motif that is so difficult to produce is not clear. All the other patterns employed are comparatively simple to form. The tightly packed lines of the Concentric Circles motif are the exception. It seems likely that the motif therefore has some special significance beyond the merely decorative.

Fig. 515 *Circular Motifs on Incised Polished Ware of the Early Bronze Age.*

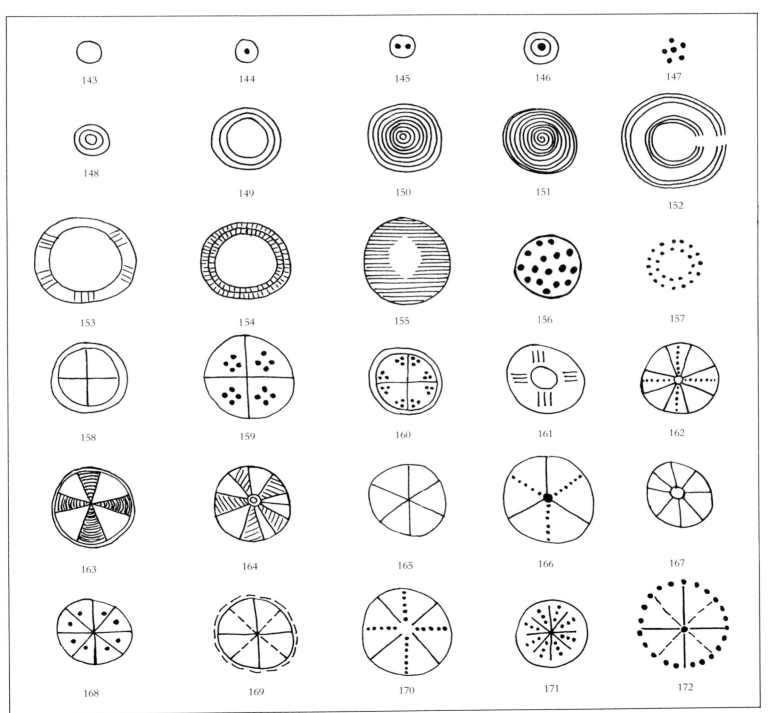

Fig. 515

Fig. 516 *Split Circles on Incised Polished Ware of the Early Bronze Age.*

9 Split Circles (Fig. 516)

The second most popular circular motif is the split or divided circle. Nearly always, the circular motif in question is the Concentric Circles type, with nos. 174 and 175 being most popular. When this type of motif appears near the rim of a bowl, it forms a *Pendant Concentric Semicircles* motif (nos. 181-3). These are most commonly seen on tulip bowls.

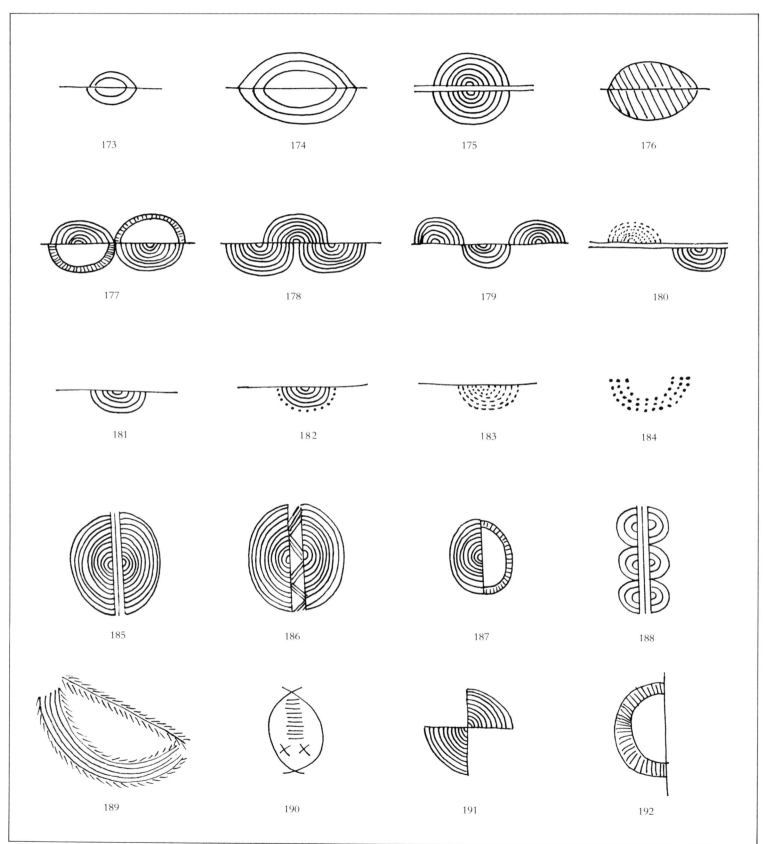

Fig. 516

10 Checkerboard Motifs (Fig. 517)

Check patterns are moderately common, usually in a fairly simple design with blank squares or rectangles alternating with cross-hatched ones, sometimes closed by a single border-line (nos. 193, 197 and 201) and sometimes open (nos. 194 and 196). They occur as horizontal bands (nos. 199 and 200) or as vertical stripes (no. 202), but more often as larger patches of 'display motif'.

11 Cruciform Motifs (Fig. 518)

Crosses of any kind are rare in the Early Bronze Age. The cruciform shape that dominated the human figurines of the earlier Chalcolithic period appears to have no echo here. There is a single example of a vertical cross (no. 212) on one vessel and another case where there is an incipient swastika (no. 211). Apart from those, there are a few diagonal crosses (nos. 205-10), but these are also rare. Nos. 205 and 206 are, in reality, mutilated diamond motifs, where the diamond shape has been sliced in two and then stuck together again, top-point to bottom-point.

12 Rectangular Motifs (Fig. 518)

These are also rare as specifically designed motifs. Rectangles may sometimes arise, as it were, by accident, through the enclosing of a 'display panel', which then assumes a rectangular shape. But deliberately formed rectangles are few and far between. Examples are given in nos. 213-20. The interior of no. 218 creates another meander motif.

13 Other Motifs (Fig. 518)

Other shapes, too isolated to be classed as distinct categories, include a *Parallelogram* (no. 221) that is rather common; two chevron patterns (nos. 222 and 223); a 'bridge' shape of multi-linear construction (no. 224); a necked-rectangle shape, reminiscent of the 'brush pattern'; a branching-tree motif; and finally two starburst patterns.

Fig. 517 *Checkerboard Motifs on Incised Polished Ware of the Early Bronze Age.*

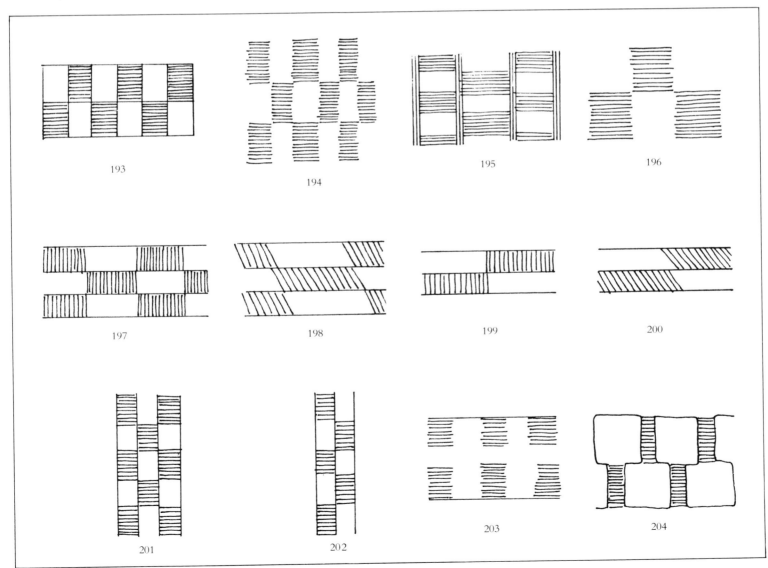

193   194   195   196

197   198   199   200

201   202   203   204

Fig. 517

Fig. 518 *Cruciform Motifs, Rectangular Motifs and Other Motifs on Incised Polished Ware of the Early Bronze Age.*

These, then, are the 228 incision-pattern motifs that can be collected from the decorations of the known Polished Ware pottery of the Early Bronze Age. Undoubtedly many more minor variants will be unearthed as time passes, but it is unlikely that future excavations will substantially alter the basic repertoire presented here.

One of the hazards of producing such a classification of motifs is that it is frequently difficult to know where to stop in distinguishing between minor elements. As the pottery was decorated by freehand, there are many small variations with each of the 'identified motifs' illustrated here. To include them all would be unwieldy and confusing. On the other hand, too much 'lumping' will throw together patterns and motifs that belong to different epochs. For instance, it is essential to consider motifs in their horizontal and vertical modes as separate entities. Failure to do this would conceal the fact that, for example, the horizontal zigzag is replaced by the vertical zigzag as one moves from central regions up into the extreme north-east peninsula.

The ideal solution to aim for is a compromise that produces a motif repertoire classification that is useful for typifying a particular ware and for understanding the way in which the pottery artists set about combining elements to create their decorations.

White Painted Ware

1 Horizontal Bands (Fig. 519)

As before, these are extremely common as borders for other motifs, but the favoured patterns are different in some respects. The dominant pattern, that of the *Plain Multilinear Band* (no. 2) remains the same, but the *Thick Single Plain Band* (no. 13) is also popular. This thick band, easy to produce with paint, was highly unsuitable for incision-decorated vessels. Bands of hanging 'cords' (nos. 9-11) also appear on the scene, and thick vertical bars (nos. 14 and 16) are used in a way that again favours paint over incision. The production of wavy lines has become so profuse that a special new category has been needed for these (see below).

Fig. 519 *Horizontal Bands on White Painted Ware of the Middle Bronze Age.*

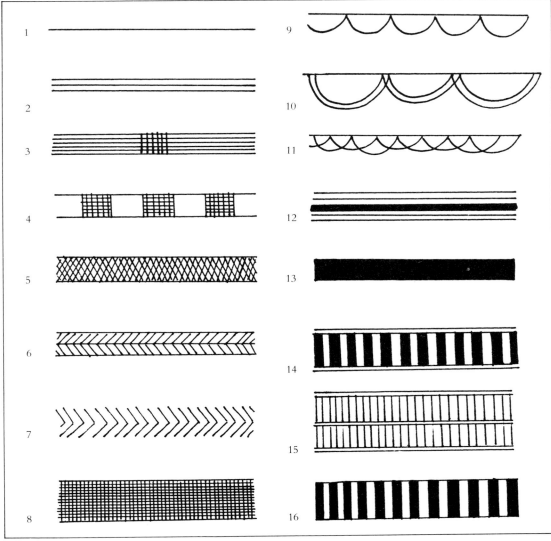

Fig. 519

2 Vertical Stripes (Fig. 520)

Here the *Plain Multi-linear Stripe* (no. 18) is the most popular vertical motif, with *Cross-hatched Stripes* (nos. 20 and 21) as a second favourite. The 'hanging cord' motif has also been up-ended to produce a variety of combinations with vertical lines (see nos. 23-6).

3 Horizontal Zigzags (Fig. 521)

The most favoured version of the zigzag is the *Hatched-below/Plain-above Zigzag* (nos. 45-8), which creates the effect of a row of triangles, pointing upwards. Occasionally, the hatching is above the zigzag line, when the triangles hang downwards (no. 51). This type of zigzag was virtually absent from the Incised Ware of the Early Bronze Age, but one style which is shared by both epochs is the *Plain Multi-linear Horizontal Zigzag* (no. 34). Even here there is, however, a detectable difference. In the White Painted Ware the number of lines per multi-linear motif is smaller—typically only two or three.

Fig. 520 *Vertical Stripes on White Painted Ware of the Middle Bronze Age.*

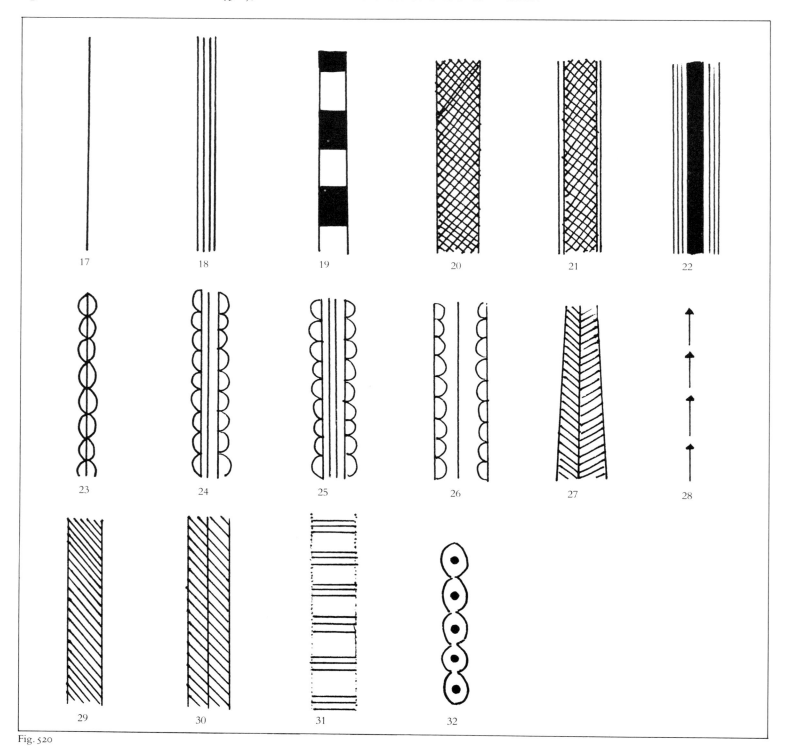

Fig. 520

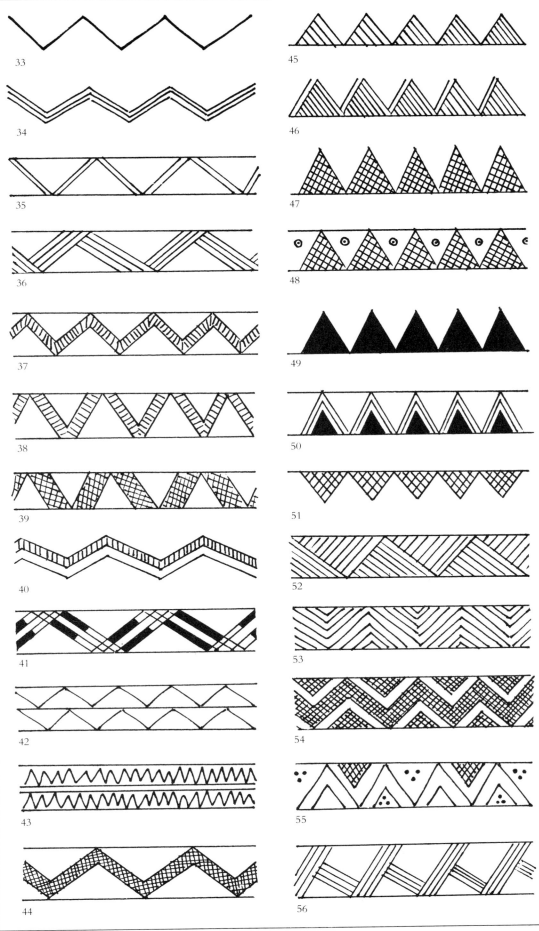

Fig. 521 *Horizontal Zigzags on White Painted Ware of the Middle Bronze Age.*

Fig. 521

Fig. 522 *Vertical Zigzags on White Painted Ware of the Middle Bronze Age.*

Fig. 523 *Horizontal Diamonds on White Painted Ware of the Middle Bronze Age.*

4 Vertical Zigzags (Fig. 522)

These are rare in the White Painted Ware decorations, and when they occur they are usually of a simple type—plain multi-linear, with only two or three lines.

5 Horizontal Diamonds (Fig. 523)

There is a marked increase in horizontal diamond bands. These are mostly *Hatched Horizontal Diamonds* (nos. 70 and 72) and *Cross-hatched Horizontal Diamonds* (nos. 71 and 74). The cross-hatched version is a new introduction, hardly detectable in the Early Bronze Age, but immensely popular with the paint-brushes of the Middle Bronze Age.

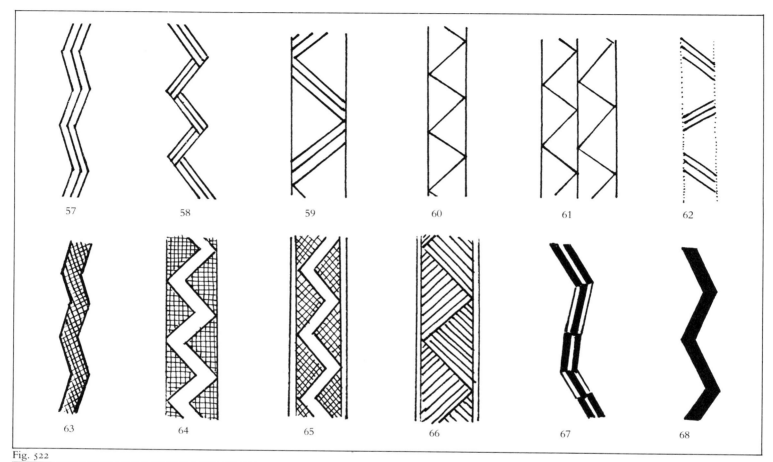

Fig. 522

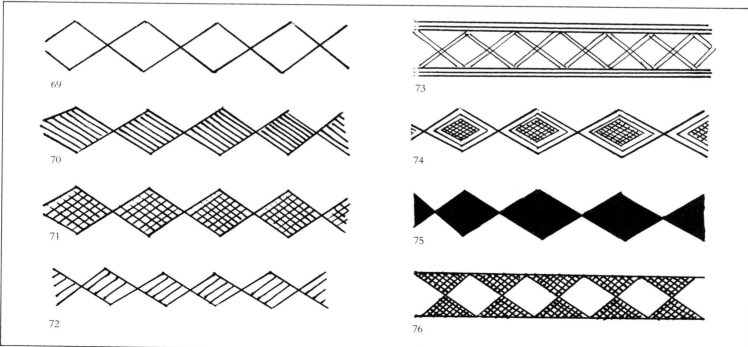

Fig. 523

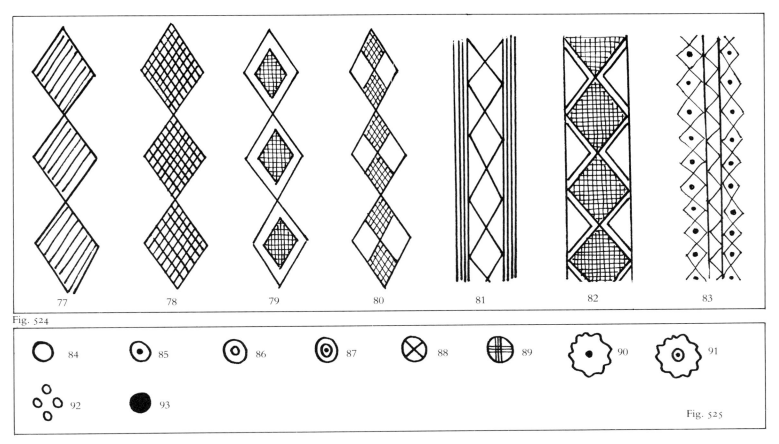

Fig. 524

Fig. 525

6 Vertical Diamonds (Fig. 524)

These remain rare and there are fewer varieties than in the earlier incised ware. Only seven distinct types were detected, as against twenty for the Early Bronze Age vessels. Hatched and cross-hatched examples were the most frequently seen.

7 Isolated Diamonds

Special diamond motifs presented as separate display units seem to vanish in the Middle Bronze Age, as do nearly all kinds of 'special motif'. Highly differentiated or isolated decorative devices appear to be foreign to the Middle Bronze Age artists' thinking. They concentrate instead on repeated patterns that tend to cover almost all of the vessel surfaces, giving the superficial impression of 'a bottle in a net bag', when seen from a distance.

8 Circular Motifs (Fig. 525)

The characteristic Concentric Circles of the Early Bronze Age also vanish. White Painted Ware does, however, offer two new kinds of circular motif—the 'paired eyes' pattern, and the basal circle. The 'eyes' appear on the bellies of vessels, often separated from one another by vertical Wavy Lines. Each 'eye' consists of either a plain circular line (no. 84), a circle with a dot in it (no. 85), a circle with a smaller circle inside it (no. 86), or one with

both a smaller circle and a dot inside it (no. 87). Sometimes these 'eyes' appear in groups of four, two-above-two, or in a ring of motifs around the belly, and this suggests that they are probably not the 'apotropaic eyes' they have sometimes been called. The basal circles are motifs which appear on the bottom of vessels—a new feature introduced in the Middle Bronze Age. Any kind of markings are rare on the bottoms of Early Bronze Age pottery, where incision patterns usually end at the 'lower belly' of the vessels, leaving the base plain. (Exceptions to this rule are certain shallow basins of Red Polished Ware and some small Philia Ware bottles (see p. 18).) The basal region of White Painted Ware, by contrast, is frequently decorated. A popular device here is the Filled Circle (no. 93), which appears centrally as a large black spot on the bottom of a variety of jugs and flasks. Another is the Crossed Circle (nos. 88 and 89).

9 Split Circles

These have vanished along with the multi-concentric circles of the Early Bronze Age. The Middle Bronze Age artist is either ignorant of or has deliberately abandoned this specialized motif of the Incised Polished Ware.

Fig. 524 *Vertical Diamonds on White Painted Ware of the Middle Bronze Age.*
Fig. 525 *Circular Motifs on White Painted Ware of the Middle Bronze Age.*

10 **Checkerboard Motifs** (Fig. 526)

There is no change in frequency here, the check patterns remaining moderately common. The big difference lies in the method of production of the dark squares (or rectangles). In the Early Bronze Age, hampered by the technique of incising closely bunched lines in soft clay, the artists made all their dark squares by simple hatching. This type of check is rare in the Middle Bronze Age, where criss-cross hatching or fully blacked-in squares become the norm (see nos. 94–109, with 110 the only exception).

11 **Cruciform Motifs** (Fig. 527)

As already mentioned, when dealing with circular motifs, the Middle Bronze Age sees the innovation of basal decorative patterns, and the most common of these is the cross. The variety is great and those shown here (nos. 111–38) doubtless represent only a part of the total repertoire of this type of motif.

Fig. 526 *Checkerboard Motifs on White Painted Ware of the Middle Bronze Age.*

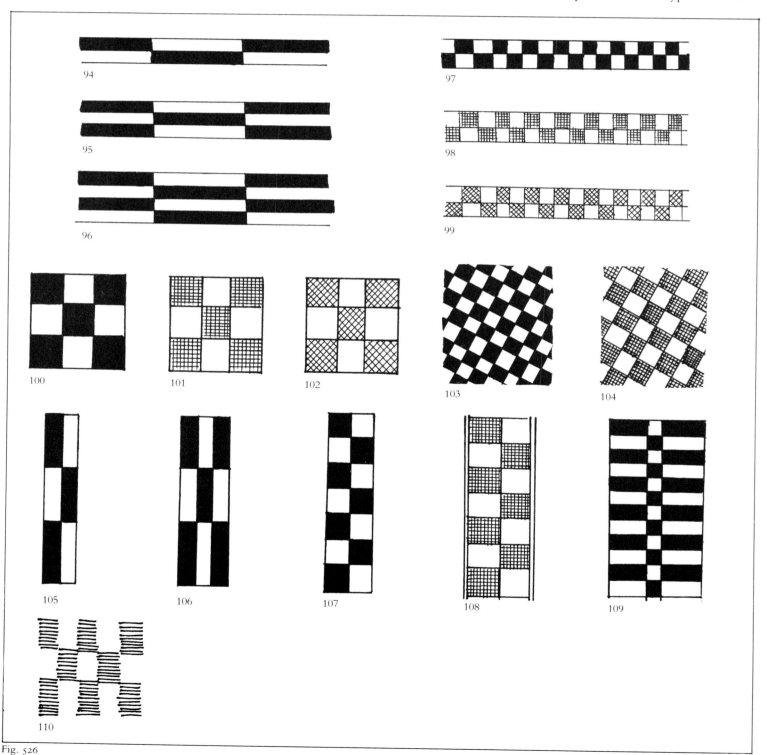

Fig. 526

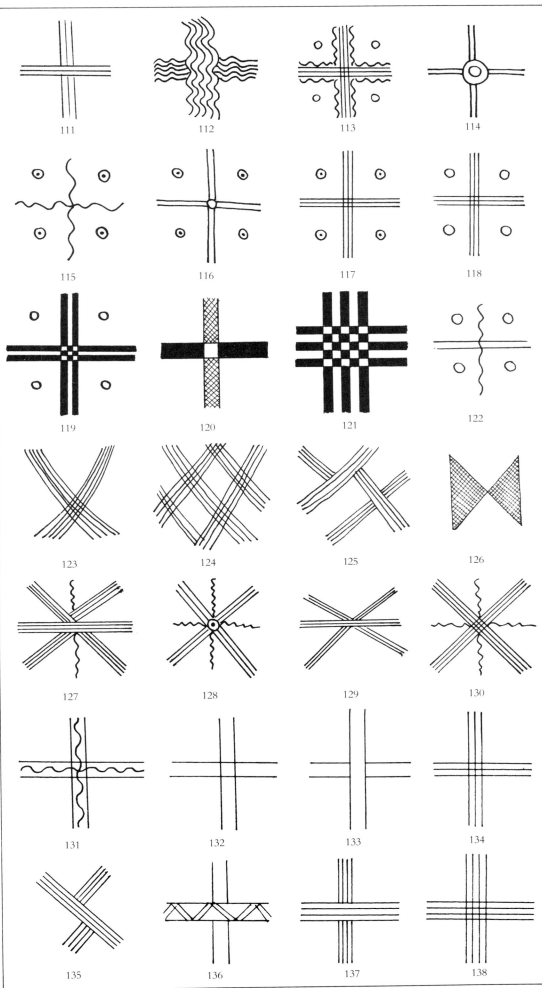

Fig. 527 *Cruciform Motifs on White Painted Ware of the Middle Bronze Age.*

Fig. 527

Fig. 528 *Wavy Lines on White Painted Ware of the Middle Bronze Age.*

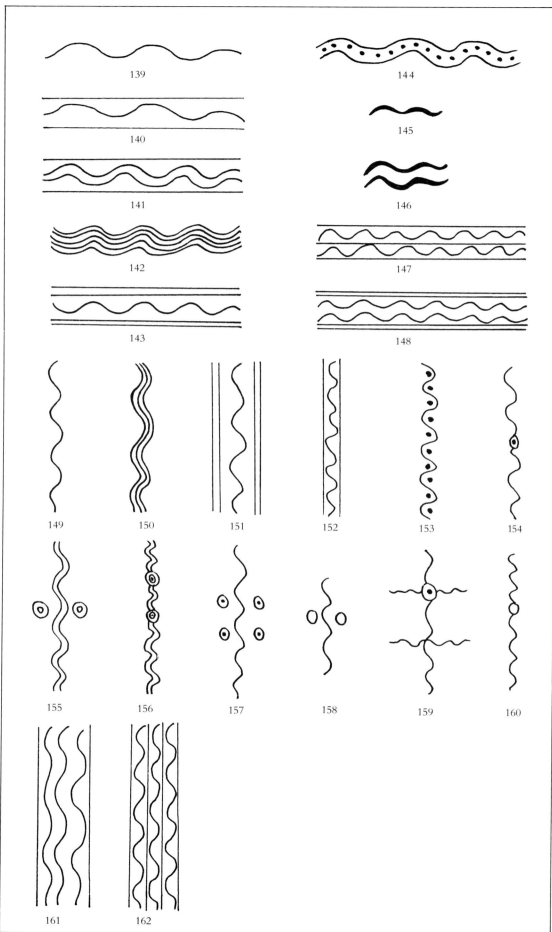

Fig. 528

12 Rectangular Motifs and **Other Motifs**

These have virtually disappeared from the Middle Bronze Age, as part of the general trend away from isolated special motifs as differentiated 'display units'.

13 Wavy Lines (Fig. 528)

One new category has to be added to complete the repertoire of the Middle Bronze Age. A few wavy lines appeared among the incision patterns of the earlier period, but not enough to justify a separate category there. Here, however, undulating lines become so common that they demand a section to themselves. Twenty-four examples have been traced. The most common form is the *Single Vertical Wavy Line*. This is usually depicted as if hanging down the belly of the vessel, like a string or tape suspended from the base of the neck. Its waviness, on the other hand, makes it look snake-like, and small circles that sometimes appear on or near it could be interpreted as eyes or even snakes' heads. But the question of string versus snake is best left for the present. For now, the wavy line can best be viewed as just another abstract motif in the Middle Bronze Age repertoire.

These are the 162 painted motifs that appear on the White Painted Ware of the Middle Bronze Age. Visually, they make a very different impact from the incision patterns of the Early Bronze Age, but this has more to do with their mode of production and the background on which they are applied, than with major differences in the two motif repertoires. Horizontal bands, vertical stripes, zigzags, diamonds, circles and checkerboard patterns appear commonly in both epochs. The only important shifts involve the fading out of the isolated diamonds, the multicircles and split circles of the Incised Polished

Ware, and the dramatic increase in basal motifs, mostly crosses, and in wavy lines, on the White Painted Ware. Apart from those, the changes are largely in detail, or of a quantitative kind.

To test this, fifty vessels of each type—Incised Polished and White Painted—were selected at random from the author's collection and analysed for motif repertoire differences. Here in crude figures are the results of this test:

Class of Motif	Incised Polished Ware (EBA)	White Painted Ware (MBA)	
1 Horizontal Bands	100%	96%	
2 Vertical Stripes	48%	52%	
3 Horizontal Zigzags	72%	74%	
4 Vertical Zigzags	22%	14%	
5 Horizontal Diamonds	12%	22%	
6 Vertical Diamonds	2%	2%	
7 Isolated Diamonds	32%	0%	★
8 Circular Motifs	18%	26%	
9 Split Circles	10%	0%	★
10 Checkerboard Motifs	24%	12%	
11 Cruciform Motifs	8%	58%	★
12 Wavy Lines	2%	32%	★

(The figures show the percentages of vessels in the samples that carried the particular class of motif. Those asterisked are the major shifts at this crude level of analysis.)

To seek further differences it is necessary to examine changes *within* each class of motifs. When this is done, twelve significant shifts can be detected at a 'lower-order' level. These are shown in the histogram (Fig. 529), where the height of each column represents the percentage of vessels carrying a particular motif. The Incised Polished Ware of the Early Bronze Age is indicated by the solid columns, and the White Painted Ware of the Middle Bronze Age by the hatched columns. The twelve selected motifs are as follows.

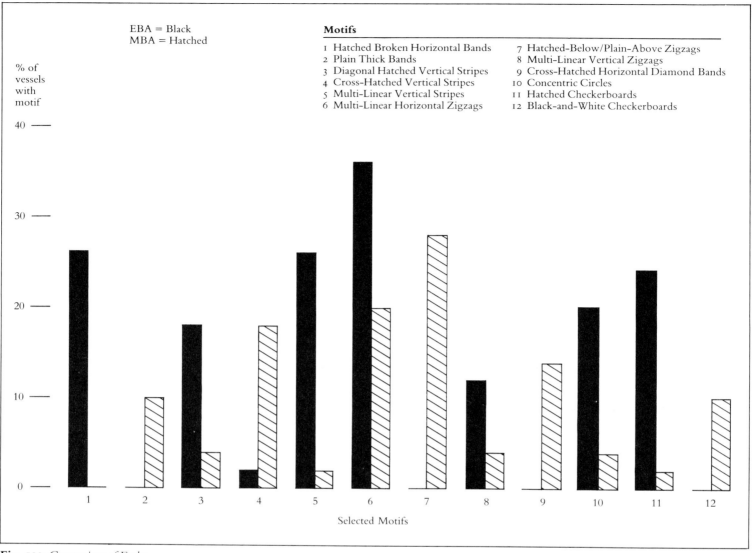

EBA = Black
MBA = Hatched

Motifs

1 Hatched Broken Horizontal Bands   7 Hatched-Below/Plain-Above Zigzags
2 Plain Thick Bands   8 Multi-Linear Vertical Zigzags
3 Diagonal Hatched Vertical Stripes   9 Cross-Hatched Horizontal Diamond Bands
4 Cross-Hatched Vertical Stripes   10 Concentric Circles
5 Multi-Linear Vertical Stripes   11 Hatched Checkerboards
6 Multi-Linear Horizontal Zigzags   12 Black-and-White Checkerboards

% of vessels with motif

Selected Motifs

Fig. 529 *Comparison of Early Bronze Age Incision Motifs and Middle Bronze Age White Painted Motifs.*

White Slip Ware

1 Horizontal Bands (Fig. 530)

These occur with an even higher frequency on the White Slip Ware, and it is impossible to find an example of this ware without at least one horizontal band. The most popular forms here are the *Cross-hatched Horizontal Band* (especially no. 7) and the *Multi-linear Horizontal Band*. The hanging 'cord' design that appeared in the Middle Bronze Age survives here (see nos. 24-7), but is now marked with dots in most instances. This tendency to 'dot' the decorative bands also spills over into other patterns, such as nos. 16-19.

2 Vertical Stripes (Fig. 531)

Here there is a major change from the previous decorative arrangements. In both the Incised Polished Ware and the White Painted Ware, vertical stripes appeared on only about half the vessels studied. With White Slip this

rises dramatically to virtually 100 per cent. This doubling of popularity of vertical stripes reflects a basic change in decorative style. What happens is that the White Slip artists reject 'overall coverage' as a pattern-plan. They show a sudden and rather sophisticated 'spatial restraint'. As if wishing to show off their new creamy-white background surface, they leave large areas of it unpainted. Above and below the ubiquitous horizontal bands it is rare to find broad panels of painted lines. Instead the spaces are decorated with widely separated vertical bands or other 'tall-and-narrow' vertical motifs such as vertical diamonds. This basic plan favours vertical bands to such an extent that they have become the dominant theme of the White Slip Ware. The most popular versions, as with the horizontal bands, are the cross-hatched and the multi-linear.

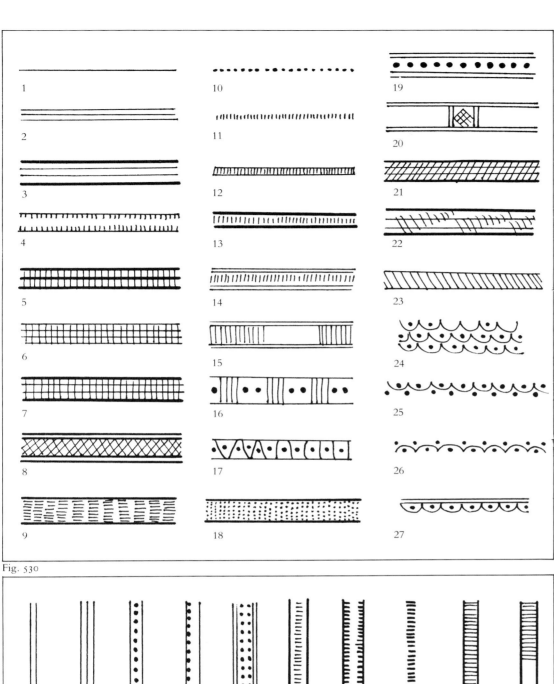

Fig. 530

Fig. 530 *Horizontal Bands on White Slip Ware of the Late Bronze Age.*

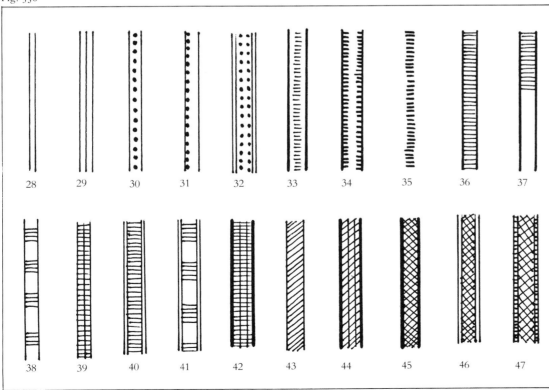

Fig. 531

Fig. 531 *Vertical Stripes on White Slip Ware of the Late Bronze Age.*

Fig. 532

3 Horizontal Zigzags (Fig. 533)

Another major change is the widespread suppression of the horizontal zigzag. This was so popular in the earlier repertoires that it figured in about three-quarters of the vessels, but here it all but vanishes, and it was only possible to locate a few rare instances (nos. 48-50). The demise of the zigzag is partly due to the 'emptying of the display panels', which leaves only narrow vertical motifs, but its disappearance goes further than this. It would be perfectly possible, for instance, for the horizontal bands that so typically lie just below the rim of many White Slip vessels to incorporate zigzag elements of some kind,

no. 31, Fig. 26). Previously it had been called Proto-White Slip Ware, but they refer it instead to White Painted IV. Significantly it not only has 'filled-in' panels typical of the Middle Bronze Age, with very little white space left open, but it also displays both vertical and horizontal zigzags—motifs that also place it firmly in the earlier period (see Fig. 532).

5 Horizontal Diamonds (Fig. 534)

Horizontal diamonds retain their popularity here, with the most favoured form being the *Cross-hatched Horizontal Diamonds* (nos. 52-5, with 52 being the favourite). The simpler

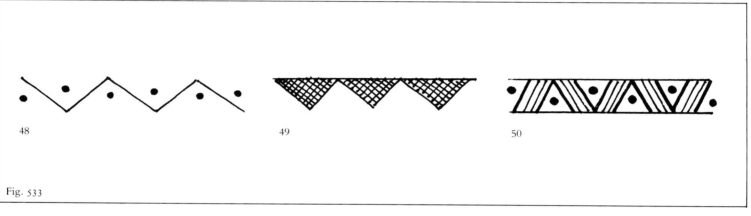

48   49   50

Fig. 533

Fig. 532 *An intermediate vessel—a jug with a rich, creamy slip typical of White Slip Ware, but with decorative motifs of the earlier White Painted Ware. Magounda. Ht. 17.8 cm. Brown and Catling. 1980, no. 31.*

Fig. 533 *Horizontal Zigzags on White Slip Ware of the Late Bronze Age.*

but they do not. It is as if the zigzag really has become a 'taboo motif' at this stage.

4 Vertical Zigzags

Here the disappearance is even more complete, and a fairly extensive survey of the literature failed to reveal a single example of this motif on any White Slip vessel. Even if a few rare examples eventually turn up, its suppression remains remarkable. We saw how, in the Early Bronze Age, the Incised Polished Ware of the central regions strongly favoured the Horizontal Zigzag, while that of the north-east peninsula favoured the Vertical Zigzag to the almost complete exclusion of the Horizontal. With the arrival of the White Painted Ware of the Middle Bronze Age, both types of zigzag were once again popular, but now, with the later White Slip Ware, both types are suppressed. There appears to be nothing haphazard about the artists' decisions to use or not to use the zigzag pattern. This suggests that it may carry some special significance for the Bronze Age artists.

An interesting 'intermediate' vessel, halfway between White Painted and White Slip Ware, appears in Brown and Catling (1980,

Hatched Horizontal Diamonds motif which was also common in the Middle Bronze Age (see White Painted Motifs nos. 70 and 72) does not, however, survive into the White Slip repertoire. A popular newcomer is the *Small Linked Horizontal Diamonds* (no. 56).

6 Vertical Diamonds (Fig. 534)

Rare in the Early and Middle Bronze Age periods, these now show a marked increase in popularity, as part of the shift from broad panels to narrow vertical motifs. There are many different versions (see nos. 58-82) but the Cross-hatched is the favourite and there is a general tendency to make the diamond units smaller, with fewer criss-cross lines inside them. Sometimes, the vertical chain of diamonds is reduced to only two or three units (see nos. 74-81), these abbreviated vertical motifs hanging in space below horizontal bands.

7 Isolated Diamonds (Fig. 534)

Missing in the Middle Bronze Age, these reappear here (nos. 83-6), but in a much smaller and simpler form than in the Early Bronze Age.

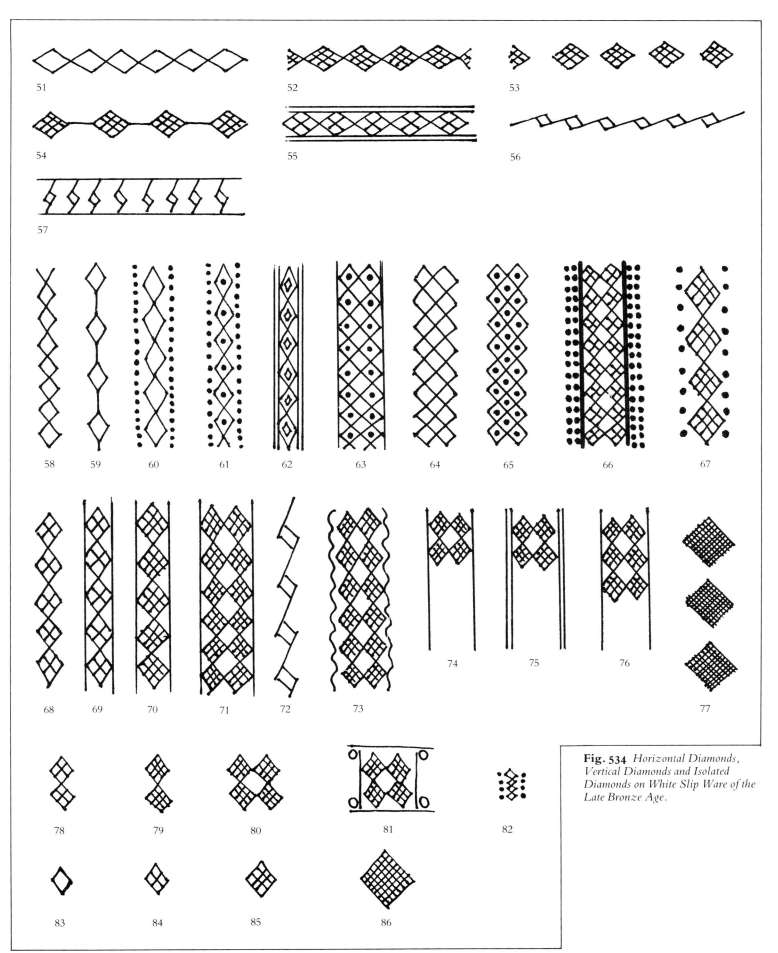

Fig. 534 *Horizontal Diamonds, Vertical Diamonds and Isolated Diamonds on White Slip Ware of the Late Bronze Age.*

Fig. 534

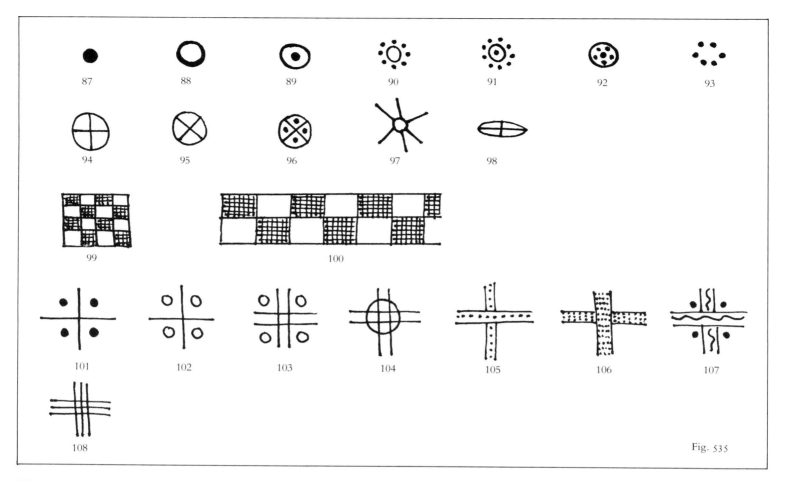

Fig. 535 *Circular Motifs, Checkerboard Motifs and Cruciform Motifs on White Slip Ware of the Late Bronze Age.*

8 Circular Motifs (Fig. 535)

There is little change here from the Middle Bronze Age, Circular motifs remain small and rather simple, but they are less common. Paired 'eye' circles, first seen in the White Painted Ware, survive into the Proto-White Slip Ware, but then disappear in the later vessels (but see section 15 below).

9 Split Circles

As in the Middle Bronze Age, these are missing from the repertoire of the White Slip Ware.

10 Checkerboard Motifs (Fig. 535)

These become extremely rare on the White Slip vessels and only one or two isolated examples could be found (nos. 99 and 100). Their demise is largely due to the removal of all broad panels of decoration.

11 Cruciform Motifs (Fig. 535)

Crosses persist in the White Slip phase, but are less frequent. As with the White Painted Ware, they appear most often as basal motifs, but occasionally are seen on the sides of vessels, where they are usually formed by the intersection of an isolated Horizontal Band and Vertical Stripe.

12 Rectangular Motifs (Fig. 536)

These are rare because of the general restriction of White Slip patterning to bands and stripes, but there are exceptions, where dotted, barred, or cross-hatched rectangles can be seen.

13 Other Motifs (Fig. 536)

Odd shapes sometimes appear as very small 'punctuations', on their own in otherwise open white spaces, but they are by no means common, the six examples shown here being the only ones located in a wide search of White Slip Ware material.

14 Wavy Lines (Fig. 536)

Wavy lines persist, but the most popular version of the Middle Bronze Age, the *Single Vertical Wavy Line*, has vanished, except for a few embellished forms, with added dots (nos. 133 and 134) or dashes (no. 139), or straight-line borders (no. 131). *Single Horizontal Wavy Lines* are the favourites, with or without borders (nos. 126-9). *Paired Vertical Wavy Lines* are also favoured, usually with dotted embellishment (nos. 135-8).

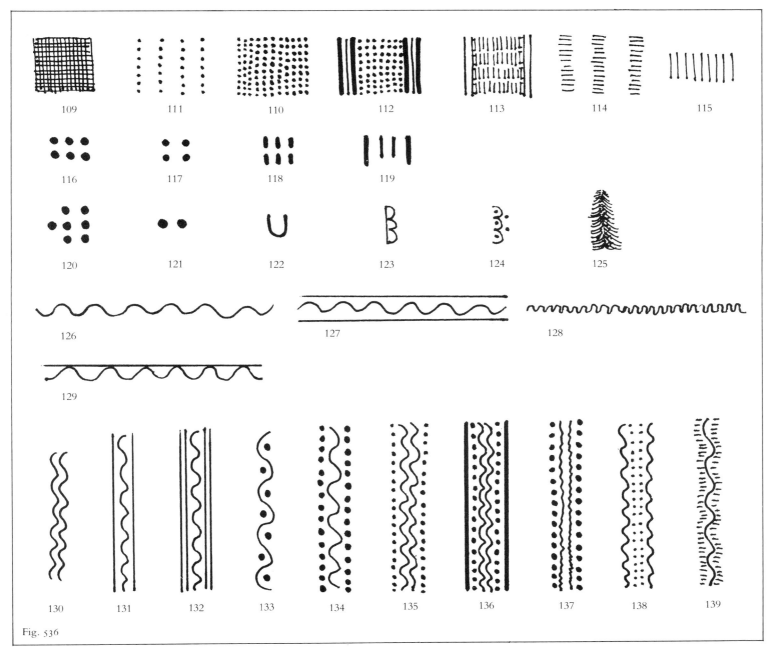

109 111 110 112 113 114 115

116 117 118 119

120 121 122 123 124 125

126 127 128

129

130 131 132 133 134 135 136 137 138 139

Fig. 536

15 Horned Motifs (Fig. 537)

A special feature of White Slip Ware, absent from the previous two repertoires, is a vertical element, usually paired, surmounted by 'horns'. Forty-two variations of this theme are shown here, but more will probably be found as further White Slip Ware is unearthed because it is with this motif that the White Slip artists seem particularly intent on 'ringing the changes'. It is rare to find precisely the same horned pattern on more than one vessel. They are always given 'pride of place' in the overall decoration, being placed in isolation, usually at the front (opposite the handle) or the centre of the side of the vessel. They are plàced below a horizontal band and are often framed, at a distance, by two verti-

cal stripes. They provide the White Slip decoration with its special focus of attention. They are unique to this ware, although it is possible to see a precursor in the White Painted Ware of the Middle Bronze Age. There, vertical wavy line motifs are sometimes flanked by a pair of small circles, looking like eyes (see White Painted motifs nos. 155 and 158). In the earliest examples of the horned motif, on Proto-White Slip Ware, similar wavy lines with paired circles appear (White Slip motifs nos. 140-2). But already here there is a crucial difference, namely that at the tops of the wavy lines there is a divergence of direction, creating the horned effect.

It has been argued that the paired circles in these Proto-White Slip examples are not ab-

Fig. 536 *Rectangular Motifs, Other Motifs and Wavy Lines on White Slip Ware of the Late Bronze Age.*

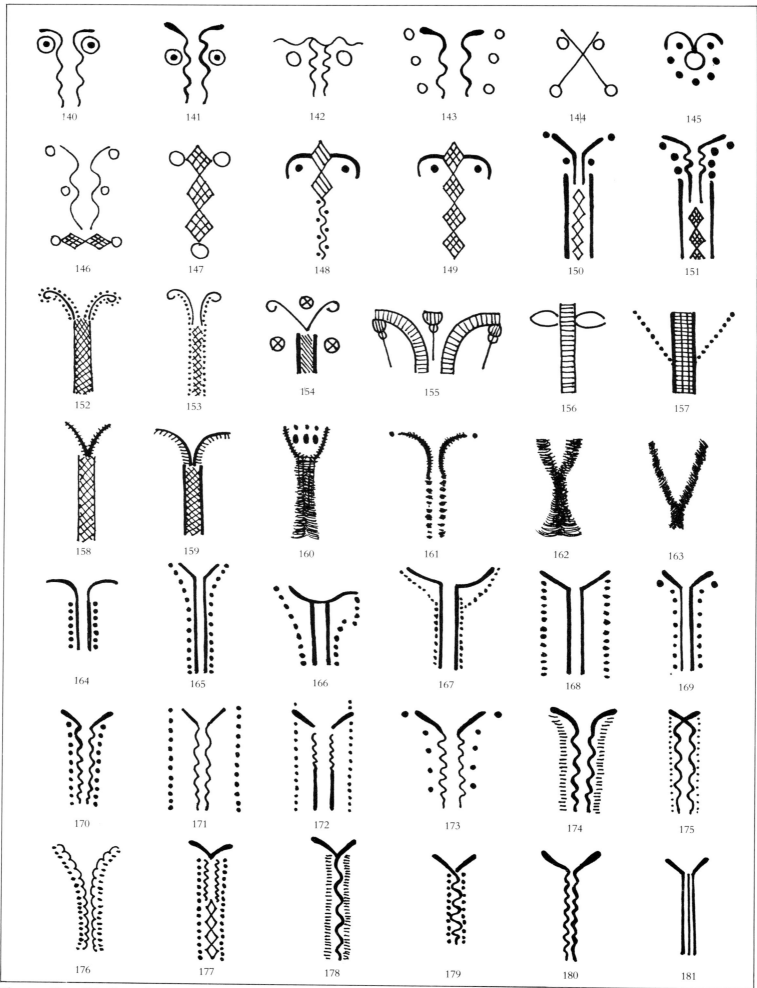

Fig. 537 *Horned Motifs on White Slip Ware of the Late Bronze Age.*

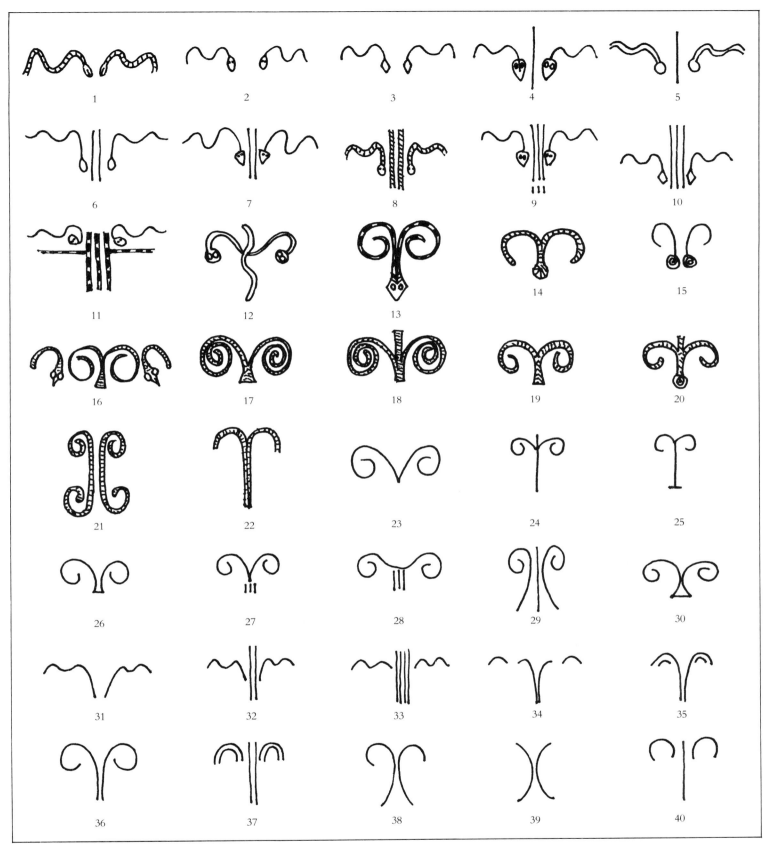

Fig. 538 *Paired Snake Motifs on Base Ring Ware of the Late Bronze Age.*

stract but part of a deliberately representational image. Combined with the vertical lines, they are seen as making up a stylized face, placed apotropaically on the vessels to ward off evil; in other words, to outstare the evil eye. It is easy to understand this view since undeniably eye-like motifs do appear, from the Chalcolithic onwards, on ancient artefacts from the nearby mainland. But if this is the case with the Cypriot White Slip Ware, then the direction taken by the increased stylization of the motif on later vessels is hard to understand. The essential feature of protective eye motifs is that they should retain the paired spots, rings or blobs that signal 'eyeness', and this is quickly lost after the Proto-White Slip phase. Nearly all later examples omit the 'eyes' but retain the 'horns'. An alternative explanation could be that the image being 'abstracted' is that of a horned head. At first this is seen as horns + eyes, but then, later on, only the horns survive, in *their* protective role (as already discussed on pp. 196-7). A third interpretation might be to see them as paired snakes, rearing up with their heads apart. This is most strongly suggested by nos. 141 and 143, and is supported by the presence of paired snakes on the contemporary Base Ring Ware, discussed on p. 233. If paired snakes became a powerful symbol in the Late Bronze Age, this would make sense, but there are no clearly representational images of snakes with detailed eyes and heads, as there are on the early Base Ring Ware vessels (see Fig. 538). The snake interpretation therefore remains tenuous. A fourth hypothesis is that these painted lines represent 'stitching'. This view has been put forward by those who feel that the higher frequency of 'dot-edged' or 'dash-edged' motifs on White Slip Ware vessels requires an explanation. This interpretation is presumably based on the idea that the pottery vessels were derived from stitched-leather originals and were, in a sense, funerary replicas of those. But with such high-quality pottery available, it seems odd that laboriously stitched leather should have been used at all.

Because no dominant symbolic theme has yet emerged, it is best for the present to continue to view these 'horned' motifs as yet another abstract decoration, although in this case it has to be admitted that the oddity of the motif, and the extent to which it differs from all the other hundreds of Bronze Age

motifs, does set it aside from the rest and place it in a special category of 'probably symbolic'. Perhaps further research will unearth vital, unstylized examples that will settle the question.

These, then, are the decorative motifs of three of the most important wares of Bronze Age Cyprus. If the manner in which they are applied to individual vessels is studied, it soon becomes clear that there are two underlying aesthetic rules in operation. These are as follows:

The first rule, operating *within* a particular decorative style, is conformity to a repertoire of motifs, with inventive variation expressed in two main ways: the selection from the motif-repertoire of the specific motifs to be used on a particular vessel, and the way in which these selected motifs are combined to produce the overall pattern of decoration.

In other words, the artist is conservative in the general range of geometric elements exploited, but anti-conservative in motif-combination. This gives rise to vessel-to-vessel *thematic variation*, which is the subject of the next chapter.

The second rule, operating *between* one decorative style and another, is that there should be changes at the level of the motif-repertoire itself. Certain elements disappear; others emerge. Still others show major shifts in popularity, from rare to common or vice versa. These switches occur both at different places at the same time and at different times at the same place, and, as *regional and temporal shifts of decorative emphasis*, they require some kind of explanation. One or more of the following factors may be involved:

1 *Creative Innovation*. Individual, exploratory inventiveness can easily account for the introduction of a new motif, which subsequently spreads and becomes commonplace. This process undoubtedly plays a part, but seems to find its major expression at the level of motif-combination rather than the motifs themselves.

2 *Error Magnification*. If unskilled copying takes place, with certain motifs lazily repeated, or modified to make them easier to incise or paint, these 'decayed' elements can become the basis for a new norm. If skill is then re-applied to their execution they may become re-elaborated, but in a way that makes them different from the original versions. Repertoire shifts that result from copy-

ing ineptitude of this kind do not, however, seem to be a major factor in the Cypriot Bronze Age.

3 *Technical Opportunism*. This is the adapting of motifs to new materials. Certain lines, for example, are easy to incise but hard to paint and vice versa. A change from incision to painting may therefore lead to adaptive shifts in the repertoire of motifs. To give one example: wavy lines are easier to paint than to incise, with the result that their frequency increases with the arrival of the White Painted Ware of the Middle Bronze Age.

4 *Aesthetic Drift*. This is the process by which old traditions fade away with the death of individual artists or the decline of artistic centres. When new motifs emerge they do so, not as a positive act of opposition to the old patterns, but simply because the old ones are no longer available as aesthetic influences. It is, in other words, a passive change brought about by poor continuity of tradition.

5 *Emblem Opposition*. If a particular motif or combination of motifs is used in one place or at one time with great frequency it will inevitably become emblematic of a particular artist or community. Regardless of whether it has a special symbolic meaning or is merely an abstract decoration, it will become entrenched as a 'label' of those who repeatedly employ it. If others wish to separate themselves from the 'labelled' group, then they must carefully avoid their decorative motifs. In modern times the swastika motif is a good example of this. Widely used in the past, with a variety of meanings, its recent association with Nazi atrocities will make it taboo as a decorative element for many years to come. Some of the shifts in Bronze Age Cyprus may reflect Emblem Oppositions of this kind, with one community actively shunning the motifs of another.

6 *Symbol Shift*. It has always been assumed by archaeological investigators that the decorative patterns incised and painted on the ancient Cypriot vessels have no specific symbolic meaning. Even in the unusual cases where snake elements are clearly present, as with the Base Ring Ware motifs shown on p. 319, the emphasis has been put on decoration rather than symbolism. The suggestion that a set of concentric circles, a multiple zigzag or a hatched diamond might be susceptible to symbolic interpretation has been completely shunned. This does not mean that it has been

carefully investigated and then rejected, but rather that it has been totally ignored. If this proves to have been an error and there *are* symbolic meanings embedded in the geometric patterns, then it would follow that a shift from one motif to another over time or space could reflect a move from one symbolic statement to another.

It looks as though several of these processes have been operating in ancient Cyprus, and provide explanations for the various motif-changes observed, from ware to ware and style to style. At this stage of our knowledge it is hard to pinpoint the relative importance of the different processes. In particular, the question of Symbol Shift remains problematical. We simply have no way of testing whether a geometric motif is symbolic or abstract. The way the motifs are combined on each vessel to create an overall pattern, each visual unit becoming a dependent element in the general effect rather than retaining an isolated independence, suggests that specific symbols are not involved. The geometric units do not have about them the flavour of discrete 'signs' or hieroglyphs. Groups of lines abut and intersect repeatedly, transforming one another in the process, with triangles growing out of zigzags and vice versa, circles splitting into arcs and semicircles, and multiple lines crossing to form diamonds or rectangles. The merging of one pattern into another in this way blurs the sharpness of the motifs as separate entities and reduces their symbol power. Because of this, it is easy to see why archaeologists have been loath to consider them as specific symbols, and they are probably right not to do so. However, a word of caution is necessary.

Anthropologists studying the apparently abstract patterns of various forms of tribal art have been surprised how rare truly 'abstract' motifs are. Even the most geometric of designs seems to carry hidden symbolic messages. To illustrate this, two examples are given here. The first (Fig. 539) is a Tahong, a piece of bamboo covered with incised geometric designs not unlike those found on Bronze Age Cypriot vessels. It is worn by the women of the Orang Semang in Malacca, hidden under their girdle during pregnancy. The upper zigzag lines act as a charm against nausea. The columns of the lower part represent the various states through which the pregnant woman passes, from conception to

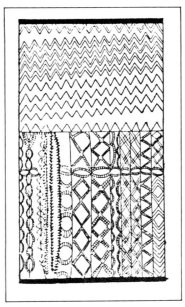

Fig. 539 *Incised bamboo Tahong from Malacca. The apparently abstract decorations are in reality highly symbolic. (For details see text.) After Ploss and Bartels 1935, Vol. II, Fig. 654.*

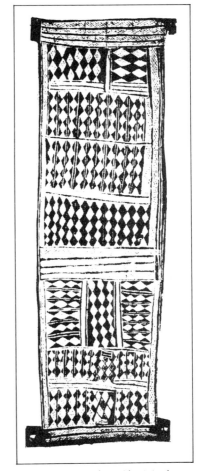

Fig. 540 *Australian Aboriginal bark painting. The apparently abstract decorations are in reality highly symbolic. (For details see text.) After Groger-Wurm 1973, Pl. 101.*

birth. The Tahong, which is carved by the woman's husband, must not be seen by strange men. (It is impossible not to be reminded of the Cypriot Plank Figures here, and wonder whether their flattened shape was due to their being worn in a similar way.)

The second example (Fig. 540) is an Australian aboriginal bark painting which to Western eyes appears to be totally abstract. Nothing could be further from the truth. In fact, the more abstract such paintings appear, the more sacred and significant is their symbolic content. This particular example depicts a fish trap made by ancestral beings with (from top to bottom) mud and grass (the upper diamond motif), water flowing through saplings (the three sets of vertical diamonds), tree logs (four cross-hatched white bars), sections of the fishtrap (horizontal diamonds) on either side of flowing water (the central section of vertical diamonds) and the basket of the trap (the small rectangle). As Groger-Wurm (1973) points out, 'the whole surface of the bark sheet is covered by designs of cross-hatchings, diamonds, lozenges, chevrons, etc., all of which have symbolic meanings based on mythology.'

Comments such as these create a feeling of unease about the archaeological rejection of possible symbolism in the decorative patterns on ancient vessels. Looking at the two tribal examples illustrated here, even the argument that the geometric units on the ancient vessels lack independence and must therefore be seen as part of a general pattern rather than as separate 'signs', begins to look a little shaky. Tribal artists, it seems, are quite able to combine elements into an overall decorative scheme, without losing sight of the symbolic 'reading' of the different parts of the pattern. If they can do this, why not the ancient

Cypriots? In future perhaps we should keep a more open mind about the significance of the incised and painted lines on the Bronze Age vessels.

Two examples deserve brief mention. On p. 141, Pl. 176 shows examples of Red Polished Ware incised motifs in the shape of a brush/comb/figure. Knowing of the terracotta models of this shape and of the presence of such figures 'worn' on Plank Figures, it was easy to see these examples as symbolic rather than abstract. As motifs, this makes them something of a rarity—one of the few cases where such an interpretation could be considered respectable. But it is almost certain that, if the terracottas and other clues had not existed, these incised motifs on otherwise apparently abstractly decorated vessels would have themselves been labelled as indisputably abstract.

The second example concerns the concentric circle motif so popular with Early Bronze Age artists. This is incised with great skill and care (and it is not an easy pattern to produce, as anyone who has tried to copy it in ink will have discovered) and appears in several forms. In the most popular version, the concentric circles rise and fall as they encompass the vessel in a decorative band. In another version, they are split into concentric semicircles, again rising and falling alternately around horizontal bands. Where such images appear in tribal art they always relate to the rising and falling of the sun or the moon. Smeets (1975) gives examples of this and other similar symbolic equations connected with the passage of time and astronomical shifts. It is just possible that the Early Cypriot artists were making similar statements, and we would be wise not to allow appropriate caution to lead to totally closed minds on this subject.

Thematic Variation

One of the fundamental principles of aesthetics is that works of art are subjected to the process of thematic variation (see Morris, 1962, 1977). Art thrives on basic themes which are subjected to repeated, minor variations. This satisfies the intense *taxophilic* urge—the human brain's love of classifying the input it receives through its sense organs. Looking back to our primeval past, it is clear that the need to classify information became so important to us as *nouveau riche* hunting primates, that our ancestors became almost obsessively taxophilic. Even when the demands of survival were easing off, we could not switch off our passion for classification. Just as a well-fed domestic cat cannot resist pouncing on a bird, we could not resist 'inventing' classificatory activities. One of these was what we today call 'art'. The root of aesthetics lies in the pleasure we take from learning a particular creative theme and then studying the skilful ways in which artists can devise variations on it. One of the great losses we have suffered aesthetically, with the passage of time, is the increasing encroachment of mass production into our creative spheres. Mass production involves aesthetic blunting on a huge scale through the elimination of the personal, minor variations imposed on works of art by individual artists. A person who picks up a coffee cup today knows that there are thousands of other cups exactly like it. The only aesthetic statement in relation to the cup was buying that design rather than some other. But the choice was a crude, not a subtle one. The sharp edge of early man has become the blunt instrument of modern technology. Efficiency has come to dominate personal aesthetics.

In the art of ancient Cyprus the first step towards this aesthetic blunting process took place at the end of the Bronze Age, with the introduction of the potter's wheel. Vessel-production became a business and the individual vessels lost a great deal of their beauty and individual charm. The handmade ware of the Bronze Age is therefore more like modern sculpture than modern crockery. Each piece follows a conservative theme, but each is slightly different in shape, size and decoration. Some of these variations may be accidental, but most were almost certainly the result of a deliberate process of thematic variation on the part of the prehistoric artists. Nowhere is this more evident than in the incision patterns of the Early Bronze Age, and two examples of this will now be examined in detail.

The first example concerns the small Red Polished Ware 'gourd juglets' of which several hundred have been excavated from sites in many parts of Cyprus. Whether they were all made in one centre and then transported to different communities as part of an intra-island trading system, or whether they were spread by an out-breeding system which involved female potters marrying outside their own villages and taking their ceramic skills and traditions with them to their new homes, or whether they spread in some other way, we do not know. But they certainly represent a highly conservative theme in shape, size, colour, polish and clay. These vary only slightly, even when vessels come from sites as much as sixty-four miles apart. At this level, then, we are dealing with a highly homogeneous group, but when it comes to the incised decoration on their surfaces, we witness thematic variation at its most active. Although there is a severe, self-imposed restriction on the number of geometric motifs employed, the way in which the artists ring the changes on motif-combination is remarkable. It is as if they are playing a game the rules of which demand that the decoration on every individual vessel shall be as different as possible from all others, while at the same time sharing with them as many individual elements as possible.

To demonstrate how this works, the exact patterns, line for line, were copied from a sample of 171 juglets (either published or ones in the author's collection). For simplicity, the patterns were drawn on a standard outline of a typical juglet, and the attractive but slight shape variations were ignored. Concentrating in this way entirely on the pattern variations, it is possible to arrange the juglets in groups according to a crude classification system, as follows:

A typical juglet is shown in Fig. 542, its decorative pattern divided into ten *incision*

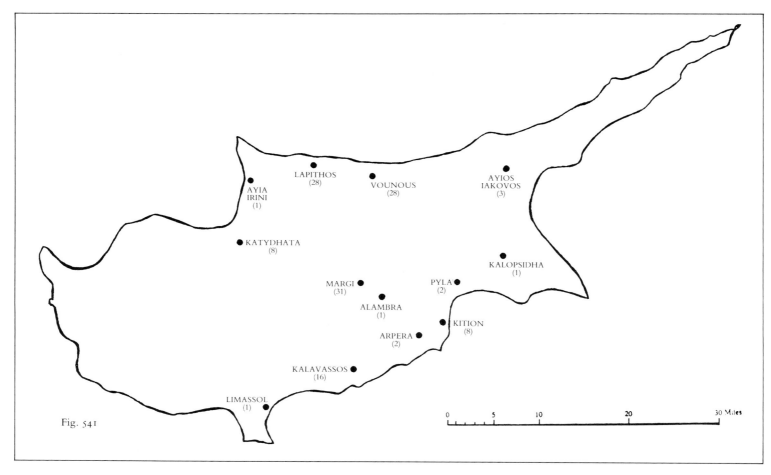

LAPITHOS
(28)

VOUNOUS
(28)

AYIA
IRINI
(1)

AYIOS
IAKOVOS
(3)

KATYDHATA
(8)

KALOPSIDHA
(1)

MARGI
(31)

PYLA
(2)

ALAMBRA
(1)

ARPERA
(2)

KITION
(8)

KALAVASSOS
(16)

LIMASSOL
(1)

0   5   10   20   30 Miles

Fig. 541

Fig. 541 *Sites for gourd juglets (showing numbers found at each location).*

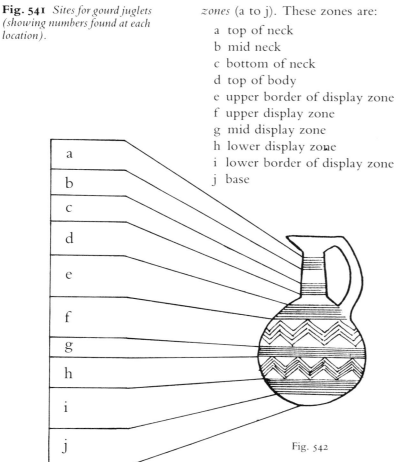

Fig. 542

zones (a to j). These zones are:

  a top of neck
  b mid neck
  c bottom of neck
  d top of body
  e upper border of display zone
  f upper display zone
  g mid display zone
  h lower display zone
  i lower border of display zone
  j base

Each of these zones behaves in a slightly different way, under the influence of thematic variation. Zones a and c act as the upper and lower 'borders' of the neck region. Each nearly always consists of a band of multiple horizontal lines. These two bands provide a 'frame' for zone b, where an incised motif may appear if a particular neck is long enough. In the majority of cases, however, the neck is too short for this 'central' motif and zone b remains blank. If the neck is unduly short, however, then zone b becomes the *only* incised neck-zone, with a and c remaining blank.

On the body of the juglets, zones d and j are nearly always blank. Inside them, zones e and i act as the borders for the vessels' main *display zone*, which is f, g and h, combined. As the main 'bulge' of the body, f, g and h provide the best area for special motifs, and it is here that the bulk of the thematic variation ocurs. In many cases, f, g and h act as a single unit, without any subdivision. A single 'display motif', such as multi-zigzag, covers the whole region. Alternatively, there may be two bands of 'display motif', one above the other (f and h) leaving the mid-zone (g) blank. Or the mid-zone g may be marked with a dividing band of some kind (as in this juglet in Fig. 542), separating the two 'display motifs' from one another.

In some juglets the display zone motif spreads much further up and down the body surface of the vessel, obliterating the usual border bands e and i, or one of them. This is common when the display motif is based on strong vertical elements.

Considering how few main motifs are employed, it is remarkable how many variations the Early Bronze Age artists manage to contrive. Two devices they call upon to help in creating this variability are *in-fillers* and *intervening motifs*. In-fillers usually take the form of short ticks or bars which are placed in the spaces created by such main motifs as zigzags. Between each zig and zag there is a triangular space, and the artist marks each of these with a few dots or dashes. Intervening motifs are introduced as 'alternators' between the elements of a main motif, creating another useful form of pattern variation.

It is difficult to visualize all these details when expressed purely verbally, but they soon become clear when line-accurate drawings of the patterns are presented, arranged in classified groupings. There are twenty-eight types recognized here, most of them with a number of sub-types. Sometimes a particular vessel appears more than once in the classification. This occurs when there are, for example, two different 'main motifs' in zones f and h. For instance, juglet 4-b1 is the same as juglet 11-12 because its zone f motif is a zigzag band, while its zone h is a diamond band. It can therefore be classified under either zigzags or diamonds. In order to avoid an arbitrary decision about where to place it, it is included in both categories. This method is preferred because the function of this classification is not to provide a unique label for each vessel, but to elucidate the relationships between the decorative patterns used. Only by grouping the juglets in this manner can we hope to comprehend the way in which the mind of the Early Bronze Age artist was working, as she obeyed her particular rules of thematic variation. Here are the twenty-eight types:

Type 1 Multi-Linear Horizontal Zigzags.   a Central band, plain.

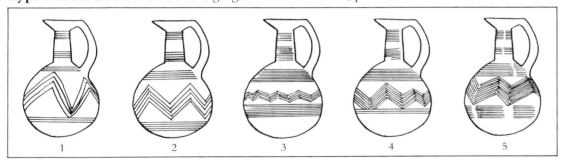

Type 1 Multi-Linear Horizontal Zigzags.   b Central band, with in-fillers.

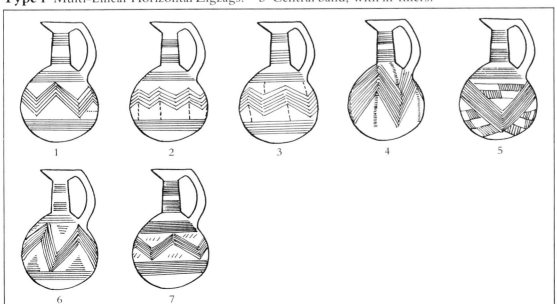

Type I Multi-Linear Horizontal Zigzags.   c Central band, with motif-borders.

Type I Multi-Linear Horizontal Zigzags.   d Double band, plain.

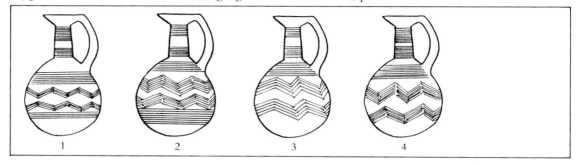

Type I Multi-Linear Horizontal Zigzags.   e Double band, with dividing line.

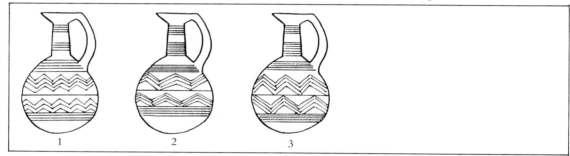

Type I Multi-Linear Horizontal Zigzags.   f Double band, with dividing lines.

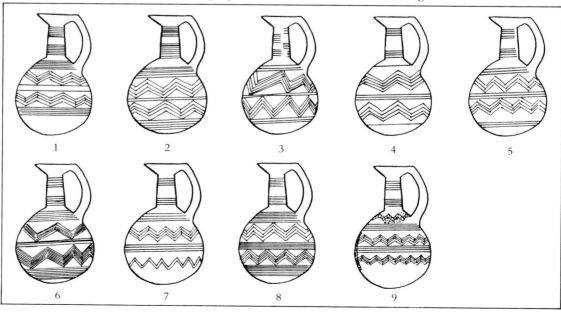

Type 1 Multi-Linear Horizontal Zigzags.   g Double band, with dividing lines and in-fillers.

Type 1 Multi-Linear Horizontal Zigzags.   h Double band, with dividing motif.

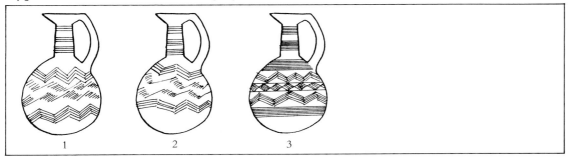

Type 1 Multi-Linear Horizontal Zigzags.   i Double band, with alternating motifs.

Type 1 Multi-Linear Horizontal Zigzags.   j Overlapping bands, plain.

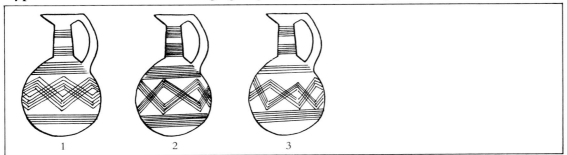

Type 1 Multi-Linear Horizontal Zigzags.   k Lower band, with upper motif.

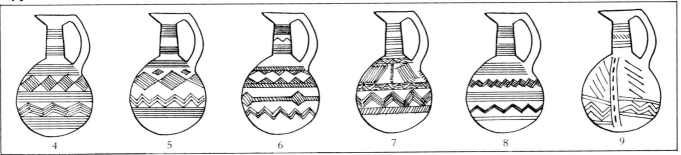

Type 1 Multi-Linear Horizontal Zigzags.   1 Upper band, with lower motif.

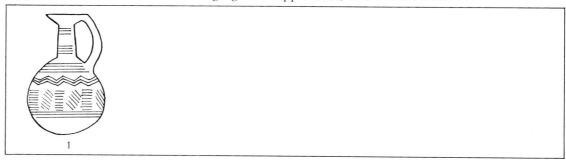

Type 2 Fragmented Horizontal Zigzags.
a Central band, plain. b Double band, with intervening motifs. c Lower band, with upper motif.

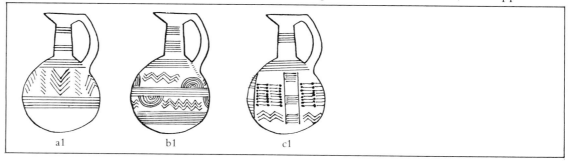

Type 3 Herring-Bone Horizontal Zigzags.   a Central band, plain.

Type 4 Uni-Linear Horizontal Zigzags.
a Lower band, with upper motif.   b Upper band, with lower motif.

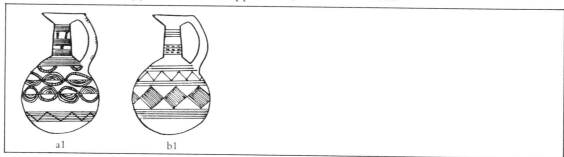

Type 5 Half-Diamond Horizontal Zigzags.   a Central band, with in-fillers.

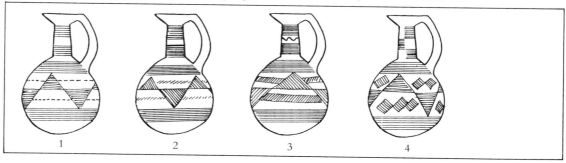

Type 6 Thick/Thin Horizontal Zigzags.   a Central band, plain.

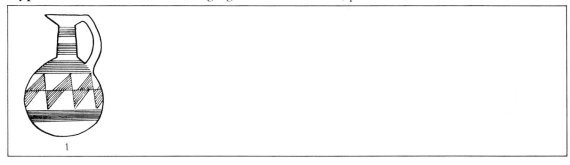

Type 6 Thick/Thin Horizontal Zigzags.   b Double band, plain, with zigzag borders.

Type 7 Hatched Horizontal Zigzags.   a Central band, with in-fillers.

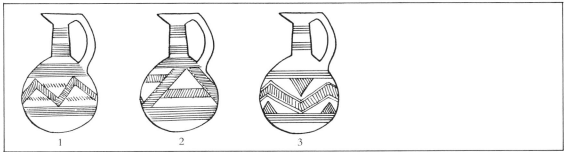

Type 7 Hatched Horizontal Zigzags.   b Double band, with dividing lines.

Type 8 Negative Horizontal Zigzags.   a Double band.

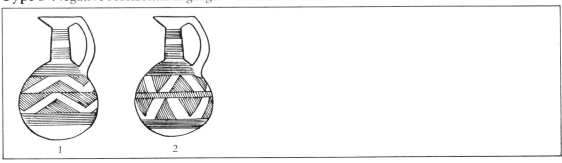

Type 9 Multi-Linear Vertical Zigzags.   a With intervening motifs.

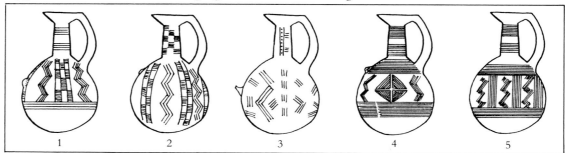

Type 10 Hatched Vertical Zigzags.   a With intervening motifs.

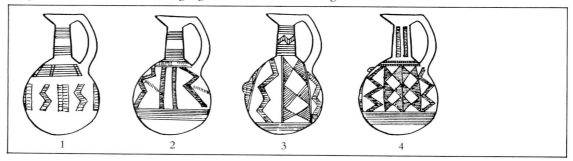

Type 11 Hatched Horizontal Diamonds.   a Central band, plain.

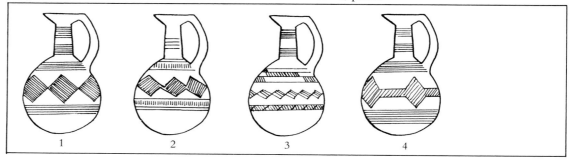

Type 11 Hatched Horizontal Diamonds.   b Central band, with in-fillers.

Type 11 Hatched Horizontal Diamonds.   c Double band, plain

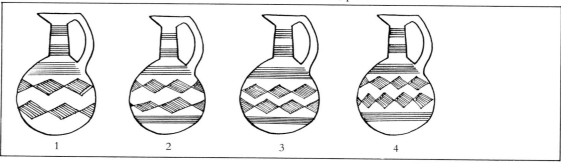

Type II Hatched Horizontal Diamonds.　d Double band, with in-fillers.

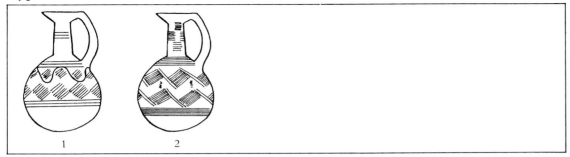

Type II Hatched Horizontal Diamonds.　e Double band, with dividing line.

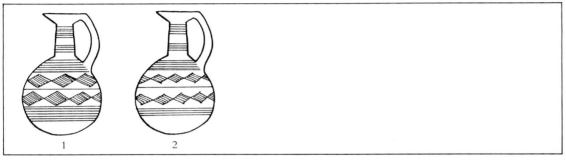

Type II Hatched Horizontal Diamonds.　f Double band, with dividing lines.

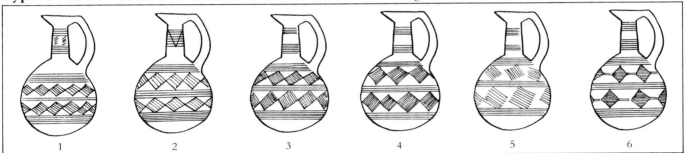

Type II Hatched Horizontal Diamonds.　g Double band, with dividing motif.

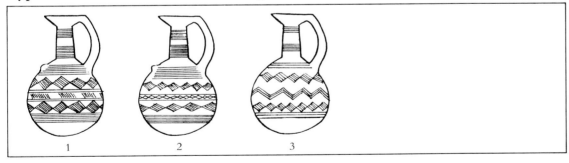

Type II Hatched Horizontal Diamonds.　h Double band, with alternating motif.

Type 11 Hatched Horizontal Diamonds.   i   Lower band, with upper motif.

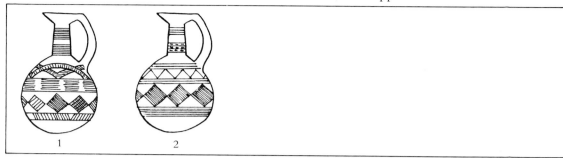

Type 11 Hatched Horizontal Diamonds.   j   Upper band, with lower motif.

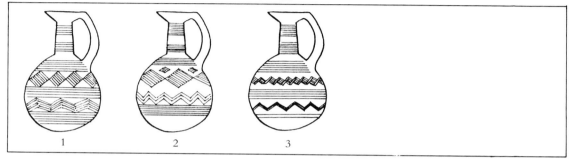

Type 12 Fragmented Horizontal Diamonds.   a   Central band, with intervening motifs.

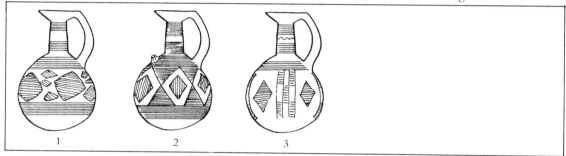

Type 13 Split Horizontal Diamonds.   a   Central band, with intervening motifs.

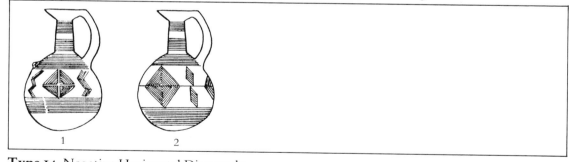

Type 14 Negative Horizontal Diamonds.
a   Central band, plain.   b   Upper band, with lower motif.

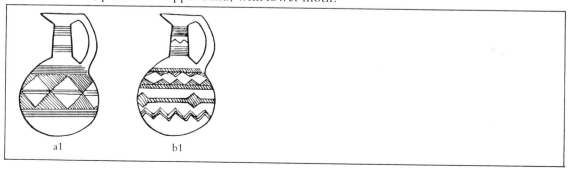

Type 15 Hatched Vertical Diamonds.   a With intervening motifs.

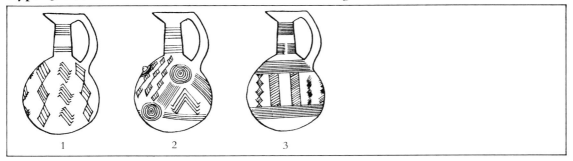

1   2   3

Type 16 Negative Vertical Diamonds.   a With intervening motifs.

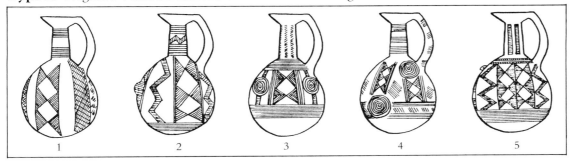

1   2   3   4   5

Type 17 Linked Concentric Circles.   a Zigzag band, with ladders.

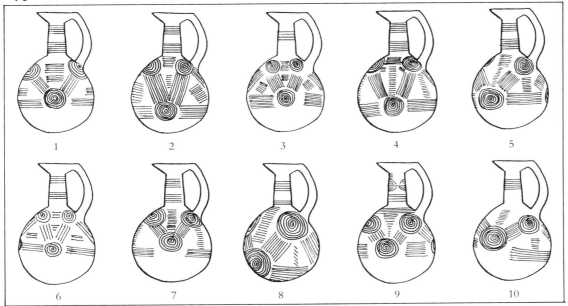

1   2   3   4   5

6   7   8   9   10

Type 17 Linked Concentric Circles.   b Zigzag band, with chevrons.

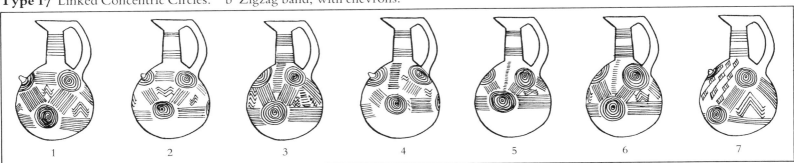

1   2   3   4   5   6   7

Type 17 Linked Concentric Circles.   c Zigzag band, with in-fillers.

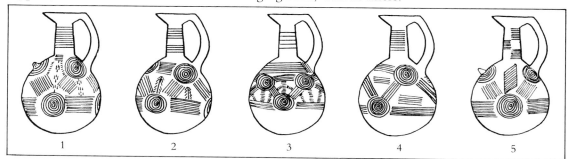

Type 18 Unlinked Concentric Circles.   a Zigzag band, with in-fillers.

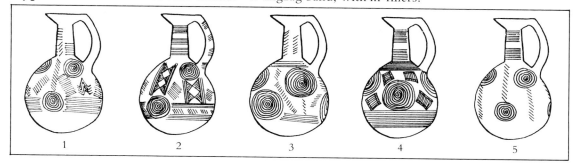

Type 18 Unlinked Concentric Circles.   b Zigzag band, with dividing lines.

Type 18 Unlinked Concentric Circles.   c Central band, plain.

Type 18 Unlinked Concentric Circles.   d Central band, with intervening motifs.

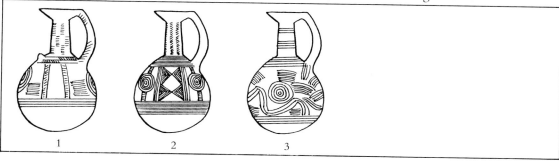

Type 18 Unlinked Concentric Circles.   e Upper band, with intervening and lower motifs.

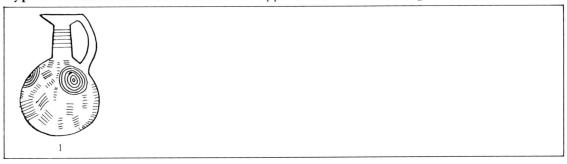

Type 19 Horizontally-Split Concentric Circles.   a With intervening motifs.

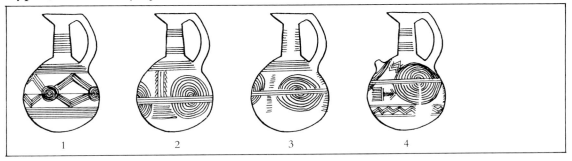

Type 20 Vertically-Split Concentric Circles.   a With intervening motifs.

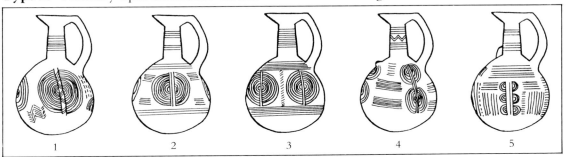

Type 21 Horizontally-Split Concentric Semi-Circles.   a Central band, with in-fillers.

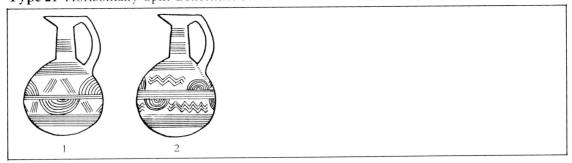

Type 21 Horizontally-Split Concentric Semi-Circles.   b Double band, with in-fillers.

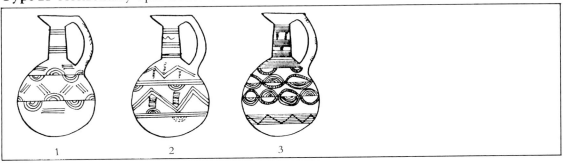

Type 22 Vertically-Split Concentric Semi-Circles.   a With in-fillers.

1

Type 23 Hatched Checker-Boards.   a Plain.

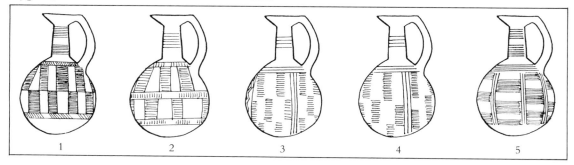

1   2   3   4   5

Type 23 Hatched Checker-Boards.   b With in-fillers.

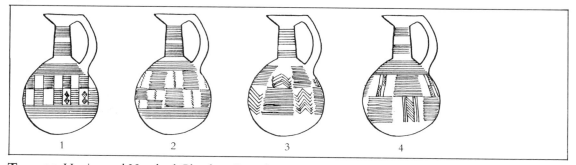

1   2   3   4

Type 24 Horizontal Hatched Checker-Boards.
a Double band, with dividing zigzag.   b Upper band, with lower motif.

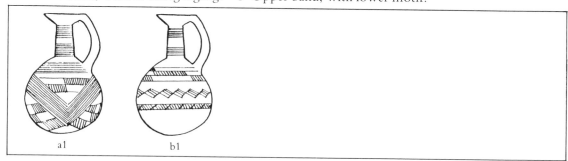

a1   b1

Type 25 Vertical Hatched Checker-Boards.   a With intervening motifs.

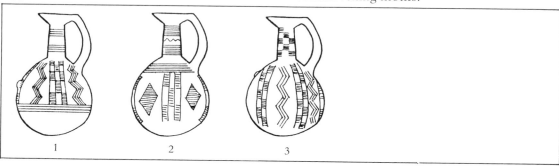

1   2   3

Type 26 Modified Hatched Checker-Boards.

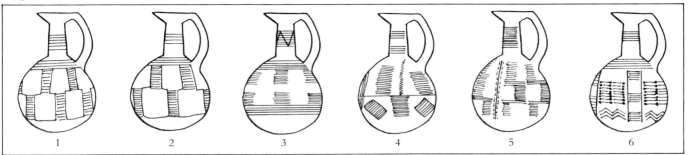

Type 27 Horizontal Bands.

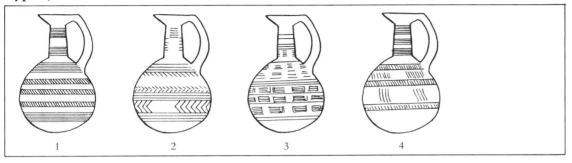

Type 28 Vertical Stripes.   a Plain.

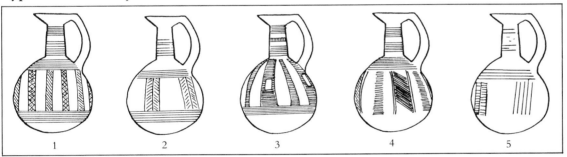

Type 28 Vertical Stripes.   b With intervening motifs.

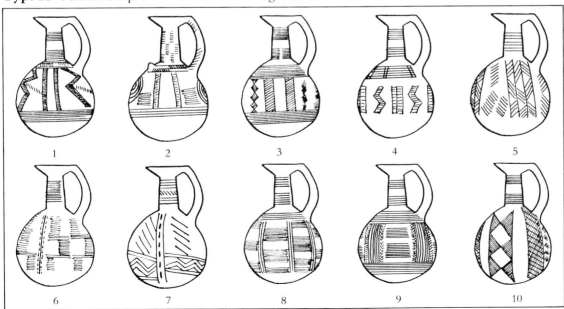

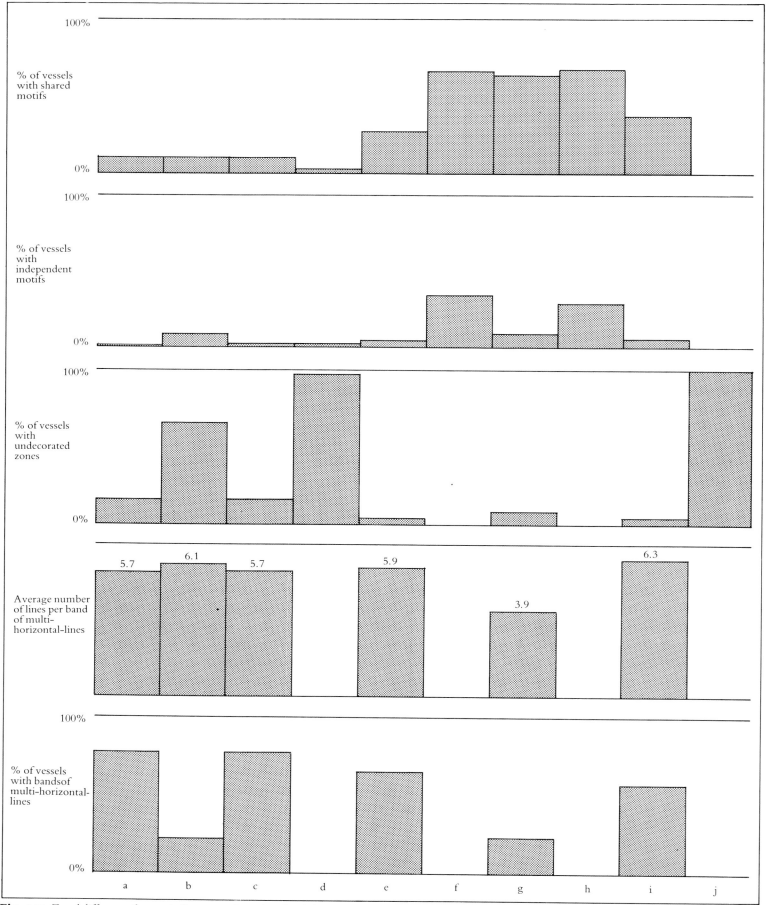

Fig. 543 *Zonal differences for certain features on Incised Red Polished gourd juglets. Based on 171 vessels (left-hand column is 'top of neck', across to right-hand column, 'base of juglet') (See Fig. 542 for zonal divisions)*

Examining the thematic variation in the incision patterns on these juglets, it is clear that certain rules are operating, both with regard to the similarities between the individual patterns and to their differences. To understand this, it helps to consider the patterns, zone by zone. The chart opposite summarizes some of the zonal features.

The histograms in this chart represent the percentages of juglets which display a particular property in a particular zone (features 1, 2, 3, and 5). Also included is a set of average figures for the number of lines per band of multi-horizontal-lines (feature 4).

The chart tells its own story, with each zone behaving in a special way, but a few additional comments may be useful.

Feature 1 A shared motif is one which spreads over more than one zone. This tendency to break through zonal barriers, to create a major display motif, is strongest in zones f, g and h. These constitute the widest part of the vessels and provide the largest 'canvas' for the major display motif. This may seem an obvious step for the artist to take, but it is not. It would be just as easy to keep the main display panel on the body of the vessels as a repetitive, uniform pattern, and to add individuality by varying small details on, say, the neck or the handle. (The use of small pot-marks on other ancient wares to establish differences between vessels falls into this second category.)

Feature 2. An independent motif is one which is restricted to a particular zone. Here, only special motifs are being considered and the simple bands of multi-horizontal-lines which act as 'borders' are omitted. When this is done, it is clear that there is a moderate tendency to split the major display area (f-g-h) into two sections (f and h) and to offer a 'double pattern', rather than a single, large one. The tendency to take this further and provide a 'triple pattern' is much weaker, as the low figure for g indicates.

Feature 3 Undecorated zones, with no incision marks, reveal the artists' recognition of the need to provide 'spacers' to highlight the motifs. A compulsive, overall coverage of the vessel surface with a network of lines quickly leads to visual indigestion, and this is avoided by keeping certain zones largely (b and d) or completely (j) free of incision lines. The principle of 'optimum heterogeneity' (see Morris, 1962) is employed with great

effect on these small juglets, where an attractive balance is achieved between the vacant boredom of a blank, undecorated surface, on the one hand, and the crowded confusion of the *horror vacui* compulsion, on the other.

Feature 4 The bands of multi-horizontal-lines employed as border framers or dividers in the overall decoration of the vessels have a characteristic width. Although examples can be found with anything from one to thirteen lines, there is a strong tendency to produce a band-width of between five and six lines (5.6 being the general average for all bands). This 'typical intensity' in band formation is a strong factor in providing juglet decoration uniformity, and in giving the vessels their characteristic identity as a group. How this typical band-width is achieved is hard to say, because there is no fixed rule about how many lines must be given to each band. The histogram (Fig. 546) on p. 341 reveals that, although there is a powerful peak in the 4-5-6 region, the tails of the histogram are far from insignificant. This suggests that the artists were not *counting* as they applied their lines, but instead were satisfying a *gestalt* image of their decorative tradition. In other words, they were aware of the 'visual melody' of their design without analysing the individual notes. To extend this analogy, they were rather like jazz musicians who, although not reading music, were able to recreate a favourite tune time and again, always varying it slightly by improvisation.

Feature 5 The frequency of appearance of the bands themselves varies greatly from zone to zone. They are common as the upper and lower *borders* of the neck and the body (zones a and c, and e and i), but also occur at moderate levels in the mid-neck and mid-body zones (b and g) as *dividers*.

Up to this point, the 171 juglets have been treated as a single group without reference to geographical distribution. Some of them have no provenance, but a total of 130 do come from known sites, as shown on the map on p. 324 (Fig. 541). If these are crudely classified as coming from the north (Ayia Irini, Lapithos, Vounous and Ayios Iakovos), central (Katydhata, Margi, Alambra, Pyla and Kalopsidha), and south (Kition, Arpera, Kalavassos and Limassol) regions of the island, then it is possible to examine the distribution of the three most popular motifs—the *zigzag*, the *diamond* and the *circle*. Expressed as percentages of their total frequency of occurrence at known sites, they are as follows:

	Zigzags	Diamonds	Circles
North	36	33	74
Central	34	33	23
South	29	33	3

It is clear from this that, although zigzags and diamonds are in widepread use, the more difficult 'concentric circles' motif is a northern speciality. It is centred on Lapithos and Vounous and can reasonably be described as a local speciality.

Looking at individual vessels, however, it is clear that very similar designs can come from very different localities. Type 5a, to take one example, shows four juglets each with a highly characteristic 'half-diamond zigzag' motif. The differences between them are restricted largely to the kind of 'in-filler' used between the zigs and the zags. It would be reasonable to suppose that they came from one locality and were the work of one group of potters, or perhaps even a single artist. Yet their distribution is as follows:

5a1 Limassol
5a2 Kition
5a3 Kalavassos
5a4 Vounous

This is far from being an exception. Pairs of vessels having very similar designs, but coming from widely separated sites, include the following:

1a4 (Kalavassos) and 1a5 (Vounous)
1j2 (Kition) and 1j3 (Ayia Irini)
8a1 (Katydhata) and 8a2 (Lapithos)
11f1 (Kalavassos) and 11f3 (Lapithos)
13a1 (Vounous) and 13a2 (Margi)
17a5 (Lapithos) and 17a8 (Margi)
19a2 (Margi) and 19a3 (Vounous)
23a1 (Kalavassos) and 23a2 (Margi)

These examples indicate either that there was a remarkably efficient island transportation and ceramic distribution system in operation in the Early Bronze Age, or that popular

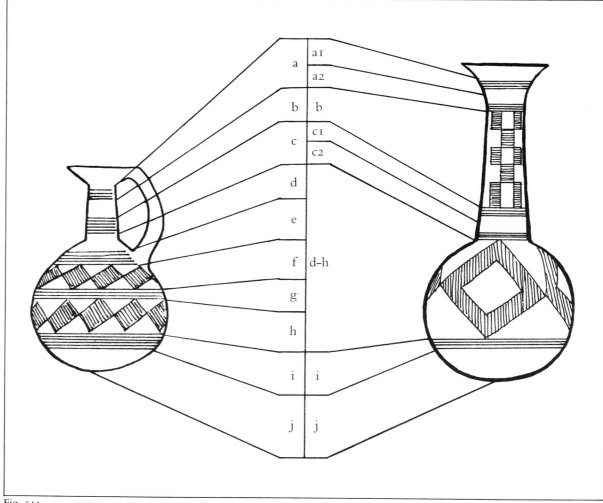

Fig. 544

motifs were so widely known that they were in use simultaneously in different parts of the island and shared by many different communities.

The second category of vessel to be examined in detail was the long-necked bottle of Karpasian Red-and-Black Polished Ware. This ware replaces the ordinary Incised Red Polished Ware in the north-eastern peninsula of Cyprus. Apart from its different coloration, it also displays a distinctive set of incision motifs. Large, complex diamond motifs appear in many forms. Circular motifs disappear completely, as do horizontal zigzags. The incised lines become finer, the hatching much denser. Although individual vessels still show much variation, the dominant themes become more heavily imposed.

Despite these differences, there are a number of similarities between the two classes of vessel. For example, both juglets and bottles display the tendency to use multi-horizontal-lines as borders of the main display panels. Fig. 544 shows examples of typical specimens of the two classes, with the zonal areas compared.

Zone a, at the top of the neck, is frequently more complex on the long-necked bottles. Because of the greater length of the neck region, this zone often becomes subdivided into two bands of horizontal lines, as shown here (a1 and a2).

Zone b, the mid-neck region, becomes a second major display panel on the long-necked bottles. On a typical panel there are four vertical motifs, usually arranged in two opposing pairs, but there are many variations of this arrangement.

Zone c, the bottom of the neck, is treated in a similar way to zone a.

Zone d to h, is treated as a single, major display panel on the body of the bottle. It is never subdivided horizontally into zones, as is the case on the Red Polished juglets. This region is usually decorated with four large, diamond-shaped motifs, but again there are many variations. The number of motifs varies from three to as many as eight on a single vessel, and in-fillers are common.

Zone i, the lower border of the display area, is treated in the same way in both juglets and bottles. It always shows a horizontal band, usually of horizontal lines, but sometimes with hatching.

Zone j, the base of the vessel, is left undec-

Fig. 545 *Comparison between the heights of Incised Red Polished gourd juglets and Incised Red-and-Black Polished long-necked bottles, showing that although there is considerable variation, the artists in both cases were working to a 'norm', revealed here as two distinct peaks.*

Fig. 546 *Comparison between the band-widths on Incised Red Polished gourd juglets and Incised Red-and-Black Polished long-necked bottles, showing that, although the bottles are taller, the artists decorating them favour narrower bands. They also adhere more closely to their 'norm' than do the juglet artists. Based on 171 juglets and 100 bottles.*

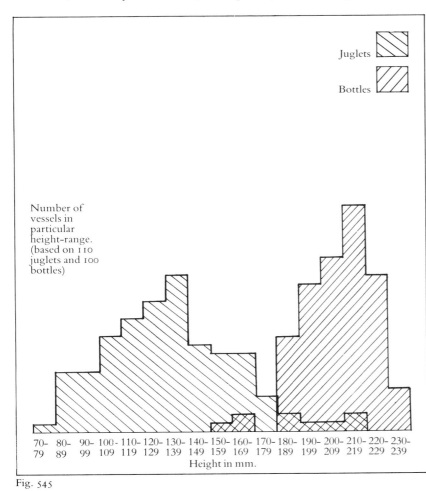

Juglets

Bottles

Number of vessels in particular height-range. (based on 110 juglets and 100 bottles)

70-79   80-89   90-99   100-109   110-119   120-129   130-139   140-149   150-159   160-169   170-179   180-189   190-199   200-209   210-219   220-229   230-239
Height in mm.

1   2   3   4   5   6   7   8   9   10   11   12   13
Number of lines per band of multi-horizontal-lines.

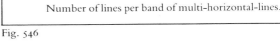

Fig. 545

Fig. 546

orated in 99 out of the 100 complete bottles in the author's collection. In the exception, there is a pair of crossed linear zigzags.

In many respects the incision patterns on the long-necked bottles are of a finer quality than those on the juglets. The lines are more carefully executed and the hatching is often meticulous. Hatching can be graded by measuring the number of lines per centimetre in a number of incised patches and then taking averages. The juglets show an average of approximately five lines of hatching per centimetre. The long-necked bottles give figures ranging from 8 to 13 per centimetre. In other words, the bottle hatching is roughly twice as dense as the juglet hatching. This means that much longer was taken over the decoration of the bottles and that more precision and skill were employed.

Because the bottles are taller than the juglets (see Fig. 545), it might be expected that the artists would adapt to this greater area by increasing the size of the bands of multi-horizontal lines. In fact the reverse is the case (see Fig. 546). The number of lines per band is smaller in the bottles. Also, the variation in band-width is much lower. The bottle decorators have a tighter control over their designs. They are not simply enlarging Red Polished Ware styles to fit their taller vessels.

Thematic variation is put to a severe test on these bottles because the range of main motifs employed is so restricted. There are only six of them:

1 HORIZONTAL BANDS which appear on 100% of the bottles, a total of 442 times on the sample of 100.

2 CHECKS on 85%, a total of 190 times.

3 DIAMONDS on 99%, a total of 398 times.

4 'FIR-TREE MOTIFS' on 9%, a total of 16 times.

5 VERTICAL ZIGZAGS on 87%, a total of 309 times.

6 RECTANGLES on 1%, a total of 1 time.

With this self-imposed, highly conservative repertoire, the artists then proceed to make visual music. They do this by (a) developing variants of each of the main motifs; (b) combining these variants in many different ways; and (c) adding small 'in-fillers', in the shape of tiny zigzags, short slopes, horizontal and vertical dashes and dots, and little areas of hatching.

The number of distinctive variants for each main motif is as follows: Horizontal Bands: 3; Checks: 5; Diamonds: 16; 'Fir-Tree' mo-

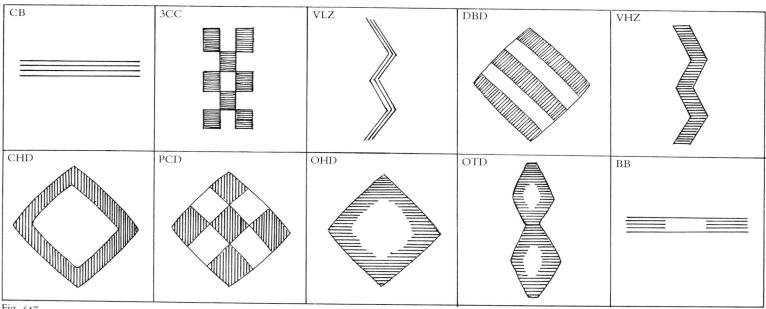

Fig. 547

Key: CB = Continuous Bands (of Multi-Horizontal-Lines)
       3CC = Three-column Closed Checks
       VLZ = Vertical Linear Zigzag
       DBD = Diagonally Banded Diamonds
       VHZ = Vertical Hatched Zigzags
       CHD = Closed Hatched Diamonds
       PCD = Plain Check Diamonds
       OHD = Open Hatched Diamonds
       OTD = Open Tiered Diamonds
        BB = Broken Bands (of Multi-Horizontal-Lines)

Ten
Main
Motifs

CB

3CC

VLZ

DBD

VHZ

CHD

PCD

OHD

OTD

BB

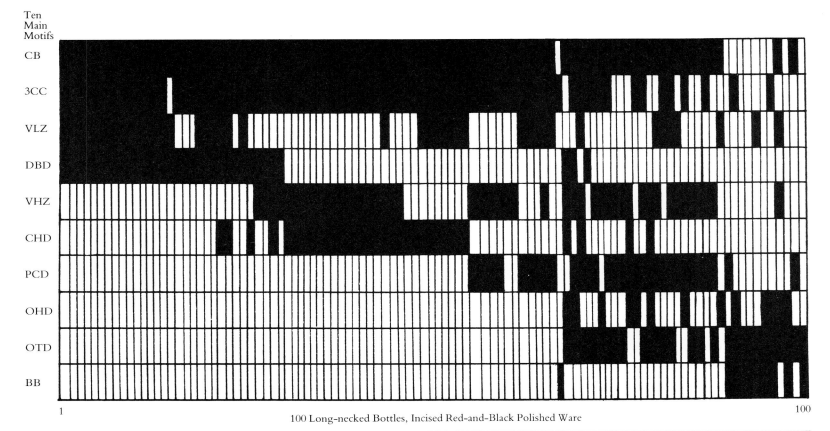

1　　　　　　　　　　　　　　　　　　　　　　　　　　　　　　　　　　　　　　　100

100 Long-necked Bottles, Incised Red-and-Black Polished Ware

Fig. 548

tifs: 5; Vertical Zigzags: 8; Rectangles: 1.

Of these variants, ten are popular enough to appear on ten per cent or more of the 100 bottles studied. These ten are shown in Fig. 547. If individual vessels are examined, it emerges that these 10 popular elements are found in forty different combinations. The details of this analysis are shown in the chart in Fig. 548. The 100 vertical 'slices' in this diagram represent the 100 bottles. The ten bands represent the ten motif-variants. Black rectangles show where the particular motif-variants are present on particular vessels.

A study of this diagram reveals, not only the way in which the different visual 'chords' are played by the artists by combining different 'notes', but also that each element has an *incompatibility factor* in relation to every other element. These vary greatly from high compatibility, where two elements nearly always occur together on vessels, to total incompatibility, where they never do so. It is possible to measure these differences in 'motif co-existence', and when this is done, two conclusions emerge.

First, it is clear that these ten motifs are liberally mixed. Total incompatiblity is extremely rare. In other words, the decorative themes are largely communal and traditional rather than private and personal. Assuming that these bottles were produced by a group of artists, then they all share in the main motifs, instead of different individuals having their own separate ones.

Second, it is clear from the various ways in which the motifs are combined, with considerable differences in degrees of incompatibility, that personal preferences *are* at work in the way the elements are assembled into the overall decorative pattern of each individual vessel.

A further personal touch is added by the use of certain idiosyncratic in-fillers, but the most useful method of detecting the work of individual artists is by their motif 'calligraphy'. Herscher (1973) has already touched on this in her initial study of this Red-and-Black Polished Ware, but she was severely limited in scope by the fact that, at that time, she was only able to assemble a total of twenty-two pieces. Even so, she was able to identify three individual potters, whom she labelled A, B and C. With the 100 bottles of this ware available for analysis, side by side, it has now been possible to extend her list of three. Space does not permit the inclusion of all 100 bottles, arranged artist by artist, but a large enough sample of them can be given to illustrate the way in which it is possible to distinguish specific prehistoric artists whose work was completed several millennia ago.

Identifiable artists are as follows:

Pl. 304 The Fine Line Artist. Style A. *The most accomplished and prolific of all the Red-and-Black Polished artists (= Herscher, Artist A). Always shows meticulous line control and very fine hatching. The major patterns rigidly standardized. Always five horizontal bands, each* triple-lined, four on neck and one on body. On neck, eight-unit checks alternating with triple-lined linear zigzags. On body, three large, banded diamonds, with the bands sloping top left to bottom right. The diamond hatching lines slope top right to bottom left. All hatchings *enclosed by borders. The only pattern variations, from vessel to vessel, are in the small in-fillers on the body. These variations are summarized in Fig. 549, below. There are 14 examples in the collection of 100 complete bottles, of which four are shown here.*

Left to right
a *Ht. 19.4 cm (DM-RBP-18).*
b *Ht. 21.4 cm (DM-RBP-21).*
c *Ht. 21.2 cm (DM-RBP-20).*
d *Ht. 21.6 cm (DM-RBP-13).*

Bottle No. DM-RBP-11   DM-RBP-13, DM-RBP-14   DM-RBP-12, DM-RBP-20   DM-RBP-15

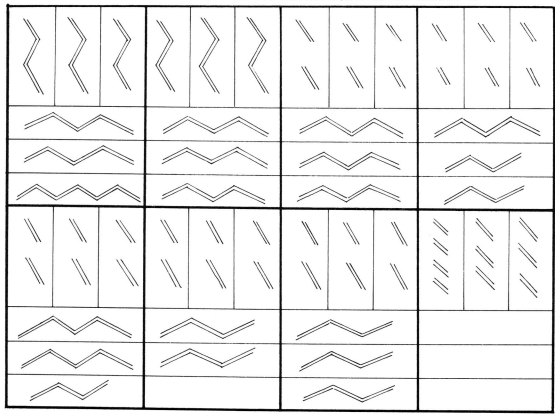

Fig. 549 *In-filler motifs on 14 otherwise identically decorated long-necked bottles, in Incised Red-and-Black Polished Ware, by the 'Fine-line Artist'. The main display panels show the same motifs in each case, but the vessels carry carefully differentiated in-fillers between the large diamond motifs on their bodies. It is as if they are being 'labelled' in batches.*

DM-RBP-16, DM-RBP-19   DM-RBP-17   DM-RBP-18, DM-RBP-23   DM-RBP-21
DM-RBP-22, DM-RBP-24

Pl. 305

Pl. 306

Pl. 305 The Fine Line Artist. Style B. *This variant differs from Style A in the following details: The horizontal bands and the linear zigzags are all quadruple-lined. On the body there are four large, closed-border diamonds, with vertical hatching lines. In-fillers are rare.*

Left to right
a *Ht. 18.4 cm (DM-RBP-63).*
b *Ht. 18.2 cm (DM-RBP-60).*
c *Ht. 18.1 cm (DM-RBP-61).*
d *Ht. 19.7 cm (DM-RBP-62).*

Pl. 306 The Fine Line Artist. Style C. *This variant has vertical zigzags on the neck which are hatched instead of linear. The horizontal bands, of which there may be four or five, are quadruple-lined. On the body, there may be either four banded diamonds or four closed-border diamonds, or two-and-two. Body in-fillers are absent.*

Left to right
a *Ht. 20.3 cm (DM-RBP-38).*
b *Ht. 20.1 cm (DM-RBP-45).*
c *Ht. 20.2 cm (DM-RBP-39).*
d *Ht. 18.8 cm (DM-RBP-37).*

Pl. 307 The Fine Line Mimic Artist. *This artist copies the patterns of the Fine Line Artist, but with less meticulous control. For example, the number of hatching lines per centimetre is between 11 and 14, compared with 15 to 20 in the case of the Fine Line Artist. Another difference is that this artist only uses*

three horizontal bands, one on the body and one at the top and bottom of the neck. These bands are always triple-lined. The vertical zigzags on the necks are usually hatched but may also be linear. The body always has four large, closed-border diamonds, with vertical hatching. There may be zigzag in-fillers on the body, but

these differ in detail from those of the Fine Line Artist.

Left to right
a *Ht. 20.3 cm (DM-RBP-10).*
b *Ht. 21.2 cm (DM-RBP-54).*
c *Ht. 21.4 cm (DM-RBP-43).*
d *Ht. 21 cm (DM-RBP-53).*
Note: It is possible that these bottles represent the work of the Fine Line

Artist at a time when her skill was below par.

Pl. 308 The Skew Hatch Artist. *This artist is closely related to the previous one, but has a highly distinctive idiosyncrasy: the hatching of the closed-border diamonds is*

vertical on the left-hand side of each diamond and then changes to horizontal on the right-hand side. This occurs whether the border is thick (see the two bottles on the left) or thin

(see the two bottles on the right).
Left to right
a *Ht. of surviving part: 15.9 cm (DM-RBP-112).*
b *Ht. 16.9 cm (DM-RBP-41).*

c *Ht. 19.9 cm (DM-RBP-44).*
d *Ht. 20.8 cm (DM-RBP-46).*

**Pl. 309 The Horizontal Hatch
Artist.** *This artist is similar to the
previous one, but employs a characteristic horizontal hatching inside the
closed-border diamonds (= Herscher,
Artist B). Also, the incisions are
heavier and cruder. Small 'joiners' of
multi-horizontal dashes are used to
connect the large motifs on the body.*
a(left) *Ht. 19.4 cm
(DM-RBP-56).*
b(right) *Ht. 20 cm
(DM-RBP-55).*
*A third example of this artist's
work is shown in Herscher, 1973
Pl. IV,9.*

**Pl. 310 The Broken Check
Artist.** *The diagnostic feature here
is found in the check pattern on the
necks, where the vertical lines of the
pattern are broken up and do not flow
continuously from the top of the
design to the bottom. Other characteristics include a heavy, bold incision
style; no more than three horizontal
bands; hatched zigzags alternating
with the checks; four closed-border
diamonds on the body, with vertical
hatching; and thick, tubular necks.*
Left to right
a *Ht. 20.4 cm (DM-RBP-49).*
b *Ht. 20.3 cm (DM-RBP-51).*
c *Ht. 19.9 cm (DM-RBP-50).*
d *Ht. 20 cm (DM-RBP-52).*
*Herscher calls this Artist B, lumping
her with the previous one.*

Pl. 309

Pl. 310

Pl. 311

Pl. 312

Pl. 311 The Narrow Check Artist. *The central column of the check pattern on the neck is extremely narrow. In addition, the check diamonds on the body possess short zigzags inside the hatched areas.*
a(left) *Ht. 21.2 cm (DM-RBP-70).*
b(right) *Ht. 22.2 cm (DM-RBP-69).*

Pl. 312 The Crude Hatch Artist. *The diagnostic feature of this artist's work is the carelessness of the hatched lines. Inside the closed-border diamonds, the direction of the hatching switches clumsily at the top of the motif, and the incision work in general demonstrates a looseness and lack of control unusual for this ware. The vessels themselves are unusually small, almost as if they are the work of a child or a beginner.*
a(left) *Ht. 16.8 cm (DM-RBP-59).*
b(right) *Ht. 15.8 cm (DM-RBP-58).*

Pl. 313 The Open Zigzag Artist. *The signature of this artist consists of hatched zigzag in-fillers which uniquely lack any borders (= Herscher, Artist C). Other features include five horizontal bands—four on the neck and one on the body. Hatched diamonds have inner borders open and sharp upper and lower points to the outer border.*
Left to right
a *Ht. 22.2 cm (DM-RBP-78).*
b *Ht. 21.7 cm (DM-RBP-82).*
c *Ht. 23.2 cm (DM-RBP-80).*
d *Ht. 19 cm (DM-RBP-83).*

Pl. 314 The Branched Zigzag Artist. *This artist shows the same details as the last one, but with one important difference. In place of the open hatched zigzags, there are in-fillers of a unique kind. They hang like small branches from the corners of the vertical zigzags on the body. Each small branch consists of a single diagonal line attached to the large zigzag, with short, open-hatched lines at its distal end. This may be no more than a variant of the last type, and the Open Zigzag and Branched Zigzag artists may be one and the same.*
Left to right
a *Ht. 20.3 cm (DM-RBP-94).*
b *Ht. 23.5 cm (DM-RBP-96).*
c *Ht. 23 cm (DM-RBP-97).*
d *Ht. 22.2 cm (DM-RBP-95).*

Pl. 313

Pl. 314

Pl. 315

Pl. 315 The Fine Fir-tree Artist. *Several artists include a neck motif with an accidental (?) resemblance to a fir-tree, but only this one incises the pattern with fine-line precision. Other features include: three banded diamonds on the body, with hatching lines applied in the vertical plane; check motifs on neck, with five units instead of the usual eight; five horizontal bands, four on neck and one on body.*
a(left) *Ht. 22.1 cm (DM-RBP-28).*
b (right)*Ht. 19.7 cm (DM-RBP-27).*
Herscher lumps this one with Artist A because of the fine lines.

Pl. 316 The Big Body Artist. *This artist employs a highly distinctive vessel-shape, using a bulbous body that is both wider and taller than usual in relation to the neck. Here the height of the neck for example, is little greater than the height of the body, whereas with other artists the neck is normally about 1½ times the height of the body. The check motifs on the neck have five units rather than eight. On the body, check diamonds alternate with long, linear zigzags. These zigzags are highly characteristic of this artist, having a large number of zigs and zags for their length. Also, the angles between the zigs and zags tend to be inconsistent.*
Left to right
a *Ht. 21.3 cm (DM-RBP-91).*
b *Ht. 19.1 cm (DM-RBP-75).*
c *Ht. 22.4 cm (DM-RBP-90).*
d *Ht. 21.2 cm (DM-RBP-92).*

Pl. 316

Pl. 317 The Tiered Diamond Artist. Style A. *This artist has a distinctive calligraphic quality, the lines being heavily and boldly incised. There are two styles. In both, the characteristic element is the blunt-* *ended hatched diamond, with an open inner border. These diamonds are placed one on top of the other, in tiers. The horizontal bands are thick, with six to seven lines, and they are broken into segments instead of run-* *ning continuously around the vessels. In Style A, there are horizontal bands at the base of the neck which act as lower borders to the tiered neck-diamonds.*

Left to right
a *Ht. 18.4 cm (DM-RBP-101).*
b *Ht. 19.5 cm (DM-RBP-106).*
c *Ht. 20.6 cm (DM-RBP-109).*
d *Ht. 20.1 cm (DM-RBP-107.*

Pl. 318 The Tiered Diamond Artist. Style B. *The same as Style A with one important exception, namely, that the tiered diamonds run down the neck and onto the body without the usual borderline* *division at the base of the neck. This spilling over of a neck motif onto the body is found hardly anywhere else in this class of vessels. The most common 'tier' in Style B consists of three diamonds, two on the neck and* *one on the body, but in a single exceptional case the motif runs riot and displays six tiered diamonds, four on the neck and two on the body (DM-RBP-100).*

Left to right
a *Ht. 21 cm (DM-RBP-110).*
b *Ht. 21.2 cm (DM-RBP-104).*
c *Ht. 21.9 cm (DM-RBP-100).*
d *Ht. 18.4 cm (DM-RBP-102.*

Pl. 319

Pl. 320

Pl. 321

Pl. 322

Pl. 319 The Closed Double-Diamond Artist. *This artist is known from a single vessel only, but the calligraphy is distinctive enough to allocate it to a separate category of its own. On the neck are two pairs of closed-border hatched diamonds. Interspaced between them are a five-unit check pattern and a vertical linear zigzag. There are five horizontal, triple-line bands, four on the neck and one on the body, also three banded diamonds, crudely shaped, on the body. Of particular interest is a unique motif which looks like a formalized human 'match-stick' figure, with arms and legs held apart. Ht. 21.9 cm (DM-RBP-31).*

Pl. 320 The Open Check Artist. *Again, this artist is known from a single, but highly distinctive vessel. The hatched check pattern on the neck is unique among these bottles in having no borders. The five horizontal bands are unusually thick, as is the vertical linear zigzag motif on the neck. On the body, two blunt-ended hatched diamonds, similar to those used by the Tiered Diamond Artist, alternate with two diamonds which contain diagonal-cross patterns. The most unusual aspect of this vessel is its contour. The body is unusually flattened in the vertical plane, to the extent that the bottle will stand up without support on a flat surface. Also, there is no defined angle between the base of the neck and the top of the body. The neck flows out into the body in a smoothly curved line. Ht. 21.7 cm (DM-RBP-99).*

Pl. 321 The Bilateral Diamond Artist. *The complex diamond favoured by this artist contains hatched bands in the shape of inverted Vs. In addition, there is a central vertical element inside the diamond. The neck design is also strange, stopping unusually short of the top of the neck, with a horizontal band containing broken hatching. Only two vessels by this artist are known, the complete one shown here and a fragmentary one with body only. Ht. 20.5 cm (DM-RBP-66).*

Pl. 322 The Basal Zigzag Artist. *Of all the long-necked bottles known from this ware, this is the only one with an incised motif on the base. It consists of crossed, linear zigzags, each double-lined. Other motifs include eight-unit checks on the neck alternating with fir-tree patterns; four horizontal bands; on the body, four banded diamonds; and several short zigzag in-fillers. Ht. 22.1 cm (DM-RBP-34).*

Check-list of the Author's Collection

This check-list is arranged in wares, for convenience, since the objects illustrated photographically in the book are thematically organized. Without this list it would be difficult to trace, for example, all the Base Ring Ware pieces included in this study, because some would appear under 'wares', some under 'shapes' and others under 'representations'.

Each entry below gives the reference number for the object concerned (DM for Desmond Morris Collection; initials to indicate the ware of the piece; and a number). These same numbers are used in the captions throughout the book. There then follows a brief description of the object and its major dimension in centimetres. This dimension is always the height, except for bowls and dishes, where the diameter is given, and boxes and certain figurines, where the length is given (signified by L). When measuring heights, the maximum figure is shown. If, for instance, a handle rises higher than the body of a vessel, then the height to the top of the handle is given. With diameters of bowls and dishes, the figure shown is for the outer edges of the rim.

When an object is illustrated in the book, the Plate number and page number are provided.

In several instances, large numbers of almost identical vessels have been collected, as part of a study of Thematic Variation of decoration motifs. In such cases, the vessels are recorded in groups to avoid endless entry-repetitions.

Where handles are referred to as vertical or horizontal, this relates to the plane of the points of attachment.

1a Philia Red Polished Ware

	Maximum dimension (cm)	Plate number	Page number
DM-PHRP-01 Jug, flat base, beak spout, incised	19.5	8b	18
DM-PHRP-02 Bottle, round base, incised	10.9	8c	18
DM-PHRP-03 Bottle, flat base, plain	12.3	8a	18

1b Plain Red Polished Ware

	Maximum dimension (cm)	Plate number	Page number
DM-PRP-01 Jug, round base, round spout	40.3	44b	50
DM-PRP-02 Jug, round base, round spout	12.6	9a	18
DM-PRP-03 Jug, round base, squat neck, side spout	7.2		
DM-PRP-04 Jug, round base, cutaway-beak spout	36.1	64c	56
DM-PRP-05 Jug, round base, cutaway-beak spout	25.5	65b	56
DM-PRP-06 Jug, round base, cutaway spout	17.8	9e	18
DM-PRP-07 Jug, nipple base, cutaway spout	26.5	78a	60
DM-PRP-08 Jug, nipple base, cutaway spout	32		
DM-PRP-09 Jug, nipple base, cutaway spout	28.1	78b	60
DM-PRP-10 Jug, nipple base, cutaway spout	37.1	78c	60
DM-PRP-11 Jug, nipple base, cutaway spout	24.4	78d	60
DM-PRP-12 Jug, nipple base, cutaway spout	27.5	9c	18
DM-PRP-13 Jar, round base	11.6		
DM-PRP-14 Jar, nipple base	63.5	106	68
DM-PRP-15 Jar, tripod base	13	9d	18
DM-PRP-16 Jar, tripod base	16.5		
DM-PRP-17 Bowl, round base, one lug	9.6		
DM-PRP-18 Bowl, round base, one lug	7.7		
DM-PRP-19 Bowl, round base, one lug	8.3		
DM-PRP-20 Bowl, round base, one lug	8.8		
DM-PRP-21 Bowl, round base, one lug	13.4		
DM-PRP-22 Bowl, round base, two lugs	9.5		
DM-PRP-23 Bowl, round base, two lugs	18.2		
DM-PRP-24 Bowl, round base, two lugs	10.9		
DM-PRP-25 Bowl, round base, two lugs	9.1		
DM-PRP-26 Bowl, round base, three lugs	37.2		
DM-PRP-27 Bowl, round base, four lugs	8.9		
DM-PRP-28 Bowl, round base, trough spout, one lug	45.7		
DM-PRP-29 Bowl, round base, trough spout, one lug	10.8	9b	18
DM-PRP-30 Bowl, round base, trough spout, one lug	16.1		
DM-PRP-31 Bowl, round base, horizontal handle	13.7		
DM-PRP-32 Bowl, round base, horizontal handle	13.5		
DM-PRP-33 Bowl, round base, horizontal handle	6.9		
DM-PRP-34 Bowl, flat base, one lug	11.2	123	72
DM-PRP-35 Bowl, flat base, round spout, one lug	37		
DM-PRP-36 Dipper	9.4		
DM-PRP-37 Twin-bowl vessel, round spouts, loop handle	12.4	164	101
DM-PRP-38 Nine-bowl vessel, lugs, central handle	25.1	163	101
DM-PRP-39 Vessel-attached bull figures, bowl, stem base	30	219	190

Note: 'Plain' vessels may have minor incisions on handles or legs.

1c Incised Red Polished Ware

	Maximum dimension (cm)	Plate number	Page number
DM-IRP-01-34 Jugs, round base, round spout ('gourd juglets')	7.4–17.3	176e	141
DM-IRP-35 Jug, round base, round spout	12.6		

	Maximum dimension (cm)	Plate number	Page number
DM-IRP-36 Jug, round base, round spout	11.8	46b	50
DM-IRP-37 Jug, round base, round spout, wide neck	13.5	55a	53
DM-IRP-38 Jug, round base, round spout, squat neck	12	56c	53
DM-IRP-39 Jug, round base, round spout, squat neck	7.4	56b	53
DM-IRP-40 Jug, round base, beak spout	28	60	55
DM-IRP-41 Jug, round base, beak spout	12.1	61a	55
DM-IRP-42 Jug, round base, beak spout	11	61b	55
DM-IRP-43 Jug, round base, cutaway-beak spout	14.1	65a	56
DM-IRP-44 Jug, round base, cutaway-beak spout	17.5	65c	56
DM-IRP-45 Jug, round base, cutaway-beak spout	28.6	63c	55
DM-IRP-46 Jug, round base, cutaway-beak spout, side spout	25.2	67	57
DM-IRP-47 Jug, round base, cutaway spout	15.1	69	57
DM-IRP-48 Jug, round base, cutaway spout	29.3	68	57
DM-IRP-49 Jug, flat base, cutaway-beak spout, side spout	30.5	10a	19
DM-IRP-50 Jug, tripod base, cutaway-beak spout	14.5	10e	19
DM-IRP-51 Bottle, round base, one lug	4.8	10d	19
DM-IRP-52 Bottle, flat base, two lugs	10	97a	65
DM-IRP-53 Jar, round base, vertical handles	26.3	101a	67
DM-IRP-54 Jar, round base, vertical handles	22	102a	67
DM-IRP-55 Jar, round base, vertical handles	27.3	102b	67
DM-IRP-56 Jar, flat base, vertical handles	32.1	10c	19
DM-IRP-57 Bowl, round base, one lug	9	10b	19
DM-IRP-58 Bowl, round base, one lug	10.7		
DM-IRP-59 Bowl, round base, one lug	11.5		
DM-IRP-60 Bowl, round base, one lug	12.9		
DM-IRP-61 Bowl, round base, four lugs	18.5	117a	70
DM-IRP-62 Bowl, round base, four lugs	14.5		
DM-IRP-63 Bowl, round base, two trough spouts, two lugs	19.8		
DM-IRP-64 Bowl, round base, two vertical handles	18.4	122	71
DM-IRP-65 Bowl, stem base, four lugs	9	129	73
DM-IRP-66 Box, egg-shaped, two lugs	L24.2	139	75
DM-IRP-67 Box, egg-shaped, horizontal handle	L15.1	140	75
DM-IRP-68 Box, egg-shaped, two lugs, figures attached	32.7	141	75
DM-IRP-69 Box-lid, rectangular	12.9	141	75
DM-IRP-70 Box-lid, oval	18.6	143	75
DM-IRP-71 Box-lid, rectangular-oval	12.5	142	75
DM-IRP-72 Dipper	38.5	144a	76
DM-IRP-73 Twin-bodied jug (vertical), cutaway spout	27.3	158b	99
DM-IRP-74 Twin-bodied jug (vertical), cutaway spout	28.6	158a	99
DM-IRP-75 Four-bodied jug (pyramid), cutaway spout	24	159a	99
DM-IRP-76 Four-bowl vessel, central handle	31.5	167a	103
DM-IRP-77 Four-bowl vessel, central handle	32.2	166	102
DM-IRP-78 Handle from four-bowl vessel	21.4	167b	103
DM-IRP-79 Human plank figure, shoulder figure	20.3	177	146
DM-IRP-80 Human plank figure, shoulder figure	12.5	179	147
DM-IRP-81 Human plank figure, shoulder figure	10	178	147
DM-IRP-82 Human plank figure, slab figure	6.9	182b	150
DM-IRP-83 Human plank figure, slab figure	18.8	181a	150
DM-IRP-84 Human plank figure, slab figure	19.4	181b	150
DM-IRP-85 Human plank figure, slab figure	17.6	181c	150
DM-IRP-86 Human plank figure, slab figure	4.4	182a	150

	Maximum dimension (cm)	Plate number	Page number
DM-IRP-87 Vessel-attached human figure, jug	21.2	183a	151
DM-IRP-88 Vessel-attached human figure, jug	18.5	183b	151
DM-IRP-89 Vessel-shaped human head, tulip bowl	10	188a	159
DM-IRP-90 Deer figure from large vessel	9.6	216b	186
DM-IRP-91 Deer figure from large vessel	5.7	216a	186
DM-IRP-92 Bull figure	L 11.6	221	192
DM-IRP-93 Vessel-shaped bull figure, jug	24	220	191
DM-IRP-94 Bird figure from large vessel	L 8.3	248a	222
DM-IRP-95 Bird figure from large vessel	L 8.2	248b	222
DM-IRP-96 Vessel-attached bird figure, jug	21.6	252	224
DM-IRP-97 Vessel-attached bird figures, tulip bowl	17.4	251	223
DM-IRP-98 Vessel imitating leather bag	30.8	284a	258
DM-IRP-99 Spindle whorl	4.9		
DM-IRP-100 Spindle whorl	4.1		
DM-IRP-101 Horn	10.2	287	263

1d Relief-Decorated Red Polished Ware

	Maximum dimension (cm)	Plate number	Page number
DM-RRP-01 Jug, round base, round spout	36.3	261	230
DM-RRP-02 Jug, round base, round spout	38.3	44a	50
DM-RRP-03 Jug, round base, round spout	18.4	45b	50
DM-RRP-04 Jug, round base, round spout	52.1	262	231
DM-RRP-05 Jug, round base, round spout, side spout	19.8	53	53
DM-RRP-06 Jug, round base, cutaway-beak spout	44.4	64b	56
DM-RRP-07 Jug, round base, cutaway-beak spout	33	63b	55
DM-RRP-08 Jug, round base, cutaway-beak spout	27	11a	19
DM-RRP-09 Jug, round base, cutaway-beak spout	37.2	64a	56
DM-RRP-10 Jug, round base, cutaway-beak spout	28.1	63a	55
DM-RRP-11 Jug, pointed base, cutaway-beak spout	41.8	76	60
DM-RRP-12 Jug, nipple base, beak spout	29.3	77	60
DM-RRP-13 Jug, nipple base, cutaway-beak spout	28	11c	19
DM-RRP-14 Bottle, round base, round spout	16.2	93a	65
DM-RRP-15 Jar, round base, vertical handles	29.3	101b	67
DM-RRP-16 Bowl, round base, four lugs	34.3	11b	19
DM-RRP-17 Bowl, round base, round spout, handle	30.5		
DM-RRP-18 Vessel-attached human figure, jug	51	187	158
DM-RRP-19 Scenic composition, perimeter figures, bowl	37.5	292-302	270-1

2 Mottled Red Polished Ware

	Maximum dimension (cm)	Plate number	Page number
DM-MRP-01 Jug, round base, round spout	34.2	45a	50
DM-MRP-02 Jug, round base, round spout	16	46c	50
DM-MRP-03 Jug, round base, round spout	14.4	46a	50
DM-MRP-04 Jug, round base, round spout, squat neck	11.8	56a	53
DM-MRP-05 Jug, round base, squat neck, side spout	13.5	57a	54
DM-MRP-06 Jug, round base, squat neck, side spout	11.5	57b	54
DM-MRP-07 Jug, round base, squat neck, side spout	14.1	12c	22
DM-MRP-08 Jug, pointed base, cutaway-beak spout	18.2	12d	22
DM-MRP-09 Bottle, round base, two handles, two lugs	15.1	93c	65
DM-MRP-10 Bowl, round base, one lug	15.3	115a	70
DM-MRP-11 Bowl, round base, one lug	10.2		
DM-MRP-12 Bowl, round base, one lug	9.7	12b	22
DM-MRP-13 Bowl, round base, one lug	82		
DM-MRP-14 Bowl, round base, four lugs	14		
DM-MRP-15 Bowl, round base, four lugs	18.7	117b	70
DM-MRP-16 Bowl, round base, four lugs	18.4		
DM-MRP-17 Bowl, round base, trough spout, three lugs	16.8		
DM-MRP-18 Bowl, round base, horizontal handle	16.8		
DM-MRP-19 Bowl, round base, horizontal handle	16.5		
DM-MRP-20 Bowl, flat base, one lug	13.6	12a	22
DM-MRP-21 Bowl, flat base, trough spout, one lug	30.6		
DM-MRP-22 Bowl, stem base, four lugs	16.2	12e	22
DM-MRP-23 Bowl, stem base, two handles	10.3	131	73
DM-MRP-24 Bowl, tripod-stem base, two lugs	14.3	133	73
DM-MRP-25 Dipper	25	144b	76
DM-MRP-26 Twin-necked jug, round base, round spouts	23	154	96
DM-MRP-27 Four-bowl vessel, stem-tripod base	25.4	165	101
DM-MRP-28 Subsidiary-unit vessel, bottle, one bowl, one jug	48.1	172	111
DM-MRP-29 Vessel-attached human face, bowl	23.2	184	151
DM-MRP-30 Vessel-shaped bird, jug, cutaway spout	11.6		
DM-MRP-31 Vessel-shaped bird, jug, beak spout	14.5		
DM-MRP-32 Funnel	15.7	284b	258

3 Black-Topped Red Polished Ware

	Maximum dimension (cm)	Plate number	Page number
DM-BTRP-01 Bottle, round base	13	13d	22
DM-BTRP-02 Bottle, round base	12.1		
DM-BTRP-03 Bottle, round base	12.2	92e	65
DM-BTRP-04 Bottle, round base	14		
DM-BTRP-05 Bottle, round base	12.2		
DM-BTRP-06 Bottle, round base	15.8	92d	65
DM-BTRP-07 Bottle, round base	17	92c	65
DM-BTRP-08 Bottle, round base	13.4		
DM-BTRP-09 Bottle, round base	16.7	12f	22
DM-BTRP-10 Bowl, round base, no lugs	9.6	114	70
DM-BTRP-11 Bowl, round base, one lug	12.2		
DM-BTRP-12 Bowl, round base, one lug	12.2	12e	22
DM-BTRP-13 Bowl, round base, one lug	9.6		
DM-BTRP-14 Bowl, round base, one lug	12.8		
DM-BTRP-15 Bowl, round base, one lug	10.5	115b	70
DM-BTRP-16 Bowl, round base, one lug	14.8	13c	22
DM-BTRP-17 Bowl, round base, one lug	8.4		
DM-BTRP-18 Bowl, round base, two lugs	10.1		
DM-BTRP-19 Bowl, round base, horizontal handle, one lug	15	119	71
DM-BTRP-20 Bowl, tulip base, two lugs	11.5	13a	22
DM-BTRP-21 Bowl, tulip base, four lugs	14.2	125b	72
DM-BTRP-22 Bowl, tulip base, trough spout, one lug	11	125a	72
DM-BTRP-23 Bowl, stem base	11.6	13b	22
DM-BTRP-24 Bowl, tripod base	10.4	134	73
DM-BTRP-25 Multi-handled bowl, tulip base	16.3	168	103
DM-BTRP-26 Vessel-attached bulls' heads, tulip bowl	16	222	194
DM-BTRP-27 Sheath-knife	21	286	262
DM-BTRP-28 Knife-sheath	21.6	286	262

4 Red-and-Black Polished Ware

	Maximum dimension (cm)	Plate number	Page number
DM-RBP-01 Jug, round base, round spout	13.8	14b	23
DM-RBP-02 Jug, round base, round spout	15.5		
DM-RBP-03 Jug, round base, round spout	11.1		
DM-RBP-04 Jug, round base, round spout	9.7		
DM-RBP-05 Jug, round base, round spout	9.7		
DM-RBP-06 Jug, round base, round spout	9.2		
DM-RBP-07 Bottle, round base, two lugs	12.5	93b	65
DM-RBP-08 Bottle, round base, no lugs	16.5	92b	65
DM-RBP-09 Bottle, round base, no lugs	12.2	92a	65
DM-RBP-10-115 Bottles, round base, no lugs, tall neck	15.8-23.5	14f 266	23 236
DM-RBP-116-33 Bottles (tall neck only)	8-13.7		
DM-RBP-134-49 Bottles (body only)	7.1-10.4		
DM-RBP-150 Bottle, round base, two lugs, tall neck	24.4	14e	23
DM-RBP-151 Bottle, round base, two handles, tall neck	25.2	14d	23
DM-RBP-152 Bottle, round base, two handles, tall neck	22.3		
DM-RBP-153 Bottle, round base, two handles, tall neck	22.7		
DM-RBP-154 Bowl, round base, one lug	12		
DM-RBP-155 Bowl, round base, two lugs	10		
DM-RBP-156 Bowl, round base, two lugs	9.4		
DM-RBP-157 Bowl, round base, two lugs	10.7	116b	70
DM-RBP-158 Bowl, round base, two lugs	11.4		
DM-RBP-159 Bowl, round base, two lugs	10.6		
DM-RBP-160 Bowl, round base, two lugs	10.1	14c	23
DM-RBP-161 Bowl, round base, two lugs	18.4	116a	70
DM-RBP-162 Bowl, round base, two lugs	14		
DM-RBP-163 Bowl, round base, trough spout, one lug	17.2	118b	71
DM-RBP-164 Bowl, round base, trough spout, one lug	22.2	118a	71
DM-RBP-165 Bowl, tulip base, two lugs	9.9		
DM-RBP-166 Bowl, tulip base, trough spout, one lug	10.7	14a	23
DM-RBP-167 Bowl, pointed base, plain	11.2	126	72
DM-RBP-168 Horn (fragment from large vessel)	17.5		
DM-RBP-169 Horn (fragment from large vessel)	16.9		
DM-RBP-170 Horn (fragment from large vessel)	11.7		
DM-RBP-171 Horn (fragment from large vessel)	13		

5 Black-Bottomed Red Polished Ware

	Maximum dimension (cm)	Plate number	Page number
DM-BBRP-01 Bottle, round base, two lugs	18.7	15a	23
DM-BBRP-02 Bowl, round base, spout, two lugs	27.7	15b	23
DM-BBRP-03 Bowl, round base, twin spout, two lugs	27.5	162	100

6 Reserved Slip Ware

	Maximum dimension (cm)	Plate number	Page number
DM-RS-01 Bowl, round base, one lug	11.1	18	26

7 Black Polished Ware

	Maximum dimension (cm)	Plate number	Page number
DM-BP-01 Jug, round base, round spout, plain	9.5		
DM-BP-02 Jug, round base, round spout, incisions	12.3	19g	26
DM-BP-03 Bottle, round base, incisions	6.1	19a	26
DM-BP-04 Bottle, flat base, incisions	9	19f	26
DM-BP-05 Bottle, flat base, incisions	11.2	97b	65
DM-BP-06 Bottle, flat base, incisions	5.4	19b	26
DM-BP-07 Bowl, round base, one lug, incisions	8.6	19d	26
DM-BP-08 Bowl, round base, one lug, incisions	10.2	19c	26
DM-BP-09 Bowl, round base, one lug, incisions	10.6	19e	26
DM-BP-10 Mouth-cover, oval shape, incisions	10.1	288	263

8 Handmade Black Slip Ware

	Maximum dimension (cm)	Plate number	Page number
DM-HBS-01 Jug, round base, round spout	17.5	20b	27
DM-HBS-02 Jug, round base, round spout	12.4	47a	51
DM-HBS-03 Jug, round base, round spout	10	48a	51
DM-HBS-04 Jug, round base, round spout	10.1		
DM-HBS-05 Jug, round base, round spout, wide neck	21.5	20a	27
DM-HBS-06 Jug, round base, round spout, wide neck	26	20c	27
DM-HBS-07 Jug, round base, round spout, wide neck	27.8	55b	53
DM-HBS-08 Jug, ring base, pinched spout	15.9	84c	63
DM-HBS-09 Bowl, flat base	9.2	123b	72
DM-HBS-10 Strainer, jug, round base	19	149	77
DM-HBS-11 Twin-necked jug, round base, cutaway-beak spouts	19	155	96
DM-HBS-12 Vessel-shaped human figure, bottle	12	188b	159
DM-HBS-13 Spindle whorl, incised	4		
DM-HBS-14 Spindle whorl, incised	4.5		

9 Drab Polished Ware

	Maximum dimension (cm)	Plate number	Page number
DM-DP-01 Jug, round base, round spout	10.2	47b	51
DM-DP-02 Jug, round base, round spout	8.5	48b	51
DM-DP-03 Jug, round base, round spout, squat neck	12.3	21b	27
DM-DP-04 Jug, round base, squat neck, side spout	20.4	58b	54
DM-DP-05 Jug, round base, squat neck, side spout	17.9	58a	54
DM-DP-06 Jug, round base, cutaway-beak spout	23.4	21c	27
DM-DP-07 Jug, round base, cutaway-beak spout	32.3	21a	27
DM-DP-08 Jug, round base, cutaway-beak spout	34.7		
DM-DP-09 Jug, nipple base, round spout	8.9		
DM-DP-10 Jug, nipple base, round spout	9.3		
DM-DP-11 Jug, nipple base, round spout, side spout	18.5		
DM-DP-12 Jar, round base, vertical handles	23.2	103b	67
DM-DP-13 Jar, round base, vertical handles	21.3	103a	67
DM-DP-14 Twin-necked jug, beaked spouts, attached birds	38.6	156	97
DM-DP-15 Subsidiary-unit vessel, jug + two bowls	44.3	169	106
DM-DP-16 Subsidiary-unit vessel, jug + two bowls, one jug	48	170	107
DM-DP-17 Subsidiary-unit vessel, jug + one bowl, one jug	37.3	171	110
DM-DP-18 Vessel-attached human heads, jar, round base	31.6	186	155
DM-DP-19 Spindle whorl, hour-glass shape, incised	5.5	285	259
DM-DP-20-35 Sixteen spindle whorls, incised	3–4.5	285	259
DM-DP-36 Scenic vessel, jug, deer-milking scene	44	215	186
		290	266
		291	267

10 Red-on-Black Ware

	Maximum dimension (cm)	Plate number	Page number
DM-ROB-01 Jug, round base, round spout	9.9	22b	30
DM-ROB-02 Jug, round base, round spout	14	49b	51
DM-ROB-03 Jug, round base, round spout	20.3	49c	51
DM-ROB-04 Jug, round base, round spout	17.8	49a	51
DM-ROB-05 Jug, round base, round spout	16.3		
DM-ROB-06 Jug, round base, round spout	20.5	23b	30
DM-ROB-07 Jug, flat base, round spout, wide neck	28.9	23a	30
DM-ROB-08 Jug, flat base, round spout, wide neck	26.6	23d	30
DM-ROB-09 Bowl, round base, trough spout, one lug	19.7	22a	30
DM-ROB-10 Bowl, round base, trough spout, vertical handle	30	23c	30
DM-ROB-11 Vessel-shaped human figure, jug	19.6	188c	159
DM-ROB-12 Bull figure	L18.4	228	199
DM-ROB-13 Camel figure	L19.5	244	215

11 Handmade White Painted Ware

	Maximum dimension (cm)	Plate number	Page number
DM-HWP-01 Jug, round base, round spout	22.5	50a	52
DM-HWP-02 Jug, round base, round spout	19.5	50c	52
DM-HWP-03 Jug, round base, round spout	15	50b	52
DM-HWP-04 Jug, round base, round spout	19.2	51a	52
DM-HWP-05 Jug, round base, round spout	17.7	51c	52
DM-HWP-06 Jug, round base, round spout	9.2	51b	52
DM-HWP-07 Jug, round base, round spout, side spout	14	54	53
DM-HWP-08 Jug, round base, round spout, wide neck	22.3	55c	53
DM-HWP-09 Jug, round base, round spout, side hole	19	59	54
DM-HWP-10 Jug, round base, beak spout	14.2	62c	55
DM-HWP-11 Jug, round base, beak spout	16.8	62b	55
DM-HWP-12 Jug, round base, beak spout	12.7	62a	55
DM-HWP-13 Jug, round base, beak spout	13.3	24b	31
DM-HWP-14 Jug, round base, beak spout	12.6		
DM-HWP-15 Jug, round base, beak spout	14.6		
DM-HWP-16 Jug, round base, cutaway-beak spout	16.1	66a	56
DM-HWP-17 Jug, round base, cutaway-beak spout	23.3	66b	56
DM-HWP-18 Jug, round base, cutaway-beak spout	15.1	66c	56
DM-HWP-19 Jug, round base, pinched spout	11	71a	58
DM-HWP-20 Jug, round base, pinched spout	13.7	71b	58
DM-HWP-21 Jug, round base, pinched spout	16.4	70a	58
DM-HWP-22 Jug, round base, pinched spout	13.5	70b	58
DM-HWP-23 Jug, flat base, round spout	10.2	72a	58
DM-HWP-24 Jug, flat base, pinched spout	10	74a	59
DM-HWP-25 Jug, flat base, pinched spout	14.7	74b	59
DM-HWP-26 Jug, ring base, pinched spout	14	84b	63
DM-HWP-27 Jug, ring base, pinched spout	13.7	84a	63
DM-HWP-28 Jug, tripod base, round spout, side hole	18	91	64
DM-HWP-29 Jug, quadrupod base, cutaway spout	20	24a	31
DM-HWP-30 Bottle, round base, two lugs	7.4	24e	31
DM-HWP-31 Bottle, round base, two lugs	9	94c	65
DM-HWP-32 Bottle, round base, two lugs	9.8	94a	65
DM-HWP-33 Bottle, round base, two lugs	7	94b	65
DM-HWP-34 Flask, round base, beak spout	24	98b	66
DM-HWP-35 Flask, flat base, round spout	21.5	100c	66
DM-HWP-36 Flask, flat base, round spout	21.5	24c	31
DM-HWP-37 Flask, flat base, round spout	9.9	100b	66
DM-HWP-38 Flask, flat base, round spout	9.3	100d	66
DM-HWP-39 Flask, flat base, round spout	6.7	100a	66
DM-HWP-40 Bowl, round base, trough spout, lug	34	24g	31
DM-HWP-41 Bowl, round base, vertical handle	11.5	121a	71
DM-HWP-42 Bowl, round base, vertical handle	8.7		
DM-HWP-43 Bowl, round base, vertical handle	5.9	121b	71
DM-HWP-44 Bowl, round base, horizontal handle	9.3		
DM-HWP-45 Bowl, round base, horizontal handle	15.2		
DM-HWP-46 Bowl, round base, horizontal handle	8.4		
DM-HWP-47 Bowl, round base, horizontal handle	8.2		
DM-HWP-48 Bowl, round base, horizontal handle	10.6	24d	31
DM-HWP-49 Bowl, round base, horizontal handle	7.8	24f	31
DM-HWP-50 Bowl, stem base	6.9	130	73
DM-HWP-51 Dipper	9	145a	76
DM-HWP-52 Dipper	10	145b	76
DM-HWP-53 Twin-necked jug, fused, cutaway spout	35	157	98
DM-HWP-54 Triple-bodied jug, fused, round spout	15.7	159b	99
DM-HWP-55 Human plank figure, shoulder figure	14.8	180	147
DM-HWP-56 Human plank figure, five small bowls	29.8	185	154
DM-HWP-57 Vessel-shaped human figure, flask	26.1	189b	159
DM-HWP-58 Vessel-shaped human figure, jug	16.8	189a	159
DM-HWP-59 Vessel-shaped human figure, jug	14.8	189c	159
DM-HWP-60 Human figure from jug handle	6.2	182c	150
DM-HWP-61 Deer figure	15	217a	187
DM-HWP-62 Stag's head	5.3	221b	187
DM-HWP-63 Bull figure	15.6	227	199
DM-HWP-64 Bull figure	14	225	198
DM-HWP-65 Bull figure	17.8	226	198
DM-HWP-66 Bull figure	8.6	224	197
DM-HWP-67 Ram figure	12.1	245	217
DM-HWP-68 Bird figure	11.6	256b	226
DM-HWP-69 Bird figure	13.5	256a	226

12 Base Ring Ware

	Maximum dimension (cm)	Plate number	Page number
DM-BR-01 Jug, round spout, painted	28	25b	34
DM-BR-02 Jug, round spout, 'bucchero' relief stripes	14.2	80a	61
DM-BR-03 Jug, round spout, traces of paint	10.2	81d	61
DM-BR-04 Jug, round spout, relief-decorated	26.4	25g	34
DM-BR-05 Jug, round spout, relief-decorated, white	14.7	25d	34
DM-BR-06 Jug, round spout, relief-decorated	13.3	80c	61
DM-BR-07 Jug, round spout, relief-decorated	14.5	80d	61
DM-BR-08 Jug, round spout, relief-decorated	11.5	80b	61
DM-BR-09 Jug, round spout, relief-decorated	11.5	267	237
DM-BR-10 Jug, round spout, incised	14.7	25a	34
DM-BR-11 Jug, round spout, plain	13.1	79d	61
DM-BR-12 Jug, round spout, plain	14.9		
DM-BR-13 Jug, round spout, plain	13.7	79a	61
DM-BR-14 Jug, round spout, plain	13.8	79c	61
DM-BR-15 Jug, round spout, plain	15.9	79b	61
DM-BR-16 Jug, round spout, painted	14.6	25c	34
DM-BR-17 Jug, round spout, painted	12.2	81a	61
DM-BR-18 Jug, round spout, painted	12.8	81b	61
DM-BR-19 Jug, round spout, painted	15.4	81d	61
DM-BR-20 Twin-bodied jug, round spouts, plain	10.2	160	100
DM-BR-21 Jug, round spout, bucranial side-spout, painted	20.8	230	201
DM-BR-22 Jug, round spout, wide neck	17.3	25e	34
DM-BR-23 Jug, round spout, wide neck	10.9	82a	62
DM-BR-24 Jug, round spout, wide neck, painted	10.9	82b	62
DM-BR-25 Jug, cutaway spout, relief-decorated	61.3	25h	34
DM-BR-26 Jug, cutaway spout, relief-decorated	39.8	83a	62
DM-BR-27 Jug, cutaway spout, relief-decorated	27.9	83b	62
DM-BR-28 Flask, round base, plain	13.4	98a	66
DM-BR-29 Jar, three handles, painted	11	110	69
DM-BR-30 Bowl, horizontal handle, plain	13		
DM-BR-31 Bowl, horizontal handle, plain	16.6		
DM-BR-32 Bowl, horizontal handle, plain	10.3		
DM-BR-33 Bowl, horizontal handle, plain	10.5	128b	73
DM-BR-34 Bowl, one lug, plain	10.7	128a	73
DM-BR-35 Bowl, horizontal handle, relief-decorated	16.7	25f	34
DM-BR-36 Human figure, headgear type	19.1	193	168
DM-BR-37 Human figure, headgear type (legs missing)	9	191	168
DM-BR-38 Human figure, headgear type (feet missing)	13.5	192	168
DM-BR-39 Human figure, earring type (head missing)	14.6	194	170
DM-BR-40 Human figure, earring type	11.5	197	172
DM-BR-41 Human figure, earring type	19.2	198	172
DM-BR-42 Human figure, earring type (legs missing)	11.2	196	172
DM-BR-43 Human figure, earring type	20.7	195	171
DM-BR-44 Bull figure, painted	17.7	232	202
DM-BR-45 Bull figure, painted	10.3	229b	200
DM-BR-46 Bull figure, nose ring, painted	15.1	231	202
DM-BR-47 Bull figure, nose ring, painted	13.2	229a	200

13 Cypro-Mycenaean Ware

	Maximum dimension (cm)	Plate number	Page number
DM-CM-01 Bottle, ring base, two vertical handles	17.1	95	65
DM-CM-02 Bottle, ring base, two vertical handles	13.6	26d	35
DM-CM-03 Jar, ring base, three horizontal handles	16	108a	69
DM-CM-04 Jar, ring base, three horizontal handles	16.2	108b	69
DM-CM-05 Jar, ring base, three horizontal handles	15.9		
DM-CM-06 Jar, ring base, three horizontal handles	15.2	26a	35
DM-CM-07 Jar, ring base, three horizontal handles	14.4	109a	69
DM-CM-08 Jar, ring base, three horizontal handles	12.7	109b	69
DM-CM-09 Jar, ring base, three horizontal handles	11.6		
DM-CM-10 Jar, ring base, three horizontal handles	17.7	26c	35
DM-CM-11 Jar, ring base, three horizontal handles	17.3	108c	69
DM-CM-12 Jar, flat base, three horizontal handles	7	26b	35

14 Cypro-Palestinian Bichrome Ware

	Maximum dimension (cm)	Plate number	Page number
DM-CPB-01 Jug, flat base, round spout	41.7	268	238
DM-CPB-02 Jug, ring base, round spout, wide neck	30.5	27	35

15 White Slip Ware

	Maximum dimension (cm)	Plate number	Page number
DM-WSL-01 Jug, ring base, round spout, wide neck	20.3	30a	38
DM-WSL-02 Jug, ring base, round spout, wide neck	25.8	31b	39
DM-WSL-03 Bowl, round base, horizontal handle	16.3	29b	38
DM-WSL-04 Bowl, round base, horizontal handle	17.6	29a	38
DM-WSL-05 Bowl, round base, horizontal handle	18.5	30b	38
DM-WSL-06 Bowl, flat base, horizontal handle	14.3	124	72
DM-WSL-07 Bowl, round base, horizontal handle	18.6	120	71
DM-WSL-08 Bowl, round base, horizontal handle	14.9		
DM-WSL-09 Bowl, round base, horizontal handle	17.7	31a	39

16 Wheelmade Red Lustrous Ware

	Maximum dimension (cm)	Plate number	Page number
DM-WRL-01 Jug, ring base, round spout	33.1	32b	39
DM-WRL-02 Flask, round base, round spout	33.3	32c	39
DM-WRL-03 Flask, round base, round spout	24.4	32a	39

17 White Shaved Ware

	Maximum dimension (cm)	Plate number	Page number
DM-WSH-01 Jug, pointed base, pinched spout, plain	17.2	28	37
DM-WSH-02 Owl-shaped rattle, pointed base, painted	9.8	254	225

18 Wheelmade White Painted Ware

	Maximum dimension (cm)	Plate number	Page number
DM-WWP-01 Jug, round base, round spout	8.5		
DM-WWP-02 Jug, round base, round spout	8.2	52b	52
DM-WWP-03 Jug, round base, round spout	8.6		
DM-WWP-04 Jug, round base, round spout	15		
DM-WWP-05 Jug, round base, round spout	11.8		
DM-WWP-06 Jug, round base, round spout	12.4	52a	52
DM-WWP-07 Jug, round base, round spout	10.3		
DM-WWP-08 Jug, round base, round spout	22		
DM-WWP-09 Jug, round base, round spout	10.4		
DM-WWP-10 Jug, round base, round spout	19.1		
DM-WWP-11 Jug, round base, round spout	9	52c	52
DM-WWP-12 Jug, flat base, round spout	8		
DM-WWP-13 Jug, flat base, round spout	17.8		
DM-WWP-14 Jug, flat base, round spout	9.7		
DM-WWP-15 Jug, flat base, round spout, side spout	11.5	278	248
DM-WWP-16 Jug, flat base, round spout, side spout	11.6	73a	59
DM-WWP-17 Jug, flat base, pinched spout	13.3		
DM-WWP-18 Jug, flat base, pinched spout	12.3	283b	249
DM-WWP-19 Jug, flat base, pinched spout	16.3	280	249
DM-WWP-20 Jug, flat base, pinched spout	12.7	282	249
DM-WWP-21 Jug, flat base, pinched spout	13.8	283a	249
DM-WWP-22 Jug, flat base, pinched spout	14	273	242
DM-WWP-23 Jug, flat base, pinched spout	15.1		
DM-WWP-24 Jug, flat base, pinched spout	13		
DM-WWP-25 Jug, flat base, pinched spout	13.5		
DM-WWP-26 Jug, flat base, pinched spout	22		
DM-WWP-27 Jug, flat base, pinched spout	12.7	74c	59
DM-WWP-28 Jug, flat base, pinched spout	11		
DM-WWP-29 Jug, flat base, basket handle	16		
DM-WWP-30 Jug, ring base, round spout	8.7		
DM-WWP-31 Jug, ring base, round spout	8.7		
DM-WWP-32 Jug, ring base, round spout	22.4	260	228
DM-WWP-33 Jug, ring base, round spout	27		
DM-WWP-34 Jug, ring base, round spout, carrying handles	22.2		
DM-WWP-35 Jug, ring base, round spout, side spout	15.1		
DM-WWP-36 Jug, ring base, pinched spout	25.5	281	249
DM-WWP-37 Jug, ring base, pinched spout	21		
DM-WWP-38 Jug, ring base, pinched spout	18.3		
DM-WWP-39 Jug, ring base, pinched spout	18.3		
DM-WWP-40 Jug, ring base, pinched spout	14		
DM-WWP-41 Jug, ring base, pinched spout	15.2		
DM-WWP-42 Jug, ring base, pinched spout	18.2		
DM-WWP-43 Jug, ring base, pinched spout	16.8		
DM-WWP-44 Jug, ring base, pinched spout	15.1		
DM-WWP-45 Jug, ring base, false spout, side spout	10.2	86	63
DM-WWP-46 Jug, ring base, basket handle, side spout	13.8	87	63
DM-WWP-47 Jug, ring base, basket handle, side spout	12.6	33b	42
DM-WWP-48 Jug, ring base, basket handle, side spout	20.8		
DM-WWP-49 Jug, ring base, basket handle, side spout	15.6		
DM-WWP-50 Jug, barrel base, round spout	39	88	64
DM-WWP-51 Jug, barrel base, round spout	9.6		
DM-WWP-52 Bottle, flat base, spindle shaped	27.1		
DM-WWP-53 Bottle, flat base, cylindrical	15.2		

	Maximum dimension (cm)	Plate number	Page number
DM-WWP-54 Flask, round base, round spout, two handles	13.9	99b	66
DM-WWP-55 Jar, flat base, two horizontal handles	33.2		
DM-WWP-56 Jar, flat base, two horizontal handles	28.1	104	68
DM-WWP-57 Jar, flat base, two vertical handles	13.2		
DM-WWP-58 Jar, flat base, two vertical handles	16		
DM-WWP-59 Jar, flat base, two vertical handles	17.8		
DM-WWP-60-94 Jars, ring base, two vertical handles	10.1-15.6		
DM-WWP-95 Jar, ring base, two vertical handles	44.8	113	69
DM-WWP-96 Jar, ring base, two vertical handles	26.3	275	243
DM-WWP-97 Jar, ring base, two vertical handles	51	263	234
DM-WWP-98 Jar, ring base, two vertical handles	34.2		
DM-WWP-99 Jar, ring base, two horizontal handles	19.2	33a	42
DM-WWP-100 Jar, ring base, two horizontal handles	35.9		
DM-WWP-101 Jar, ring base, two horizontal handles	39.5	111	69
DM-WWP-102 Jar, ring base, two horizontal handles	45.3		
DM-WWP-103 Jar, ring base, two horizontal handles	33.8		
DM-WWP-104 Jar, ring base, two horizontal handles	22		
DM-WWP-105 Jar, ring base, two horizontal handles	26		
DM-WWP-106 Jar, ring base, two horizontal handles	18.1	33c	42
DM-WWP-107 Bowl, round base, one horizontal handle	12.4		
DM-WWP-108 Bowl, round base, two rim-holes	10.2		
DM-WWP-109 Bowl, flat base, plain	14.5		
DM-WWP-110 Bowl, flat base, two horizontal handles	23.7		
DM-WWP-111 Bowl, flat base, two horizontal handles	11.8		
DM-WWP-112 Bowl, flat base, two horizontal handles	12.3		
DM-WWP-113 Bowl, flat base, two horizontal handles	11.3		
DM-WWP-114 Bowl, ring base, two horizontal handles	23.6	127	73
DM-WWP-115 Bowl, ring base, two horizontal handles	25.7		
DM-WWP-116 Bowl, ring base, two horizontal handles	20.3		
DM-WWP-117 Bowl, ring base, two horizontal handles	13.7	279	249
DM-WWP-118 Bowl, ring base, two horizontal handles	15.3		
DM-WWP-119 Bowl, ring base, two horizontal handles	10.3		
DM-WWP-120 Bowl, ring base, two horizontal handles	15.8		
DM-WWP-121 Bowl, ring base, two horizontal handles	14.6		
DM-WWP-122 Bowl, ring base, two horizontal handles	16.2		
DM-WWP-123 Bowl, ring base, one vertical handle	11.6		
DM-WWP-124 Bowl, stem base, two horizontal handles	15.7		
DM-WWP-125 Bowl, stem base, two horizontal handles	15.6		
DM-WWP-126 Dish, three handles	51.1	135	74
DM-WWP-127 Dish, three handles	27		
DM-WWP-128-71 Dishes, three handles	8.3-35	137	74
DM-WWP-172 Dish, one handle, spike	15.6		
DM-WWP-173 Dish, one handle, spike	19	138	74
DM-WWP-174 Dish, one handle, spike	15.9		
DM-WWP-175 Dish, two lugs	8.3		
DM-WWP-176 Dish, two lugs	8.2		
DM-WWP-177 Pottery basket	27	146	77
DM-WWP-178 Strainer, ring base, round spout, side spout	15.8	147b	77
DM-WWP-179 Strainer, ring base, round spout, side spout	14.1	147a	77
DM-WWP-180 Ring vessel, horizontal, bucranial spout	21.3	150	83
DM-WWP-181 Ring vessel, horizontal, bucranial spout	20.8	151	83
DM-WWP-182 Ring vessel, vertical, round spout	16	153	85
DM-WWP-183 Human figure, warrior	12.7	200	176
DM-WWP-184 Deer figure	15	218	187
DM-WWP-185 Bird figure, wing stumps	L22.7	255	225
DM-WWP-186 Bird figure, three legs	L16.5	257a	226
DM-WWP-186 Bird figure, three legs	L16.5	257a	226
DM-WWP-187 Spindle whorl	3.6		
DM-WWP-188 Spindle whorl	3.6		
DM-WWP-189 Spindle whorl	3.6		

19 Bichrome Ware

	Maximum dimension (cm)	Plate number	Page number
DM-BI-01 Jug, flat base, round spout	9.2	72d	58
DM-BI-02 Jug, flat base, round spout	8.3	72b	58
DM-BI-03 Jug, flat base, round spout	12.7	72c	58
DM-BI-04 Jug, flat base, round spout	21.3		
DM-BI-05 Jug, flat base, round spout	16.5		
DM-BI-06 Jug, flat base, round spout	21.2		
DM-BI-07 Jug, flat base, round spout	6.7		
DM-BI-08 Jug, flat base, round spout, side spout	10.3	73b	59

	Maximum dimension (cm)	Plate number	Page number
DM-BI-09 Jug, flat base, pinched spout	30.6		
DM-BI-10 Jug, flat base, pinched spout	19.5		
DM-BI-11 Jug, flat base, pinched spout	21		
DM-BI-12 Jug, flat base, pinched spout	12.3	75a	59
DM-BI-13 Jug, flat base, pinched spout	11.1	276	248
DM-BI-14 Jug, flat base, pinched spout	15.5		
DM-BI-15 Jug, flat base, pinched spout	12.6	75b	59
DM-BI-16 Jug, flat base, pinched spout	10.6	75c	59
DM-BI-17 Jug, flat base, pinched spout	17.8	277a	248
DM-BI-18 Jug, flat base, pinched spout	16.7	277b	248
DM-BI-19 Jug, ring base, round spout	26.3		
DM-BI-20 Jug, ring base, round spout	9		
DM-BI-21 Jug, ring base, pinched spout	24	85a	63
DM-BI-22 Jug, ring base, pinched spout	22.8		
DM-BI-23 Jug, ring base, pinched spout	19.1		
DM-BI-24 Jug, ring base, pinched spout	15		
DM-BI-25 Jug, ring base, pinched spout	20		
DM-BI-26 Jug, ring base, pinched spout	33	34a	42
DM-BI-27 Jug, ring base, pinched spout	24.5		
DM-BI-28 Jug, ring base, pinched spout	22.5	85c	63
DM-BI-29 Jug, ring base, pinched spout	31.3	85b	63
DM-BI-30 Jug, barrel base, round spout	10.3		
DM-BI-31 Jug, barrel base, round spout	20	90	64
DM-BI-32 Jug, barrel base, round spout	33.7	89	64
DM-BI-33 Flask, round base, two vertical handles	9.6	99a	66
DM-BI-34 Jar, flat base, plain	6		
DM-BI-35 Jar, flat base, two horizontal handles	13.3		
DM-BI-36 Jar, flat base, two horizontal handles	10.3	105a	68
DM-BI-37 Jar, flat base, two horizontal handles	10.1	105b	68
DM-BI-38 Jar, flat base, two horizontal handles	10.8		
DM-BI-39 Jar, pointed base, two vertical handles	18.5	107	68
DM-BI-40 Jar, ring base, two vertical handles	13.5		
DM-BI-41 Jar, ring base, two vertical handles	21.5		
DM-BI-42 Jar, ring base, two vertical handles	22.8		
DM-BI-43 Jar, ring base, two vertical handles	15.5		
DM-BI-44 Jar, ring base, two vertical handles	21.5		
DM-BI-45 Jar, ring base, two vertical handles	18	112	69
DM-BI-46 Jar, ring base, two vertical handles	25.2	264	235
DM-BI-47 Jar, ring base, two horizontal handles	39.7		
DM-BI-48 Jar, ring base, two horizontal handles	42.5		
DM-BI-49 Jar, ring base, two horizontal handles	42.8		
DM-BI-50 Jar, ring base, two horizontal handles	36.6	269	239
DM-BI-51 Jar, ring base, two horizontal handles	32	34c	42
DM-BI-52 Jar, ring base, two horizontal handles	10.8	274	242
DM-BI-53 Jar, ring base, two horizontal handles	7.3	34b	42
DM-BI-54 Bowl, flat base, two horizontal handles	12.3		
DM-BI-55 Bowl, flat base, two horizontal handles	12		
DM-BI-56 Bowl, flat base, two horizontal handles	11.1		
DM-BI-57 Bowl, ring base, two horizontal handles	13.6		
DM-BI-58 Bowl, stem base, two horizontal handles	12.2	132	73
DM-BI-59 Bowl, stem base, two horizontal handles	14.3	271	242
DM-BI-60 Bowl, stem base, two horizontal handles	20	272	242
DM-BI-61 Bowl, stem base, two horizontal handles	18.7		
DM-BI-62 Dish, two handles	13.4		
DM-BI-63 Dish, two handles	20.3		
DM-BI-64 Dish, two handles	13.7		
DM-BI-65 Dish, two handles	14.4		
DM-BI-66 Dish, two handles	17.5		
DM-BI-67 Dish, two handles	24.5		
DM-BI-68 Dish, two handles	14.4		
DM-BI-69 Dish, two handles	10.2		
DM-BI-70 Dish, two handles	13.4		
DM-BI-71 Dish, one handle	9		
DM-BI-72 Dish, one lug	9.1		
DM-BI-73 Dish, two rim holes	22.5		
DM-BI-74 Horizontal ring vessel, pomegranates, goat	22.8	152 / 246	84 / 219
DM-BI-75 Triple-bodied flask, six vertical handles	9.7	161	100
DM-BI-76 Human figure, arms upraised	18	199b	176
DM-BI-77 Human figure, arms upraised	17.7	199a	176
DM-BI-78 Human figure, arms upraised	16.7	199d	176
DM-BI-79 Human figure, arms upraised	16.5	199e	176
DM-BI-80 Human figure, arms upraised	11.3	199c	176
DM-BI-81 Human figure, arms outstretched	14.5		
DM-BI-82 Human figure, arms outstretched	14.5		

Catalogue	Description	Maximum dimension (cm)	Plate number	Page number
DM-BI-83	Human figure, arms to chest	14	202a	178
DM-BI-84	Human figure, arms to chest	14.7	202d	178
DM-BI-85	Human figure, arms to chest	14.2	202e	178
DM-BI-86	Human figure, arms to chest	13.5	202b	178
DM-BI-87	Human figure, arms to chest	13.1	202c	178
DM-BI-88	Human figure, one arm to chest	14	203a	178
DM-BI-89	Human figure, one arm to chest	16	203b	178
DM-BI-90	Human figure, necklace	19	204a	178
DM-BI-91	Human figure, necklace	17.6	204b	178
DM-BI-92	Human figure, tambourine	15.5	205f	179
DM-BI-93	Human figure, tambourine	16	205e	179
DM-BI-94	Human figure, tambourine	15	205b	179
DM-BI-95	Human figure, tambourine	14.1	205c	179
DM-BI-96	Human figure, tambourine	15.2	205a	179
DM-BI-97	Human figure, tambourine	17.6	205d	179
DM-BI-98	Human figure, tambourine	13.7	206	179
DM-BI-99	Human figure, playing flute	6.2	205g	179
DM-BI-100	Human figure, warrior	10.3	207	180
DM-BI-101	Human figure, warrior	10.2	208	180
DM-BI-102	Human figure, warrior with shield	12.8	209	181
DM-BI-103	Human figure, mounted in chariot	23.2	211	182
DM-BI-104	Bucranial plaque	17.1	234	203
DM-BI-105	Horse figure, three legs	10	237b	207
DM-BI-106	Horse figure, three legs	12.3	237a	207
DM-BI-107	Horse figure, three legs	10		
DM-BI-108	Horse figure, four legs	20.5	238	207
DM-BI-109	Horse and rider	13.8	210a	181
DM-BI-110	Horse and rider	12.5	210b	181
DM-BI-111	Horse and rider	14	210c	181
DM-BI-112	Horse and rider	20	236	206
DM-BI-113	Horse and rider	19.5	235a	206
DM-BI-114	Pig figure	L 7	240	212
DM-BI-115	Bird figure, three legs	L16.5	257b	226
DM-BI-116	Bird figure, no legs, wing spikes	L15.8	257c	226
DM-BI-117	Bird figure, no legs, no wings	L20.8	257d	226
DM-BI-118	Boat model	L 9.7	289	263

20 Black-on-Red Ware

Catalogue	Description	Maximum dimension (cm)	Plate number	Page number
DM-BOR-01	Jug, flat base, round spout	13.6	35f	43
DM-BOR-02	Jug, flat base, round spout	8.5		
DM-BOR-03	Jug, flat base, round spout	9.8		
DM-BOR-04	Jug, flat base, round spout	9		
DM-BOR-05	Jug, flat base, round spout	12.4	35a	43
DM-BOR-06	Jug, flat base, round spout	8.5	35b	43
DM-BOR-07	Jug, flat base, round spout	11.5		
DM-BOR-08	Jug, flat base, round spout	9.7	35e	43
DM-BOR-09	Jug, ring base, pinched spout	26.7		
DM-BOR-10	Jug, ring base, pinched spout	21		
DM-BOR-11	Jug, ring base, pinched spout	12.5	35d	43
DM-BOR-12	Jug, barrel base, round spout	11		
DM-BOR-13	Jug, barrel base, round spout	12.8	35c	43
DM-BOR-14	Bowl, ring base, two horizontal handles	22.6		
DM-BOR-15	Bowl, ring base, two horizontal handles	10.4		
DM-BOR-16	Bowl, ring base, two horizontal handles	22.8		
DM-BOR-17	Bowl, ring base, two horizontal handles	23.4		
DM-BOR-18	Bowl, stem base, two horizontal handles	13.3		
DM-BOR-19	Bowl, stem base, two horizontal handles	13	258	227
DM-BOR-20	Dish, two lugs	12.2		
DM-BOR-21	Vessel-shaped figure, strainer jug	23	148	77

21 Bichrome Red Ware

Catalogue	Description	Maximum dimension (cm)	Plate number	Page number
DM-BIR-01	Bowl, ring base, one horizontal handle	15.1	36d	43
DM-BIR-02	Bowl, stem base, two horizontal handles	18.5	36a	43
DM-BIR-03	Dish, ring base, two rim holes	20.7	36b	43
DM-BIR-04	Vessel-attached human figure, jug	15.1+	36c	43

22 Wheelmade Black Slip Ware

Catalogue	Description	Maximum dimension (cm)	Plate number	Page number
DM-WBS-01	Jug, ring base, round spout	9.6	37b	44
DM-WBS-02	Jug, ring base, round spout	15.5		
DM-WBS-03	Jug, ring base, pinched spout	15		
DM-WBS-04	Jug, ring base, pinched spout	16.4		
DM-WBS-05	Jug, ring base, pinched spout	12.5		
DM-WBS-06	Jug, ring base, pinched spout	15.5	37c	44
DM-WBS-07	Jug, ring base, pinched spout	12.5		
DM-WBS-08	Jug, ring base, pinched spout	19.5		
DM-WBS-09	Jug, ring base, pinched spout	18.6		
DM-WBS-10	Jug, ring base, pinched spout	22.2		
DM-WBS-11	Jug, ring base, pinched spout	24.6		
DM-WBS-12	Jug, ring base, pinched spout	21.2		
DM-WBS-13	Jug, ring base, pinched spout	12.6	37a	44
DM-WBS-14	Jug, ring base, pinched spout	16.3		
DM-WBS-15	Jug, ring base, pinched spout	15.8		
DM-WBS-16	Jug, ring base, pinched spout	20.7	37d	44
DM-WBS-17	Jug, ring base, pinched spout	23		
DM-WBS-18	Jar, ring base, two vertical handles	18.2		
DM-WBS-19	Jar, ring base, two vertical handles	23.1	37e	44
DM-WBS-20	Jar, ring base, two vertical handles	12.5	37f	44
DM-WBS-21	Bowl, ring base, two horizontal lugs	12		
DM-WBS-22	Bowl, ring base, two horizontal lugs	11.1		
DM-WBS-23	Bowl, ring base, two horizontal lugs	13		
DM-WBS-24	Bowl, ring base, two horizontal lugs	12		

23 Wheelmade Black Slip Painted Ware

Catalogue	Description	Maximum dimension (cm)	Plate number	Page number
DM-WBSP-01	Jar, ring base	17.8	38	45

24 Plain White Ware

Catalogue	Description	Maximum dimension (cm)	Plate number	Page number
DM-PW-01	Jug, flat base, round spout	12	39d	45
DM-PW-02	Jug, flat base, round spout	14	39a	45
DM-PW-03	Jug, ring base, round spout	14.3	39b	45
DM-PW-04	Bottle, flat base, spindle shaped	20	96b	65
DM-PW-05	Bottle, flat base, spindle shaped	17.2	96a	65
DM-PW-06	Bottle, flat base, spindle shaped	10		
DM-PW-07	Jar, pointed base, torpedo shaped	46.2	39f	45
DM-PW-08	Jar, pointed base, torpedo shaped	36.7	39g	45
DM-PW-09	Jar, pointed base, torpedo shaped	29.9	39e	45
DM-PW-10	Bowl, round base, plain	10.4		
DM-PW-11	Bowl, flat base, plain	11.7		
DM-PW-12	Bowl, flat base, plain	11.3		
DM-PW-13	Bowl, flat base, plain	11	39c	45
DM-PW-14	Bowl, flat base, plain	12.4		
DM-PW-15	Bowl, flat base, plain	10		
DM-PW-16	Bowl, flat base, two horizontal handles	11.4		
DM-PW-17	Bowl, flat base, two horizontal handles	11.6		
DM-PW-18	Bowl, ring base, two rim holes	23.5		
DM-PW-19	Dish, two handles	8.4		
DM-PW-20	Dish, round base, plain	18.7		
DM-PW-21	Dish, flat base, plain	10		
DM-PW-22	Dish, flat base, plain	14.1		
DM-PW-23	Dish, flat base, two rim holes	16.7		
DM-PW-24	Group of three human figures sitting by wall	11		
DM-PW-25	Donkey figure, with pannier	L12.3	239	211
DM-PW-26	Pig-shaped rattle, short nose	L15	242a	213
DM-PW-27	Pig-shaped rattle, long nose	L15	242b	213
DM-PW-28	Dog figure	L10.5	247	221
DM-PW-29	Dog's head bell	8		

25 Wheelmade Red Ware

Catalogue	Description	Maximum dimension (cm)	Plate number	Page number
DM-WRS-01	Jug, ring base, round spout	19.7	41c	46
DM-WRS-02	Jug, ring base, round spout	10	41a	46
DM-WRS-03	Jug, ring base, round spout	8.7	41d	46
DM-WRS-04	Jug, ring base, round spout	8.5	41b	46
DM-WRS-05	Jug, ring base, round spout	7.4		
DM-WRS-06	Jug, ring base, round spout	26.4	42c	47
DM-WRS-07	Jug, ring base, round spout	21.2	42a	47
DM-WRS-08	Jug, ring base, round spout	15.2	43	47
DM-WRS-09	Jug, ring base, pinched spout	17.2	40b	46
DM-WRS-10	Jug, ring base, pinched spout	15	42d	47
DM-WRS-11	Jug, ring base, pinched spout	12.7	42b	47
DM-WRS-12	Bottle, round base, one lug	7.6		
DM-WRS-13	Flask, flat base, round spout, one lug	10.6		
DM-WRS-14	Flask, flat base, round spout, one lug	10.9		
DM-WRS-15	Jar, ring base, two vertical handles	14	40a	46
DM-WRS-16	Bowl, round base, plain	10.8		
DM-WRS-17	Bowl, flat base, two horizontal handles	9		
DM-WRS-18	Bowl, ring base, two vertical handles	10.8		
DM-WRS-19	Bowl, ring base, two horizontal handles	27		
DM-WRS-20	Bowl, ring base, one horizontal handle	12.4		

	Maximum dimension (cm)	Plate number	Page number
DM-WRS-21 Dish, flat base, two rim holes	10.2		
DM-WRS-22 Dish, flat base, two rim holes	20.4		
DM-WRS-23 Dish, flat base, two rim holes	16.2		
DM-WRS-24 Dish, flat base, two rim holes	21.8		
DM-WRS-25 Pig-shaped rattle	10.3	241	213

26 Bone Objects

	Maximum dimension (cm)	Plate number	Page number
DM-BO-01 Human figure, incised long bone	14.6	190a	165
DM-BO-02 Human figure, incised long bone	16.5	190c	165
DM-BO-03 Human figure, incised long bone	17.9	190b	165

27 Stone Objects

	Maximum dimension (cm)	Plate number	Page number
DM-ST-01 Hand axe	15.7	1	8
DM-ST-02 Hand axe	7.5	2	8
DM-ST-03 Hand axe	8	3	8
DM-ST-04 Spherical grinder/pounder	6.9		
DM-ST-05 Pierced stone ball, traces of red paint	8		
DM-ST-06 Pierced stone ball	5.6		
DM-ST-07 Picrolite cruciform pendant	4	173	125
DM-ST-08 Picrolite 'comb-figure' pendant	4.4	175	138
DM-ST-09 Pierced circular stone	7.3		
DM-ST-10 Conical pestle	5.5		
DM-ST-11 Conical pestle	8		
DM-ST-12 Conical pestle	6.6		
DM-ST-13 Conical pestle	8.8		
DM-ST-14 Mortar dish, three legs	16		
DM-ST-15 Mortar dish, ring base	16.7		
DM-ST-16 Mortar dish, ring base	14.3		
DM-ST-17 Mortar dish, ring base	11.7		
DM-ST-18 Mortar dish, flat base	10.5		
DM-ST-19 Marble L-shaped grinder/pounder	6.9		
DM-ST-20 Picrolite incised dish, pierced centrally	11		
DM-ST-21 Picrolite pierced disc	2.7		
DM-ST-22 Spindle whorl	4.2		
DM-ST-23 Human figure, arms to sides	18.2	201	177
DM-ST-24 Marble octagonal tile, Greek inscription	21		
DM-ST-25 Marble hand holding bowl, fragment from statue	7.2		

28 Metal Objects

	Maximum dimension (cm)	Plate number	Page number
DM-ME-01 Socketed spearhead	30.4		
DM-ME-02 Rat-tanged spearhead or knife-blade	32.7		
DM-ME-03 Rat-tanged spearhead or knife-blade	29.3		
DM-ME-04 Rat-tanged spearhead or knife-blade	27.9		
DM-ME-05 Rat-tanged spearhead or knife-blade	27.5	4a	10
DM-ME-06 Rat-tanged spearhead or knife-blade	22.4	4b	10
DM-ME-07 Three-pinned spearhead or knife-blade	21.5	6a	11
DM-ME-08 Three-pinned spearhead or knife-blade	14		
DM-ME-09 Three-pinned spearhead or knife-blade	13.8		

	Maximum dimension (cm)	Plate number	Page number
DM-ME-10 Two-pinned spearhead or knife-blade	13.2		
DM-ME-11 One-pinned spearhead or knife-blade	12.1		
DM-ME-12 Three-pinned spearhead or knife-blade	11.5		
DM-ME-13 Two-pinned spearhead or knife-blade	11.1		
DM-ME-14 Three-pinned spearhead or knife-blade	10.6	6b	11
DM-ME-15 Three-pinned spearhead or knife-blade	8.7	6c	11
DM-ME-16 Segment of spearhead or knife-blade	12.4		
DM-ME-17 Pinch-spring tweezers	14.1	5	10
DM-ME-18 (Broken) tweezers	8.4		
DM-ME-19 (Broken) tweezers	7.6		
DM-ME-20 (Broken) tweezers	7.3		
DM-ME-21 Long pin with flat head	21	7c	11
DM-ME-22 Long pin	17.9	7a	11
DM-ME-23 Long pin	12.5		
DM-ME-24 Long pin	16.2		
DM-ME-25 Long pin	15.9	7b	11
DM-ME-26 Long pin	13.4		
DM-ME-27 Long pin	7.3		
DM-ME-28 Long pin	9.3		
DM-ME-29 Long pin	11		
DM-ME-30 Pin with central band	8.5		
DM-ME-31 Pin with central slit	6.3		
DM-ME-32 Pin with central slit	8.1		
DM-ME-33 Pin with central slit	10		
DM-ME-34 Needle	8.4		
DM-ME-35 Needle	11.6		
DM-ME-36 Needle	10.8		
DM-ME-37 Needle	9.9		
DM-ME-38 Miniature bowl with relief ridge on underside	2.7		
DM-ME-39 Bowl, round base, plain	13.8		
DM-ME-40 Spiral ring	1.9		
DM-ME-41 Spiral ring	2		
DM-ME-42 Child's bracelet	4.2		
DM-ME-43 Lead spindle whorl	2.5		
DM-ME-44 Lead spindle whorl	2.5		
DM-ME-45 Human foot, wearing sandal	8.5		
DM-ME-46 Human foot, wearing sandal	8.5		
DM-ME-47 Human foot, wearing sandal	8.5		
DM-ME-48 Strigil	21.5		

29 Miscellaneous

	Maximum dimension (cm)	Plate number	Page number
DM-GL-01 Eagle-shaped dish, coloured glazed ware	19.7	259	227
DM-GL-02 Bowl, round base, trough spout, lug, faience	7.8		
DM-GP-01 Jug, flat base, pinched spout, grey polished	7.7		
DM-GP-02 Jug, flat base, pinched spout, grey polished	7.5		
DM-GW-01 Bowl, flat base, vertical 'ribbing', grey ware	11.5		
DM-RT-01 Human head, terracotta	30	212	183
DM-RT-02 Pomegranate-shaped rattle	11.5	265	235

Bibliography

RDAC = Report of the Department of Antiquities, Cyprus

Adelman, C. M. 1976. 'Cypro-geometric Pottery: Refinements in classification.' *Studies in Mediterranean Archaeology* XLVII. Göteborg.

Admiraal, S. L. 1982. 'Late Bronze Age Tombs from Dromolaxia.' *RDAC* pp. 39-59.

Alastros, D. 1955. *Cyprus in History—A Survey of 5,000 Years*. Zeno, London.

Ambraseys, N. N. 1963. *The Seismic History of Cyprus*. Imperial College Publication, University of London.

Amiran, R. 1970. *Ancient Pottery of the Holy Land*. Rutgers University Press, New Jersey.

Annual Report of the Director of the Department of Antiquities. 1915; 1949–present day. Nicosia.

Argoud, G. et al. 1973. *Salamine de Chypre IV. Anthologie Salaminienne*. De Boccard, Paris.

Artzy, M., I. Perlman and F. Asaro. 1976. 'Wheel-made pottery of the M.C.III and L.C.I periods in Cyprus identified by neutron activation analysis.' *RDAC* 1976, pp. 20-25.

Astrom, L. and P. Astrom. 1972. *The Swedish Cyprus Expedition. IV, 1d. The Late Cypriote Bronze Age. Other Arts and Crafts. Relative and Absolute Chronology, Foreign Relations, Historical Conclusions*. Lund.

Astrom, P. 1966. 'Excavations at Kalopsidha and Ayios Iakovos in Cyprus. *Studies in Mediterranean Archaeology* II. Lund.

Astrom, P. 1968. 'L'Art et la Culture Antiques de Chypre.' *Civilisations Anciennes du Bassin Méditerranéen* (Thimme, J. et al.) Albin Michel, Paris. pp. 57-88.

Astrom, P. 1972. *The Swedish Cyprus Expedition. IV, 1b. The Middle Cypriote Bronze Age*. Lund.

Astrom, P. 1972. *The Swedish Cyprus Expedition. IV, 1c. The Late Cypriote Bronze Age. Architecture and Pottery*. Lund.

Astrom, P. 1973. 'Comments on the corpus of Mycenaean Pottery in Cyprus.' *Acts of the International Archaeological Symposium 'The Mycenaeans in the Eastern Mediterranean'*. pp. 122-7.

Astrom, P. 1974. *Cypern—Motsattniningarnas O*. Studies in Mediterranean Archaeology—Pocketbook I. Göteborg.

Astrom, P. et al. 1980. *Corpus Vasorum Antiquorum. Sweden: 1. Museum of Classical Antiquities, Lund 1*. Almqvist and Wiksell, Stockholm.

Astrom, P., J. C. Biers et al. 1979. 'The Cypriote collection of the Museum of Art and Archaeology, University of Missouri-Columbia.' *Studies in Mediterranean Archaeology* XX:2. Göteborg.

Astrom, P. and S. A. Eriksson. 1980. 'Fingerprints and Archaeology.' *Studies in Mediterranean Archaeology* XXVIII.

Belgiorno, M. R. 1980. 'Materiale del Medio Bronzo Cipriota nella Collezione Pierides di Larnaca.' In: *Studi Micenei ed Egeo-Anatolici*, Fasc. XXI, pp. 73-121.

Benson, J. L. 1972. *Bamboula at Kourion. The Necropolis and the Finds*. University of Pennsylvania, Philadelphia.

Benson, J. L. 1973. 'The Necropolis of Kaloriziki.' *Studies in Mediterranean Archaeology* XXXVI. Göteborg.

Benson, J. L. 1975. 'Birds on Cypro-Geometric pottery.' In: (Robertson, N., editor) *The Archaeology of Cyprus*. pp. 129-50.

Birmingham, J. (editor). 1973. 'The Cypriot Bronze Age. Some recent Australian contributions to the prehistory of Cyprus.' *Australian Studies in Archaeology No. 1*. Department of Archaeology, University of Sydney.

Bray, W. and D. Trump. 1970. *A Dictionary of Archaeology*. Allen Lane, London.

Brown, A. C. and H. W. Catling. 1975. *Ancient Cyprus*. Ashmolean Museum, Oxford.

Brown, A. and H. Catling. 1980. 'Additions to the Cypriot Collection in the Ashmolean Museum, Oxford, 1963-77.' *Opuscula Atheniensia* XIII:7, pp. 91-137.

Buchholz, H-G. and V. Karageorghis. 1973. *Prehistoric Greece and Cyprus. An Archaeological Handbook*. Phaidon, London. (Originally published in 1971 as: *Altägäis und Altkypros*.)

Calvert, Y. 1972. *Salamine de Chypre III. Les Timbres Amphoriques*. De Boccard, Paris.

Casson, S. 1937. *Ancient Cyprus*. Methuen, London.

Catling, H. W. 1964. *Cypriot Bronzework in the Mycenaean World*. Clarendon Press, Oxford.

Catling, H. W. 1971. 'Cyprus in the Early Bronze Age.' In: *The Cambridge Ancient History* I. Part 2. Cambridge University Press, Cambridge.

Catling, H. W. 1974. 'The Bomford Horse-and-rider.' *RDAC* 1974, pp. 95-111.

Catling, H. W. 1976. 'Prolegomena for a study of a class of Late Cypriote terracotta figures.' *RDAC* 1976. pp. 66-74.

Caubet, A. 1971. 'Terres cuites Chypriotes inedites ou peu connus de l'Age du Bronze au Louvre.' *RDAC* pp. 7-12.

Caubet, A. 1974. 'Une terre cuite Chalcolithique Chypriote au Louvre.' *RDAC* pp. 35-7.

Caubet, A. 1977. *Antiquités de Chypre. Petits Guides des Grands Musées*. Louvre, Paris.

Caubet, A. 1979. *La Religion a Chypre dans l'Antiquité*. Maison de l'Orient, Lyon.

Cesnola, A. P. di. 1881. *Cyprus Antiquities Excavated by Major Alexander Palma di Cesnola, 1876-1879*. Holmes, London.

Cesnola, A. P. di. 1882. *Salaminia (Cyprus). The History, Treasures & Antiquities of Salamis in the Island of Cyprus*. Trubner, London.

Cesnola, L. P. di. 1877. *Cyprus: Its Ancient Cities, Tombs and Temples*. John Murray, London.

Chappel, T. J. H. 1977. *Decorated Gourds*. Ethnographica, London.

Charleston, R. J. 1968. *World Ceramics*. Hamlyn, London.

Chavane, M-J. 1975. *Salamine de Chypre VI. Les Petits Objects*. De Boccard, Paris.

Chavane, M-J. and M. Yon. 1978. *Salamine de Chypre X. Testimonia Salaminia 1*. De Boccard, Paris.

Christou, D. 1972. 'A Cypro-geometric tomb from "Latsia" Rizokarpaso.' *RDAC* pp. 143-55.

Cirlot, J. E. 1962. *A Dictionary of Symbols*. Routledge and Kegan Paul, London.

Cles-Reden, S. von. 1961. *The Realm of the Great Goddess*. Thames and Hudson, London.

Clutton-Brock, J. 1981. *Domesticated Animals from Early Times*. Heinemann, London.

Colonna-Ceccaldi, G. 1882. *Monuments antiques de Chypre de Syrie et d'Egypte*. Didier, Paris.

Conrad, J. R. 1959. *The Horn and the Sword. The History of the Bull as Symbol of Power and Fertility*. MacGibbon & Kee, London.

Cook, A. B. 1914-1940. *Zeus: A Study in Ancient Religion*. Cambridge University Press, Cambridge.

Cook, B. F. 1979. *Cypriote Art in the British Museum*. British Museum, London.

Cooper, J. C. 1978. *An Illustrated Encyclopedia of Traditional Symbols*. Thames and Hudson, London.

Courtois, L. 1971. *Description Physico-chimique de la Ceramique ancienne: La Ceramique de Chypre au Bronze Recent*. Doctoral thesis.

Crouwel, J. 1978. 'Cypriote Chalcolithic figurines in Amsterdam'. *RDAC* pp. 31-8.

Davis, R. J. and T. B. L. Webster. 1964. 'Cesnola Terracottas in the Stanford University Museum.' *Studies in Mediterranean Archaeology* XVI. Lund.

Des Gagniers, J. and V. Karageorghis. 1976. *Vases et Figurines de l'Age du Bronze a Chypre. Céramique Rouge et Noire Polie*. Les Presses de l'Université Laval, Quebec.

Deshayes, J. 1963. *La Nécropole de Ktima*. Paul Geuthner, Paris.

Dikaios, P. 1934. 'Early Bronze Age cults in Cyprus as revealed by the excavations at "Vounous", Bellapais.' *Proceedings of the First International Congress of Prehistoric and Protohistoric Sciences, London 1932*. Oxford University Press, Oxford.

Dikaios, P. 1940. 'The excavations at Vounous-Bellapais in Cyprus, 1931-2'. *Archaeologia* 88, pp. 1-174.

Dikaios, P. 1953. *Khirokitia*. Oxford University Press, Oxford.

Dikaios, P. 1961. *Sotira*. University of Pennsylvania, Philadelphia.

Dikaios, P. 1961. *A Guide to the Cyprus Museum*. Nicosia.

Dikaios, P. 1962. *The Swedish Cyprus Expedition. IV, 1a. The Stone Age*. Lund.

Dikaios, P. 1969. *Enkomi. Excavations 1948-1958.* Philipp von Zabern, Mainz am Rhein. (Vol. II in 1971).

Doell, J. 1873. 'Die Sammlung Cesnola.' *Mem. l'Acad. Imp. des Sci. de St Petersbourg,* XIX no. 4, VII Series.

Dussaud, R. 1907. 'L'Ile de Chypre. Particulierement aux ages du cuivres et du bronze.' *Rev. l'Ecole d'Anthropologie de Paris,* 17, V, pp. 145-212.

Ede, C. 1976. *Cypriot Pottery, 2250-475 BC.* Catalogue IV. Ede, London.

Ede, C. 1982. *Cypriot Pottery, 2300-475 BC.* Catalogue VIII. Ede, London.

Ergüleç, H. 1972. 'Large-sized Cypriot sculpture in the Archaeological museums of Istanbul.' *Studies in Mediterranean Arachaeology* XX:4. Göteborg.

Fisher, J., N. Simon and J. Vincent. 1969. *The Red Book. Wildlife in Danger.* Collins, London.

Flourenzos, P. 1975. 'Notes of the Red Polished III plank-shaped idols from Cyprus.' *RDAC* pp. 29-35.

Frankel, D. 1974. 'Middle Cypriot White Painted Pottery. An analytical study of the decoration.' *Studies in Mediterranean Archaeology* XLII. Göteborg.

Frankel, D. 1974. 'Inter-site relationships in the Middle Bronze Age of Cyprus.' *World Archaeology* 6, no. 2, pp. 190-208.

Frankel, D. 1974. 'A Middle Cypriot vessel with modelled figures from Politiko, Lambertis.' *RDAC* 1974, pp. 43-50.

Frankel, D. 1975. 'The pot marks of Vounous—Simple Clustering techniques, their problems and potential.' *Opuscula Atheniensia* XI, pp. 37-51.

Frankel, D. 1978. 'Pottery decoration as an indicator of social relationships: a prehistoric Cypriot example.' *Art in Society* pp. 147-60.

Frankel, D. 1983. 'Corpus of Cypriote Antiquities 7. Early and Middle Bronze Age material in the Ashmolean Museum, Oxford.' *Studies in Mediterranean Archaeology* XX:7. Göteborg.

Frankel, D. and A. Tamvaki. 'Cypriot shrine models and decorated tombs.' *Australian J. Biblical Archaeology* 2, no. 2, pp. 39-44.

Gardner, E. A. et al. 1888. 'Excavations in Cyprus, 1887-8. Paphos, Leontari, Amargetti.' *J. Hell. Stud.* 9.

Gejvall, N. 1966. 'Osteological investigation of human and animal bones from Kalopsidha.' In: P. Astrom, 'Excavations at Kalopsidha and Ayios Iakovos in Cyprus.' *Studies in Mediterranean Arachaeology* II, Appendix IV.

Gjerstad, E. 1926. *Studies on Prehistoric Cyprus.* Uppsala.

Gjerstad, E. 1948. *The Swedish Cyprus Expedition. IV,2. The Cypro-Geometric, Cypro-Archaic and Cypro-Classical Periods.* Stockholm.

Gjerstad, E. 1977. 'Greek Geometric and Archaic pottery found in Cyprus. *Skrifter Utgivna av Svenska Institutet I Athen, 4° XXVI. Acta Instituti Atheniensis Regni Sueciae 4° XXVI.* Stockholm.

Gjerstad, E. 1980. 'The origin and chronology of the Early Bronze Age in Cyprus.' *RDAC* pp. 1-16.

Gjerstad, E., J. Lindros, E. Sjoquist and A. Westholm. 1934-1937. *The Swedish Cyprus Expedition. Finds and Results of the Excavations in Cyprus, 1927-1931.* Stockhom. (Vol. I: 1934; Vol. II: 1935; Vol. III: 1937.)

Grinsell, L. V. 1975. *Barrow, Pyramid and Tomb.* Thames and Hudson, London.

Groger-Wurm, H. M. 1973. *Australian Aboriginal Bark Paintings and their Mythological Interpretation.* Vol. 1. Australian Institute of Aboriginal Studies, Canberra.

Grunwald, C. 1976. *Schätze aus Zypern.* Kunstmuseum der Universität, Bonn.

Halstead, P. 1977. 'A preliminary report of the faunal remains from Late Bronze Age Kouklia, Paphos. *RDAC* pp. 261-75.

Haltenorth, T. 1961 'Lebensraum, Lebensweise und Vorkommen des Mesopotamischen Damhirsches, *Cervus mesopotamicus* Brooke, 1875.' *Saugetierkundliche Mitteilungen BVL-Verlagsgellschaft München* 3, 9. Jhg., Heft 1, pp. 15-39.

Harrison, J. 1903. *Prolegomena to the Study of the Greek Religion.* Cambridge University Press, Cambridge.

Hennessy, J. B. 1964. *Stephania. A Middle and Late Bronze-Age Cemetery in Cyprus.* Quaritch, London.

Hennessy, J. B. 1979. *Masterpieces of Western Ceramic Art. Vol. 1. Ancient Near Eastern Pottery.* Kodansha, Tokyo.

Herscher, E. 1973. 'Red-and-Black Polished Ware from the Western Karpas.' *RDAC* pp. 62-71.

Hill, G. 1940. *A History of Cyprus. Volume 1; To the Conquest by Richard the Lion Heart.* Cambridge University Press, Cambridge.

Hogarth, D. G. 1889. *Devia Cypria.* Frowde, London.

Hutchinson, R. W. 1962. *Prehistoric Crete.* Penguin, London.

Jehasse, L. 1978. *Salamine de Chypre VIII. Le Ceramique à Vernis noir du Rempart Meridional.* De Boccard, Paris.

Johnson, J. 1980. 'Maroni de Chypre.' *Studies in Mediterranean Archaeology* LIX. Göteborg.

Karageorghis, J. 1977. *La Grande Déesse de Chypre et son Culte.* Lyon.

Karageorghis, V. 1958. 'Finds from Early Cypriot Cemeteries.' *RDAC* 1940-1948, pp. 115-52.

Karageorghis, V. 1962. *Treasures in the Cyprus Museum.* Nicosia.

Karageorghis, V. 1963. *Corpus Vasorum Antiquorum. Cyprus: 1. Cyprus Museum (Nicosia); Larnaca District Museum.* Department of Antiquities, Nicosia.

Karageorghis, V. 1964. *Sculptures from Salamis I.* Department of Antiquities, Nicosia.

Karageorghis, V. 1965. *Nouveaux documents pour l'Etude du Bronze Récent à Chypre.* Ecole Française d'Athènes. Etudes Chypriotes III. De Boccard, Paris.

Karageorghis, V. 1965. *Corpus Vasorum Antiquorum. Cyprus: 2. Private Collections.* Department of Antiquities, Nicosia.

Karageorghis, V. 1967. *Excavations in the Necropolis of Salamis.* Vol. I. (Vol. II: 1970; Vol. III: 1973; Vol. IV: 1978). Nicosia.

Karageorghis, V. 1968. *Mycenaean Art from Cyprus.* Department of Antiquities, Nicosia.

Karageorghis, V. 1969. *Archaeologia Mundi: Cyprus.* Nagel, Geneva.

Karageorghis, V. 1969. *Salamis in Cyprus. Homeric, Hellenistic and Roman.* Thames and Hudson, London.

Karageorghis, V. 1970. *Annual Report of the Director of the Department of Antiquities.* Nicosia.

Karageorghis, V. 1970. *Excavations in the Necropolis of Salamis II.* Nicosia.

Karageorghis, V. 1971 *Annual Report of the Director of the Department of Antiquities.* Nicosia.

Karageorghis, V. 1972 *Annual Report of the Director of the Department of Antiquities,* Nicosia.

Karageorghis, V. (editor) 1973. *Acts of the International Archaeological Symposium 'The Mycenaeans in the Eastern Mediterranean'.* Department of Antiquities, Nicosia.

Karageorghis, V. 1973. *Cypriote Antiquities in the Pierides Collection, Larnaca, Cyprus.* Endotiki Hellados, Athens.

Karageorghis, V. 1974. *Cyprus* (In Greek). Athens.

Karageorghis, V. 1974. *Excavations at Kition. I. The Tombs.* Department of Antiquities, Nicosia. (Vol. II in 1976.)

Karageorghis, V. 1975. *Annual Report of the Director of the Department of Antiquities.* Nicosia. (See Pl. 57).

Karageorghis, V. 1975. *Alaas. A Protogeometric Necropolis in Cyprus.* Department of Antiquities, Nicosia.

Karageorghis, V. 1975. *Ancient Cypriote Art.* National Archaeological Museum, Athens.

Karageorghis, V. 1975. 'Kypriaka II' *RDAC* pp. 58-68.

Karageorghis, V. 1975. *Cyprus Museum and Archaeological Sites of Cyprus.* Ekdotike Athenon, Athens.

Karageorghis, V. 1976. *Kition. Mycenaean and Phoenician Discoveries in Cyprus.* Thames and Hudson, London.

Karageorghis, V. 1976. *The Civilization of Prehistoric Cyprus.* Ekdotike Athenon, Athens.

Karageorghis, V. 1977 *Annual Report of the Director of the Department of Antiquities,* Nicosia.

Karageorghis, V. 1977. *The Goddess with Uplifted Arms in Cyprus.* CWK Gleerup, Lund.

Karageorghis, V. 1978. 'A "Favissa" at Kazaphani.' *RDAC* pp. 156-96.

Karageorghis, V. 1979. 'Two pictorially decorated vases of the Cypro-Archaic period.' In: *Studies Presented in Memory of Porphyrios Dikaios.* Lions Club, Nicosia.

Karageorghis, V. 1979. 'Cyprus. 4,000 years of an island's rich prehistory.' *Popular Archaeology* 1, no. 4. October 1979.

Karageorghis, V. 1980. 'Fouilles à l'Ancienne-Paphos de Chypre: Les premiers colons Grecs.' *Comptes Rendus de l'Academie des Inscriptions.* pp. 122-36.

Karageorghis, V. 1980. 'Kypriaka V'. *RDAC* pp. 128-35.

Karageorghis, V. 1981. *Annual Report of the Department of Antiquities.* Nicosia. (See Pl. 53).

Karageorghis, V. 1981. *Ancient Cyprus*. Louisiana State University Press, Baton Rouge.

Karageorghis, V. 1982. *Cyprus, from the Stone Age to the Romans*. Thames and Hudson, London.

Karageorghis, V. et al. 1971. *Studi Ciprioti e Rapporti de Scavo*. Biblioteca de Antichita Cypriote I, Roma.

Karageorghis, V. et al. 1979. *Studies Presented in Memory of Porphyrios Dikaios*. Lions Club, Nicosia.

Karageorghis, V., D. A. Amyx et al. 1974. 'Cypriot antiquities in San Francisco Bay area collections.' *Studies in Mediterranean Archaeology* XX:5. Göteborg.

Karageorghis, V. and A. Christodoulou. (editors) 1972. *Proceedings of the First International Cyprus Congress, Nicosia, 1969*. Nicosia.

Karageorghis, V. and J. des Gagniers. 1974. *La Ceramique Chypriote de Style Figure. Age du Fer. (1050-500 Av J-C)*. Istituto per gli Studi Micenei ed Egeo-Anatolici. Edizioni dell'Ateneo, Roma. (Supplement in 1979).

Karageorghis, V. and C. C. Vermeule. 1966. *Sculptures from Salamis II*. Department of Antiquities, Nicosia.

Kenna, V. E. G. 1971. 'Catalogue of the Cypriote Seals of the Bronze Age in the British Museum.' *Studies in Mediterranean Archaeology* XX:3. Corpus of Cypriote Antiquities 3. Göteborg.

Lacey, A. D. 1967. *Greek Pottery in the Bronze Age*. Methuen, London.

Lawler, C. A. 1979. *Treasures from the Nicholson Museum*. David Jones' Art Gallery, Sydney.

Leach, M. (editor) 1975. *Folklore, Mythology and Legend*. NEL, London.

Leipen, N. 1966. *The Loch Collection of Cypriote Antiquities*. Royal Ontario Museum, University of Toronto Press, Toronto.

Lienard, J. 1972. *Cyprus, The Copper Island*. MAM, Nicosia.

Lloyd, S. 1967. *Early Highland Peoples of Anatolia*. Thames and Hudson, London.

Lorblanchet, M. 1977. 'From naturalism to abstraction in European prehistoric rock art.' In: *Form in Indigenous Art* (editor P. Ucko). Duckworth, London.

MacLaurin, M. L. G. 1980. *Cypriote Red Polished Pottery and its Regional Variations*. Ph.D. thesis. Institute of Archaeology, University of London.

Mellaart, J. 1966. *The Chalcolithic and Early Bronze Ages in the Near East and Anatolia*. Khayats, Beirut.

Mellaart, J. 1967. *Çatal Hüyük. A Neolithic Town in Anatolia*. Thames and Hudson, London.

Mellaart, J. 1974. 'A note on Cypriote Early Bronze Age chronology.' *RDAC* pp. 38-42.

Merrillees, R. S. 1965. 'Reflections on the Late Bronze Age in Cyprus.' *Opuscula Atheniensia* 6, pp. 139-48.

Merrillees, R. S. 1968. 'Two Late Cypriot vases.' *Opuscula Atheniensia* 8, pp. 1-10.

Merrillees, R. S. 1968. 'The Cypriote Bronze Age pottery found in Egypt.' *Studies in Mediterranean Archaeology* XVIII. Lund.

Merrillees, R. S. 1975. 'Problems in Cypriote History.' In: (N. Robertson, editor) *The Archaeology of Cyprus*. Noyes Press, New Jersey.

Merrillees, R. S. 1976. 'Vassos Karageorghis, Darrell A. Amyx and Associates, Corpus of Cypriote Antiquities 5. Cypriote Antiquities in San Francisco Bay Area Collections. A review article.' *RDAC* pp. 98-142.

Merrillees, R. S. 1977. 'The absolute chronology of the Bronze Age in Cyprus.' *RDAC* pp. 33-50.

Merrillees, R. S. 1980. 'Representation of the human form in prehistoric Cyprus.' *Opuscula Atheniensia* 13, 12. pp. 171-84.

Merrillees, R. S. (In press). How Cyprus gave its name to copper.

Michaelidou-Nicolaou, I. et al. 1980. *Studi Micenei ed Egio-Anatolici* XXI. Ateneo & Bizzarri, Rome.

Morris, D. 1962. *The Biology of Art*. Methuen, London.

Morris, D. 1977. *Manwatching; A Field-guide to Human Behaviour*. Cape, London.

Morris, D., P. Collett, P. Marsh and M. O'Shaughnessy. 1979. *Gestures: their Origins and Distribution*. Cape, London.

Morris, D. and R. Morris. 1965. *Men and Snakes*. Hutchinson, London.

Munro, J. A. R. 1890. 'Excavations in Cyprus, 1889. Second season's work—Polis tes Chrysochou—Limniti.' *J. Hell. Stud.* 11.

Munro, J. A. R. 1891. 'Excavations in Cyprus, 1890. Third season's work. Salamis.' *J. Hell. Stud.* 12.

Murray, A. S., A. H. Smith and H. B. Walters. 1900. *Excavations in Cyprus*. British Museum, London.

Myers, J. L. 1914. *Handbook of the Cesnola Collection of Antiquities from Cyprus*. The Metropolitan Museum of Art, New York. (Reprinted by Arno Press, 1974.)

Myres, J. L. and M. Ohnefalsch-Richter. 1899. *A Catalogue of the Cyprus Museum*. Clarendon Press, Oxford.

Neuburger, A. 1930. *The Technical Arts and Sciences of the Ancients*. Methuen, London.

Nicolaou, K. 1970. 'Antikes Zypern.' *Du*. Zurich.

Nicolaou, K. 1976. 'The historical topography of Kition.' *Studies in Mediterranean Archaeology* XLIII. Göteborg.

Nicolaou, K. 1979. 'Minoan survivals in Geometric and Archaic Cyprus.' *Acts of the International Archaeological Symposium 'The Relations Between Cyprus and Crete, ca 2000-500 BC'*. pp. 249-56.

Ohnefalsch-Richter, M. 1891. *Ancient Places of Worship in Kypros*. Hermann, Berlin.

Ohnefalsch-Richter, M. 1893. *Kypros, the Bible and Homer*. Asher, London.

Organ, J. 1963. *Gourds*. Faber and Faber, London.

Overbeck, J. C. and S. Swiny. 1972. 'Two Cypriot Bronze Age sites at Kafkallia (Dhali). *Studies in Mediterranean Archaeology* XXXIII. Göteborg.

Oziol, Th-J. 1977. *Salamine de Chypre VII. Les Lampes du Musée de Chypre*. De Boccard, Paris.

Oziol, Th-J. and J. Pouilloux. 1969. *Salamine de Chypre I. The Lamps*. De Boccard, Paris.

Pecorella, P. E. 1977. 'Le tombe dell'eta del Bronzo Tardo della necropoli a mare di Ayia Irini "Palaeokastro".' *Biblioteca di Antichita Cipriote* 4★.

Peltenburg, E. J. 1975. 'Ayios Epiktitos Vrysi, Cyprus: preliminary results of the 1969-1973 excavations of a neolithic coastal settlement.' *Proc. Prehist. Soc.* 41, pp. 17-45.

Peltenburg, E. 1977. 'Chalcolithic figurine from Lemba, Cyprus.' *Antiquity* LI, pp. 140-43.

Peltenburg, E. 1979. 'The prehistory of West Cyprus: Ktima Lowlands investigations 1976-1978.' *RDAC* 1979, pp. 69-99.

Peltenburg, E. 1980. 'The Lemba Lady of Western Cyprus.' *Illustrated London News*, Feb., 1980, pp. 57-8.

Peltenburg, E. 1981. *Cypriot Antiquities in Birmingham Museum and Art Gallery*. Birmingham..

Peltenburg, E. 1982. 'The Evolution of the Cypriot Cruciform Figurine.' *RDAC* pp. 12-14.

Peltenburg, E. 1984. 'Lemba archaeological project, Cyprus, 1982, preliminary report.' *Levant* XVI, pp. 55-65.

Peltenburg, E. and V. Karageorghis. 1976. 'Some Cypriote vases in Glasgow.' *RDAC*, pp. 84-91.

Perrot, G. and C. Chipiez. 1885. *History of Art in Phoenicia and its Dependencies*. Chapman and Hall, London.

Pierides, A. G. 1971. *Jewellery in the Cyprus Museum*. Nicosia.

Pieridou, A. 1966. 'A tomb group from Lapithos "Ayia Anastasia".' *RDAC* pp. 1-12.

Pieridou, A. 1967. 'Pieces of Cloth from Early and Middle Cypriote Periods.' *RDAC* pp. 25-9.

Pieridou, A. 1971. (Greek paper on ring vessels). *RDAC* pp. 18-26.

Ploss, H. H., M. Bartels and P. Bartels. 1935. *Woman: an Historical, Gynaecological and Anthropological Compendium*. Heinemann, London.

Popham, M. R. 1972. 'A note on the relative chronology of White Slip Ware.' In: Astrom, *The Swedish Cyprus Expedition IV*, 1d. Lund.

Regaldi, G. 1879. *Le Antichita di Cipro e Il Generale di Cesnola*. Tipografia del Senato, Roma.

Report of the Department of Antiquities, Cyprus. Department of Antiquities, Nicosia. (Published in the years 1937-9; 1940-8; 1963-present day).

Robertson, N. (Editor) 1975. *The Archaeology of Cyprus. Recent Developments*. Noyes Press, Park Ridge, New Jersey.

Rochetti, L. 1978. 'Le tombe dei Periodi Geometrico ed Arcaico della necropoli a mare di Ayia Irini "Palaeokastro".' *Biblioteca di Antichita Cipriote* 4★★.

Russell, C. 1981. 'Kinship symbols and their Evolution.' *Social Biology and Human Affairs* 45 (no. 2), pp. 119-44.

Savory, H. N. 1968. *Spain and Portugal. The Prehistory of the Iberian Peninsula*. Thames and Hudson, London.

Schaeffer, C. F. A. 1936. *Missions en Chypre,*

1932-1935. Paul Geuthner, Paris.

Schaeffer, C. F. A. 1948. 'Enkomi.' *Amer. J. Arch.* LII, no. 1, pp. 165-76.

Schaeffer, C. F. A. 1952. *Enkomi-Alasia.* Klincksieck, Paris.

Singer, C., E. J. Holmyard and A. R. Hall. 1954. *A History of Technology.* Clarendon Press, Oxford. (Vol. I).

Sjoqvist, E. 1940. *Problems of the Late Cypriote Bronze Age.* Swedish Cyprus Expedition, Stockholm.

Smeets, R. 1975. *Signs, Symbols and Ornaments.* Van Nostrand Reinhold, New York.

Spiteris, T. 1970. *The Art of Cyprus.* Weidenfeld and Nicolson, London.

Stanley Price, N. P. 1979. *Early Prehistoric Settlements in Cyprus.* BAR, Oxford.

Stavrou, P. et al. 1967. *Trésors de Chypre.* Musée des Arts Décoratifs, Palais du Louvre, Paris.

Stewart, J. R. 1962. *The Swedish Cyprus Expedition IV, 1a. The Early Bronze Age in Cyprus.* Lund.

Stewart, E. and J. Stewart. 1950. *Vounous 1937-1938.* Lund.

Strand, W. E. 1974. *Voices of Stone: The History of Ancient Cyprus.* Zavallis Press, Nicosia.

Swiny, H. W. and S. Swiny. 1983. 'An anthropomorphic figurine from the Sotira area.' *RDAC* pp. 56-9.

Swiny S. 1981. 'Bronze Age settlement patterns in Southwest Cyprus.' *Levant* XIII, pp. 51-87.

Tatton-Brown, V. 1979. *Cyprus BC. 7000 Years of History.* British Museum, London.

Thimme, J. 1977. *Art and Culture of the Cyclades.* University Press, Chicago.

Todd, I. A. 1979. 'Vasilikos Valley Project, 1977-1978; an interim report.' *RDAC* pp. 13-68.

Todd, I. A. 1982. 'Radiocarbon dates for Kalavassos-Tenta and Kalavassos-Ayious.' *RDAC* pp. 8-11.

Ucko, P. J. 1968. *Anthropomorphic Figurines.* Szmidla, London.

Ucko, P. J. (Editor). 1977 *Form in Indigenous Art.* Duckworth, London.

Vagnetti, L. 1974. 'Preliminary remarks on Cypriote Chalcolithic figurines.' *RDAC* pp. 24-34.

Vagnetti, L. 1975. 'Some unpublished Chalcolithic figurines.' *RDAC* pp. 1-4.

Vagnetti, L. 1979. 'Two steatite figurines of Anatolian type in Chalcolithic Cyprus.' *RDAC* pp. 112-14.

Vagnetti, L. 1980. 'Figurines and minor objects from a Chalcolithic cemetery at Souskiou-Vathyrkakas (Cyprus).' *Studi Micenei ed Egeo-Anatoici XXI,* Roma.

Vermeule, C. 1972. *Art of Ancient Cyprus.* Museum of Fine Arts, Boston.

Vermeule, C. 1974. 'The Ram Cults of Cyprus: pastoral to paphian at Morphou.' *RDAC* pp. 151-6.

Vermeule, C. 1976. *Greek and Roman Cyprus: Art from Classical Through Late Antique Times.* Museum of Fine Arts, Boston.

Vermeule, E. T. 1974. *Toumba tou Skourou. The Mound of Darkness.* Museum of Fine Arts, Boston.

Vermeule, E. and V. Karageorghis. 1982. *Mycenaean Pictorial Vase Painting.* University Press, Harvard.

Vessburg, O. and A. Westholm. 1956. *The Swedish Cyprus Expedition. IV,3. The Hellenistic and Roman Periods in Cyprus.* Stockholm.

Villa, P. 1969. 'Early and Middle Bronze Age pottery of the Cesnola collection in the Stanford University Museum.' *Studies in Mediterranean Archaeology* XX:1. Lund.

Vincentelli, A. et al. 1976. *Studi Ciprioti e Rapporti di Scavo.* Biblioteca de Antichita Cypriote II, Roma.

Watson, J. P. N. and N. P. Stanley-Price. 1977. 'The vertebrate fauna from the 1972 sounding at Khirokitia.' *RDAC,* pp. 232-60.

Weinberg, S. S. 1966. 'Ceramics and the supernatural: cult and burial evidence in the Aegean World.' In: *Ceramics and Man* (Editor: F. R. Matson). Methuen, London.

Westholm, A. 1936. *The Temples of Soli.* Swedish Cyprus Expedition, Stockholm.

Yon, M. 1971. *Salamine de Chypre II. La Tombe T.I. du XI^{e}s. av. J.C.* De Boccard, Paris.

Yon, M. 1974. Salamine de Chypre V. *Un Dépôt de Sculptures Archaiques.* De Boccard, Paris.

Yon, M. 1976. *Manuel de Céramique Chypriote. I. Problèmes Historiques, Vocabulaire, Méthode.* Collections de la Maison de l'Orient Méditerranéen Ancien. no. 1. Série Archéologique: 1. Institut Courby, Lyon.

Zeuner, F. E. 1958. 'Animal remains from a Late Bronze Age sanctuary on Cyprus, and the problem of the domestication of Fallow Deer.' *J. Palaeont. Soc. India. Lucknow.* 3, pp. 131-5.

Zeuner, F. E. 1963. *A History of Domesticated Animals.* Hutchinson, London.

Acknowledgements

The collection of Cypriot antiquities on which this book is based was begun in 1967, but it was not until 1973 that it occurred to me that it should be published. I am grateful to Angela Tamvaki for first suggesting this to me, when she visited the collection to make drawings for her study of human representations of the Bronze Age. She felt that the collection had grown to a point where it deserved publication and I set about outlining a book on the subject. It soon became clear to me that there were many gaps in the collection and that a great deal of research was needed to prepare such a volume. I therefore spent the next ten years filling those gaps and making special studies of Cypriot archaeo-aesthetics. During the course of research I was greatly helped by a large number of people and, in particular, I would like to thank the following:

David Attenborough, James Bomford, Ann Brown, David Brown, Richard Burleigh, Hector Catling, Annie Caubet, Ted Colman, Sheena Crawford, Bernard Dod, Charles Ede, James Ede, John Evans, David Frankel, Liselore Hassenberg, John Hayes, Basil Hennessy, Linda Hulin, Tony Hunt, Vassos Karageorghis, Kathleen Kimber, Lucy MacLaurin, Gilbert Manley, Tom Maschler, Barbara Mercer, Robert Merrillees, Michael Morey, Christine Morris, Jason Morris, Ramona Morris, Felicity Nicholson, Kenneth Oakley, Alan Peatfield, Jean Claude Peissel, Eddie Peltenburg, George Riches, Bill Russell, Claire Russell, Doreen Stoneham, Stuart Swiny, David Symons, Angela Tamvaki, Veronica Tatton-Brown, Peter Ucko, Sarah Vaughan, Michael Vickers and William Waldren.

Restorations

The cleaning, repair and conservation of the ancient objects illustrated photographically in this book have been carried out by KATHLEEN KIMBER, and for the immense care she has taken in this task I owe her my special thanks. After working through my collection—over a period of more than ten years—her specialized skill at restoring early Cypriot artefacts is second to none. Several hundred of the vessels and figures have now passed through her hands and the problems she has encountered are as follows:

1 *Clinging surface deposit.* Encrustations of various kinds often obscure the surface decorations of the objects. With some wares (especially those of the Iron Age period) it is possible to remove this deposit by soaking in a weak acid solution. Other, earlier wares from the Bronze Age cannot always be treated in this way and there it becomes necessary to remove the deposit manually, fragment by fragment, using fine instruments.

2 *Surface wear.* Repeated earthquakes in Cyprus have led to the formation of cracks in the rock-cut tombs, through which rainwater has found its way. This flooding has happened repeatedly, year after year, often for millennia, with the result that the vessels and figures have frequently been rubbed against one another and surfaces damaged. In many cases this had led to the loss of decorative detail, but this usually only applies to one side of the vessel or figure, giving it a 'good side' and a 'bad side'. Only in very rare cases have restoration attempts been made to correct such damage because it is always dangerous to guess the details of an Early Cypriot decoration pattern.

3 *Ancient breakage.* Either because they were (a) shaken by earthquakes, (b) swirled about by flood-water, or (c) crushed by the weight of other tomb-contents, or by tomb collapse, certain objects were broken in antiquity. Subsequent movement and wear often led to the rounding off of the broken edges. This means that they can no longer be joined cleanly and now require special treatment to re-fix them.

4 *Ancient repair.* In rare cases there is evidence of ancient 'restoration' work. This always takes the same, clumsy form, namely the drilling of pairs of large holes along the fracture lines. Out of the hundreds of vessels in the collection, only four showed ancient restoration work of this kind. No trace of the material used to tie the holes together was found. One of the four examples was from the Middle Bronze Age (see Pl. 23) and the others were from the Iron Age (see Pl. 135). In each case, during modern restoration, the holes were left in their ancient condition and no attempt was made to conceal them.

5 *Modern Breakage.* A number of vessels showed recent damage caused by modern accidents. Such fractures were easy to deal with, having clean break-lines which became almost invisible after restoration.

6 *Amateur restorations.* Some vessels, especially when purchased in the salerooms, showed signs of having been poorly restored in recent times by inexpert hands. This nearly always involved the excessive use of glues and other adhesives which left unsightly marks and lines. Three common 'tricks of the trade' were also encountered. The first was the smearing of a pseudo-encrustation over fractures to conceal their presence. This was to give the false impression that, once cleaned, the objects would prove to be perfect. The second device was to leave a small flaw conspicuously unconcealed to distract from a major flaw that was carefully covered up. The third was to assemble 'hybrid' objects using parts from different originals. The body of one fragmentary vessel would be married to the neck of another, for example, and the line of the join concealed with an artificial encrustation.

All these 'improvements' had to be removed so that serious restoration work could begin. Frequently the removal of the bad restoration was a greater problem than the positive repair work. In the case of the hybrid vessel, of course, the assembled object had to be dismantled and then kept as separate fragments.

7 *Missing parts.* A number of objects were incomplete. Frequently, it was obvious what the missing segment would have been and, in such instances, it was replaced with modern materials. A chip out of a rim of a bowl, for instance, could be replaced without any risk of error. In some cases, however, replacement of a missing piece involved guesswork and, in almost all such instances, the object was left in its incomplete state (see for example the headless figure in Pl. 194). This rule was broken only twice. The nine-bowl vessel shown in Pl. 163 lacked a handle. Because this major imperfection spoiled the shape and balance of the piece, a modern handle was added, based on the known, ancient handles of other similar multi-unit vessels. In the second case, the Scenic Composition vessel referred to as the Deer-milking Jug, the head of the human figure was missing. It had been substituted by a modern one of poor design and this was replaced with one based on the heads of other Early Bronze Age figurines. Although this involved guesswork it was considered the lesser of two evils, since it completed the overall impression of the scenic composition as intended by the original artist.

Index

*This refers to the text only and not
to the illustrations and captions.
The checklist on pp. 353 - 359
provides an index for the
photographic illustrations.*

A

abstraction, 6,117,127,138,224,240,
293,320,322
Aegean, 11
Aghios, 214
alabaster, 142
Alambra, 324,339
Allard Pierson Museum, Amsterdam,
125,132
Amathus, 214,237
Ambraseys, N.N., 10
Amiran, R., 33,240
amphora, 48-9
Anatolia, 9,13-14,189,196,223; Çatal
Hüyük, 196,223; interaction with,
8-10,20,24,37,41,126,135-6,192,
196
andesite, 118-20
animal-shaped vessels, 113,200,233
animals: deities, 196,217,232,281,283;
depicted, 11-12,32,40-1,48,75,79,
81,113-5,141,156,167-9,174,180,
184-235,249,265,292; domestic,7-8,
10,116,184,189,192,204-5,212-22,
249; marine, 233; masks, 180,217;
pelts, 113,188,215,252; suckling,
185,268; unidentified, 272,274-6
anthropology, parallels in, 15-16,
321-2
Archaic Period, 12-13,41,164-5,174-5,
213,233,240,292
Arpera, 324,339
artistic aims, 12,15-16,21,25,48,136,
215,219-20,283,323
artistic effects, 6,16,20-1,28,36,41,
47,78,112,116-7,124,129,135,174,
248,288,291-2,299,320-1,342
artistic composition, 29,156-7,264,
276-7,282,293,303,307,312,320,
323,339-43
artistic innovation, 6,9-10,13,20,24,
47,78,112,119,132,141,144,162,228,
240,292,320-1,323,343
artistic traditions, 6,20,29,36,48,
112,116,130,145,237,264,292-3,
320-1,323,339,342-3
artists, identity of, 15-16,21,29,
281-2,292,323,343-52
Artzy, M., 33
Ashmolean Museum, Oxford, 192,204,
214-5,269
Assyria, 12
Astarte, 12,166-7
Astrom, P., 25,28-9,32-3,37,77,166,
214,217
Australia, 322
Ayia Irini, 324,339-40
Ayia Mavri, 120
Ayios Epiktitos-Vrysi, 8,119,190
Ayios Iakovos, 21,324,339

B

babies, 16,116,127,130-1,145,149,
152,156,160,162-3,166-7,170,174,
180,275,277-8,280,282,286;
suckled,116,149,166-7,170
band motifs, 29,36,113,292-3,303,
312,324-5,339,341-2
Bartels,M.& P.;Ploss &, 122
Base Ring Ware, 11,25,32-3,44,47,79,
81,85,166,200,205,219,233,236-7,
250,291,319-20
baskets, 48-9,77,252
Benson, J.L., 228
Bichrome Red Ware, 41,228
Bichrome Ware,12,40,47,74,77,79,81,
85-6,180,200,210,213,217,219-20,
225,228,233,237
birds, 12,40,75,79,81,113,184,214,
222-9,248-9,277,279,287-8,292;
named 184,196,222-3,225
Birmingham Museum, 121,265
Black Polished Ware,24-5,47,85,251-3
Black Slip Painted Ware,wheelmade,44
Black Slip Ware, handmade, 10,24-5,
28,32,74,81,85,160,163,220
Black Slip Ware, wheelmade, 44,291
Black-bottomed Red Polished Ware,21,
86
Black-on-red Ware, 41,81,228
Black-topped Red Polished Ware,20,86
boats, 114,250-1,260,264-5,287
bone, 250; figures, 139,164-5,254
bones, animal, 185,190,192,214,216,
220,222
bottles, 20-1,48-9,65,167,307,341-3
bowls, 20-1,36,44,48-9,70-3,75,79,
81,141,192-3,222,228,232,240,252,
264,288; complex, 79,86,104,112,
156,196,233; milk, 70,268;scenic,
78,265,269-79,281-3; tulip,21,70,
156,162,300
boxes, 48-9,75,142,153,156,288
Boysset Collection, 280
branch motifs, 301
Bray, W., 250
bread making, 264,269,272-81
bronze, 9-10,12,165; artefacts, 174,
180,200,250,256
Bronze Age, 6,9-11; artefacts, 70,76,
78-80,81-111 *passim*,113,116,174,
184,188-90,204-5,217,220; *see also
under* Early, Middle, Late
Brown, A.C., 14,192,205,249,253,314
Bucchero Ware, 44,46
bucranials, 193,196-7,200,217,232-3,
254,265,282-4
buildings, 7-8,10-11,32,119
bulls, 75,81,167,169,192-200,232,
274-6,282-4,292
burial customs & beliefs, 15-6,79,
112-6,149,211,214,233,250,253,·
260,264,272
burial goods & offerings, 6,9-10,15
-17,21,40,70,78,80,112-6,133,138,
149,152,161-2,165,177,180,211,
213-4,223,250-4,256,264,269,272,
283,285,320
burial sites, 8,10,116
burnishing, 17,33,37

C

camels, 184,214-5
Canary Islands, 136
carnelian, 8
Catling, H.W., 14,20,192,205,210,
233,249,253,314
cattle, 10,75,81,167,169,184,189,
190-203,205,232,274-6,279,282-4,
286
Caubet, A., 133
Cesnola, A.P.di, 160,213-4; *Cyprus
Antiquities*, 121,213
Chalcolithic, *see* Copper Age
chameleon, 233
Chappel, T.J.H., 236
chariots, 181,205,210; models, 114,
181,250-1,260
Charleston, R.J., 112
checkered motifs, 29,40,113,301,308,
312,316,342
chevron motifs, 301
childbirth, 122-3,152,162,277-8,281,
321
Chipiez, C., 236
Christie's Salerooms, London, 139,
265,268
chronology, 7-8,10,13-14,17,21,29,
32,164-5
circle motifs, 40-1,113,145,292,299-
300,307,312,316,320,322,339-41
Cirlot, J.E., 79
Classic(al) Period, 13,41,200
clay, 17,25,33,40-1,323
Cles-Reden, S. von, 136
clothing: decoration of, 15,292; depicted, 120,127-9,138-42,152,157,
161-2,167,174-5;decay of original,
115,142; manufacture, 253-4;
washing, 16,264,276-81,286-7
Clutton-Brock, J., 204,211,214,218
comb figures, 138-42,161-2,322
combed wares, 8
Conrad, J.R., 196
Cook, A.B., 196
Cooper, J.C., 131,237
copper, 8,165; industry, 9-12,273-4,
290; leaching, 9,273-4,276-7,
280-1,290
Copper Age, 8-9,13-14; artefacts,10,
17,78,80,85,116-24,126,131,133,
135-6,139,141,162,184,213,291,320
corn-grinding,16,264,272-8,281,286-7
Crete, 78,115,175
Crouwel, J., 132
cruciform figures, 9,116,121-32,162
cruciform motifs, 301,308-9,316
cultural interaction, 8-13,20,24,33,
40,46-7,112,121,124,126,135-6,
166,183,192,196-7,217,228,233,
240,292,320
cups, 48-9,70
Cycladic artefacts, 124,126,132,136

Cypro-Archaic, *see* Archaic
Cypro-Classical, *see* Classical
Cypro-Geometric, *see* Geometric
Cypro-Minoan script, 11
Cypro-Mycenaean Wares, 33,65,81,292
Cypro-Palestinian Bichrome Ware, 33,240
Cypro-Phoenician Ware, 41
Cyprus Antiquities (Cesnola,1881), 121,213

D

D(h)ali, 214
dating methods, 8,13-14,165,218
Decorated Gourds of North-Eastern Nigeria (Chappel, 1977), 236
decoration, 12,16-7,20-1,28-9,32,36, 40-1,48,78-9,113,120,127-9,142, 165,181,236,260,291-352;classifi- cation,323-4; non-pottery,15,120, 127,133,164-5,236,292
deer, 75,184-93,196,248,272-3,292; meat,8,189,216;milking,189,265-9, 273,364
deities, 12,114-6,122-3,126,135, 166-7,175,177,189,196-7,217,232, 281,283
Des Gagniers, J., 40,138,188,200, 228,233,253,265
Dhali-Agridhi, 190
diabase, 118
diamond motifs, 29,40,113,294,306-7, 312,314,339-42
Dikaios, P., 8,33,138,216,220,232, 281,285-6
dippers, 48-9,76
dishes, 44,48-9,74,177
dogs, 184,213,216,220-1,233,272-3
Drab Polished Ware, 25,28,81,85, 104,264-5

E

Early Bronze Age, 10-11,13-14; arte- facts,16-25,47,49,65-7,75,135-6, 142,144-5,152,161-2,165,192,197, 213-5,222-3,232,236,251-4,264-88, 291,293-303,322,325
Ede, C., 24
Egypt, 7,11,36,115,237,250,272-3; interaction with, 20,121-3,133, 217,223,240
Eibl-Eibesfeldt, I., 133
ejaculation figure, 134-5
Enkomi, 11,37,200,253
environment, natural, 7-10,116,214
equines,11,75,181,184,204-11,285,292
Erimi, 188,190,212,218
Etruscans, 44; Bucchero Ware, 44,46
Evans, Sir Arthur, 114

F

faience, 11
farming, 7-8,10-11,16,169,193,196, 212-7,256,264-5,268,272-9,285-7, 290
feather motifs, 293
fertility,114-32,135,139-40,145,149, 152,161-2,166,174,192-3,196,200, 210,232,237,240,281-2

figurines,114-183; depicted,126,139- 42,322; roles of,114-6; worn,116, 120,122-6,138-42,161-2,322; *see also* human figures
firing, 15-17,20-1,24-5,32-3,48
Fisher, J., 216
flasks, 37,48-9,66,164
Flourenzos, P., 135-6
food, 269,272-7; bread, 264,269,272- 81; offerings, 15,70,114,174,177, 180,214
formalization, 117,124-5,130,138, 141-2,204,211,219,222,224,237,276
fortification, 10-11
Frankel, D., 29,138,205,214
frogs, 233
functionality, 32,37,41,48-9,66,70, 78-80,104,115,126,152,162,174, 224,237,256,264
funnels,215,250,252
furniture,114,122,135,167,250-3,260, 268,282-3,285

G

Gejvall, N., 217
Geneva Art Museum, 205
geometric decoration, 12,40-1,113, 161,240,291-3,320-3
Geometric Period, 12,40-1,44,74,174, 177,260,292
Gjerstad,E., 14,17,40,77,214,237,240
Glasgow Museum, 260
goats,81,181,184,190,192,218-9,233; meat, 8,216
goblets, 49,70
gold, 200,250,253
Goudhi, 213
gourds, 236,250,252
Greece,7; interaction with, 11-13, 33,36,40,46,49,74,77-8,115, 183,233,293
Greek language, 11,48-9
greenstone, 9
Groger-Wurm, H.M., 322
gypsum, 138

H

Hadjiprodromou bowl, 265,278
Hadjiprodromou Collection, Famagusta, 278
Halstead, P., 189
Harrison, J., 78,232
headgear, 142,157,161,164,166-70, 174,177,277-82,286,288
hedgehog, 233
Hellenistic Period, 13,46,65,213,292
herringbone motifs, 293
Herscher, E., 20-1,343
Hill, G., 214
horn, 139,196,250
horned motifs, 317-20
horns,114,180,192-3,196-7,200,216-9, 233,251,254-6,317-20
human figures, 16,40-1,75,79,104, 113-6,116-83,292; modelled,41,75, 81,104,113,136,145,157,162,181, 264,268-9,272-88; mounted, 75, 169-70,174,181,205,210-11,219; on vessels, 41,81,113,139,141,153-7, 161,264,268-75;*see also* figurines

humour, sense of, 6,41,48,78-80,112, 130,132,141,160-1,174,228,292
hunting, 216-7,220,256,273,290
Hutchinson, R.W., 232

I

Iberia, 136
Incised Polished Wares, 292-303, 311-2
Incised Red Polished Ware, 20-1,25, 75,81,85-6,104,161,215,253-4, 290,307,322,323-41
incision decoration, 15,20-1,24-5, 28,32,75,81,85-6,104,113,133, 137-41,144-5,153,157,160,167,188, 213,217,236,253,268,291-4,299- 303,321-3,339-42; non-pottery, 120,127,164-5,236
incomers, 7-12,20,33,188-9,192,196, 216,218,220,228,233
interpretation,78,138-9,143,149,152, 161-2,169,181,197,210,213,240, 252,256,268-9,273-4,277,281-3, 286-7,293,311,321-2
Iran, 185,214
Iraq, 185
iron, 12
Iron Age, 11-13; artefacts, 40-7,49, 65-7,74,77-81,85-6,116,174,180, 188,200,205,210-1,213,217,219-20, 225,233,237,249,251,260,292
ivory, 11

J

jars, 44,48-9,67-9,79,81,141,200, 213,220,222,237,264; complex, 79,104; depicted, 280,283-4; human-shaped, 162-3; scenic, 78,280-1
jugs, 20,25,32,36-7,41,44,46,48-64, 79,81,139,153,156,193,218,220, 222-5,232-3,237,240,288,290; complex, 41,79,85-6,104,168,288; depicted, 180,268,279-80,286,288; gourd-shaped,153,224,236,250,323- 42; imitative,163-4,200,236-7, 252,292;scenic, 78,265-9,286,290
Johnson, J., 233

K

Kalavassos bowl, 265,269,278-9
Kalavassos-Tenta, 7-8,13,122,264-5
Kalavassos village, 278,324,339-40
Kalopsidha, 217,284,324,339
Karageorghis, V., 14,16,28,32,37,40, 125,135,138,141,156,160,166,169, 188,200,205,213,218,220,228,233, 237,253,260,265,274-5,284
Karpasian Peninsula, 28-9,294
Karpasian Ware, 21,341
Katyd(h)ata, 214,324,339-40
kernos, 78-9
Khirokitia, 8,10,117-8,188,190,212, 216,218
Kimber, K., 364
Kissonerga Mylouthkia, 121,128
Kition, 11-12,141,200,253,324, 339-40
Klavdhia, 120

Kochati, 219,253,265,283
Kouklia, 189
Kourion, 37
Kyrenia mountains, 7,10
Kythrea, 124

L

Lacey, A.D., 78
lactation figures, 133
ladles, 48-9,76
Lapithos, 144,264-5,288,324,339-40
Late Bronze Age,11,13,25,32-9,47,49,
   65-7,77,116-7,136,160-1,166,180,
   188-200,205,219,233,237,240,251,
   253-60,312-20
Leach, M., 237
leather, 32,36,250-2,320
Lemba, 120-1
'Lemba lady', 119,129
Levant,interaction with, 7-8,216,232
Light-on-dark Ware, 28
Limassol, 324,339-40
limestone, 119-20,129,143
lions, 233
Lloyd, S., 24
Lorblanchet, M., 117
lotus, 12,40,113,237,240-8,292
Louvre Museum, Paris,133,174,265,287

M

MacLaurin, M.L.G., 17,20,24
Malacca, 321
Malta, 196-7,284
Margi, 141,193,264-5,269,274,277-8,
   283,286,324,339-40
'Margi bowl', 205,265,274-5,287
Maroni, 120,233
masks, 124,160,174,180,217
meander motifs, 293,301
Mellaart, J., 13-14,24,196,223
Merrillees, R.S., 9,11,14,20,29,32,
   123,138,143,236-7,273-4,276,279-
   81,290
Mesaoria, plain of, 7
Mesopotamia, 10,166,184-5,189
metals, 8,10,165,250-1;imitation of,
   25,32,44,250,253-4
Metropolitan Museum, New York, 160
Middle Bronze Age, 11,13-4,25,28-31,
   47,49,65-7,75,135-6,142,145,149,
   152,156-7,160-3,188,200,205,
   214-5,260,264,287,291,303-11
milking animals, 265-8
Minoans, 11,175,228,232
modelled decoration,41,78,157,192-3,
   197,233,264-5,268-9,274-81,288,
   290
models, 32,114,181,193,250,254,
   260-3,283,290
moon, 322
Morris, D., 117-8,196,232; & Morris,
   R., 232
Mother Goddess, 114-5,122-3,133,
   135,138,149,152,166,281
motifs, 291-352; classified,303,311;
   regional, 29,293-4,299,303,321,
   340-1; significance of, 293,299,
   303,314,321-2,343
Mottled Red Polished Ware, 20,85-6,
   104,279

mourning, 115,133,149,162,166,177
multi-unit vessels, 48,78-80,85-103,
   112,156,364
Murray, A.S., 253,260
musicians, 116,174,177
Mycenae, interaction with, 11,33,40,
   65,81,113,136,175,228,292
Myres, Sir J.L., 14,17,24,32,36,
   116-7,236

N

Neolithic, see Stone Age
Neuberger, A., 272
Nicolaou, K., 174

O

objects, inanimate: depicted,36,114,
   232,250-63,290
obsidian, 8
opium, 32,236-7
Organ, J., 236
ornaments, 8,11,122-6,137,141-5,152,
   157,161-7,170-4,177,200,237,
   251-3,286
Ovgos river, 9
oxen, 193,196,205,279,282,286
Oxford bowl, 265,269-74

P

pack animals, 204-5,211,214,275,277,
   279,285,287
painted decoration, 12-16,28-9,32,36,
   40-1,44,113,167,180,188,224-5,228,
   236-7,240,248,291,303,321
Palaeolithic, 7-8,117
Palestine, 10,33,36-7,41,77,115,165,
   240
Palestinian Bichrome Ware, 33,240
Paphos, 11,120,124,213-4,216
Pappara, 274
patterns,12,15,20-1,25,28-9,32-3,36,
   232-3,240,291-2; analysed, 21,29,
   292-323,343-52; on bottles,341-3;
   on juglets,323-41
Peltenburg,E.J., 13-14,119-21,128-9,
   192,260
Perrot, G., 236
Peru, pottery from, 156
Petra tou Limniti, 8,120
Philia Culture, 9,13-14
Philia Red Polished Ware, 14,20,32,
   104,293,307
Philistines, 228
Phoenicians, 12,41,46
Photios, 214
picrolite, 118,120-2,124,129,132,
   136,139,213
pictorial decoration, 12,33,40-1,
   113,188,200,213,225,228,233,249,
   292-3,320
Pierides bowl, 265,277-8,288
Pierides Collection, Larnaca, 163,
   253,265,277
Pierides figurine, 233
Pieridou, A., 233,254
pigs, 184,212-3; meat, 8
Pitt Rivers Museum, Dorset, 213
Plain Red Polished Ware, 9,20,81,
   85-6,104

Plain White Ware, 44,220
plank figures, 13,116,135-62,164-5,
   253,264,322; categorized, 136,161
plants, 12,40-1,79,81,234-49; food,
   8,78,116
Ploss, H.H.; & Bartels, 122
ploughing, 193,196,264,275,285-6
Politico, 29
pomegranates, 79,81,237
Popham, M.R., 36
poppies, 32,236-7,250
pot marks, 37,339
potter's wheel, 10-12,15-16,29,33,
   37,40,44,292,323
pottery: classification of, 17,20,
   24-5,29; imitations in, 16,25,32,
   36,44,113,188,215,236,250-9,287,
   320; impressed marks on, 269;
   significance of, 8,10,12,15-16
Proto-White Painted Ware, 40,205,
   225,233
Proto-White Slip Ware, 36,314,316-7,
   320
pubic triangle figures, 116,160,
   166-74
Pyla, 324,339
pyxis, 48-9,75

R

realism, 116-7,124,129,135,145,160,
   185,233,288
realistic figures, 182-3
rectangular motifs, 40,301,311,316,
   342-3
Red Book, The (Fisher, Simon &
   Vincent, 1969), 216
Red-&-Black Polished Ware, 20-1,
   341-52
Red-on-Black Ware, 10,28,47,85,163,
   200,215,291
Red-on-Red Ware, 28
Red-on-White Ware, 80,85
Red Polished Ware,10,14,17-23,25,28,
   32,47,76-81,86,136,139,141-2,144,
   152-3,156-7,162,188,192-3,204,
   213,217,220-5,236,251-2,264-5,
   269,274,276-8,281-8,307,323,342
   see also black-bottomed,black-
   topped,incised,mottled,Philia,
   plain,relief-decorated
Red Slip Ware, 46
Relief-decorated Red Polished Ware,
   20,81,85-6,104,113,140-1,218,232
relief decoration, 20,32,78,81,85-6,
   104,113,126,129,136,139-42,153,
   156-7,174,188,218,232-3,272,276-7,
   291-2
religions & cults, 9,12,79,114,116,
   133,135,175,177,189,197,217,232,
   264,268,281-4,287,292
Reserved Slip Ware, 24,86
restorations, 74,268-9,285-6,364
ribbed decoration, 44,46,81
riding, 75,169-70,174,181-205,210-1,
   219
ring vessels, 48,78-85,112,200,219,
   237
rituals: depicted, 197,264,268,281-2;
   existence of, 112-3,135,169,181,
   197,278-9,281-4,287,322; interpretation of, 79-80,115-6,141,

196-7,232-3,281-3,320; objects in,
   48,78-80,120,144,174,196,248,252-3,
   256,268,272-3,290,322; offerings
   at, 78,80,104,114,116,133,169,174,
   177,180,214,250,272,287,290
Roman Period, 13,46
Rome, interaction with, 13,46,183
ropes, 20,232,274-7,282,303,311-2
rosettes, 237,240
Russell, C., 131

S

Salamis, 11,164,213,220,248
Savory, H.N., 136
scenic vessels, 10,12,16,157,162,188,
   192-3,196,200,232-3,250,264-90;
   list, 265
Schaeffer, C.F.A., 218
schematization, 6,32,117-8,135-6,139,
   145,152,183,213
sculpture, 9,12-13,15,25,124,129,323
sea creatures, 233
'Sea Peoples', 11
Sèvres bowl, 265,276-7
Sèvres jar, 265,280-1
Sèvres Museum, Paris, 162,265,276,280
sexes, differentiation between: in
   animals,185,192-3,268; in figures,
   118,128,130-1,138,145,149,157,160,
   164,166,169,272-4,280-2,288; in
   society, 15-16,174,272-3,280-2,
   290,292,323
sheep, 184,190,216-7; meat, 8
Simon, N., 216
Singer, C., 254
skeuomorphs, 16,138-9,141,250-9
Smeets, R., 322
snakes, 32,81,184,210,230-3,282-3,
   303,320
snowman figures, 13,116,174-83
Soloi, 11
Sotheby's Salerooms, London, 143,213
Sotira, 8,118-9,188,190,212,218,220
Souskiou, 125
Souskiou-Vathyrkakas, 120,125,127,132
spoons, 48,250,252-3
Stanley-Price, N.P., 9,189,216
starburst motifs, 301
steatite, 118,131
Stewart, J.R., 20-1,24,214
stereotyping, 117
stone: artefacts, 8,118-36,138,142,
   254; buildings, 10-11
Stone Age, 7-8,10,13; artefacts, 17,
   116-21,162,184,188-9,196,212,218,
   220,222,291

strainers, 48-9,77
Strand, W.E., 233
stripes motif, 113,293-4,304,312
stump figures, 116-25,162
stylization, 6,9,104,116-9,127,130,
   135,145,152,157,183-4,214-5,220,
   224,233,240,252,320
subsidiary-unit vessels, 48,78,80,
   104-12,265,268,288
Sumerians, 196-7
sun, 322
Swiny, S., 25
Sydney University, 237
symbolism, 6,32,78-80,114-9,122,125-
   32,136,138,145,149,161-2,164,167-
   70,177,180-1,192-3,196-7,200,210-
   13,223,232-3,237,240,252-6,284,288,
   293,320-2
Syria, 7,10-11,33,36-7,41,115,166-7,
   217,228
Syro-Palestinian, 33,40

T

Tahong, 321-2
Tamvaki, A., 138,364
tankards, 49,77,220
Tatton-Brown, V., 14
tendrils, 237
Tenta, 7,8,13,122
Terra Sigillata, 46
terracotta, 113,133,136,138-9,145,
   160,174,225,233,250-2,254,256,
   260,264,283-5,292,322
Thimme, J., 128-9,132
tin, 10
Todd, I.A., 7,13,278
tools, 8,10,16,21,114,138-41,250-4,
   256,260,268,272,274,279
torpedo-shaped vessel, 44
tortoise, 233
Toumba tou Skourou, 214,220
toys, 114-5,161,213,237,250
trading: external, 8,10-12,20,24,
   32-3,36-7,41,48-9,74,126,135,174,
   183,192,228,240,292; internal, 11,
   29,323,340-1
trees, 40,248,293,342
Troodos mountains, 7,9,124
Trump, D., 250
Turkey, 7
Tyre, 12

U

Ucko, P.J., 114-5,133,149
urban development, 11-12,33,114

utensils, see tools

V

Vagnetti, L., 120,124,126-7
Vermeule, C., 217
Vermeule, E.T., 220,228
vessel-shaped figures, 162-4,167
village life, 10-11,16,264,269-90
village sites, 10,115,162
village traditions, 21,29,197,293,
   321
Vincent, J., 216
Vounous, 138,192-3,196,213,217-8,232,
   253-4,256,264-5,285-6,290,324,
   339-40
Vounous bowl, 232-3,265,281-3

W

warfare, 10-12,116,180,210,290
warriors, 16,174,180-1,210,256,290
water-carts, 251,260
Watson, J.P.N., 189,216
wavy-line motifs, 29,311,316,321
weapons, 8,10,16,114,116,177,180,211,
   216-7,249,251-2,256
Weinberg, S.S., 16
Wheelmade Red Lustrous Ware, 37
Wheelmade Red Ware, 46
White Painted Ware, handmade, 10,28-9,
   33,47,65,75-6,79,81,85-6,136,142,
   145,152,156-7,160,163,188,200,205,
   214,217,220,225,254,287,291-2,303-
   12,314
White Painted Ware, wheelmade, 12,
   40-1,44,47,74,77,79,81,85-6,210,
   219,225,228,237,260,292
White Polished Ware, 86
White Shaved Ware, 37,225
White Slip Ware, 11,32,36,47,291-2,
   312-20
wine-skins, 113,188,215,252
Witkowski, G.J., 122
wood, 10,36,139,250-4,285
writing, emergence of, 11

XYZ

Xenophon, 211

Yon, M., 14,24
Yortan, 24

Zeuner, F.E., 189,204,214,216-7
zig-zag motifs, 29,293-4,304-6,312,
   314,325,339-43